THE GENERALS' WAR

THE GENERALS' WAR

The Inside Story of the Conflict in the Gulf

by Michael R. Gordon *and*
General Bernard E. Trainor

Little, Brown and Company

Boston   New York   Toronto   London

To our wives, Cheryl Gordon and Peggy Trainor, and to Matthew
Gordon, for their patience, encouragement, and support

First Edition

Library of Congress Cataloging-in-Publication Data
Gordon, Michael R.
    The generals' war : the inside story of the conflict in the Gulf /
by Michael R. Gordon and Bernard E. Trainor. — 1st ed.
        p.   cm.
    Includes bibliographical references and index.
    ISBN 0-316-32172-9
    1. Persian Gulf War, 1991.   I. Trainor, Bernard E.
II. Title.
DS79.72.G67   1994
956.7044'2 — dc20   94–27144

10   9   8   7   6   5   4   3   2   1
MV-NY

*Published simultaneously in Canada
by Little, Brown & Company (Canada) Limited*

Printed in the United States of America

Contents

List of Maps

Preface

WHEN COLIN POWELL entered the Oval Office on the afternoon of February 27, 1991, the question was on the table. The United States and its allies had spent five months planning how to defeat Iraq and had waged an intensive six-week campaign of day-and-night warfare to destroy Saddam Hussein's military machine and — Washington hoped — the regime itself. With the Iraqis in rout, President Bush needed to know how and when to end the fighting.

Now, the president was stating the issue in its simplest form. Sitting in his customary white chair to the right of the fireplace, which was dominated by a portrait of George Washington, the chief executive said that Iraq had indicated that it would meet the allies' demands.

"What do you need?" the president asked, according to the notes of the meeting taken by a participant.[1]

It was the sort of question that Powell specialized in, and all eyes turned to him. Vice President Dan Quayle, Bush's loyal backup, sat on the white couch to the president's right, along with James A. Baker, Mr. Bush's longtime friend and secretary of state, and Dick Cheney, the conservative secretary of defense.

Sitting on straight-back chairs were Brent Scowcroft, the president's soft-spoken but hard-line national security adviser; Robert M. Gates, the ambitious deputy national security adviser; and John Sununu, the blunt-spoken White House chief of staff.

British Foreign Minister Douglas Hurd was also there, along with lower-ranking American and British aides. Mr. Hurd was in Washington for consultations and before Powell's arrival had said that the war should probably be brought to a close in the next two days. Bush, however, had given the generals enormous leeway in prosecuting the war, and he was now asking Powell to make the call.

Powell was accustomed to operating in this kind of rarefied atmosphere. The chairman of the Joint Chiefs of Staff embodied the new breed of American commander, a politically attuned officer as skilled in testifying before Congress on national security questions as in orchestrating a battle. As a former national security adviser to President Reagan, Powell was wise in the ways of Washington. He was brilliant in dealing with the media and a respected figure on Capitol Hill.

Among the Joint Chiefs, Powell was the dominant presence. To overcome the failure of the services to work together, Congress had passed legislation in 1986 strengthening the powers of the chairman of the Joint Chiefs of Staff, and Powell used them to the hilt, wielding power and influence beyond that exercised by any previous chairman. Throughout the Gulf War, his fellow members of the JCS, the chiefs of the four services, were relegated to the status of observers who simply provided forces for the conflict. While Powell kept them informed, he did not need their approval.

As with many generals of his generation, Powell's formative experience was the Vietnam War, and the conflict colored his advice on the weighty matters of war and peace. If force was to be used, it should be overwhelming, and its application should be decisive and preferably short. Military intervention should not be undertaken unless the outcome was all but guaranteed. The aims in using force needed to be precisely defined beforehand, and as soon as they were achieved American forces should be quickly extracted, lest the Pentagon risk sliding into a quagmire. American casualties had to be held to a minimum.

This view was based on Powell's reading of politics, as much as on his sense of American military capabilities. It maximized the chances of victory and reflected the military leaders' fears that American public opinion could turn against the armed forces, as it did during the Vietnam War, if their operations were open-ended.

The view was not Powell's alone. Indeed, it reflected the conventional wisdom among much of the military leadership, particularly in the Army. But the JCS chief's convictions on this count were applied so systematically, and expressed so articulately, that Pentagon hands dubbed them the "Powell doctrine."

The purest expression of the Powell doctrine had been the lightning invasion of Panama, in which the Army and Marines quickly overpowered an overmatched Panamanian force. But Powell had applied his doctrine to the Persian Gulf as well, sometimes with contentious results.

Based on his exacting criteria for using force, Powell had rebuffed suggestions by civilian Pentagon and State Department officials before Iraq's invasion of Kuwait that American warships be dispatched to the Persian Gulf to signal American resolve. And it was Powell who had argued within the Bush administration and, surprisingly, outside administration councils with allied officials, against even going to war to liberate Kuwait. With the Pentagon's overgenerous estimates of Iraq's military prowess, Powell's concern was that the liberation of Kuwait, noble goal that it was, might not produce the speedy and decisive victory his doctrine required.

Once the decision to go to war had been made, Powell was the politico-military maestro, playing a pivotal role in shaping the war plan in light of his doctrine of decisive military force. For Powell, victory was ultimately guaranteed by massive land power. It was Powell who cautioned President Bush against relying on airpower to carry the day and who fought Cheney's idea to launch a military operation in the far western reaches of Iraq to neutralize the Scud missile threat, threaten Baghdad, and try to turn the tables on Saddam Hussein. And it was Powell who pressed for the massive and time-consuming military buildup, which saw American forces in the Gulf rise to more than 500,000, and who guided Gen. H. Norman Schwarzkopf, the commander of the United States Central Command (CENTCOM), in developing his celebrated left hook — the Army's flanking attack on the Republican Guard.

The underlying logic of the military planning was as important as the tactics. Americans would enter the enemy's territory in force and leave as soon as possible, with no entangling occupation duties or alliances with Iraqi insurgents who might take up arms against the Iraqi dictator. The stain of Vietnam would be removed by a rapid victory, and American forces would exit swiftly. Anything else was a potential snare. Even the code name of the military campaign — Desert Storm — expressed the philosophy of the war plan. Like a thunderstorm, the attacks would be furious while they lasted but limited in duration.

Now, as Bush and his aides listened for the chairman's response, Powell made the case for ending the war the next day. Speaking without notes, Powell said that he had talked to Schwarzkopf. The volatile Schwarzkopf was not Powell's equal in acumen or bureaucratic skill, but he intuitively shared the JCS chairman's philosophy of military power. Concerned that the bombardment of Iraqi forces escaping from Kuwait City would tarnish the American military's lopsided victory, Powell had prodded Schwarzkopf to think about ending the war, and Schwarzkopf had gone along. The two generals agreed that the allies were, at most, twenty-four hours away from achieving their war aims, Powell reported. The Army was still engaged in a fight with a Republican Guard division and wanted to finish the battle, but that would not require fighting much past midday the following day, the JCS chairman advised.

"We are in the home stretch," Powell told the president. Today or tomorrow by close of business, the allies would meet their objectives. There was not a great deal of significance either way, Powell advised.

"Norm and I would like to finish tomorrow, a five-day war."

The president was impressed by Powell's presentation.

"We do not want to lose anything now with charges of brutalization," Bush said. "We do not want to screw this up with a sloppy, muddled ending. A speech could do it."

Then the president turned to Scowcroft.

"You are going to work on it," Bush said with a smile.

It was one of the crucial decisions of the war, made on the basis of incomplete intelligence and guided by Powell's desire to protect the image of the American military and withdraw American forces as quickly as possible.

The meeting broke up at 2PM. Seven hours later, Bush told the nation in a television address that he was ordering a cease-fire after a hundred-hour ground war.

After a spy plane canvassed the battlefield on March 1, the Central Intelligence Agency determined that half the Republican Guard forces in the Kuwaiti theater of operations, the most powerful element of the Iraqi army and a force that CENTCOM had earmarked for destruction, had escaped. Most of the Iraqi forces that got away had been south of the Euphrates River and squarely in the path of the allied attack when it was brought to a halt. Over the next few days and weeks, the forces would cross the Euphrates, be reorganized, and join Saddam Hussein's effort to quash the Shiite and Kurdish rebellions that challenged his rule. Nearly four years later, the Iraqi president's hold on power would be as firm as ever.[2]

The Persian Gulf War is without precedent in the annals of warfare. It was the dawn of a new era in which high technology supplanted the bayonet, a war in which one side had a clear picture of events while the other floundered deaf, dumb, and blind. It was a war that saw a new breed of highly skilled professional soldiers victorious over a traditional army bred to blind obedience. It was also the first war in history in which airpower, not ground forces, played the dominant role.

Equally important, it was a test of Powell's doctrine of decisive force, of joint warfare, and of Congress's attempt to reform and reorganize the military to avoid the pitfalls of the Vietnam War. Once the political objectives were set, this had been the generals' war to win or lose.

Under the guidance of Powell and Schwarzkopf, each service was given the opportunity to apply its own ethos to the war, with few restraints from on high. To apply their doctrine of strategic bombing, the Air Force generals who ran the bombing campaign used virtually every tool in their kit save for nuclear and chemical weapons — and developed new ones that did not even exist when Iraq invaded Kuwait. Unlike Vietnam, there would be no gradual escalation to give the enemy a chance to recover. From the first moments of the campaign, American planes and missiles would bring the war home to downtown Baghdad.

The Army saw the Gulf War as an opportunity to apply its "Air-Land Battle" doctrine of maneuver warfare, devised to defeat a numerically superior Warsaw Pact on the plains of Europe. Drawing on the best-prepared troops ever to wear an Army uniform, equipped with the most modern armor and attack helicopters, and supplied with ample ammunition, it launched a powerful offensive to flank the enemy defenses.

The Marine Corps approached the Gulf with a long history of expeditionary warfare and the aggressiveness associated with amphibious assaults. Using speed, stealth, and decentralized command and control, it burst through the Iraqi defensive lines, creating and expanding its "beachhead" in Kuwait. Denied an opportunity to carry out an amphibious landing, it nonetheless exceeded CENTCOM's expectations by racing to the gates of Kuwait City in three days.

The Navy, as in the past, settled into a pattern of studied aloofness from CENTCOM. But with a force of six aircraft carriers and a large supporting cast of warships, it imposed a tight quarantine on Iraq and joined in the Air Force–dominated air war against Iraq while its battleships pummeled the coast of Kuwait. Even its submarines got into the action, joining Navy ships in firing Tomahawk cruise missiles to demonstrate the Navy's capabilities in precision-guided warfare.

The fighting itself was short, violent, and one-sided. Over a million men faced off in battle, but only one side sustained grievous loss. When the Bush administration called a cease-fire after forty-three days of war, most of Saddam Hussein's residences and military command centers had been destroyed. Iraq's electrical grid had been shut down. Its telecommunications links were largely severed and its bridges dropped. Many of the country's nuclear, chemical, and biological warfare installations were bombed. The Iraqi army had been routed, and Kuwait had been liberated. Thousands of tanks and guns had massed in the desert, but half of them provided little more than target practice for the other side.

But Saddam Hussein remained unbowed. Iraq had preserved enough of its nuclear, biological, and chemical weapons programs to necessitate an open-ended program of United Nations inspections. Much of Iraq's Scud missile force was unaccounted for. Half its Republican Guard forces had escaped.

Almost four years after the United States achieved a "decisive" victory over Iraq, the American military still finds itself engaged in an open-ended police action, flying air patrols in northern and southern Iraq and occasionally bombing targets inside Iraq. Three and a half years later, some of the same Republican Guard forces that Powell thought had been largely destroyed again menaced Kuwait. And in October 1994, some of the same American units that took on the Iraqis in 1991 were ordered back to the Gulf to prevent a possible second Iraqi invasion. Perhaps Iraq was not the tar baby the American military feared, but neither had the United States been able to cleanly extract itself from the region, as it had hoped.

The military's planning had been meticulous. The performance of its weapons and tactics exceeded any reasonable expectation. The soldiers, sailors, Marines, and airmen had been courageous. The Persian Gulf War had been an impressive demonstration of American military power and was heroically executed. But it was an incomplete success.

Why?

We began this project four years ago to get at the "ground truth" of the war. Interviews with senior officials on three continents and access to classified and recently released government documents enabled us to uncover some little-known facets of the Persian Gulf War, which allowed us to assess the conflict in an entirely new way.

Based upon our research, we have tried to see the conflict through the eyes of all the services — and their commanders in Washington — and to analyze the planning and execution of the campaign. In an event as large and politically charged as a war, the memories and accounts of participants often vary. The reality of war is complex, and decision makers, and the bureaucracies they serve, are often inclined to present history in a self-serving way. To the extent possible, we have sought to resolve the inconsistencies and identify the sources of our information. In our account, there is no attempt to create an omniscient narrator. When top officials have presented irreconcilable accounts, we have noted the differences.

Our effort yielded a simple but important conclusion: the way the war was planned, fought, and brought to a close often had more to do with the culture of the military services, their entrenched concept of warfare, and Powell's abiding philosophy of decisive force than it did with the Iraqis or the tangled politics of the Middle East.

In that sense, our examination of the war is more than an inside account of a specific conflict, its origins, battles, turning points, and the particular personalities, prickly and otherwise, that populated the high command. It is also a case study of the nature of American warfare in the 1990s: an assessment of the guiding principles, bureaucratic forces, and doctrines that shaped American military planning during the most important conflict since the Vietnam War and will continue to do so in the next major conflict.

Several points are clear.

The war was a stunning failure of America's policy of trying to deter war. Deterrence is made up of two elements, capability and credibility. Capability is the raw military power that can be brought to bear against an enemy. Credibility is the willingness to use that power.

But the Bush administration's reluctance to concede the failure of its policy to moderate Iraq's behavior and Powell's caution disadvantaged the United States. Using the military to send political signals did not fit comfortably with Powell's theory of military power, and the United States failed to take any significant steps prior to Iraq's August 2, 1990, invasion of Kuwait to strengthen its military position in the region to deter aggression.

Another point is that the defense of Saudi Arabia was more problematic than is generally acknowledged. Despite CENTCOM's early efforts to come up with a plan for the defense of Saudi Arabia, the plan was incomplete in several key respects. To maintain harmony among the Arab and Western members of his eclectic command, Schwarzkopf adopted a decentralized leadership style. He set the strategy, and his disparate subordinates were free to operate according to their own precepts as long they conformed to that strategy. That approach soothed the political sensitivities, but technical and operational differences between the Army and the Marines and friction among the nations lingered. Had the Iraqi attacked Saudi Arabia in 1990, they would have been defeated, but CENTCOM's defensive scheme would have been severely stressed.

With an event as complex as the Persian Gulf War, there is no singl answer to why the American military failed to reap the full measure its victory. But by addressing the generalship of the air and land car paigns in detail, we were able to draw some broad judgments.

The victory in the Persian Gulf War has been portrayed as a vindic tion of the military's efforts to reform itself following Vietnam, the sastrous 1978 failed Iranian hostage rescue attempt, and the flaw invasion of Grenada four years later by revising its fighting strateg buying advanced weaponry, and carrying out dogged and highly rea tic training. In particular, the war has been hailed as a demonstratio

Congress's wisdom in strengthening the power of the JCS chairman and the theater commanders to ride herd over the disputatious services and wage joint-service warfare. Operation Desert Storm, Powell later wrote in the JCS's new manual on joint warfare, demonstrated the "richness of the joint operational art."[3]

In fact, the American military fell short of its goals. The campaign was "joint" more in name than in fact. Each service fought its own war, concentrating on its own piece of the conflict with a single-minded intensity, and the commanders in Washington and Riyadh failed to fully harmonize the war plans. In this sense, the Gulf War shows that there is much to be done if the American armed forces are to operate in a truly coordinated and integrated manner.

The American military also failed to achieve a complete victory because of the failure by top commanders to decipher the mind of the enemy and reliably estimate Iraqi military capabilities. Viewing the Iraqi armed forces as a force of battle-hardened Saladins, and not the dispirited and poorly led force they were shown to be in the Gulf War, American military commanders assumed the Iraqis would stand and fight.

The battle of Khafji gave reason to question that assumption. As allied ground forces prepared for the upcoming offensive, doubts began to arise within the Iraqi high command over the Iraqi army's ability to successfully use the same type of defense it employed during the Iraq-Iran War against the coalition. The air campaign was far longer and more effective than they had anticipated, but Baghdad still believed that the United States was loath to suffer heavy casualties in a ground war for the sake of Kuwait. Saddam Hussein decided to start the ground war by launching a limited offensive into Saudi Arabia. This, he anticipated, would lead to an antiwar outcry in the United States as U.S. casualties mounted.

On January 29, 1991, Iraqi forces attacked at four points along the Saudi border. They found themselves unable to maneuver on the battlefield in the face of American airpower and were dealt a stunning defeat by allied forces.

But Schwarzkopf all but ignored what happened at Khafji and failed to appreciate the message it sent about Iraq's inability to carry out its defensive plans for Kuwait; no provisions were made for the collapse of the Iraqi army. Like Gen. George Meade at the battle of Gettysburg in the Civil War, Schwarzkopf defeated his enemy, but allowed him to escape to make future mischief.

Finally, with the emphasis on a quick victory and speedy exit, the generals supported the premature decision to bring the war to a close with surprisingly little planning for the termination or the possible re-

verberations within Iraq. As policy-makers struggled to respond to the upheaval that swept Iraq after the war, the generals blocked plans to create a demilitarized zone in southern Iraq to weaken the surviving Saddam Hussein regime. They also successfully resisted (until the 1992 presidential election season) providing any measure of protection for the Shiites, who had been encouraged to battle Saddam Hussein, thus diluting the moral force of the allied victory.

The undermining of the post–Gulf War Saddam Hussein regime — an implicit goal of the allied military campaign — was contradicted by the impulse to quickly withdraw, disengage, and avoid any military links to the insurgents. The disconnect between the military and political aims resulted in a confusing end.

This is not to say that some things were not done right. On the positive side, Iraq's aggression was not tolerated. Few would have thought in July 1990 that the Bush administration would send half a million troops to the Gulf and assemble the most elaborate political and military coalition since the Napoleonic Wars. The allies showed remarkable cohesion. The power and effectiveness of American troops, weapons, and equipment were so impressive as to leave no doubt that the United States was the most powerful nation on earth. The United States brought to the battlefield an integrated system of sensors, stealth technology, and precision munitions designed to counter Soviet-style warfare on the European continent. And Washington had a competent and proficient military to use them.

But even as the war drew to a close, there were matters left unfinished.

The first few weeks after the war were filled with victory parades, but then a lingering unease set in. President Bush sensed something was awry, although he could explain it only by comparison with the defining war of his generation: World War II.

Two days after he announced the cease-fire, an observant questioner at a White House press conference put the matter to the president.

"I'm struck by how somber you feel. And I was wondering, aren't these great days?" the reporter asked.

Bush replied, "You know, to be very honest with you, I haven't yet felt this wonderfully euphoric feeling that many of the American people feel. And I'm beginning to. I feel much better about it today than I did yesterday. But I think it's that I want to see an end. You mentioned World War II — there was a definitive end to that conflict. And now we have Saddam Hussein still there — the man that wreaked this havoc upon his neighbors."[4]

It was a surprisingly candid admission. The generals' war, triumph though it was, had not been so decisive after all.

Demere rebus tumultum.
— *Seneca*

PART ONE
Preparing for War

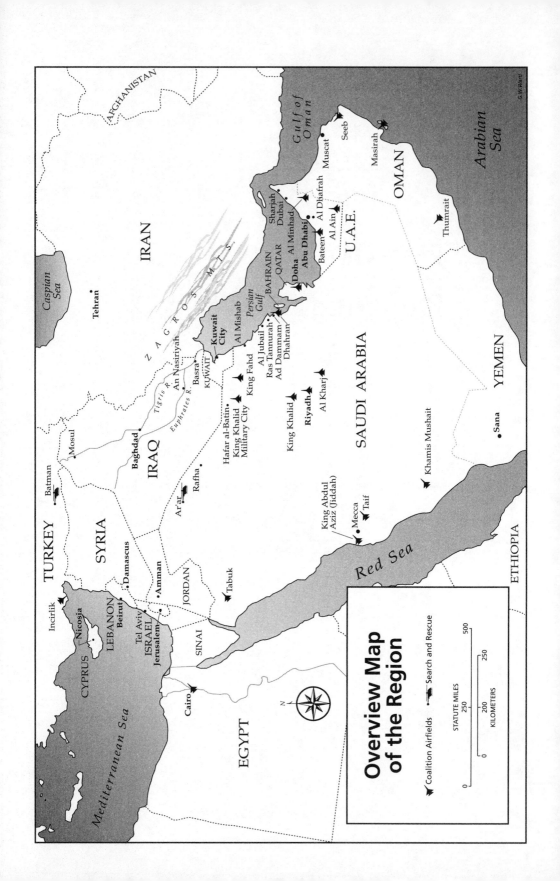

Overview Map
of the Region

Coalition Airfields ◆   Search and Rescue ◆

STATUTE MILES
0   250   500

KILOMETERS
0   200   250

G.W. Ward

AFGHANISTAN

IRAN

Tehran

Caspian Sea

Z A G R O S   M T S.

TURKEY

Batman

Mosul

Baghdad

IRAQ

An Nasiriyah

Basra

Tigris R.

Euphrates R.

SYRIA

Damascus

Amman

JORDAN

Tabuk

Ar'ar

Rafha

Hafar al-Batin

King Khalid Military City

KUWAIT

Kuwait City

Al Mishab

Persian Gulf

Al Jubail

Ras Tannurah

Ad Dammam

Dhahran

King Fahd

BAHRAIN

QATAR

Doha   Abu Dhabi

Al Minhad

Bateen   Al Dhafrah

Al Ain

Sharjah
Dubai

U.A.E.

Gulf of Oman

Muscat

Seeb

Masirah

OMAN

Thumrait

Arabian Sea

King Khalid

Riyadh

Al Kharj

SAUDI ARABIA

Khamis Mushait

YEMEN

Sana

King Abdul Aziz (Jiddah)

Mecca   Taif

Red Sea

ETHIOPIA

Incirlik

CYPRUS

Nicosia

LEBANON

Beirut

Tel Aviv

ISRAEL

Jerusalem

SINAI

Cairo

EGYPT

Mediterranean Sea

N

1

War by Miscalculation

We must not only be able to defend the interests of Kuwait, Saudi Arabia and ourselves against an Iraqi invasion or show of force, we should also make manifest our capabilities and commitments to balance Iraq's power — and this may require an increased visibility for US power . . . If the US were to intervene at all, it would be desirable to do so early in the crisis, before hostilities began, and while escalation might still be avoided.

> — "Capabilities for Limited Contingencies in the Persian Gulf"
> Office of the Secretary of Defense
> June 15, 1979

Let me reassure you, as my Ambassador, Senator Dole and others have done, that my Administration continues to desire better relations with Iraq. We will also continue to support our other friends in the region with whom we have had long-standing ties. We see no necessary inconsistency between these two objectives.

> — President Bush
> Message to Saddam Hussein
> July 28, 1991
> Classified "Secret"

WHEN CHARLIE ALLEN saw the satellite photos on the morning of August 1, 1990, he knew that it was time to sound the klaxon. For a week, Allen had been warning that Iraq would probably attack Kuwait, only to be told by most of his colleagues in the intelligence world that Iraq's muscle flexing was a bluff. But now the invasion preparations were undeniably clear. Overnight Iraq had moved its tanks and artillery close to the Kuwaiti border and flown Frogfoot ground-attack planes to airfields in southern Iraq. Not only did the Iraqis have the military capability to take Kuwait, Baghdad had amassed enough of a force to press on into Saudi Arabia as well. If the Bush administration was going to do anything at all to head off the invasion, it would have to act now.

Rumpled, disorganized, but fiercely independent, Charles E. Allen was a thirty-two-year veteran of the Central Intelligence Agency who had barely missed becoming a casualty of Washington's bureaucratic wars. Allen had the dubious distinction of being the only CIA analyst to figure out that Oliver North was diverting money from the sale of American weapons to Iran and sending the proceeds to the Contras.

Allen's role in bringing the scandal to light had not done him any good. After the Iran-Contra affair broke, his superiors considered sending him on a sabbatical to the Naval War College. Allen balked and was eventually made the National Intelligence Officer (NIO) for Warning. If it looked like a crisis was about to break, it was Allen's job to sound the alert.

To the uninitiated, the job sounded important, but the post was a bureaucratic Siberia. Originally, the main purpose of the CIA was to warn the government about impeding crises and prevent a repetition of Pearl Harbor. Over time, however, warning had become progressively less important a mission for the agency. With the United States and the Soviet Union in a nuclear arms race, warning had become more a technical matter and less a matter for the CIA analysts. Warning was a function performed by American spy satellites and NORAD (North American Aerospace Defense Command), the underground complex that scanned the skies looking for a Russian missile and bomber attack.

The NIO for Warning had a tiny staff, but Allen was an unconventional bureaucrat and used the post to challenge some of the establishment's deeply held assumptions. Allen had questioned the Pentagon's precept that it would have only two weeks' warning of a Soviet attack on Europe. He had predicted that the Soviet withdrawal from Afghanistan would produce a deadly stalemate and not the quick victory for the CIA-backed rebels that the White House envisioned. But warning was a tricky business. Allen had told the White House that a Soviet military crackdown on Lithuania was imminent in February and March 1990. The Soviet forces — nine special operations groups — were active in or near Lithuania but no incursion occurred.

This time Allen was sure. When it came to the Persian Gulf, Allen was neither in the mainstream nor a major player. The big guns were Brent Scowcroft, the national security adviser and former Air Force general; Defense Secretary Dick Cheney; Gen. Colin L. Powell, the chairman of the Joint Chiefs of Staff; Secretary of State James A. Baker; their aides; and, of course, the president himself.

The Bush administration had been pursuing a policy of bringing Iraq back into the family of nations, through diplomacy and economic aid. And the Bush administration's reading of Middle East politics had persuaded it that a full-scale Iraqi invasion of Kuwait was unlikely. Arab countries did not invade other Arab countries, the policy-makers had argued. Iraq did not need to invade Kuwait to wring economic sanctions from the Gulf state. Neither the Egyptians nor the Saudis were alarmed, so why should the Americans be unduly concerned? So went the administration's litany of inaction. The Bush administration was looking at the Gulf through the prism of its diplomacy. It was trying to explain away the obvious.

Allen was not on a first-name basis with the Egyptian or Saudi leaders the Bush administration relied on to gauge Iraqi intentions. He just kept thinking about the Iraqi forces that had taken up positions near the Kuwaiti border. For the past few weeks, there had been a steady escalation of Iraqi war preparations. Now the Iraqis were in the starting blocks, ready to go. The satellite intelligence showed that eight of Iraq's Republican Guard divisions, some 120,000 men and 1,000 tanks, were stationed just north of the Kuwaiti border, including Iraqi Special Forces.

Gathering his staff together later that morning, Allen issued a new "warning of attack," raising the possibility of an Iraqi invasion to at least 70 percent. The highly classified memorandum stated that Saddam Hussein's objective could be to invade Kuwait City and depose the Al-Sabah ruling family.

Then Allen drove down to the White House to personally deliver the message to Richard Haass, the top official on the National Security Council staff for Middle East policy. With his voice rising, Allen warned that the White House had received its final warning. Iraq was going to attack by day's end.

After returning to the Central Intelligence Agency, Allen worked his other contacts as well. Allen called Powell's office to pass the word to the chairman of the Joint Chiefs of Staff. Allen was told that Lee Butler, the three-star aide to Powell, was in a briefing on NATO issues and could not be disturbed. But Allen insisted that Butler be pulled out of the meeting. Then he alerted Richard Clarke, the director of politico-military affairs at the State Department.

In bureaucratic terms, it was a bold, almost reckless move for an intelligence officer who had his share of enemies. But the stakes were high. The Bush administration — and its Arab allies — had yet to issue a stern warning to Baghdad not to invade Kuwait. But Allen's warning on that August day was one that the White House, State Department, Defense Department, and even some of Allen's superiors in the intelligence agencies would find hard to accept. For it meant that the Bush administration's policy toward Baghdad had been an utter failure.

After hearing Allen's presentation, Haass passed the warning to Scowcroft. A high-level meeting was convened late in the afternoon, but the White House was still not in a crisis mode. That meant that if Iraq attacked and the United States launched a military response, it would proceed under the most disadvantageous set of circumstances. The bulk of American troops and warplanes that could be used to defend the Arabian Peninsula were more than 7,000 miles away, and Saddam Hussein's troops would have an enormous head start. With only token American forces in the Gulf, the American military was already way behind the curve.[1]

"WAR WEARY IRAQ"

One of the larger ironies of the Persian Gulf War is that the threat of an Iraqi invasion of Kuwait, which seemed so unthinkable to most of the top echelon of the Bush administration in August 1990, had been anticipated by some of the administration's top national security hands more than a decade earlier.

Led by Paul D. Wolfowitz, a Pentagon analyst who later became undersecretary of defense for policy during the Bush administration, a small group of up-and-coming Defense officials prepared a top secret Pentagon study that underscored the emerging Iraqi threat and outlined a series of possible military responses.

The drafters of the 1979 study, which has never been made public, included some of the brightest and most ambitious young officials in the Pentagon. Dennis B. Ross, who served as Secretary of State Baker's director of policy planning during the Bush administration, was among the authors, as was Geoffrey Kemp, who later worked as a Middle East analyst on the staff of the Reagan administration's National Security Council. The study carried the anodyne title "Capabilities for Limited Contingencies in the Persian Gulf," but it saw Iraq for what it was: a growing menace to the Persian Gulf states.

That Iraq had long coveted Kuwait was clear. When the British granted independence to its protectorate of Kuwait in July 1961, Iraq's strongman, Abdul al-Karim Qassim, claimed sovereignty over the tiny Gulf state. A harbinger of events to come, the 1961 Kuwaiti crisis contained many elements of the Persian Gulf crisis that was to follow almost thirty years later. Qassim wanted Kuwait for its oil fields and long coastline, an attractive prize for Iraq, whose only access to the sea was a waterway, the Shatt al-Arab, whose sovereignty was a regular source of contention with its Persian enemy to the east, and a naval base at Umm Qasr, which was wedged in a sliver of territory between Kuwait and Iran.

In 1961, however, Kuwait asked for British protection before the Iraqis mounted a military threat. British forces were quickly dispatched, and an Arab peacekeeping force took the place of the British several months later and stayed until 1962. To smooth over the affair, the Kuwaitis made substantial loans to the Iraqis, which were never repaid.

Qassim was killed in a coup attempt the next year, but the bloody change of government did not put an end to Iraq's interest in Kuwait.

What made Iraq a growing worry for Wolfowitz and his fellow Pentagon analysts was not just Baghdad's historic designs on its neighbor. Rather, the Pentagon was also worried about several new developments: the fall of the Shah of Iran, Washington's proxy in the turbulent Gulf; the withdrawal of British military power from the region; and the steady buildup of Iraq's armed forces.

Baghdad's campaign to assume a radical leadership role in the Arab world and among the nonaligned nations was another factor. After Egypt and Israel signed the Camp David accords, Iraq mounted an effort to expel Egypt from the Arab League, holding meetings in Baghdad to rally Arab states against the accord. To the dismay of Washington, Saudi King Fahd yielded to Iraqi pressure and signed an anti-Egyptian communiqué during a visit to Baghdad. It was clear that Iraq, with a 280,000-man military, not only was the dominant regional force, but could also use its power to coerce moderate Arab regimes in the Gulf.

"It seems likely that we and Iraq will increasingly be at odds," the 1979 Pentagon study predicted.

To restrain Iraq from expanding its reach into the Arabian Peninsula, the study recommended that the United States make clear that it was prepared to respond to Iraqi aggression with military force, much as the British had done when Iraq threatened to attack Kuwait in 1961. "We must not only be able to defend the interests of Kuwait, Saudi Arabia and ourselves against an Iraqi invasion or show of force, we should also make manifest our capabilities and commitments to balance Iraq's power — and this may require an increased visibility for U.S. power," it said.

If the United States' warnings and occasional muscle flexing were not enough to keep the Iraqis at bay, the United States needed to act fast to send combat forces to the region. The Iraqi troops were on the doorstep of the oil-rich states in the Gulf while American forces were half a world away.

"If the U.S. were to intervene at all, it would be desirable to do so early in the crisis, before hostilities began, and while escalation might still be avoided," the 1979 study advised. The speedy dispatch of Air Force and Navy warplanes and Marine amphibious forces would signal American resolve and deter the Iraqis. At a minimum, an aircraft carrier should be moved into the region when tensions heated up, the study noted.

The costs of delay, the secret report warned, could be high. If Iraqi forces launched a surprise attack, they would be "totally dominant" for the first few weeks and could capture Kuwait, Saudi Arabia's oil fields, and critical airfields and ports in the Saudi kingdom within a week or two. Assuming that the Iraqis refrained from seizing the key facilities, it would still take ten to twenty days for the Americans to move substantial ground forces to the region, leaving the Iraqis with a two to one advantage for at least twenty-five days.[2]

Not everyone in the Pentagon shared the analysts' concerns. When Wolfowitz presented his study on Persian Gulf contingencies to then Defense Secretary Harold Brown, Brown was dismissive. How many times did he have to explain to conservative analysts who seemed to have their own foreign policy that they should not cast Iraq as a major threat? Brown complained in the margin of Wolfowitz's study. To Brown, revolutionary Iran was a greater worry than Baathist Iraq.[3]

The assumption that Iran was the real menace also colored American policy throughout the Carter and Reagan administrations. Iraq's decision in 1980 to launch a bloody, and ultimately futile, war with Iran was seen by top officials in both administrations, not as a confirmation of the expansionist and aggressive nature of the Baathist regime, but as a move that could check the power of revolutionary Iran.

To help the Iraqis, the Reagan administration shared intelligence on Iranian troop dispositions. The Saudis also supported the Iraqi war effort financially and permitted Iraqi combat planes to launch surprise attacks against Iranian targets from Saudi airspace.

The end of the Iran-Iraq War provided the Bush administration with a natural opportunity to reassess Washington's tilt toward Iraq. During the transition from the Reagan to the Bush administration, Zalmay Khalilzad, a member of the State Department's policy planning staff who later worked on Cheney's Pentagon staff during the Gulf War, wrote a memo that portrayed Iraq as a growing threat. Khalilzad urged that Washington respond by strengthening its military position in the region or broadening relations with Iran. With Wolfowitz and Ross occupying top positions in the Bush administration, Washington might have been expected to rethink policy toward Iraq. But instead of challenging the assumptions behind the Reagan administration's approach, the Bush administration ignored the analysis in the 1979 study and expanded the Reagan administration's policy.[4]

After the war, Ross said that bureaucratic considerations had led the State Department to play down the growing Iraqi threat. As the head of the agency's policy planning staff and an aide to Baker, Ross was immersed in the effort to broker a peace settlement between Israel and its Arab neighbors. In order not to usurp all the duties of the State Department's Middle East hands, Ross recalled, he was careful to let the department's Bureau of Near Eastern and South Asian Affairs assume primary responsibility for the Persian Gulf.[5]

But the Bush administration's reluctance to cast Iraq as an adversary actually stemmed from more deep-seated intelligence assumptions and foreign policy calculations. Its fundamental mistake in its dealings with Baghdad, intelligence analysts now concede, was its failure to understand the explosive relationship between the deterioriating Iraqi economy and its outsize military.

Virtually until the day of Iraq's invasion of Kuwait, the Bush administration's policy toward Baghdad was guided by two basic and related assumptions. The first was that Baghdad, having battled Iran to a standstill at great cost in lives and treasure, was a punch-drunk fighter who was tired of war and needed a respite to rebuild. Iraq would continue to update its arsenal of conventional weapons and try to develop weapons of mass destruction, but diplomatic coercion and subversion would be its primary levers of power, not war.

That assessment was outlined in a highly classified National Intelligence Estimate entitled "Iraq: Foreign Policy of a Major Regional Power," which was prepared in 1989 by the CIA and other key intelligence agencies. Its conclusions were seen as almost routine. Normally, an NIE is formally approved by the National Foreign Intelligence Board, a panel of high-level intelligence officials. But the NIE was seen as so noncontroversial that a meeting was never convened and the document was approved in a round of telephone calls, recalled Richard Kerr, the deputy director of the CIA at the time.

"It was kind of a sloppy NIE. There was no debate of senior people," said Kerr. "The estimate did not do a good job of looking to the future. The respite was seen as more temporary."[6]

Sloppy or not, the broad conclusions of the assessment were echoed by civilian Pentagon officials and senior military officers. A classified Pentagon paper prepared during the first year of the Bush administration on "The Rise of Third World Threats" is a case in point.

> Iraq had emerged from the Iran-Iraq war with the largest, most experienced, and best-equipped standing armed forces in the Arab world. Iraq possesses long range strike aircraft, surface-to-surface missiles, a well-developed CW [chemical weapons] program, and the demonstrated capability to use CW. In the next five years Iraq will reduce the size of its ground forces, but will continue to modernize its long range strike aircraft, surface-to-surface missile systems, and CW capability. Iraq is dedicated to acquiring an indigenous ballistic missile production capability. It has, with foreign assistance, extended the range of its Soviet-supplied SCUD SSMs [surface-to-surface missiles], and may be able to begin prototype production of a 1,000 km-range missile in the early 1990s. It is developing biological weapons, and would need five to ten years to develop a nuclear weapon. War weary Iraq will pose a military threat to small neighboring states during this period but will be reluctant to engage in foreign military adventures. It is more likely to resort to diplomacy and subversion to achieve its goals. Attacks against US forces coming to the aid of US allies in the region are unlikely.

Supporting the analysis of a moderate Iraq, the paper predicted a steady reduction of the Iraqi Army and provided a detailed chart ("Iraq's Significant Military Strike Assets"; see p. 11) on Iraq's current and projected military capability.

The second key assumption, encouraged by Middle East specialists and supported by lawmakers from wheat-exporting states, like Sen. Bob Dole of Kansas, held that Saddam Hussein's behavior could be moderated through diplomacy and by encouraging American companies to become involved in rebuilding Iraq. The idea was that Saddam Hussein

Iraq's Significant Military Strike Assets[7]

		1989	1994
Armed Forces:	Personnel	1,200,000	450,000
	Reserves/Militia	500–600,000	50,000
Army	Divisions/Brigades	45/125	25/75
Navy	Surface Combatants	5	4
	Missile Attack Boats	9	15
	Submarines	0	0
Air Force	Bombers	17	17
	Fighter/Bombers	280	300–325
	Fighters	350	350–375
	Attack Helicopters	135	140–150
Missiles	Surface-to-Surface		
	(Scud Launchers)	22	22–25
	Antiship (Launchers)	4	4–6
	Surface-to-Air (Tels)	550–600	650–700

would emerge as a ruthless but pragmatic leader who would deal with Washington out of self-interest.

During a September 1989 National Security Council meeting, President Bush asked Kerr if it was possible that Saddam Hussein could really change.

"The leopard does not change its spots," Kerr replied, noting that the Iraqi leader had taken brutal measures to suppress dissent and was continuing with programs to develop nuclear, chemical, and biological weapons. But Brent Scowcroft, the national security adviser, summed up the consensus by saying that there was little to be lost by trying to build ties with the Saddam Hussein regime, and the president accepted that analysis.

The administration's policy reflecting these twin assumptions was codified in National Security Directive 26, a presidential order on foreign policy, which was signed by Bush in October 1989.

Normal relations between the United States and Iraq would serve our longer-term interests and promote stability both in the Gulf and the Middle East. The United States should propose economic and political incentives for Iraq to moderate its behavior and to increase our influence with Iraq. . . . We should pursue, and seek to facilitate, opportunities for U.S. firms to participate in the reconstruction of the Iraqi economy. . . . Also, as a means of developing access to and influence with the Iraqi defense establishment, the United States should consider sales of non-lethal forms of military assistance, e.g., training courses and medical exchanges, on a case-by-base basis.[8]

The idea of conducting military exchanges with the Iraqis had been promoted in the summer of 1989 when the American embassy to Baghdad sent a message to Washington arguing that the Iraqi government had demonstrated "a modicum of political maturity" by publicly renouncing the use of chemical weapons and offering to compensate Washington for the 1987 attack against the USS *Stark*, an attack Iraq insisted was a mistake.

Supporting the proposal, Gen. H. Norman Schwarzkopf's Central Command, which was responsible for military operations in the Gulf, proposed ten possible initiatives, including training the Iraqi military in disabling mines and aerial reconnaissance and outfitting Saddam Hussein's personal aircraft with flares and others devices to protect it against missile attacks by coup plotters or insurgents. Before the program could be proposed to the Iraqis, the State Department put the plan on hold because of concern over congressional reaction. Eight months later, as Iraqi forces crossed into Kuwait, the command could only be grateful that its program to assist the Iraqi military had fallen through.[9]

All in all, the analysis behind the Bush administration's policy was not without its logic, but it was an exercise in what intelligence analysts call "mirror imaging," a projection of one's own values and attitudes onto a potential adversary. The United States military had gone through a painful contraction after the Second World War, the Korean War, and the Vietnam War, as the Pentagon budget was cut and the country began to attend to its domestic needs, and it seemed reasonable for Iraq to do the same.

In fact, Iraq's deteriorating economy created an incentive for it to keep its military strong. Unemployment was high, and Iraq's economy could not easily accommodate the strains of a large-scale military demobilization, which also threatened social unrest. As the economic vise tightened, Iraq began to view its military might not as an impediment to the rebuilding of the country, but as a way to compel its neighbors to contribute to Iraq's reconstruction and economic development or to grab their wealth if they resisted.

Early in 1990, American and Iraqi relations began their downward spiral. First, Saddam Hussein proclaimed that Iraq needed fifty infantry and armored divisons to guard its security, the number it had during its war with Iran. Then, Iraq demanded that the American Navy leave the Gulf and shortly afterward called in the American chargé d'affaires in Baghdad to protest the flight of an American AWACS plane over Turkey, near the Turkish-Iraqi border. The flight had been part of a NATO exercise and was not directed against Iraq, but the Iraqis nonetheless accused the Americans of spying.

In March, American intelligence confirmed that Iraq had deployed stationary Scud missile launchers within range of all of Israel and Syria, and Baghdad subsequently threatened to "burn half of Israel" with chemical weapons. American intelligence had first detected the Scud missile launchers in the fall of 1989, but imagery analysts had difficulty in persuading the office that oversees the use of spy satellites to arrange for American reconnaissance satellites to look for them. There were many potential dangers to spy on, and the emerging Iraqi missile threat to Israel was not a priority item for Washington.

American customs agents also ran sting operations, catching Iraqi middlemen trying to purchase triggering devices for Baghdad's nuclear weapons program. British customs agents, for their part, intercepted shipments of components for the "Supergun," a huge artillery piece capable of firing rocket-propelled ordnance more than sixty miles.

Despite worldwide appeals for clemency, Iraq also hanged Farzad Bazoft, a reporter for the *London Observer,* as a spy. On Iraq's Armed Forces Day, representatives were invited from around the region to view an ostentatious display of Iraqi military might, an unsubtle way of suggesting that Iraq's neighbors would be safer if they bent to Baghdad's will.

With Iraq rattling the saber and amid allegations of corruption involving the provision of U.S. commodity credits to encourage Iraqi purchases of American grain, the Bush administration launched a review of policy in May 1990. The Bush administration suspended the commodity credits program, which guaranteed $500 million a year in grain sales. Richard Haass and John H. Kelly, the assistant secretary of state for Near Eastern and South Asian Affairs, went to Baghdad to tell the Iraqi government that the future of American-Iraqi relations was in its hands. The administration's policy of trying to moderate Iraq's behavior was faltering, but Washington did not have a new policy of containing Iraqi power to replace it.

Iraq's bellicose behavior was chronicled in the daily intelligence assessments. Worried that Iraq might do something precipitous, particularly against Israel, Allen complained to his staff that the intelligence community was not taking Iraq seriously.

Certainly, the top CIA hierarchy was more relaxed about the Iraqi threat. Not once did CIA Director William Webster and Defense Secretary Dick Cheney discuss the possibility of an Iraqi attack on Kuwait during their weekly meetings of the spring and early summer, according to an aide to the defense secretary. Much of the discussion between the Pentagon chief and the CIA director focused on fears of a war between India and Pakistan. To the extent that Iraq was discussed, the issue was Iraq's efforts to build up its weapons of mass destruction, not its territorial designs to the south.[10]

At the United States Central Command, an Iraqi threat to the Arabian Peninsula was also seen as more theoretical than real. "Iraq is not expected to use military force to attack Kuwait or Saudi Arabia to seize disputed territory or resolve a dispute over oil policy," CENTCOM intelligence experts wrote in a classified assessment of the "Security Environment" in the year 2000.[11]

By July 1990, however, Iraq's bullying behavior had crossed a new threshold even by the Bush administration's standards. On July 16, Tariq Aziz, the Iraqi foreign minister, sent a blistering letter to the Arab League. Even against the backdrop of the ongoing dispute between the Iraqis and the Kuwaitis over boundaries and loan repayments, Aziz's letter was a thunderclap. The Iraqi foreign minister charged that Kuwait's refusal to resolve the border disputes with Iraq, its rejection of Iraqi demands that its multibillion-dollar debt be canceled, and its insistence on pumping oil in excess of OPEC quotas were tantamount to military aggression. Aziz made a similar threat against the United Arab Emirates, which were also exceeding the OPEC production quotas. Kuwait had been a source of soft loans throughout the Iran-Iraq War, and Iraq, $80 billion in debt from the war, was thinking about robbing the bank.

The Bush administration, however, still did not understand the forces that were driving Baghdad. Instead of taking the long view, it treated the Iraqi threats as a short-term disruption that its mid-level diplomats were perfectly capable of handling.

WARNING OF WAR

The task of expressing the Bush administration's concern over the Iraqi threats was left initially to a mid-level State Department official: David Mack, the deputy assistant secretary of state for Near Eastern and South Asian Affairs and a former ambassador to the United Arab Emirates, who complained to Mohammad al-Mashat, Iraq's ambassador to Washington, about the threats at a previously scheduled meeting.

It was not a productive session. Iraq had sent some of its more astute and capable diplomats to Washington, such as Nizar Hamdoon, who by 1990 was a senior official in Iraq's foreign ministry. Ambassador al-Mashat was not among them.

Soon after arriving in Washington, al-Mashat had held a luncheon in honor of Richard Haass. Al-Mashat was late to his own luncheon and then explained that he had been giving an interview to an American television network. When the ambassador was asked about Iraq's mistreatment of the Kurds, he responded that what Iraq was doing was not as bad as the United States' decision to incarcerate Japanese-Americans during the Second World War. Haass responded that al-Mashat had something to learn about diplomacy. Rebuffing charges with invective was the way Baathists brawled in Iraq, but it was not a good way to make inroads in Western public opinion.

True to form, the ambassador confessed to Mack that he had no instructions from Baghdad on the Aziz letter. And then after exposing his ignorance, al-Mashat offered the assurance that Iraq would never make war on another Arab country.

Mack gave the ambassador a copy of the State Department press guidance on the Iraqi threats, which was to be used that day at the department's daily noon briefing. When asked about the Iraqi threats to Kuwait and the UAE, State Department spokesmen were to respond: "I do not have any specific reaction to these statements. However, let me take this opportunity to repeat U.S. policy in the Gulf. We remain determined to ensure the free flow of oil through the Strait of Hormuz and to defend the principle of freedom of navigation. We also remain strongly committed to supporting the individual and collective self-defense of our friends in the Gulf with whom we have deep and long-standing ties."

After the meeting, Mack drafted a classified cable for Secretary of State Baker to send to American embassies in the Middle East recounting the meeting with al-Mashat. The American embassy in Kuwait was to assure the Kuwaitis that the Americans had expressed their unhappiness with Saddam Hussein's threat to Baghdad. American ambassadors in other Gulf states were to query officials as to what actions the Gulf Coordination Council, an association of Gulf states, might take. Baker instructed the embassies in Cairo and Amman to approach the governments there and get their views "as to what the Iraqis hope to accomplish and where this initiative is likely to lead."[12]

April Glaspie, the American ambassador in Baghdad, was also instructed to press for a clarification of Iraq's intentions. Glaspie went to see Hamdoon, but he had nothing to say. Glaspie went back seven straight days in a fruitless attempt to implement her instructions. The Iraqis had, in effect, taken the phone off the hook. But while the State Department was not alarmed, Charles Allen was on the lookout for signs that Iraq was involved in war preparations for an attack on Kuwait. They were not long in coming.

Allen was visiting his wife at the hospital on the morning of July 21 when he received a telephone call from John McCreary, director of the Pentagon-based National Warning Staff.

"They've arrived," McCreary said, speaking cryptically over the nonsecure phone line. Allen knew what he meant. The Republican Guard troops he had been expecting had finally begun arriving at Basra.

Days later, Allen received a report, provided by the British military attaché to Baghdad, who had traveled on July 23 from Kuwait City to Baghdad. Between Basra and Baghdad, the British officer had counted 3,000 vehicles, some from civilian ministries, rapidly moving war matériel toward the Kuwaiti border. Cash-strapped countries did not take steps that could interfere with their economy just for a bluff, he figured.

On July 25, Allen issued a "warning of war" stating that there was a 60 percent chance that Iraqi forces would attack Kuwait. Making predictions about the actions of third world despots was a tricky business. In an age of high-technology surveillance, the United States had the means to monitor troop movements, but seeing was not necessarily believing. Adversaries could still achieve a measure of surprise by creating an alternative explanation for their war preparations and masking the movement of forces with a web of words. In essence, Allen was hedging his bets, but in forecasting a better-than-even chance that Iraqi forces would cross the Kuwaiti border, he was discounting the dominant argument within the administration that Saddam Hussein was posturing to obtain economic concessions from Kuwait. Only after the invasion would the intelligence community learn a final incriminating bit of information. Before moving its troops to the Kuwaiti border, Iraq had ordered satellite photos of Kuwait and northern Saudi Arabia from SPOT, the French commercial satellite reconnaissance service. The photos had been provided with no questions asked. On July 26, Allen visited Haass to underscore his warning, bringing along one of the intelligence community's top imagery analysts, Thomas Lewis. The analyst graphically laid out the rapidity and magnitude of the Iraqi buildup, but Allen left feeling that Haass had not been persuaded.

While Allen and his staff had worked on their warning, officials from the Defense Intelligence Agency had also been monitoring the situation at the National Military Intelligence Center at the Pentagon. At the

DIA, Walter P. Lang, the agency's senior Iraq analyst, also found himself ahead of the crowd. Like Allen, Lang was concerned that the Iraqis might lash out, but his superiors tended to discount Iraq's moves as a bluff. The DIA's National Military Intelligence Center at the Pentagon provided an escalating series of warnings, or "watch notices," to American forces. The warnings were not as clear as Lang would have liked, but the increasing Iraqi military preparations were clear.[13]

On July 21, the DIA declared "WATCHCON III," the lowest level of alert, noting that elements of the Republican Guard had been deployed close to the Kuwaiti border. The classified notice read:

This latest development is probably a continuation of Saddam Husayn's campaign of intimidation and force posturing designed to raise oil prices and end cheating on oil production quotas. However, this relocation does significantly reduce warning time if the Iraqis were to decide to conduct cross border operations.

Three days later, the DIA raised the alert level to "WATCHCON II."

Iraqi ground force strength opposite the Kuwaiti border has attained roughly corps level. Necessary logistics infrastructure is assessed by DIA to be in place and fully functional. These forces would initiate military operations against Kuwait at any time with no warning. The threat to U.S. citizens and regional interests arising from this rapid military buildup is significant. DIA continues to closely monitor the situation and to task collection assets as necessary.

With the NIO for Warning and the DIA underscoring the Iraqi presence near the Kuwaiti border, Central Command's planners drew up a list of steps the Bush administration could take to signal its determination to defend the Gulf, measures that closely resembled the thinking in the 1979 Pentagon study.

The United States could speed up the USS *Independence,* an aircraft carrier that was in the Strait of Malacca en route to the North Arabian Sea after training near Diego Garcia, an island in the Indian Ocean. It could begin to move the Maritime Prepositioning Ships (MPS) filled with tanks and other equipment for the Marines, from Diego Garcia to Al Jubail, Saudi Arabia. The Air Force could send a squadron or so of F-15s to Saudi Arabia if permitted. The planes were bound to be picked up by Jordan's radar stations as they flew across Egypt, and Jordan would have quickly told Iraq that the United States was sending forces to the region.

The fourth option was to send B-52 bombers to Diego Garcia, load them up with bombs, and have them ready to go.

The options went up to the JCS and that was the last the CENT-COM staff heard of them. In meetings of the Deputies Committee, a high-level group of interagency officials, Robert M. Kimmitt, the undersecretary of state for political affairs, suggested to Wolfowitz and Adm. David Jeremiah, the vice chairman of the Joint Chiefs of Staff, that the Pentagon accelerate the deployment of a carrier to the North Arabian Sea. Wolfowitz, in keeping with the recommendations of his 1979 study, also suggested moving the MPS ships.

But with moderate Arab states making encouraging statements about the prospect of a diplomatic resolution to the dispute between Iraq and Kuwait, neither Kimmitt nor Wolfowitz pressed the White House to support their recommendations.

Nor was Colin Powell, the JCS chairman, eager to send forces. Powell distrusted hard-nosed civilians who were quick to deploy forces without a clear idea of where the crisis could lead. "I was not reluctant," Powell insisted after the war. But he acknowledged: "Clearly, I did not leap on it and say 'let's do this right away.' "

But the end result was that the Bush administration separated diplomacy from the threat of American military power.[14]

The Bush administration did take one small step at the suggestion of the UAE. Unlike his Gulf neighbors, Sheikh Mohammed bin Zayed, the defense chief for the Emirates, was inclined to take Iraq's threats seriously. During the Iran-Iraq War, Iraq had struck an offshore oil drilling platform that belonged to the Emirates. The Iraqis had said that the attack was a mistake, but the Emirates were not so sure. The UAE wanted the United States to send them two KC-135 refueling tankers. The refueling planes would extend the range of the Emirates' Mirage 2000 planes and enable them to stay on station longer, thus helping the tiny Gulf state fend off an air attack. More important, the American planes would be a signal that the Emirates had a powerful friend in their corner.

That was not the only thing the Emirates wanted. In a part of the operation that has never been made public, the Sheikh sought a ground link to American AWACS and E-2C Hawkeye radar planes so that they could monitor the air traffic in the Gulf.

Although the dispatch of the planes and the radar would be a modest gesture, even that was not a foregone conclusion. Norman Schwarzkopf, the CENTCOM commander, strongly supported the request, not as a way to demonstrate resolve against Iraq, whose saber rattling he was inclined to discount, but, he recalled, as a means of forging closer ties to the Emirates. The Defense Department's civilians supported the request, but the State Department's Bureau of Near Eastern and South Asian Affairs initially opposed it, arguing that the Emirates would be better advised to work with the Saudis. Even a modest show of American force would draw protests from some of the deeply conservative states in the region and thus complicate American diplomacy there. The Saudis, however, had no interest in participating in such an exercise with the Emirates. After a Saturday night telephone call between Wolfowitz and Kimmitt, the State Department's Near Eastern Bureau was overruled.

The operation was code-named Ivory Justice. On July 24, two KC-135 refueling planes and one C-141 arrived in Al Dhafrah. Rear Adm. William Fogarty, the commander of the American Middle East fleet, set up a zone defense in the Gulf, deploying his ships so their radars could give early warning. The operation did not go smoothly. The refueling probes on the KC-135 were not compatible with the Emirates' French-made Mirage planes, and the Emirates' pilots had no previous experience with refueling operations.

Politically, there were some rough times as well. The Emirates were insistent that the Bush administration not publicize the dispatch of the planes. Even with the Emirates' apprehensions about Iraq, the ideal American force was an unobtrusive one. When word of the "exercise" got around Washington and was confirmed by Pentagon spokesman Pete Williams, the Emirates angrily denied that anything other than routine training was taking place.

For his part, Prince Bandar bin Sultan, the Saudi Arabian ambassador to Washington, quietly complained about the move. The United States was right to honor the request of its friends, the prince said, but the Emirates should not have asked.

Nor was Riyadh alone. Egyptian President Hosni Mubarak told President Bush that the Arab states were capable of working out a diplomatic solution and that the United States should keep a low military profile in the Gulf. Even with Iraqi forces gathering on the Kuwaiti border, the dispute looked to Riyadh and Cairo like something that could be handled within the Arab family.

Despite the technical and political difficulties, Ivory Justice established a basis for future cooperation with the Emirates. It also set the stage for the final diplomatic exchanges between Washington and Baghdad. After officially notifying Iraq of the exercise, Glaspie and the UAE ambassador to Baghdad were called to a midnight session at the

Foreign Ministry. Ivory Justice demonstrated that even minor American deployments in the Gulf could get Baghdad's attention. But the forces sent to the region were essentially symbolic. Iraq would have no problems bending Kuwait to its will as long as the American military presence was not expanded. To make sure it was not, Saddam Hussein summoned Glaspie to an impromptu July 25 meeting.

SADDAM HUSSEIN'S MESSAGE OF FRIENDSHIP TO THE AMERICAN PEOPLE

When Glaspie was ushered into the Presidential Palace, the Iraqi leader was accompanied by two notetakers, an interpreter, and his office director.

A career foreign service officer who had been born in the Middle East, Glaspie had ascended step-by-step through the ranks at a time when diplomacy was a man's preserve and had made it her life. She had been posted in Amman, Kuwait City, Beirut, Cairo, Tunis, and Damascus and had headed the State Department's office of Arabian Peninsula Affairs before taking up her ambassadorial post. She was fluent in Arabic and a whole-hearted supporter of the administration's strategy to use its influence to "moderate" Saddam Hussein. Unmarried, she lived unostentatiously in Baghdad with her mother and dog.

Glaspie saw her role as keeping open the channels of communication between Washington and the Iraqi leadership, but this was the first time that she had ever been invited for a solo audience with the Iraqi president. The request came so suddenly that Glaspie did not have time to arrange to bring a notetaker or an interpreter of her own, but she did not feel that she needed one.

Nor did Glaspie have time to ask for fresh instructions, but she was not operating without guidance from Washington. The day before, a State Department cable had gone out under Baker's name providing American embassies with guidance on "US Reaction to Iraqi Threats In the Gulf."

> The U.S. is concerned about the hostile implications of recent Iraqi statements directed against Iraq's neighbors, Kuwait and the United Arab Emirates. While we take no position on the border delineation issue raised by Iraq with respect to Kuwait, or on other bi-lateral disputes, Iraqi statements suggest an intention to resolve outstanding disagreements by the use of force, an approach which is contrary to UN-Charter principles. The implications of having oil production and pricing policy in the Gulf determined and enforced by Iraqi guns are disturbing.[15]

According to Glaspie's diplomatic cables, which have never been officially released, Saddam Hussein began the meeting by telling the ambassador he wanted better relations with Washington and launched into a long monologue. Seeking to justify Iraq's pressure campaign against Kuwait and the UAE, the Iraqi leader argued that they were engaging in economic warfare against Iraq by maintaining a high rate of oil production. The "maneuvers" that the United States was conducting with the Emirates and Kuwait were encouraging those states to be intransigent, he said, assuming incorrectly that Kuwait was participating in Ivory Justice.

The Iraqi leader next spoke bluntly about the possibility of a new Gulf war. "Do not push us to it; do not make it the only option left with which we can protect our dignity," he said.

Accentuating the positive, Glaspie said that President Bush had instructed her to broaden American relations with Iraq, a commitment Bush had demonstrated by opposing economic sanctions.

"Is it not reasonable for us to be concerned when the president and the foreign minister both say publicly that Kuwaiti actions are the equivalent of military aggression, and then we learn that many units of the Republican Guard have been sent to the border? Is it not reasonable for us to ask, in the spirit of friendship, not confrontation, the simple question: what are your intentions?" Glaspie asked.

Saddam Hussein said that it was a reasonable question but complained that Iraq was in such difficult financial condition that pensions for widows and orphans would have to be cut, at which point the interpreters and one of the notetakers broke down and wept, an elaborate piece of political theater that Glaspie reported without comment.

Before the meeting ended, the Iraqi leader left the room to take a telephone call from Egyptian President Hosni Mubarak, who informed him that the Kuwaitis had agreed to a round of negotiations over their disputes with the Iraqis. Returning, he reported that he had told Mubarak that "nothing will happen until the meeting." And nothing would happen after the meeting if the Kuwaitis "give us some hope," added the Iraqi leader, leaving open the possibility of military action against Kuwait.

After the meeting ended, Glaspie hurried back to her office and fired off the first of two cables to the State Department. The first one was a brief summation of the meeting and was marked "NODIS," meaning distribution of the communication was to be severely limited even among officials with clearances for classified and diplomatically sensitive information.

Speaking of his conviction that our Governments do not sufficiently understand each other, especially since "some circles" of the USG continue to work to undermine his Government and his policies, Saddam stressed that he put his hope in President Bush and Secretary Baker, who are fine and honorable men, as is NEA Assistant Secretary Kelly. He asked me to return to the U.S. to explain Iraq's concerns to the President, who he supposed might have questions.

Comment: Saddam, who in the memory of the current diplomatic corps, has never summoned an ambassador, is worried. He does not want to further antagonize us. With the UAE maneuvers, we have fully caught his attention, and that is good. I believe we would now be well-advised to ease off on public criticism of Iraq until we see how the negotiations develop.[16]

After Iraq's invasion of Kuwait, Glaspie would be assailed as an accommodationist who failed take a tough stand with Saddam Hussein when it mattered most. In fact, the ambassador was operating within the Bush administration's policy framework. Her real failing was her recommendation to avoid tough talk, which reinforced the administration's inclination to see Iraq's military preparations in the most benign possible light. There were few officials in the American government who understood how far Saddam Hussein was prepared to go to fulfill his ambitions, and for all her erudition Glaspie was not among them.

At the Pentagon, Wolfowitz was not pleased by Glaspie's performance. Traveling with Secretary of State James Baker for a meeting with Soviet Foreign Minister Eduard Shevardnadze, Dennis Ross was not impressed either. Glaspie had violated Henry Kissinger's dictum that one should never come out second best in one's own cable, Ross quipped. Glaspie's meeting, however, was not the last word. A presidential reply would have to be sent to the Iraqi leader, and the Pentagon saw that as an opportunity to send a tougher message.

The task of drafting President Bush's reply was assigned to the Middle East specialists at the State Department and the White House's National Security Council staff. And unlike Wolfowitz and Ross, they were not unhappy with the way Glaspie had handled the issue.

As Richard Haass, the senior NSC aide on Middle East issues saw it, the crisis had passed. Iraqi troops continued to mass on the Kuwaiti border, but the Saudis were hosting a meeting in Jiddah to adjudicate the dispute between Iraq and Kuwait. Egypt's Mubarak and Jordan's King Hussein had told the White House that the crisis could be solved within the Arab family. Prince Bandar was telling everyone that there was nothing to worry about. The Kuwaitis had not asked for help. Haass saw the presidential message as an opportunity to acknowledge the easing of the tensions and reaffirm the policy of moderation.

Not surprisingly, the moderate theme prevailed. The draft message began by welcoming all of Saddam Hussein's encouraging statements about seeking a peaceful solution to the "tensions" between Iraq and Kuwait, as if both nations were responsible for the crisis. It did not condemn the Iraqi threats that were the source of those tensions. Nowhere did it warn Saddam Hussein that the United States would regard an attack on Kuwait as a threat to American vital interests. The Iraqi leader's threats against Israel and the Gulf states, his dismal record on human rights, and Baghdad's efforts to acquire weapons of mass destruction were referred to elliptically as "certain Iraqi policies and activities" that were of concern to the United States, but not to the extent that they would interrupt efforts to strengthen relations between Washington and Baghdad. The message itself was all of three paragraphs:

I was pleased to learn of the agreement between Iraq and Kuwait to begin negotiations in Jeddah to find a peaceful solution to the current tensions between you. The United States and Iraq both have a strong interest in preserving the peace and stability of the Middle East. For this reason, we believe that differences are best resolved by peaceful means and not by threats involving military force or conflict.

I also welcome your statement that Iraq desires friendship, rather than confrontation with the United States. Let me reassure you, as my Ambassador, Senator Dole and others have done, that my Administration continues to desire better relations with Iraq. We will also continue to support our other friends in the region with whom we have had long-standing ties. We see no necessary inconsistency between these two objectives.

As you know, we still have fundamental concerns about certain Iraqi policies and activities, and we will continue to raise these concerns with you in a spirit of friendship and candor, as we have in the past both to gain a better understanding of your interests and intentions and to ensure that you understand our concerns. I completely agree that both our governments must maintain open channels of communication to avoid misunderstanding and in order to build a more durable foundation for improving our relations.

This was not the rap on the knuckles that Cheney's aides had in mind. The Defense Department got a look at the message when Arthur

G. Hughes, a deputy assistant secretary of defense for Near East Affairs who served as Cheney's point man on the Middle East, attended a reception for a visiting delegation of Egyptian defense officials at the Navy Museum in southeast Washington. Milling with the guests, Hughes was approached by Jock P. Covey, a top official in the State Department's Bureau of Near Eastern and South Asian Affairs, who used the chance meeting to show Hughes a copy of the communication.

Hughes did not like what he saw. With his mustache and quiet manner, Hughes had a professorial demeanor. But the long-time foreign service officer and former Army intelligence officer fit in well with his conservative Defense Department superiors. To Hughes, the almost obsequious tone of the draft defeated the whole purpose of sending a presidential message. The Defense Department's tactics had backfired. It had sought a presidential message to toughen the American stance toward Baghdad and instead the White House was echoing Glaspie's line.

Hughes consulted briefly with Henry S. Rowen, the assistant secretary of defense for International Security Affairs, who was also at the reception, and they both agreed that there was only one thing to do. Hughes asked Covey to hold up the message while the Defense Department prepared an alternative.

The next day, however, when Hughes called over to the White House he learned that the request had been for naught. The presidential message had been sent out, dispatched to Glaspie in a July 28 cable from Lawrence Eagleburger, the deputy secretary of state, who was running the department while James Baker was in Siberia with Soviet Foreign Minister Eduard Shevardnadze.

Glaspie was instructed to deliver the message orally before she departed Iraq on home leave on July 30 or, if that was not possible, to deliver its main points in a "non-paper," a unofficial diplomatic communication that Washington could disown if it somehow leaked. The ambassador was to tell Saddam that Bush's message was "in the nature of an interim reply." There would be time to prepare a more comprehensive message, or so it appeared at the time.[17]

Eagleburger himself had read neither the message nor the instructions that went out over his name. He was convinced that the crisis in the Gulf would blow over and had delegated the whole matter to his subordinates.

Nor was Eagleburger alone. Except for Charles Allen, the CIA was providing mixed messages. On July 30, many of the agency's top experts met to discuss the tense situation in the Gulf and a pending report by the National Intelligence Council, a top-level body of intelligence officials, on Iraq's intentions. It was clear that Allen's assessment was a minority view. When his staff argued that Iraq was preparing a major attack, their views were shunted aside.

The next day, the council completed its memorandum on the situation in the Gulf. Drafted by the National Intelligence Officer for the Near East and South Asia on behalf of the entire intelligence community, the report said that military action was likely unless Kuwait made rapid concessions. But the report went on to say that a major attack to seize most or all of Kuwait was unlikely. In essence, the threat identified was a limited attack to seize the Rumaila oil field or Kuwait's islands and buttress Baghdad's position in the talks. It was a variation on the theme that the Iraqi troops were part of a bluff designed to extract economic concessions from Kuwait.

Rarely were the predictions of the agency's Middle East hands so quickly overtaken by events. Copies of the assessment were still in the council's official registry of documents, awaiting dissemination to policy-makers on August 1. Shortly after Iraq attacked, David Gries, the vice chairman of the council, quickly withdrew the assessment.

Then in the weeks following the invasion, CIA analysts prepared a new analysis of the Iraqi leader's decision making on war and peace. Studying Saddam Hussein's decision on the Iran-Iraq War, it concluded that the Iraqi leader was impulsive and prone to strategic miscalculation.[18]

WARNING OF ATTACK

August 1 was Eagleburger's birthday, and the deputy secretary of state was enjoying the day at his family farm in Charlottesville, Virginia, leaving the State Department in the hands of Robert Kimmitt, the third-ranking State official.

At the White House, Brent Scowcroft was focusing on plans to announce a 25 percent cut in American forces and restructure the military. Bush was to announce the plan, intended to rebut congressional criticism that the Bush administration was moving too slowly to adapt to the end of the cold war, at an August 2 speech in Aspen, Colorado. Scowcroft planned to fly to Aspen, along with Cheney, to background the White House press corps.

At the Pentagon, Schwarzkopf met with Cheney, Powell, and the JCS to go over the plan the command had been working on for the defense of Saudi Arabia and discuss the military's options for responding to an Iraqi attack.

By this time Schwarzkopf was persuaded that the Iraqis were planning some kind of military operation. CENTCOM's intelligence experts had told Schwarzkopf that Iraqi marines, outfitted with bridging equipment, were near Bubiyan Island. Still, CENTCOM's chief was persuaded by the majority view within the intelligence community that Iraq's main aim was coercion, not occupation.

After the session, Cheney asked Schwarzkopf for his assessment. "I said I think they are going to attack. But they are going to take Rumaila and Bubiyan and then stop," Schwarzkopf recalled after the war. "Somebody said: 'if that happens what do we do?' I said not a damn thing. The world will not care. It will be a fait accompli."[19]

Most of Washington's Arab allies were not alarmed, either. Prince Bandar had been exultant when Iraq and the Kuwaitis agreed to meet in Jiddah for talks and departed for London, the first stop on his summer vacation. Kuwait's ambassador to Washington, Sheikh Saud Nasir al-Sabah, had been receiving regular intelligence briefings on the Iraqi troop deployment but was powerless to act. The emir and the top officials of the Kuwaiti Foreign Ministry were convinced that the Iraqis were bluffing.

At the CIA, however, Allen was becoming more and more concerned. The latest satellite photos showed the dramatic overnight movement of Iraqi armor and artillery forces closer to the border with Kuwait and the sudden movement of Soviet-made Frogfoot, Fitter, and Flogger ground-attack aircraft to airfields in southern Iraq. The Iraqis had also moved Hip and Hind helicopters to southern Iraq. Allen and John McCreary, the director of the National Warning Staff, thought the Iraqis could use the helicopters to carry Republican Guard special forces to assault Kuwait City. Those sorts of preparations, Allen concluded, were not part of a bluff but final invasion preparations. Not only did the Iraqis have the military capability to take Kuwait, they could move into Saudi Arabia as well. The military actions came against the backdrop of the collapse of the talks between Iraq and Kuwait.

Allen issued a new "warning of attack," raising the possibility of an Iraqi attack to at least 70 percent, and then began to work his contacts within the administration. The warning memorandum stated that Saddam Hussein's objective could be to take Kuwait City and depose the Al-Sabah ruling family.

Then Allen tried to mobilize the administration, visiting the White House to talk to Haass and phoning the Pentagon and the State Department. After Allen talked to Richard Clarke, the director of politico-military affairs at the State Department, Clarke called Kimmitt, who had been chairing the Deputies Committee meeting on Iraq while Gates was on vacation, hiking in the Pacific Northwest. Kimmitt decided to hold a meeting at the State Department later that afternoon. At the CIA, Allen also contacted the National Intelligence Officer for Near East/South Asia, who was preparing the talking points for Kerr's presentation at the deputies meeting later that afternoon. Allen said that Saddam Hussein had moved his forces to final attack positions and that an offensive was only hours away. That ran counter to the basic analysis by the NIO for the Near East that Baghdad's goal was economic concessions.

Meanwhile, the DIA, at Lang's prodding, echoed Allen's alarm. It went to "WATCHCON I," the highest level of alert.

> Talks between Kuwait and Iraq, which began on 31 July, broke down today after Iraqi negotiators refused to soften their hardline positions. Both delegations have reportedly returned home . . . The talks collapsed due to unspecified territorial demands and a tone of threats by the Iraqi representatives. Iraqi press had earlier implied that Baghdad would demand that Kuwait withdraw from disputed territory, pay $2.4 billion to Iraq for stolen oil, and cancel war debts (estimated at $10 billion). . . . Iraq demanded as much as $27 billion in compensation. Kuwaiti negotiators reportedly proposed consideration of the border issue by an international body similar to that created to resolve the Israeli-Egyptian Taba territorial dispute. Iraq reportedly agreed, on the condition that all the meetings of such an arbitration body be held in Baghdad. When Kuwait refused this Iraqi demand, the Iraqi negotiators reportedly angrily stormed out of the room, and returned to Baghdad. Iraqi press has been pessimistic about the talks, and a leading Iraqi newspaper stated on 1 August that a breakthrough in Jeddah is impossible.

After taking note of Iraq's latest military preparations, the DIA watch notice continued:

> Although there is as yet no evidence of a direct move against Kuwait, the combination of the breakdown in the talks, the latest Iraqi military moves, and the resumption of harsh Iraqi rhetoric all point toward military action by Iraq, although these developments may only be part of an escalation in psychological pressure by Baghdad. Saddam is undoubtedly prepared to cross the border in force. In fact, the Iraqi force now assembled is sufficient not only to overrun all of Kuwait, but the Eastern Province of Saudi Arabia if necessary.[20]

Kimmitt convened the deputies meeting at 5PM — ten hours after Allen had called on Haass to warn him that an Iraqi attack was likely. The United States was not working from a position of strength. Nothing had been done to strengthen the American military position in the Gulf. The Saudis, whose facilities the United States would need to mount a major military response in the region, were not taking the threat seriously. What the United States could have done unilaterally it had not done. No bombers had been dispatched to Diego Garcia. The Maritime Prepositioning Ships had not been sent toward the Gulf. There were no amphibious forces in the region; the 2,000-man Marine Expeditionary Unit, which might have been sent to the Gulf, was in Subic Bay, as a hedge against instability in the Philippines. The *Independence* was still four days away from the Gulf in terms of steaming time. Indeed, early that day Kimmitt had received a State Department memo indicating that the JCS continued to oppose expediting moving the carrier to the North Arabian Sea because it would interfere with the training program the Navy planned near Diego Garcia.

When the meeting got under way, Kerr provided an analysis that reflected the yet-to-be-disseminated paper by the National Intelligence Council. Kerr indicated that an attack was likely, but discounted a major attack.

"Our formulation on this was that at a minimum they would take the oil field and the islands but they had the capability to do more than that," Kerr recalled.

Kimmitt and other participants, however, recall that the scenario Kerr emphasized was a limited land grab, not an all-out invasion that would bring Saddam Hussein's Republican Guard to the frontiers of Saudi Arabia.

"Why would Iraq do just that?" Kimmitt recalled asking. "If the oil fields and the islands are what Saddam Hussein wants, why wouldn't he take more so that he could bargain back to what he wants?"[21]

As Kimmitt brought the meeting to a close, it was agreed that Haass should meet with Scowcroft and consider sending a stronger message to Saddam. Meanwhile, Sandra L. Charles, another NSC aide on the Middle East, would draw up talking points for a presidential phone call to Saudi King Fahd to get his latest assessment of the situation.

But there was no longer time to send a new message or to ask the Saudis for their view of the matter. At 5PM, Saad Nasir, Kuwait's Washington ambassador, was advised by the Americans that the Iraqis were about to cross the border and immediately called Kuwait. The ambassador was told that there was no confirmation of an attack and there was no request for assistance. By 7PM EST, he received an urgent phone call. Iraqi forces were deep inside Kuwait.

In Tampa, CENTCOM planners had been on an invasion watch since mid-July, doing one what-if exercise after another. What if Saddam just takes the Rumaila oil field? What if his troops kill the emir of Kuwait but do not continue south? What if the Iraqi forces continue into Saudi Arabia? What if the Iraqis attack oil tankers carrying Kuwaiti crude but do not attack Kuwait? Round and round they had gone, but no instructions had come from Washington to make any military preparations. Exhausted and frustrated after weeks of long hours, Schwarzkopf allowed the staff to go home early to get some rest. It was not clear if Saddam Hussein was going to strike Kuwait or if the United States would respond if he did. The planners left about 3PM.

Six hours later, one of CENTCOM's planners received a call from headquarters. "You are not going to believe this, but it has started. You better get back here," he was told.

After the war, lawmakers and pundits assailed the Bush administration for its efforts to build a bridge to the Saddam Hussein regime. But both the administration and its critics missed the point. The problem was not so much with the effort to "moderate" Iraqi behavior as it was with the failure to make clear the costs of Iraqi aggression should the policy of working with the Iraqis fail.

The invasion of Kuwait might have been averted. The 1979 Pentagon study had advised that the military needed to flex its muscles early in a crisis to deter an Iraqi invasion. But the administration never acted on that recommendation. It had not been so much a failure of intelligence as a failure to act on available information. An elementary lesson of deterrence had been lost. The Bush administration drew a line in the sand in firm, deep strokes, but not until the Iraqis had already crossed it.

The Bush administration's commitment to its Baghdad policy was one reason. Instead of seeing Iraq's war preparations for what they were, it had embraced the most benign explanation of the Iraqi moves. Only those outside the policy consensus, such as Allen, could see the Iraqi moves for what they were.

The Bush administration's desire not to cross the moderate Arabs, who also misread Iraq's intentions, also encouraged a policy of inaction.

Powell's aversion to using American military to send diplomatic signals also contributed to the administration's failure to act. In effect, Powell's reluctance to shift an aircraft carrier toward the Gulf or break out the Maritime Prepositioning Ships had deprived the administration of the tools it needed to hedge its bets. Ironically, Powell's efforts to avoid an ill-considered use of force actually increased the prospects for American military involvement in the region.

But Baghdad had miscalculated, too. Given Iraq's military, economic, and territorial ambitions, Washington and Baghdad were bound to find themselves at odds sooner or later, and from Iraq's standpoint later should have been better than sooner.

In that sense, the Bush administration's policy failure worked to the United States' advantage. The military confrontation would take place at a time of American strength and Iraqi weakness. It would occur before the cuts in American military forces were too far along, at a time when the end of the cold war had freed up American military resources around the world and before Iraq had developed a nuclear bomb. But first Washington would have to scramble to defend Saudi Arabia and to determine whether it wanted to try to roll back the Iraqi invasion of Kuwait.

2

Drawing the Line

We are the only ones who can tell the President what to do. He will look to us. The others can't do it. So what do we do?

— Defense Secretary Richard Cheney
August 2, 1990

We must start with policy and diplomatic overtures. We can't make a case for losing lives for Kuwait, but Saudi Arabia is different. I am opposed to dramatic action without the President having popular support.

— Gen. Colin L. Powell
Chairman, Joint Chiefs of Staff
August 2, 1990

THE AFTERNOON following Iraq's invasion of Kuwait, Dick Cheney, Colin Powell, and their top aides gathered in the secretary of defense's conference room at the Pentagon to figure out what to do. Even as the battle lines were being drawn in the Gulf, they were being drawn in the administration as well. But the lineup ran counter to what most of the public would have expected. The civilians were looking for a way to roll back the Iraqi gains while the military was urging caution.

By any measure the problem was an imposing one. When the Iraqis attacked, they did so with the cream of their army, the Republican Guard, and their special operations forces. An armored and mechanized division crossed the Kuwait-Iraq border and headed south to Al Jahrah at the head of the Gulf of Kuwait. It then wheeled to the east to occupy Kuwait City.

At the same time, helicopters carried special forces directly to the city while commandos made an amphibious landing from the sea, in an attempt to seize key government facilities in the city and capture the emir of Kuwait, Sheikh Jaber al-Ahmed al-Sabah. The Iraqis failed to capture the emir, who escaped to Saudi Arabia, but did kill his younger brother, Sheikh Fahd, who was still in the palace when the commandos attacked it, a disturbing sign for the conservative monarchs and sheikhs in the Gulf.

Meanwhile, a second Republican Guard armored division swept south below the Gulf of Kuwait to dispose of the remaining feeble resistance by the Kuwaiti army. The well-coordinated offensive also quickly captured the Kuwaiti airfields at Ali al Salem, Al Jaber, and Kuwait City. Kuwaiti aircraft that made it into the air fled to bases in Saudi Arabia. Adding to the worry, Iraqi T-72 battle tanks were also rolling toward the Kuwaiti border with Saudi Arabia, where they would be dug into defensive positions hastily prepared by combat engineers.

All in all, it was an impressive performance by the Iraqis notwithstanding the fact that they had met negligible resistance. Of further concern, Iraqi reinforcements for the assault force were pouring into Kuwait from their assembly areas in southern Iraq.[1]

In the weeks leading up to Iraq's invasion of Kuwait, the Bush administration had never confronted the question of whether it would go to war for Kuwait or what military steps it would take to defend the rest of the Arabian Peninsula. Now Cheney and Powell were struggling to come up with the answers.

A former Republican congressman from Wyoming and White House chief of staff for President Ford, Cheney had never met a weapon system he didn't like. Cheney had never served in the military, a point of some sensitivity for the defense secretary. With strong conservative credentials, Cheney had been criticized as an unreconstructed Cold Warrior, but he saw a role for himself in making sure that the arms cuts Congress was pressing on the Pentagon did not go too far too fast. Cheney had always thought the Persian Gulf was important. And he did not like the idea of Saddam Hussein's troops occupying Kuwait and sitting astride the Gulf oil supply. It would give Baghdad political influence, if not outright physical control, over the Saudi oil flow.

Cheney had planned to accompany President Bush, who was scheduled to deliver a major speech that day in Aspen, Colorado, outlining a new Pentagon plan to cut American forces by 25 percent and shifting the focus of American military planning from the Soviet Union to regional threats. But the defense secretary had decided against the trip in order to try and get the Pentagon's recommendations in order. Cheney was not looking just to stop the Iraqis, he was searching for a way to reverse the invasion.

But Cheney was only one half of the Pentagon team. Powell, the chairman of the JCS and a former national security adviser to President Reagan, was a powerful voice in the Defense Department's military and political policies. Powell cut an imposing figure, but behind the scenes he defined American military objectives in terms of what the public was prepared to stand for and the all-but-certain likelihood of success.

Most of the time Powell and Cheney worked as a team, and when they had their differences, they settled them behind closed doors. But this was different. The exchange between Cheney and Powell — recorded in previously undisclosed notes taken by an aide — was one of the clearest signs of the military's reluctance to take on the mission of liberating Kuwait.

Cheney was thinking big. "We need an objective," he said. Should it be to get the Iraqis out of Kuwait or topple Saddam Hussein himself? And would the American people support military action to put Kuwait's emir back on his throne? Cheney asked.

But Powell was trying to redirect the debate to the more limited task of defending Saudi Arabia. He predicted that the Iraqis would withdraw their troops and that the American public would not support military action to force the Iraqis out if they did not.

"The next few days Iraq will withdraw, but Saddam Hussein will put his puppet in. Everyone in the Arab world will be happy," Powell said. "I don't see the senior leadership taking us into armed conflict for the events of the last twenty-four hours. The American people do not want their young dying for $1.50 gallon oil, and the Arabs are not happy about cutting their lines off."

Powell was being very cautious. He was wary of the civilians' impulse to use military power to reverse Iraq's invasion of Kuwait and was concerned that they would use half measures to do the job.

The JCS chief recognized that the Bush administration had sent mixed signals to the Iraqis about Kuwait and did not want them to get the idea that they could move on Saudi Arabia, as well.

"We were late last night in having the president call Hussein," Powell said, referring to the White House's failure to send a tough warning to the Iraqi leader. "We must communicate to Saddam Hussein that Saudi Arabia is the line."

As the Pentagon officials struggled to figure out how to respond, they complained about the intelligence reports they had received.

"We had an intelligence community failure," said Pete Williams, Cheney's loyal spokesman.

"They told me they were saber-rattling," Cheney added.

"Only in the last two days, did the CIA say the Iraqis might attack," Powell said.

The criticisms roughly characterized the dominant view within the intelligence agencies. But they overlooked Allen's repeated warnings and sidestepped the JCS reluctance to send forces to the Gulf to signal Iraq not to attack.

Then the Pentagon officials discussed the possibility of cutting off Iraq's oil supply, while Rear Adm. William A. Owens described what forces were available for deployment.

The top Pentagon officials and their aides talked about the difficulties in deploying a large force to Saudi Arabia.

"We need nineteen days," said Paul Wolfowitz, the undersecretary of defense for policy, referring to the time needed to deploy a major ground force to the Gulf.

"What if there is no Saudi support?" Cheney asked.

Powell said that the United States had to tell the Iraqis in no uncertain terms that the loss of Saudi Arabia was unacceptable and pressure the Saudis to let the American forces in. Air strikes launched from a distance would not be good enough to defend Saudi Arabia. The United States needed to have aircraft and troops in the kingdom.

Referring to the plan developed by the United States Central Command for the defense of Saudi Arabia, Powell added, "We have plans for 100,000 soldiers, but we need a national sense."

Cheney responded that the Pentagon leadership had the responsibility to advise the president; they could not take their cues from public opinion. "We are the only ones who can tell the president what to do," Cheney said. "He will look to us. The others can't do it. So what do we do?"

"We must start with policy and diplomatic overtures," Powell said. "We can't make a case for losing lives for Kuwait, but Saudi Arabia is different. I am opposed to dramatic action without the President having popular support."[2]

At the State Department, Deputy Defense Secretary Lawrence Eagleburger was also playing catch-up. Eagleburger had raced back from his farm in Charlottesville, Virginia, the day after the invasion took place, using his radar warning receiver to avoid being flagged down by state troopers. But the real diplomatic action was in Russia, where Secretary of State Baker was meeting with Eduard A. Shevardnadze.

Shortly before the invasion, Robert Kimmitt had alerted Baker that it looked like Saddam Hussein's forces were headed south, and Baker had passed it on to his Soviet counterpart during a meeting in Siberia. But Shevardnadze had discounted the warning. He, too, had thought the Iraqis were bluffing.

Now Baker and his deputy, Dennis Ross, wanted the Soviet Union to pressure Baghdad. Ross flew on to Moscow and huddled with one of Shevardnadze's assistants. The two aides cobbled together a statement condemning the Iraqi invasion and calling for an immediate arms embargo on Iraq.

It would be an important message. Iraq's longtime patron and arms supplier would be on record as assailing the action; Baghdad would be isolated diplomatically. The plan was for the United States and the Soviet Union to issue the joint declaration after Baker wrapped up his talks in Siberia.

After a basic text was agreed upon, the statement was watered down by the Middle East hands at the Soviet Foreign Ministry, who were concerned about the fate of thousands of Russian advisers and their families in Iraq and were not happy to take on an old friend. After hours of wrangling, the matter was still not settled. When Baker's plane arrived in Moscow, Ross met him at the airport and explained that the matter had to be bumped up to Shevardnadze.

Shevardnadze agreed to the tough wording but was concerned that Washington would use the statement as a justification to attack the Iraqi occupation force in Kuwait. Baker said that Washington wanted to solve the dispute peacefully but reserved the right to use force if Baghdad harmed the hundreds of Americans trapped in Kuwait and Iraq. The tough wording was restored even though there was little military force in the area to back it up.[3]

Ross, for his part, felt that Iraq's invasion had revealed Saddam Hussein to be a clear and present danger to the Middle East. Ross told Jack F. Matlock, the American ambassador to Moscow, that if military force was used it would have to get at the root of the problem, Matlock later recalled. Saddam Hussein's regime would have to go.[4]

At the White House, President Bush was trying to think through the problem. By the morning, the White House had prepared an executive order freezing Kuwait's financial assets before Baghdad could seize control of them and had pushed an urgent resolution through the United Nations Security Council demanding the unconditional withdrawal of Iraqi troops. It was clear that that was just the beginning, but it was not clear what the end would be.

Before leaving for Aspen, Bush had presided over a rambling National Security Council meeting at which Powell had again stated his recommendation that the administration's policy should concentrate on the defense of Saudi Arabia, not the liberation of Kuwait. Powell's recommendation brought a rejoinder from Thomas Pickering, the U.S. ambassador to the United Nations. He argued that American credibility in the Middle East would be damaged if it acquiesced in the invasion of Kuwait.[5]

With the administration's top officials at odds, Bush told the press that he was not contemplating military action. But the trip to Aspen also gave the president an opportunity to consult with the leader of the United States' most important Western ally: British Prime Minister Margaret Thatcher, who was also in Aspen to deliver a speech and was staying just outside the city in the house of Henry Catto, the former ambassador to London.

For Iraq, the timing of the Bush-Thatcher meeting was unfortunate. As the former colonial master of Kuwait, the British had long since let the United States assume the primary responsibility for defending the Gulf, but it maintained its interests in the region, and the fate of Kuwait was one of them.

Before the meeting, Bush's aides furiously rewrote the talking points, which had been drafted earlier in the week by State Department officials in the Bureau of Near Eastern and South Asian Affairs, that portrayed Iraq's military moves along the border as a bluff.

Bush was already inclined to take a tough line. Of all the leaders in the Western alliance, however, Thatcher was the most resolute when it came to the Iraqis, and she reinforced Bush's determination to take a firm stand. In their meeting, Thatcher compared Iraq's attack on Kuwait to Nazi Germany's 1930s aggression in Europe. Raising the specter of an Iraqi attack on Saudi Arabia, Thatcher said the West simply could not tolerate Baghdad's control over the Persian Gulf oil supply. When Bush noted that Egyptian President Hosni Mubarak and Jordan's King Hussein were urging Washington to give the Arabs a chance to fashion a diplomatic solution, Thatcher argued against any Arab-brokered compromise. The two leaders discussed using their navies to impose a trade embargo against Iraq, persuading Saudi Arabia and Turkey to shut down their oil pipelines and moving the MPS ships from Diego Garcia.[6]

After returning to Washington, Bush convened an August 3 National Security Council meeting to decide on a political and military course of action. Cheney, Powell, Eagleburger, and all the other top hands were there. Bush deliberately refrained from laying out his view at the start of the meeting. Once the president declared himself, debate was inhibited.

Protocol dictated that the State Department representative go first, and Eagleburger took the floor. Although he had paid little attention to the Gulf in the weeks leading up to the crisis, he now delivered a rousing call to action. Eagleburger said that the issue before them was far more important than the invasion of Kuwait. If Washington accepted the Iraqi takeover of Kuwait, it would send all the wrong signals to the Qaddafis and Kim il Sungs of the world. They would get the idea that the end of superpower competition had created power vacuums around the globe that the most ruthless and powerful despots in the third world could exploit.

Even if Iraq did not attack Saudi Arabia, its occupation of Kuwait would put its army astride the Gulf oil supply. That alone would give Baghdad greater political as well as economic power, which it was bound to use for no good. Sooner or later, a strengthened Iraq would confront Israel and then Washington would find itself drawn into a war in the Middle East.

"Under these circumstances, it is absolutely essential that the U.S. — collectively if possible, but individually if necessary — not only put a stop to this aggression but roll it back," Eagleburger said.

Eagleburger's presentation was a virtual echo of Cheney's thinking, as well as that of Brent Scowcroft, the national security adviser, but it went far beyond what Powell had in mind. The most important member in the audience was receptive.[7]

The debate over administration policy was, in essence, a battle for the mind of the president. And fresh from his meeting with Margaret Thatcher, Bush was tilting toward rollback, not containment.

The administration had been fortunate. It had been ill-prepared to respond to the Iraqi invasion, but coincidence had placed the president and the secretary of state with British and Russian leaders, two of the allies who mattered the most.

But there was another ally that needed to be consulted, the Saudis. It was clear that, at a minimum, Washington needed to protect Saudi Arabia. It was also clear that Riyadh's backing was essential for a defensive or offensive strategy. Unless the Saudis accepted the deployment of American troops, there was no real prospect of protecting the Saudi oil fields or reversing the Iraqi invasion of Kuwait.

Persuading the Saudis to accept the American troops was a top White House priority, and when it came to dealing with Riyadh, Washington relied heavily on Saudi Arabia's flamboyant ambassador to Washington, Prince Bandar.

THE SAUDI CONNECTION

The son of Prince Sultan and a commoner from Saudi Arabia's southern Asir province, the dark-skinned Bandar had to depend more than most members of the royal family on his wits to survive. A British- and American-trained fighter pilot, Bandar had survived the crash of an F-5 that gave him years of back problems and had gone on to fly F-15s in the Royal Saudi Air Force, where he deepened his fascination with military affairs. Appointed by King Fahd in 1983 as Saudi Arabia's ambassador to Washington, Bandar had decorated his office with symbols of both his Arab heritage and his more worldly ambassadorial role: crossed sabers mounted next to a wall full of television sets, so that the prince could monitor every conceivable news broadcast.

Bandar had been involved in some of the kingdom's most sensitive diplomatic operations. When William Casey, Ronald Reagan's CIA director, wanted to share sensitive satellite intelligence with the Iraqis during the Iran-Iraq War, Bandar made available his Washington home overlooking the Potomac for the meeting. In 1985, Bandar had worked with the Americans, arranging for Saudi funds to be channeled to the Nicaraguan Contras. But he could just as easily go behind Washington's back if it suited the king. When the Saudis decided to buy Chinese medium-range missiles in 1988, it was Bandar who secretly negotiated the deal in Beijing. Washington was not informed and American intelligence was caught by surprise.

For all his sophistication, Bandar was shocked by the Iraqi attack on Kuwait. After Saddam Hussein threatened to attack Israel with chemical weapons in March, Bandar had flown to Baghdad to meet with the Iraqi leader and later provided Washington with his analysis of the situation. Bandar knew that the Iraqi leaders could be brutal — during his March visit, the Iraqi leader boasted that he had launched several attempts to assassinate an exiled Iraqi officer — but not in his wildest dreams did Bandar think the Iraqis would take all of Kuwait.

The initial discussions between Washington and Riyadh following Iraq's invasion of Kuwait had been anything but definitive. The Saudis had long been ambivalent about American military support. They had built new, outsize airfields and ports so that American forces could pour in during a crisis, but unless the fate of the regime was at stake, the Saudis kept an arms-length relationship. When Iran started attacking Kuwaiti oil tankers in the Persian Gulf in 1988 and the United States responded by putting them under American flags and providing military protection, neither the Saudis nor the Kuwaitis would allow CENT-COM to base American special operations helicopters on their territory. While CENTCOM had developed plans to protect the Saudi oil fields against an Iraqi attack, it had never discussed the planning with the Saudis. The assumption was that the issue was too sensitive to be broached in peacetime and that the Saudis would let the Americans in once they perceived a mortal danger. But even with thousands of Iraqi troops just north of their border, it was not clear that the Saudis wanted to confront Iraq.

The night of the invasion, the Bush administration offered the Saudis a tactical fighter squadron. It was essentially a symbolic gesture to demonstrate the American commitment to defend the Saudi Kingdom while the Pentagon struggled to come up with a more comprehensive response. But the Saudis never replied to the offer.

On Friday, August 3, Bandar went to the White House to meet with Scowcroft and other top officials. But the results were initially no more conclusive. Scowcroft wanted to know if the Saudis would accept a major deployment of American forces before the administration laid out the details of its military plan, and Bandar wanted to know what the United States was prepared to do before saying yes to anything.

As the two sides went round and round, John Sununu, the White House chief of staff, quietly left the room. Soon after, President Bush appeared and asked if the prince and the national security adviser had reached agreement on the deployment of American troops.

Bush appeared distressed that Bandar and Scowcroft were playing Alphonse and Gaston. It hurts when your friends don't trust you, Bush told the Saudi prince, according to a participant. The president said that he was offering his word of honor: if American forces were sent to Saudi Arabia, the United States would go all the way. Saudi Arabia would not be abandoned.

Bandar told the president that his assurance had transformed the situation, but that it would help if the Saudis were briefed on the American defensive plan. The White House authorized Cheney to show Bandar CENTCOM's plan, which had been marked "NOFORN," meaning that it was not to be shared with officials outside the American government.

When Bandar entered Cheney's expansive Pentagon office later that day, he was met by the defense secretary, Powell, and Wolfowitz. Bandar was shown classified satellite photos of the Iraqi forces in Kuwait. Then the JCS chairman began to take the prince through the plan. When Bandar saw the dimensions of the plan, he seemed to catch his breath; the Pentagon was talking about a massive ground presence.

Bandar asked Powell how many troops he was talking about, and the JCS chairman pegged the number at around 100,000.

"Colin, now I know you are not bullshitting me," Bandar said. "Now you know why we did not want a tactical fighter squadron."

Bandar indicated that he thought the Saudis would agree to accept the forces, but he was not in a position to make such a momentous decision. Later, Bandar telephoned King Fahd to report on the meeting, and the monarch asked his ambassador for his assessment of the Iraqi threat. Bandar told the king he should ask for the intelligence reports and judge for himself. A Saudi team could come to Washington or a team of American military briefers could go to Saudi Arabia. The Saudis were beginning to come around, but they had not given a definitive answer.[8]

The administration was making headway with the Saudis, but this was only the first inning. The military mission was being entrusted to an untested command that had long been seen as having one of the weakest staffs in the military — the United States Central Command — which was led by one of the Army's most volatile commanders, H. Norman Schwarzkopf. As the Iraqis tightened their grip on Kuwait, Schwarzkopf was summoned to an August 4 meeting at Camp David to present his plan to defend Saudi Arabia against any further encroachments.

THE LOST COMMAND

Schwarzkopf was a complicated man. The son of a famous father and an alcoholic mother, he cast his self-image in terms of his father's rectitude and sense of purpose. He wanted to measure up as a man of character, honor, and accomplishment. He accepted his mother's alcoholism with the stoicism of his generation for such "family" problems. The fiction of family normalcy was maintained, and the accompanying dismay and anger were kept submerged. Military life, which he dearly loved for both its pomp and challenges, was his passion. It provided structure and purpose to his life.

Schwarzkopf ran the Army race well, but never as a front-runner. In his early years as an officer, he was diligent and obedient, unquestioning of authority. His experiences in Vietnam were the defining factors of his career, as they were for many of his generation of officers. He was an adviser to the South Vietnamese paratroopers during his first tour in 1965 and relished his role. Like most Americans who went to Vietnam early in the war, he felt ennobled by the part he was playing to stop the advance of communism. But that had all changed by 1969, when he returned for a second tour of duty. The war was floundering along with little sense of purpose and rising casualties. The crusade had turned into an ordeal.

During his second tour in Vietnam, Schwarzkopf saw the results of indifferent and callous leadership. His rage was always close to the surface. Periodically, he would be unable to contain it and would explode. Like the benign Dr. Jekyll, the normally charming and affable future four-star general could become a tempestuous and nasty Mr. Hyde under the proper stimulus. Schwarzkopf's violent temper became well known in the Army as he made his way up the ladder to senior rank. Lt. Gen. Calvin Waller, as big a man as Schwarzkopf himself, who served under him four times, including as his deputy in the Gulf, never took it seriously — "It was just Norm's way." But there is no doubt that Schwarzkopf terrorized some of his subordinates, who never knew what would set him off or when it would happen. Few in the Army felt neutral about Schwarzkopf. They either liked him or loathed him. To his admirers, Schwarzkopf was a warrior. To his detractors, and there were many, he was a bully, who commanded through intimidation and was too eager to grab the credit that belonged to others.

After Vietnam, Schwarzkopf touched all the bases. He served in the airborne, infantry, and mechanized infantry. He attended the Army War College and served in the civilian Army secretariat, on a Navy-dominated staff in the Pacific, and on the Army staff at the Pentagon. He gained momentary fame, if questionable celebrity, as the ranking Army officer during the clumsy 1983 Grenada invasion.

Along the way, he made one star and then a second. He also acquired a sponsor in the person of Gen. Carl Vuono, one of his former commanders who knew Schwarzkopf from their days at West Point, and who in his own race with his peers made it to the top as chief of staff of the Army. Vuono pulled Schwarzkopf behind him and gave him the most prestigious staff job in the Army, operations deputy. It carried with it three stars and entrée to the tight circle of the Joint Chiefs of Staff.

As Vuono's operations deputy, Schwarzkopf had a solid reputation as a competent officer, but he was not considered vintage stock. Most of those who knew him professionally doubted he would have made the rank of lieutenant general if it had not been for Vuono. But the power of a service chief is not to be underrated. Vuono was in his last posting, and before he stepped down he did one last favor for his protégé by nominating Schwarzkopf to head the Central Command.

The origins of CENTCOM went back to the old Rapid Deployment Joint Task Force, which had been promoted by Zbigniew Brzezinski, President Carter's hawkish national security adviser, to contest Moscow's continuing military buildup and growing Soviet influence in the developing world. The Joint Chiefs had only reluctantly accepted the creation of a joint task force for the Middle East, fearing that its establishment would heat up the rivalry between the services. Having become accustomed to sharing authority for the Middle East, neither the Army-dominated European nor the Navy-dominated Pacific command was eager to relinquish its respective responsibility for the Persian Gulf region. And if a new command was established, which service would control it?

When President Reagan was elected, his administration was amenable to creating new symbols of military power. Defense Secretary Caspar W. Weinberger pressed the chiefs to replace the task force with a more permanent command on an equal footing with the European and Pacific commands. Sensitive to Arab concern that the United States was seeking dominion over the Middle East, the chiefs chose the most innocuous name possible for the new command: the United States Central Command.

CENTCOM had geographic responsibility for United States military operations in most of the Middle East and Southwest Asia. The European Command managed to hold onto the "confrontation states" — Israel, Lebanon, and Syria — while the Pacific Command continued to hold onto the Indian Ocean and the Arabian Sea. The decision to leave Israel outside CENTCOM's area of operation allowed the European Command to keep its hand in the Middle East. But it also deprived CENTCOM of interchange with Israeli officials, who wielded the most powerful military in the Middle East and the only one willing to overtly align itself with the Americans. The greatest anomaly with CENTCOM was that it consisted only of a planning headquarters in Tampa. It had no forces assigned to it. If CENTCOM went to war, it would have to "borrow" forces earmarked for Middle East contingencies but actually under other geographic commands.

Although CENTCOM had been formally elevated in status, the chiefs were skeptical that the call to battle would ever come for the command. Not even the Reagan administration's costly military buildup enabled the military to field enough forces to fight simultaneous conflicts in Europe, the Pacific, and the Middle East with any hope of success. Although they never officially wrote off the Gulf, the chiefs knew that the defense of Europe would take priority. Defend Europe first and liberate the Gulf later was the unspoken credo, only it was important that the Soviets not know it.

Gen. Jack Vessey, chairman of the Joint Chiefs of Staff, expressed the dominant view. After being briefed during the Reagan administration on CENTCOM's plan to defend Iran against a Soviet attack, Vessey blew a big cloud of cigar smoke and delivered his verdict. "You know, that is nothing more than a big deception plan," Vessey said.

But CENTCOM had enormous appeal for Schwarzkopf. While Lt. Gen. Schwarzkopf was not a Middle East expert, he was fascinated with the region. Schwarzkopf's father, Col. H. Norman Schwarzkopf, who had graduated from West Point in 1917, was sent to reorganize the Iranian national police force during World War II when the United States was using Iran as a corridor to resupply the Russians. Colonel Schwarzkopf had taken his family with him and the experience had been a deep influence on his son.

Although the CENTCOM post had considerable drawbacks, getting the command turned out to be somewhat problematic. William Taft, the acting secretary of defense, was inclined to see the post go to Adm. Hank Mustin, the Navy candidate, concluding that it was a way to get the Navy involved in joint military operations. But Richard Armitage, the powerfully built and bureaucratically skillful assistant defense secretary for international security affairs, argued that the job should go to Schwarzkopf. Armitage had never found Mustin to be an enthusiastic backer of the American effort to protect Kuwaiti oil tankers from Iranian attack by putting them under an American flag. Moreover, the Persian Gulf was, first and foremost, a theater for land warfare, Armitage told Taft.

Adm. William J. Crowe, Vessey's successor and the JCS chairman during the Reagan administration, had seen Schwarzkopf for a year and a half at JCS meetings and did not have much of an impression of him one way or another. As far as Crowe was concerned, the nominee was a general of no special distinction for a post of no great importance. Schwarzkopf was Vuono's choice and under an informal understanding among the services, it was the Army's turn to run CENTCOM. As far as Crowe was concerned, Schwarzkopf could have the job. Nobody anticipated at the time that Schwarzkopf and his bastard command would end up leading a shooting war.

Schwarzkopf's first challenge when he got to CENTCOM in 1989 was to establish a new rationale for his command, whose very survival was coming under increasing challenge with the demise of the Soviet threat. The challenge came from the highest level. Two months after Schwarzkopf went down to Tampa, Admiral Crowe issued a slim, classified report on the "National Military Strategy," an annual strategy statement that provided a general ordering of the United States military priorities to guide Pentagon planning. Not only was the Gulf at the bottom of the list but it barely rated a mention.

In discussing the region, Crowe's August 25, 1989, report stated tersely: "Access to Arabian Peninsula oil and the critical natural resources of South America and Africa will also be a high priority." It was a throwaway line, which signaled the opposite of what it said. The fact that the JCS was equating the protection of the West's oil supply with the need to ensure access to resources in South America did not bode well for CENTCOM.[9]

However one might disagree with Crowe's assessment, it raised a valid question. If the Soviets no longer presented a serious threat to the Persian Gulf, and the Iranians were down, if not out, following their calamitous eight-year war with Iraq, what was CENTCOM's raison d'etre?

To maintain its standing, CENTCOM needed some new allies at the Pentagon and a new foe abroad. The command soon found the allies it needed. Neither Cheney nor Wolfowitz was yet prepared to entirely write off the Soviet threat, and they were not comfortable with Crowe's downgrading of the Persian Gulf. When Cheney issued his first Defense Planning Guidance — a classified statement intended to guide the services in their budget preparations — he stressed the importance of protecting the Persian Gulf oil supply against a Soviet-led attack or a "robust regional threat," an allusion to Iraq.

A terse footnote at the bottom of page 22 of the guidance made it clear that Crowe had been overruled. "The Secretary has increased the relative priority of Southwest Asia by making explicit that the region ranks above South America and Africa in terms of global wartime priorities and by outlining an initial theater strategy," it read.[10]

Crowe's successor, Powell, took relatively little interest in the command, Schwarzkopf recalled. Unlike in Europe or the Pacific, the United States had few formal military commitments in the region. But Powell nonetheless encouraged Schwarzkopf to overhaul the war plan with focus on regional, non-Soviet threats to the oil supply.

The new foe was not hard to identify. Since the fall of the shah, Tehran had been Washington's nemesis in the region, but following the devastating Iran-Iraq War, the Iranian military was not in a position to threaten anybody. Syria had a large military, but it was primarily a threat to Israel, and CENTCOM did not cover Israel. That left Iraq as the potential adversary.

Assuming a twenty-two-division Iraqi threat to Saudi Arabia, CENT-

COM launched an effort to develop a new three-phase plan to deter, defend, and then go on the offensive to seize any lost ground.

Substantively and bureaucratically, fashioning such a war plan was a huge undertaking. A total revamping of a war plan, including the TPFDL (Time Phased Force Deployment List), a computerized list for dispatching forces to the area, generally took several years. As the command updated its planning, the work moved at a deliberate pace. There were meetings and draft plans to circulate for comment, and then more meetings. Barring any delays, CENTCOM planned to submit the final version of its new plan to the JCS in April 1991, some twenty-two months after work on the plan began.

As with the old plan to defend against a Soviet thrust to the Gulf, putting a credible defense in place depended heavily on advance warning of an attack. CENTCOM assumed, optimistically, that it would have twenty-one days of warning, although the National Warning Staff, the group of intelligence officials who monitored the war preparations of potential adversaries, thought ten to twelve days was more like it.[11]

With strains developing in Washington's relations with Baghdad, the State Department became uneasy with CENTCOM's war planning. But it was not the methodical pace of the planning that bothered the diplomats. Rather, the department was disturbed that CENTCOM was portraying Iraq as the enemy in its war games. The State Department's Bureau of Near Eastern and South Asian Affairs was not diplomatic about expressing its reservations.

On one occasion, recalled Joseph P. Hoar, Schwarzkopf's chief of staff and eventual successor, a senior State Department official protested CENTCOM's decision to portray Iraq as the enemy in a major war game dubbed Internal Look.

"Somehow, in the process of all this, a State Department official had been invited to come on down," recalled Hoar. "Somehow he wandered into the tactical aspects of the planning and went home and told his boss that Central Command was getting ready to go to war with Iraq. An assistant secretary called me and we had a long discussion about this. He wanted to point out to me that we were not at war with Iraq, that Iraq was not an enemy of ours, and that it was entirely inappropriate for CENTCOM or anybody else to be planning to fight a country with which we were not at war."[12]

When it came time to conduct Internal Look, Gordon Brown, a career foreign service officer attached to CENTCOM as Schwarzkopf's foreign policy adviser, came up with a solution. The war game would proceed, but CENTCOM would have a cover story in case news of the exercise leaked — what Brown called "plausible deniability." If Internal Look became public, the command would explain that the adversary was not Saddam Hussein's regime but a future Iraqi regime that was hostile to Western interests. It was a thin cover story, but it was the only way to reconcile the State Department's concerns with CENTCOM's new mandate.[13]

For all the work, as Iraqi forces began to menace Kuwait, there was plenty of unfinished business. There was no doubt about the first units to be deployed. But the command had only a rudimentary idea of how to set up its ground defenses and a limited notion of how to use airpower. The list of forces to be deployed had not been updated. Work had also been deferred on an offensive plan in case the Iraqis beat Washington to the punch and their gains had to be rolled back.

Just days after Iraqi Foreign Minister Tariq Aziz threatened the Kuwaitis, CENTCOM began to circulate the second draft of its plan — "Operations to Counter an Iraqi Regional Threat to the Arabian Pensinsula" — to senior officers in the Pentagon and in the field. The comments were due on September 14.

One of the most vexing riddles had to do with intelligence. The only sure way to get a defense in place before Iraqi forces swept into Saudi Arabia was to send American forces there before Baghdad launched its attack. Not only would the president have to receive adequate warning of an Iraqi invasion, but he would have to act on the basis of that intelligence and persuade the conservative rulers of the Gulf states to accept American forces on their territory.

The problem was driven home when Lt. Gen. John Yeosock, CENTCOM's top Army commander, met with his fellow Army generals on August 1 to discuss the latest version of the command's defensive plan.

"It was a shoulder-shrugging briefing," recalled one participant at the Pentagon meeting. "Yeosock was laying out the timelines of when we would have to move, and they went so far back that it looked like a situation where we could not get there in time. The message was that getting the forces depended on the president making an early decision and nobody thought that was likely."

The Army generals agreed they should meet in a few weeks to discuss the issue further. "Let's peel the onion some more," said Gordon Sullivan, the four-star vice chief of staff of the Army, using one of his favorite expressions for intractable problems. Hours later Iraqi forces invaded Kuwait.[14]

Preparing for his August 4 Camp David presentation, Schwarzkopf had a lot of work to draw on. But the Iraqis had gotten the jump on the Americans and Schwarzkopf had something less than a completed plan.

★   ★   ★

Schwarzkopf arrived at Camp David with Lt. Gen. Charles Horner, who would command American warplanes in the Gulf. The CENTCOM commander outlined the Iraqi threat and identified the American units that would be sent to defend Saudi Arabia.

Like most of the American military, Schwarzkopf tended to be impressed with the quantitative measures of Iraqi military power: the number of divisions and tanks.

The Iraqis had taken Kuwait in four days — not the seven days that CENTCOM had assumed would be necessary. That meant that the Americans would have three fewer days to ready a defense of Saudi Arabia. CENTCOM's intelligence officers had told Schwarzkopf that the Iraqis could continue the march on twenty-four to forty-eight hours' notice. But given the Iraqis' limited logistics and their need to pause and regroup, it seemed likely that the Americans would have more time than that to get their first forces to the Gulf.

If Iraq decided to press on, CENTCOM's ability to repulse the invaders would depend on Iraq's ability to manage logistics and the killing power of American warplanes, Schwarzkopf reasoned. He had no sense of how well the Air Force and Navy might do against an Iraqi invasion force. The Air Force always talked a good game, but like many Army officers, Schwarzkopf had come away from Vietnam with the impression that the fly-boys promised more than they could deliver.

Schwarzkopf said it would take a minimum of a month to get a capable defense in place, and he highlighted the 82nd Airborne, whose deployment was to send a signal of American resolve. Horner then outlined a plan to use allied aircraft primarily to attack Iraqi ground forces and suggested that the United States bomb only targets deep in Iraq if the Iraqis resorted to chemical weapons.

The plans for an offensive operation to kick the Iraqis out of Kuwait were really no more than an educated guess. Asked about offensive options, Schwarzkopf said that building up the necessary force to evict the Iraqis from Kuwait would take eight to ten months. Some of the president's men were taken aback by the estimate, but it reinforced Powell's case that the administration should limit itself to the defense of Saudi Arabia.[15]

But from the start, the White House was thinking about a potential offensive for evicting Iraqi forces from Kuwait and was sizing the American deployment to Saudi Arabia accordingly, recalled Brent Scowcroft, President Bush's national security adviser, though not even the hawks in the administration fully appreciated the number of forces that would ultimately be required.

"What happened at Camp David was that there were two different figures that were discussed: what we would have to put in there to stop a further advance and what it would take to keep our options open. The latter figure was about 100,000," recalled Scowcroft. "As the Iraqis kept putting in more forces, that figure kept changing."[16] The major problem, however, was still the uncertain attitude of the Saudis.

That day, Mubarak told Bush in a telephone call that the Saudis would find it difficult to accept the deployment of American troops. Having advised Bush before the Iraqi invasion that Arab states in the region were confident of a negotiated solution and that Washington should avoid a provocation, the Egyptian president's assessments had been somewhat less than prescient. But the observation worried the White House. Having failed to sound the alarm before the Iraqi invasion of Kuwait, William Webster, the CIA director, was now warning that Iraqi forces were likely to cross into Saudi Arabia.

Following his discussion with Mubarak, Bush telephoned Fahd and indicated that Washington was prepared to do whatever was necessary to help the kingdom.

Referring to his earlier conversation with Bandar, Fahd said that he would wait to hear the plan from the American team that was coming to brief him. With that comment, the discussions of sending a delegation to brief the Saudis went into high gear.

Sending a team was not such a simple matter. There was considerable deliberation among the Americans over whom to send. Perhaps Schwarzkopf should lead the delegation. He knew the plan best and would oversee any operation in the Gulf. But the White House decided that the team should be headed by a civilian. Maybe Robert M. Gates, the deputy national security adviser, who had rushed back from vacation, should head the group. Gates had led a team to Pakistan and India earlier in the year when the intelligence community had forecast that there was a fifty-fifty chance of another Indo-Pakistani war. But that suggestion was also put aside. The White House wanted higher-level representation.

Eventually, it was agreed that Cheney would lead the mission and that Gates and Schwarzkopf would go too, along with a large retinue of top administration officials and CENTCOM officers. Powell would stay behind at the Pentagon in case the Iraqis started heading south while the defense secretary was en route. Bandar would fly back first in his private plane to lay the groundwork for the meeting.

Bandar arrived in Jiddah on Sunday following a grueling twelve-hour flight. Situated near the Red Sea, Jiddah was cooler than Riyadh and served as the summer capital for the Saudi leadership. Soon after arriving, Bandar received a call from Scowcroft, who wanted to know if the king had agreed to the deployment of American forces. The national security adviser was concerned that if Cheney came and went without an agreement to dispatch American troops, Saddam Hussein might interpret this as dissension between Riyadh and Washington and try to take advantage of the situation. Bandar raised Scowcroft's concerns with King Fahd, and his response was a simple one.

"Let the guests come," Fahd said. That fell short of the guarantee Scowcroft was looking for. The Saudis were accustomed to operating on the basis of promises and signs; the Americans on the basis of legal contracts and treaties.

Bush decided to send the team anyway. On Sunday, as Cheney led his team to the Gulf, Bush returned by helicopter from Camp David and bluntly declared to the television cameras that the Iraqi aggression "would not stand." Bush had been quiet in his August 3 National Security Council meeting, but his public comments tipped his hand. In the debate between Cheney and Powell, Bush was in Cheney's corner. Whatever it took, he wanted the Iraqis out of Kuwait.

"I had decided in my own mind in the first hours that the Iraqi aggression could not be tolerated," Bush recalled after the war. "During my press remarks at the outset of the first NSC meeting, I did say that I was not contemplating intervention that perhaps inadvertently led to some confusion about my intent. I did not intend to rule out the use of force. At that juncture I did not wish explicitly to rule it in. But following the series of meetings, I came to the conclusion that some public comment was needed to make clear my determination that the United States must do whatever might be necessary to reverse the Iraqi aggression. I don't know that I had determined at that point that force would be required, but I had decided that that would be up to Saddam."

President Bush's tough words before the television cameras caught some of the members of his own administration by surprise. Margaret Tutwiler, the chief spokesperson for Secretary of State Baker, was struck by the categorical tone of Mr. Bush's remarks. "What's got into him?" she wondered.

As the Saudis and the Americans went through their diplomatic dance, Alfred Gray was concerned that Washington was losing valuable time. A stocky, tobacco-chewing general, the Marine Corps commandant was not involved in the talks with the Saudis. But he knew what had to be done to get a defense in place and that Washington was not doing it.

The Pentagon had spent billions of dollars to store a Marine brigade's worth of tanks, artillery, and other heavy weapons on climate-controlled Maritime Prepositioning Ships stationed at the tiny British island of Diego Garcia in the middle of the Indian Ocean, seven sailing days from the modern Saudi ports in the Gulf, which the Saudis had expanded for just such an eventuality. Gray and Hoar, who by then had left CENTCOM and was serving as Marine Corps deputy chief of staff for plans, policy, and operations, believed that CENTCOM had to get the ships at Diego Garcia under way — and fast. Gray estimated that it would take the Iraqis at least a week to organize themselves for a thrust into Saudi Arabia. If the president had ordered the MPS squadron to sail on August 2 or 3, the ships could be there within a week's time and the United States could deploy a substantial ground force around the ports and oil complexes in the Eastern Province of Saudi Arabia. If the president changed his mind after the MPS ships set sail, they could quietly return to Diego Garcia and nobody would be the wiser.

But the Marines could not get the Bush administration to act. There was a case for not sending the ships, but if it figured in the administration's thinking, nobody shared it with the Marines. If the Saudis somehow found out that the ships had been dispatched, it could indicate a presumptuous attitude. The United States would be sending forces before the Saudis had agreed to take them, and that might queer the whole deal.

The Marines believed, however, that the White House had simply let the matter slip through the cracks. When the White House thought about deploying forces, it seemed to focus on aircraft carriers, the paratroopers of the 82nd Airborne, and tactical fighter wings, not the floating warehouses in the Indian Ocean.

"We would have gained time had those ships been moved earlier. But it was a decision that had to be made at the highest level, and it was a decision that got lost in the background music as best we can determine. It was lost in the sense that it was on a list of items that went forward to the Secretary of Defense, to the President, but was not made," Hoar observed after the war. "But it's an important lesson for us as Marines that when a crisis begins that we, and our Navy partners, do not have to wait until the same day that aviation and ground forces are loaded into the theater; that naval ships, MPS ships, can be moved before the decision is made. And it is a very prudent decision, in our belief, to move those forces earlier so they are available to the National Command when the time comes. We believe that we would have been better positioned to have operated had those ships been moved, say, on the second or third day of August."[17]

Added Gray: "We wasted time in not doing so and ended up with only the lightly armed paratroopers on the ground at a critical time."

Without a green light from the White House, there was little the Marines could do on their own. The Marines did manage to turn around one of the MPS ships that had left Diego Garcia for routine maintenance in Jacksonville, Florida, and send it back to the Indian Ocean. But it would be August 15 before the first of the ships began unloading in Saudi Arabia. The Bush administration's failure to anticipate the invasion of Kuwait had cost the military valuable time. And the delay in activating the MPS ships meant that the window of vulnerability would be open that much longer.

After arriving in Jiddah on August 6, Cheney, Gates, Schwarzkopf, and the rest of their entourage were taken to the king's marble palace, where they were served tea laced with cardamom. Although the Americans did not fully understand it at the time, they were pushing on an open door.

By the time Cheney arrived in Saudi Arabia, five Iraqi armored, two Iraqi mechanized, and four Iraqi infantry divisions were in Kuwait. Of these, an armored and mechanized division were positioned opposite the Saudi border. While insufficient to invade Saudi Arabia, they were enough to worry Riyadh. Iraqi infantry units were en route to the border to occupy defenses to free up the Republican Guard heavy units to assume a defensive counterattack role against a Western effort to evict the Iraqis out of Kuwait or to head south for further offensive action against the Saudis.

The Saudi dealings with the Iraqis following the invasion had also done little to reassure them. According to a senior Saudi official, the Iraqis sent patrols to probe the Saudi border on three occasions. The first time it happened, the chief of staff of the Saudi military called Baghdad on a hot line (which had been installed between Riyadh and Baghdad during the Iran-Iraq War) to protest the action. The Iraqis immediately apologized and promised that it would not happen again. The second time a complaint was made over the hot line, an officer in Baghdad informed Riyadh that no senior officials were there to take the call. The third time the Saudis sought to use the line, they discovered that it was dead. The Saudis had misjudged Saddam Hussein's intentions regarding Kuwait and the cost of another miscalculation could be huge.

When it came time to meet the king, Cheney gave a low-key presentation, outlining the threat but not exaggerating it. Unless the Saudis agreed to the deployment of American forces, the Saudi kingdom risked becoming another Kuwait, the defense secretary said. After the crisis, the Americans would take steps to build up the Saudi defensive capabilities, an allusion to arms sales. It would also help if the Saudis would take steps in the future to make it easier for the kingdom to receive friendly forces, a reference to the American desire to store heavy ground equipment on Saudi territory. As for the American forces that were to be deployed, they would stay only as long as they were wanted. The United States was not interested in permanent bases. Then Schwarzkopf ran through CENT-COM's defensive plan.

After hearing the Americans' presentation, the king and other members of the royal hierarchy discussed it in Arabic, which Charles Freeman, the American ambassador to Riyadh, strained to understand, hampered by his limited command of the language. Freeman later told the American team that there had appeared to be some dissension among the Saudis, but the king quickly put an end to any debate. The Kuwaitis that had fled south had been put up in luxury hotels in Saudi Arabia. What country would put the Saudis up in their hotels? Fahd asked rhetorically.

The king gave his assent. The Saudis asked the Americans to keep the deployment secret until the U.S. troops were on the ground. They did not want to tempt the Iraqis to preempt. But the Americans said that would be all but impossible to do. Once the American forces started to head out, it was bound to make the news.

After the meeting broke up, Schwarzkopf told Horner, Yeosock, and Lt. Gen. Dale Starling, the command's top logistician, that they were staying in Saudi Arabia to oversee the deployment. The burly CENTCOM commander was emotional and teary-eyed. It looked like a lot of soldiers, marines, and airmen might have to die, the commander exclaimed to one member of Powell's staff.

Cheney telephoned the White House to inform President Bush that King Fahd had agreed to receive the troops and secured Bush's go-ahead to launch the deployment. Then Cheney called Powell, telling him to begin flowing the forces. Respecting the principle of civilian control of the military, Powell had done nothing to set the deployment in motion and there was an enormous amount to do.

Powell started calling the commanders. The process of moving the forces began so late in the day that, for all intents and purposes, the following day, August 7, became C day, the deployment day for sending forces to the region.

At the headquarters of the United States Transportation Command at Scott Air Force Base in Illinois, Tom Wellmon responded quickly to Powell's order. A civilian in the command's International Operations Division, Wellmon had the job of requesting clearances for the American transport and refueling planes that were to fly through the airspace of friendly nations. The first few days of the crisis had been confusing ones for the command. It had been alerted by the JCS days before the

Iraqi invasion of Kuwait to be prepared to send forces to the Gulf and then told to stand down. Now that Powell had given the go-ahead, Wellmon rushed out cables to American embassies, asking them to secure the necessary permission.

When Powell learned of the messages, he was irate. The White House had not officially announced the dispatch of American forces to the Gulf. Yet the whole operation was being telegraphed by routine requests for flight clearances, as if the Gulf deployment was some kind of military exercise.

"We were directed to plan the mission, and Mr. Wellmon sent out the appropriate dip[lomatic] clearance messages, and all of a sudden the embassies around the world figured out what we were doing. General Powell was somewhat excited about that but got over it fairly quickly," Hansford T. Johnson, the head of the Transportation Command, recalled after the war.

"Looking back, if we had been more careful, we might have gone through more secure channels with the embassies," Johnson added. "We told the embassies before the State Department did that we were going to go to war."[18]

Schwarzkopf later recommended that the operation be dubbed Peninsula Shield, the name of the small Gulf Arab force that protected the Arabian Peninsula. But the Pentagon wanted something more dramatic. So Schwarzkopf's planners came up with Desert Shield.

In a matter of days, Washington had laid the basic foundation of a military and political strategy to defend Saudi Arabia and wrest control of Kuwait. Powell had sought to focus the mission on the defense of the Saudi kingdom and was now the head of a military buildup that would send hundreds of thousands of Americans to the Gulf. The JCS chief had not been successful in heading off talk of an offensive operation to kick the Iraqis out of Kuwait. Still, there was no commitment to launch an offensive, either.

The immediate problem was not liberating Kuwait, but protecting Saudi Arabia. The Bush administration's watch-and-wait approach had opened an enormous window of vulnerability. While the Iraqi forces in Kuwait caught their breath and menaced the Saudi frontier, American forces had to begin from a standing start. Powell's line in the sand had been drawn, but given the Saudis' defensive philosophy, the situation was more problematic than it sounded. Schwarzkopf's ability to manage the logistics and set up an effective command structure for his diverse coalition would be the first test of his generalship.

3

Crossed Swords

The division issued its first operational plan of Operation Desert Shield, OPLAN 90-1, on 11 September, 1990. The mission statement read: "when directed 101st Airborne Division (Air Assault) (-) defends King Fahd International Airport (KFIA) to protect the airport and key facilities. . . . The 101st would have probably been hard pressed to support this defensive plan due to the lack of adequate ammunition stockages and late echelonment of Corps and EAC combat service support elements into the theater."

— 101st Airborne Division
"History for Operation Desert Shield/
Operation Desert Storm"

W HEN COL. RON ROKOSZ stepped off a giant C-141 transport of the Military Airlift Command at the vast Dhahran airfield on August 8, he was not expecting a welcoming committee. The 2nd Brigade of the Army's 82nd Airborne had been on call as the "ready brigade" when the Iraqis invaded Kuwait, which meant that it had to be prepared to deploy anywhere in the world on several hours' notice.

The soldiers of the brigade had achieved glory in 1944 by parachuting into Normandy on D Day, but this time there would be no parachute drop. The lead elements of Rokosz's brigade had left Fort Bragg, North Carolina, the day before and, as the first American ground troops reaching Saudi Arabia, had the job of protecting the airfield and ports American forces needed to deploy in Saudi Arabia.

The first Air Force planes — a C-141 carrying Air Force logistics and communications gear and twenty-four F-15 fighters from Langley, Virginia — had arrived at the sprawling Dhahran Air Base just the day before. In a matter of hours, the F-15s were flying combat air patrols with Saudi aircraft over northern Saudi Arabia, while AWACS radar planes dispatched from Tinker Air Force Base in Oklahoma provided continuous air surveillance.

Meanwhile, the aircraft carrier *Dwight D. Eisenhower* had moved through the Suez Canal into the Red Sea while the USS *Independence* sailed toward the Gulf of Oman. The Navy's warplanes were spared the problem of deploying to poorly equipped Saudi airfields, but they were hundreds of miles from their potential targets. Navy ships in the theater were equipped with cruise missiles, but none of the weapons had Iraqi targets programmed into their computerized brains, further blunting the Navy's striking power.

While the Air Force and Navy planes could take care of themselves in the skies, only a lightly armored Saudi Arabian National Guard Brigade stood astride the six-lane coastal highway to the key airfields, ports, and oil facilities in the Eastern Province of Saudi Arabia. That meant that the gateway to the economic heart of the Saudi Kingdom was essentially wide open. After crushing the Kuwaiti army, Iraq's Republican Guard divisions were poised to head south. Traveling time from the Kuwaiti border to the vital region along the coast, even with Saudi opposition, was no more than twelve hours.

As the transport planes carrying the brigade approached, Colonel Rokosz expected to arrive in a country that was tense and on the edge of war. He ordered his troops to prepare to defend the airfield the minute they stepped off the plane. Soldiers smeared camouflage paint on their faces, put on their kevlar helmets, and swallowed as much water as they could.

Instead of battle-hardened Iraqis, however, they were met by an American Army officer with a soft cap, who directed them to waiting buses to be taken to a nearby workers camp. Company commanders were relieved because the brigade was only lightly armed and woefully short of artillery and antitank ammunition. It would take four days for all the troops in the brigade to deploy to Saudi Arabia.

It soon became clear to the Americans that the fears that led King Fahd to accept foreign forces were not shared by all the members of the political structure in the oil-rich Eastern Province. Rokosz told the Saudis he needed to move his troops through the desert to train, conduct reconnaissance, acclimate to the Saudi blast furnace, and set up defensive positions. But the local Saudi officials were more apprehensive about the influx of foreigners than the Iraqi Republican Guard divisions to their north.

When Rokosz wanted to conduct a reconnaissance mission to the Al Jubail port area, where the huge Maritime Prepositioning Ships full of Marine weapons and supplies were to be unloaded, the Saudis told the soldiers that it would be best to take civilian vehicles instead of their green Humvees, which were equipped with TOW antitank guns.

After four days, Rokosz's brigade was granted permission to move to Al Jubail, and the Saudis arranged for the troops to move into another trailer complex near the port city. The Americans were unsure why they were there in a compound when an Iraqi attack appeared imminent. They told the Saudis the static defenses were absurd. The 82nd needed to get out of their camps, train, and familiarize themselves with the desert terrain.

"Though these guys seemed to know Americans were coming, they had no idea of the scope, and they wanted us to be kind of low-key, low profile, and don't upset the population," recalled Rokosz. "It was screwy."[1]

Gradually, numbers overwhelmed policy. Within a week the escort system began to break down as the Saudi minders were overwhelmed by the flood of Americans troops. Still, the 82nd was more a symbol than a real capability.

"The 82nd was nothing more than a trip-wire force. It was a show of resolve, a way to say to the Iraqis if you run down the highway by the way you are at war with the United States. I never believed for one minute that it could do anything against a sustained offensive armored onslaught," Schwarzkopf recalled after the war.[2]

The 82nd's experience exemplified CENTCOM's initial defensive strategy. In his 1979 Pentagon study, Paul Wolfowitz had warned that, given the vast distance American troops had to travel, the United States needed to get a running head start to prepare a defense of Saudi Arabia if the Iraqis were about to attack. But there was a big difference at the Pentagon between theory and practice. The Bush administration had allowed the Iraqis to get a jump on the Americans, and CENTCOM was facing precisely the situation it had hoped to avoid.

Schwarzkopf's solution was to create the impression that Saudi Arabia was well defended until the heavy reinforcements arrived. To try to fool the Iraqis, Schwarzkopf ordered that the deployment of combat forces be given precedence over the dispatch of ammunition, spare parts, and logistics. The number of American combat units that were seen arriving on the television news seemed impressive, but the deployment was essentially a bluff.

The name of the defensive deployment was Desert Shield, but in the early weeks of the deployment, much of CENTCOM's defense was a hollow force incapable of moving very far and shooting for very long. Schwarzkopf himself recalled that it was not until September 24 — when the first of the heavy armored divisions was deployed to the desert — that he was confident he could repulse an Iraqi attack. Even when the forces took up their positions, the Americans and the Saudis — and within the U.S. command, the Army and the Marines — were often at odds about the tactics to use to defend the kingdom. While CENTCOM held its breath, moving the American forces to the Gulf took longer and proved to be harder than anyone had anticipated.

GETTING THERE IS HALF THE FUN

Schwarzkopf's problems were long in the making. Logistics had always been CENTCOM's Achilles' heel. The problem was that the United States needed a force that would arrive in the region fast enough to fight but heavy enough to survive.

The task was so daunting there was not a single answer. Sealift could deliver the punch, but did not have the speed to get to the crisis area early. Airlift could provide the speed, but could not move heavy forces. Storing heavy equipment in the region helped. Thanks to efforts launched during the Carter administration, the Marines had enough weapons and supplies on the huge Maritime Prepositioning Ships to equip 17,000 men. And $1 billion worth of Air Force fuel and munitions was stored in Oman, Bahrain, and on ships at Diego Garcia. Still, there were only so many weapons stationed in the region.

Given the billions the Pentagon had received during the Reagan administration, it seemed logical that the Defense Department should have expanded its capability to move its forces to the battlefield. But that was not how the Pentagon worked. Logisticians were second-class citizens. Their programs took a back seat to the push to buy new stealth bombers, attack submarines, and other high-tech weapons. The failure to allocate sufficient funds for mundane programs like transport ships, mine-clearing gear, and field radios was one of the major flaws of the Reagan military buildup. The Pentagon behaved like a bachelor who owned a Porsche but forgot to pay his electric bill.

There was no clearer example of the military's neglect of essential but unglamorous logistical programs than ocean transport. During the Vietnam War, 95 percent of all weapons and supplies moved by sea. And while $7 billion had been expended on transport ships during the 1980s, sealift did not have much of a constituency.

The Navy was reluctant to spend more than it was required to buy ships to move the Army. With a declining Pentagon budget, neither Cheney nor Powell had pushed to purchase more and better ships. When Congress appropriated $592 million in funds to buy additional fast ships, Cheney recommended that the funds be rescinded. He shifted $217 million of the money for a military health care program.

Reflecting sealift's low priority, the administration of the program was also a bureaucratic thicket. In peacetime, the ships were operated and maintained by the Maritime Administration, an arm of the Department of Transportation. The civilian agency was familiar with the shipping industry, but not inclined to spend its relatively small budget on military readiness. In wartime, it came under the control of the Navy's Military Sealift Command, which in turn reported to the United States Transportation Command, based at Scott Air Force Base in Illinois, a new command set up to manage troop deployments.

The cream of the fleet were eight SL-7 fast sealift ships. Capable of sustained speeds of 30 knots, each was more than 1,000 feet long and could carry 15,000 tons of equipment — equivalent to the cargo carried by 230 flights of C-5 cargo planes. Together, they could move one heavy Army division. Maintained at a reduced operating status with partial crews, they were expected to be ready to sail within four days. To complement the SL-7s, the United States had ninety-six older and considerably slower ships designated as a "Ready Reserve Fleet." Laid up in inactive status, two-thirds of the ships were to be under way in five days after sailing orders were received; the remainder were to be ready for sea duty within ten to twenty days. The average age of the vessels in the reserve fleet was twenty-seven years, and some were as old as forty-seven years. Eighty percent of the ships had antiquated steam propulsion systems. Only seventeen of them were "Ro-Ro" ships, meaning that they were designed so that vehicles could be driven on and off.

Because the ships were so old it was important that they be regularly tested. But to hold down costs, only twenty-one of the ninety-six ships participated in exercises at sea, and these tended to be the ones that were the most seaworthy. Some vessels sat in port for as long as thirteen years without a test run.

When the United States began to deploy its troops, it paid the price for the years of neglect. The order to activate the first seventeen ships in the reserve fleet was not given until the evening of August 10, a Friday, when union halls were closed. A nationwide call went out for longshoremen, but finding the crews to load the ships was not easy. In the South Port–Wilmington, North Carolina, region, the union could supply only 300 of the 450 to 600 dockworkers that were needed. Assembling the crews to operate the antiquated vessels was no easier. Because of the decline of the American merchant marine, the pool of American labor that could be called on to operate the ships had shrunk. Many sailors had been called out of retirement, and Filipinos were used to man one of the ships. All told, seventy-two of the ninety-six ships in the reserve fleet were eventually activated, but only about a third of them moved on schedule.[3]

The Pentagon's problem in finding ocean transport was a boon to commercial charters, who were quick to profit from the crisis. Some commercial "Ro-Ro" ships were hired at as much as $35,000 a day, double the normal rate. As of mid-October, fifty-seven vessels had been chartered, thirty-three of which operated under a foreign flag.

The Egyptians also benefited handsomely. To persuade Egyptian forces to join the anti-Iraq coalition, President Bush cancelled Egypt's multibillion-dollar debt. But that did not stop Egypt from cashing in on the deployment: it charged $200,000 for each transport ship that transited the Suez Canal, well over the average fee.

Flying cargo by air presented a different set of problems. As in the case of ocean transport, there was a shortage of transport planes to move troops and equipment to the Gulf. Unlike sealift, the Air Force had a healthy commercial industry to fall back on.

Under the Civilian Reserve Air Fleet program, created by the Truman administration to speed the deployment of reinforcements to Europe, civilian airlines committed themselves to furnish cargo- and troop-carrying planes in wartime in return for preferential military contracts in peacetime. With the skies filled with summer travelers, the Transportation Command was worried that airline companies might not respond to the call to action, but the system worked well. Ultimately, 115 planes were requisitioned under the program. Additional civilian planes were voluntarily supplied to the Pentagon under contract. By the war's end, the civilian requisition program was credited with transporting 20 percent of the cargo sent by air and 64 percent of the troops.

While some of Washington's allies helped transport the gear to the Gulf, they did so in a way that maximized their advantages in the commercial market. Japan, which was heavily dependent on Persian Gulf oil, paid American charter companies to fly cargo to the Gulf instead of offering its own planes, thus enabling Japan to keep its profitable commercial routes over the Pacific.

The principal limitation on flying in troops and equipment, however, was not the number of planes but the limited capacity of the airfields in the Gulf. Although the Dhahran and Riyadh air bases were large, combat planes occupied much of the space and used much of the fuel and servicing.

The cargo haulers' second-class status in the military's warrior culture was an added burden. Cargo pilots who refueled at the American air base at Torrejon, Spain, received only perfunctory cooperation from their Air Force colleagues. "The Spanish commander moved his forces before the US commander moved his to give us more space," recalled Gen. Hansford Johnson, who led the Transportation Command. "We were treated worse than any foreign country would have treated us." In Dhahran, cargo pilots were not allowed to eat in the dining hall used by the fighter pilots, and some had to go to the 82nd Airborne to find sleeping quarters, Johnson added, "so I was very disappointed about how the Air Force treated us."[4]

As the cargo planes and ships streamed toward the Gulf, the building blocks of the defense gradually fell into place. While the lightly armed 82nd Airborne was the first ground force to arrive in the Gulf, it was the 7th Marine Expeditionary Brigade that provided CENTCOM with its first substantial ground force.

Commanded by Brig. Gen. John Hopkins, the brigade was based at the Marine Corps training base at Twenty-nine Palms, California, where George S. Patton had trained his armored forces in the early days of World War II. The brigade was the leading edge of the First Marine Expeditionary Force, which was earmarked for deployment to the Gulf.

A 235-pound former Naval Academy football player from Brooklyn who had served two tours in Vietnam, Hopkins was not known for his patience. He was miffed about the delay in sending the Maritime Prepositioning Ships that held the brigade's arms, until King Fahd formally assented to the deployment of American troops.

The first Marines from the brigade arrived by air at Al Jubail on August 14, just in time to greet the first three MPS ships, which arrived the following day with the brigade's tanks, artillery, equipment, and thirty days' ammunition, food, and water.

To achieve a high level of readiness, the equipment in the ships' climate-controlled holds was to be maintained so that vehicles, tanks, radios, and other war matériel could immediately go into action after it was unloaded. But when the Marines began to unload the three ships at Al Jubail, they were dismayed at the poor state of some of the vehicles. Some had no oil while others had an improper weight of oil for the hot desert climate. The biggest problem was batteries. Many of the vehicle batteries were dead, and the Marines were forced to scour the local commercial market for replacements and order emergency shipments from the United States. The unloading of the ships was also hindered by the priority given to the movement of combat troops over support troops. Infantrymen soon found themselves doing engineering and longshoreman work until the deployment plan was modified to bring in more logistical and maintenance teams.

The M-60 tanks that rolled off the ships were far better than the 82nd Airborne's light, antiquated Sheridan tanks, but they were less capable than the Army's new M-1 tanks and there were only 123 of them. The tanks also needed to be test-fired so that the M-60 crews could adjust the sights. Artillery and other major weapon systems also needed to be fired to ensure that they were in proper working condition and to iron out bugs. The Saudis, however, were reluctant to let the Americans turn stretches of the desert into military firing ranges, and the Marines' live-fire exercises were repeatedly postponed. However great the Iraqi threat, the Marines would not get to fire their tanks until mid-October.

The tanks, however, were not the main problem. In keeping with its fighting doctrine, Hopkins's Marine brigade depended heavily on its Harrier attack planes, FA-18 fighter-bombers, and helicopter squadrons. But Marine aircraft flying from the United States were delayed as the Air Force used the tankers to refuel its own planes in flight.

"We had the attack helicopters, the Hueys, and the transports. The helicopters were coming in by Air Force C-5s. We had them all. They were coming in fine. But the fixed-wing was stalled," Hopkins recalled after the war. "The Air Force didn't give us the tankers that we needed to get across the Atlantic."

Lt. Gen. Walter Boomer, the top Marine commander in the Gulf, appealed to Washington, and Schwarzkopf also intervened. The first complement of Marine aircraft, Marine Air Group 70, finally completed its long transoceanic journey to bases in Saudi Arabia and Bahrain on August 24.[5]

As formidable a force as the brigade represented, it was small compared with the Iraqi troops massed in Kuwait. The heavy punch had to come from the Army. But, unlike the Marines, the Army had to ship all its armor and heavy weapons from the United States.

The 24th Mechanized Division at Fort Stewart, Georgia, was the first heavy Army unit to go to the Gulf. Equipped with 1,574 armored vehicles, the 24th Mech had long trained for war in the Middle East and was led by Maj. Gen. Barry McCaffrey, the youngest division commander in the Army and one its most aggressive generals.

To get the divisions to the Gulf as soon as possible, CENTCOM arranged for the unit to be transported via fast sealift ships, which performed reasonably well but were not without their problems. When the division began loading its equipment onto the *Capella* in Savannah harbor on August 12, the vessel became stuck in the mud. The division's logisticians had estimated the weight of the equipment to be put on the ships without taking into account the fuel and ammunition, and the oversight did not become apparent until the tide receded.

Three of the fast sealift ships were delayed an average of ten days because of unscheduled repairs. The most notorious case, however, was the *Antares,* which was undergoing maintenance for engine and boiler problems at the time of the Iraqi invasion but was pressed into service. McCaffrey's planners concentrated much of the division's helicopter brigade and its maintenance and supply system on the ship and were caught short when the vessel broke down in the middle of the Atlantic. After the *Antares* was towed to Rota, Spain, the division's equipment was then loaded on another fast sealift ship, which did not arrive in Saudi Arabia until September 23, a full month from the day the *Antares* left the United States.[6]

Maj. Gen. Binford Peay's 101st Airborne Division also had its share of difficulties. Flush with tank-killing helicopters, the 101st had long figured prominently in CENTCOM's defensive plan. But the Pentagon's failure to make any military preparations until King Fahd agreed to the presence of American troops complicated the division's deployment. Based at Fort Campbell, Kentucky, the 101st was in the middle of its training program when the Iraqis invaded Kuwait and had units in Honduras, Panama, and West Point.

The 101st dispatched its first troops — an aviation task force and an air assault brigade by air to Saudi Arabia — on August 17. Consisting of almost three thousand soldiers and 117 helicopters, the unit provided the initial American force with much-needed mobility and firepower.

Ammunition, however, soon became a big problem. The 101st kept only enough ammunition for one brigade at Fort Campbell. Additional ammunition was to be brought to Jacksonville, Florida, and loaded on the ships that carried the bulk of the division to Saudi Arabia. But the United States Forces Command, which oversees the training and readiness of American-based troops, failed to deliver it.

The division's problems were only compounded by Schwarzkopf's decision to step up and expand the deployment of combat units at the expense of badly needed spare parts and ammunition. Schwarzkopf was hoping to impress the Iraqis with a conspicuous display of American firepower, but the troops in the field felt squeezed. If the Iraqis attacked, they needed to be able to do more than put on a brave front; they needed the logistics to maneuver and fight.

By the 101st Division's own account, the "Screaming Eagles" would have found it difficult to defend their sector "due to the lack of adequate ammunition stockages" and the late arrival of logistics units. "This late arrival strained the ability of combat forces to sustain themselves through the first few months of Operation Desert Shield," the division's command history noted.[7]

To compensate for the slowly arriving ground units, CENTCOM depended on airpower. While the warplanes provided most of the command's striking power in the early weeks, there were limited supplies of spare parts, bombs, and fuel.

A-10 tank-killing planes arrived at the unfinished King Fahd Airport near Dhahran on August 16 with half a tank of fuel only to learn that the nozzles on their fuel tanks were incompatible with the ones at the Saudi base. The planes' cannons were armed with 30mm ammunition, but the Maverick tank-killing missiles they fired needed to be shipped separately. In mid-August, flights of F-15E Strike Eagles were curtailed when a shipment of tires failed to arrive.[8]

Eighteen F-117s left for Saudi Arabia on August 20, each carrying two bombs. Most, if not all, of the bombs were GBU-10s, which were less accurate than the GBU-27s the stealth fighters used during the war. Arriving at Khamis Mushait near the Red Sea, the F-117s did not receive any additional ordnance for about three weeks, when a convoy of flatbed trucks arrived with bombs, bomb finds, and guidance units. The trucks, operated by local drivers, had driven all the way from the east coast of Saudi Arabia escorted by two junior Air Force NCOs armed with a couple of M-16s and a Saudi road map.[9]

As in the case of the ground forces, the Saudis put constraints on the pilots' training. In order not to alarm the Saudi population, CENTCOM agreed to prohibit practice bombing runs and low-level training flights. The Saudis also balked at stationing B-52s at their Jiddah airport, which was close to Mecca. Instead, the B-52s were stationed at Diego Garcia, more than 2,000 miles away from Kuwait.

Another problem was the handful of Patriot anti-missile systems in the Army inventory. CENTCOM needed the missiles to protect Saudi

Arabia's airfields and ports from Iraq's Scud missiles and keep up its flow of reinforcements. But during the first week in August, the Army had only three PAC-2 Patriot missiles, the type that was designed to intercept incoming missiles. A crash program was launched to increase production of the weapons, and as the missiles rolled off the assembly line they were loaded on C-5 planes and rushed to Saudi Arabia. Meanwhile, the Patriot batteries in Saudi Arabia were conspicuously displayed to the press, the military's version of the Potemkin village the Russian czars used to build to impress foreign visitors.[10]

For all of CENTCOM's early vulnerabilities, the Iraqis never learned of one of its greatest pressure points. The command was heavily dependent on the civilian communications satellite network even for sending and receiving coded messages. Even after the Iraqi invasion of Kuwait, much of the communications was routed over land lines to a commercial satellite terminal in Kuwait City and then broadcast back to the United States. There was a satellite terminal in Saudi Arabia, but it could not carry all the message traffic.

"If we lost the downlink in Kuwait City, it would have significantly reduced our capability. The vast majority of our calls on the STU-3 went through Kuwait City," one senior intelligence official said, referring to the device that electronically encodes telephone communications. "Saddam could have totally disrupted our communication capability and forced us to spend an exponential amount of money to rebuild satellite terminals for those communications had he known."[11]

By late August, it was time for Schwarzkopf to move his headquarters from Tampa to Riyadh. As the American troops began to set up their defenses, the American consulate in Dhahran assured American workers at ARAMCO, the Saudi oil company, there was no reason for alarm. The Saudi oil was important to the war effort, and to the world oil supply, and Washington was determined to keep it flowing.

But Schwarzkopf was still worried. The Iraqi forces in Kuwait were continuing to swell. The White House had won United Nations support for an economic embargo, and American and allied ships had begun stopping ships going in and out of Iraq. A skirmish at sea, Schwarzkopf feared, could trigger an Iraqi land attack.

American intelligence also kept him on edge. Iraqi MiGs had strayed over the Saudi border on several occasions, and on August 23 CENTCOM reported that chemical decontamination equipment was located near two Iraqi artillery battalions. It was the first of many intelligence reports that predicted, erroneously, that Iraq intended to use poison gas.

The commander gave particular credence to an intelligence report indicating that the Iraqis had a plan for an offensive into the oil-rich kingdom. "Before the Marines ever got there," Schwarzkopf later said, "we had a defector come in and give us the attack plan." According to the defector, the Iraqis had three options: an attack straight down the coast toward Dhahran, one launched from the western desert aimed at Riyadh, and an attack between the other two routes coming at Dhahran from the northwest.[12]

There is no other evidence that Baghdad ever intended to do anything more than hold what it had already captured. Republican Guard units raced to the Saudi border on the second day of the invasion, but within a matter of days they were replaced by Iraqi infantry units and engineers who began to build a series of defensive positions along the border. The defector's report may have been a ruse to intimidate the Saudis. More likely, it was genuine, but was nothing more than a contingency plan. But it nonetheless contributed mightily to Schwarzkopf's sense of apprehension.

Before leaving for Saudi Arabia, Schwarzkopf stopped in Washington to see Powell on August 24. During the weeks following Iraq's invasion of Kuwait, Powell complained privately to Schwarzkopf that James Baker had all but disappeared, leaving Powell to address diplomatic as well as military issues.

When are we going to hear from the secretary of state? Powell said, referring disparagingly to Baker. Baker and his State Department were not playing the role that they should, and Powell was being forced to pick up the slack, the JCS chief griped. Baker went on a working vacation and assumed a low profile after his return from Moscow. But as a former national security adviser Powell had his own sense of how the Gulf crisis was going to play out and was not hesitant to pass his guidance to Schwarzkopf.

Powell told Schwarzkopf that no more than 150,000 troops would be sent to the Gulf, Schwarzkopf recalled. Echoing the comments he had made to Cheney on the day of the invasion, the JCS chairman said he was concerned the American public would not support keeping a larger force in the inhospitable Saudi desert. Schwarzkopf's own estimate required 216,000 troops, and the CENTCOM commander was determined to deploy every last one of them. As it turned out, the American defensive deployment totaled about 265,000 troops, only to double again when the United States began preparing to launch its offensive.

Powell also pushed Schwarzkopf to continue his offensive planning but told him that he doubted President Bush would sacrifice American lives to wrest Kuwait from Saddam Hussein. The remark said more about Powell's thinking than about that of the president, but it was comforting to the CENTCOM commander, who was consumed with the problems of defending Saudi Arabia and found the idea of an offensive almost too terrible too contemplate.[13]

Several days after arriving in Saudi Arabia, Schwarzkopf echoed Powell's assessment in an August 31 news conference at the Dhahran International Hotel. "There is not going to be any war unless the Iraqis attack," Schwarzkopf said.[14]

That was not the way the president and his White House aides were talking in Washington, but Schwarzkopf did not want to give the Iraqis any incentive to preempt. Until the defense was set, he planned to avoid any talk of an offensive, and Schwarzkopf still was not certain he had the wherewithal to stop the Iraqis dead in their tracks. When asked if the United States and its allies could successfully defend the kingdom, the otherwise voluble CENTCOM commander sidestepped the question. "If the Iraqis are dumb enough to attack, they are going to pay a price," he declared.

But getting the defense in place was more than a matter of sending troops. It was also a question of setting up a command structure and agreeing on strategy and tactics.

THE "DESERT INN" SHOWDOWN

The way Schwarzkopf dealt with the military services in Saudi Arabia said much about his style of generalship. Thoughout the history of warfare, field marshals and generals have confronted the problem of how to lead their subordinate commanders and what to do when they disagreed.

The public perception of Schwarzkopf was that he knocked heads and ruled by decree. But the record is more complicated. Schwarzkopf ranted and raved when his frustrations boiled over. His nickname, "Stormin' Norman," was well earned. But at the same time Schwarzkopf placed enormous confidence in his field commanders and gave them considerable flexibility. Throughout the Gulf War, he never rammed a plan down the throat of any of his Army, Marine, Air Force, or Naval commanders. Nor did he fire a single officer despite his angry threats to do so.

In organizing the defense of Saudi Arabia, Schwarzkopf adopted a decentralized approach. The northeastern sector was divided between the Marines and the Army. Each was free to develop its own war plans as long as they broadly supported his overall strategy. CENTCOM hands dubbed Schwarzkopf's command a "federated system." The approach kept a relative peace among the services, since they all had a piece of the action and the freedom to fight as they saw fit.

But though their plans looked good on paper, the Marines and the Army cast a nervous eye on each other's deployments and tactics. Each service was worried the other might not be able to hold up its end.

Deployed in a ten-mile stretch near the coast, the Marines' initial defense was tied to the terrain. Even before he left the United States, Hopkins began to devise his defensive plan. There were salt marshes — or "sabkah" areas — on both sides of the highway that ran along the Saudi coast and a rock quarry forty miles north of the port of Al Jubail.

If the Marines could force the Iraqis off the highway, Hopkins figured, the Iraqi attack would stall. To block an Iraqi attack down the highway, the Marines planned to mine the road, blow up gas stations along the road, and explode highway culverts. They also planned to harass the Iraqi advance with a light armored infantry battalion and pummel the Iraqis with air and naval gunfire.

The final defensive line would be at the quarry, which the Marines called "Cement Factory Ridge." On a coastal plain that was as flat as a pool table, the quarry represented the only defensible high ground in their sector.

The dispute between the Army and the Marines was less a difference of style about how to fight a defensive battle than a disagreement over how it would develop and the way to deal with it. Both services agreed that the triangle formed by the intersection of the Tapline Road and the coastal highway at Abu Hanifah was critical. But each service was looking at the threat from a different direction. Their swords were crossed.

The Army was concerned that the Iraqis might attack down the coastal highway in the Marine sector and wanted the Marines to meet the Iraqis near Manifah, north of Cement Factory Ridge, where the Iraqis had anchored their defenses. The Marines were concerned that the Iraqis would come down the Tapline Road across the Army sector and then head directly south from An Nuayriyah, flanking the Marines from the west.

Despite the Army plans to cover this route, Boomer and Maj. Gen. James M. "Mike" Myatt, the commander of the 1st Marine Division, to this day maintain that the Army had only paper plans to stop the Iraqis

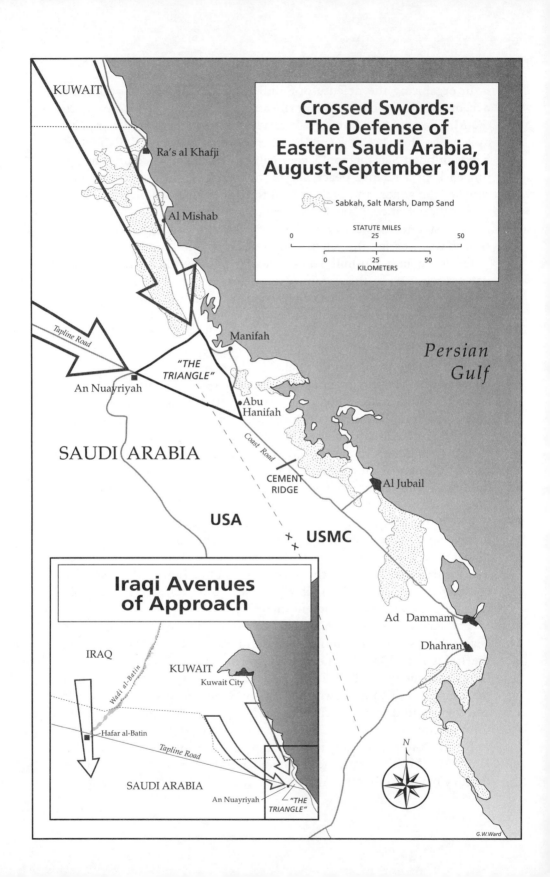

Crossed Swords:
The Defense of
Eastern Saudi Arabia,
August–September 1991

Sabkah, Salt Marsh, Damp Sand

STATUTE MILES
0   25   50

0   25   50
KILOMETERS

KUWAIT

Ra's al Khafji

Al Mishab

Manifah

Persian
Gulf

Tapline Road

"THE
TRIANGLE"

An Nuayriyah

Abu
Hanifah

SAUDI ARABIA

Coast Road

CEMENT
RIDGE

Al Jubail

USA

USMC

Ad Dammam

Dhahran

Iraqi Avenues
of Approach

IRAQ

Wadi al-Batin

KUWAIT

Kuwait City

Hafar al-Batin

Tapline Road

SAUDI ARABIA

An Nuayriyah

"THE
TRIANGLE"

N

G.W.Ward

and did not have the combat power in place to do the job. For that reason, they wanted the Marine zone to include the triangle until the Army had enough forces in Saudi Arabia to support its defensive strategy.

Further, the Marines were being reinforced by the British 7th Armored Brigade, known by its World War II nickname, "The Desert Rats." The deployment of the British force doubled the number of tanks in the Marine area and, as the Marines saw it, strengthened their case for expanding their turf.

The Army, however, was not impressed with the Marines' arguments. With their armor and helicopters, the Army generals believed that the Army was the premier service for land warfare.

Army commanders also thought that the more lightly equipped Marines would have their hands full protecting their narrow sector. And while the Army was short of supplies, Army commanders argued that shifting their divisions farther west to accommodate the Marine commanders would only lengthen the supply lines and make a difficult situation worse.

"The Marines were worried they were so light they needed more tank killers. They wanted the 7th Brigade and we gave it to them. Our notion was to put the 7th Brigade in there to thicken up the tank killers. But then they wanted to widen the sector for more maneuver," recalled Brig. Gen. Steven L. Arnold. "We did not want an open flank or to have our ports cut off from us. We told them, 'Please use the same area that you have.'"[15]

The dispute between the services surfaced when Schwarzkopf assembled his top Army, Air Force, Marine Corps, and Navy commanders in mid-September at the "Desert Inn."

What CENTCOM called the Desert Inn was in reality a mess hall at a Saudi military base at Dhahran. It was a good place for meetings of this sort. Security was tight. It was, more or less, equidistant between the Marine command in Al Jubail, the Navy command in the Persian Gulf, and the Army and Air Force headquarters in Riyadh, yet far enough away from the press headquarters at the Dhahran International Hotel that the media could not see the senior officers come and go. CENTCOM could have a MAP-X, or major review, of its plans there and nobody would be the wiser.

Schwarzkopf said little as Lt. Gen. Boomer and Lt. Gen. Gary E. Luck, commander of the Army's XVIII Corps, explained how they planned to repulse the Iraqis. But as the commanders went through their briefs, it became clear that the command had a problem on its hands. The Marine and Army forces were aligned side by side, but there was a major disconnect between the tactics in the Marine and Army defensive plans.

After the meeting broke up, Luck cornered Boomer. Luck, who held an advanced degree, often played the role of a soft-spoken country boy from Kansas. Some of his Army colleagues would chuckle when he adopted his "Country Gary" mode to pacify the opposition. Now, however, Luck was visibly irritated.

"Goddam, Walt. I thought we had this agreement about how to fight. I thought you were going to do a covering force fight."

"Well, I am," Boomer replied in his tidewater drawl.

After about twenty minutes of discussion, it was apparent that the dispute revolved around doctrinal differences about how to conduct a defense.

The Army and Marine commanders agreed to work out their differences, but they did not work them out. The dispute later came to a boil at a dinner hosted by Luck. Myatt and Luck got into an argument over Myatt's insistence that the boundary be shifted west, which culminated in Luck calling Myatt "a little shit."[16]

Despite the continued friction, Schwarzkopf never intervened to resolve the dispute once and for all. When the Marine-Army boundary dispute was raised at an October 6 briefing at XVIII Corps headquarters, Schwarzkopf ended the discussion by saying, "You guys work it out." While Myatt's relations with Luck were poor, they were good with Barry McCaffrey, whose 24th Mech would bear the brunt of the Iraqi attack along with Myatt's 1st Division. Still, the Marines continued to stress the threat from the northwest and press for more maneuver room.

Recalling the debate, Schwarzkopf later brushed it off saying, "I never had to step in and say, 'I decree this is it.' As I recall the border thing, the border was settled by moving the Marines to the west. We did not give them everything to the west. But they did move to the west."[17]

As the emphasis shifted from defensive to offensive operations, the dispute between the Marine and Army commanders faded into the background.

The Americans, however, were not the only ones who were worried about an Iraqi attack. The Israelis and the Saudis each had serious concerns, and meeting them would not be easy.

COALITION MEMBERS AND OTHER STRANGERS

While Schwarzkopf was trying to build a defense of Saudi Arabia, it was up to Washington to deal with another major player in the area: Israel. Trying to divide the United States from its Arab allies, Iraq had repeatedly threatened to strike Israel if CENTCOM launched an offensive to liberate Kuwait. It was a threat that the Israeli military took seriously.

Five days after the Iraqi invasion, Israel quietly asked the Pentagon to begin joint military planning and establish a command and control link between the two countries in case the Jewish state was attacked. But fearful of upsetting the Arab members of the coalition, the National Security Council staff and the State Department refused to allow the Pentagon to meet with Israeli officials. Finally, however, the Americans agreed to a meeting. If Washington wanted to keep the Israelis out of the war, the Americans at least had to listen to their concerns.

On August 25, David Ivri, the director general of the Israeli Defense Ministry, led a team of Israeli officials to Washington to meet with Paul Wolfowitz, Robert Kimmitt, Richard Haass, and other senior officials. It was an eye-opening meeting for both sides. The Israelis were adamant that Iraq would fire Scud missiles at Israel if the United States and the Iraqis came to blows. They appeared startled to find out in their discussions how little American armor had been deployed to the Gulf. State Department and NSC officials argued that it was not clear that the Iraqis would launch Scuds against Israel and urged the Israelis not to consider a preemptive strike to try to neutralize the Iraqi missile threat.

During the talks, Wolfowitz asked Ivri how Israel might respond if it was hit by Scuds. Ivri gave a qualified response: it would depend on whether the Scud hit an empty parking lot or a crowded section of downtown Tel Aviv and whether Israel felt that the United States had done everything possible to prevent it, a pointed complaint about the perceived lack of U.S.-Israel cooperation.

After the meeting, Cheney recommended that Washington offer to send Patriot antimissile batteries to Israel. The Pentagon wanted to ship the missiles by September 30, the end of the fiscal year, when $75 million of congressional authority that would cover arms transfers to Israel would expire.

Secretary of State Baker, concerned about the appearance of any American-Israeli cooperation, resisted the move. Baker's resistance, however, melted when Cheney reminded him of the political costs. If Israel was attacked and Congress held hearings, the Bush administration would have to explain why it had not done anything to help protect its ally, Cheney argued.

The Pentagon offered to supply the Patriots, but the offer fell short of the cooperation the Israelis had in mind. Israel did not say yes or no to the idea, but at least Washington and Jerusalem had begun a dialogue.[18]

While the Bush administration was willing to cooperate in only the most minimal way with the Israelis, it needed to work closely with the Saudis. The Saudis had no experience in land warfare. Still, the Saudis were supplying the military bases and, possibly, the battlefield, and their views could not be ignored.

To maintain harmony among the Arab and Western members of his eclectic command, Schwarzkopf sought to preserve the fiction that the Americans and Saudis were operating as equals. Schwarzkopf would command the American, British, and other multinational ground forces. Prince Khalid Bin Sultan al-Saud would lead the Arab forces and, initially, the French 6th light division, as Paris was at first reluctant to place its forces under the authority of a U.S. general.

The son of the Saudi defense minister, Khalid had degrees from Sandhurst, the British military academy, and Auburn University. He also was familar with Western ways. One of his favorite forms of relaxation was to watch taped episodes of *Family Feud*. But while Khalid appeared to have the credentials needed to lead the Arab forces, he had little appreciation for American fighting doctrine.

While Schwarzkopf intimidated his staff, he was circumspect with ranking officers from other countries. Powerful constituencies in Riyadh, London, and Paris were watching every move he made, and Schwarzkopf had no intention of adding unnecessary political battles to the military one he faced. Those Americans who were on the receiving end of the beefy general's tantrums marveled at his forbearance with the Arabs and wished that he would extend some of it their way.

In Schwarzkopf's first weeks in the Gulf, however, it became clear that beneath the veneer of unity the Americans and the Saudis disagreed about how to repel an Iraqi attack, and dealing with Khalid sometimes meant finding a polite way to say no. The strategic and operational differences between the two militaries were profound. For the Americans, protecting Saudi Arabia did not entail a commitment to secure every square inch of the kingdom, or even the towns and cities in the north. The Marine and Army defenses were geared to safeguarding the economic heart of Saudi Arabia — the enclave of ports, airfields, and oil complexes strung along the coast from Al Jubail to Dhahran — and the Abqaiq oil province just to the south.

But while Saudi Arabia's northern cities had little significance for CENTCOM, they were important to King Fahd, who had invited in foreign forces to protect his subjects. Khalid argued that the cities should be ringed by troops and the border defended.

Khalid was also worried that the Iraqis might ignore the coastal enclave altogether and drive through the central Saudi town of Hafar al-Batin directly south to Riyadh. The Hafar al-Batin attack route had long been a worry for the Saudis, who at great expense had built a huge military base, King Khalid Military City, just south of the town, complete with airfield and marble dormitories. (Because of its green-domed mosques, the American military irreverently referred to the base as "The Emerald City.")

Khalid stacked his forces near the border, grouping them in two clusters. Saudi and Gulf Arab forces near the coast were organized as the Eastern Province Area Command. As Egyptian and Syrian armored units arrived in the kingdom, Khalid organized them and the remnants of the Kuwaiti army into the Northern Province Area Command and stationed them near Hafar al-Batin. The relatively small and ill-prepared Arab forces belied the grandiloquent titles Khalid had bestowed on them. In deploying his army, Khalid had also left a large gap between his forces that the Iraqis could easily exploit.

"They had taken the national guard and stuck them in the north," Schwarzkopf said. "That way Arab blood would be the first to be shed. Also, the king ordered Khalid not to give up one square inch of Saudi Arabia."[19]

The main issue was not what Khalid was doing with his forces, since the Americans never viewed the Arab forces as anything more than a trip wire. Khalid's plan also had the virtue of keeping the Arab forces clear of the area where the Americans expected the real fighting to take place.

The problem was Khalid's insistence that American forces be moved from the coastal enclave to join the Arabs in protecting the northern cities and blocking the supposed attack route through Hafar al-Batin to Riyadh. Khalid's worst fear was actually the Americans' hope. If an attack was to come at all, the U.S. commanders prayed that the Iraqis would be so foolish as to launch it in the west where they would be battered from the air for its 400-mile length to Riyadh.

"They felt like we gave it lip service," said Arnold. "We felt that it was not a big worry militarily. Most of us had in mind that the Iraqi objectives were clearly Saudi Arabia's oil fields. To the Saudis, it was not."[20]

The Americans tried to assure the Saudis they would never let the Iraqis reach Riyadh and made a few gestures to try to mollify them. When the 1st Cavalry Division was deployed in October, the Saudis were told that it had a secondary mission to block a thrust toward Riyadh. Later, soldiers from the lightly armed 82nd were shifted from Al Jubail to Riyadh, where they were ordered to defend the city and protect against a terrorist attack.

As the 82nd moved south, Col. Ron Rokosz discovered once again that the anxieties at the highest levels of the Saudi government had not trickled down to the locals. After guarding the Al Jubail area, Rokosz was assigned to protect Abqaiq, an ARAMCO oil complex northeast of Riyadh. Rokosz soon learned that while the American and British employees of the company were helpful, the Saudi officials who ran the company were more afraid that the presence of the soldiers would make the company a target for Muslim fundamentalists than they were that the Iraqis would arrive.

Company officials refused to let the soldiers connect their field telephones to the ARAMCO phone lines or help the 82nd in other ways. "At the official ARAMCO level, they wouldn't do a goddamn thing for the U.S. Army," Rokosz recalled. "I mean nothing unless the Army made sure the request came from a Saudi prince." It was not the last time that the Saudi oil company refused to cooperate with the American troops that had been dispatched to protect the free world's oil supply.[21]

Over the next few months, the top American and Saudi command would work relatively well together. But the secret of their success lay more in keeping a respectful distance than in lockstep teamwork.

Schwarzkopf's philosophy of command worked during the early months of the American deployment because it was never seriously tested. His penchant to allow each service to fight the war as it saw fit minimized the political headaches. But his failure to harmonize the Marine and Army plans left some critical strategic and tactical issues unresolved. If the Iraqis had attacked, its inherent flaws might have been exposed.

Because the Iraqis never attacked, the disagreements over the defense of Saudi Arabia soon became a moot issue. But Schwarzkopf's proclivity to stand back while his commanders clashed established a pattern that would come back to haunt the command when it planned its offensive.

4

Instant Thunder

What it is: a focused, intense, air campaign designed to incapacitate Iraqi leadership and destroy key Iraqi military capability in a short period of time. And it is designed to leave basic Iraqi infrastructure intact.

What it is not: a graduated, long-term campaign plan designed to provide escalation options to counter Iraqi moves.

> — Instant Thunder plan
> Presented to Gen. H. Norman Schwarzkopf
> August 17, 1990

It sounds like a "decapitate the snake plan." I don't see it as a slick plan, but as a "hit him in the face plan."

> — Lt. Gen. Charles Horner
> Response to Instant Thunder plan
> August 20, 1990

WHILE SCHWARZKOPF was busy overseeing the defense of Saudi Arabia, he worried about how he would strike back at the Iraqis if they began to harm the American citizens who were being detained in Kuwait and in Iraq. The CENTCOM staff was working on possible retaliatory options, but Schwarzkopf was not happy with any of them. Several revolved around the use of cruise missiles. But at that point, a cruise missile had never been fired in anger, and Schwarzkopf was not sure they would get off the ship, let alone hit targets in Iraq. Other options included blowing up Iraqi dams, a violation of the Geneva convention, and even a threat to use nuclear weapons. A ground attack was out of the question — for the moment. Schwarzkopf had estimated that it would take eight to ten months to amass enough force for a land offensive.

Clearly, better ideas were needed, and it did not appear that anyone at CENTCOM was capable of coming up with them. Lt. Gen. Charles Horner had not taken air-war planning very far, and he was in Saudi Arabia overseeing the deployment of American forces. CENTCOM's staff included Lt. Gen. Craven C. Rogers, the deputy commander, and Maj. Gen. Burton Moore, Schwarzkopf's J-3, or chief operations officer. They had been sent to CENTCOM as a reward for their long years of loyal Air Force service. They were not strategists. Schwarzkopf was afraid that the president would demand retaliation only to find the quiver empty.

"It was about a week into war. They had all the hostages and guests. There was a lot of rhetoric on how they better not hurt our guys or else," Schwarzkopf recalled. "I am thinking retaliation. I want a list of options, minimal up to full-scale attack. If the president comes to me and says 'I have to retaliate,' I have got a platter to pick from."[1]

Schwarzkopf called Powell and told him he needed help from the air staff at the Pentagon, he recalled. Then, with Powell's permission, Schwarzkopf called Gen. John M. "Mike" Loh, the Air Force vice chief of staff, on August 8 and asked for headquarters' help in "showing him what air could do in Iraq."

If it had been almost any other time of the year, Schwarzkopf's request would have been relayed by Loh to Lt. Gen. Jimmie V. Adams, a staunch advocate of Tactical Air Command's position that the main contribution of airpower was to interdict enemy ground forces, not undertake strategic bombing campaigns to win the war. But Adams was on a long, scheduled leave. So the request trickled down to Col. John A. Warden III, who ran a highly classified war-gaming office known as Checkmate. In less than ten days, Warden had developed an air-war plan. Warden's plan was skeletal and overambitious, but it provided the conceptual underpinning of CENTCOM's strategic air campaign.

There are many secrets of the Gulf War, but one of the most sensitive episodes concerns the genesis of the air-campaign plan. The official mythology of the war holds that Congress had been so successful in strengthening the role of the theater commands through defense reform legislation that CENTCOM had the expertise and resources to do the war planning on its own and that civilian and military officials in Washington, mindful of the errors of the Vietnam War, took a virtual hands-off approach toward the planning of the war in the Gulf.

Like most myths, it contains elements of fact mingled with self-serving omissions. The fact is that Schwarzkopf opened the door for the planning of the air campaign almost without knowing it, and, initially, his top Air Force commander had nothing but contempt for the idea. The initial plan, which the Air Force would later tout as a revolution in warfare, was a hard sell even within the Air Force.

The allied air campaign to take the war to downtown Baghdad from the opening moments of the Persian Gulf conflict was one of the military's most important strategic innovations. But it almost did not happen.

CHECKMATE

John Warden was on a Caribbean vacation, relaxing on a cruise ship steaming south of Cuba when Iraqi forces invaded Kuwait. There was no way to get off the ship before it docked in Miami. Warden would not be back at the Pentagon until Monday morning, August 6, and he spent the time at sea thinking about what sort of air campaign would be needed to beat back the Iraqis.

An iconoclast to his critics, a visionary to admirers, Warden was passionate about strategic bombing to the point of zealotry. He was virtually unknown outside the Pentagon, and his career had had its ups and downs.

An OV-10 pilot in Vietnam and the director of operations in an F-4 wing, Warden had made his mark as a strategist. But he ran into problems when he was promoted to be a wing commander in Europe. Gen. William L. Kirk, the commander in chief of the U.S. Air Force in Europe, sent Warden back to Washington after only six months as a wing commander, ostensibly to oversee a study on how to operate air bases while under enemy attack. Warden's supporters say that Kirk was uncomfortable with Warden's insistence on pushing the envelope while critics say the episode showed that Warden was a better theorist than a commander. In the military, where careers are built by command, not by desk work at the Pentagon, the abrupt transfer was an unusual setback for the officer. Warden ended up with an office in the basement of the Pentagon, but only weeks after arriving there he found a kindred spirit in Michael Dugan, then Air Force deputy chief of staff for plans and operations, whose star was continuing to ascend. Like Warden,

Dugan believed that the Air Force was too preoccupied with new weaponry at the expense of strategy. Dugan ordered that a new strategy office be created. He made Warden its director.

Warden set out to make people rethink how to use airpower, developing his "five rings" paper in 1988. Throughout the cold war, the Air Force had focused on two types of airpower: strategic and tactical, each of which had its own bureaucracy and doctrine. Strategic airpower was largely identified within the Air Force as nuclear firepower for deterring a Soviet nuclear strike and turning the Soviet Union into a radiating ruin if deterrence failed. It was overseen by SAC, the Strategic Air Command, based in Omaha, Nebraska.

Tactical air operations, on the other hand, focused on using fighter and ground attack planes to gain air superiority and then interdict enemy forces on their way to the battlefield. It was the province of the Tactical Air Command, located at Langley, Virginia. TAC's approach fit nicely with the American cold war policy of containing the expansion of Soviet power, which in military terms meant keeping Soviet military forces within the borders of the Soviet Union and its satellite nations. If the Soviet forces launched an invasion of Western Europe or Iran, American warplanes would knock out their airfields, achieve air superiority, and destroy advancing enemy columns, supply lines, and depots. TAC was planning a war of attrition.

Warden found both concepts of air warfare too limiting, and his "five rings" paper sought to rehabilitate and update the old arguments that a war could be won by aerial bombing raids with non-nuclear weapons against key "centers of gravity" in the enemy homeland or in the field if attacks deep in enemy territory were not feasible. The object of an air campaign, Warden reasoned, should be to convince the enemy leadership to do what you want them to do. That meant you had to see things from their standpoint: what were the enemy's instruments of internal control; what political, economic, and military assets allow the enemy to stay in power and command their forces.

Warden depicted the modern battlefield as a dartboard. In the bull's-eye was the command, control, communications, and decision-making capability of the enemy. It was the prime target for any air campaign, and a direct hit could put an end to the enemy regime's ability to stay in power or run the affairs of state, including its war effort.

The first ring around the bull's-eye represented the enemy's military and economic production capability, its factories, electrical grids, power plants, refineries, and the like — all essential to a sustained war effort and modern life. Cripple this and the enemy lost the ability to function.

The third ring held the means of transportation, movement, and distribution — bridges, highways, airfields, and ports. Destroy these and military and civilian traffic would be paralyzed.

The fourth outward circle is the population and its food sources. Giulio Douhet, the early Italian airpower theorist, had advocated attacking these targets to break a population's will to resist. But Warden reasoned that the moral implications of hitting this ring were repugnant to most states and argued that hits on this ring would be unlikely to pay big dividends even if it were ethical.

The fifth and outermost ring was the least important of the target array: the enemy's military forces. Warden reasoned that these existed only to protect the inner rings — particularly the decision-making capabilities in the bull's-eye — and to pose a threat to the attacker.

When Dugan was promoted to be the top Air Force commander in Europe, Warden lost an ally and protector. Jimmie Adams was Dugan's successor as the Air Force deputy chief of staff for plans and operations. Adams was TAC through and through, a protégé of Gen. Robert D. Russ, the TAC commander at Langley, who believed that the Air Force's main role was to support the Army. Adams let the strategist know that he thought his theorizing was radical.

Warden's fortunes improved when Dugan returned in 1990 as the four-star chief of staff of the Air Force, and the colonel's perspective also was in accord with that of Donald B. Rice, the former president of the Rand Corporation, who became secretary of the Air Force in the Bush administration. Rice was a strong advocate of the proposition that the Air Force could do much more than just support the Army.[2]

Even before Schwarzkopf's call to Mike Loh on August 8, Warden had Checkmate working on a war plan. Housed behind cipher-locked doors in the basement of the Pentagon, Checkmate had been created by David Jones, the Air Force general whom Jimmy Carter later selected to be chairman of the Joint Chiefs of Staff, to assess how the Air Force would stack up against the Soviets during a big war in Europe. The information fed into Checkmate's computers included classified data on the performance of American aircraft and weapons systems as well as intelligence estimates about the Soviet air force and other potential adversaries. But Checkmate was more than a computer program; it was a means of drawing on intelligence experts, targeteers, and weapon specialists throughout the government to analyze and simulate air campaigns as realistically as possible.

Warden presented an initial brief of his plan to Loh, incorporating some of the general's suggestions. Reflecting Warden's concept of the five rings, the aim of the plan was to persuade Saddam Hussein to pull his troops out of Kuwait and sue for peace — without a ground war. Or, if that did not happen, the air strikes would create the conditions for his overthrow.

American air strikes would not concentrate on the Iraqi troops occupying Kuwait, not even on Saddam Hussein's Republican Guard, which had spearheaded the invasion. That would be like aiming for the outer ring of the dartboard. The bull's-eye was Saddam's command and control facilities in and around Baghdad, his political headquarters, his secret policy network, even statues of the Iraqi leader. They were all instruments of Saddam's control over Iraq or visible symbols of his power. Simultaneously, the air attacks would go after the second and third rings: Iraq's weapons factories, its electrical grid, its oil refineries, as well as the transportation system to move vital military commodities. The political objective of these strikes would be to make it impossible for Saddam Hussein to run his country and to drive a wedge between the Iraqi leadership and the Iraqi people by bringing home the costs of war. The military objective would be to knock out that portion of the national infrastructure that was essential for the war effort.

Warden dubbed the plan Instant Thunder. It was a play on the Rolling Thunder campaign of the Vietnam War, the bombing attacks that Lyndon Johnson had launched to reverse the United States' declining fortunes in the deltas and jungles of Vietnam. To airpower advocates like Warden, Rolling Thunder was a virtual prescription for how not to use airpower. The campaign had been long and drawn out, interrupted by pauses that gave the enemy a chance to recover and adapt. Its objectives constantly changed, oscillating from the tactical to the strategic. It never focused on the most important objective of all: command, the "center of gravity" of the enemy war effort. By contrast, Instant Thunder was a massive and concentrated six-day-long aerial coup de main.

Dugan was a strong supporter of Instant Thunder and believed strategic airpower could prove itself in the Gulf. Clausewitz, the Prussian military strategist, had argued that war went from the outside in. Armies would clash on the periphery of each side's territory and then penetrate to the interior. This time, the Air Force would wage war from the inside out, the first truly strategic air war.

But Dugan also knew what it would take to sell the plan. He telephoned Schwarzkopf and reported that the air staff at the Pentagon had put together a plan to defeat Iraq. If Schwarzkopf liked the plan, it would be his, not the Air Force headquarters', plan, Dugan explained.

It was critical that CENTCOM, including its senior Air Force representatives, overcome the "not invented here" syndrome.[3]

RENDEZVOUS WITH THE CINC

On August 10, Maj. Gen. R. Minter Alexander, the head of the plans directorate under Adams and Warden's direct superior, led a briefing team to CENTCOM, flying down on an Air Force C-21. Other members of the team included Warden; Lt. Col. Ben Harvey, the acting director of the Air Force's "Skunk Works," or strategy division, and a former EC-135 pilot; Maj. Larry Eckberg, an Air Force intelligence officer; and Lt. Col. Ron Stanfill, a scholarly-looking officer who had over 2,500 hours flying the F-111 and who helped plan Eldorado Canyon, the Air Force raid against Libya.

Warden had never met Schwarzkopf before, but he knew what buttons to push. Schwarzkopf was a four-star Army general, and Warden was careful to explain his plan using ground force metaphors. Instant Thunder, Warden explained, was the aerial equivalent of the old First World War Schlieffen plan, with which every West Point graduate was familiar.

Count Alfred von Schlieffen rose to become chief of the German general staff. Schlieffen's planning was imbued with an offensive spirit that aimed at a decisive victory. In 1905, Schlieffen drafted a daring plan to envelop and destroy the French army in the event of war with France. Seven German armies would be divided into two wings: a left wing consisting of two armies and a right wing made up of five armies. While the left wing blunted an anticipated French offensive, retreating slowly if necessary, the more powerful right wing would outflank the French, marching into the rear of the French army, taking Paris, and depriving the French forces of their support base. Even after his retirement, Schlieffen was persuaded that the only way to defeat the French was through strategic maneuver and his dying words in 1913 as World War I approached were "See that you make the right wing strong!" But Schlieffen's advice was rejected by his successor, Helmuth von Moltke, who took forces from the right wing to strengthen the left. The results were disastrous. When the war erupted, the attack by the German right wing stalled at the Battle of the Marne.

For Warden, the analogy between the Schlieffen plan and the air campaign was uncannily apt, and the colonel used his hands to demonstrate the connection in his brief for Schwarzkopf. The aerial attacks on Baghdad and points deep in Iraq were the vertical equivalent of

Schlieffen's right wing ground assault to defeat the enemy in his rear, Warden said, extending one hand as if it were a formation of warplanes heading toward Baghdad. Close air support and interdiction of advancing armies were the equivalent of Schlieffen's left wing and were needed only to hold the enemy in place or blunt his ground offensive, Warden added, keeping his other hand close to his chest. The air campaign could be decisive if Schwarzkopf, in effect, kept "the right wing strong," putting the emphasis on attacking Baghdad and targets deep in Iraq. But if CENTCOM diverted aircraft from the deep strikes to attack the Iraqi ground troops, it would repeat von Moltke's error of cautiously guarding against an enemy breakthrough while sacrificing the opportunity for a decisive offensive blow. Warden had taken his belief in strategic airpower to its logical extreme. Instant Thunder called for attacks deep in Iraq, but no attacks were planned on Iraqi forces or targets in Kuwait.

Then, having explained the concept, Warden used a more up-to-date analogy to heighten the appeal of the plan to Schwarzkopf, recalling Douglas MacArthur's bold decision during the Korean War to bypass the advancing North Korean armies with the surprise Marine landing at Inchon, a move recorded in the annals of military history as exemplary generalship. The air campaign, Warden told the commander, would be an opportunity to achieve the greatest military victory since Inchon.

Schwarzkopf, a man of no small ego, was impressed. For the first time, he had a plan to call on in case the White House wanted to take action against Iraq. But Schwarzkopf also confided that, even if war came, he did not think CENTCOM would ever get a chance to conduct an extended bombing campaign. After three or four days of bombing, the war would probably be brought up in the United Nations, Schwarzkopf said. Even if Iraq attacked first, the idea that the world community would sit idly by and watch American airpower pulverize Iraq for six days was unlikely. By the end of the fifth or sixth day, Schwarzkopf said, there would probably be a UN call for a cease-fire and Washington would have little choice but to go along. Schwarzkopf told Warden to brief the plan to Colin Powell and then return in a week's time when the plan had been fleshed out. Warden was on his way.

The next day, August 11, Warden and a group of senior Air Force officers crowded into Powell's first-floor office at the Pentagon. Equipped with a sofa, several armchairs, and a coffee table, the chairman's office was not the place for a large meeting. But more than a dozen senior military officers and their aides were there at 9:25AM to discuss the plan, some of whom were kneeling in a half-crouch as if they were in a football huddle because there were not enough chairs to go around. Also attending the meeting was Adm. David Jeremiah, the vice chairman of the JCS; Lt. Gen. Thomas Kelly, the J-3, or chief operations officer for the JCS; and Lt. Gen. Lee Butler, the J-5, or Powell's chief planning officer.

Based on his experience in Vietnam, Powell was skeptical of the claims made by airpower enthusiasts and had set in motion a huge deployment of ground troops. It was a view that Powell would carry with him throughout the planning and conduct of the war. But in the first month or two of the deployment, there was little choice but to rely heavily on airpower.

"This is not Rolling Thunder. It is Instant Thunder," Warden began his brief, according to then top secret minutes of the meeting taken by one of the participants. The colonel was drawing the philosophical distinction for Powell. Instant Thunder still needed to be fleshed out, but Warden said that he was planning seven hundred attacks per day for six days. Warden's Air Force superiors spoke up to demonstrate their support of the plan.

The plan "could not be done in pieces," Alexander said.

"That is right. This is a highly integrated plan," added Loh.

Powell's response was generally positive. He described Instant Thunder as a good plan, a fine piece of work. But it was clear that the JCS chairman still had some serious questions. What would happen after the six-day campaign was executed?

Loh responded that the United States would have air supremacy. The six days of air strikes would take a tremendous psychological toll on the Iraqi leadership. The Saddam Hussein regime would be incapable of continuing its current course of action. Alexander was somewhat more cautious in promising results: Instant Thunder was a good plan, but there were no guarantees.

The discussion then turned to what fuel and munitions would be required to support Instant Thunder. This was a discussion about logistics, but also a measure of Powell's enthusiasm for the air-war plan. The preparations for an air campaign could be accelerated if the logistical flow was tilted more in favor of the Air Force. The Air Force generals said that the plan could be carried out in about a month under the current logistical assumptions, but the preparations could be speeded up if more transport was made available to the Air Force. Powell indicated that he did not want to interfere with the current deployment plan. Getting the forces to the Gulf was hard enough without trying to redo the transportation plan to support Instant Thunder. It was apparent that Powell's enthusiasm for Instant Thunder went only so far. If there was any misunderstanding about where Powell stood, he made things clear, bluntly stating that he could not recommend to the president that the United States rely exclusively on airpower to defeat the Iraqis. Whatever campaign was launched would have to be backed up by ground troops.

Then Powell honed in on his principal concern with Instant Thunder. The plan had a serious omission: it did not call for any strikes on the Iraqi ground troops that had invaded Kuwait and which, he thought, could threaten the region for years to come. The strategic air plan aimed to cut out the enemy's guts and heart, but did not touch his hands and feet, the troops in the field. Unlike Warden, Powell had focused on Iraq's ground forces from the beginning of the crisis. If Iraq salvaged its prime ground-combat forces, the United States would have a long-term problem on its hands. It would have to worry about tying down its forces defending the Saudi kingdom, whose terrain and climate were forbidding and which might not welcome a long-term American presence. Soon after the invasion, Powell had told Kelly that if war broke out, Iraq's army of 1 million men and 5,000 tanks needed to be reduced once and for all so that it could never again be a threat to the region. Powell thought that an army of 100,000 men and 1,000 tanks would suffice to guarantee Iraq's defense. Powell did not repeat those figures to the Air Force, but he made clear that he wanted some of the airpower directed at the Iraqi armor.

Powell was a reluctant warrior, but if there was to be war, it was clear what he considered the major criterion for success. From the start, Powell defined victory in terms of destroying Iraq's potent ground forces, a goal CENTCOM would never fully achieve.

Warden was more concerned with destroying Iraq's weapons of mass destruction, but he promised that the air campaign would induce Saddam Hussein to pull his forces out of Kuwait. But Powell did not want the Iraqis to withdraw with their equipment, he wanted their invasion force to be destroyed.

"I won't be happy until I see his tanks destroyed," Powell said. "I want to leave their tanks as smoking kilometer fence posts all the way back to Baghdad."

Loh, Warden, and Kelly agreed that tanks were not hard to kill. It would be left to the air-war planners to work out the details.

Powell gave Warden the green light to proceed but ordered that the planning effort be expanded to include representatives from all the services and be conducted under the auspices of the JCS. Maj. Gen. J. W. Meier, a deputy operations officer on the JCS staff, would be in charge. Powell also asked Warden to condense the briefing so that he — Powell — could give it to "senior officials." And the following week, he went over it with the most senior official — President Bush.[4]

There was still a lot of work to do before Instant Thunder was ready for prime time. Warden had yet to specify a full list of targets, required munitions, and supporting aircraft. Warden was over another hurdle, but he was not there yet. He still had to sell the fleshed-out plan to Schwarzkopf. Nor was he without critics in his own service.

As Instant Thunder was developed in Checkmate's warren of offices in the Pentagon basement, planners at the Tactical Air Command at Langley, Virginia, began to snipe at the plan. Adams's absence in early August had enabled Warden to launch his efforts without objection from the TAC community, which believed in hitting what the Army asked it to hit. But now that the Instant Thunder plan was starting to get around, the TAC planners were unhappy. TAC had sent three colonels to "observe" and "assist" in the planning. But rather than help, they questioned why the effort was under way.

Although their objections were primarily military, TAC officers couched much of their complaining in terms of command prerogatives. Pentagon officials in Washington should not be in the business of devising an air campaign for CENTCOM to carry out 7,000 miles away, TAC officers argued. That violated one of the cardinal lessons from the Vietnam War. Congress had passed the 1986 Goldwater-Nichols Defense Reorganization Act, which strengthened the authority of the theater commanders, or CINCs, precisely to stop the kibitzing colonels and generals in Washington from trying to run the show. The TAC planners had a few ideas of their own about how to wage an air campaign. While some were similar, most differed markedly from Warden's plan. The ideas were put down in a briefing that was sent back up to circulate at the Pentagon. TAC was not trying to win the war single-handedly; it would support the Army's troops. Nor did the TAC planners foresee a violent spasm that would bring the brunt of the air strikes to downtown Baghdad. Instead, it envisoned several bombing pauses to give Saddam a chance to seek a diplomatic solution, reprising the graduated escalation concept that had failed in Vietnam. That was a surprising feature, given the military's oft-stated complaints that it had had one hand tied behind its back during the Vietnam War. The proponents of Instant Thunder had stolen a march on the TAC mafia during the first two weeks of August, but it was clear that there were Air Force critics ready to put forth their own plan at the first opportunity, should Warden be rebuffed.

On August 17, Meier led Warden and a multiservice team of planners to CENTCOM to give Schwarzkopf and his staff the expanded Instant Thunder brief. This time Warden was playing to a larger audience. The briefing was to be given in a small auditorium. Most of the top CENTCOM planners would be present. The definition of the campaign, the opening slide in the presentation, drew a sharp distinction between Instant Thunder and the Vietnam-era bombing attacks, an appealing point for Schwarzkopf, who had been seared by his Vietnam experience.

> What it is: a focused, intense, air campaign designed to incapacitate Iraqi leadership and destroy key Iraqi military capability in a short period of time. And it is designed to leave basic Iraqi infrastructure intact.

> What it is not: a graduated, long-term campaign plan designed to provide escalation options to counter Iraqi moves.

Instant Thunder, the briefing slides continued, would enable the United States to seize the initiative, to attack the heart of the problem, the Saddam Hussein regime, and could be executed in the near term, which was critical. The briefing suggested that time was on Saddam Hussein's side, as it would allow him to strengthen his hold on Kuwait while the allies' resolve might falter.

At this early stage, there were eighty-four targets in all, broken down as follows:

Strategic Air Defense:	10
Strategic Chemical:	8
National Leadership:	5
Telecommunications:	19
Electricity:	10
Oil (internal consumption):	6
Railroads:	3
Airfields:	7
Ports:	1
Military production and storage depots:	15

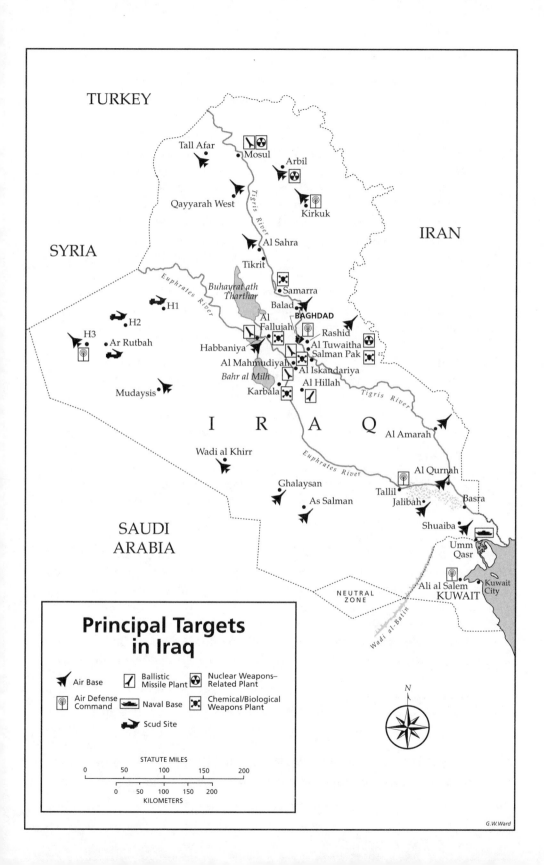

TURKEY

Tall Afar

Mosul

Arbil

Qayyarah West

Kirkuk

IRAN

SYRIA

Al Sahra

Tikrit

Tigris River

Buhayrat ath Tharthar

Samarra

H1

Balad

BAGHDAD

H2

Al Fallujah

Rashid

H3

Euphrates River

Ar Rutbah

Habbaniya

Al Tuwaitha

Salman Pak

Al Mahmudiyah

Al Iskandariya

Bahr al Milh

Al Hillah

Mudaysis

Karbala

Tigris River

I R A Q

Al Amarah

Wadi al Khirr

Euphrates River

Ghalaysan

Al Qurnah

As Salman

Tallil

Basra

SAUDI ARABIA

Jalibah

Shuaiba

Umm Qasr

NEUTRAL ZONE

Ali al Salem

Kuwait City

KUWAIT

Wadi al-Batin

Principal Targets in Iraq

Air Base

Ballistic Missile Plant

Nuclear Weapons– Related Plant

Air Defense Command

Naval Base

Chemical/Biological Weapons Plant

Scud Site

STATUTE MILES

0   50   100   150   200

0   50   100   150   200

KILOMETERS

N

G.W.Ward

The most important targets were the leadership and telecommunications centers that enabled Saddam Hussein to run his country. Although the briefing did not say so, the Warden team had, in some cases, pinpointed the location of Iraq's leaders and command centers down to the office, window, and floor. To do this they had drawn on the knowledge of members of the diplomatic corps and intelligence experts. The attacks on Baghdad, the briefing stated, would be accompanied by a psychological operations campaign to deny Saddam Hussein popular support and encourage his overthrow. There would be radio and TV broadcasts and leaflet drops in Baghdad. The United States would tell the Iraqi people why it was bombing their capital and what they needed to do to bring an end to the conflict. Iraq's electrical grid and oil-refining capability would be attacked, as would its railroads and airfields. Its nuclear, biological, and chemical weapons production and storage capabilities, deemed to be a threat to American troops and Iraq's neighbors, would be targeted.

Operationally, the attacks would be carried out over a six-day period of around-the-clock attacks, day and night. On the first two days, American aircraft would attack all the strategic targets on the list. The simultaneous attack on all targets was a radical departure from American wartime operations, when aircraft were massed to strike key targets sequentially, starting with the enemy air defenses. On days three and four, American planes would reattack targets that had not been destroyed, based on initial bomb damage assessments, with an emphasis on destroying what was left of the Iraqi air force. Given the problems that the Air Force would later experience in getting timely and accurate intelligence to determine which targets were not destroyed, the notion of carrying out effective restrikes on the third and fourth days of the war was considerably optimistic. On the final two days, the air attack would concentrate on chemical weapons production facilities and other military-industrial targets. It would be an intense campaign with no letups. No fewer than 1,200 total sorties, 700 of which would be bombing sorties, would be flown the first day, and 900 total sorties would be flown each day for the remainder of the campaign.

To carry out the attack, the Warden team worked with the scheduled Air Force deployments. But CENTCOM's initial list of planes to be sent to the region was decidedly defensive in character. It included air superiority fighters and A-10 antitank planes, but no B-52 bombers, stealth F-117A fighters, or F-111Fs, which had the capability to deliver precision-guided munitions but which were assigned to defend

NATO. The list would not do for Instant Thunder. The United States would need the strike planes, as well as Tomahawk sea-launched cruise missiles.

The Instant Thunder briefing contained a long list of anticipated results:

Strategic Air Defense: Destroyed
Strategic Chemical: Long-Term Setback
National Leadership: Incapacitated
Telecommunications: Disrupt/Degrade
Electricity: 60 percent Baghdad, 35 percent country (Destroyed)
Oil (internal consumption): 70 percent (Destroyed)
Railroads: Disrupt/Degrade
Airfields: Disrupt/Degrade
Ports: Disrupt
Key Military Production/Storage: Disrupt/Degrade

Warden relegated attacks on Iraq's ground forces to a subsequent phase of the attack plan. Although Powell wanted to destroy Iraqi tanks, Warden did not want to dilute the bombing attacks against Iraqi command centers by diverting a lot of sorties to attacks on Iraqi ground troops. On strategic airpower he was a purist. Warden did not think the United States would ever need to go beyond the strategic air campaign, but he later drafted a plan for a several-phase attack: phase one would be the Instant Thunder plan; phase two would be a one-day effort to achieve air superiority over Kuwait; phase three would be attacks on the Iraqi ground forces — a plan that Schwarzkopf appropriated as his own.[5]

After the briefing, there was a discussion of the inevitability of civilian casualties and the detailed plans for targeting the Iraqi leadership and psychological operations that would accompany such attacks. There was a brief discussion of who might take over Iraq if Saddam Hussein was killed or overthrown.

Meier also reported Dugan's assessment on the feasibility of the plan. The Air Force chief of staff was putting his weight behind the plan, certifying that it was not overly optimistic and could be executed in mid-September, perhaps earlier with some additional risk. Like Powell, Schwarzkopf was not interested in the Air Force suggestion that air and sealift plans be rejiggered to accelerate the deployment of Air Force munitions and logistics.

"I cannot flow air and land simultaneously," Schwarzkopf said.

Meier responded that he was not telling Schwarzkopf what to do. He was just offering him an option.

Maj. Gen. Robert B. Johnston, the Marine Corps officer who served as Schwarzkopf's chief of staff at CENTCOM, mounted the strongest challenge to the plan. Johnston wanted to know if the Air Force had a plan to logistically support a longer air campaign, and suggested that CENTCOM might want to take a longer time to destroy the air defenses before tackling all the targets deep in Iraq. Warden's team was surprised at the point. The idea of drawing out the campaign ran counter to the whole simultaneity concept of the Instant Thunder plan. Schwarzkopf, however, was not interested in pursuing the point. He quickly dismissed the comment, referring to the lessons of Vietnam.

As the discussion continued, it centered on the attrition the coalition could suffer. One CENTCOM official estimated that 10 to 15 percent of the attacking aircraft might be lost, but Warden indicated that he thought that was far too high, and estimated that ten to fifteen planes might be lost the first day, no more than forty over the entire six-day period. The Air Force would use mass, shock, and the destruction of enemy command centers to gain air superiority and keep American casualties low. "I am a volunteer to fly," said Warden, dramatically underscoring his claim.

As the meeting came to a close, Schwarzkopf said that his intention was to continue the air-war planning. He wanted Warden to present the Instant Thunder plan to Horner in Riyadh. Meier asked when Schwarzkopf wanted that done.

"The sooner the better," Schwarzkopf shot back. "We are at war."[6]

Warden believed that he had sold Schwarzkopf on the plan. But like Powell, the CENTCOM commander was never persuaded that airpower could triumph on its own. Additionally, even in dispatching Warden to Saudi Arabia, Schwarzkopf did not fully grasp the essence of the Warden plan.

After the war, Schwarzkopf said he thought Warden's plan fulfilled two functions. It was, he said, a "Chinese menu," a list of target categories such as leadership, transportation, and logistics that CENTCOM might use a basis for launching retaliatory strikes. Alternatively, Schwarzkopf saw the Instant Thunder plan as "a precursor to an offensive plan," a way to reduce Iraqi strength prior to a ground war. Both views ran counter to Warden's idea that Instant Thunder was a recipe for victory. The most innovative and important part of the American war plan had been launched, but there was no agreement at the highest levels what it was all about.

RIYADH SHOWDOWN

The cover story for Warden's August 19 trip to Riyadh was that he was heading a study team to examine the lessons learned from the deployment to the Gulf. In addition to Warden, the delegation included three bright lieutenant colonels who had been involved in the planning of Instant Thunder from the very beginning: David Deptula, a member of Secretary Rice's staff and a fighter weapons instructor who would later direct the targeting of Iraq; Ben Harvey of the Air Force strategy division; and Ron Stanfill, the F-111 pilot who worked in Checkmate. Warden took the package of slides from the briefing to Schwarzkopf and an inch-thick draft "Op Order," the operational order to turn the briefing into formations of airplanes headed deep into Iraq. If the briefing to Horner went well, Warden hoped to stay on and oversee the air-war planning in Riyadh.

Even before the Pentagon briefing team arrived, Horner knew what was coming. Schwarzkopf had told Horner that he was soliciting ideas from the air staff, that the focus was retaliation, and that there was no doubt that Horner would be the man in charge of the air war if and when it was launched. Despite Schwarzkopf's reassurance, Horner had been angry at the development, complaining that it smacked of Vietnam, when officials in Washington picked the targets.

Deptula had provided a draft copy of Instant Thunder to Lt. Col. Steve Wilson, an aide to Adams who had been dispatched to Riyadh a week earlier, so that he could show it to Horner. Horner, in a fit of disdain for the Instant Thunder campaign and the officers he regarded as renegade planners, threw the briefing against the wall. Wilson gathered up the slides only to have Horner hurl the charts against the wall yet again.

Since arriving in Saudi Arabia, Horner, who was serving as the acting theater commander pending Schwarzkopf's arrival in Riyadh, had faced continual challenges. Every day, Horner spent his time trying to make arrangements to "bed down" the steady stream of aircraft headed to the Gulf and keep up the flow of ground forces to the Saudi kingdom. Every night he went to sleep thinking about what he would do if the Republican Guard drove south into the oil-rich Eastern Province of Saudi Arabia. His main worry was that Iraqi forces would take the oil fields and stop, forcing the Western nations and the Arabs to negotiate. Getting a defense in place was a tricky business. Now, a colonel from the Pentagon had arrived to tell him to stop worrying so much about the Iraqi forces in Kuwait and to start planning strikes against downtown

Baghdad. To Horner, the pitch that he was about to receive seemed shockingly theoretical and naive, and competed with the more traditional plan he had sketched to attack the invading Iraqi forces.

When Warden showed up at the Royal Saudi Air Force headquarters in downtown Riyadh on August 20, Horner was loaded for bear. To break the ice, Warden started out by telling Horner that he had brought packages of sunscreen and other supplies from Adams, but Horner rejected the offering, pushing them across the table. Horner's back was turned to Warden as the colonel began his presentation. No sooner had Warden begun the briefing than Horner began to assault him with criticism, complaints, and questions, deriding the advice he was getting from armchair generals in Washington. As the briefing went on, it was clear that the two Air Force officers were talking past each other.

Horner began with minor objections and built to a crescendo. Warden's discussion of precision-guided munitions was off base, Horner complained. Instead of talking about smart weapons, Warden should be talking about the precision-guided delivery of weapons. That was a reference to the F-16, one of Horner's favored weapons, which did not have the capability to deliver laser-guided bombs, but which had the supposed capability to drop its dumb bombs with great accuracy at low altitude using its radar bombing system. Warden's analysis of Iraq's command and control system needed more work, Horner continued. Warden had made an academic study; Horner had to make the destruction of the command system a reality.

As the discussion turned to the aircraft that would be used, Warden and his aides told Horner that they projected a 3 percent loss rate the first day and a 0.5 attrition rate thereafter. Horner asked if Warden had done a system-by-system analysis, including the F-117 stealth fighter. The F-117 had made its combat debut in the 1989 invasion of Panama. But the Panamanians had virtually no air defenses and the mission of the two F-117s used in the invasion had been marred when they dropped their bombs off target.

Instant Thunder depended to a considerable extent on the performance of the F-117, and although Horner did not confide his reservations to Warden, the general simply did not believe that the F-117s would be as radar-evading as advertised. The analysis Warden relied on was based on historical data from previous air wars.

Then Horner got to the heart of the matter. He was uncomfortable with Warden's philosophy of Instant Thunder, which, contrary to a traditional plan, did not provide for any attacks on targets in Kuwait or Iraqi ground forces, and he thought that Washington was minimizing the defensive problem confronting the command. Horner needed an air plan to take on the Iraqis and it needed to go beyond six days.

"It sounds like a 'decapitate the snake plan.' I don't see it as a slick plan, but as a 'hit-him-in-the-face plan,' " Horner said. Warden's plan left a number of key issues unsettled, the general continued. How would the air campaign work in conjunction with a land offensive? How would CENTCOM respond if an air campaign triggered an Iraqi ground assault?

"We could be looking out the window right now and see the Iraqi tanks come into Riyadh," Horner said at one point.

Warden believed that Horner was exaggerating the problems of defending Saudi Arabia and underestimating the potential of a strategic air campaign.

"You are being overly pessimistic about those tanks," Warden bluntly told Horner. Iraq's ground forces were just not that important a target for the air campaign, and Warden did not believe that the Iraqis had the logistics to mount a deep push into Saudi Arabia. There was no way the Iraqis could go far in the face of American air superiority, the colonel told the three-star general.

The already tense room built to a boiling point. Horner and Warden were heading for a head-on collision. Horner turned to an aide and jested sarcastically about Warden's persistence.

"And you didn't think I could hold my temper, did you?" Horner asked mockingly.

Warden quickly recognized his error and offered an apology, which Horner accepted. Then Horner summed up his critique.

"If folks in Washington want to fight this war, tell them to come to the theater. Jimmy Adams knows that you don't fight from Washington," Horner said, invoking Warden's boss and nemesis.[7]

Horner's tolerance, however, extended only so far. Determined that Warden would not be a player in Riyadh in any air campaign against Iraq, Horner sent him back to Washington, where he would support the air campaign through Checkmate. But Horner asked the lieutenant colonels who came with Warden to remain. What was Horner up to? Did Horner intend to use Warden's team to take over Instant Thunder and put his own imprint on the plan? Or was Horner trying to separate Warden from his team in order to frustrate the colonel's efforts to develop and market a competing air campaign? How could there be a strategic air campaign if the general who was to carry it out was among the sharpest critics?

That afternoon, Warden's team saw him off as he hitched a ride on an

RC-135 flight back to Offut Air Force Base. One of the lieutenant colonels who were left behind dubbed the group "the exiles." Morale was low. The team of planners had worked day and night for two weeks to develop Instant Thunder. For their efforts they had been virtually branded as outcasts. Their only hope, the officer confided in his diary, seemed to be to get Schwarzkopf's attention and be moved from Horner's office at the Royal Saudi Air Force Headquarters to the Saudi Ministry of Defense and Aviation (MODA), where Schwarzkopf and his staff had set up shop. He wrote:

> I came [to Saudi Arabia] with a perception of service and value to my country and fellow aviators. Unless Schwarzkopf positions us at MODA or in a satisfying role, our purpose here is ended and we must go. I feel a loss learning that our mission was misguided, unappreciated. I do not want to leave in a mental body bag (castrated).

He and the other lieutenant colonels, except one, returned to the Pentagon within ten days.[8]

THE BLACK HOLE

The man Lt. Gen. Charles Horner chose to develop the air campaign was Buster Glosson. An Air Force brigadier general who served as the deputy commander of Rear Adm. William Fogarty's Middle East task force, Glosson was almost the antithesis of Warden.

With his white hair swept back, his North Carolina accent, and his sense of complete conviction about whatever task he had undertaken, Glosson was one of the few larger-than-life personalities that could be found at the Pentagon, an institution where many officers seemed to lose their edge as they served on interdepartmental policy-making committees or managed multibillion-dollar weapons programs. Confident to his admirers, cocky to his critics, Glosson was a hard-charging, operationally oriented officer. He could be a demanding superior, but he was also a boss that a lower-ranking officer could differ with and survive, a virtue missing in some of the general officer corps.

Unlike Warden, Glosson had a rapport with Horner and with Schwarzkopf. He was well connected where it counted the most. While Warden had made his reputation as a theorist in the bowels of the Pentagon, Glosson was a skillful politician and was good at getting things done.

Born in Greensboro, North Carolina, Glosson was given the name Buster and it seemed a perfect fit. He joined the Air Force out of college, flew F-4s in Vietnam, was a squadron commander at the Air Force weapons school at Nellis Air Force Base, and commanded two fighter wings, including the Air Force's premier 1st Tactical Fighter Wing at Langley, Virginia, generally the first to deploy in a crisis.

Glosson had risen to the grade of brigadier general and was working as the principal deputy to the assistant secretary of defense for legislative affairs, troubleshooting congressional problems with the Pentagon budget, when Dick Cheney came to the Pentagon. When it came time to leave legislative affairs, Gen. Larry Welch, the Air Force chief of staff, asked Glosson to accept the post of deputy commander of the Joint Task Force Middle East, the small fleet that steamed around the Persian Gulf. It was not a highly coveted position. The deputy did not command any forces; his office was on a ship, the USS *LaSalle*. The weather was oppressively hot in summer, sometimes reaching 120 degrees. Since the end of the Iran-Iraq War, and the tanker war in the Gulf, the mission for the task force had shrunk. It was not where the action was, a dead-end street for a general hoping to head for the top. Glosson soon began to think about retirement.

When the Iraqi invasion took place, Glosson knew that if the United States mounted any kind of response it was going to be a big Air Force show and wanted badly to be part of the action. Even before Warden arrived in Riyadh, Glosson hoped to be in charge of the air campaign. Glosson's thoughts about retirement gave him a sense of independence as he planned the war. It looked like the end of the line anyway, so what did he have to lose?

On August 21, Deptula and Harvey gave the Instant Thunder briefing to Glosson and Brig. Gen. Larry Henry, who would take over the electronic warfare programs in the Gulf. Later that evening, the lieutenant colonels learned that Glosson would oversee the planning of the air campaign. The planning was to be a highly compartmentalized operation. The name of the team was the Special Planning Group, but shortly before the war it became known simply as the Black Hole. The team set up shop in a third-floor conference room at the Royal Saudi Air Force building in Riyadh. The room was spartan, containing one large table, one secure phone back to Washington, and another phone for operating in the Arabian theater.

Although Warden's team had been kept on for the time being, Horner made clear that Glosson was not to be captured by Warden's concepts. When Glosson asked Horner where he wanted them to start, the three-star general held up a sheet of paper. It was blank on both sides.

When he first heard Deptula's brief of the Instant Thunder plan, Glosson expressed interest but thought it needed more work. For one thing, it did not explain how airpower should be used if the six days of bombing did not produce the victory that Warden promised. CENTCOM, Glosson told Deptula, needed an air campaign that would last for fifteen rounds, not two or three. The air war would be a marathon, not a dash. They would be attacking a country that had fought Iran for eight years. Nor did the plan provide for attacks against the Republican Guard.

Glosson had never read Warden's books and papers. Still, he had read Billy Mitchell and he had an instinctive sympathy for many of the concepts in the Instant Thunder plan. Glosson liked the idea of taking the war to Baghdad at the outset and striking deep into Iraq instead of focusing on bombing troops in the field, as Horner was inclined to do. Nor did he have much time to invent a new plan from scratch. Schwarzkopf was moving his headquarters in late August, and Horner needed to have something to show him.[9]

Glosson kept Deptula as his principal planner, but eventually sent the other lieutenant colonels back to Washington. Of all the planners in Riyadh, Deptula alone could bridge the gap between the Washington planners and the Air Force officers in Riyadh. Deptula had previously worked for both Warden and Horner and had a pipeline to his current boss, the secretary of the Air Force. In a couple of weeks, Glosson and Deptula put together an air campaign that embodied the same principles as Instant Thunder.

There was still the problem of winning Horner over — or, at least, getting him to acquiesce in the plan. On August 26, Glosson and Deptula met with Horner and presented a reworked version of Warden's plan entitled "Instant Thunder: Concept of Operation and Execution."

Horner grumbled that he never wanted to hear the words "Instant Thunder" again, but he grudgingly accepted the overall thrust of the plan. Horner asked that the first twenty-four hours of the attack plan be put into an Air Tasking Order, a formal directive to units in the field, so that it could be quickly executed in case "Hussein puts a bullet through the head of our ambassador."

The strategic air campaign, however, soon had a new adversary: the U.S. Navy. Virtually from the start, it was clear that Air Force planners in the Black Hole and their Navy counterparts had competing visions of what airpower could accomplish and how to use it. The Navy planners had their own name for Warden's plan. Comdr. Donald W. "Duck"

McSwain, the Navy representative in the Black Hole, called it Distant Blunder, "distant" because it had been drafted at the Pentagon and "blunder" because of its emphasis on attacking Baghdad at the outset of the campaign. The idea of single-handedly winning the war with air-power was not a new one, the Navy planners argued. It had not worked before, and there was no reason to think that it would work now, even with the improvements in precision-guided weapons.

The dispute was a matter of war-fighting philosophy. With its tradition of strategic bombing and assumed access to the considerable logistics and munitions that are stored at land-based airfields, the Air Force thought in terms of campaigns, extended air operations to defeat an adversary. The Navy had a very different concept of war. Before the Gulf, Navy planners had, in effect, two models of conflict: the short, one-day attacks off the coast of Libya or an all-out war with the Soviet Union. In neither case was Navy aviation viewed as the decisive force for winning a large conventional conflict. But the dispute also revolved around tactics and weaponry. For years, pilots at the Navy's Strike University in Fallon, Nevada, had been taught that the way to defeat the enemy was to first take down his air defenses and only then attack objectives deep in the enemy interior. That, the Navy argued, was the lesson of the Israeli attacks on the Bekaa valley, when the Israelis took out the Syrian missile defenses in Lebanon and then scored a lopsided victory over Syrian MiGs. To attempt simultaneous attack on air defenses, command centers deep in Iraq, and infrastructure targets would be to court unacceptably high loses, the Navy planners argued. Instant Thunder was prepared with only the barest understanding of Iraq's dense air defenses, they insisted, and based on the dubious assumption that any targets missed on the first two days of the campaign could be retargeted and hit on days three and four based on reconnaissance photos.

In its original form, Instant Thunder was "a prescription for disaster," recalled Vice Adm. Stanley Arthur, who took over the naval forces in the Gulf in December. "It was a very shallow effort. The Navy folks took a look and said this stuff does not make sense."[10]

The dispute escalated to the point of confrontation after Glosson and Deptula flew out to the *LaSalle* on August 30 to brief Vice Adm. Henry H. Mauz Jr., Arthur's precedessor as the commander of Navy forces in the region. Glosson explained that the Black Hole planned to go to Baghdad on the first day of the war and that Navy A-6 bombers and Tomahawk sea-launched cruise missiles were to be used in the attack. Mauz argued for a traditional roll-back campaign, concentrating on

Iraqi air defenses for two to three days and only then sending warplanes deep into Iraq. The Navy was more concerned with the problem that faced it immediately than with any ultimate war aims. The threat was in front of them, not in Baghdad. Given the distances that Navy planes had to travel and the Navy's reliance on the limited supply of land-based Air Force refueling tankers, it was also the best way to optimize the Navy role. The Navy did not have a plane like the F-117.

Maj. Gen. Royal Moore, the commander of the Marine warplanes in the Gulf, was also skeptical. The F-117, he told Glosson and Deptula, had failed to hit its targets during the invasion of Panama and would not do much better in the Gulf.

Glosson rejected the Navy proposal for a roll-back campaign. The Navy did not have a strong institutional power base to press its position. The strategic air campaign plan had been an Air Force show from the beginning and had been presented to Schwarzkopf before the Navy had much of a chance to get into the act. The Navy's years of disdain for CENTCOM and its independent — critics would say arrogant — attitude came at a cost. Mauz was based on the *LaSalle,* and Timothy W. Wright, Mauz's senior Riyadh-based liaison officer, was only a one-star. The debate over the concurrent versus the rollback campaign was not the last time that the Air Force would roll over the Navy.

On September 3, Glosson outlined the campaign to Schwarzkopf, who approved the plan. Then, after dismissing the other officials in the room, Schwarzkopf privately told the Air Force general that he worked for him, not Horner, and then went over the gamut of planning issues, including special operations, amphibious operations, and the Republican Guard. Schwarzkopf told Glosson to be sure not to let the services in Washington get involved. Now that the CENTCOM commander felt he had a good thing going, he was determined to guard it from any encroachments from Washington. He wanted total control.

Schwarzkopf called Powell. "I told him if the President decides to act you have a huge list of options and the force in place to do it. And by the way, you also have the first phase of an offensive to execute as a stand-alone or to incorporate with a ground plan," he recalled.

Despite his embrace of the plan, Schwarzkopf had trouble thinking of airpower as anything more than a list of options or a prelude to a ground war. "I had never felt you were going to eject the Iraqis out of Kuwait short of ground action. I did feel there was a possibility that you could launch and as a result Iraq would make a decision to pull out, but I did not think it was likely," he said.

Glosson, however, hoped that airpower alone could bring an end to Saddam Hussein. When Powell visited Riyadh on September 12, Glosson showed him a chart. Air strikes, it stated, would destroy Iraq's military capability, eliminate the Iraqi government's control, and generate internal strife. The result, it bluntly predicted, would be to "decapitate [the] Saddam regime." If airpower failed to encourage Saddam Hussein's overthrow, Glosson believed it would limit an allied ground attack to a police action.

There were still what the Air Force called "limfacs," limitating factors, on what airpower could do, given the continuing problems with intelligence and logistics. The F-117 stealth fighters, on which Glosson was counting, suffered from shortages of spare parts, which reduced the F-117 flying by 20 percent. The satellite photos of Baghdad that the pilots needed in order to conduct pinpoint strikes were not supplied until October.

The first F-111Fs, which would carry out the lion's share of the strikes using precision-guided weapons during the Gulf War, flew to Saudi Arabia on August 25 with their initial load of ordnance under their wings. Settling into their base at Taif, they experienced considerable teething pains.

Deploying ahead of their logistics units, the planes arrived at Taif without supplies of coolant for the Pave Tack targeting system, which was used to guide their laser-guided bombs. Fuel was also a problem. The Taif base had spanking new aircraft shelters, but there were no refueling vehicles or storage bladders for the jet fuel.

"The bottom line was that jet fuel was in critical shortage and would have severely hampered combat operations if they were requested in the first weeks," the wing said in its after-action report.[11]

The F-15Es did not yet have LANTIRN targeting pods, necessary to conduct pinpoint attacks at night, and lacked good intelligence about the location of Scud launchers in the west.

On September 22, Horner sent Schwarzkopf a message saying that he had enough logistics for a seven-day conflict, but cautioning that his supplies for fighting a thirty-day war were "marginal." Donald Rice later observed that it was not until early October that the Air Force had what it needed to carry out a strategic air campaign.[12] While the Air Force boasted that it could strike virtually at a moment's notice, getting ready for a sustained bombing campaign was still a time-consuming undertaking.

Nonetheless, Glosson's assessment was, taking into account the "limfacs," that the strategic air campaign was doable by mid-September.

When Glosson briefed Powell, he told him the air-war plan could be executed the next day, if necessary. So far, the debate over airpower as a "stand-alone" option" had stayed under wraps. But then the air campaign was given a premature airing by the Air Force chief of staff.

DUGAN'S DEMISE

Michael Dugan had been the Air Force chief for only two months when the crisis in the Gulf developed. He had not been Cheney's first choice to head the Air Force but his appointment had been approved by Rice.

Shortly before Powell was briefed, Dugan passed through Riyadh. Initially, Schwarzkopf had declined to give Horner and Glosson permission to brief Dugan. But after some importuning by Horner, Schwarzkopf told Glosson that he could brief the Air Force chief on the first twenty-four hours only. That was all Dugan needed to establish that the basic philosophy of Instant Thunder was still intact.

In hours of interviews with accompanying journalists on the way over and back from Saudi Arabia, Dugan did some proselytizing for airpower. Ground commanders and CENTCOM officials were uneasy with the coalition's defensive capabilities, fearful of giving Saddam Hussein any additional incentive to launch a preemptive attack, and were playing for time. But Dugan was confident that strategic airpower provided Washington a near-term offensive option. Given the American advantage in the air, Dugan had no apprehensions about talking publicly about the possibility of offensive action.

"If push comes to shove, the cutting edge would be in downtown Baghdad," Dugan said. "This wouldn't be a Vietnam-style operation, nibbling around the edges. The way to hurt you is at home, it's not out in the woods somewhere. We're looking for the centers of gravity where airpower could make a difference early on," he said.

"Hussein ought to be at the focus of our efforts," said Dugan, who added that Israeli officials had suggested that the coalition target Saddam Hussein, his family, personal guard, and mistress. Some of Dugan's comments were off base. But in the main, Dugan had given a vivid account of the strategic air campaign. Coming at a time when virtually every facet of CENTCOM's operations was under wraps, however, Dugan's comments made headlines.[13]

When Powell saw the Sunday press accounts of the Dugan interview, he was furious. Powell twice called Dugan at home that Sunday, accusing him of leaking secret information and misrepresenting the plans.

The JCS chairman seemed to be particularly upset by comments attributed to Dugan that suggested that the Air Force could win a war single-handedly. Dugan denied the charges. The Air Force chief felt he had been talking theoretically about the nature of a strategic air war.

The next day, Dugan was summoned to Cheney's office. Cheney complained that Dugan had said that the plan had been decided on by the JCS, but Dugan said that he had skirted the subject. Cheney said that Dugan had forecast that an offensive campaign would involve massive bombing in Baghdad. Dugan denied using the word "massive." Cheney said that Dugan had given out operational details. Again, Dugan rejected the charge. Cheney was not persuaded. He read the rest of his bill of particulars and told Dugan that he wanted his resignation by noon. Dugan thought about saying that he had been appointed by President Bush, not by Cheney, but held his tongue.

In its efforts to distance itself from Dugan's comments, the Bush administration suggested that he was freelancing. "General Dugan is not in the chain of command and does not speak for the administration," Brent Scowcroft said, when asked about the morning headlines. In fact, when the air campaign was launched, it went pretty much as Dugan had said.[14]

But while the basic plan was set, there was still plenty of work to be done before the air campaign was ready for prime time. In particular, Glosson still had to perfect the plan to take down the Iraqi air defenses.

5

Kari

Growing airspace surveillance and protection requirements and the need to make decisions quickly and reliably on the basis of real-time data has driven the development of comprehensive detection systems offering end-to-end continuity — a field in which Thomson–CSF has a reputation for technological excellence and unparalleled systems availability.

— Thomson–CSF
Annual Report, 1990

TO WIN SUPPORT for the air campaign, Buster Glosson and much of the Air Force hierarchy at the Pentagon had virtually promised that American warplanes could range freely over Iraq with relatively small risk to airmen's lives. But the projections were mainly a reflection of the Air Force generals' confidence in their own capabilities and their intuitions about the mind and capabilities of the enemy. American intelligence had only a crude understanding of Iraq's air defense system at the time of Iraq's invasion of Kuwait. As the intelligence specialists began to focus on the Iraqi defenses, it soon became clear that winning command of the skies was a trickier problem than had been expected.

Iraq had got a taste of what enemy air strikes could accomplish when the Israelis launched a surprise 1981 attack on Iraq's Osirak nuclear reactor, located at the Tuwaitha nuclear facility south of Baghdad. To ensure that no enemy aircraft could again penetrate into the Iraqi military-industrial heartland, Iraq had gone on a multibillion-dollar spending binge in the world arms bazaar, acquiring modern radars, military communications equipment, computers, antiaircraft missiles, and guns from obliging Western, East European, and Asian nations.

Now Iraq planned to use the system to extract a greater price in downed American pilots and aircraft than the Bush administration was willing to bear. Just how high that price would be depended on the United States' success in deciphering Iraq's air defense network.

The plan to take down the Iraqi air defenses was one of the war's most highly guarded secrets. Even after the war, the Pentagon never made public much of the story. The classified nature of some of the programs involved inhibited discussion, because much of what the coalition did to gain air superiority over Iraq is applicable to future conflicts. So did the Defense Department's proselytizing for stealth technology — in the budget debates, a superlative weapon demands an undiminished enemy. With an eye to adversaries in Congress and, more important, potential enemies abroad, the plan to achieve air superiority was one of the few Gulf War stories that the Pentagon found too good to tell.

SPEAR

One of the first military officials to tackle the Iraqi air defense network was a Navy captain who ran an intelligence cell in a federal office complex in Suitland, Maryland. At six feet six inches, Mike "Carlos" Johnson stood out among a crowd. Johnson had made a solid reputation for himself within the Navy as a tactician and understood the value of knowing the enemy's antiaircraft capabilities. During the Vietnam War, Johnson flew 120 missions, during which seventeen aircraft in his air wing were shot down over North Vietnam. More recently, he had been the deputy air wing commander when American warplanes launched from the USS *John F. Kennedy,* in January 1989, shot down two Libyan MiGs that appeared to menace American warships in the Mediterranean.

When it came time for Washington assignment, Johnson was made the director of SPEAR, which is Navy-speak for Strike Projection Evaluation and Anti-Air Research. SPEAR had been established by the Navy to improve the service's tactical intelligence on Soviet and third world threats after the Navy had lost two airplanes and had a third badly damaged while penetrating a relatively thin set of air defenses during a 1983 raid in Lebanon.[1]

Past intelligence had placed too much emphasis on the technical performance of enemy weapons and had not paid sufficient attention to the training, doctrine, and capabilities of the enemy soldiers who operated them. SPEAR was the Navy's attempt to right the balance. The idea was to take airmen, Marines, and sailors and put them into a highly classified intelligence cell. They would work closely with intelligence agencies to produce information that would be useful to warriors going into harm's way, instead of the standard intelligence data, which was useful only to the policy-makers.

SPEAR had only recently begun to focus its attention on Iraq when Saddam Hussein's forces invaded Kuwait. But the cell immediately spun into high gear, expanding its team to include Air Force and Army experts on Iraqi equipment, and sharing information with the Air Force's Checkmate planning office in the Pentagon. Some of SPEAR's team were sent to Western and Eastern Europe to get the details about the antiaircraft, radar, computer systems, and training Iraq had acquired. It did not take long for the intelligence cell to determine that the Iraqi air defense system was more sophisticated than the national intelligence community has assumed.

The problem was not the Iraqi air force. In terms of equipment, the Iraqis had some of the most modern planes in the world: French-made Mirage F-1s and Soviet-made MiG-29 fighters and SU-24 Fencer fighter-bombers. Iraq's air force was deployed at twenty-four main operating bases and thirty dispersal bases, many of which had multiple runways and Yugoslavian-designed aircraft shelters hardened to NATO standards.

The Iraqis did not have the capability to refuel their planes from large tankers in flight when they invaded Kuwait. But that deficiency was remedied in the months leading up to the Gulf War when several military transport planes were dispatched to Libya and transformed into tankers by Muammar Qaddafi's military, a move that extended the potential reach of the Iraqi air force well into Saudi Arabia.

Some Iraqi pilots were capable of impressive aerial exploits. During the war with Iran, four Mirage F-1s flew a grueling 1,100-mile mission, refueling from other F-1s with fuel pods, to bomb four Iranian tankers, an impressive strike even by American standards.

But that was the exception rather than the rule. The vast majority of Iraqi pilots had relatively little flight experience. Even as war neared, the average pilot was receiving about one flight a week — and often less than one night flight a month. More important, the Iraqi pilots were not trained to take independent action and were, for all intents and purposes, tethered to the ground, dependent upon instructions from ground controllers. Imbued with Soviet-style tactics, Iraqi pilots received explicit directions from ground-based officers who monitored the air war on radarscopes and directed the Iraqi interceptors toward their prey. So dependent were the Iraqi airmen on the ground controllers that the Iraqi air force could be largely neutralized as a defensive force by destroying or jamming its ground-based command centers.

Nor did the Iraqis have much of an airborne early warning capability. The Americans and the Saudis had sophisticated AWACS planes, Boeing 707s filled with rows of computer equipment that tracked friendly and enemy aircraft and helped direct the air battle. In a crude effort to create an airborne early warning capability, the Iraqis had taken French-made ground-based Tiger radars and installed them on Soviet-supplied IL-76 transport planes. The earliest version of the plane crashed on its initial takeoff because the Iraqis had put the radar dome too far to the rear of the plane, making it unstable. The remaining two planes — which the Iraqis dubbed Adnan I and Adnan II — were deemed to have little capability. Even if the equipment worked beyond expectation, the Iraqis had flown the Adnan aircraft so sparingly that they had little to no proficiency in using it as an airborne command post. American AWACS and E-2C controllers spent hundreds of hours in the air, practicing their skills. According to American intelligence, the Iraqis had not flown the Adnan planes more than twenty times before the Gulf War.

Although SPEAR was not overly impressed by the Iraqi air force, it was fascinated by the Iraqi ground-based air defense system, the likes of which were unknown anywhere else in the third world. Like a mansion that had been enlarged by different builders, the system boasted an enormous variety of technologies. The Iraqis had purchased six Chinese Nanjing low-frequency radars, some of which the Iraqis had not deployed but held in reserve. The radars were deemed by American intelligence officials to be the most important radar in Iraq because its low frequency made it relatively impervious to jamming and enabled it, in principle, to detect stealth aircraft. They also had a variety of modern French and Italian long-range and short-range radars, including Tiger and Pluto short-range radars capable of detecting aircraft flying as low as fifty to one hundred feet.

One of Iraq's more unusual systems was acquired from the Japanese: the RM-835 was a sophisticated ground-based system that was used to track electronic emissions. The system could be used to pinpoint emissions from enemy aircraft so that they could be jammed or targeted by antiaircraft systems. American intelligence, however, also believed that the system was used by the Iraqi security forces to monitor electronic emissions within Iraq, presumably to help track down and eradicate subversive groups.

But the heart of the system was Kari. Completed in 1988, Kari was Iraq spelled backward in French. Driven by a mainframe computer and designed by the French aerospace firm Thomson–CSF, Kari represented the best 1970s technology that a third world power could buy. To achieve early mastery of the skies, the coalition needed to learn Kari's secrets.

SPEAR and other intelligence agencies exploited their contacts with Thomson and French air defense commanders. But it took months of lobbying in Paris and intelligence gathering in the Gulf to pry loose many of Kari's mysteries. According to a senior American official, the United States had to seek the intervention of the top officials in the French government to persuade Thomson to disclose some of Kari's capabilities, because the firm apparently calculated that to provide technical data on the system's capabilities so that it could be destroyed by the Americans would devalue the product to its extensive market in the third world. Even with war clouds gathering in the Gulf, the culture of arms sales held a tenacious grip.

As the Bush administration pressed the French for data, American aircraft flew along the Iraqi border in an effort to activate the Iraqi air defenses. Meanwhile, satellites and Rivet Joint RC-135 aircraft and Compass Call EC-130s packed with special equipment recorded the spasm of Iraqi emissions that followed, allowing intelligence officers to map Kari's structure.

One senior Air Force official described the process this way: "We watched to see at what altitude he could see things, what motion he reacted to, which SAM, or surface-to-air missile, sites got activated." On one occasion, American intelligence even monitored the Iraqis as they issued a sample firing order to one of their SAM batteries. As the war approached, the Iraqis stopped talking in an effort to frustrate American intelligence. But by then, American intelligence had already learned many of Kari's secrets.[2]

The breadth and sophistication of the Kari system was detailed in a series of highly classified studies that SPEAR shared with Checkmate and sent to the Joint Chiefs of Staff. The network was more than a means to repulse individual air attacks. Kari enabled the Iraqi leadership to determine the scale and origin of an air strike so that it could marshal its defenses. In psychological terms, Kari provided Baghdad with its "situational awareness." Its destruction would be a disorienting blow to an Iraqi leadership that insisted on tight central control.

Kari had a pyramidal structure. At the base were more than four hundred observation posts. The observers at a post were equipped with hand-held controls that automatically fed tracking data into the Kari system. All the observer had to do was push buttons that sent signals to a command post, giving the presumed heading, altitude, and size of an aircraft. Key tracking data was also provided by seventy-three radar reporting stations.

The observation posts and radar stations, in turn, fed their information to seventeen Intercept Operations Centers (IOCs), regional command posts spread throughout the country. A hardened concrete shelter, often built by Yugoslav and Belgian contractors, served as the shell of the command post. Inside were two mobile vans packed with electronic equipment and manned by air defense officers, which could drive away on short notice in case the command post came under attack. Equipped with radarscopes, the officers in the command centers could direct Iraqi fighters to intercept attacking planes as well as pass targeting information to batteries of surface-to-air missiles and to anti-aircraft artillery. In most cases, all an air defense officer had to do to transmit his targeting data was to touch a light pen to the aircraft track on a radar screen. Exploiting computer technology, Thompson had devised an automated system that third world officers with as little as a sixth-grade education could operate.

Like spokes of a wagon wheel, the Intercept Operations Centers, in turn, led to regional Sector Operations Centers (SOCs). Three-story command centers built of reinforced concrete, they orchestrated the air defense of huge areas of Iraq.

There were four SOCs in Iraq, three to control the outlying regions and one to oversee the defense against any intruders that made it through to the country's center. Situated at the H-3 airfield in western Iraq, just east of the border with Jordan, the western SOC served as the primary command post for blunting Israeli air strikes. Based at the Tallil air base, the southern SOC was responsible for the defense of the Basra area against Iranian air attacks in that area. At Kirkuk, the northern SOC guarded against attacks emanating from northern Iran and also provided protection against air strikes from Turkey or

Syria. The SOC that oversaw the air defense of Iraq's interior and of Baghdad itself was located at the Taji military base, just north of Baghdad. American intelligence initially believed that the Iraqis had established a fifth SOC, at the Ali al Salem air base, but later concluded it was not fully operational.

All the SOCs fed their information to Air Defense Headquarters in Baghdad, thereby providing the Iraqi high command with a nationwide air picture. Terminals depicting the information were also situated in the presidential palace, presidential bunker, intelligence headquarters, defense headquarters, and a hotel used by the Iraqi leadership in Baghdad. From their well-defended sanctuary in Baghdad — American intelligence reports indicated that the city was surrounded by sixty SAM batteries and 1,800 or more antiaircraft guns — Saddam Hussein and top Iraqi commanders could monitor the air war over Iraq, allocating resources as needed.

The entire system was tied together by buried land lines, microwave relay stations, field radios, and telephone, thus providing the Iraqis with backup communications links if any one of them was severed in a bombing raid. Much of the microwave and fiber-optic material was of Western origin, including some from the United States. Many of the radios were of German, British, French, and Swedish origin. Kari was also tied into a computerized battle management system, called ASMA, that the British had helped develop. Housed in a government ministry in Baghdad, the ASMA system provided the Iraqis with the ability to manage their war stocks and oversee the distribution of logistics. But it apparently had the potential to serve as a backup for some of the Kari capabilities. The French informed American intelligence that many of the Iraqi air defense officers it trained had been educated in computer technology and electrical engineering in the United States. The Iraqi air defenses constituted a prominent, but not the only, example of a case in which the West had helped erect a system it was later obliged to destroy.

Kari had its limitations. The system was designed to counter small raids of between twenty and forty aircraft, such as would be expected in an attack by Israel or Iran, not the huge massed attack that the coalition was preparing. According to the French, each command center could track 120 aircraft under optimal conditions. Nonetheless, the system enhanced the performance of Iraq's belts of surface-to-air missiles. Turning on a SAM radar was like shining a flashlight in a dark room. It illuminated the enemy but also disclosed the presence and location of the defender. The longer Iraq's SAM radars were turned on, the more

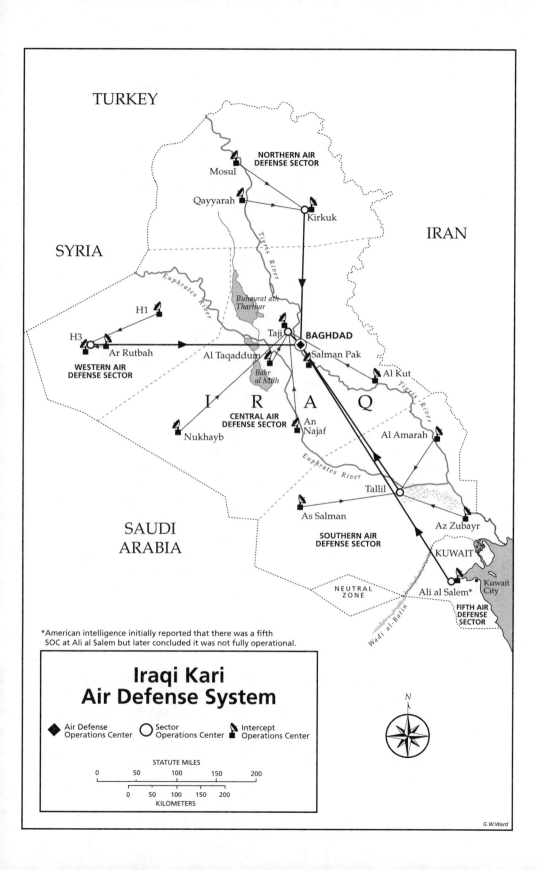

TURKEY

SYRIA

IRAN

NORTHERN AIR
DEFENSE SECTOR

Mosul

Qayyarah

Kirkuk

Buhayrat ath
Tharthar

H1

H3

Ar Rutbah

Taji

BAGHDAD

Salman Pak

Al Taqaddum

WESTERN AIR
DEFENSE SECTOR

Bahr
al Milh

Al Kut

I   R   A   Q

Nukhayb

CENTRAL AIR
DEFENSE SECTOR

An
Najaf

Al Amarah

Euphrates River

Tigris River

Tigris River

Euphrates River

Tallil

SAUDI
ARABIA

As Salman

SOUTHERN AIR
DEFENSE SECTOR

Az Zubayr

KUWAIT

NEUTRAL
ZONE

Ali al Salem*

Kuwait
City

FIFTH AIR
DEFENSE
SECTOR

Wadi al-Batin

*American intelligence initially reported that there was a fifth
SOC at Ali al Salem but later concluded it was not fully operational.

Iraqi Kari
Air Defense System

◆ Air Defense
Operations Center

○ Sector
Operations Center

■ Intercept
Operations Center

N

STATUTE MILES

0   50   100   150   200

0   50   100   150   200
KILOMETERS

G.W.Ward

they risked attack by antiradiation missiles, which guided themselves to their targets by homing in on the energy of the radar beam. By providing targeting information to the Iraqi missile batteries, Kari made it easier for the missile batteries to acquire their targets and minimized the time they needed to use their radars.

In theory, an adversary could try to skirt the Kari system by flying low. That would enable the attacking planes to delay detection by Iraq's long-range radars and most of its surface-to-air missiles, which engaged at medium altitude.

The Iraqis, however, had tried to seal off the low-level attack route by complementing the Kari system with hundreds of foreign-made anti-aircraft guns. The Iraqi military was equipped with Soviet SA-7, SA-9, SA-13, and SA-16 missiles, which homed in on the heat of jet engines; SA-6 and SA-8 Soviet low-altitude SAMs, which were radar-guided; and 200 to 300 French-made Roland surface-to-air missiles, a relatively low-level system that the Iraqis later used to shoot down a Navy A-6E on the second night of the war. Iraq had also purchased 150 to 400 Swedish-made Orelikon guns. Captured weapons added to Iraq's firepower. The Iraqi forces that invaded Kuwait captured five to ten Amnon systems, a unique weapon that combined American surface-to-air Sea Sparrow missiles with an Italian radar and Orelikon guns. The Italian-manufactured weapon had been designed originally for Egypt by Italy and sold to Kuwait. American intelligence was also concerned that the Iraqis had captured American-made Hawk antiaircraft missiles in Kuwait and might have acquired a small number of American shoulder-fired Stinger missiles by purchasing them on the black market and stealing them from Kuwait.

Even poorly aimed antiaircraft artillery was bound to hit something if it was fired in sufficient abundance. To counter enemy planes, Iraq used the Soviet technique. They did not try to track and shoot down a plane. Instead, all guns in a battery set up a wall of fire in their sector and let the plane run into it.[3]

POOBAH'S PARTY

SPEAR's role in deciphering the Iraqi defensive network was one of the most important contributions that the Navy made to the air war. The air-war commanders had other means of learning about the system. Glosson met with some of the engineers who built and installed the system during a secret trip to Europe. Once the system was deciphered, the air-war commanders still had to come up with an answer.

Part of the solution was knowing what not to do. Armed with intelligence about the Iraqi air defenses, the air-war planners ordered a wholesale revision of tactics. Low-level attacks were a staple of American airpower. It was the way the Navy intended to carry out surprise strikes against third world nations, and it reflected the Air Force's long experience in training for the big war in Europe. By flying at low altitude a pilot could gain some protection against antiaircraft defenses by maneuvering around the rolling terrain. Low-altitude flying was also helpful where persistent cloud cover hampered precision-guided strikes at medium altitude with laser-guided weapons. But low-level tactics could be costly. Air Force and Navy statistics showed that 85 percent of all the aircraft lost since World War II were lost to antiaircraft artillery and shoulder-fired SAMs, most of them within twelve miles of their targets. And the proliferation of Iraqi antiaircraft artillery promised more of the same.

Glosson ordered that the majority of night missions for the first two days be carried out at low altitude — with the exception of the F-117s. Daytime missions were mostly conducted at medium altitude. But on the third day, the vast majority of the raids would be conducted at medium and high altitude, out of the range of the Iraqi gunners. While not all the pilots in the field agreed, SPEAR reinforced the message. Dispatched by the JCS in October to brief air commanders and aircrews on the Kari system, Mike Johnson advised that low-level tactics could prove to be extremely costly to aircrews.

That left the problem of dismembering and destroying the Kari system to create a medium-altitude sanctuary. The military had a name for that: it was called SEAD, for suppression of enemy air defenses.

Even before all the intelligence was in on the Kari system, Glosson, David Deptula, and Brig. Gen. Larry Henry, Glosson's deputy for electronic warfare, hammered out the basic principles of the SEAD campaign. The objectives were put in a classified memorandum on "efforts in support of potential interdiction tasking," which was sent to Schwarzkopf, senior commanders in the Gulf, the Joint Chiefs of Staff, and the chief of staff of the services.

As the memo explained, the SEAD attack on the Iraqi air defense system would have five objectives:

Destroy/Disrupt C2 Nodes
Disrupt EW/GCI Coverage And Communications
Force Air Defense Assets Into Autonomous Modes
Use Expendable Drones For Deception
Employ Maximum Available HARM Shooters[4]

In plain English, the plan was to break Iraq's centralized air defense system into chunks and then smash the pieces. The major SOCs and IOCs that ran the Iraqi air defense network would be bombed by F-117s at the outset of the war. Key early warning radars, like the ones Iraq had strung along the border with Saudi Arabia, and communications links would also be attacked.

If properly executed, the attacks would have two effects. Without the targeting data from the Kari system, Iraq's surface-to-air missile batteries would be forced to use their radars for a longer period of time to track allied planes, making them more vulnerable to attack by American and British anti-radiation missiles. Cut off from the ground controllers who guided them into battle, Iraq's pilots would be easy prey for the Americans.

The idea in the memo of using drones to fool the Iraqi defenses was a tactic that Warden's Checkmate office had suggested and which Henry favored. A salty-tongued officer, Henry had served two tours in Vietnam, rising through the ranks, not as a pilot but as a WSO, or weapon system officer. Henry was the first nonpilot to command a wing — a unit of F-4G Wild Weasels — in the history of the Air Force. During a stint at the National War College, Henry had studied one of the greatest SEAD campaigns of all time: Israel's lopsided June 1982 destruction of Syrian surface-to-air missile batteries in the Bekaa valley of Lebanon. The Israelis had launched drones to fool the Syrians into firing their SAMs at phantoms. After the batteries had expended their missiles, the Israeli F-16s dropped cluster bombs on them.

Taking a page from the Israeli book, Henry planned to fire drones and decoys deep into Iraq to simulate an attack. F-4G Wild Weasels, EA-6Bs, A-6Es, and FA-18s, which carried high-speed antiradiation missiles (HARMs) would follow. As soon as the Iraqis turned on their missile radars to track the decoys, they would find a HARM flying back at them. It would be the Bekaa valley all over again, but on a much grander scale.

Of all the missions developed by the air-war planners, the SEAD attacks in the Baghdad area would be among the most difficult. More heavily defended than Hanoi during the Vietnam War, Baghdad was the hub of the Kari system and contained command centers, communications facilities, and electrical plants that the air-war commanders were determined to destroy on the first night of the war. Beckoning and forbidding, the Iraqi capital would be the most demanding test of the campaign to win control of the skies.

★   ★   ★

The principles Glosson and his deputies outlined looked good on paper. But making the preparations for Kari's destruction was not as simple as it seemed.

As important as SEAD was to the success of the air campaign, it was one of those essential but unglamorous areas that the American military had not generally treated as a top funding priority. The lack of an effective drone, for example, was particularly disconcerting.

The Navy had purchased a derivative of the Israeli Samson drone, which the acronym-happy American military dubbed TALD, for Tactical Air Launched Decoy. Launched by planes as they ventured toward their target, the Navy drones glided to earth, drawing away enemy fire. The decoys could be equipped with various devices to simulate American aircraft, including emitters that replicated their electronic signatures. But they were unpowered and had a range of only thirty to forty miles. As for the Air Force, for all the billions it had spent on nuclear missiles and bombers, it did not have a suitable decoy. Still, Checkmate had been looking into the drone possibilities.

The task of coming up with a drone to spoof the Iraqi defenses fell to Mark "Buck" Rogers, an up-and-coming major who was working for John Warden at Checkmate. A barrel-chested fighter pilot, Rogers was one of the few airmen to eject from an F-4 and live to tell about it. The impact of the ejection had compressed his spine, shortening his height by about an inch. But at six feet two inches, Rogers was still an imposing presence.

Consulting with experts at the Northrop Corporation and officers at the Tactical Air Command, Rogers arrived at an ad hoc solution. The Navy had BQM-74 drones, long-range radio-controlled platforms that it used for target practice. These drones' gyroscopes were not designed for long, uncontrolled flight, and they would probably stray off course if they were fired deep into Iraq. By affixing reflectors on them, the BQM-74s could be adapted to simulate the radar cross section of coalition aircraft.

Rogers's idea was initially not well received by the Air Force hierarchy. After Warden and Rogers briefed Jimmie Adams on the plan, the deputy Air Force chief of staff for operations told them he was tired of majors in the basement of the Pentagon coming up with new schemes to win the war. But after a formal request for a drone was sent to the Pentagon from CENTCOM, the Air Force blessed the effort, which was code-named Scathe Mean.

Finding an Air Force team to fire the drones was almost as hard as finding the decoys. The Air Force's experience with ground-launched missiles was limited to the nuclear-tipped cruise missiles, which were being eliminated under the 1987 Intermediate-Range Nuclear Forces Treaty that the United States had concluded with the Soviets. The Air Force, however, still maintained a training unit for ground-launched cruise missiles, under the command of Col. Douglas Livingston, at Davis Montham Air Force Base in Arizona.

Soon, Rogers was on his way to California to meet with the cruise missile team, which had been ordered to book into a hotel close to a Northrop warehouse where the drones were kept. There was more than one member of Livingston's team who concluded that the Bush administration had decided to use nuclear cruise missiles against the Iraqis. But the next day Rogers dispelled the mystery. Livingston and his men were told that they would be leaving in a matter of days but could not tell family members that they were deploying to the Gulf. If the Americans were going to fool the Iraqis, the drones needed to remain a secret. There were also some political considerations in the Gulf to think of: it would not do to let word get around that the crews for nuclear-armed cruise missiles had been dispatched to Saudi Arabia. After a brief training session at the naval air station at Point Magu, California, where it was determined that the gyroscope problem was not as bad as was originally feared, Livingston and his team were dispatched to Saudi Arabia and began surveying launch sites under Larry Henry's command.

Henry approved two launch points for the drones — one near King Khalid Military City, a huge Saudi military base just south of Hafar al-Batin, and one near Ar'ar, a western Saudi Arabia town that was eventually turned into a staging area for American special forces.

In addition to numerous Navy TALDs, the plan was to fire all thirty-nine of the BQM-74 drones on the first day of the war in and around Baghdad and Basra, as well as at Iraq's H-3 airfield close to the Jordan border. In Riyadh, the air-war commanders developed their own informal code name for the operation. Whenever Henry was out in the field he identified himself by his call sign — "Poobah." Thus it came to be that the drone program was known as "Poobah's Party."[5]

Other problems were more political in nature. When Glosson and Deptula first prepared the war plan, it called for sending a combination of stealthy and nonstealthy aircraft to Baghdad. While most aircraft carried their munitions under their wing, all of the F-117's bombs were stowed inside a bomb bay. The design contributed to the radar-evading quality of the plane, but it limited the aircraft's payload to two 2,000-pound bombs. To attack the full range of Baghdad targets, Glosson and Deptula planned to send Air Force F-111s and Navy night and all-weather A-6s to Baghdad along with the radar-evading F-117s. The Navy had one mission: six A-6s would attack a target on a river west of downtown Baghdad.

The plan tested the already strained relations between the Air Force, which ran the air campaign, and the Navy. SPEAR supported the idea of abandoning low-level tactics, but not sending aging Navy bombers to Baghdad. On the advice of the intelligence cell, neither Vice Adm. Henry Mauz, the senior Navy commander in the Gulf, nor Rear Adm. Timothy Wright, the senior Navy commander in Riyadh, approved of the plan to send A-6s to Baghdad. The top Navy commanders were convinced that the A-6 was too vulnerable to the dense air defenses surrounding Baghdad and that the additional targets to be attacked by the Navy bomber were not worth the potential cost in lives and aircraft. If the air-war planners wanted the Navy to hit targets in Baghdad, Wright argued, they should rely on Tomahawk cruise missiles.

Following the Navy's complaints, Glosson ordered that a series of computer simulations be carried out to assess the risks of sending non-stealthy planes to Baghdad. The war game showed that about half of the F-111Fs and A-6s would be lost, a rate of attrition that would be hard for Washington to accept and which Saddam Hussein could use to advantage in his propaganda campaign against the West. That was enough to persuade Glosson that the idea of using cruise missiles instead of non-stealthy planes was a good one if the technical and political questions could be worked out.

The Navy had long trumpeted the capabilities of the Tomahawk. Programmed into the computer brain of each Tomahawk was a digitized map of the terrain over which it was to fly. By using a radar altimeter to scan the ground and comparing the returns with the map, the missile's guidance system, dubbed TERCOM, for terrain contour mapping, kept the weapon on course.

The cruise missiles also had some unique capabilities, which made them well suited to the Baghdad mission. During the 1980s the Navy had experimented with a bomb that would dispense thousands of pieces of chaff to confuse enemy air defense and had stumbled onto a surprising discovery. During a major exercise, the chaff from the experimental bomb drifted over southern California and landed on power lines there, short-circuiting them and blacking out much of Orange County. After the embarrassing episode was over, the Navy had a new weapons system. By packing spools of carbon filament into bombs or the warheads of cruise missiles, the Navy could incapacitate enemy electrical facilities. The filament-spitting cruise missile, called KIT-18, was not, strictly speaking, a SEAD program, but it could be woven into the attacks on Baghdad as part of a general effort to cut off electrical power and create confusion in the minds of the Iraqi commanders.

Powell, however, was skeptical about the Tomahawk, which had never been fired in anger. When he visited Riyadh in September, he insisted that Glosson have a backup if the Tomahawks failed, which was why F-111Fs were assigned to attack Baghdad until late October.

Apart from residual qualms at the Pentagon about the missile's capabilities, however, there was a complication. The missile's guidance system worked best over rough ground, where it could easily identify differences in terrain. But as Navy officials scrambled to develop the maps for the weapons from satellite photos it became clear that the smooth terrain in much of southern Iraq was difficult for the computerized brain in the missile to distinguish, and some of the features that were readily detectable, such as sand dunes, shifted over time. For the cruise missile, navigating over southern Iraq was like driving down a highway without road signs. There was a solution, but it was a diplomatically sensitive one. Tomahawks could be routed along the eastern side of the Iraqi-Iranian border, allowing the missile guidance system to fix its position by flying up the spine of Iran's rugged Zagros Mountains before swinging west. Cruise missile targeteers knew Iran's terrain well; during the cold war, routes were planned that would take the missiles over Iran to targets in the Soviet Union.

The Pentagon viewed the issue as more of a military than a legal issue. If flying over Iranian territory was the surest route to Baghdad, so be it. Iran had long been Washington's nemesis, but it was Iraq's traditional enemy. If most of the cruise missile attacks were concentrated during the first few days of the war, the Iranians might turn a blind eye. They might not even notice. Either way, it would be incumbent on the United States to give the Iranians the opportunity to pretend they did not know what was going on by keeping the routes secret. The overflight was quietly approved by Dick Cheney and known to only a handful of officers.

Ironically, almost as soon as the issue was settled, the Navy cast a cloud over the mission. The maps that were to be electronically inserted into the Tomahawk's brain had been prepared at the Navy's Pacific Command headquarters in Hawaii. But when cruise missile planners at the Atlantic Command in Norfolk reviewed them, they concluded that half of them were flawed and would not work for the time of day that the missiles were scheduled to fly. The maps would have to be redone. It was an embarrassing setback for the Navy. After weeks of lobbying on behalf of the Tomahawk, the plan to use them was placed on hold while the cruise missile planners furiously reworked the digital maps and conducted a secret series of tests to ensure that the fix was valid. In all, it had taken months to ensure that there was a place for the Tomahawks in the war plan. The Tomahawks had been instrumental in holding down American casualties. But they had not proved to be weapons that could be rapidly taken out of the quiver and fired.[6]

Even with the tools in hand, blazing a path through the Iraqi defenses to Baghdad was not an easy problem. The decision to use the Tomahawks in the Baghdad raids left the stealthy F-117 as the only aircraft that the air-war planners intended to regularly send over the Iraqi capital. While the plane's designers assured the pilots that the aircraft's stealth technology would enable it to avoid the Iraqi radars, Baghdad was still viewed with apprehension by F-117 pilots, who knew they would be conducting the first true, operational test over a critical target surrounded by all the surface-to-air missiles and antiaircraft guns the Iraqis could muster.

Since the Gulf War, the public debate over stealth technology has become sharply polarized. In seeking congressional funding for the stealthy B-2 at a time of declining defense budgets, the Air Force has implied that the F-117s were unaided in their attacks on Baghdad. Congressional critics, meanwhile, have charged that claims of the plane's stealthiness have been vastly exaggerated.

But while Glosson was bullish on the F-117s, Horner reinforced the stealth pilots' apprehensions. During a September visit to Khamis Mushait, the secret F-117 base in Saudi Arabia, Horner called the F-117 pilots a bunch of prima donnas and made it clear that he was not impressed with the black jets. The F-117s were going to hit the targets he wanted them to and some of the planes probably would not come back. Despite their stealthiness, the F-117 pilots expected to take some hits and lose some planes during the war.

The issue of jamming support for the F-117s was among the most contentious questions to be fought out within the Air Force family. Glosson did not think that the F-117s needed jamming support and was afraid that sending the non-stealthy EF-111s — electronic jamming planes — would backfire by telegraphing the attack to the Baghdad gunners. Either the Iraqis would detect the EF-111 Ravens as they streaked across Iraq or the jamming itself would announce the presence of the F-117.

The F-117 commanders, for their part, took the pragmatic position that the aircraft's "low observable" design made it extremely difficult, but not impossible, for the enemy to detect. After the Kari system was dismembered, operating in Iraqi airspace would be less of a worry. And the Scathe Mean drones and TALDs would sow confusion and afford a measure of protection to some F-117 pilots: the second wave of F-117 attacks was scheduled to come on the heels of the drone firings. But the first wave of attacks on Baghdad, which would require the stealth pilots to fly through the undiminished Iraqi air defenses, was a concern for the F-117 pilots. The F-117 commanders pressed Glosson to send EF-111 and EA-6B electronic warfare planes to jam the enemy radars during the stealth raids.

Lt. Col. Ralph W. Getchell, an F-117 squadron commander, explained the thinking of the "stealth community" in an unpublished paper he wrote after the war as a student at the Air War College at Maxwell Air Force Base, Alabama. On the basis of exercises, F-117 pilots knew that enemy radar operators often tried to minimize the disruptive effects of electronic jamming on their system by adjusting their radars so that they would be less sensitive. If the air defense radars in Baghdad were jammed, and if the Iraqis compensated by turning down their radars, American jamming might make an occasional blip of an F-117 on a radarscope disappear altogether, Getchell wrote. It was a form of insurance to help ensure the destruction of a critical set of targets.

Col. Alton C. Whitley Jr., the F-117 wing commander, had a simpler way of expressing the concept. Electronic jamming was to the stealthy F-117s as an outgoing wind was to a batter at home plate, Whitley recounted in an interview at Nellis Air Force Base after the war. A batter might be able to hit a home run without the wind, but if the wind was blowing out to center field, it was that much easier. Perhaps the F-117s did not need the jamming, but what was the harm in using it anyway? During the Gulf War, Whitley wanted the wind to go his way as much as possible.

Reluctantly, Glosson agreed to the request. If jamming support was what the F-117 pilots thought they needed, it was what they would get, at least in moderation. The first wave of F-117s to hit Baghdad would have jamming support from EF-111s.[7]

That still left the problem of cutting a hole in the network of early warning radars the Iraqis had strung across the border. Code-named Spoon Rest, Squat Eye, and Flat Face, these radars covered the attack routes to central and western Iraq. Operated from mobile vans in the open desert and deployed along with a microwave system to relay communications, the radars enabled the Iraqis to peer as much as 150 miles into Saudi territory at high altitude and 30 miles at low altitude. The radars, and their operators, were clearly not expected by the Iraqi authorities to have a long life expectancy during wartime but to provide the first alert of timing and size of an air attack so that Iraq could blunt the assault.

In addition to sitting astride the routes the Ravens needed to support the F-117s over Baghdad, the radars also blanketed the corridor that the F-15E Strike Eagles planned to use to hit the fixed Scud launchers in western Iraq at the outset of the war. The trick was to find a way to get the EF-111s, as well as the F-15Es, through the Iraqi early warning network without tipping off the Iraqis.

It was a young Air Force captain who first suggested that American special operations forces be used to blow a hole in the Iraqi defenses without tipping off Baghdad that the air war was under way. Decorated for flying Pave-Low helicopters during the invasion of Panama, Randy O'Boyle served as a planner before the Gulf crisis for the Air Force's 1st Special Operations wing at Hurlburt Field, Florida. After the crisis began, he volunteered to join the Black Hole planners and served as Glosson's liaison to Col. Jesse Johnson's special operations forces in Saudi Arabia.

O'Boyle's main job was to set up search and rescue operations for downed pilots, but taking out the radars looked like a natural mission for special operations — and one that would give them a prominent role in the war. If American commandos went in on the ground and blew up the installations, the twin radar complexes would go off-line simultaneously and without warning. As far as Baghdad was concerned, it would be as if someone had pulled the plug on the radars. The radars would simply cease functioning and the Iraqi air defense commanders in Baghdad would not be the wiser. Assigning the mission to special operations also meant that more aircraft would be available for other bombing missions. Henry liked the idea. He accompanied Johnson, O'Boyle, and Deptula to the Saudi-Iraq border to look over a typical radar site. Some of the entourage even crossed over the border to take some souvenir Iraqi sand — some of which found its way to Donald Rice's desk at the Pentagon. (Henry also used the opportunity to scout areas for the Scathe Mean drones, careening across the desert in a Chevy Suburban at eighty-five miles an hour.)

O'Boyle's plan also appealed to Glosson, and the Air Force general assigned the mission to special operations in early September, leaving the details of the mission up to Johnson. But while the special operations forces were confident of their ability to deal with the Iraqis, they were on more dangerous footing with Schwarzkopf, who wanted to avoid any actions that would risk American lives, spark an international incident, or even provide the Iraqis with a pretext to attack. To the special operations forces, the mission to neutralize Iraq's early warning radars seemed to be well within Schwarzkopf's guidance: it was a commando strike that would start the war, not a cross-border operation to be carried out in advance of it.

But that was not how Schwarzkopf saw it. Concerned that CENTCOM be able to respond quickly to any Iraqi provocation, Schwarzkopf had stipulated that Glosson be able to execute his plan on sixty hours' notice. But on September 20, a planning officer for special forces sent out an impolitic message. In order to guarantee that the early warning radars would be destroyed, special operations forces used their newfound importance to requisition more equipment, more antitank missiles, more vehicles, more of just about everything. It was the type of request that was designed to catch the eye of officials at CENTCOM and ensure that the group's needs were met.

When the message crossed Schwarzkopf's desk three days later, the commander was furious. He had sought to provide the White House with an offensive option that it could quickly execute. Now the special operations forces were saying they did not have the wherewithal to carry out the first SEAD attack of the war. And when they were ready, they were planning to send commandos across the border.

Schwarzkopf called Glosson to his office and asked if he could execute the mission with helicopters and include the Army. Glosson said he could. "I'll take care of Jesse," the CENTCOM commander added.

Schwarzkopf then summoned Johnson from his headquarters at King Fahd Airport outside Dhahran to a short-notice Sunday meeting the next day in Riyadh. Schwarzkopf railed that he knew nothing of the operation to take out the radars. He told Johnson that he thought he had made it clear there were to be no cross-border commando operations.

To make the operation work, militarily as well as politically within CENTCOM, the special operations forces joined with the conventional Army and turned the commando operation into a helicopter raid. Air Force special operations Pave Low helicopters equipped with sophisticated avionics, including terrain-following radar that enabled them to sneak in low over the desert at night and global positioning systems that allowed them to pinpoint their position by interrogating navigational satellites, would lead Apache helicopters to the radar sites so that the Apaches could blast the radar vans with their Hellfire missiles.

The decision to go for a helicopter option seemed to be confirmed when the Iraqis moved their early warning radars ten miles back from the border on October 10, reestablishing them at two large sites sixty kilometers apart. But the original concept had evolved from a clandestine commando mission to knock radars off the air without alerting Baghdad to an attack to obliterate the radars with firepower.

To ensure that the Hellfire missiles, which were designed to destroy tanks, could be used to knock out mobile radars, the Army took buses and vans that had similar dimensions to the radars and blasted them. The Army dubbed its helicopter attack force Task Force Normandy. There was no question the Apaches could reduce the Iraqi early warning radars to a pile of smoking rubble, but by the time the mission was launched it was problematic as to whether it would be possible to carry out the raid without word of the attack making its way to Baghdad.

O'Boyle told Glosson that the operation would not be as neat and clean as if commandos snuck across the border and attacked the radars. The Iraqi commanders might get a radio call that the radar sites had been attacked. But the Iraqis would probably be confused as to what was actually happening and the helicopter attacks would prevent detailed information from being passed on and probably save some aircraft.

A subsequent plan to use special operations AC-130 gunships to destroy all of the seventy-odd border radar sites during the first three days of the war was vetoed by Horner as too risky, and was later carried out by A-10 planes.

A final touch was the creation of a deception plan. Launching a surprise strike against the Iraqi radars and targets in Baghdad would not be easy. It was not, after all, Pearl Harbor. The air campaign would not be launched until UN ultimatums had been exhausted. Some preparations could not be hidden: a notice had to be issued before the war, advising civilian aircraft not to fly across Saudi Arabia so that they would not collide with the massive air armada that was headed north.

Looking for a way to stop civilian flights without tipping off the Iraqis on the timing of an attack, the Americans needed a cover story, a benign interpretation of the war preparations that the Iraqis might accept even as the coalition was drawing its fist. Working with the special operations planners, the Air Force's Tactical Deception Office devised an elaborate plan to cover the closing of the civilian airway and throw off the Iraqis.

Hours before the air campaign, an AWACS would begin sending messages in the clear that a "special aircraft" had crashed in far western Saudi Arabia, suggesting that a hunt was under way for the downed F-117. Air Force and Navy helicopters would be launched to simulate the search. The loss of an F-117 would be a sufficiently troubling event that it would explain a decision to put Saudi Arabia off limits to civilian air traffic as well as any increased helicopter activity that might be detected by the Iraqi early warning radars as the Pave Lows and Apaches in Task Force Normandy headed north.[8]

The deception had an ironic circularity to it. The false story of a downed F-117 would be disseminated in part to mask the helicopter attack that could cut a radar-free corridor for the Ravens and the F-15Es that would attack the Scud sites in the west. The Ravens, in turn, would jam for the F-117s that attacked over Baghdad, as well as the F-15Es. In one sense, the F-117 pilots would be on their own. They would be flying solo, without escort. If something went wrong with the Raven mission, the stealth fighters would carry out their mission anyway. In another sense, they would benefit from the Ravens, "Poobah's Party," Army attack helicopters, special operations Pave Low helicopters, and the AWACS and other planes involved in the deception operation.

Schwarzkopf and Powell, for all intents and purposes, had subcontracted the air-war planning to the Air Force, and the plan had been crafted in great detail. The enemy's defenses had been deciphered, and the opening night attacks had been structured so that the stealth technology would derive support from the less-heralded players in the plan. There were still some issues to iron out, but the plan had basically passed muster with Powell and Schwarzkopf, two Army generals. The land campaign, however, was another story. The ground war would be one of the most trying tests of their generalship and would provoke considerable concern on the part of the civilian leadership in Washington.

6

"High Diddle Diddle"

Offensive Ground Plan Not Solid. We Do Not Have The Capability To Attack On The Ground At This Time.

— CINC's assessment
October 11, 1994

L T. COL. JOSEPH PURVIS had just been transferred to Hawaii when he was told to catch a September flight to the Persian Gulf. Purvis was being posted to Bahrain to work on military assistance issues — military jargon for arms sales and training foreign armies. Even though Bahrain was host to the Navy's Middle East Task Force, the tiny Gulf state liked American servicemen to keep a low profile. Purvis would not be wearing his uniform there.

Military assistance was not the most logical assignment for Purvis, a graduate of the Army's School of Advanced Military Studies at Fort Leavenworth, Kansas, known within the Army simply as SAMS. Leavenworth was where majors and lieutenant colonels went to deepen their grasp of military tactics and strategy. The school had been created as part of the Army's post-Vietnam reforms, after critics complained that the service was top heavy with weapons managers and short on war fighters. Some of the most influential generals in the Army had been involved in the school's creation and curriculum. Its graduates were supposed to be the best and brightest in the Army. But Purvis had been in the Army long enough to know that it sometimes works in strange and bureaucratic ways. It would not be the first time that the Army put a square peg in a round hole.

Purvis went out and bought some shirts and slacks at the local PX and began to bone up on military assistance issues. A few days later, Purvis got a call. The Bahrain assignment had all been a misunderstanding. Purvis was going to the Gulf all right, but to work for CENTCOM. That sounded more like it, although when Purvis arrived in Riyadh on September 14 nobody at the command could tell him what he was supposed to be doing. Purvis kept himself busy by going through intelligence reports and "Sit Reps," but he was somewhat out of place, walking the halls in his green Army camouflage uniform while virtually everyone else at CENTCOM was wearing desert fatigues.

Finally, four days after he arrived in the country, Purvis was ushered into a well-appointed conference room in the Saudi Ministry of Defense to meet with Schwarzkopf. In addition to Purvis, the group included Maj. Gregory Eckert, an armor official from Fort Carson, Colorado; Maj. William Pennypacker, an infantryman from Fort Riley, Kansas; and Maj. Daniel Roh from the 8th Infantry Division in Europe, a logistics specialist. None of the team members knew each other until they were brought together in Riyadh.

Then, the CENTCOM commander sat the young officers down and dispelled the mystery. Purvis would head up a special team that would plan the ground offensive to evict the Iraqis from Kuwait. The entire exercise would be extremely close held. Unsure that its shield was in place, CENTCOM saw no sense in brandishing a sword. That meant that everything the planners did was subject to stringent security procedures.

The planners would be known as the Special Plans Group, and they would report through CENTCOM's J-5 staff, the directorate headed by Adm. Grant Sharp that was nominally in charge of military planning, but only a handful of top CENTCOM officials would know of the effort. By design, the group was to be a self-contained planning effort that included a cross section of Army expertise. The Marines would not be included. Nor was the team to have direct contact with Colin Powell's staff in Washington.

Schwarzkopf told the team that they should draw up a plan entirely on the basis of what made the most military sense, not on the basis of what was needed to keep all the services, or coalition partners, happy. But Purvis was not starting with a blank sheet of paper.

Taking out a small map, the burly commander laid it on the floor, knelt down, and put his broad hand on a point just north of Kuwait City, where the two highways ran north from the Kuwaiti capital to Basra. That, Schwarzkopf explained, was the military objective for the

American ground forces. American forces, the commander explained, were not to go into Kuwait City. With that, the planners were sent on their way. CENTCOM had a code name for the land offensive: Eager Anvil.

More than any other facet of the conflict, the land war would test Schwarzkopf's skill as a strategist. Although the air campaign, for all intents and purposes, had been turned over to the Air Force, it was Schwarzkopf who determined the military objective for the first ground offensive plan.

In developing a ground-war plan, however, Schwarzkopf started with several handicaps. Virtually no work on offensive planning had been done at CENTCOM before Iraq invaded Kuwait. The planning had centered on ways to deter and defend, not on seizing lost territory. Nor was the command well endowed with senior ground-war strategists. The top officers on the CENTCOM staff in charge of planning and operations were a sailor and an airman: Admiral Sharp was the chief planning officer while Air Force Maj. Gen. Burton Moore was in charge of operations. Neither had the expertise to plan a land campaign, and although their staff contained a few able planners, they were burdened with the job of managing the deployment of forces to the Gulf and getting a defense in place. Lt. Gen. John Yeosock, the head of the Third Army and the commander of Army forces in the Gulf, worked long hours managing the buildup, the movement of logistics, and adjudicating disputes between lesser-ranking Army officers.

Schwarzkopf had his CENTCOM staff draft a provisional plan, which he showed to Powell before leaving for the Gulf. It called for racing to the high ground north of Kuwait City and cutting off the Iraqi army in southern Kuwait. But as far as Schwarzkopf was concerned, it was nothing more than a back-of-the-envelope sketch, and the commander was never comfortable with the plan. Schwarzkopf hoped that his new planners could do better.

Purvis and his team set up shop in a small office in the Saudi Ministry of Defense across the hall from the war room. The office was swept for electronic bugs and its television was unhooked so that its antenna could not function in the unlikely event that Iraqi intelligence had penetrated to the basements of the Saudi ministry and secretly transformed the TV into a transmitter. The planners disposed of their own "burn bag," the respository for classified scrap, and stored their papers in a separate security vault at the Saudi Ministry of Defense. They crunched their own numbers, using hand-held calculators, avoiding the military's computers. The group lived together, and no shop talk was allowed in their residence. War plans were to be discussed only in their cramped work-space or when traveling by car. If anyone asked what they were working on day and night, the team would give the cover story: the group was a special cell that had been assembled to study desert warfare. The team's disciplined aloofness was a tip-off to some on the CENTCOM staff that the group was doing more than that and initially was the cause of some resentment. As the rumor spread that the officers were planning a land offensive, Army officers dubbed them the Jedi Knights, a term of re-spect laced with more than a touch of sarcasm.[1]

In drawing up their plan, the Jedis operated with several key assump-tions. One central presupposition was that the coalition ground forces should not waste men and material fighting nondecisive battles; military power was to be conserved for a possible fight with the Republican Guard, which Iraq was holding in reserve, and not weakened in unnec-essary engagements with Iraq's regular army forces. December 18 was seen as the first possible D day, since all the forces from the United States would be in place and acclimated to the Gulf by then. A rule of thumb was that the last man to get off the boat must have been in the Gulf for three weeks before the attack. All the planning assumed a twelve-hour "intelligence action" cycle for the Iraqis, meaning that it would take no more than half a day for the Iraqis to react to their reports about American military operations, a level of efficiency that Iraq never came close to achieving during the Gulf War.

In accordance with military doctrine, the Jedis developed three possi-ble courses of action: an up-the-middle attack and two variations of a left hook. The first and favored option was for the coalition to attack just east of the Wadi al-Batin. To throw the Iraqis off, the attack would be preceded by several deceptions. West of the Wadi al-Batin, special oper-ations forces or helicopter units would fake an attack. The main attack would begin at night, the better to take advantage of the United States' superior night-fighting equipment.

The main attack would be carried out by the Army's 1st Cavalry Divi-sion, the 24th Mechanized Division, and the 3rd Armored Cavalry Reg-iment. The Marines' role would be to break through the Iraqi forward defenses, then protect the right flank of the armored advance. To beef up the Marine ground force and give it more mobility, the Jedis planned to move most of the amphibious Marines ashore. If CENTCOM wanted the attack to have the veneer of Arab participation, the Saudis could also guard the right flank.

By daylight, the American Army forces were to be about thirty kilometers north of Kuwait City, astride the highways running north of it. If need be, the 101st Airborne would mount an air assault to control the escarpment west of Kuwait City. The Iraqi army units in Kuwait would have been bypassed and cut off while the American Army would have preserved its strength for a clash with the Republican Guard, which was deployed along the Kuwait-Iraq border. Once the lines of communication had been secured, the American Army units would proceed to the Kuwait-Iraq border and invite the Iraqis to attack them. If the Republican Guard tried to flee, CENTCOM would go after it with airpower.

The second and third options involved attacks west of the Wadi al-Batin. But they were ruled out because they were seen as too demanding logistically and because the Jedis were worried that the Army's supply lines would be vulnerable to a counterattack from Iraqi mechanized reserve divisions. If the Iraqis cut off the American supply columns, the entire Army force would be at risk. There would be two Army divisions and an armored cavalry regiment ninety miles deep in enemy territory with the Republican Guard in front of them and the Iraqi mechanized reserves on their flank or behind then. It could be one of the greatest military disasters of modern American history, the Jedis feared.[2]

The Jedis thought that the Saudis might have problems with all three plans, as massing the American forces for the attack would leave the border wide open. But Schwarzkopf said that their planning should not be restricted by political considerations and the Jedis were taking him at his word.

On October 5, Purvis briefed Schwarzkopf on the plan. Schwarzkopf observed that Purvis did not appear to be comfortable with any of the options, and Purvis confessed that he was not. The coalition was outnumbered. Even taking the conservative approach of attacking east of the wadi, the colonel thought the plan was too risky. If CENTCOM was ordered to mount a land attack, this was how it should do it, but the command needed another Army corps to do it right, Purvis said. Schwarzkopf nodded affirmatively, but did not say much more.[2]

Two days after Purvis briefed Schwarzkopf, a huge explosion rocked the ammunition depot at As Shuaybah, which the Iraqis were using to supply their troops in southern Kuwait. Nine revetted storage bunkers were blown up and eight storage buildings were destroyed. The rail spur there was turned into a tangle of twisted metal and the nearby petroleum refinery received damage. According to estimates by American intelligence experts, at least 10,000 metric tons of ammunition were blown up, enough to sustain six Iraqi heavy divisions for three days of medium- to high-intensity conflict. There was plenty of ammunition in

Iraq to make up for the loss. But the episode, never publicly disclosed by CENTCOM or by the Iraqis, could have done little to instill confidence in the Iraqi ranks.[3]

But Schwarzkopf and the Jedis were reluctant to generalize from the trickle of intelligence reports about rot and incompetence in the Iraqi military. The CENTCOM commander and his planners were impressed by the sheer mass of the Iraqi forces and worried about the possibility of poison gas attacks. And whatever problems the front-line forces had, they were not the Republican Guard.

Soon after the briefing, Schwarzkopf received a telephone call from Powell. A secure line had been set up between Powell's second-floor office at the Pentagon and Schwarzkopf's office in the Saudi Ministry of Defense. The two generals usually talked several times a day. This time, Schwarzkopf reacted as if Powell had bad news.

Powell told Schwarzkopf that he was under a lot of pressure from the hawks in the White House and had to give them something to get them off his back and give the president a warm feeling that the military had the situation under control. The JCS chairman said that the air campaign was in good shape and that Buster Glosson should come back and brief it. But Powell wanted CENTCOM to present its ground plan as well. If Cheney and the JCS were happy with the plan, it might go to the White House.

Schwarzkopf had been caught short. The Army officers involved in the ground-war planning did not have anyone like a Warden, with a bold vision for victory, or a Glosson to make it happen. Schwarzkopf's ground-war planners had gotten a late start in devising an offensive campaign and did not have much to show for the effort — at least nothing that Schwarzkopf was happy with. The Jedis were supposed to be the best and brightest of the Army, but they had essentially come back with the same thing Schwarzkopf had sketched out a month and a half before. Schwarzkopf said after the war that he considered the Jedi plan "garbage," but he had not produced a better plan. Much of Schwarzkopf's energy had gone into getting a ground defense in place and working out arrangements with the Saudis. The CENTCOM commander was not eager to go on the offensive and did not have any particularly good ideas for how to go about it.[4]

Schwarzkopf protested to Powell that he had not had enough time to work on the land offensive. There was no offensive land campaign. Powell knew Schwarzkopf was a volatile commander and reasoned with him. CENTCOM might lose the opportunity to brief Washington on the ground-war plan unless it sent its plan forward now, warts and all. Schwarzkopf quieted down and later confided to senior officials that Powell had a point.

Schwarzkopf wanted to go to Washington to give the brief himself. But Powell vetoed the idea, saying he was needed in Saudi Arabia. So Schwarzkopf decided that Robert Johnston, the Marine major general who served as Schwarzkopf's chief of staff, would lead a briefing team. Glosson would brief the air campaign, Purvis the land offensive. Richard Francona, a Defense Intelligence Agency officer attached to CENTCOM, would give the briefing on the Iraqi threat. Ready or not, the Jedi plan was going to make its Washington debut.

Before the team left, Schwarzkopf hurriedly dictated a final slide, to be shown at the end of the briefing. Dubbed the "CINC's Assessment," it stated that Schwarzkopf felt comfortable with the air campaign but did not feel at ease with the land offensive. To guarantee success another corps was required. Before he dispatched the team, Schwarzkopf sent Powell a classified cable reinforcing his message. If Washington was to take the offensive, Schwarzkopf wanted another corps of Army forces.

Schwarzkopf had a last piece of guidance for some members of his briefing team. They were to stick to their brief and not offer personal opinions. If they went off on their own, they would not only be thrown out of the Gulf, they would be out of the military.[5]

The CENTCOM commander hoped for the best, but the mission was doomed from the start. While the air campaign was in good shape, Schwarzkopf was sending Washington a ground-war plan he himself did not believe in, to be briefed by a staff that would be too scared to do anything but give a literal reading of the strategy.

DOUBT AT THE TOP

Of all the commanders involved in running the Gulf War, none was more skilled in the ways of Washington than Powell. Schwarzkopf commanded through intimidation, but the charismatic Powell had a way of getting his subordinates to do what he wanted them to — and like it. And having served as national security adviser to President Reagan, Powell knew how to deal with the civilians as well. In his years in Washington, Powell had polished more than his military skills. He had developed his own sense of foreign policy and a doctrine for when and how to use military force.

Iraq's invasion of Kuwait, deplorable though it was, did not quite cross the threshold for the JCS chairman. Powell and Schwarzkopf had the same position as Sen. Sam Nunn and many of the Democrats. Schwarzkopf's ground-war plan, unsatisfactory though it was, had some advantages for Powell's effort to slow the rush to war. It showed the civilians that an early war could be a tough affair — assuming that the air campaign did not produce the sort of result that Col. John Warden and the other airpower zealots were promising, and Powell was assuming it would not.

While Powell hid his dissent from the administration's hawkish line from public view, he shared it with one allied official. Whether it was a matter of letting his hair down among trusted allies or an effort to encourage skepticism within the coalition was not clear. What was clear was that the top American military man had his doubts.

On October 9, the day before Johnston's briefing team arrived in Washington, Powell held an unusually frank meeting with Sir Patrick Hine. Britian's air chief marshal, Hine was in Washington for the long-scheduled "airmen to airmen" talks between the Royal Air Force and the United States Air Force. Since the Gulf crisis, Hine also was doubling as the London-based commander of British forces in the Gulf region. As he was in Washington, Hine wanted to use his meeting to get Powell's take on the Gulf; but he was startled by Powell's analysis.

Britain was the United States' closest military ally in peacetime and its strongest and most militarily effective partner in the anti-Iraq coalition. From the start, Britain had sent Tornado fighters, Jaguar bombers, and a brigade of armored forces to the Gulf; and with Margaret Thatcher in charge, it was clear that London was prepared to do much more. Sir Charles Powell, Thatcher's national security adviser, used to opine that British officials were treated like virtual members of the Bush administration. Hine was a top member of the British military structure and someone the JCS chairman could talk to in confidence.

Sitting alone with Powell in his Pentagon office, Hine asked him how he saw the Gulf crisis and was struck by his extreme caution on the use of military force. Powell was making the case for relying on economic sanctions. War with Iraq, Powell argued, would be politically damaging to Western interests in the Middle East. It was not clear where it would lead; you could win the victory and lose the peace. The JCS chairman, Hine recalled more than a year later at his home in London, was also concerned that a Gulf conflict could entail heavy loss of life. Nobody could be sure that air operations could reduce the combat effectiveness of Iraqi forces. "There was uncertainty in his mind. You could not be sure how it was going to go. You could well get involved in a battle of attrition, and then lack public support. That was part of it, but not the only aspect," recalled Hine.[6]

Surprised by Powell's arguments on behalf of economic sanctions, Hine asked the chairman if he would be willing to wait twelve to fifteen months to see if sanctions would work, the period of time the American intelligence indicated might be needed. Powell indicated that he would. Hine then asked if Powell thought sanctions should be given as long as two years to work. Possibly, Powell responded.

It was not a view that Hine felt had much to recommend it, and the British commander argued the opposite case. There was a winter window of opportunity for taking military action, Hine insisted. It would be difficult to mount a major operation in the summer months, when the desert became a veritable blast furnace, particularly as the Iraqis were expected to use chemical weapons, forcing the coalition forces to don heavy protective gear. If the coalition did not force the issue by March 1991, it would have to think about thinning out its forces, since it was not possible to keep hundreds of thousands of troops in the inhospitable Gulf region indefinitely. And once it started to thin out the forces, the prospect of getting them all back there for a military confrontation with Iraq was pretty remote. The Western public would lose interest. The Saudis and other Arab members of the coalition would begin to lose confidence in the West's resolve to take on Saddam.

Powell argued otherwise, insisting that the coalition would maintain a long-term military presence and then reconstitute what it needed if war could not be avoided. The chairman never breathed a word to Hine about Johnston's upcoming brief on the air and land campaigns. Nor did Powell betray any reservations about a military offensive when Johnston arrived to give him a preview of the briefing planned for the next day. Powell well knew that you could share some information with your allies, but not with your own subordinates, and vice versa.

Defense Secretary Cheney, Powell, and the service chiefs of staff were in the JCS conference room, known as the Tank, when Johnston and his briefers entered the room. Short, with close-cropped hair and in starched camouflage field uniform, Johnston did things by the book. He was very military in his bearing, a model of efficiency, a solid chief of staff who was loyal to Schwarzkopf. But he had little experience in dealing with the officials who populated the upper reaches of the Bush administration and was stiff in their presence.

Johnston did not plan on delivering a take-charge briefing. He would sit back as his team outlined CENTCOM's plans and then come in at the end to provide the "CINC's Assessment." Francona would go first to brief the threat, then Glosson would present the air campaign, followed by Purvis, speaking on behalf of the Jedis.

Glosson was cut from a different mold than Johnston — and showed it when it came time to outline the air campaign. Glosson knew much of the Cheney team from his days as a top aide for David Gribben III, the assistant defense secretary for legislative affairs, and his demeanor radiated confidence. In a sense, Glosson's attitude reflected the difference in the situations confronting the Air Force and the land forces. The Air Force believed that it had the assets it needed to conduct a full-fledged strategic air campaign. The Army, in contrast, was still nervously looking to add more forces. But it was also a matter of personality. Glosson was loose and blunt-spoken.

Standing before his high-level audience, Glosson explained that the air campaign could be executed in fourteen to twenty-one days, given good weather. The laser beams that the American pilots used to direct their precision-guided bombs could not penetrate through cloud cover, and Glosson was assuming that less than 7 percent of the time would be lost for bad weather. Glosson forecast that the United States would lose forty to fifty aircraft. By the end of the campaign, Iraq would have capitulated or the Iraqi army would be so weakened that the Army could run over them.

Adm. David Jeremiah, the vice chairman of the Joint Chiefs of Staff, reacted skeptically. "Is that an optimistic or a pessimistic analysis?" Jeremiah asked rhetorically.

"It is worst case," Glosson shot back.

Al Gray, the scrappy and blunt-spoken Marine commandant, also reacted somewhat skeptically, but by and large Glosson went unchallenged. In the tank, at least, the air campaign plans did not take any hits.

After Glosson's brief, Purvis took the floor, unraveling a roll of acetate and placing the transparent covering on a map of the region. The arrows on the plastic depicted the ground campaign, standard operating procedure for depicting land operations. Purvis began by showing a series of slides that outlined the guiding principles of the campaign. Airpower would be critical to making the plan work because American forces would be outnumbered, the slide stated without further elaboration. The assault on the Iraqi front-line fortifications would be preceded by a withering barrage of air and artillery attacks. Purvis did not provide any casualty estimates. It was just as well that no one asked. Using standard models, the Jedis had projected that there would be about 10,000

American casualties, 1,500 of whom might be killed in action. It was a crude guesstimate based on computer projections, but a sobering one. It was well understood within the American military that holding down casualties was a political prerequisite for launching a military offensive.

Even without the casualty estimates, it was as if the Army colonel had set a bomb off in the Tank. Gray objected vehemently to the plan, which had been prepared without consulting the Marines. The Jedis had essentially eliminated the Marine amphibious capability so that the Marines could breach the Iraqi fortifications on behalf of an Army land offensive, Gray complained. Marines would be lost in the wire, added Gray, who was aghast at the idea of plunging through the heart of the Iraqi defenses in southern Kuwait. After repeated outbursts, Powell intervened to calm Gray down.

"Let's wait for the chief," Powell said, referring to Johnston. Alone among the Pentagon officials in the tank, Powell knew that Johnston would present the "CINC's assessment" expressing Schwarzkopf's reservations about the plan.

But Powell registered his own criticism of the plan. Powell asked how long it would take the American forces to pass through the Iraqi frontline fortifications, and Purvis said that it would require several hours. The response appeared to alarm Powell; he seemed concerned that the Jedis were making the breach look too easy.

"Let me understand what you are saying: air creates a breach?" Powell asked in a tone of incredulity.

"No sir, I did not say that," Purvis replied. Purvis's protestations were in vain. Powell started relating his Vietnam experience, how American airpower pounded the enemy trenches. Then an American soldier stood up and took a bullet in his shoulder. For not the first time, Powell was arguing that airpower had its limits.

Purvis concluded that some of Powell's criticism was the result of a miscommunication. Purvis thought Powell was asking how long it would take to move the lead troops through the breach site, once the minefields had been cleared, the obstacles knocked down, and the frontline Iraqi defenders neutralized — not how long it would take to complete the entire process of breaching the defenses and moving the follow-on forces through. But Purvis kept his thoughts to himself. Powell's comments on the difficulty of the breach, Purvis thought, were partly intended for effect, to make sure that nobody in the tank got the idea that a ground war would be an easy proposition.

At the end of Purvis's brief, Johnston took the floor to present the "CINC's Assessment." The commander was comfortable with the air campaign, but not with the ground-war plan. If an attack was to be launched soon, the ground plan was the one that Schwarzkopf would go with, but it was not his recommended course of action. The ground plan lacked the forces to guarantee success and relied very heavily on airpower and on the collapse of the Iraqi forces. It ran the risk of not accomplishing the mission and generating unacceptable casualties. It would take at least another corps to ensure that the United States could attack the Iraqis on the ground and defeat them.

After the briefing, Powell conferred privately with Johnston, who was scheduled to take his team to the White House the next day to brief the president. While Purvis waited for Johnston in a small conference room down the hall, Gray sat down, put his feet up on the table, and continued his critique of the Jedi plan.

"If you dismount the MEB, I am going to send another MEB," Gray matter-of-factly stated, referring to the Jedi plan to disembark most of the Marine amphibious brigade afloat in the Arabian Sea. The Marine commandant was determined to give the Marines an alternative to a casualty-producing plunge up the middle, whatever the bright Army colonels and majors in Schwarzkopf's planning cell decided.[7]

Powell's concerns went beyond tactics. Although the "CINC's Assessment" was replete with caveats and disclaimers, Powell was concerned that the White House might act on the plan — or at least the air campaign portion. When Johnston rejoined Glosson and Purvis, he told them to be sure not to oversell the plan the next day at the White House.

Shortly after that, Powell and Michael P. C. Carns, an Air Force lieutenant general who worked for Powell as the director of the Joint Staff, separately made the same point to Glosson. Relating Powell's concerns, Carns told Glosson that the air campaign was too smooth, too attractive to a White House that was losing patience with Saddam Hussein. Glosson should condense his presentation and avoid making the air campaign look too easy.

Then, there was a fourth warning in a telephone conversation with Schwarzkopf himself. Powell had called the commander after the session in the tank to give him a report. The ground campaign had raised a lot of questions, but Powell was concerned that the air-war plan might be too attractive.

"Buster, the chairman is afraid that if the brief goes to the president like this, the president will execute the air campaign," Schwarzkopf told Glosson.

Glosson was angry. He was a one-star general propelled by events to his first audience with the president. He did not want to pull his punches. Schwarzkopf tried to calm Glosson and smooth over the situation. Glosson did not have to censor his convictions, he should simply condense the presentation.

"I said, 'Buster, when you get over there just stick to the facts. Let's not be too enthusiastic.' I said be like Sergeant Friday. Just given them the facts," Schwarzkopf recalled.[8]

After the telephone call, Glosson met with Donald Rice, the secretary of the Air Force, and related the guidance he had received. Rice, an unabashed proponent of airpower, advised Glosson to give the best briefing he could and let the chips fall where they may. Later, Glosson was informed that there would be only forty-five minutes for the briefers' White House presentation. But when the CENTCOM briefers walked into the White House situation room, it soon became apparent that the president and his top advisers were prepared to spend hours going over the campaign plan.[9]

DAY OF DECISION

The October 11 White House meeting was a defining moment in the evolution of the ground- and air-war plans. President Bush was there, along with Vice President Quayle, Secretary of State Baker, Cheney, Powell, National Security Adviser Scowcroft, White House Chief of Staff John Sununu, and Robert M. Gates, the deputy national security adviser, who took a seat along the back wall. The briefing lineup was the same. Francona would give the standard threat brief. Then Glosson was to give a condensed version of his air campaign brief, to be followed by Purvis and Johnston. The difference was that this time President Bush would be asking the questions, and unlike Powell, Bush was not reluctant to force a military confrontation with Saddam. What follows is drawn from the notes of the participants at the meeting.

Francona's brief was uneventful. But Glosson's presentation soon became a three-way discussion among Glosson, the air-war proponent; Powell, the air-war skeptic and reluctant warrior; and Bush, the former World War II Navy aviator and commander in chief in search of a workable military option.

Glosson walked the president through the opening days of the air war, and Bush asked a series of technical and strategic questions. The initial attacks would involve F-117 and F-111F strikes against Iraq's Kari command centers, explained Glosson, brandishing a satellite photo of a command center. The Air Force and Navy would also use drones to spoof the Iraqi defenses, he said, referring to the secret "Scathe Mean" program and the Navy TALDs. F-15E Strike Eagles would go after the Scud launchers in the west. There would be strikes against chemical and biological weapons sites at Karbala and Salman Pak.

Turning to the planned attacks on downtown Baghdad, Glosson ran through the list of leadership, command and control, and communications targets that were to be bombed and struck by Tomahawk cruise missiles. The Baghdad attacks, which included raids on Saddam's residences and Iraq's political institutions, had the greatest political sensitivity and potential for controversy. There could be no misunderstanding in Washington about what the Black Hole was planning to do. The strikes, Glosson explained, were intended to "decapitate" the Saddam Hussein regime and included the International Communications Center, the Presidential Palace, Presidential Retreat, Presidential Residence and Bunker, Baath Party headquarters, National C3 Bunker, Government Control Center, Royal Palace, and Telecommunications Center. The Iraqi power grid would be struck by air-launched and sea-launched cruise missiles and by F-111Fs. Iraqi airfields would be hit by F-111Fs, British and Saudi Tornados, and B-52 bombers. The Republican Guard would be attacked by F-16s, A-6s, and FA-18s. There would be attacks on Iraq's military industry, on its bridges, its railroad yards, its television transmitters.

Bush was comfortable with the strategic air campaign and questioned only one of the proposed targets in downtown Baghdad: the Royal Palace. The president wanted to know if the structure had symbolic value to the Iraqi people. Glosson replied that it had no religious value. Bush told Powell to make doubly sure that no targets of religious or historic significance were on the target list. Bush had no apparent reservations about going after the Iraqi leadership or the Baath Party headquarters, but wanted to ensure that the American air strikes would not anger the Iraqi people or the Arab masses.

Baker, however, was concerned about the way Glosson described the objective of the Baghdad raids. The secretary of state did not like the reference to "decapitating" Saddam's government, military jargon for severing a regime's ability to command its forces or eliminating it altogether. Blunt talk like that was a red flag for Baker, who had the task of holding together the anti-Iraq coalition. Baker suggested that a more politic way to express the objective of the Baghdad raids was "incapacitating" Saddam's regime. Glosson indicated that Baker's suggestion could be accommodated.

The most important question on the president's mind, however, was not one of semantics but the question of what the strategic air campaign would accomplish. Glosson told the president that as a result of the air war Saddam Hussein would not be able to communicate effectively with his people or his military forces. Nor would he be able to reinforce his army in Kuwait. There would be disruption throughout Iraq.

Bush then raised the critical question: What if the coalition mounted an air campaign and then waited seven to ten days for the Iraqi government to give up or collapse? What would be wrong with that? It was a decisive point in the discussion. If airpower could shut down the Iraqi government and cut off the Iraqi army in Kuwait, the United States would not need to send massive troop reinforcements to the Gulf and the military option could be exercised sooner rather than later.

Powell quickly preempted Glosson's response, as if he was concerned that the Air Force general might use his audience with the president to sell Bush on the idea of starting the air campaign soon instead of waiting for the ground troop buildup. Bombing was a politically inviting solution. It held out the promise of a defeat of Saddam with little risk of sizable American casualties, and Powell did not want the president to be seduced by the Air Force.

"I have to tell you, Mr. President, that it will not meet your objectives. I cannot assure you that Iraqi ground forces will be out of Kuwait, just because we do an air campaign," Powell said.

Bush kept on with his questioning. What did Glosson say to the critics who predicted that Saddam would rise out of the rubble in Baghdad and broadcast to his people and the world on national television? Bush did not say so, but he appeared to have his former nemesis, Manuel Antonio Noriega, in mind. It had taken the United States days to knock out the Panamanian television station that was broadcasting Noriega's defiance, and the United States was operating from bases in that country. Glosson gave a confident reply.

"He might be able to do that, Mr. President, but it would not be on his television network," Glosson said.

Again, Powell felt that the Air Force was making promises it could not fulfill. "But we have got to be ready for that. We can't let people think that Saddam will not survive this," Powell interjected.

Glosson responded that there was a high probability that the Iraqi leader would in fact survive, since the United States was not making a determined effort to target him. There was a difference between shutting down Saddam's command centers, creating the conditions for his overthrow, and guaranteeing the death of the Iraqi leader.

"Buster's correct," Cheney chimed in. "We have got to make sure that we do not lead people to expect that Saddam will be eliminated."

But that did not mean that CENTCOM would be precluded from trying.

The remainder of the session dealt with more technical questions. Bush wanted to know why the Navy aircraft carriers were deployed so far away from Kuwait when the battleships were stationed in the Gulf. The map that Glosson presented showed the Navy's three carriers in the Red Sea and the Arabian Gulf. The Air Force general said that the Navy was concerned about the vulnerability of its carriers. Powell quickly intervened with a more charitable response: a heavily armored battleship could withstand more punishment than an aircraft carrier.

Baker wanted to know how the Air Force could be sure that the Iraqis would not detect the stealth F-117, which figured so prominently in the air campaign. Glosson explained that he had ordered a secret test mission: an F-117 had flown along the Saudi-Iraqi border. The Iraqis often responded to American fighter patrols near their territory by activating their radars and dispatching their interceptors to the border. But this time there was no response.

Did CENTCOM plan to launch strikes out of Turkey? Baker asked. Glosson responded that they had no current plans to do so. Would it help if the Air Force could do so? Baker asked. Yes, Glosson responded. CENTCOM would like to open a second front.

John Sununu was reading budget documents throughout the meeting and had only one question. Glosson had stated that the strategic air campaign would take ten to fourteen days. If that campaign did not win the war outright, it was to be followed by seven to ten days of attacks on Iraq's ground forces, to weaken the Iraqi army for the ground war to come. That meant that the air war could last nearly a month, Sununu observed.

"A real rocket scientist," Baker jested.

Then discussion shifted to the ground offensive. Purvis talked through the plan to attack through the Iraqi defenses. Brent Scowcroft was nonplussed. The national security adviser had heard nothing about the reception the plan had received the day before in the Tank, and he was concerned. Why was the American Army attacking into the strength of the Iraqi defense? Why wasn't the Army hitting the Iraqis on their western flank? Scowcroft asked.

Purvis began to answer, but then Powell took the floor. The stakes were too high to leave the answers to a lieutenant colonel from CENTCOM. Powell told Scowcroft that the Army could not logistically sustain an attack from the west and did not have an adequate-size force. Powell's comment appeared to dispose of Scowcroft's proposal, disguised though it was in the form of a question. But it immediately became clear that this was the starting point, not the end, of the debate over plans for a ground war.

What would it take to mount an attack from the west? President Bush asked. It would take one more corps, Powell explained.

But that might give the coalition force too much of an American cast, Baker observed. There would not be enough Arab forces to credibly argue that Saddam was being opposed by an international coalition. Washington had to watch that, Baker said.

Bush did not appear to be perturbed by Baker's concern. How long would it take to deploy an additional corps? the president asked Powell. Powell said that the corps could be in place by January 1.

Where would they come from? Bush asked again. Powell said that he would get the additional forces from Europe.

Cheney interjected that this was a discussion that should be held in a smaller group. After the meeting, Scowcroft telephoned Cheney. The CENTCOM plan for a ground offensive was awful, Scowcroft complained. The Pentagon would have to do better than that. Cheney concurred.[10]

The White House meeting was a turning point that foreshadowed all the key decisions in planning the war. President Bush and his top advisers had concluded that military action, and not sanctions, would almost certainly be needed to evict the Iraqi forces from Kuwait, even as the press and the public were debating the efficacy of sanctions. The president and his men had also accepted Powell's argument that airpower was not sufficient to do the job. If Washington had been convinced of the ability of American airpower to cut the Iraqis down to size, the Army's plan would not have mattered that much and the reaction to the Jedi strategy would not have been as severe as it was.

The Jedis' one-corps plan had been deemed unacceptable. The president and his national security adviser had pointed the way to a two-corps plan involving an attack in the west. Although the final decision to dispatch the forces had yet to be made, a tentative date for deploying the force had even been identified. The exact size of the reinforcement package to be deployed and its deployment schedule were to be worked out by Powell during a trip to Saudi Arabia.

"I never considered seriously the possibility of an 'air-only' campaign," Bush recalled after the war. "There was much discussion about what an air campaign might accomplish — and that it might be enough to convince Saddam to pull out. But from the outset, I thought we should plan on the assumption that Saddam would resist to the end and develop our force requirements on that basis."[11]

Politically, however, the session was a calamity for Schwarzkopf. Schwarzkopf's monopoly of the ground-war planning had ensured secrecy and made it easier for him to test ideas without intervention from Washington. It was not the way the theater commander for Central and South America, Gen. Maxwell Thurman, had done things when he worked with Powell and the JCS to develop a plan to invade Panama. The close-hold approach fit Schwarzkopf's imperious command style, but it also meant that the ground-war plans were seen as uniquely Schwarzkopf's.

Schwarzkopf and his aides would argue later that he was not recommending an up-the-middle attack in Kuwait. Quite the contrary, he had insisted that the plans were the best he could do with the available forces and was making the case that more forces were needed. Strictly speaking, that was true. But while the CENTCOM commander had indicated that another corps was needed to guarantee success, he had failed to explain in his briefing how it might be used. Two months after the Iraqi invasion of Kuwait, CENTCOM still did not have a clue how ground forces should be used to evict the Iraqis from Kuwait.

At the Pentagon, officials were concerned that Schwarzkopf just wanted more men to throw at the Iraqis and lacked a vision for how to evict them from Kuwait. "You know I can't draw a picture and say at the bottom this ain't my picture," said one three-star general who was present for the Washington briefing of Schwarzkopf's plan. "For anybody to come with that construct said to me that they don't know what they were doing. A lot of the national leaders lost a lot of confidence in the CINC."[12]

The word at the White House was that Schwarzkopf was unimaginative; indeed, that the entire American military had let the president down. In conversations with senior administration officials, Scowcroft made unflattering comparisons between the CENTCOM plan and the bloody battles of the Civil War, which had been recounted months before in a long television series on Public Broadcasting.

While the White House did not know that Powell was privately arguing with his British counterpart against forcing a military confrontation with Iraq, the JCS chairman had let a plan be presented to the White House that it could not accept.

The morning after the briefing at the White House, Cheney, Powell, Carns, and Rear Adm. Mike McConnell, the chief intelligence official for the JCS, met to review the bidding. Cheney was clearly troubled.

"Colin, I have been thinking about this all night. I can't let Norm do this high diddle diddle up-the-middle plan," Cheney said, according to one participant in the meeting. "I just can't let him do it."[13]

While the public debate was focused on the efficacy of sanctions, the momentum for war was well along within the administration. President Bush was prepared for a forceful conclusion to the crisis. But with the White House rejection of the one-corps ground plan, a rift was developing between the military and the civilians. Cheney had differed with Powell on the day of the invasion, when the general argued that the United States ought to focus on the defense of Saudi Arabia, not the liberation of Kuwait. Since then, the tensions between the two had been submerged in the background. But now Cheney sensed that the military was again dragging its feet.

"There was constant friction between Cheney and Powell, which was extremely healthy," observed an aide to Powell. "Cheney always wanted to do it now. He did not always understand the monstrosity of the buildup. But we probably would not have been ready as soon as we were if it had not been for Cheney's pressure."

Powell told Cheney that he would stay on top of the situation and get back to him, but Cheney did not intend to wait for an answer. The defense secretary was already beginning to formulate his own plan to turn the tables on the Iraqis.

7

"The Western Excursion"

I think it is fair to say the Washington pressure led us to look farther to the west than we were looking.

— Gen. H. Norman Schwarzkopf
April 1993 interview

I N RIYADH, Washington's dismissive reaction to Schwarzkopf's ground-war plan grated on the commander. Schwarzkopf felt abused and misunderstood. The best talent Schwarzkopf could muster had produced a plan that was being ridiculed by top officials in Washington. He was being second-guessed by the secretary of defense, the president's national security adviser, and the chairman of the Joint Chiefs of Staff. Everyone seemed to have his own plan, including one scheme that Schwarzkopf ridiculed as the "great Trojan horse plan," in which commandos would hide in an oil tanker sent into Kuwait harbor and then fan out into Kuwait City.[1]

Schwarzkopf's therapy was to take his frustration out on his staff. He was like a man who came back from a bad day at work and kicked the dog. It was not the best way to inspire his planners to help CENTCOM extricate itself from a sticky situation. The Jedis did not like the commander's tirades, but they were becoming used to them.

When the Jedis met with Schwarzkopf to pick up the pieces shortly after Johnston's trip to Washington, it was clear that the commander's frustration was spilling over. The Jedis were briefing the latest iteration of the ground-war plan when Schwarzkopf started complaining about Bush administration officials who seemed to think that there was a hidden Inchon that CENTCOM was unable to find. Well, there was no Inchon, he said.

As the meeting went on, Schwarzkopf was interrupted by a call from Powell. After the call ended, the Jedis started to resume the briefing, but Schwarzkopf slammed down his fist.

"You can't brief me on this, because we don't have an approved concept. We don't have a concept at all!" he shouted. The meeting later went down in the Jedi lore as the "Tuesday night massacre."[2]

Schwarzkopf's monopoly on the land-war planning had been broken by Washington. He was still the commander, but with the White House rejection of the one-corps ground plan, the development of the strategy was becoming a three-way game involving Schwarzkopf, Powell, and Cheney.

Cheney got the idea for his offensive plan from the most unlikely of sources: a donnish civilian official who had come to the Pentagon from the Stanford University Graduate School of Business. Tall, lean, and professorial in bearing, Henry Rowen served as the assistant defense secretary for international security affairs. Rowen had held a succession of senior government posts and academic positions.

Rowen's geographic area of responsibility at the Pentagon included the Middle East and all of Southwest Asia, to include arms sales, the overseas deployment of American forces, and the proliferation of nuclear weapons and other means of mass destruction. Rowen found the subject matter engaging, but he was not trying to use the post as a stepping stone to more high-ranking administration appointments. He planned to return to Stanford, and he approached his Pentagon post with a kind of academic detachment. After Iraqi forces invaded Kuwait, Rowen worked day and night along with other Pentagon officials. But Rowen, who was older than many of his Pentagon counterparts, concluded the affair would drag on for months, and he kept to his plans to take a short September vacation in France.

True to his academic temperament, Rowen used some of his vacation time to read the *History of the Arab Peoples* by Sir John Bagot Glubb. Glubb was a legend in the annals of Middle East military history. A British officer who was wounded three time during the First World War, Glubb later led several campaigns in Transjordan and Iraq, which was a British dominion. During his service in the Middle East, Glubb led the Arab legion in Transjordan, helped defend Iraq from the tribes in what is now Saudi Arabia, put down a pro-Axis uprising in Iraq during the Second World War, and fought with the Arabs during the 1948 war with

Israel. Later, he settled in Britain and wrote several books on his two decades of military adventures in the Middle East.

In reading Glubb, Rowen saw that Arab armies had moved across the desert with incredible freedom. The lessons Rowen extracted from reading Glubb were reinforced by conversations he had during his vacation with a neighbor, a former diplomat who had served in the British embassy in Baghdad when pro-German Iraqis overthrew the British-supported ruler in Baghdad in 1941. It had taken the British a matter of weeks to put down the rebellion by launching a two-pronged attack, from Basra and from Transjordan. If Arab and British forces could sweep through western Iraq, why could not American troops, which had the advantage of air superiority and mobile ground forces, do the same? Although transporting and sustaining a division in the far western desert would be a demanding task, logistics was an American strength.

Rowen had picked up a rumor that Schwarzkopf's plan was to launch a ground attack straight at the Iraqi forces in Kuwait, a plan Rowen later derided to Cheney as like the "charge of the light brigade into the wadi of death."

Instead of plunging into the thick of the Iraqi defenses in Kuwait, Rowen thought CENTCOM should send a division or two to occupy the far western part of Iraq. Unlike the British, the Americans could not go through Jordan. But the American forces could be sent down the Tapline Road — a two-lane east-west route that went through Hafar al-Batin and continued across the Saudi frontier — from their bases in Saudi Arabia and dropped by parachute.

Upon returning from France, Rowen discussed his ideas with Wolfowitz, who took Rowen to present them to Cheney. The defense secretary thought that Rowen's concept was better than going "high diddle diddle, right up the middle."

To develop the plan, Wolfowitz created a small group of retired and active-duty military officers, led by ret. Army Lt. Gen. Dale Vesser, who had served as a J-5, or planning officer for the Joint Chiefs of Staff, before joining Wolfowitz's staff. It was not the orthodox way of doing business. Military planning was the province of the theater commander and the JCS chairman, not the civilian bureaucracy at the Pentagon. But Cheney wanted to ensure that the plan was properly developed and not dismissed out of hand. The planners were instructed not to discuss their work with anyone else in the Pentagon. As difficult as it would be for the military commanders to accept an idea from Cheney, plans that were believed to have been spawned by lower-ranking civilians were sure to be rejected. Vesser was initially skeptical of Rowen's idea, but changed his mind as he studied it.

Vesser developed a detailed plan, expanding the list of potential forces, and dubbed it Operation Scorpion. The purpose of the plan was severalfold. Strategically, the sudden arrival of coalition forces in the far western desert would be a shock to the Iraqi high command, creating an actual or perceived threat to Baghdad. That, the planners theorized, could lead to "regime collapse." Even if the Bush administration decided not to use the western territory as a springboard to launch an attack on Baghdad, American forces could occupy the territory and pressure the Iraqi leaders into a political settlement on the coalition's terms. From a tactical standpoint, if Iraq tried to move forces to the west to take on the Americans, they would become easy targets for allied airpower. Instead of using airpower to prepare for a ground assault, a ground attack would be used to facilitate air strikes. Politically, the occupation of western Iraq would protect Israel from Scud attacks launched from the area and thus help keep the Jewish state out of the war. From an economic standpoint, it would cut the road from Amman to Baghdad, which Iraq was using to get supplies despite the United Nations imposed embargo.

Once he had fleshed out the plan, Vesser briefed it to Cheney. And while Cheney was not interested in surrounding Baghdad, he liked and adapted the concept, referring more colloquially to it as "the Western Excursion."[3]

Cheney had good reason to anticipate that his plan would be rebuffed by the generals. Powell's philosophy of warfare was evident in the invasion of Panama, where the United States neutralized the hapless Panamanian Defense Force with one massive blow. When it came to distant reaches like the Gulf, it was an approach that took time. Continuing the troop deployment to build an invincible force would delay an offensive for months. But since Powell's political analysis held that it would be best to avoid a military confrontation, that was a plus, not a liability.

When Cheney was pressing the Western Excursion, Powell launched his own planning effort, turning to Lt. Gen. Thomas Kelly, the Army officer who served as the J-3, or chief operations officer on the JCS staff, and Lt. Gen. Martin Brandtner, a Marine who was to succeed Kelly.

Powell instructed them to assemble a team of planners and develop a land campaign. There could be no possibility of failure. Powell did not care what it took. The plan would use overwhelming force. The White House response to the Jedi plan had been so negative that it was clear that the starting point for Powell's planning effort was a large flanking move in the west.

Powell's planners represented a cross section of military expertise. The team also brought in logistics experts and worked quietly with a handful of specialists at the Army's European Command. The JCS planning cell was sworn to secrecy. Outside the planners themselves and the handful of officials who were briefed on their efforts, the planning effort simply did not exist. "The plan did not have a name. It met in a room that did not exist. It was held very, very, very closely," said one ranking member of the planning cell.[4]

The team's first planning exercise was a crash effort carried out the weekend after Johnston's team returned to Riyadh. It produced six options, some of which the planners regarded as credible and others that were included to demonstrate that the team had left no stone unturned. One option was to launch an expeditionary attack through Jordan, but that was rejected on political and logistical grounds. The same went for the option of attacking through Turkey. Cheney's Western Excursion, which the defense secretary asked the planners to consider, was considered, but discounted as out of synch with the JCS chairman's maxim to build an invincible force, logistically difficult, and of dubious strategic benefit. The planners also considered a more conventional armored thrust in the far west, which would be mounted from Ar'ar, a Saudi town that later became a base for the special forces. Logistically, that too was a bridge too far.

That left two options: huge multidivisional sweeps through the desert that would send the Army west of the Wadi al-Batin and have them turn east to envelop the Republican Guard. One of the plans developed by Powell's team had the Army stretched along the Saudi frontier from the Wadi al-Batin to as far west as Ar'ar while a more conservative approach strung the deployment out to Rafha. The American Army forces would seize the Tallil Air Base, which Powell planners saw as a major road and communications junction, and seal off the escape route of the Republican Guard. Then the Army would destroy the premier Iraqi force. A forward operating and supply base, which the planners dubbed Cobra, would be established in western Iraq. Cobra could be used as a staging area to send American troops even deeper into Iraqi territory to cut communications lines, go after Scud launchers, or block the escape of Iraqi forces along Highway 8 paralleling the Euphrates River in the event the Iraqis tried to bolt down that road. The Marines did not have much of a role in the plan: essentially, they were to draw Iraqi attention east.

These flanking movements, the planners felt, had much to recommend them. They would enable Army forces to circumvent the Iraqi defenses. Logistically, they could be supported by using the Tapline Road. Politically, the sweep across western Iraq would enable the military to buy off Cheney and defuse the pressure to implement the Western Excursion.

The early intelligence reports fielded by Powell's planners raised doubts about the feasibility of a huge left hook through the desert. Defense Intelligence Agency experts said that the Arabian Peninsula was entering the rainy season and questioned whether the desert terrain in the west would support tanks. But after intelligence officials in the Gulf talked to bedouins and oil companies, it was determined that the Tigris and Euphrates had flood control systems and that the desert terrain would not be an impenetrable obstacle.

When Powell took the overlays of the Joint Staff's left hook with him on his October trip to Saudi Arabia, it was clear that the JCS chairman intended to quietly go over the Washington-generated ideas with Schwarzkopf.

WESTWARD HO

Schwarzkopf knew that Powell's trip would be a milestone. Schwarzkopf was the theater commander, but his plans would never be accepted in Washington unless they passed muster with Powell. Powell had embraced the Air Force's air-war plan in September, and it had been relatively smooth sailing from then. Now Schwarzkopf and Powell needed to get their heads together and form a united front. Otherwise, the civilians would try telling them what to do.

In anticipation of Powell's visit, Schwarzkopf ordered the Jedis to draft a new land-attack plan that would involve two Army corps. Schwarzkopf did not tell them what he had in mind, and he also told them to continue working on the one-corps plan that had been rebuffed in Washington. Unless CENTCOM received additional forces, it had to be prepared to fight with what it had.

Finally, Schwarzkopf told the Jedis that from now on they would be reporting to Army commanders in Riyadh. Like a boulder rolling down a hill, the planning of the offensive was gathering momentum by the day, and the close-hold nature of the Jedi planning had produced an odd state of affairs. It was time to integrate the Jedi and the Army planning in the Gulf.

Brig. Gen. Steven Arnold, the Army's chief operations officer in Riyadh, was ordered to oversee the Jedi planning effort. A one-star general, Arnold was the assistant commander of the Army's 2nd Division along the demilitarized zone in Korea when the Gulf crisis developed. But on Labor Day, he received a call from Army headquarters ordering him to leave for Saudi Arabia within twenty-four hours. A West Point graduate and thirty-year Army veteran who had served two tours in Vietnam, Arnold was needed to help strengthen Lt. Gen. John Yeosock's Third Army headquarters. A soft-spoken general with an avuncular style, Arnold got on well with Lt. Col. Purvis and the rest of the Jedis and did not much care for Schwarzkopf's management style. Arnold evinced a quiet competence and sought to lead by example. He thought that Schwarzkopf's fear-inducing tirades were unnecessary, even counterproductive. After assuming his new role, Arnold described his briefings to Schwarzkopf as "reconnaissance by fire." The CENTCOM commander's volcanic eruptions were sometimes the only guidance he and the Jedis had to go by.

The Jedis began by reviewing satellite photos that showed the Iraqi defense was focused on the tri-border area, where the Iraq, Kuwait, and Saudi borders met, as if the Iraqis were expecting the coalition forces to drive up along the Wadi al-Batin. The Tawakalana Division, the southernmost of the three armored Republican Guard divisions deployed in the theater, was positioned to move in various directions to blunt an attack. Intelligence estimates showed that there were up to ten armored divisions from Iraq's regular army and increased artillery in southwest Kuwait in a mutually supporting position with the Tawakalana Division. The reconnaissance photos of the Republican Guard showed that they had not dug themselves into defensive positions. Instead, the Republican Guard divisions were laagered up in battalion circles as if they intended to move quickly — to take on the Americans or to escape. Only after the war would American intelligence learn that the Iraqis had concluded that the Americans were planning to launch a fall offensive.

In developing a two-corps plan, Arnold and the Jedis considered three options, which roughly paralleled the earlier work they had done on their rejected one-corps plan. But the Jedis' favored option was to mass two Army corps and the British forces as the main attack in the flat seventy-mile stretch of desert just west of the Wadi al-Batin, which the CENTCOM staff called the "bowling alley." The force would then rush up to the Euphrates River and attack the Republican Guard. The Marines and Arab members of the coalition would provide the supporting attack, going west of Kuwait City to hold the Iraqi forces in position. Schwarzkopf had been adamant in his meetings with the Jedis that the Republican Guard were not merely to be forced out of Kuwait, they were to be destroyed. Sending both Army corps, and whatever allies might accompany them, up the bowling alley would enable the force to sidestep the Iraqi front-line defenses and concentrate the coalition's striking power on their principal objective.

The Jedis saw little reason for stretching the attack farther west, as Powell was suggesting from Washington. To the immediate west of the bowling alley, the Iraqi desert looked a little like a moonscape. After thirty miles or so of difficult terrain, the desert smoothed out again. But there were no forces there to attack, and putting American troops there would simply divert combat power from the main attack. The Jedis' two-corps plan was a left hook, but not the roundhouse punch that Powell's team had secretly prepared and far different from Cheney's Western Excursion.

When the Jedis briefed the plan in an October 21 meeting, Schwarz-kopf seemed to be in agreement, at least measured by his mood. The commander was calm and the meeting went smoothly.[5]

But even while Schwarzkopf was drawing up a plan to send a massive army to destroy the Republican Guard, he was doing his best to slow the push toward war. Like Powell, Schwarzkopf favored giving sanctions a chance and was unhappy with the administration hawks who argued that it was politically naive to think the polyglot anti-Iraq coalition could hold together for another year or two and that it was important to force the issue. Unlike Powell, he laid his cards on the table, making his case in an interview with the *Atlanta Journal and Constitution*.

"Now we are starting to see evidence that the sanctions are pinching," Schwarzkopf told the newspaper. "So why should we say, 'Okay, gave 'em two months, didn't work. Let's get on with it and kill a whole bunch of people'? That's crazy."

If the alternative to bloodshed was having American troops sit in the Saudi desert for another summer, Schwarzkopf continued, that was not such a bad alternative.

Some of the Army's senior field commanders privately echoed Schwarzkopf's sense of caution. When Paul Wolfowitz visited Saudi Arabia that month, Gen. Gary E. Luck, the XVIII Airborne commander who would help lead the attack against the Republican Guard, and later become the top commander of American forces in Korea, told him bluntly that the liberation of Kuwait simply was not worth the lives of American servicemen.

But the White House had made it clear that the planning was to go ahead, and on October 22 Powell came calling.

★   ★   ★

After arriving in Riyadh, Powell met privately with Schwarzkopf. Powell also met separately with the Jedis, although when he did he kept his ideas to himself. An astute politician, the JCS chief knew better than to get between Schwarzkopf and his planners.

"Pretend we are just a couple of tactics instructors," Powell said, as he began his meeting with the Jedis.

Purvis went through the one-corps plan in excruciating detail with Powell challenging him at every turn. Powell seemed determined to satisfy himself that there was not a war-winning strategy Schwarzkopf's planners had missed before endorsing the flanking attack and the massive buildup it required.

After running through the one-corps plan, the Jedis briefed their plan for using two corps to conduct an attack just west of the Wadi. To carry out the plan, the Jedis estimated that they needed two additional heavy divisions and an armored cavalry regiment and projected that it would take eighty days to get the force to Saudi Arabia. It had taken ninety days for the first Army corps to deploy to the Persian Gulf, and the Jedis figured that they could shave ten days off that time through various efficiencies.

"My guys told me ninety days," Powell replied. Clearly, Powell had already given some thought to conducting a ground war with two Army corps, but what precisely Powell had in mind he did not say.

But while the JCS chief was abroad, Cheney was busy, as well. Powell returned to Washington by way of NATO headquarters in Europe, and while he was on the road Cheney informed Powell's planners that he wanted to see them.

Cheney had come down to the JCS offices before. But this time Cheney was not coming to hear the latest thinking of the joint staff on the land offensive. He had come to ask Powell's aides to gussy up the Western Excursion. Then, armed with a new set of graphics, Cheney took Adm. David Jeremiah, the vice chairman of the JCS, with him to the White House to brief the Western Excursion to President Bush and his top aides.

It was an extraordinary development. Cheney had concluded that the Western Excursion had been given short shrift by Powell and had decided to take matters into his own hands — and to do so without telling Powell what he was up to.

That was not the only surprise that Cheney had for Powell. As the JCS chairman prepared to return to Washington he was shocked to hear news reports quoting Cheney as saying that the Bush administration was planning to send more forces to the Gulf. Cheney had made the comments during a morning television news show and had weighed his words carefully. What Cheney had actually said was that the administration had never set an upper limit on Gulf deployment, that more forces were on the way, and that the number of additional troops could reach 100,000. But Cheney measured his words carefully and always said less than he meant. This was Cheney's way of preparing the American public for the reinforcements to come. Powell was supposedly on a mission to decide what additional forces were necessary and how they should be used. Cheney was acting as if the reinforcment decision had already been decided in principle.

Powell was furious when he learned that Cheney had gone behind his back. By taking a plan that Powell did not approve to the White House while the JCS chairman was out of town, the defense secretary had short-circuited the process. Cheney's actions could be interpreted as a lack of confidence in the military leadership.

After returning to Washington, Powell complained to Schwarzkopf about Cheney's move. " 'I can't go out of town anymore. When I go out of town things get out of control,' " Schwarzkopf recalls Powell as saying. " 'I've got to get this thing back in the box.' " Schwarzkopf and Powell needed to combine forces to regain control of the land-war planning.[6]

Powell asked for a CENTCOM assessment of the Cheney plan, and Schwarzkopf was more than happy to oblige. Schwarzkopf also thought the Western Excursion was crazy. Cheney envisioned the plan as a way to hold Iraqi soil as a bargaining chip to pressure Saddam Hussein to order his forces out of Kuwait, as well as a means of neutralizing the Scud missile threat to Israel. But the idea of bargaining chips had little appeal for the generals. Nor did Schwarzkopf consider the Scud missile threat to Israel that much of a problem. The Air Force was persuaded that it could take care of that. The Western Excursion looked like too much risk and too much trouble for too little return. It was a distraction from the main event: the destruction of the Republican Guard.

Schwarzkopf ordered Arnold to evaluate the plan, working with planners from the XVIII Airborne Corps. And Arnold dutifully produced an analysis, assailing the idea, which Schwarzkopf forwarded back to Washington.[7]

Meanwhile, the left hook was pushed farther west, partly as a sop to Cheney. Schwarzkopf and Powell repeatedly discussed how far west to conduct the flanking attack, with Schwarzkopf stressing the logistical problems of going too far west and Powell pushing the CENTCOM commander to think big and recommending an attack that would string the Army out all the way to Ar'ar.

"It was something so that he could say to Cheney we are far enough out west so that Cheney did not look like he made a mistake by running over and briefing the president without Colin being there," Schwarzkopf recalled. "I kept saying we don't have to go way out there."[8]

Schwarzkopf asked the Jedis to determine how far the two-corps attack could be stretched to the west while being supported logistically. Schwarzkopf told the Jedis they should develop a plan that would have American forces attacking as far west as As Samawah in the Euphrates River valley.

The Jedis, however, did not agree with the idea of pushing the flanking attack out west. Logistically, they concluded, it would stretch the coalition's capabilities to the breaking point and perhaps beyond. Strategically, it undercut the Jedi concept of massing the entire coalition force for an attack on the Republican Guard. Schwarzkopf initially had not expressed any problems with their two-corps plan to concentrate the coalition force in the seventy-mile stretch east of the Wadi al-Batin, but now he was throwing out some new ideas.

But there was no discussing the idea. The Jedis guessed that Washington was exerting its influence, but they could not be sure. The Jedis began to modify their plan.

"Still looking at far west options (i.e. As Samawah)," the Jedis noted two days later in an entry in their classified log. "Although there are periodic discussions of attacks to Baghdad nothing is planned due to the size of the coalition force and logistics constraints. It is too far to successfully attack and hold ground."[9]

Cheney, for his part, handled the whole affair with his customary discretion. Rowen was never told that his Western Excursion had a White House debut. The defense secretary was philosophical about the affair. Even if the Western Excursion was not the perfect plan, it had already accomplished one of Cheney's goals: it had lit a fire under the military. They would not be coming back with any more "high diddle diddle plans."

There was a convergence between Schwarzkopf and Powell over how to attack, but there was also continuing static between the civilian and military leaders of the Pentagon and a lingering unease with Schwarzkopf at the White House. The next month looked like a difficult period, indeed.

DOUBLING THE FORCE

On October 31, President Bush convened a meeting of the National Security Council to formally decide the question of whether to continue the buildup. Powell and Baker had been voices of caution, but there had never been much of a debate. The president had been pushing the military option from the beginning. He was the most hawkish of the White House hawks.

By late October, the weight of opinion within the administration was against waiting for the sanctions to work. The administration was concerned that it would be impossible to hold together the anti-Iraq coalition for the twelve to eighteen months that the intelligence community predicted would be needed for the sanctions to start hurting Iraq in a serious way.

Cheney, in particular, was worried that a recent clash between Israeli soldiers and rock-throwing Palestinians at the Temple on the Mount in Jersualem boded ill for the coalition.

The British were concerned that Ramadan, which fell in March, and the Haj, which came in June, would interfere with the allied war effort. Once Muslim pilgrims came to Mecca for the Haj, all the kingdom's transportation would be tied up and the threat of terrorism would increase. Powell's argument to Sir Patrick Hine about delaying the war had not had any impact on British policy. London was arguing that the Islamic holidays, plus the prospect of having allied forces endure another broiling summer, indicated a winter war.

Baker led off the meeting by noting that the trade sanctions had not been effective so far. There were two courses of action before the administration: an enhanced package of sanctions or an ultimatum to Saddam Hussein that Iraq order its forces out of Kuwait or face attack.

As the discussion turned to the military option, Powell presented a list of forces that he said were required. Schwarzkopf had requested two additional armored divisions to carry out the flanking attack, as well as some additional Marine troops and another aircraft carrier and the deployment of more Air Force planes.

Powell's request, however, went well beyond what the CENTCOM chief had sought. Powell was proposing that a second Army corps be sent, to include the 1st Infantry Division at Fort Riley, Kansas, a doubling of the Marine forces in the Gulf, three additional aircraft carriers, and a virtual doubling of the number of Air Force planes. It was Powell's overwhelming force, a long list of units designed to scare Saddam Hussein out of Kuwait and prevent the war, which Powell still believed was ill-advised, or guarantee a decisive victory if the Iraqi leader decided to call the coalition's bluff.

White House officials were struck by the size of the force that Powell was requesting. Was the military proposing such a large reinforcement in the hope that the president would balk? Was it Saddam Hussein or Bush that Powell was trying to scare?

"The White House had been accustomed over the years to the military coming in with very large force requirements for contingency plans. This was clearly partly out of caution, but there was also the perception that at times it was to disuade the President from action," recalled Robert M. Gates, then deputy national security adviser.

"What was striking about this episode was that the military put their gigantic requirements on the table — moving the VII Corps from Europe, six carrier battle groups, activating more reserves — and Bush did not blanch."[10]

If the military was bluffing, the White House would call the bluff. However the war went, no one could accuse Bush of shortchanging the military.

"I was not gaming him," Powell insisted after the war. "Anybody who has the ability to generate overwhelming force should do so. We bought it to fight wars. There was no other crisis. This was the obvious place to pile on. We were getting ready to win as quickly, as overwhelmingly as we could."[11]

Bush, for his part, acknowledged that there was disagreement over the request, but stressed that he was determined to provide the military with everything it needed.

"Scowcroft did observe that the forces requested seemed excessive for the mission," Bush recalled after the war. "But I was determined not to haggle. The important thing was to be able to get the job done without leaks about divided views on force requirements which might tend to reinforce concerns on the part of the doubters."[12]

The administration calculated that if it could get the UN Security Council to endorse military action, it could persuade Congress to support the international consensus. Under the system of rotation established by the Security Council, November was the United States' turn to chair the body. If an ultimatum was to be sent, it would have to be approved then, months before the coalition was ready for a ground war.

Baker, it was agreed, should fly to Saudi Arabia to get King Fahd's permission to launch the offensive and also consult with other nations in the Middle East. Then Baker would fly to Moscow, Paris, and London to discuss the buildup and lay the basis for a Security Council resolution authorizing the use of force.

In Germany, word was quietly passed to the VII Corps to start planning for a Persian Gulf mission. Col. L. Donald Holder, the commander of the 2nd Armored Cavalry Regiment, which would be at the forefront of any VII Corps attack into Iraq, was told that his units would be deploying to the Gulf. Two days later, the notification was abruptly cancelled without explanation.

A formal announcement of the reinforcement decision would not be made until after the November 7 congressional election. That meant that the Soviet president would know of the American reinforcement plan before the American public and virtually all of the VII Corps forces that would be ordered to destroy the Republican Guard.

During his trip to the Middle East, the secretary of state began to let the Arab members of the coalition know that the air campaign was not going to be a three- or four-day affair, a message Baker expanded on during later trips. Arab members of the coalition had to understand that so that they could manage public opinion at home.

Baker also took up another sensitive issue on this and other trips: Israel's role. Before the war, Israeli Prime Minister Yitzak Shamir assured the administration that Israel would not launch a preemptive attack. That still left the question of what Israel would do if it was attacked, but it enabled Baker to assure the Arabs that Israel would not strike the first blows.

The message was generally well received by the Arabs. Egyptian president Hosni Mubarak told Baker that Egypt would remain with the coalition even if Iraq provoked Israel into responding. To prepare his own public for such a possibility, Mubarak said publicly on the eve of the war that Israel would have the right to retaliate, like any other nation, if it were attacked. But the Egyptian president added there would be no need to because there would not be anything left in Iraq worth attacking.

The Moscow portion of the trip was more tricky. The Soviet president had complained that he had not been consulted about the initial deployment of American forces to the Gulf. Moscow was not a member of the military coalition, but Gorbachev was basically supporting the Gulf operation and the Bush administration wanted to keep the Soviets on board.

During the Moscow deliberations, Soviet foreign minister Eduard Shevardnadze argued that it was premature to commit the coalition to a military offensive. Baker responded that force might not be necessary but that only a credible threat of military action would scare the Iraqis into leaving Kuwait. It was not practical for the American forces to play a waiting game, Baker argued. The Muslim holidays in the spring, the difficulty of sustaining a large force in the desert, and the unwelcome prospect of seeing the troops through another broiling Saudi summer meant that Washington needed to bring the crisis to a head sooner rather than later.

When Baker talked to Gorbachev, the Soviet leader proposed that there be two resolutions: one to authorize military action and another to implement the threat.

Baker proposed one resolution that would authorize an offensive only after a certain date. That would give the Russians the "pause" they wanted to seek a diplomatic settlement. The Russians did not commit themselves, but it looked like they would go along.[13]

The decision to send the reinforcements escalated the political stakes at home. There had been widespread support for sending troops to defend Saudi Arabia, but the administration's decision to prepare for an offensive split the Congress.

As the domestic debate heated up, retired Adm. William J. Crowe, the former chairman of the Joint Chiefs of Staff, had lunch with his successor. Crowe told Powell that he intended to tell the Senate Armed Services Committee that he favored giving economic sanctions more time to work and opposed the rush to war. Powell listened carefully. He made no effort to discourage Crowe from arguing for delaying the war and said that he, too, believed economic sanctions were the right approach. "I don't think I encouraged him," Powell said. "I didn't discourage him either. My own view is that I hoped sanctions would work, but by December it was less likely that it would."[14]

Crowe made headlines with his November 28 testimony advocating that the United States wait a year or more to see if sanctions worked. But the White House was well along in its campaign to line up the support it needed to go to war. The next day, with Baker in the chair, the Security Council passed UN Resolution 678 authorizing military action against Iraq.

The United States had sought UN blessing for a January 1 deadline but in a compromise accepted January 15. Instead of an explicit reference to military action, the resolution authorized the coalition to evict Iraqi troops by "all necessary means."

Days later, Iraq announced it was releasing the Western hostages it had kept in Baghdad and at weapons sites around Iraq to deter an American attack. The move was intended to slow the momentum toward war, but it actually had the opposite effect. The Bush administration had talked bravely of targeting Iraq without concern for the hostages, but in fact Buster Glosson had made contingency plans to avoid the sites where the "human shields" were kept. The Iraqi leader's decision gave the Americans one less problem to worry about.

After the announcement that the American forces were being doubled was made, Lt. Gen. Frederick Franks, the VII Corps commander, and most of his division commanders took a quick trip to the Gulf to look over the terrain and meet with Schwarzkopf. When Schwarzkopf met with Army corps and division commanders in Dhahran, he outlined the attack plan. He told the commanders that there were three centers of gravity: the Republican Guard, Iraq's nuclear and chemical capability, and Saddam Hussein himself. Schwarzkopf said the Iraqi leader had to go or be discredited, recalled Maj. Gen. Ronald Griffith, the commander of the Army's 1st Armored Division.

Schwarzkopf told the commanders that the strategic air campaign would last six days, the number set in Instant Thunder. Air strikes on the Iraqi ground forces would last another twelve days.

After the meeting, the Jedis recorded the plan in their log. The XVIII Airborne Corps would attack in the west, seizing As Salman, where intelligence reports indicated that Iraq had deployed Scud missiles. Then the XVIII Corps would move up Highway 8, seizing the towns of As Samawah and An Nasiriyah, which was situated along the Euphrates River. This would stop Iraq from sending reinforcements down from Baghdad and would prevent the Republican Guard from escaping to the west.

Of the XVIII Airborne forces, the 101st would be the first to cut off the highway. But Barry McCaffrey's 24th Mechanized Division would be right behind in case the 101st ran into trouble and would serve as an "exploitation force" to press the attack against the Republican Guard. The plan also provided Schwarzkopf with a way to use the 82nd Airborne, which he had been planning to keep in reserve. It would take As Salman and serve as the left flank guard. The 82nd commanders were constantly pressing Schwarzkopf to include in his war plans an air drop or at least a jump along the border as a show of force. But Schwarzkopf saw no need for a parachute assault; he planned to send the division by truck.

The VII Corps would be the main effort against the Republican

Guard. The 1st Cavalry Division would be held in reserve, mainly to help the Arab members of the coalition if they ran into trouble. The British forces were to be assigned to the Marines, who would plan an attack in the east. The allied ground forces were to be ready to attack by mid-January.[15]

By November, Cheney's Western Excursion was all but dead, but some of its spirit lived on. Even some of the plan's staunchest critics conceded that it had an influence in Riyadh. By proposing his own plan, Cheney had raised the question of military action in far western Iraq and, in effect, challenged the military to accept the plan or develop an imaginative alternative.

Some significant adjustments were made to the left hook as the war approached. The two commanders, for example, later decided to direct that American troops avoid the towns along the Euphrates so as not to get bogged down in street fighting. But the main outlines of the plan stayed remarkably intact.

"I think it is fair to say the Washington pressure led us to look farther to the west than we were looking," Schwarzkopf said after the war.

But when the land war was launched, much of the XVIII Airborne Corps would find itself traversing empty desert or fighting marginal Iraqi units. The French 6th Light Regiment and the 82nd Airborne, which would be positioned on the left flank of the left hook, never played an important role in the land offensive. And while the left hook swept farther west than it needed to attack the Republican Guard, it did not go far enough west to solve the Scud problems, one of the major motivations for Cheney's plan. Nor was Baghdad directly threatened, a fateful decision that made it easier for Saddam Hussein to hold onto power.

Schwarzkopf and Powell were right to insist that a military land attack be decisive. But they were wrong to think that there was nothing to be gained by deploying troops in the far western Iraqi desert to help stop the Scud firings. CENTCOM would later concede as much by belatedly deploying special operations forces in the far west.

The Army's flanking attack, however, was only part of the story. CENTCOM still had to figure out what to do about the Marines.

8

Tell It to the Marines

The mission was to conduct a supporting attack and that just drove some Marines crazy. They would say, "We got to be in the main attack. We can't be in the supporting attack."

— Lt. Gen. Walter Boomer
MARCENT component commander
March 1991
Al Jubail, Saudi Arabia

WHILE THE ARMY'S flanking attack was falling into place, the Marine mission was up for grabs. The Marines had been the first ground forces to get any substantial combat power on the ground. They had, in effect, covered for the Army as the ships full of M-1 tanks slowly made their way to the Gulf.

Now that CENTCOM was looking to go north, the Jedis had concluded that the most important contribution the Marines could make was to support the Army's left hook. With their infantry-laden units, the Marines and the British brigade that was attached to them could breach the Iraqi fortifications, open supply lines for the main Army attack, and then protect the logistical trains from an Iraqi counterattack.

There was one complication. The Jedis had never consulted the Marine high command about any of this. The Jedis could go only so far in their planning without bringing the Marines into the game, and in early November the Jedis finally opened their doors to the Marines. Col. James D. Majchrzak, a hulk of a man who worked as one of Lt. Gen.

Walter Boomer's planners, was sent to the Jedi sanctuary to be briefed on the Jedis' war plan. Majchrzak did not stick around long.

Although Boomer knew the Marine attack would not be the main one, he was not aware of the Jedi team or what it had in mind for his command. While the Jedis were plotting the attack, the Marines had been struggling to come up with their own offensive plan. They planned to complement the Army attack in the west with a two-division attack in the east to penetrate the forward Iraqi defenses and race to the outskirts of Kuwait City. "We will go quickly. We will go violently," Boomer had told his staff.

What Majchrzak reported came as a shock to the top Marine commander. The Jedis, he observed, were treating the Marines as an adjunct of the Army. They wanted the Marines to knock down the door for the Army and then hold it open while they raced north. Furthermore, to do so they wanted to break up the Marine team by using the airplanes in Royal Moore's 3rd Marine Air Wing to support the Army effort. If the Jedis got their way, the offensive-minded Marines would be nothing but pawns on the Army's chessboard.[1]

Boomer was furious that Schwarzkopf's planning cell, at the CENTCOM commander's direction, had been preparing a land offensive for two months without the Marines' knowledge, let alone participation. A tall, soft-spoken man who looked like he belonged more in a farmer's bib overalls than in camouflage battle dress, Boomer had been the commander of the 1st Marine Expeditionary Force, known as I MEF, for only a few weeks before the Iraqi invasion of Kuwait. The media liked the eminently quotable general. He had come to that post from a stint as head of the 4th Marine Division but earlier had served as the chief of Public Affairs, and was never too busy to see reporters who made the one-hour drive from their hotels in Dhahran to visit him at I MEF headquarters in Al Jubail.

But while the press notices were generally favorable, the Marine commander had more than his share of problems, and the Jedis were only one source. Much of the trouble was at home. Although Boomer had extensive combat experience in Vietnam, Gen. Alfred Gray, the Marine Corps commandant, did not consider Boomer to be the man for the job. Around the Corps, there were a handful of Gray "Bubbas," protégés whom the commandant knew well and considered to be trusted executors of the newer Marine doctrine of maneuver warfare. Boomer was not one of them.

Boomer heard through the Marine grapevine that there was a lot of grousing behind his back about the unimaginative planning that was being done by the I MEF for a thrust into Kuwait and the likely casualties that would result, but Gray never directly complained to him or offered Boomer a realistic alternative. But it was a lonely feeling being in an Army-dominated command while his Marine boss was sniping at him within Marine circles. There was little to be gained by forcing a confrontation with his superiors in Washington. But there was everything to gain in taking on the Jedis, and Boomer was determined to do so.

Boomer's chance to put his foot down over the Jedis' proposed use of the Marines came on November 6 when top CENTCOM commanders gathered to hear the latest Jedi brief on the land offensive. After Brig. Gen. Steven Arnold ran through the plan, Boomer said that he could not agree with the Jedi plan for using the Marines as a battering ram for the Army. The Marines intended to go to Kuwait City. They needed to operate near the coast, close to their logistical bases, near the supporting fire of the battleships, and with their amphibious forces close by in case a landing was needed.

To the surprise and disappointment of the Jedis, Schwarzkopf agreed with Boomer. The Marines were free to come up with their own plan. Even after Schwarzkopf's ruling, the Jedis were reluctant to accept the decision. If the Marines were not to join the Army attack, there was still another way they would help the Army's left hook.

Four days later, the Jedis met alone with Schwarzkopf and presented a new plan in which Boomer's force would serve as a giant feint. The Marines, Arnold explained, could attack into the heel of Kuwait, the point where the Saudi-Kuwait border turns abruptly northwest, and then head toward a point west of Kuwait City. The purpose of the Marine attack would be to hold the Iraqi units in place so that they would not go after the Army's flank, and the pace of the Marine assault would be calibrated so as to support the Army attack. By abandoning the idea of having the Marines drive to Kuwait City, CENTCOM would also be able to use the bulk of the allied and American close air support on behalf of the Army. There was a name for the kind of operation Arnold proposed for the Marines. It was called a "fixing attack." To underscore his point, Arnold held up a map that included a large arrow signifying the Marine attack. In bold letters was the word "FIX."

Schwarzkopf was unimpressed. As far as he was concerned, the question of the Jedis and the Marines had already been resolved in Boomer's favor.

"Stop screwing with the Marines," Schwarzkopf barked.

The Marines would have a real mission, Schwarzkopf explained, and the Army should not go around calling it a fixing attack. If it was successful, the Marine attack could become the main attack. The Jedis should confine their planning to the Army sweep in the west and stop trying to do the Marines' planning for them.[2]

Schwarzkopf's handling of the Marines was one of his most important decisions and would have an enormous impact on the ground war. The Jedis were purists. They were fixated on the mission of attacking the Republican Guard. All resources should be devoted to that single objective. Anything else was a distraction from the main event and diluted the striking power CENTCOM needed to accomplish its main objective. Under the Jedis' concept of joint operations, some services were more equal than others. The Army had the main role and the Marines should be an element of the Army-dominated attack.

As in his earlier handling of the debate between the Marines and the Army over the defense of Saudi Arabia, however, Schwarzkopf was not going to have one service dominate another. As an Army general, Schwarzkopf was not steeped in the Marines' war-fighting doctrine. He had not known Boomer before the Iraqi invasion of Kuwait. But Schwarzkopf nonetheless trusted the Marine commander to develop an effective plan that would avoid excessive American casualties. As Schwarzkopf would learn later, he had more confidence in Boomer than the Marine commandant had in him.

Politically, Schwarzkopf's approach kept the Marines happy. In terms of morale, it was an important expression of confidence in his subordinates. Tactically, it gave the Marine commanders the flexibility to apply their doctrine as they saw fit. Strategically, it had the virtue of adaptability. If the Army attack slowed for any reason, the Marines could go forward.

But it was not enough to let each service plan and fight its own war. Schwarzkopf also needed to closely monitor that planning and understand how the Marine plans might enhance or conflict with the Army's strategy for destroying the Republican Guard. The ultimate failure of Schwarzkopf and Powell to do so would turn out to be one of the critical lapses in the planning of the land war.

THE SADDAM LINE

While the American war planning was shrouded in secrecy, there was little mystery about Iraq's plan to defend Kuwait. Iraq's military strategy was the embodiment of the old military axiom that when generals do not know what to do, they do what they know.

Iraq had little experience with air warfare and none fighting an enemy practiced in mobile armored tactics. Having fought the Iranians to a draw during a grueling eight-year war, the Iraqi commanders intended to fight the same type of war they waged against Iran, a grinding battle of attrition with high casualties on both sides that would nullify the American hopes to win a quick victory with high-technology weapons.

Traced on a long strip of clear acetate that hung down over a map of Kuwait at the Iraqi command post at the Al Jaber Air Base in Kuwait, the Iraqi plan was to create a three-tiered defense along the Kuwait border and along the coast as far as Kuwait City.

The function of the first defensive layer, just north of the Kuwait border, which American forces dubbed the Saddam Line, was to delay and weaken the invaders. The Saddam Line was actually made up of two parallel belts of mines, sand berms, bunker complexes, and oil-filled ditches, fed by pipes from Kuwait's abundant oil tanks, which could be turned into a flaming wall of fire. Along the coast, mines, barbed wire, pillboxes, and three Iraqi infantry divisions would greet any amphibious attack.

The Iraqis hoped to catch the coalition forces in the open as they tried to cut a path through the obstacles and turn the entire area into a killing zone. A corps' worth of artillery, more than eight hundred guns, was concentrated just north of Al Jaber Air Base in southern Kuwait, twenty-five miles north of the Saudi border. Equipped with South African 155mm guns that had a longer range than anything in the Marine inventory, the Iraqi artillery batteries could cover the likely attack routes from Saudi Arabia and smother the attackers with massed artillery fire.

The second layer of the tripartite defensive scheme was made up of armored and mechanized divisions in the interior of Kuwait. If the Iraqi experience with the Iranians was valid, the enemy would have been so disorganized by their struggle to get through the Saddam Line that they would be ripe for a counterstroke by Iraqi mechanized divisions, moving on roads that Iraqi combat engineers had built connecting the key defensive sectors.

Finally, the third element of the Iraqi defense would be brought into the fight: Republican Guards, which were deployed in southern Iraq to serve as the strategic reserve.

Boomer knew that with enough firepower and troops he could bull his way through the enemy, but the cost would be high and it was not how he had been taught to fight. While the public image of the Marines was one of casualty-inducing, head-on assaults, the Marines had embraced the newer concept of maneuver warfare. Front lines, physical objectives, and enemy combat formations were secondary to the goal of destroying the enemy's ability to react. From corporal to colonel, Marines would then exploit opportunities at their own volition. At a minimum, the aim was to ensure that the enemy commander was a step behind events, but the hope was that the adversary's command system would break down altogether. All the forces in the world were of little value if they could not be effectively controlled.

It was a sophisticated doctrine, and while the Marines had trained with it for almost ten years, it had not yet been used in actual combat. Unfortunately, until the Marines broke through the Iraqis' forward defenses, there would be precious little room to maneuver. The key was to find weak points in the Iraqi defense and break through quickly so that the war of maneuver could begin.

Boomer wanted his planners to assume that the Iraqis were tough as nails. By and large, intelligence analysts had been painting an alarming picture of the Iraqis' military might. By mid-November, American intelligence was also telling the Marines that they were outnumbered by three to one in men and by more than five to one in tanks, even with the 9,500-man British 7th Armored Brigade, which was under Boomer's tactical control, included on the Marine side.[3]

Combat Power Comparison (Marine Area of Operation)

	Iraq	Marine
Personnel	120,000	41,000
Tanks	1,455	247
APCs	1,099	521

However, a smattering of intelligence reports was already indicating that the Iraqis were suffering from desertions, poor discipline, and low morale. By late October, intelligence was coming in that the Iraqi army in Kuwait was short of food and was experiencing serious morale problems. By early November, word reached Boomer's command that Iraqi troops had begun to gather up T-shirts and other pieces of white cloth to use as flags of surrender as soon as the multinational forces crossed the border.[4]

The conflicting intelligence perplexed the Marine commander. It was only prudent for the Marines to adopt the worst-case analysis. But Boomer had fought some very tough battles in Vietnam, and the Iraqis did not remind him much of the Vietnamese adversaries. The North Vietnamese had defeated the French and taught the Americans a lesson or two. But one of Boomer's most trusted intelligence officers argued that the Iraqi military was overrated. The Iraqis were good at enforcing order at home and running roughshod over their ill-trained, overmatched neighbors like the Kuwaitis, but they had never really played in the major leagues. As time went by, Boomer came to believe his aide was right.

Boomer confided his suspicions about the Iraqis in a letter to a retired Marine friend who had been a fellow adviser to the South Vietnamese Marines during the 1973 Easter offensive after American ground forces had left the scene.

"As I study the Iraqi soldier to the best of my ability, I believe that we have a rather hollow Army facing us, despite the amount of equipment they possess," Boomer wrote. "I never underestimate my enemy, Gerry, but these guys are not in our league except in total amount of equipment. My gut feeling is that they are very shaky."[5]

Boomer had not figured out exactly how and where the Marines would attack along the Kuwaiti border, but he never doubted that the mission was doable. By the time CENTCOM would be ready to launch the ground war, Boomer would be commanding two full divisions and a heavily reinforced air wing, almost two-thirds of the Marine Corps combat power. Nor were the Marines planning on attacking alone.

Early on in the crisis, it had been agreed at CENTCOM that the Marines should be reinforced by British troops. When the British announced in November that they were increasing their contribution by sending Maj. Gen. Rupert Smith's 1st Armored Division to the Gulf, Boomer assumed that it, too, would end up under his command. The 1st Armored was a powerful force, and Boomer planned to use it to blitz the Iraqi defenders in the drive to Kuwait City after the Marines had cut through the Iraqi fortifications.

Based in northern Germany, the British division was configured to fight the Russians. It had 28,000 men, 221 Challenger tanks, 327 Warrior armored personnel carriers, and lots of artillery, including 16 new multiple-launch rocket systems. Mounted on a tracked vehicle, each MLRS contained twelve tubes, which could fire bomblet-carrying rockets with frightening rapidity. It was the perfect weapon for destroying enemy artillery positions, the main threat to the Marine effort to bust through the Saddam Line, and the Marines had nothing like it. The British division also had experienced combat engineers and its own team of intelligence officers, an area where the Marines were somewhat lean.

But the Marines were not the only ones who were eying the British.

THE BRITISH JILT

The inclusion of the British 1st Armored Division in what the Jedis persisted in seeing as essentially a diversionary Marine attack seemed like a waste to Arnold and his team of Jedi planners. To them, CENT-COM's flanking plan lacked the scientific rigor that had been instilled in them during their years at the Army's Command and General Staff College at Fort Leavenworth. With the XVIII Airborne Corps pushed farther west than the Jedis thought wise and with the Marines and the British attacking into the heart of Kuwait, the planners were afraid that the coalition's striking power against the Republican Guard was being diluted. Everybody was getting a piece of the action instead of subordinating the forces to one goal and one alone: the destruction of the Republican Guard.

The Jedis had experienced some serious reversals. By rejecting their thinking on the Marines, Schwarzkopf had effectively downgraded the Jedis from a team that was devising a theater-wide land campaign for the entire coalition to one that had responsibility only for the Army's flanking attack. Coming on top of Schwarzkopf's rejection of the Jedis' plan to pack all the Army forces into the seventy-mile stretch west of the Wadi al-Batin, it reflected Schwarzkopf's growing disenchantment with his own planners, whom the commander somewhat unfairly blamed for the up-the-middle plan that had led to ridicule in Washington.

But the Jedis had other ways to work the problem. The Jedis were virtual unknowns in Washington, and they were on a weak footing with Schwarzkopf, but they had friends within the coalition.

Six feet six inches tall, Tim Sulivan came from a long line of British Army officers. Sulivan had been slated for promotion to brigadier, a rank that has no exact parallel in the American military but is somewhere between a colonel and a one-star general. Sulivan's promotion was put on hold by the Gulf crisis, and the British officer pressed to be deployed to the Gulf.

On November 7, he became the only non-American member of the Jedis. Discarding his green British military fatigues, Sulivan donned an American desert camouflage uniform to indicate that he was part of the team, but he had a dual loyalty: he was a member of the Jedi planning team, but he also served as the eyes and ears for Sir Peter de la Billière, the senior British commander in the Middle East.

Even though he was a foreign military officer, Sulivan had more in common with the Jedis than the Marine planners on Boomer's staff.

Through NATO, the British high command was accustomed to the American Army's operating style for fighting Soviet-trained armies, but was relatively unfamiliar with the Marines.

Sulivan did not like the idea of putting Smith's 1st Armored Division under Marine control any more than the American members of the Jedis did. By its standards, Britain was making a major military contribution to the Gulf operation. The British wanted to participate in the main flanking attack, not a secondary attack, particularly one they feared would be a bloody charge into Iraqi fortifications.

Arnold and Sulivan agreed that the 1st British Armored Division should join the VII Corps attack on the Republican Guard. It was not as good as putting all of Boomer's forces at the service of the Army, but it was the next best thing. Arnold and Sulivan began to work up a briefing for de la Billière to present to Schwarzkopf on November 24.

Not all the British commanders liked the the idea of switching the British forces from the Marines to the Army. Brig. Patrick Cordingly, commander of the Desert Rats already with the Marines, was strongly opposed. He had developed working ties with the Marines and knew that Boomer was counting mightily on the British forces to help rout the Iraqis. To Cordingly, leaving the Marines just after they had succeeded in securing the mission of attacking into Kuwait was a little like abandoning a friend in a time of need. It was almost ignoble, which was not how the British officer class fancied itself.

But de la Billière wholeheartedly approved of the idea of his countrymen joining the main effort, as did Smith, the British 1st Armored Division commander, and virtually all of the British military establishment in London. De la Billière pressed the matter with Schwarzkopf, and the British military in the Gulf went roundabout to London, anticipating that her majesty's government would press the issue with Washington. To buttress his case with Schwarzkopf, de la Billière arranged a special briefing to ease concerns that the British logistics were not up to the more demanding flanking movement in the west. The British Challenger tank, which London was trying to market around the world and hoped to show off in the Gulf, broke down regularly. To ensure that it could support an armored thrust across the Iraqi desert, the British cannibalized their tanks in Western Europe so that each Challenger tank could have a spare engine, a move that the Thatcher government was prepared to take because of the reduced Soviet threat.

There was no question that Britain was the United States' most loyal ally. Prime Minister Margaret Thatcher was the only leader who had a tougher position on Saddam Hussein than Washington. With its

Tornado bombers, minesweepers and destroyers, and ground troops, the British force made a more important military contribution than any other member of the coalition except the Americans.

CENTCOM had not heeded every British recommendation. As CENTCOM refined its air-war plan, a team of officials from the British Ministry of Defense went to Riyadh to argue that the air attacks should focus on Iraq's oil production capability. By destroying Iraq's ability to produce and refine oil, the British officials argued, the coalition would reduce the ability of the Iraqi military to operate in the desert. Buster Glosson and his air-war planners politely rebuffed the idea. The Bush administration wanted to avoid lasting damage to Iraq's oil infrastructure, and since Iraq's army was hunkered down in the desert it was unclear that concentrating attacks on its oil installations would be decisive.

But the British request to shift their troops from the Marines to the Army was different. It was a high priority for London and reflected a concern over the welfare of its troops. The duties of the CENTCOM commander were political as well as military. Part of Schwarzkopf's job was to help hold the coalition together. While Schwarzkopf did not agree with the British request, he felt he had little choice but to accept it.[6]

On December 17, Boomer was notified that the British ground forces would be leaving the Marine sector by mid-January. The Marines' reaction was one of bitter betrayal. The Army had three times the number of tanks as the Marines in the theater. The Army was going to avoid the teeth of the Iraqi defenses by going around most of them while the Marines were going through them. Now the Army would be getting the British 1st Armored Division. How many troops did the Army need anyway? It looked like a case of Robin Hood in reverse, robbing the poor to give to the rich.

In the months that they had labored in Riyadh, the Jedis had evolved from Schwarzkopf's elite planning staff to a bureaucratic force in their own right, with diminished authority but with their own agenda. On the question of the British force, the alliance between the Jedi cell and the British planners in Riyadh had proven to be more powerful than the CENTCOM commander himself.

Even after losing a round to the Jedi planning team, Boomer did not intend to go quietly. Soon after the Marines were notified about the decision to shift the British forces, Boomer met with Schwarzkopf and Lt. Gen. John Yeosock to try to limit the damage.

If the British were determined to jilt the Marines for the prestige of the main attack, the Marines wanted an American armored Army unit and additional artillery as compensation. The Iraqi artillery, possibly chemically armed, posed the greatest threat to the Marine regiments that would be cutting through the Iraqi fortifications. Coalition artillery was one way of silencing the Iraqi guns, both during the push into Kuwait and in artillery raids before the offensive, and the British had the best artillery in the Marine area. Schwarzkopf agreed to Boomer's request. He ordered Yeosock to transfer an Army unit of equal capability to the Marines.

"Like force, John," Schwarzkopf admonished Yeosock, leaving it up to the Army to define what a "like force" was.

Despite Schwarzkopf's instruction, the Army did not intend to be generous with its forces. The point of switching the British over to the Army was to add to the combat power to be used in the left hook, not merely to substitute British forces for American ones. Unless the Army gave the Marines less than they were taking away from them, there was little sense in shifting the British forces over in the first place.

Yeosock initially decided to send the Marines one of the VII Corps brigades that had been brought over to Europe to round out the 1st Infantry Division from Fort Riley, Kansas. But Lt. Gen. Frederick Franks, the VII Corps commander, said that he needed all three brigades in the 1st Infantry Division to breach the Iraqi defenses. Franks suggested a compromise. Why not give the Marines a brigade out of those Army units held in reserve to back up the coming offensive? That way the Army's offering would not come out of the VII Corps's hide. CENTCOM accepted the suggestion.

The Army informed the Marines that they would be getting the Tiger Brigade, commanded by Col. John Sylvester, which had recently arrived from Fort Hood, Texas. Boomer believed that the Army knew that it was not a fair trade, since the unit did not nearly match the combat and support capabilities of the British unit it was to replace. He protested vigorously that he was being shortchanged. Eventually, Boomer improved on the deal by also acquiring an artillery battalion equipped with the MLRS, capable of firing a lethal rain of bomblets. But that was about all that the Army was prepared to give.

Even as they assigned the Tiger Brigade to Boomer's command, the Army commanders were nervous about the shotgun marriage between the Tiger Brigade and the Marine forces. It had been a long time since a Marine general had command over an Army unit, and not all the precedents were good ones.

During the Pacific campaign of World War II, the Army's 27th Division, a National Guard division led by Maj. Gen. Ralph C. Smith, had been placed under the operational control of Gen. Holland M. "Howling Mad" Smith, the Marine commander of the island-hopping offensive. Following the invasion of Saipan, the Marine commander relieved the Army general, complaining that the Army's slow pace had left the Marine forces vulnerable. The action ignited an angry response at the highest levels of the Army, which believed that Holland Smith's action was both embarrassing to the Army and unfair.

While neither Boomer nor Yeosock referred to the episode, it soon became clear that the forty-five-year-old fracas cast a shadow over the Gulf. When it came time to work out the command relations for the Tiger Brigade, Yeosock insisted that the unit be placed under the "tactical" control of the Marines. It was a matter of semantics, but an important one. Tactical control meant that Boomer could direct the Tiger Brigade in battle but had no right to decide who should command the unit or to divvy up the brigade and use it piecemeal to reinforce the Marine attack, another Army worry. "Operational" control would mean that Boomer had the same authority over the Tiger Brigade in battle as he would over a Marine unit.

Eventually, the issue was bumped up to Schwarzkopf, who decided the question in the Marines' favor. It may have made sense for the British, a foreign army, to be under the tactical control of the Marines, but there was no similar concept in American doctrine. The Tiger Brigade was formally made "OPCON" to the Marine command.

When it finally came time for the Tiger Brigade to join the Marines, it arrived with no small sense of trepidation. "Sylvester had a long face. He expected to ride into the valley of death," recalled Boomer. Boomer sought to assure Sylvester that the Marines did not plan to use his brigade as an expendable drill bit. The dirty work of breaching the Iraqi defenses would be left to the Marines.[7]

Despite the anxiety that surrounded the Tiger Brigade's subordination to Marine control, it formed a surprisingly successful and fruitful alliance with the Marines.

KHALID RULES

The problem between the Marines and the British was not the only one the Marines had with other members of the coalition. Boomer's opinion of the Arab forces was almost as low as his view of the Iraqis. Boomer did not invest much time in solidifying ties with the Saudis, nor did the Saudis fully trust the Marines. Boomer's forces had liaison officers with the Arab armies, but they could not compensate for the lack of trust at the top. The strain complicated relations between the Marines and the Saudis throughout the war and hampered Marine planning when it came time to pick a point of attack.

The Marines' first thought was to take the shortest and most direct route to Kuwait City by attacking at the "elbow," where the Kuwaiti border sharply angles westward. If the attack was successful, the Marines would arrive at Kuwait City before the Iraqis knew what had hit them. But the Iraqis, too, understood the strategic significance of the area and kept their mechanized reserves close to the elbow. As soon as the Marine forces pushed through the defensive barriers, the Marine planners reasoned, Iraq's mechanized reserve would be right on top of them, setting back the offensive before it could build up steam. This was not what Boomer wanted as he searched for a soft spot. The elbow attack, which would be well inland, also looked problematic for the amphibious logisticians, who were organized to support an attack within fifty miles of the shore.

Turning away from elbow, the Marines began to look at an attack up the coast. The plan had several things going for it. The logisticians loved it. Supplies could be sent up a paved highway or sent in by sea, instead of being moved by long, interior lines. The Marines could be supported by the sixteen-inch guns of the Navy's two battleships, assuming the success of mine-clearing operations off the coast of Kuwait. If necessary, Maj. Gen. Harry Jenkins's amphibious forces, deployed on assault ships in the Gulf, could be brought into play, landing behind the Iraqi front-line defenders and opening a port for resupply as they approached Kuwait City.

But the eastern sector of the border from which the Marines wanted to attack was occupied by troops from the Saudi National Guard and the Persian Gulf states, which made up the Eastern Province Area Command. The command reported to Prince Khalid, son of the Saudi defense minister and the senior commander of Arab forces in the coalition.

If Boomer wanted to attack up the coast, the Saudis would have to agree to move out of their positions and follow the Marines in trace. As Boomer saw it, the plan made sense for the Saudis as well as the Marines. The Saudis had no experience in breaching obstacle belts, no training in handling mine-clearing equipment, and no mine-clearing equipment. They would be better off if the Marines carried out the breach for them. But the trick was persuading the Saudis of that.

Boomer explained the idea to the Saudi National Guard commanders, who seemed amenable to the plan. But it was not up to them. The plan would have to be presented to Prince Khalid for a decision.

At the Marines' request, Schwarzkopf agreed to handle the matter personally. Schwarzkopf, who kept an office just down the hall from Khalid's spacious office at the modern Saudi Ministry of Defense, had worked hard to maintain a good working relationship between the Americans and the Saudis. Schwarzkopf had pretty much dictated the defense plan for Saudi Arabia despite Saudi objections. But it was sometimes important to respond to Khalid's wishes even at the cost of the tactical considerations.

In a meeting in Khalid's office, Schwarzkopf gingerly presented Boomer's plan for a coastal attack. Khalid rejected the Marine plan out of hand. The Saudi forces did not need the Marines to breach the Iraqi fortifications for them. Even without training or mine-clearing equipment, they would conduct their own breach, thank you.

Sitting in an overstuffed chair in his office after the war, Khalid recalled the episode. His veto of Boomer's plan, the prince explained, could be summed up in one word: "Pride."

Schwarzkopf responded as if he had expected Khalid to reject the idea and did not press the point. " 'I didn't think you would accept it,' " Khalid recalled Schwarzkopf as saying.[8]

While Schwarzkopf failed to persuade the Saudis to go along with the Marine plan, he did better for the French. The French initially put their 6th light division under Gen. Khalid's command, but after a few weeks changed their mind and appealed to Schwarzkopf. As much as Paris chaffed at the thought of putting French soldiers under American command, Khalid's limited military experience was a greater worry.

To help ease the French out of the jam, Schwarzkopf told Prince Khalid that the French division would have to join the XVIII Airborne Corps attack because its armament made it best suited to protect the allies western flank. Khalid's chief operations deputy, Schwarzkopf recalled, became "unglued" at the notion that the Saudis would now lose the only Western force under their command, but Khalid accepted the argument. As in the case of the British, meeting French concerns was a political prerequisite.

But while the Marines failed to win Saudi acquiescence, Boomer was actually relieved. The Marine commander had been driven to the coastal option primarily by logistical considerations and had not been persuaded that the plan was such a good idea in the first place. While the coastal highway was an advantage, there was little maneuver room due to oil installations and civilian communities. With a coastal attack out, he moved the attack inland, opposite the Wafra forest in Kuwait.

PROBLEMS AT HOME

At the Marine Corps headquarters just across the road from Arlington National Cemetery, all of Boomer's options looked equally bad to Al Gray. A feisty commander, Gray was not used to sitting on the sidelines. With his irreverent style and his blunt comments, the Marine commandant had attracted something of a following in Washington. But shaping the Marine offensive was harder than working the Congress. With Congress's efforts to strengthen the role of the theater commander, it was generally agreed that the service chiefs were not to get heavily involved in the planning process. Although as Marine commandant, Gray could not tell Schwarzkopf, or even Walt Boomer, what to do, he was determined to influence CENTCOM's planning if he could.

Gray thought that Boomer's rush into the teeth of the Iraqi defenses in Kuwait would produce enormous Marine casualties, and he sent Dick Cheney a paper suggesting that the Marines open a "second front" instead. Under the plan — urged upon Gray by Robert F. Milligan, the three-star commander of the Marine forces in the Pacific, who was one of the commandant's protégés — the Marines could come at Iraq from Turkey, Syria, western Jordan, or the Red Sea, moving through Saudi Arabia and into western Iraq.

Strategically, the plan had some similarities with Cheney's Western Excursion. Politically, the idea had a fanciful quality. The idea of launching a ground assault from the north was a nonstarter. Turkey's and Syria's cooperation with Washington was limited. Jordan, with a large Palestinian population, was not a member of the coalition and was sympathetic to Iraq. American diplomacy was oriented at keeping Jordan out of the war, not enlarging the battlefield to include it. But Gray had never developed a reputation in Washington for his insights into international politics. The "second-front" plan was dead on arrival, but it amounted to a vote of no confidence by the Marine commandant in the top Marine commander in the field.

That was not the only plan Gray set in motion. Marine planners at the corps' war-fighting center at Quantico were told to think of alternative ways to outflank, outsmart, or leverage the Iraqis, by land or sea. It was a closely held effort. Gray, the paperwork read, had commissioned an "Ad Hoc Study Team" at Quantico to prepare a Battle Requirements Study. If the team could come up with a winning combination, Gray would look for a way to import it into the Gulf, suggesting it to Boomer and letting it bubble up to Schwarzkopf from below. It would be a variation of the way Col. John Warden had sold his air plan.

The head of the Quantico team was Maj. Gen. Matthew P. Caulfield, a company commander in Vietnam and graduate of the Harvard Business School, who pursued his assignment with a missionary zeal. Like Gray, Caulfield and his team of planners believed that a Marine charge through the Iraqi defenses in southern Kuwait could be extremely costly. War-gaming such an attack at the Center for Naval Analyses, computers predicted about 10,000 casualties over seven days. These distressing conclusions were shared with the British planners in London, who did their own estimates. This could only have fortified the resolve of the British leadership to wrest the British ground forces from Marine control and join the American Army attack in the west.

Caulfield and his planners began to focus on another way of avoiding the Iraqi defenses in southern Kuwait: a major amphibious operation. Although the Gulf coastline from the Saudi-Kuwaiti border to its head at the Al Faw peninsula offered few opportunities for brilliance on the same scale as Douglas MacArthur's Inchon, Caulfield believed that the Marines could pull off a bold strategic stroke that would collapse the structure of the Iraqi defenses. By the end of December, the team was putting the finishing touches on Operation Tiger.

As the Quantico team conceived of the plan, Basra, where the Euphrates River feeds into the Shatt al-Arab bordering Iran, was the key. Most of the Iraqi defenses were south of the city, including those to counter an amphibious landing. If the Marines went north and threatened the Iraqi command and control hub at Basra, the entire Iraqi defense would unravel. The Army would have a left hook, and the Marines would have a comparable right hook. It would be a huge pincer, a two-pronged strategic envelopment.

The operation itself needed to be carefully timed. The Marines would wait for the Republican Guard forces to be engaged by the Army's VII Corps in the west and then mount an attack in the Iraqi rear. The ambitious plan required a wholesale restructuring of the Marine forces in the Persian Gulf. The Marines had five regiments ashore and two afloat. Caulfield planned to reverse the ratio. The idea would be to leave a small force in northern Saudi Arabia to hold the Iraqis in place and help defend the kingdom. The rest of the force would undertake a massive amphibious assault, as tens of thousands of Marines were moved from Saudi Arabia to the Iraqi coast.

There were some serious logistical obstacles as well as political problems implicit in a military operation that would take place close to the border with Iran. Caulfield believed they could be overcome with innovative amphibious techniques and some aggressive diplomacy. After all, the Marines were experts at amphibious operations and the State Department was supposed to be expert in diplomacy.

Gray was briefed on the plan in December. Although the commandant had reservations about Operation Tiger, he decided to allow the plan to be transmitted to the theater. Col. Martin Richard Steele, the deputy director of the war-fighting center, had the dubious honor of presenting Operation Tiger to Boomer and Vice Adm. Stanley Arthur, the senior Navy commander in the Gulf. No approach would be made to Schwarzkopf, who would have been enraged to think that strategists at Quantico were devising a new war plan for him just a few weeks from the start of the air war. If Operation Tiger was to go anywhere, Steele would have to convince Boomer and Arthur to adopt the plan as their own and present it to the CENTCOM commander. But given Boomer's planning, the lateness of the Quantico planning, and Schwarzkopf's and Powell's fear that amphibious operations would mean high casualties, it was clear to Steele that selling the plan was going to be an all-but-impossible task. Boomer's planners and Gray's team were on different tracks.[9]

When Gray planned a December visit to the Gulf, it looked as if the long-simmering dispute between the Marines' home office and Boomer's command would finally come to a head. Soon after arriving in Saudi Arabia, Gray was whisked to the command post for Task Force Ripper. Ripper was the mechanized combat team that was to spearhead the Marine attack, and its "CP" was a logical place to get briefed on the latest iteration of the Marine plan.

To Gray, the plan looked like a recipe for disaster. Myatt's 1st Marine Division was to attack head-on the Iraqi fortifications between the Wafra forest and the heel, where the Saudi-Kuwait border angles sharply northwest. Then Bill Keys's 2nd Marine Division, including the Tiger Brigade, would pass through the gap in the Iraqi defenses and attack the Iraqi mechanized forces just behind the front line.

After that phase of the attack was completed, the two divisions would switch places yet again. The 1st Division would pass through the 2nd Division to attack and seize Al Jahrah, the high ground outside Kuwait City, and block the withdrawal of Iraqi forces. The Marines had never attempted a passage of lines on that scale before, and the plan called for two of them. But the Marine command did not have much choice. Iraq had purchased thousands of mines, and for all the billions spent on the military buildup during the Reagan administration, relatively little had been spent for mine-clearing equipment. The Marines would be hard put to clear the mines in front of one division, much less two. It appeared there was no other choice but to attack one division behind the other.

After hearing the plan, Gray paused and rendered his verdict, which surprised the Ripper briefers, who were unaware of Gray's months-long effort to overturn the Marine plan.

"This is going to be another Tarawa. You are going right into their teeth," Gray protested.

The comparison was one that every Marine understood. The 1943 assault on Tarawa, a tiny, heavily defended, Japanese-held Pacific atoll, had resulted in appallingly high casualties — 1,113 Marines and Navy personnel killed and 2,290 wounded — as wave after wave of Marines was cut down by dug-in Japanese troops. Only after the attack was it revealed that the commander of the Marine force in the island invasion was opposed to the operation but was ordered to carry it out.

To Gray, the attack into Kuwait looked to be every bit as grisly, only the politics were worse. The Tarawa mission was forced on the Marines against their best judgment. This time, it was the Marine field commander who was pushing for the headlong assault against the advice of the Marine commandant and the Army planners in Riyadh.

"There must be a way for technology to help us," he added.

The case for shaking up the Marine command seemed to the commandant to be clearer than ever. After hearing the brief, Gray returned to Al Jubail and spent the day with Boomer, during which he never directly expressed any dissatisfaction. Then he flew to Riyadh to meet with Schwarzkopf and press his plan for overhauling the Marine command.

Meeting privately with Schwarzkopf, Gray told him that he had lost confidence in Boomer and had an idea for restructuring the Marine hierarchy in the Gulf. Boomer had the dual responsibility of serving as the commander of the Marine troops in the field and as the top Marine official at CENTCOM. Gray's plan was to put a three-star Marine general senior to Boomer in Riyadh and leave Boomer as the field commander. Gray did not say who might fill the billet, but his protégé Milligan seemed a logical candidate.

Schwarzkopf was taken aback by the eleventh-hour proposal. He had given Boomer enormous leeway to fashion a Marine plan. Now Boomer's superior was suggesting that the Marine commander in Saudi Arabia needed expert supervision.

Schwarzkopf had no intention of adding another layer to his command. During a break in the conversation, Schwarzkopf made a call to Boomer in Al Jubail. Was Boomer aware of Gray's proposal? What did he think of it? Schwarzkopf asked.

Boomer had not been informed by his Marine superior of the plan and was surprised by the question. Sidestepping the issue of what he had and had not been told by Gray, Boomer told Schwarzkopf that he saw no need for it.

Then Schwarzkopf went back to his meeting with Gray and turned him down.

Gray returned to Al Jubail in a black mood and all but ignored Boomer that evening. But the next day he was over his pout. He asked Boomer what he needed and catalogued his request. The two Marine generals never directly discussed the issue of command, and the matter never arose again. Instead, Gray settled for seeding the Marine force with some of his most promising colonels and young generals. For better or worse, Boomer would be the man to command them. A lot of lives were at stake, and Gray would help make the Marine headquarters the best it could be. The commandant lacked Boomer's confidence in the campaign plan. But after a rocky few months, at least relations between the Marines in the field and the home office were being smoothed out. Time would prove that Boomer's understanding of the Iraqis had been accurate despite Gray's grousing.[10]

After months of jockeying and intrigue between the Marines and the Army, Boomer had finally secured a piece of the war plan and had the confidence of Schwarzkopf. But there was plenty of unfinished business.

As D day approached, CENTCOM did not have a truly integrated offensive plan. There were three of them. Buster Glosson's special planning group had overseen the development of the air campaign. The Jedis, under Schwarzkopf's tutelage, were refining the plan for the flanking attack against the Republican Guard. Boomer was planning a thrust into the heart of Kuwait.

But the parallel development of the air- and land-war plans also meant that some long-standing differences between the services were sidestepped. How long should the air campaign run before the land offensive was launched? How much destruction could air strikes do to the Republican Guard? Could there be an air war without a ground war? And could Iraq do anything to frustrate the strategy?

9

"The Mailed Fist"

*Expected Results: Iraqi Army in Kuwait Effectively Destroyed.
Re-occupation Met with Minimal Resistance. Could Be Desirable (and
May Be Possible) with Kuwaiti and Arab Ground Forces. U.S. Ground
Forces Could Be Held in Reserve as a 'Cocked Fist.' Near Certain
Achievement of President's Objectives Without Significant Casualties to
Ground Troops.*

> — Col. John Warden
> Classified briefing to
> Defense Secretary Dick Cheney
> on the expected results of the air
> campaign
> December 11, 1990

*Many experts, amateurs and others in this town, believe that this can be
accomplished by such things as surgical air strikes or perhaps a sustained
air strike. And there are a variety of other nice, tidy, alleged low-cost,
incremental, may-work options that are floated around with greater
regularity all over this town. One can hunker down, one can dig in, one
can disperse to try to ride out such a single-dimension attack. Such
strategies are designed to hope to win, they are not designed to win.*

> — Gen. Colin L. Powell
> Chairman, Joint Chiefs of Staff
> Testimony to the Senate Armed Services
> Committee
> December 3, 1990

O N DECEMBER 3, Colin Powell and Dick Cheney went up to Capitol Hill to testify about the administration's plans to evict the Iraqis from Kuwait. With the momentum toward war building by the day, the Senate Armed Services Committee had reserved a cavernous room in the Dirksen Senate Office Building to accommodate the crush of observers, reporters, and television cameras.

Powell used the occasion to outline his philosophy of overwhelming force and to underscore the potential costs of going to war. The allied offensive ultimately had to be guaranteed by ground power; Washington would not rely on airpower alone to defeat Iraq, he asserted. Powell directed his remarks to the experts at the think tanks and the lawmakers who were urging that airpower be used as an alternative to the ground war, and it seemed to many in the Air Force that Powell was speaking to them as well.

"Many experts, amateurs and others in this town, believe that this can be accomplished by such things as surgical air strikes or perhaps a sustained air strike," Powell said. "And there are a variety of other nice, tidy, alleged low-cost, incremental, may-work options that are floated around with greater regularity all over this town. One can hunker down, one can dig in, one can disperse to try to ride out such a single-dimension attack. Such strategies are designed to hope to win, they are not designed to win."[1]

After Powell's testimony, David Deptula, Buster Glosson's main planner, who had returned to Washington for a brief visit, sent Air Force Secretary Donald Rice a memo expressing alarm about Powell's statement. Iraq, Deptula wrote, had no experience with modern air warfare, and Saddam Hussein had discounted the threat of an allied bombing campaign. The U.S. military should be touting its airpower to persuade Baghdad to pull its troops out of Iraq. Instead, he continued, the top American military man was reinforcing the Iraqis' belief that they would weather the air campaign. Powell was talking to an audience in Washington, but his statements rebounded around the world.[2]

Rice was also concerned. Schwarzkopf and Powell's almost single-minded focus on the left hook concerned the Air Force secretary. Was it possible that the United States could double its ground forces and *not* put them to use? If so, what would be the purpose of the air campaign? Would the United States make a genuine effort to wring the maximum possible benefits from airpower before sending in the ground forces? Or would the Air Force and the Navy merely be prepping the battlefield for the Army?

The Air Force was confronting a two-front war. It was preparing for war with the Iraqis and trying to outmaneuver two Army generals who commanded the allied war effort. For Rice, the Air Force's success in the bureaucratic battle, as much as its strategy and tactics, would determine what it could accomplish in the Persian Gulf War.

Cheney and Powell were planning to go to Riyadh in late December to make one final review of the war plan. As a civilian service secretary, Rice was outside the chain of command. But Rice had a pipeline to Cheney, and he decided to use it. As the January 15 deadline approached, the jockeying between the services heated up. Meanwhile, the Iraqis began making their final preparations for the war. And they had their own ideas about what air strikes could accomplish.

THE VIEW FROM BAGHDAD

Iraq's strategy reflected a dim view of airpower and was rooted in a kind of cultural chauvinism. The West had its high-tech military toys and was good at bombing raids, but it lacked the determination to pay the ultimate price of going to war, or at least of finishing the job if it did. But Iraq, the Iraqis told themselves, was a nation inured to sacrifice.

Iraq did not have to defeat the allies or even come out ahead in the body count. There was no hope of that. But if Iraq could not scare the American-dominated coalition out of attacking in the first place, it had to cause the coalition enough pain so that the popularly elected Western governments would seek a compromise.

The Americans hoped their offensive would be decisive and short; Iraq would make it long and drawn-out. The Americans hoped that their airpower would enable them to weaken their opponent without mixing it up on the ground; Iraq would ride out the air war and then use its large army to slug it out on the ground. The Americans wanted to make the Gulf War another Panama; Iraq would make it another Vietnam.

"The U.S. depends on the Air Force," Saddam Hussein told an Iraqi newspaper in an August interview. "The Air Force has never decided a war in the history of war. In the early days of the war between us and Iran, the Iranians had an edge in the air. They had approximately 600 aircraft, all U.S.-made and whose pilots received training from the U.S. They flew to Baghdad like black clouds, but they did not determine the outcome of the battle . . . The U.S. may be able to destroy cities, factories and to kill, but it will not be able to decide the war with its Air Force."[3]

Secrecy, deception, and dispersion were the Iraqis' main tactics for countering the West's bombing strikes and dragging out the war. With a military complex as vast as Iraq's, there was a lot to hide.

Iraq's air defenses were an obvious target, so the Iraqis stripped some of their command posts of computers and other vital gear. The Sector Operational Center at Tallil, the most southern command post in the Kari system, was turned into an empty shell. That would diminish the capability of the Kari system against the allied attacks from Saudi Arabia, but Iraq's plan was to endure the bombardment, not defeat the allies in the skies. Iraqi warplanes took refuge in hardened bunkers, while Iraq flew transport planes to Iran to move them out of harm's way.[4]

To protect its oil industry, Iraq removed computer equipment from its oil refineries. One of the most ingenious dodges was at Diyala, a small town on the outskirts of Baghdad, where the Iraqis emptied one of their water reservoirs and filled it with oil. Communications equipment was removed and dispersed from telephone exchanges in southern Iraq, and Iraq's Ministry of Defense and Ministry of Military Industry were evacuated.

Shielding its development programs for weapons of mass destruction was one of Iraq's highest priorities, as well as one of its greatest challenges. The potential vulnerability of Iraq's weapons complex had been shown by the 1981 Israeli bombing raid against the Iraqi nuclear reactor at Tuwaitha. But the Iraqis had years of practice.

To hide its nuclear weapons program from the prying eyes of international inspectors and American spy satellites, Iraq launched a clandestine nuclear program following the Israeli attack based on the use of highly enriched uranium.

In addition to developing centrifuges for uranium enrichment, Iraqi scientists copied the technology the United States had pioneered at its Oak Ridge Plant in Tennessee to produce its first nuclear bomb. The Iraqis built huge machines — called calutrons — for enriching uranium to weapons-grade levels. Components of the calutrons were manufactured at Za' Faraniyah south of Baghdad. The machines were assembled at Tuwaitha and moved to secret locations in the north.

An elaborate complex for developing and testing the high-explosive trigger of the bomb, which included filters, procedures for air handling, and isolated areas, was built at Al Altheer. The cover story was that Al Altheer was a research facility for carrying out advanced work on composite materials.

As the two sides girded for war, the CIA picked up clues that the scope of the Iraqi nuclear program exceeded anything the United States had imagined. After Iraq released its Western hostages, administration experts examined their clothing. The clothes worn by the hostages kept at Tuwaitha contained radioactive elements that suggested some sort of uranium enrichment program. But American intelligence experts never thought Iraq would go so far as to build its own calutrons.

Armed with fragmentary intelligence about the Iraqi nuclear program, only a small number of Iraqi nuclear sites were targeted. "Prior to Desert Storm, little was known about Iraq's highly compartmented nuclear weapons program," the Defense Intelligence Agency concluded in a classified assessment after the war.[5]

Iraq's efforts to hide its germ warfare program were equally prodigious. The Iraqis constructed a large installation at Salman Pak, twenty miles southwest of Baghdad, and filled it with equipment for fermentation, laboratory research, and aerosol testing of biological weapons. Baghdad said the plant analyzed foods to study ways to prevent contamination.

Salman Pak was well known to American intelligence, but other such plants were not discovered until UN weapons inspectors visited them after the war. When the war began, the Iraqis were in the process of building a seven-square-mile complex at Al Hakem, an isolated stretch of desert south of Baghdad. The ostensible purpose of the Al Hakem facility was to conduct research on the production of animal feed. But it had the telltale markings of a military installation, including underground warehouses, dummy facilities, and barbed-wire fences. It was also administered by the Center for Technological Research, the same Baghdad-based organization that oversaw Salman Pak.

To keep the existence of the Al Hakem facility secret, equipment purchased for the complex was first sent to other facilities. When the Iraqis bought fermenters from a Swedish company, it arranged for the equipment to be delivered to facilities at Taji and Latifiyah in the Baghdad suburbs and then secretly moved the equipment to Al Hakem. Taken in by the Iraqi deception, the Americans targeted the Taji and Latifiyah facilities, although they were largely empty by the time of the Gulf War. Al Hakem, however, was never identified by American intelligence as a suspicious site until the war was well under way and was not put on the target list.

While Western intelligence failed to uncover Al Hakem, it misidentified some commercial companies as war plants. The Defense Intelligence Agency listed the Al Kinde veterinary company in Abu Ghurayb as a suspected biological warfare facility. The plant was funded by a grant from the United Nations Food and Agriculture Organization, which maintained an office in the same building, and was later determined to be legitimate by UN inspectors.

The biggest intelligence error had to do with the weapons bunkers that American intelligence believed were used to house germ weapons. Using spy satellites, the CIA identified four bunkers near Salman Pak as refrigerated storage sites for biological weapons. Seventeen other bunkers of this same type were also pinpointed throughout Iraq. On the basis of this and other intelligence, the CIA concluded that Iraq had not only developed biological weapons but had stored them for use in the Gulf War. Only after the war would United Nations inspectors learn that the bunkers were air-conditioned storage sites designed to protect conventional munitions and their sensitive electronics from the searing desert heat. Iraq had a biological warfare program, but the UN inspectors found no evidence that it had turned its biological agents into actual weapons.[6]

Of all the weapons programs, Iraq's production of chemical weapons was the most difficult to hide. Iraq's drive to make poison gas was not so much a program as a country-wide industry. The program was headquartered at the State Establishment for Pesticide Production at Al Muthanna, a vast complex surrounded by electrified fences near the town of Samarra, north of the capital. There, the Iraqis manufactured two types of poison gas: Sarin, a nerve agent, and mustard gas, which were inserted inside bombs, artillery shells, and rockets. The ingredients for the poison-gas program were manufactured at three plants at Habbaniyah, a town west of Baghdad.

All told, Iraq had 46,000 filled chemical munitions and 97,000 unfilled munitions, which gave it one of the largest chemical arsenals in the world. Unknown to American intelligence, Iraq also had more than seventy Sarin warheads for its Scud missiles.[7]

To protect their chemical arsenal, the Iraqis dispersed equipment for making poison gas throughout the country. At least one of the three buildings at Muthanna used to fill chemical munitions may have been empty at the time of war and a mechanical press used to make chemical bombs was moved to a sugar factory at Mosul. Meanwhile, the Iraqis dispersed their weapons to some twenty locations, including air bases and storage sites. One of the largest was just south of An Nasiriyah, technically puncturing the claim made by CENTCOM after the war that no chemical munitions were located within the Kuwaiti theater of operations.

To protect its missile force, Iraq began dispersing its Scuds from the missile production plant at Taji in August, moving mobile launchers out into the desert.

Unlike its weapons of mass destruction, Iraq could not hide its troops in out-of-the-way installations. Its plan to frustrate the allies was simply to have the soldiers dig in, endure the allied bombing, and then dust themselves off when it came time for the ground war — all of which depended on retaining the loyalty of the Iraqi army and maintaining its morale.

The Iraqi military did not have moral qualms about the invasion of Kuwait. Iraqi general officers had nothing but contempt for the Kuwaitis and resented the prosperity the Kuwaitis enjoyed. Nor was there any question that higher-ranking officers benefited from their loyalty to Saddam Hussein. A division commander received a new car every year, which he could sell for profit if he wished; a brigade commander was given a car every two to three years. Senior officials received land and soft loans to build new homes.

But the realities of the desert duty were more arduous than many in the lower ranks of the "battle-hardened" Iraqi army could bear. The rank and file, as well as some generals, had less faith in the Iraqi strategy than the authorities in Baghdad. The irony is that Iraq's ground power, which Saddam Hussein saw as his trump card, was weakened by cronyism within the officer ranks and an astonishing disregard for the welfare of the average soldier.

The deterioration of the Iraqi army was well documented after the war in several reports by the U.S. Army's 513th Military Intelligence Brigade that have been kept classified, apparently out of concern that the unflattering portrait of its adversary would diminish the Army's victory in the Gulf.

The experience of Iraq's 27th Infantry Division was typical of many of the units that were deployed as Iraq's first line of defense. Stationed near Saiyid Sadig, along Iraq's border with Iran, the division was at 76 percent of its authorized strength when it was notified in early November that it would be heading south. To bring its brigades up to 90 percent strength, the 27th needed six hundred men, but received none.

As the division headed toward the Saudi frontier, it did not have enough trucks to take more than the basic essentials. The division had only one bulldozer to prepare its defensive positions. Once in the desert, supplies were hard to come by. The division's defensive positions were 80 miles away from the Iraqi army's corps logistics at Az Zubayr, which meant that to get supplies the division had to send a truck on a 160-mile round-trip. The Americans were new to the Saudi desert, but they were closer to their logistics bases than the first line of Iraqi defense was to its stocks of spare parts.

"Regardless of how difficult and frustrating the mobilization and deployment of U.S. and coalition forces may have seemed to us, ours was a clockwork operation compared to that of the Iraqi Army," the intelligence brigade noted in a classified report. "Iraqi units called up after the August 2 invasion were hastily thrown together, reorganized, and manned with a combination of career officers pulled from other sectors and retired officers who were reactivated from the reserves. With the exception of Republican Guard units, most infantry divisions were sent to the Kuwaiti theater undermanned, short of equipment (or with poor equipment), and with little or no idea of what they were to do upon arrival in their areas of responsibility, other than to dig in and await orders. Each division was different, with little regard to T O & E [or authorized] structure while Soviet and Chinese equipment pulled out of warehouses was sometimes issued without required overhaul and maintenance."

According to Army intelligence, front-line and second-echelon units deployed at no more than 80 percent, and in some cases 50 percent, of their authorized strength. After taking up their positions, morale was low and front-line commanders had no reliable intelligence on the American troop position. The commanders on the front lines had little autonomy. Orders came directly from Baghdad; there was no theater headquarters that was deployed close to the troops and which could understand their problems. Rarely did senior Iraqi officers visit their troops. As a result of a liberal leave policy, desertions, and the ragtag nature of the Iraqi deployment, the Iraqi army never approached CENTCOM's public estimates of 540,000.[8]

Living under onerous desert conditions, many Iraqi commanders simply refused to believe that war was possible. "This conviction was expressed by most of our sources, who simply accepted the fact that they were pawns in a gamble that would not result in hostilities, rather than commanders of units about to engage in the 'Mother of Battles,' " the report stated.

"Saddam Hussein, the man is a gambler. He was certain that you would not attack, and if you did, it would only be by air," one captured Iraqi general told American intelligence after the war. "He kept telling the Iraqi people that airpower had never won a war in the history of warfare, and that the Americans would never have the nerve to engage the Iraqi army on the ground. I remember him saying that Americans would not be able to stand the loss of even hundreds of soldiers, that Iraqis were prepared to sacrifice thousands. Our soldiers heard this too. It had a very bad effect you see, for they figured out that he was talking about them — and they weren't ready to sacrifice for Kuwait."

At bottom, Iraq's efforts to hide much of its war machine would make bombing more difficult for allied warplanes, but Saddam Hussein's strategy to tout the indomitable will of its army asked too much of his own soldiers. Iraq's strategy also reflected an underestimation of the West's airpower and the allies' willingness to use it over an extended period.

But in December, just how long the air campaign would last was a matter the United States had yet to decide.

THE 50 PERCENT SOLUTION

From his vantage point at the Pentagon, Rice thought the answer was straightforward. The civilian secretary of the Air Force, Rice was not lacking in self-confidence. Rice had served as president of the Rand Corporation, the government-funded think tank, and was well connected with lawmakers on both sides of the aisle on Capitol Hill.

At the Pentagon, he had been an active proselytizer for airpower. When some of Cheney's systems analysts circulated budget-planning documents early in the Bush administration that treated the Air Force as largely a supporting arm of the Army, Rice fired off a March 28, 1990, memo to Cheney on "The Potential of Air."

"Considering air forces only together with land forces as a single entity precludes a variety of force structure, fiscal, and power projection options which may be desirable," Rice wrote in the memorandum, which was drafted by John Warden and David Deptula. Instead, Rice argued, the Pentagon should develop an "Air Option," capitalizing on the use of long-range bombing and other aircraft to serve as the primary service in some conflicts. Three months later, Rice went public with the argument, using the Persian Gulf as an example.[9]

Now that the issue had been transformed from a theoretical debate over airpower to a practical debate over war planning, Rice was no less determined to press his case. Powell and Schwarzkopf talked as if a land offensive would almost certainly follow the air campaign as the night follows day. But Rice wanted the Air Force to be given the chance to win the war through its "air option."

When it came time to pick a deputy CENTCOM commander, Rice tried to strengthen the Air Force's position. Asked for his recommendation, Rice urged Cheney and Powell to select Lt. Gen. Henry Vicellio, who was in charge of Air Force logistics. Rice even offered to pull Burt Moore, the CENTCOM J-3, or operations deputy, out of the post, to sweeten the arrangement and blunt any charge that CENTCOM had too many Air Force officers.

Rice was flabbergasted when Powell picked Lt. Gen. Calvin Waller, an old Army buddy of Schwarzkopf's.

Powell believed that Waller could help with the Army planning, which was eating up much of Schwarzkopf's time. But he also told Rice that Schwarzkopf was so volatile that he needed somebody who could act as a steadying influence. Yet at a time when Rice was trying to make the case for an extended air campaign, CENTCOM would be dominated by two Army generals. With Powell at the helm of the JCS, the Army controlled the top jobs.

Rice also tried to win over Cheney. The main point, Rice told Cheney in memos and private discussions, was that the decisions to launch the air campaign and the ground war should to be treated separately. The decision to bomb Iraq should not mean that a land war would follow. Nor should there be a rigid timetable for launching a land offensive. Washington should run the air war as long as it was producing measurable results and it seemed possible that the Iraqis might give up.

To buttress his point, Rice told the defense secretary that the analysis carried out by Checkmate, the Air Force's war-planning center that Warden oversaw, indicated that air strikes could be so effective against Iraq's army that the Kuwaitis and the other Arab members of the coalition could reoccupy Kuwait by themselves. American ground forces could be held in reserve as a mailed fist, to be employed only if the Arab attack faltered. In making the claim, Rice assumed that the Arab coalition members would not be fighting the Republican Guard, which was deployed in southern Iraq. His larger point was that technology had changed the relative contributions of air and ground power on the modern battlefield. If airpower was effectively applied, the weakest link in the coalition could carry out its ground mission. Cheney, he said, could get the details from the inventor of Instant Thunder himself. Cheney accepted the invitation, and on December 11 he went down to the JCS warren of offices to hear Warden's assessment.

The briefing room selected for Warden's presentation was uncommonly small and could barely contain Cheney, his top aides, the Air Force officials, and the JCS staff that were present. Cheney sat at the end of a conference table as Warden went through his catechism.

Using "smart bombs," the air war would unfold in phases. The first phase was the strategic air campaign, an expanded version of Warden's Instant Thunder. It was directed at undermining the Saddam Hussein regime, knocking out Iraq's electricity, shutting down its oil production, scrambling its communications, neutralizing its air defenses and its air force, and laying waste to its program to build nuclear, biological, and chemical weapons. Rice and Warden hoped that these attacks would be enough to win the war.

Cheney was told that 4,600 sorties would be carried out over the first six days, but Warden believed that the strikes against Baghdad and other targets deep in Iraqi should continue as long as they were needed. Warden showed a slide that depicted five "Expected Results," dispensing with the antiseptic talk about "incapacitating" the Saddam Hussein regime that the Pentagon would later use to publicly describe its war aims.

National Leadership Destroyed
Iraq's Strategic Offensive and Defense Eliminated for Extended Period
Internal Economy Disrupted
Iraq's Ability to Export Oil Not Significantly Degraded
Peninsula Nations Would Have Combat Capability to Deal with Residual
    Iraqi Forces

There would be casualties, to be sure. Forty aircraft would likely be lost during the strategic air campaign and perhaps another 110 planes during the subsequent phases of the war. Using historical studies, Warden calculated that thirty to forty American pilots would be killed. The rest would be rescued or captured. There would be 400 to 2,000 direct Iraqi civilian casualties. The killing of civilians would be tragedy for their relatives and friends, but the projected losses would be a tiny fraction of the populace that was killed in the bombing of European and Japanese cities during air attacks in World War II. In terms of American and Iraqi lives lost, the campaign would be politically sustainable.

In the event that the strategic air campaign did not win the war outright, the second phase would be aimed at knocking out the Iraqi air defense in Kuwait and southern Iraq so that the allied warplanes could bombard the Iraqi troops there at will. Then, Warden argued, CENTCOM could use airpower to shatter Iraq's ground forces.

The colonel said that it would take eight days of concentrated bombing to destroy half of the Iraqi artillery in Kuwait and nine days to destroy half of its armor, which, he thought, would be sufficient to defeat the Iraqi army. But to impress the skeptics, Warden asserted that a much greater degree of destruction could, in theory, be achieved. In fifteen days, 90 percent of all of Iraq's artillery and armor in Kuwait could be wiped out. The calculation postulated good weather, an attack rate of 1,000 sorties a day, and that the pilots would have a 75 percent chance of finding their targets.

Changing the assumptions lengthened the amount of time it took to destroy the Iraqi forces but did not change the basic principles. The basic claim was that airpower could essentially win the war on its own — if CENTCOM was prepared to give it time.

Repeating the claim made earlier by Rice, Warden said the air attacks would so disable the Iraq army that "reoccupation would be met with minimal resistance." Indeed, so much damage would be done to the Iraqi army that Kuwait and other Arab members might be able to do the jobs themselves, the colonel argued. To drive the point home, Warden held up a chart innocuously labeled "Phase III: Expected Results":

Iraqi Army in Kuwait Effectively Destroyed.

Re-occupation Met with Minimal Resistance.

Could Be Desirable (and May Be Possible) with Kuwaiti and Arab Ground Forces.

U.S. Ground Forces Could Be Held in Reserve as a 'Cocked Fist.'

Near Certain Achievement of President's Objectives Without Significant Casualties to Ground Troops.

Cheney noted the claims without comment.[10]

To buttress his claims, Warden flashed a chart to show that precision-guided munitions had exponentially increased the service's striking power. The left-hand column depicted the CEP, or circle error probable, for Air Force ordnance. The CEP was the radius of the area in which a bomb was likely to land 50 percent of the time. The right-hand column showed the number of bombs that would have to be dropped to ensure the destruction of a target.

	CEP	Bombs
World War II (B-17)	3300	9070
Korea, South East Asia		
(F-104, F-105)	400	176
Desert Storm		
(F-16)	200	30
(F-117)	10	1

In Riyadh, Glosson made his own pitch on behalf of the air campaign. Like Warden, Glosson agreed that airpower could halve the Iraqi combat forces. But he was not about to tell the CENTCOM commander that the American troops that were massing in Saudi Arabia for the left hook should be considered as one big reserve force. For Glosson, as for Rice, Warden was a zealot, who carried a good thing too far.

Glosson told Schwarzkopf that the air campaign could destroy 50 percent of Iraq's ground forces in Kuwait, but never echoed Warden's claim that airpower could destroy 90 percent of the Iraqi army. Schwarzkopf was dubious: a 50 percent "attrition rate" had never been achieved by any air force on so grand a scale. Still, airpower was CENTCOM's best hope to hold down American casualties if and when the ground war was launched. Overcoming his skepticism, Schwarzkopf made the goal a fundamental assumption of CENTCOM's war plan.

Tying together its air- and land-war plans, Schwarzkopf's staff prepared a top secret OPLAN, or operations plan, that spelled out its strategy. The command assumed that the entire war would be over in less than a month. One step followed quickly after the other, and the culmination was not an open-ended bombing campaign that brought about the fall of the Saddam Hussein regime, but the Army's left hook.

The first phase of the bombing campaign was aimed squarely at the Saddam Hussein regime. It would lead, the plan stated, to "loss of confidence in the Government," the "disruption of Iraqi command and control," and a "significant degradation of Iraqi military capabilities."

According to the order, seven to eleven days into the air war, the focus of the bombing would shift. The aim would be "to open a window of opportunity for initiating ground offensive operations by confusing and terrorizing Iraqi forces in the [Kuwaiti Theater of Operations] and shifting combat force ratios in favor of friendly forces." During the war, CENTCOM said that it had no interest in body counts, but the operations order bluntly stated that one aim was to "inflict maximum enemy casualties."

To block the Iraqi escape routes to the north, "the bridges, roads and rail line immediately south of Basra will be cut to block withdrawal of [Republican Guard forces] and to form a kill zone north of Kuwait," it stated.

The land offensive would take about eight days. The Arab members of the coalition and the Marines would launch the "supporting" attack. Their role would be, first, to fool the Iraqis into thinking the main attack was aimed at the Iraqi forces in Kuwait and, second, to liberate Kuwait.

The Saudi, Egyptian, and Syrian forces would have the honor of attacking first. The Marines would began their thrust an hour or so later, a schedule that was later revised.

After focusing the Iraqis' attention on the fighting in the east, the main Army attack in the west, aimed at destroying the Republican Guard, would not begin until the next day.[11]

Rice's idea of waging an extended air campaign and holding the American ground forces in reserve was not part of the plan drafted by the CENTCOM staff. But Schwarzkopf's mind was not fixed on the matter. And ultimately, it would be Washington that would determine the timing of the air and land offensives. Cheney had heard what Rice and Warden had to say and now he went to Riyadh to hear from Schwarzkopf and his commanders.

COMMAND PERFORMANCE

Two full days of briefings had been arranged for Cheney and Powell to review the status of the war planning during their Riyadh meeting in the war room at the Saudi Ministry of Defense. Over the five months since the invasion of Kuwait the target list had grown exponentially. Unlike Warden, the air-war commanders were not talking about winning the war by hitting eighty-four targets over a six-day period. As impressive as the increase in targets was, it would more than quadruple before the Gulf War was over. The number of targets seemed to be directly related to the time that American intelligence had to identify them and the munitions stocks set aside to destroy them (see chart on p. 192).

One pressing issue was not the number but the types of targets to be struck. Washington needed to decide if the air-conditioned bunkers that the CIA had misidentified as biological weapons storage sites should be on the "hit" or "no hit" list. The Pentagon also needed to be assured that the Air Force had a handle on the Scud missile problem.

Targeting the storage sites posed a dilemma. London and Washington were taking the threat of germ warfare seriously. British troops were being inoculated against biological warfare attack. So were some American troops. In the years of planning for a possible war in the Middle East, however, the Pentagon had not anticipated the magnitude of the threat and there was not sufficient antidote for all the American forces. The Arab allies were forced to do without the inoculations altogether.

The question was whether air strikes could be used to destroy the

	Initial list	Fall list	December 18
Strategic Air Defense	10	21	27
Chemical and Scuds	8	20	34
Leadership	5	15	27
Republican Guard	0	8	10
C3	19	26	30
Electricity	10.	14	16
Oil	6	8	8
Railroads and Bridges	3	12	21
Airfields	7	13	25
Ports	1	4	4
Military/Production			
and Storage	15	33	36
Total	84	171	238

bunkers without unleashing a plague on the Middle East. Schwarzkopf and Horner, however, wanted to attack the bunkers. Army specialists from the service's biological research center at Fort Dietrich, Maryland, believed that the risks of spreading disease were grossly overstated. But Powell was wary. Before Cheney and Powell arrived, Schwarzkopf advised Horner to brief the Pentagon chiefs together. Cheney tended to be more aggressive than Powell.

But Powell was not the only one who was worried. The British were concerned. So were the Russians, according to Yvgeni Primakov, the Russian diplomat who carried out several fruitless rounds of diplomacy with Baghdad and later was appointed by President Gorbachev to head the KGB. Moscow ordered its intelligence services to monitor the southern tier of the Soviet Union for indications that biological, chemical, or even nuclear materials had been released into the atmosphere.

As the discussion proceeded, Horner argued that the risks of bombing the biological weapons bunkers were manageable. If there was a small outbreak of disease as a result, that would be a lesson to third world nations about the risks of producing biological weapons.[12]

The officials decided to target the bunkers. During the discussions, Glosson outlined a plan to destroy the bunkers. F-117s would drop 2,000-pound bombs on the bunkers just before sunrise so that any agent that escaped would soon be exposed to the killing effects of the sun. Then F-111Fs would drop cluster bombs to prevent the Iraqis from retrieving any of the agent to use and also reduce the chances that disease could spread through contamination. F-111F pilots would try not to fly downwind of the bunkers.

The issue of the Scuds was less contentious. Cheney stressed that knocking out the Scuds early was the key to keeping Israel out of the war. Horner was confident he had the problem in hand.

When the commanders shifted to the land offensive, the Pentagon chiefs were briefed on the VII Corps and XVIII Airborne Corps plans to battle the Republican Guard. With the focus on the left hook, Brig. Gen. Steven Arnold was brought in to deliver CENTCOM's verdict on Cheney's Western Excursion. After Arnold ran through a litany of reasons why the plan would not dilute the attack the Army was planning against the Republican Guard, Powell praised the presentation as a "good brief." Cheney just smiled. With Schwarzkopf and Powell opposed to the plan, it was clear that it was going nowhere.

Throughout the discussion, the exact duration of the air campaign was not determined. Rice had talked about an open-ended air campaign, but the CENTCOM OPLAN projected an air campaign of at most nineteen days.

Like Cheney, Wolfowitz had sat through Warden's briefing, and he was worried about moving too quickly to a casualty-producing land offensive. During a break in the deliberations, Wolfowitz asked Schwarzkopf how long he thought the air war should run before CENTCOM kicked off the ground war.

Schwarzkopf quipped that he would be happy with an air campaign that ran 365 days. When the principals reassembled, Wolfowitz prompted Schwarzkopf to make the same remark again in front of Cheney, Powell, and the other participants.[13]

No firm decision on the length of the air campaign was made. But the message was clear: Schwarzkopf did not want to rush into a ground war.

Rice's theories meant nothing to Schwarzkopf, who acknowledged after the war that he assumed all along that the allies would have to take on the Iraqis on the ground. But there were other factors weighing in favor of a lengthy air campaign. The military also had a saying: amateurs talk strategy; professionals talk logistics. And in December, the logistical problems in getting ready for the offensive were greater than even the professionals had anticipated.

In drafting their OPLAN, Schwarzkopf's staff had assumed that the Army reinforcements would be in place by mid-January. But by mid-December the deployment of the VII Corps had fallen way behind schedule.

The European-based corps had a shorter distance to travel than the XVIII Airborne Corps, which provided the initial Army force in the desert, and could draw on the lessons from the first American rush to the desert. But unlike the XVIII Corps, the VII Corps had no experience in preparing for overseas deployments. And its deployment soon became a textbook example of how not to move forces to the battlefield.

Most of the planes carrying the VII Corps troops were on schedule, but a quarter of the ships were late. That meant that many of the soldiers reached Saudi Arabia only to wait for their equipment to arrive. Facing a shortage of transport ships, the VII Corps packed its vessels to the gunwales with little thought to the problem of piecing the units back together once they arrived. It was the logistical equivalent of taking the drawers out of the dresser, throwing the clothes into a suitcase, slamming it shut, and then sorting things out on the other end. On average, a combat battalion's equipment was stowed on seven vessels that reached the Saudi Arabian ports over a period of twenty-six days, according to an internal VII Corps report prepared after the war. A typical support battalion saw its equipment arrive on seventeen vessels over a period of thirty-seven days. The VII Corps 1st Maintenance Battalion had the distinction of enduring the most trouble-plagued deployment; its equipment was spread over twenty-six ships that docked over a period of forty-five days.

The delays in getting the VII Corps to the Gulf became a public sensation during Cheney and Powell's meetings in Riyadh. While they were locked in deliberations, Waller told a group of journalists traveling with Cheney that the Army would not be ready to launch a ground offensive until mid-February at the earliest.

With all eyes on the standoff in the Gulf, Waller's comments made headlines. The White House was unhappy both with the delay and with Waller's public affirmation of the problem.

The VII Corps's problem, however, meant that there was a symbiotic relationship between the Army and Air Force commanders. The Army needed time to get ready for a ground war it viewed as all but inevitable, and the Air Force needed time to prove that the ground war was unnecessary or at least a footnote to the main event. The debate over airpower's role was not so much resolved as deferred.[14]

As Cheney and Powell prepared to leave Riyadh, Wolfowitz received a message from the Pentagon. With the war fast approaching, the Israelis were apprehensive about how the war was going to go. The Israelis had promised not to preempt, but had not pledged not to retaliate.

David Ivri, the director general of Israel's Defense Ministry, was trying to get Wolfowitz on the phone.

After some consideration about the diplomatic propriety of talking to the Israelis from Saudi Arabia, Wolfowitz had the Pentagon patch the call through. Moshe Arens, the Israeli defense minister, wanted to meet with Cheney right away, Ivri explained. The meeting could be anytime, anywhere.

Cheney was concerned that meeting with Arens on the way back from Riyadh would make Israel look like an unofficial member of the coalition and rebuffed the request. But on the way back to the United States, he agreed that a high-level delegation needed to go to Israel before the January 15 deadline. Because Baker would be anxious to preserve the State Department's prerogatives, Cheney proposed sending Eagleburger and Wolfowitz to Israel with a message that the United States would do everything in its power to protect Israel from Scud attacks.

Specifically, the United States would provide warning from American satellites of any missiles launched toward Israel — the only way that Israeli civil defense could warn its population in time to get into shelters and put on gas masks — and would offer to do something the United States had never done: it was prepared to provide American-crewed Patriot batteries to protect Israel. (Because Israeli crews were still in training and could not be ready by January 15, American crews would be sent.)

As unprecedented as it was to propose sending Americans to Israel, it would be even more remarkable if Israel accepted, since self-reliance was such a central point in Israeli doctrine. Powell predicted that the Israelis would not accept the proposal, but Cheney figured that the offer would at least show that the administration was trying to be helpful.

The Americans would also offer to establish a direct, encrypted communications link, code-named Hammer Rick, between the Israeli Ministry of Defense and the Pentagon, which Cheney could use to provide Israel with advance notice of the war. As war approached, an Aegis air defense cruiser would be positioned off the coast of Israel to expand Israel's radar coverage.

The Americans were careful not to make the offer conditional on an Israeli promise not to retaliate. That sort of thing could backfire. The real point was to get the Israelis to consult with Washington before doing anything.

As the deadline approached, the Israelis welcomed the Hammer Rick communications link and the early warning of missile launches, which they had sought from the start. But while Prime Minister Shamir told Eagleburger that he would consider the offer of American-manned Patriots, Arens subsequently rejected it. Israel did not promise not to retaliate, but it did promise to consult.[15]

It was still not clear to either the United States or Iraq, however, that the war they were preparing for was unavoidable. In early January, Washington proposed a meeting between James Baker and Tariq Aziz in Geneva. The meeting, Brent Scowcroft later recalled, was intended mainly as a means of persuading Congress and the American public that the Bush administration had given the Iraqis every chance to seek a peaceful settlement before sending American troops into battle. It was not to be a forum for working out a compromise.

The Saudis, however, were aghast. They were afraid that Baghdad would read the move as a sign of weakness. It would hardly be the first time that the two sides had misread each other's intentions, but at this juncture the stakes were higher than ever before.

GENEVA RENDEZVOUS

In early January, Saddam Hussein gathered his high command in Baghdad. The Iraqi president appeared nervous and pale, a senior Iraqi official later told Primakov. As the top Iraqi officials sat in silence, the Iraqi president delivered a long lecture about how much more important Iraq was than Kuwait. The officials, he said, had an enormous responsibility for the welfare of Iraq. Whatever they decided, the Iraqi president needed the recommendation by the January 15 deadline. Because Saddam Hussein made all the decisions, some of the Iraqi officials felt as if they were being encouraged to recommend a withdrawal from Kuwait as a fig leaf to justify the dictator's retreat.

But soon after making that extraordinary statement, the Iraqi leader received a message from Gorbachev, notifying him that the Americans had proposed a meeting between Baker and Aziz.

Saddam Hussein was buoyed by the news, according to the account that Primakov later shared with a Saudi official. The Iraqi leader regained his composure. It looked like he had been right all along: the United States did not have the stomach for a real war. It was the United States that had blinked. Iraq would hang tough. The crisis of self-confidence was over. Baghdad had misread the Bush administration's gesture toward American public opinion as a sign of weakness. Aziz, Saddam Hussein instructed, was to go to Geneva and not waver.[16]

★   ★   ★

On January 9, Baker met Aziz in Geneva and opened the session by giving him a letter to pass on to Saddam Hussein. It was clear from this letter that Bush had not blinked and was ready to go to war.

Bush's letter warned Iraq of serious consequences if it did not pull its troops out Kuwait, but that was not the end of the threats. American intelligence believed that the Iraqis planned to respond to an allied offensive by launching terrorist attacks against American companies and embassies abroad, striking at American forces with chemical weapons, and, perhaps, igniting the Kuwaiti oil fields. "The American people would demand the strongest possible response," Bush warned. "You and your country will pay a terrible price if you order unconscionable acts of this sort."[17]

Although Bush's letter did not say precisely what the United States would do, Iraq later said that it took the U.S. position as a threat to overthrow the Saddam Hussein regime.

Scowcroft, however, recalled after the war that the strong response the administration had in mind was the destruction of much of the Iraqi economy and civilian infrastructure. If this led to Saddam Hussein's downfall, so much the better. "Our targets were pretty strictly military," Scowcroft said. "We would have extended them into economic targets. We would have extended the target list to oil refineries, oil fields, stuff like that."[18]

Baker handed the letter to Aziz in a sealed envelope along with a copy. The Iraqi foreign minister took five minutes to read the copy, underline sections, and then place it on the table. This was not the message the Iraqis had expected when the Americans proposed a meeting.

"I've read Bush's letter to my president," Aziz responded, according to the Iraqi transcript of the meeting. "But it is full of threats and it has a language which is not normally used in dialogue between heads of states. I cannot receive it."

Baker responded that Baghdad had made a huge miscalculation in invading Kuwait and should not miscalculate again. "The only question is are you going to leave Kuwait peacefully or are you going to be forced to do so?"

Seeking to rebut the Iraqi notion that the United States would be drawn into a long and costly war, Baker told the Iraqis that if the allies attacked, Iraq would face a kind of warfare that they had never encountered before. The United States, he said, had technological superiority and would use it to destroy the Iraqi ability to command their forces. The Iraqis would be vanquished.

If an allied offensive was launched, Baker continued, "there will be no UN truce, creating a breathing space. It will not be another Vietnam. It will be fought for a quick and decisive end."

There was little in the way of carrots. Baker assured the Iraqis that if they withdrew from Kuwait unconditionally the United States would not attack and added that Washington had no intention of keeping huge military forces in the region after Iraqi withdrawal.

Aziz reponded that Iraq knew the power of American weapons, but that the war would not be decided by high technology.

"My youngest son is eleven years old," he said. "The experiences of his lifetime are exclusively confined to war, to expecting Iranian air raids and missiles. So, war is not something alien to us."

The Iraqi foreign minister continued, "You are a power which possesses strong weapons. You have your estimates about the effectiveness of these weapons. You have your plans and you are convinced that if you start the war against Iraq you will win and you will smash us. We have a different conviction. I sincerely and without pretention tell you that the nineteen million Iraqis, including the Iraqi leadership, are convinced that if war erupts with you, we will win."

Baker tried to argue with Aziz.

"Please do not let your military commanders convince you the strategy used against Iran will succeed here. You will face a completely different force," Baker said. "Midnight of January fifteenth is a very real date."

But the Iraqi official argued that the allied coalition would collapse if Iraqi forces were attacked.

"Against the backdrop of your ties with Israel, I would like to tell you in all sincerity that if you initiate military action against an Arab country, you will be faced with hostile sentiments in the region, and in many Muslim states as well," Aziz said. "You think it will be short, but we are determined and confident that it will be long."[19]

Despite the standoff, some top Bush administration aides found it difficult to believe that the Iraqis were determined to tangle with the United States. Dennis Ross, Baker's adviser on the Middle East, predicted that the Iraqis would fight for a couple of days just to show they were not afraid of the Americans and then seek a diplomatic compromise.[20]

In Riyadh, the word spread fast that the die was cast. The avoidable war had now become the inevitable war. Saddam Hussein had decided to test the United States' mettle on the battlefield. George Bush had convinced the international community and most of the Congress that he had gone the extra mile in search of a peaceful solution and would now let the generals take the war to the Iraqis.

In early January, the Black Hole rushed to put the finishing touches on the air campaign. The air-war commanders had already begun Operation Border Look, flying large numbers of planes close to the Iraq-Kuwait border so that the Iraqis would become accustomed to the presence of aircraft and would become dull to the actual attack preparations.

Glosson wanted to launch the attack on January 18, which was Thursday, leading to the Friday Muslim sabbath, to try to maximize the element of surprise. The Bush administration, however, did not want to give the Iraqis, or faint-hearted members of the coalition, any more time for diplomatic maneuvers and decided to attack on the 17th, the earliest possible opportunity to launch a night strike following the expiration of the United Nations deadline.

The actual hour of the first attack on Baghdad, H hour, was set for 3AM, when some of the Iraqis assigned to the air defense command centers would be asleep.

Some of the final details were so sensitive they could be handled only in person. During a pep talk to F-15C pilots at Al Kharj on January 13, Glosson issued a simple order. If any Eagle crew ever heard the AWACS issue the command "Horner's Buster," they were to chase down the nearest Iraqi aircraft regardless of the type and shoot it down at all costs — even if it meant exhausting their fuel and punching out over Iraq. Glosson did not offer any further details, but he did not have to. It was understood that the Black Hole had contingency plans to send the Iraqi leadership down in flames if Saddam Hussein tried to make a beeline out of Baghdad.[21]

The day before the air war, Schwarzkopf paid a visit to Glosson's Black Hole planning team at the Royal Saudi Air Force Headquarters, accompanied by a phalanx of gun-toting bodyguards in civilian dress. It was his first visit to the team and his last chance to go over the war plan before CENTCOM kicked off the air campaign.

Schwarzkopf stationed himself in front of the large plastic-covered map of Iraq and looked at the multicolored pins that denoted the campaign targets, as Deptula outlined the first six hours of the air war.

Deptula had not gone very far before Schwarzkopf's jaws tightened. The commander was visibly upset. Where were the B-52 strikes on the Republican Guard? Schwarzkopf demanded.

For months, the CENTCOM commander had been preparing his left hook to send two Army corps after the Republican Guard. He wanted to make sure the Republican Guard did not escape before the ground war was launched by pinning them with air strikes. The air campaign, however, called for striking all manner of strategic targets, but the three armored Republican Guard divisions were not among them.

Horner tried to smooth things over. The Republican Guard would be hit by F-16s bombing from medium altitude the first day, but B-52s would not begin to bomb the Guard until the end of the first twenty-four hours of the war. The air-war planners were trying to hold down American casualties and did not intend to take the air war to the Republican Guard until the surface-to-air missile batteries that protected the forces had been attacked.

Glosson jumped into the argument to support Horner's point. "Tell me how many airmen you are willing to lose, and the air war commanders could redraft its plan to attack the Republican Guard in the first hours of the war," Glosson asked undiplomatically.

Schwarzkopf did not accept the explanation and complained that he had been misled.

"I directed as my guidance that the Republican Guard be attacked at the earliest. You told me that B-52s would be attacking the Republican Guard," Schwarzkopf exclaimed.

The air campaign was not neglecting the Republican Guard, Horner continued. A-10s would begin to work over the Tawakalna Division, one of the three heavy Republican Guard divisions, early on.

Schwarzkopf grew angrier. Horner's attempt to reason with the commander looked like insubordination. Schwarzkopf was asking for B-52 attacks and the Air Force was trying to buy him off with F-16 and A-10 raids.

Who directed the use of A-10s? Red-faced, Schwarzkopf issued the ultimate threat: the dismissal of the generals who ran the air war. The air campaign, he exploded, was going to go exactly the way he wanted it. If Horner and Glosson would not follow his guidance, he would find other generals who would and put them in charge, Schwarzkopf barked. Usually, disputes between the top commanders were confined to Schwarzkopf's inner office, not acted out in front of a room full of subordinates. The Black Hole planning staff was stunned by the eruption.

After the blow-up, Schwarzkopf and Horner met privately in Horner's office, while Glosson and Deptula thumbed through old briefings so that they could show the CENTCOM commander they had not misled him. The volcanic commander cooled down somewhat. His threat to fire the generals had been, like many of his other threats of dismissal, just so much bluster.

But the issue remained on the table. The generals discussed the pros and cons of sending the B-52s more calmly. The B-52s already had assignments for the first night. Along with British and Saudi Tornados, F-111Fs, F-15Es, and Navy A-6s, the B-52s were to attack airfields on the opening night to stop the Iraqis from flying. The first three days' worth of Air Tasking Orders had already been put to bed. Did the first-night plan need to be revised? There was no change in Schwarzkopf's position; he wanted the B-52s to attack the Republican Guard.

After Schwarzkopf left, Glosson observed to his staff that what the Black Hole had seen was a commander who was shouldering huge responsibilities, was under tremendous pressure, and was not thinking straight.

Nor, he reasoned, were B-52s that potent a weapon. They would be dropping "dumb" unguided bombs at medium-to-high altitude and there would be no telling exactly where they would land. But B-52s appeared to have made quite an impression on Schwarzkopf during his years in Vietnam and he was fixated on the weapon.

The pressure had made the CINC appear "brain dead," Glosson said in exasperation.

There were times, his staff had learned, to jump at Schwarzkopf's commands and times when the commander's intemperate demands were best ignored, or at least finessed. The Air Force generals were worried about the vulnerability of the B-52s, so this was a time to follow the spirit, but not the letter, of Schwarzkopf's instructions.

After Schwarzkopf left, Horner and Glosson ordered RF-4C surveillance planes to make a pass over the Republican Guard during the first few hours of the war to make sure they were not going anywhere, but the first B-52 attacks would not take place until eighteen hours into the war. The Black Hole would ride out Schwarzkopf's tirade and could only hope the Republican Guard would stay in its trenches and try to ride out the air war.[22]

Everyone at CENTCOM and in Washington agreed that the air-war commanders would have first crack at the Iraqis and, with the Army's logistical problems, would mount a sustained campaign. But Schwarzkopf's outburst also pointed to the deeper questions that had haunted the command from the beginning of its offensive planning and which the deliberations among the air commanders, ground commanders, and Pentagon civilians had never definitively resolved.

What was the main focus of the air campaign? Would the air-war commanders achieve a victory by launching strikes on Baghdad or by pummeling the Iraqi army so that that allied ground forces could roll over them? How long would air attacks remain oriented on Baghdad before Schwarzkopf would insist that the attacks be shifted to the Iraqi forces to the south? When differences developed between the Air Force and the Army over what Iraqi targets to strike, how would they be settled? And if the commanders were arguing under the pressure of preparing for their offensive, what would the war bring?

PART TWO
The War

10

Friction

Everything in war is very simple, but the simplest thing is difficult. The difficulties accumulate and end by producing a kind of friction that is inconceivable unless one has experienced war. . . . Countless minor incidents — the kind you can never really foresee — combine to lower the general level of performance, so that one always falls short of the intended goal. . . . Friction is the only concept that more or less corresponds to the factors that distinguish real war from a war on paper.

— *On War*
Carl von Clausewitz

SIERRA ALERT. Sierra Alert," blared the public address system at Barksdale Air Force Base in Louisiana. It was dawn on January 16, 1991, one day after the United Nations deadline for Saddam Hussein to withdraw his forces from Kuwait. An anxious nation's focus was on the coalition's forces in the Persian Gulf, not on the 596th Bomber Squadron stationed in the heart of the bayou country.

After five months of planning, Colonel Warden's Instant Thunder plan, refined and expanded by Buster Glosson and his Black Hole planners, was about to be put to the test. All the political hurdles had been crossed. Congress had passed a resolution on January 12 authorizing military force. While the measure had passed in the House by the comfortable margin of 250 to 183, the resolution passed in the Senate by the narrow margin of 52 to 47. Three days later Cheney and Powell had signed the secret order authorizing the attack and a copy was faxed to Schwarzkopf. It was to be high-tech war at its finest.

Jumping into their flight suits, the Barksdale airmen raced to the briefing room and were met by Lt. Gen. Ellie Shuler, the commander of the 8th Air Force, who sought to pump up the squadron. The mission the 596th was going on, Shuler said, would be one of the most historic strikes that the Air Force had carried out since James Doolittle attacked Toyko during World War II. It would represent the first time that an air-launched cruise missile had ever been fired in anger and the longest offensive mission in the history of air warfare.

For Lt. Col. Jay Beard, the mission was the culmination of years of training under the most stringent security precautions. The AGM-86C cruise missiles slung under the wings of the aging B-52s had been developed under a "black program" code-named Senior Surprise, which meant that it simply did not exist as far as the general public was concerned. The purpose of the program was to give the Air Force the capability to launch long-range attacks with conventional weapons. The nuclear warheads on a select number of air-launched cruise missiles had been removed and replaced with a conventional payload, a complicated procedure that cost $380,000 a missile. Shortly after Saddam Hussein's forces swept into Kuwait, the squadron had conducted several secret practice missions over the Caribbean, lining up the ungainly B-52s in launch tracks and simulating the firing of the missiles.

To preserve the secrecy of the mission, the airmen were not allowed to make any farewell calls to their wives. If any family members asked where the pilot had gone, the cover story was that the thirty-year-old B-52s were headed to an Air Force base at Loring, Maine, a possible staging area before being dispatched overseas.[1]

The planes would not land in Saudi Arabia after they fired their missiles. There were generally a few "hangers," cruise missiles that malfunctioned and, for one reason or another, simply did not launch. Even with all the controls that CENTCOM had placed on the media, it would not do to show up at a Saudi air base with a cruise missile strapped under the wing. The cruise missile attack would have to be a "round robin" mission, a thirty-five-hour nonstop ordeal that would send the B-52s from Barksdale to the Gulf and back again. The Bush administration counted on Russian support in the Gulf crisis, but not to the point where it planned to notify Moscow that air-launched cruise missiles, a system that the Soviets associated exclusively with nuclear weaponry, were going to make an operational debut.

As an added precaution, Glosson timed the Barksdale mission so that the B-52s would not reach North Africa until the first bombs had fallen on Baghdad. Glosson was concerned that the Libyans might detect the planes and tip off the Iraqis that the war was about to start.

As the B-52s lumbered toward the Gulf, a huge air armada began to gather just outside the range of the Iraqi radars. Refueling tankers — more than would have been employed in a war with the Soviet Union — flew to their "tanker tracks," their anticollision beacons twinkling in the night. Electronic surveillance planes, with code names like Rivet Joint and Compass Call, were aloft. Fighter patrols flew to four large patrol areas over northern Saudi Arabia so they could "delouse," shoot down, any Iraqi planes that followed allied planes into Saudi Arabia after their attacks on Iraq.

At Khamis Mushait, an ultra-modern air base tucked away near the Red Sea in the southwestern corner of Saudi Arabia, F-117 stealth fighters taxied to the runway without lights.

On ships in the Red Sea and the Persian Gulf, launchers equipped with cruise missiles were primed and ready to fire. Even cruise-missile-firing submarines would get a chance to join the war after the initial strikes were carried out.

In the Black Hole, the tension grew. That there would be problems with the air campaign was preordained. The great nineteenth-century Prussian strategist Carl von Clausewitz had invented the concept of "friction" to describe the inevitable snafus that occurred during war. Even small problems had a way of mounting up and interfering with the best-laid plans. That was the nature of war. The one consolation was that friction applied to both sides. The side that coped best with the problems would have an advantage.

Already, Glosson was coping with first signs of friction. At 10PM, an AWACS crew flying over Saudi Arabia was supposed to fake a conversation with the Tactical Air Control Center in Riyadh about the crash of a "special aircraft," a clear reference to the F-117, and then announce that it was beginning a search. The ruse was meant to put Baghdad's mind at rest in case Iraqi spies and radars picked up allied warplanes and helicopters in western Saudi Arabia. But the AWACS ran into mechanical problems and was forced to return to base. No other AWACS crew had been trained in the deception. The right hand did not know what the left hand was doing, Glosson complained.[2]

Other important details remained unresolved. Schwarzkopf wanted to ensure that the Saudi military was not notified about the war before King Fahd and instructed Glosson not to alert the Royal Saudi Air Force until an hour before the attack. But that posed a problem. Unless the Saudi pilots were clued in earlier, there was no way they would be able to participate in the scheduled attacks, and Saudi participation was essential.

Glosson's major worry, however, was the weather. The laser-targeting system used by the F-117s had pinpoint accuracy but only if there was no fog or clouds. The first two days were critical. That was when the allies would pound Iraq's leadership bunkers, target its communications, ground its air force, and turn out the lights in Baghdad. But now the weather was turning foul. If the clouds rolled in, Baghdad would be transformed from a bull's-eye to a haven for the Iraqi high command.

Code names had been developed to deal with the unexpected. "Bag it, bag it, bag it" would be the order to cancel an individual mission. "Razor" was how the airmen were to refer to a battle-damaged aircraft. "Golf" signified that the radar of an AWACS plane was out of commission. In the most extreme case, the air-war commanders would issue the order "Terminate Wolfpack" — true to his heritage, Glosson had derived the code from the North Carolina State basketball team — effectively putting the war on hold. But only an unexpected capitulation by Iraq or a massive midair collision could stop the war now.

As Glosson tried to iron out the last-minute problems, he got a call from Gen. Merrill McPeak, the Air Force chief of staff. McPeak was calling to pass on an unpleasant message from Donald Rice, the civilian Air Force secretary. There should be no more Panamas, an allusion to the efforts Air Force officials had made to cover up the fact that two bombs dropped by F-117s during the invasion of Panama had missed their mark. If the bombs went astray or problems occurred, the air-war planners needed to own up to them. Glosson was annoyed. He had already told the pilots that, and it was not what he needed to hear on the eve of one of the biggest air wars in history.

Glosson canceled the tactical deception plan and ordered the Saudi aircrews to report to the briefing room at Dhahran, suited up and ready to go at 1AM, without telling them what was up. As for the weather, there was nothing much he could do about that.

The air campaign looked great on paper. Now it was time to see if it would work in reality. The first shots of the war would occur in the remote and darkened desert, not on CNN. The pilots would carry a personal reminder of the risks of war: a "blood chit," a piece of cloth explaining in Arabic, Persian, Turkish, and other languages that the bearer was an American who needed assistance and offered $80 in gold coins to grease the way.   ★ ★ ★

At 1:30AM the first Tomahawk cruise missiles rocketed off their launchers in the Red Sea and Persian Gulf and began their long flight along the Iranian Zagros Mountains toward Baghdad. Unlike manned aircraft, there was no way for those weapons to be recalled. The war was on. Now it was up to the pilots.

As the Tomahawks flew toward Baghdad, Lt. Col. Dick Cody was leading Task Force Normandy north. The helicopter task force lifted off in the inky darkness at 1AM from Al Jouf, a lonely base in western Saudi Arabia. Air Force special operations Pave Low helicopters, equipped with sophisticated night-flying equipment and navigation systems, led the way, skimming over the undulating desert at 125 miles per hour while Army Apache helicopters, equipped with Hellfire laser-guided anti-tank missiles, rockets, and 30mm guns, followed behind. To dispense with the need for refueling, the Army had replaced some of the munitions with fuel tanks. Achieving surprise would be tricky enough without establishing a fuel base close to the Iraqi border.

Cody's mission was to take out two clusters of Soviet-made early warning radars just north of the Saudi-Iraqi border. Separated by sixty miles of open desert, the radars were operated from mobile vans and used a microwave system to relay communications. American intelligence figured the Iraqi radars could peer as much as 150 miles into Saudi territory at medium and high altitude and 30 miles at low altitude.

The Iraqi radars sat astride the route that the EF-111 electronic warfare planes would use to jam for the F-117s. They also blanketed the corridor reserved for the F-15E Strike Eagles' attack on the Scud sites in the west. To prevent the Iraqis from alerting Baghdad the war was under way, the two clusters were to be attacked simultaneously, so the task force had been divided into Team White and Team Red.

As the choppers flew across the Iraqi border there was a crackle of small-arms fire and shoulder-fired missiles went whizzing through the air. Team White had received the first hostile fire of the war. None of the shots hit, but the operation had not gone unnoticed. Still, there was no indication that the border incursion had been reported to the Iraqi high command. As far as the world was concerned, an uneasy peace still held.

As the Pave Lows got to within seven miles of the radars, they queried the navigational satellites overhead to pinpoint their location. Once their positions were confirmed, the crews threw small bundles of green phosphorescent lights at designated points in the desert so that the Apaches that followed behind could orient their navigation and targeting systems. The Pave Lows then pulled back and the Apaches flew ahead to the attack.

Slowing their airspeed to sixty knots, the helicopters hugged the desert floor, guiding themselves to their targets using their FLIRS, forward-looking infrared radar systems, which created images from the heat emitted by objects on the cold desert floor.

Cody, flying with Team White, could see that the Iraqis still had their lights on. But almost immediately, the Iraqis sensed they were not alone and turned them off. The FLIRS on the Apaches, however, turned the night into an eerie greenish killing zone. After hovering in place, the teams began to attack.

"Party in ten," yelled Lt. Tom Drew, breaking radio silence to give the code for Team White's attack.

"This one is for you, Saddam," said Chief Warrant Officer Dave Jones, as Team White hurled laser-guided Hellfire missiles at the generators, antennas, and command vans in the radar complex. Greenish human forms ran for cover across the FLIR screens, as the Apaches used their rockets and 30mm cannon fire to rake over the radar site.

Over a four-minute period, the helicopter teams fired more than thirty Hellfire missiles and dozens of 70mm rockets, setting off a series of explosions that lit up the horizon. American signals intelligence monitoring Iraqi communications later reported that the Iraqis got off a phone call before the radars were destroyed, alerting the Iraqi high command in Baghdad that an attack was under way. It was a wonder that anybody in CENTCOM thought the attack could remain a secret, given the fireworks that lit up the sky. The early warning radars were knocked out, but the Army had used a sledgehammer to do it.[3]

The next blow was up to Maj. Greg Feest. One of the best stealth pilots in the business, Feest had flown one of the two F-117 fighters that conducted a night attack at a troop barracks during the American invasion of Panama. His mission was intended to be a stellar debut for the F-117 but had turned into a public relations nightmare for the Air Force. Although the Air Force originally claimed that the planes had dropped their bombs with pinpoint accuracy, it later conceded that bombs had missed their targets. There had been a lot of mitigating factors. The jungle humidity had degraded the F-117's infrared targeting system — a problem happily absent in the Gulf.

Now, Feest had a chance to set things right. The Gulf War provided an opportunity for personal vindication and, more broadly, for the Air Force's new high-tech strategy of warfare.

When the helicopter task force was blasting away at the Iraqi radars, Feest and a handful of other F-117 pilots were already flying over Iraq. Feest's first target was the Nukhayb bunker in southern Iraq, one of the nodes in Iraq's Kari air defense system. Protected by two layers of reinforced concrete and filled with French-built radar and computer equipment, the Nukhayb Intercept Operations Center was used to direct Iraqi fighters to intercept intruding aircraft and to disperse targeting information to surface-to-air missile batteries in the region. Feest and a wingman, Capt. Dave "Dogman" Francis, were to take out Nukhayb and a nearby Iraqi command post that served as a backup.

Everything had gone like clockwork. This was not like flying in the massive bombing formations in World War II. The life of the modern warrior was lonely work. There was no copilot in the single-seat F-117 to talk to. Feest and the other F-117 pilots maintained radio silence. Midair collisions were avoided by assigning the pilots specific altitudes and TOTs — times on target. The pilots needed to adhere religiously to their courses. They had to reach their assigned altitudes and stay there, no matter how much fire they received from the ground.

The nearly imperceptible radar image of the black bat-wing F-117 had been further reduced by having the plane carry its bombs internally. But that also meant that each plane could carry only two bombs. The bombs would have to be dropped with precision. Sitting in the small cockpit in front of the faintly lit dials and video displays was like playing a computer game, but with enormous stakes. The engineers had assured the pilots that stealth technology would make the F-117s virtually invisible to Iraqi radar, but some of the pilots were worried. The raids against Iraq would be the ultimate operational test of stealth technology. Additionally, there was always the chance of getting hit by a barrage of unaimed fire when the Iraqis blanketed the sky. Most of the young pilots had never been to war before, and in Feest's case his combat experience was limited to the single ill-fated mission over Panama.

At 2:51AM, Feest was nervous as he turned his computer system to "weapons delivery." The night was still as he flipped the switch to open the bomb-bay doors and dropped the GBU-27. It was a 2,000-pound laser-guided bomb specially designed to crash through layers of reinforced concrete before exploding. As he directed his laser on the target, he watched the bomb fall on his cockpit display.

As soon as the bomb exploded, the video game was over. The Iraqis responded with massive barrages of triple A — antiaircraft artillery — big bursts of red and orange that lit up the sky like a fireworks display.

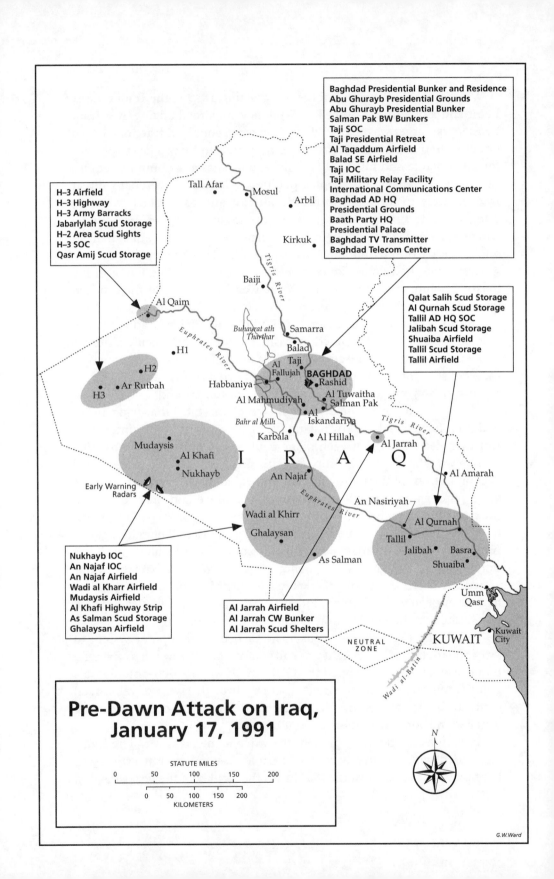

H–3 Airfield
H–3 Highway
H–3 Army Barracks
Jabarlylah Scud Storage
H–2 Area Scud Sights
H–3 SOC
Qasr Amij Scud Storage

Baghdad Presidential Bunker and Residence
Abu Ghurayb Presidential Grounds
Abu Ghurayb Presidential Bunker
Salman Pak BW Bunkers
Taji SOC
Taji Presidential Retreat
Al Taqaddum Airfield
Balad SE Airfield
Taji IOC
Taji Military Relay Facility
International Communications Center
Baghdad AD HQ
Presidential Grounds
Baath Party HQ
Presidential Palace
Baghdad TV Transmitter
Baghdad Telecom Center

Qalat Salih Scud Storage
Al Qurnah Scud Storage
Tallil AD HQ SOC
Jalibah Scud Storage
Shuaiba Airfield
Tallil Scud Storage
Tallil Airfield

Nukhayb IOC
An Najaf IOC
An Najaf Airfield
Wadi al Kharr Airfield
Mudaysis Airfield
Al Khafi Highway Strip
As Salman Scud Storage
Ghalaysan Airfield

Al Jarrah Airfield
Al Jarrah CW Bunker
Al Jarrah Scud Shelters

Tall Afar
Mosul
Arbil
Kirkuk
Baiji
Al Qaim
Buhayrat ath Tharthar
Samarra
Tigris River
Balad
H1
Taji
Al Fallujah
BAGHDAD
H2
Ar Rutbah
Habbaniya
Rashid
H3
Al Mahmudiyah
Al Tuwaitha
Salman Pak
Bahr al Milh
Al Iskandariya
Tigris River
Karbala
Al Hillah
Al Jarrah
Mudaysis
Al Khafi
I R A Q
Nukhayb
An Najaf
Al Amarah
Early Warning Radars
Euphrates River
Wadi al Khirr
Ghalaysan
An Nasiriyah
Al Qurnah
Tallil
Jalibah
Basra
As Salman
Shuaiba
Umm Qasr
NEUTRAL ZONE
KUWAIT
Kuwait City
Wadi al-Batin

Pre-Dawn Attack on Iraq, January 17, 1991

STATUTE MILES
0   50   100   150   200

0   50   100   150   200
KILOMETERS

N

G.W.Ward

The Iraqis were throwing up virtually everything they had, lacing the sky with tracer rounds.

Feest knew that the Iraqis had no idea where he was, but the detonations appeared to be going off all around him. All it took was a lucky hit. "Nothing was guided, but it was more triple A than I could ever imagine," he recalled after the war. "I was praying that I would make it through, but I had to go through it to get to my next target. I was surprised when I did and when my wingman made it through."

Feest and his wingman pressed on to their next target, the Iraqi Sector Operations Center at H-3 airfield in western Iraq. There they would have less luck. The F-117 commanders could not confirm that Feest or his wingman hit that command post.[4]

As he raced north in his EF-111, Lt. Col. Dennis Hardziej figured the jig was up. Hardziej could see the red glow on the horizon from Task Force Normandy's raid on the Iraqi radars. With the sky aglow with burning debris, he could not believe the Iraqis did not know that the first blows had been struck and that more were to come.

The commander of the EF-111 Raven electronic combat squadron based at Taif, Hardziej had flown F-4s in Korea and F-111 bombers in Europe. During the invasion of Panama, he had flown a grueling mission to jam the lone Panamanian radar station that might have picked up the flight of American troop transports. But this was different. Hardziej had been been worried about the Gulf mission from the beginning.

During peacetime, Raven crews were taken for granted by much of the Air Force. Loaded with sensitive electronic equipment to fool enemy radar systems, the EF-111 carried no air-to-air missiles or armament of any kind. It was not a "shooter," and in the Air Force caste system the EF-111 crews enjoyed second-class status compared with the pilots who flew the sexy warplanes like the F-15C and the F-117. But with war on the horizon, the Ravens found themselves in demand.

Looking for some extra insurance in case they were detected, the F-117 pilots insisted that the EF-111s jam for them during the opening strike on Baghdad. The jamming was to start two minutes before H hour, when the first bombs dropped on Baghdad. To carry out the mission, the Ravens would have to cross into Iraq a good twenty minutes before H hour.

Hardziej had asked for F-15C fighter escort. But the air-war planners in Riyadh were afraid of losing the element of surprise. The request was rejected. The Ravens would be the first nonstealthy aircraft in Iraq, except for the helicopters that crossed the border at twenty-five feet at 2:15AM, and they would be on their own.

To maximize the chances of success, Hardziej decided to lead a flight of three EF-111s to central Iraq. That way they could provide some jamming for the F-117s even if one or two Ravens were shot out of the skies. He also picked the three fastest planes in his squadron, Ravens that could fly at 590 knots without using their telltale afterburners, which would illuminate the sky like Roman candles.

To surprise the Iraqis, the Ravens had taken off from Taif, refueled over northern Saudi Arabia as if on a routine exercise, and turned back toward their base, before diving to elude the Iraqi radars. Then Hardziej and his wingmen had swung around and hurtled toward Iraq at 400 feet above the desert floor.

The plan was to head north, hugging the ground, and then ascend over "Ravenlake," the code name for the lakes just west of Baghdad and start the jamming. An AWACS orbiting over Saudi territory would alert the Ravens to any airborne Iraqi fighters. After ten minutes of jamming, the Ravens would hit the deck and escape south.

As they streaked north, several Iraqi fighters zoomed over them, heading south. The Iraqi fighters had their wing lights on to avoid mid-air collisions. Clearly, the Iraqi air force had a lot to learn about night operations.

Still, Hardziej was worried. American intelligence had indicated that the Iraqis might use their Soviet-made Fulcrum and French-made Mirage interceptors in tandem. The Fulcrum had the superior radar, and the Mirage had a French-made missile, the Super Matra. If the Fulcrums and Mirages worked together, even the ill-trained Iraqi air force might exact a toll.

Soon the AWACS saw the Iraqis on its radar screen, too.

"Bandits," the AWACS called out.

The Iraqi planes turned around and headed back north. Hardziej could not tell if the Iraqis had turned tail after detecting the F-15C fighters patrolling northern Saudi Arabia or had turned around to chase the Ravens. To be safe, he decided to go to his backup plan.

"Touchdown," Hardziej announced, sounding the prearranged code name for the plan.

The last of the Ravens ascended to draw the Iraqis' attention. It was like waving a red flag before a bull. Hardziej and his wingman pressed on, but pulled up short of "Ravenlake," seventy miles west of Baghdad. That was farther away from Baghdad than they had planned, but the

EF-111 had powerful electronic equipment. Hardziej figured that they could still effectively jam the Baghdad area.

After jamming, Hardziej descended and streaked south. By now, the Iraqis seemed to be on his trail. He saw an Iraqi fighter with a searchlight fixed on its wing. Hardziej, at full throttle, saw an Iraqi air-to-air missile explode in the desert below as he crossed back into Saudi Arabia.

After the war, the Air Force said virtually nothing about the Raven raid, and most of the details of the mission were kept classified. Touting the Ravens, the Air Force apparently calculated, might detract from the success of its stealth technology. But Hardziej was awarded the Silver Star and other Raven crew were given the Distinguished Flying Cross for their first night mission. The Ravens had to use the backup plan, but the F-117s had received the jamming they requested.[5]

Flying in his F-117, Lt. Col. Ralph W. Getchell could tell from the Iraqi reaction that the Ravens had made it close to Baghdad. Getchell had been the first F-117 pilot to enter Iraq and was well on his way to Baghdad to lead the first wave of attacks when Feest bombed Nukhayb. The call signs for the F-117s for the first wave of attacks on Baghdad were, appropriately, "Hail" and "Thunder."

None of the planes in the Baghdad attacks had a backup target to hit if their primary target was obscured. With all the pressure of the opening night attacks, the F-117 planners were keeping things simple. If the pilots were unable to drop their bombs on their designated targets, they were to bring their bombs home. To ensure that the key command posts, communications centers, and air defense centers were hit, many of them would be bombed by several F-117s before the night was over.

Getchell's flight to Baghdad had been uneventful, but as he approached the city, a malfunction developed in his targeting system. Getchell had to shut it down and then power it up again, much as one might reboot a computer. Clausewitz's friction had taken hold. It would take several minutes to get his targeting system back on line, and there was not much for Getchell to do but to take in the view. To his surprise, Baghdad was not blacked out. It was lit up like Las Vegas.

All of a sudden, the Iraqi antiaircraft artillery lit up the sky. Getchell looked at the time on the cockpit display. It was 2:58AM. It was clear to Getchell that the Iraqis had picked up the Raven jamming. Electronic warfare might help protect the F-117s against surface-to-air missiles and radar-guided antiaircraft guns, but it had also announced the attack to the rest of Iraq's defenders, just as Glosson warned the aircrews it would. Once one gun went off, they all did. The F-117s and the Ravens would have to rethink their tactics.

Even so, the Iraqis did not seem to understand what they were up against. They were firing 23mm antiaircraft artillery, as well as 37mm, 57mm, and larger-caliber antiaircraft pieces, creating a tapestry of tracers over Baghdad. The pattern of firing indicated that the Iraqis had anticipated that many of the attacking planes would be flying low-level, the way nonstealthy F-111Fs and A-6s would have attacked. For the F-117 pilots, flying over the airbursts from the triple A was like driving over speed bumps.[6]

Two minutes after the firing commenced, Capt. Paul Dolson, "Hail 01," dropped a GBU-27 bomb on the Iraqi International Communications Center, the so-called AT&T building that was used to route telephone traffic. Dolson then flew on to strike the Intercept Operations Center at Al Taqaddum.

Capt. Marcel Kerdavid, "Thunder 10," bombed the Al Kharhk Telecommunications Center, a 270-foot structure studded with microwave relay dishes for transmitting radio and television throughout Iraq and Jordan. Then he went on to strike a command bunker at North Taji.

Within minutes, Maj. Jerry Leatherman came along and dropped two GBU-10s on the AT&T building, while other stealth fighters attacked the Iraqi Air Defense Headquarters and the Baghdad Sector Operations Center, one of five major hubs of the Kari air defense system. One F-117 also bombed a long causeway to Abu Ghurayb, a palace redoubt in the middle of a man-made lake near the airport, blocking the entranceway to the presidential bunker.

The F-117s scored thirteen hits in seventeen attempts. Minutes later, Tomahawk cruise missiles that had flown up the spine of the Zagros Mountains in Iran reached Baghdad, striking the Baath Party headquarters, Scud missile plants, and electrical power facilities. Eight Tomahawks were targeted on the Presidential Palace along the Tigris River, six on the Baath Party headquarters, and twenty on the Taji missile production complex.

Eighteen Tomahawks were directed against electrical facilities in and around Baghdad. Many of the missiles carried a highly classified special carbon filament designed to short out the electrical system. In Riyadh, David Deptula let out a cheer when the CNN telecast from Baghdad went off the air. The allies had turned out the lights.

The first wave of attacks had gone well but had benefited from the element of surprise. Baghdad, however, was still defended by over sixty surface-to-air batteries and countless antiaircraft guns, none of which had been attacked. A fog bank was beginning to roll into the Euphrates River valley. The next several waves of attacks would require an entirely different set of tactics.

A SHOT IN THE DARK

As the F-117s headed south from Baghdad, Col. David Livingston's missile crews at Ar'ar and Hafar al-Batin were primed to fire. The BQM-74 target drones that were mounted on the crews' launchers were not the most sophisticated weapons that had been developed. But they did not have to be. The missiles were not meant to destroy the Iraqis, only fool them.

The plan was straightforward. Livingston's men would launch the drones while Navy A-6s fired TALDs, the unguided decoys. The hope was that the drones would look like attacking planes on the Iraqi radars and that would prompt the Iraqis to turn on their antiaircraft radars and fire their antiaircraft missiles. Like turning on a spotlight in a darkened room, activating the radars would expose them to attack by allied anti-radiation missiles, which home in on enemy radar beams. After the radars were blown up, the Iraqi ground-to-air capability would be blunted. The F-117s would then come back for another round of attacks. In essence, the aim was to get the Iraqis to fight shadows while the F-117s wound up for another punch.

At 3:48AM, Livingston's crew fired the drones toward Baghdad and Basra, while the Navy A-6s launched their decoys. Meanwhile, flights of Air Force F-4G Wild-Weasels and Navy FA-18s, A-7s, and A-6s closed in on Baghdad. Armed with HARM antiradiation missiles, the planes waited for the Iraqis to respond.

They did not have to wait long. With much of the capital in darkness and panic, the Iraqis were determined to stave off another attack. The Iraqi radars were up and running, and the missile crews began to launch their SAMs at the drones. American intelligence later concluded that the Iraqis had taken the falling drones for downed enemy warplanes. The Iraqis thought they were protecting their capital, but they were simply setting themselves up for a fall.

As the Iraqis fired off their SAMs, the HARM-carrying planes pulled up short of Baghdad and unleashed a lethal rain of antiradiation missiles. The Air Force F-4Gs alone would fire 118 HARM missiles on the first night of the war.

The tactic came at a price. During the attack on the Iraqi air defenses, three Iraqi aircraft — two MiG-25s and a MiG-29 — took off from Al Taqaddum and Kairi West at 4AM. In his haste to defend Baghdad, one MiG-25 pilot used his afterburner and was visible for miles.

Cmdr. Mike "Spock" Anderson, an F-18 pilot from the *Saratoga* aircraft carrier, saw the MiG in the distance, but he was inhibited from firing by the rules of engagement. To the layman, rules of engagement sound like a technical issue, but to a fighter pilot they define an air battle. With hundreds of planes in the air at one time, the rules of engagement are needed to strike the correct balance between aggressive pursuit of the enemy and avoiding knocking a friendly plane out of the air by mistake.

To avoid cases of friendly fire, the Air Force generals who ran the air war stipulated that a fighter that wanted to shoot at a plane that was not conducting a hostile act had to determine, using two independent means of verification, that the plane he was shooting at was hostile and that no friendly planes were in the line of fire.

It was not a coincidence that the Air Force's F-15C, its premier fighter, had the technology to do both. The Air Force figured its most modern fighters needed to be able to tell friend from foe in skies crowded with NATO and Warsaw Pact aircraft should war erupt in Europe. The F-15C was equipped with a classified piece of equipment dubbed the "noncooperative target recognition system," which used Doppler radar to distinguish a Soviet jet engine from one of Western design. The plane could also send out electronic signals that would trigger a transponder carried by allied planes. Once stimulated, the transponder sent out a coded signal that identified the plane as friendly.

The Navy, however, had never made the investment to buy both these systems and install them in a single aircraft. Its FA-18s had the radar technology to identify Soviet-made planes, while its F-14 Tomcats had the capability to trigger allied transponders.

The Navy objected before the war that the Air Force–drafted rules favored the Air Force and could cost the Navy "kills." But the Air Force would not budge, and it was the Air Force that decided the air-war plan. Navy planes that wanted to fire at aircraft that could not be identified visually would have to receive clearance from the Air Force AWACS radar planes.

Using the F-18s target-recognition system, Anderson reported that he had a "bogey" and locked onto the plane with his fire-control radar. With the MiG flying at 1.4 Mach, Anderson had at most seven seconds to fire his missile. Anderson sought clearance to fire, but the AWACS could not identify the plane.

Minutes later, there was a huge explosion. Lt. Cmdr. Michael Scott Speicher had fired a HARM antiradiation missile at the Iraqi SAM battery and was circling around to launch another missile when his plane disintegrated in midair. It was the only plane that the United States lost in a dogfight during the Persian Gulf War.

Navy intelligence analyzed the episode for months but could not reach a definite conclusion on how Speicher was blown out of the air. Navy intelligence officials concluded that one possibility is that the MiG-25 shot the FA-18 in the tail with an AA-6, a powerful air-to-air missile. But the absence of a distress call from the American pilot and the fact that the Iraqis never boasted about the "kill" also raise the possibility that the Iraqi MiG may have collided with the Navy plane in the darkness, Navy intelligence concluded.

Whether more liberal rules of engagement would have made a difference is uncertain. Under the restrictive rules, the Navy had only three confirmed "kills" during the entire war. There was, however, no case of friendly planes shooting down other allied planes.[7]

The attacks on the Iraqi air defenses were effective and paved the way for another assault by F-117 fighters. Before the Iraqi air defense crews could catch their breath, the second wave of F-117s made their way to Baghdad, pounding the city from 4:10 to 4:20AM. As Col. Al Whitley, the commander of the F-117 wing, approached the capital, he could see the Iraqis were in a panic. There were long lines of cars — bumper to bumper — streaming out of the capital. It looked, he later recalled, like the interstate from Los Angeles to Las Vegas on a Friday night.

Half of the F-117 attacks were repeat strikes on the Iraqi Air Defense Headquarters, the Baghdad Sector Operations Center, the North Taji commander centers, and telephone exchanges. But there were some new targets as well, including a television transmitter station, Rasheed Airfield, an international radio transmitter, and the presidential bunkers at Abu Ghurayb and in Baghdad.

With all the smoke from the furious barrages of antiaircraft artillery and with the weather closing in, however, the success rate was down. The second wave of F-117s scored ten hits in sixteen tries.

The third wave of F-117 strikes, which was carried out before dawn, was devoted to attacks on Iraq's biological and chemical weapons bunkers in the desert. By then the clouds were even more of a problem, and the stealth fighters scored only five hits in sixteen tries.

In an effort to promote stealth technology after the war, the Air Force kept secret virtually all the tactics used to help the F-117s get to Baghdad. The F-117 image the Air Force projected publicly was that of an invisible aircraft that flew to Iraq's capital alone and unafraid through the teeth of the Iraqi defenses.

The F-117s, in fact, benefited by the jamming, by the clever use of decoys and drones, and by the fusillade of missiles Air Force and Navy planes had unleased on the Iraqi SAM sites. Nor were they totally invisible. But the stealth technology had worked better than many, including the F-117 pilots, had expected.

American intelligence, in a highly classified assessment, later determined that Iraq's Chinese-made Nanjing low-frequency radars were able to pick up the F-117s on the first night but could not determine at what altitude they were flying. The limited tracking information from the Nanjing was passed to the SAM batteries, but their radars were not able to find the F-117s. MiG-29s were also dispatched to intercept the black jets, but they, too, could not find the F-117s. (In another indication of the limitations of the Nanjing radar, later in the war F-117s bombed a Nanjing radar near the Tallil air base, along with an SA-2 and an SA-3 surface-to-air missile battery.)

All told, the F-117s had struck about half their targets. Their grand total for the night was twenty-seven hits out of forty-nine attacks. Eighteen of the planes never attempted to drop their bombs because of bad weather. Even taking the weather into account, that was not the image that the Air Force created when it showed videotapes of its bombing runs to reporters in Riyadh.[8]

But the F-117s' success rate was an order of magnitude better than that of dropping dumb bombs, and none of them had been lost. There was plenty of bombing for the F-117s to carry out in and around Baghdad, but no more to do that night. The focus turned to the rest of Iraq.

From watching CNN, the world had the impression that the war was being fought by invisible airplanes dropping bombs on Baghdad, but beyond the city most of the war was being fought by nonstealthy planes. At H hour, twenty-two F-15E Strike Eagles soared into western Iraq to attack the stationary Scud launchers at Iraq's H-2 airfield. The planes dropped dumb bombs. The Air Force had pulled out all the stops to expedite the delivery of their targeting pods for dropping laser-guided weapons, but they had not yet arrived in Saudi Arabia.

Four additional F-15Es were kept on alert — two on ground alert and two on airborne alert over Saudi Arabia — on the theory that they could pounce on any mobile Scud launchers that Iraq might use to attack Israel.

The Iraqi airfields were attacked by a wide variety of allied planes. The Iraqis stationed F-1 and MiG-29 fighter interceptors at five heavily defended airfields in southern Iraq so that they could break up the American attacks, pick off stragglers, or make a run at the AWACS battle-management planes. Flying at a low level, B-52s dropped British 1,000-pound bombs on runways while F-15Es dropped cluster mines.

The British delivered a gutsy performance. British Tornados, hauling the JP-233 bomb-dispensing system, disgorged hundreds of little bomblets as the planes swept low across Iraqi runways. It was a dangerous mission, but it was the one that the British had prepared for throughout the cold war.

The French were more of a problem. The French had initially insisted that they needed to husband their planes and bombs during the ground war and at first declined to join the H-Hour attack. France, Schwarzkopf complained after the war, wanted to be a part of the coalition while keeping open its options to sell arms to Iraq and other Arab states after the war. "I felt they wanted to turn to the Iraqis and say 'we're not really bad guys and we'll sell you Mirages,' " said Schwarzkopf, who added that the French military played a "double dealing role."[9]

But only fifteen hours before the war was to start, a French commander flew to Doha, Qatar, and announced to the F-16 wing there that French Jaguars would participate in the coalition attack on the Al Jaber airfield. The Americans hastily provided the French with the intelligence they needed and advised them to fly high to avoid the Iraqi anti-aircraft fire. But with little time to plan their attack, the French carried out the raid at low level as they had been trained.

The Jaguars found the target by watching the stream of American bombs falling from the sky. With the element of surprise gone, the French then attacked. All the Jaguars sustained battle damage. One French pilot was struck by a bullet from an Iraqi AK-47 rifle that penetrated the cockpit, went through his helmet, and lacerated his scalp. The pilot was bleeding profusely and was almost in shock when he landed, but somehow he managed to survive. The French casualties came from Iraqi fire, but more fundamentally were the result of indecision in Paris as to whether or not to join in the allied air attacks and the failure to develop effective tactics in advance.

Saudi Tornados joined in the attack on the H-3 airfield, a base in western Iraq built by the British during their colonial occupation decades earlier. Participating in the attacks on H-3, the Saudis ironically had the mission of trying to suppress Iraqi fighter and missile attacks against their sworn enemy Israel. Other Saudi Tornados, however, dropped out of the attack on Shuaiba airfield, near Basra in southern Iraq, after they failed to link up with the refueling tankers.

In a remarkably close call that might have strained American and Saudi relations, one Saudi Tornado pilot narrowly missed being shot down. The Saudi plane became separated from his companions and was identified as an enemy plane by an American AWACS scanning the Iraqi skies from northern Saudi Arabia. The AWACS cleared an F-15C, piloted by Capt. Getnar Drummond, to fire, but the pilot was uneasy with the order and held off. At the last possible moment, the American pilot determined that the aircraft was friendly. The incident was hushed up at the time, but the American pilot was later awarded the Distinguished Flying Cross for his good judgment and restraint.[10]

Lt. Col. Denny Ertler and Maj. Keith Zuegel undertook one of the most harrowing F-111F missions on the first night of the war when they attacked a shelter at the Ali al Salem airfield in Kuwait that was suspected — wrongly it would be learned later — of holding chemical weapons.

As the airmen and five other F-111Fs flew toward the base, Ali al Salem itself was barely visible behind the barrage of antiaircraft fire. It looked like a big wall of glowing sparklers. What the Iraqis were doing was not sophisticated. They were using barrages of fire to keep out the allies. Dodging the fire would be like running through a shower without getting wet.

Three of the F-111s concluded that the Iraqi fire was too much for them and turned back. Glosson told the American pilots just before the war: "No mission was worth getting killed for. You could always come back another night." The war was a dangerous challenge for the airmen, but it was not a crusade. But Ertler and Zuegel had never been to war before and did not know what to expect. They pressed on.

Suddenly, the warbling tone of the RHAW (radar homing and warning) receiver went off. The F-111F was being tracked by a SAM battery and an SA-6 missile had been fired at the plane. The standard technique for avoiding a SAM was for the F-111F to break four to seven seconds before the missile arrived, but depth perception was difficult at night. Ertler waited and then pulled the aircraft in toward the missile at the last instant. The airmen dodged another missile as they guided a bomb to its target.

Fleeing the airfield, Ertler put the plane into a dive to avoid the Iraqi fire. Looking through his radarscope, Zuegel tried to determine the altitude. But all he saw were little green dots. It was like a cathode-ray tube had just been turned off. He had no idea of the altitude.

"You do not have a scope. Pull up," Zuegel yelled. Looking up, he saw the F-111F was streaking south at an altitude of fifty feet or maybe less.

As they headed home, the triple A created an umbrella of light that lit up Kuwait City.

"Hey, dude, we made it," Ertler said.

"We are not out of here yet," said Zuegel. Suddenly, an SA-3 came soaring toward the plane. Relying on instinct, Ertler jerked his plane away just as the SAM blew up.

Finally, Ertler flicked on the safety lights. "If they did not kill me doing this, I am going to live forever," Zuegel recalled thinking. But as they were flying back to base he thought again: "We are probably going to have to do this again tomorrow night, and maybe the night after that. It only takes one golden BB to get you. This could be a long deal."[11]

As dawn broke, Lt. Col. Jay Beard's B-52s from Barksdale arrived in the Gulf. The planes lined up in two formations and, one by one, fired their missiles. The B-52s shuddered as the missiles dropped off their pylons, fell 500 feet, spread their wings, popped up their tails, and streaked toward Iraq.

Of the thirty-nine cruise missiles carried to the Persian Gulf, thirty-five were launched toward their targets — communications sites, telephone exchanges, and electrical plants in northern and southern Iraq. Four others could not be fired because of software or hardware failures. All in all, the Air Force had expended more than half of its total inventory of non-nuclear missiles. The mission had not been essential, but it gave the Air Force an opportunity to try out one of its most secret weapons and showed that the service could reach out globally to strike an enemy from bases in the United States.

The American high command was exultant with its first night's effort. With almost seven hundred planes over Iraq in the attack, the first night's casualties were remarkably low. Many of the pilots had honored the injunction that no target was worth dying for, but most had pressed on to their targets. The FA-18 from the *Saratoga* was the only American loss. In return, the allies had dealt a crippling blow to Iraq's air defense and command and control infrastructure.

The Iraqi pilots had found it difficult to take on the allies. Before the war, American intelligence had judged that Iraq had no more than a dozen crack pilots. Modeled on the Soviet system, the Iraqi air force took its orders from controllers in ground-based command posts, which took a beating. Iraq lost eight fighters, including five MiG-29s and three F-1s, its most modern planes. By the third day of the air war, the Iraqi losses would be up to fourteen and its air force would be hiding in concrete shelters. It was the beginning of an ominous trend for the Iraqis. By the war's end, the allies had flown 69,000 fighter or bomber missions, compared to 910 for the Iraqis. Many of the Iraqi front-line fighters were destroyed in their shelters, while others were flown to sanctuary in Iran.

The allies had not accomplished all their objectives for the opening day of war. The effort to decapitate the Saddam Hussein regime had been blunted by the foul weather. The presidential compound at Abu Ghurayb near the airport had emerged unscathed. The weather precluded attacks on the American surface-to-air I-Hawk missiles that the Iraqis had captured from the Kuwaitis and moved to a test range near Baghdad. Nor were the F-117s able to completely destroy the Al Ramadi radio relay sites, which provided communication links to the Scud sites in the west. But many key sites were hit. Most of all, the United States had struck the physical and psychological blow it was seeking by taking the war to the enemy redoubt with virtual impunity.

Iraq's electrical system was severely damaged. By the end of two days, eleven of Iraq's major power plants would be down, either disabled by allied bombs or turned off by Iraqi plant managers who were afraid to make their installation a target.

Iraq's Scud missile plants and presumed biological weapons bunkers had been hit. Iraq's nuclear sites would be attacked on the second day of the war. The emphasis on the first day was on hitting weapons that posed an immediate danger to American forces, not weapons that posed the greatest long-term threat to the United States' allies in the region.

The allies' command of the skies also gave the Army the ability to begin the laborious and time-consuming process of moving undetected its thousands of men and tons of supplies into position for its left hook.

On the second night the United States opened a second front, launching F-111 strikes from Turkey, which took out the early warning stations along the Turkish border. Iraq would be hit from two sides from then on.

Still, after the long first night, the generals were divided about what had been accomplished. Glosson was exhausted but was surprised by how few glitches there had been. One of the few times he had been forced to intervene was when a few F-15Es had refused to taxi onto a runway and take off because of an alert of an imminent Scud attack. Glosson had castigated the squadron for its "peacetime" mentality and told them he wanted them in the air. On the afternoon of the 17th, Glosson sat down and wrote in his diary that the air strikes had gone even better than he had thought they would. "The war is all but over can be heard everywhere — B.S. — A good start but the war is a long way from over," he wrote.

Lt. Gen. Frederick Franks, the VII Corps commander, however, was afraid the allied warplanes had stirred up the hornet's nest and that the Iraqis would come streaming south. As the warplanes returned from the first day of strikes, Franks received an alarming report: fifty tanks were reported to be attacking the 3rd Egyptian Division. Another Iraqi column was reported to be moving from the southeast corner of Kuwait toward Log Base Alpha, the sprawling compound near Hafar al-Batin that contained the corps' supplies. Only a relative handful of 1st Infantry Division soldiers were protecting the logistics base and their tanks were short on ammunition.

Franks moved fast to fend off the blow. The 1st Infantry Division soldiers and the 2nd Armored Cavalry Regiment went to battle stations, and the 1st Cavalry Division rushed north and began furiously digging trench positions. The VII Corps also took operational control of a nearby brigade of the 101st Airborne.

Eventually, the word filtered in that the Iraqi attack was in fact a group of Egyptian tanks on the move and a Marine deception operation along the Kuwaiti border. Franks wrote the scare off as good practice. Around the VII Corps, the episode was dubbed one of the "battles that never were." But it spoke volumes about Franks's perception of the enemy.[12]

During his nightly meeting with his top commanders, Schwarzkopf was surprisingly low key after such an exciting day. It was, to his commanders, another example of his volatile moods swings. The battle was just beginning, Schwarzkopf said, and would not be over until the allies occupied Kuwait.

The Russians, however, could see where things were headed, and they did not look good for their former clients. Two days after the air war began, Soviet President Mikhail S. Gorbachev called Bush and floated the notion of ordering a pause in the bombing while Moscow made a diplomatic approach to Baghdad, according to a senior White House official. Bush brushed the suggestion off.[13]

The Russians did not get much further with the Iraqis. Gorbachev instructed the Soviet ambassador in Baghdad to encourage the Iraqis to seek a diplomatic solution, but Moscow did not receive a response. Finally, Baghdad radio said that all cease-fire proposals should be addressed to President Bush.

The Iraqis were taking a pounding. Their air force was not a factor. But they had a few tricks up their sleeve. As early as August, Iraq had threatened to draw Israel into the war by firing Scuds, and on the second day of the air campaign that is just what it did.

11

The Great Scud Hunt

This morning the United States Air Force found three mobile Iraqi launchers, with missiles on board, inside Iraq. These launchers were obviously aimed at Saudi Arabia given their positions. Those three mobile erector launchers have been destroyed. In addition to that, at the same time, we found eight more mobile erector launchers in the same location. We are currently attacking those launchers, and we have confirmed the destruction of three more of those mobile erector launchers. We are continuing to attack the others, and, I assure you, we will attack them relentlessly until either we are prevented from attacking them any further by weather or we have destroyed them all.

— Gen. H. Norman Schwarzkopf
CENTCOM briefing
Riyadh, Saudi Arabia
January 18, 1991

In spite of over a hundred claims of destroyed SRBM [short-range ballistic missile] mobile launchers, national intelligence resources did not definitely confirm any of the "kills." . . . The Coalition's inability to permanently degrade SRBM command and control is also significant, despite determined efforts to incapacitate Iraqi military and civilian national networks. Even in the last days of the war, Baghdad retained a sufficient capability to initiate firings from new launch areas and to retarget SRBMs from urban to military and high-value targets, such as the Dimona nuclear reactor.

— Defense Intelligence Agency memorandum
March 1991 (classified "secret")

MAJ. GEN. GIORA ROMM had just come on duty at the Israeli air force's underground command post in Tel Aviv in the early morning hours of January 18 when he received a warning from the Americans. An American satellite had picked up the firing of a Scud missile toward Israel.

Romm ordered that a nationwide alert be sounded. There was a pause. It would be the first time in nearly twenty years that the Israeli government had notified its people that the nation was under attack. Romm repeated the order. Moments later the first of seven Scud missiles struck Israel.

At air bases around Israel, F-16s scrambled into the air. If Scud missiles were heading toward Israel, Iraqi Su-24 fighter-bombers could be as well. The Israelis' radars were showing blips that appeared to indicate Iraqi planes flying toward the Jewish state. Only later would the Israeli military determine that the blips were a false reading.

As the Israeli F-16s patrolled the skies, Romm received a report that a tethered weather balloon had broken loose from its moorings and was drifting east. The Israelis were concerned that the balloon might drift into Jordan and inadvertently draw Amman into the war. Intercepting a weather balloon at night was not easy, but eventually the balloon crashed in Israel on its own. The Israeli military had avoided one misstep, but it had a big problem on its hands.[1]

The Bush administration had urged Israel to stay out of the war. There was no military action the Israelis could take that the Americans were not already engaged in, Washington had argued. There had been no Scud launches on the first night of the war, and the Americans were hoping that this might mean that the heavy air attacks on stationary Scud launch sites in the west — where the terrain was exposed — had been successful in neutralizing Iraq's missile threat.

But now it was clear that CENTCOM had not stopped the Scuds. Israel would have to decide whether to act on its own or give the Americans more time. And the Bush administration would have to decide what it could do to keep Israel out of the war and how it might avoid an unintended collision between Israeli and allied forces if it could not.

The Scud, not the airplane, was Iraq's primary weapon during the air war. CENTCOM's air strikes hindered the Iraqi missile crews, but they never stopped them. Schwarzkopf's failure to develop an effective plan to stop the Scud firings stemmed from faulty intelligence; an exaggerated faith in airpower; CENTCOM's traditional indifference toward Israel, a nation outside the command's area of responsibility; and the commander's skepticism about the utility of special operations forces to track down and destroy the missiles.

Even as the Scuds kept flying, Schwarzkopf regarded them as having little military significance. But a reading of the record does not support that view. The worst American losses in any engagement came when a Scud hit a barracks in a suburb of Dhahran. If one had struck the port of Al Jubail when it was jammed with troops unloading, the results would have been far worse. According to internal Marine Corps records, there was at least one such near miss. If Iraq had mounted chemical warheads on its missiles, even its primitive Scuds could have caused widespread panic among the Saudis and the allied troops sent to protect them.

What is more important, Schwarzkopf missed the point. Saddam Hussein's strategy for responding to the allied attacks was not to try to match his air force against the allies' but to stir up political problems for the coalition by firing Scuds, which was one reason Cheney had supported the Western Excursion. Schwarzkopf's failure to understand this was a persistent source of unhappiness in Washington. Following Schwarzkopf's early ground-war plan, CENTCOM's campaign against the Scuds raised the most doubts about his generalship in Washington.

THE WAR OF THE CITIES

As with many of its other tactics during the Persian Gulf conflict, Iraq's use of Scud missiles had figured prominently in its war with Iran. To try to terrorize the Iranian public, the Iraqis extended the range of their Soviet-supplied Scud-B missiles and fired them at Teheran. The longer-range variants were less accurate and carried a smaller warhead than the Scud-B. They also sometimes broke up upon reentry into the atmosphere. But the Iraqis were not after perfection, they were trying to create a weapon of intimidation.

Between February and April 1988, Iraq fired at least 189 Scuds at Teheran, according to classified American intelligence reports, more than twice the number that it would fire during the Gulf War. Iran responded with its own attacks against Baghdad. The strikes became known as the "war of the cities."

As important as the Scud missiles were to Iraq, however, American intelligence about the weapons was spotty. When Iraq strapped several Scuds together in November 1989 and launched them into space, American intelligence was caught by surprise. The launch went unnoticed until it was proudly announced by Baghdad, which proclaimed, misleadingly, that it had developed a new space rocket.

Shortly before the Gulf War, American intelligence estimated Iraq's inventory of Scud missiles at between three hundred and seven hundred, a huge disparity. Nor did American intelligence agencies know how many of these were the Soviet-supplied Scud-B missiles and how many were longer-range variants.

More important, the Americans had little understanding of how the Iraqis intended to use the weapon. While the Scud was a primitive weapon, the Iraqis' mode of operating it was sophisticated. The Iraqis built twenty-eight concrete launch pads for firing Scud missiles in the western part of their territory, which were within range of all of Israel. But the stationary launchers functioned as a diversion.

While the Americans believed the pads would be Iraq's principal means of attacking Israel, Iraq never used them. The real threat came from mobile launchers. Before the war, American intelligence estimated the number of mobile Scud launchers at thirty-six, twenty-two of which were believed to have been supplied by the Soviets and fourteen of which were thought to have been made by the Iraqis themselves. That was probably an underestimate, although even after the war Washington has been unable to develop a reliable count.[2]

Having studied the Russian military for years, the Americans also assumed it would take the Iraqis hours to set up and launch their Scuds, as was the case with the Soviets. That would give CENTCOM time to attack. But the Iraqis, the Americans soon learned, had practiced how to "shoot and scoot." The Iraqi missile crews would put their Scuds under highway culverts and in other hiding places by day and drive out into the desert at night to previously identified firing sites, fire, and then race away. To further defy detection, the Iraqis avoided the use of radios. They also made use of East German decoys, which were impossible to tell from the real thing from a distance of twenty-five yards.

CENTCOM's plan was to pound the launching pads, bomb the missile production plants, and keep a handful of F-15Es in the air in case the Iraqis popped off a missile from one of their mobile launchers. But as Washington soon began to discover, without good intelligence on where the mobile launchers were, the plan could not work.

When Iraq fired its first salvo of Scuds at Israel, the Pentagon knew it had a big problem on its hands. In the inner councils of the Bush administration, no problem worried officials more than what might happen if Israel entered the war. Given the logic of Middle East politics, the concern had as much to do with Jordan as it had to do with Israel. If Israeli warplanes retaliated, they would have to fly over Jordan or Saudi Arabian territory to get to Iraq. And given the difficulty in eradicating the Scuds, there was no reason to think the Israelis would limit themselves to a single raid.

One of the administration's greatest fears was that an Israeli attack would prompt King Hussein to send his air force to join the fray. With a large Palestinian population, the king had been sympathetic toward Iraq from the beginning. The Pentagon had little respect for the Jordanian monarch. Paul Wolfowitz's Pentagon office was filled with photographs of him and world leaders, and after the Iraqi invasion of Kuwait, his staff turned the picture of him and the king around so that it faced the wall. But the Americans figured that King Hussein was the best they could do. The Pentagon calculated that if the Jordanians entered the war they would be sorely thrashed and the moderate regime of King Hussein might be overturned in the political upheaval that was sure to follow. At bottom, Washington's campaign to stay Israel's hand was an effort to keep King Hussein in power and avoid the nightmare Middle East scenario of a war of all against all.

It was possible, of course, that the Americans had exaggerated the political risks of an Israeli strike, but nobody in Washington wanted to put that assessment to a test. While Schwarzkopf and his generals downplayed the problem of keeping Israel out of the war, there were few things the president and his top aides worried about more.

Almost as soon as word of the Scud attacks reached Washington, Cheney got a call from Moshe Arens, the Israeli defense minister, on the Hammer Rick secure phone line to Jerusalem the Americans had installed. Arens — who had resisted an earlier American offer to ship Patriot ground-to-air missiles and American crews to Israel — urgently asked that they now be shipped. That much Washington could do. But that was not all the Israelis wanted. Arens wanted the United States to make arrangements for an Israeli counterstrike. Washington should give Israel the Identify Friend or Foe (IFF) codes, which would enable the Israelis to determine whether approaching planes belonged to the Iraqis or the allies.

After talking with Arens, Cheney gave his assessment by telephone to Brent Scowcroft, who was huddling with Vice President Quayle, Deputy Secretary of State Lawrence Eagleburger, and Richard Haass, the senior specialist on Middle Eastern affairs on the NSC staff, and other top administration officials in Scowcroft's modest office in the west wing of the White House.

According to the notes taken by a White House participant in the meeting, Cheney said he doubted it would be possible to stop Israel from retaliating. A bad situation would only be made worse if Washington kept trying to stop the Israelis. Nobody wanted Israeli and coalition airplanes to attack each other by mistake. Cheney's assessment provoked consternation. Haass argued that it would be a big mistake to let the Israelis strike back. Saddam Hussein might succeed in splitting the coalition.

As the president's men wrestled with the problem, a report came in that some of the Scud missiles that had landed in Israel carried nerve gas. The room grew quiet. Then Eagleburger broke the silence. If Cheney was not correct before, it looked like he was right now. It would no longer be possible to keep Israel from striking back, Eagleburger said. He predicted that the Israelis would attack with Jericho surface-to-surface missiles, not aircraft.

The president's men discussed how best to minimize Israel's involvement if it could not be dissuaded from attacking. Perhaps the United States could persuade the Israelis to limit their attack to the H-2 and H-3 airfields in western Iraq, the area from which it was believed the Scuds had been launched, instead of going to Baghdad. Or maybe Washington could arrange for Israeli aircraft to cut across Saudi Arabia instead of overflying Jordan, thus avoiding the risk of an Israeli-Jordanian confrontation.

Meanwhile, the president's advisers decided to mount a campaign to persuade the Israelis to hold off and to see how the Arabs might respond if the Israelis did not.

Operating from the White House, the President's men could not use Cheney's Hammer Rick line. Eagleburger tried to place a call to Israeli Prime Minister Yitzak Shamir, but the White House operator could not get a line to Israel. The international telephone lines to Israel were clogged by anxious relatives and friends of Israelis who were calling Israel.

Eagleburger called Zalman Shoval, the Israeli ambassador to Washington, and asked him to relay a message to Jerusalem. The Bush administration was "devastated" by the Scud attacks on Israel. The Israeli military should do nothing; the United States would do it all.

Secretary of State Baker called the Syrian, Egyptian, and Saudi ambassadors. Prince Bandar bin Sultan, the Saudi ambassador, gave no hint of flexibility on Israeli retaliation. Israel should not be allowed to enter the war, Bandar insisted.

Using the Hammer Rick link, Cheney spoke again to Arens. The two defense chiefs agreed that the Bush administration should send a team to Israel to discuss how to cope with the Scud attacks. Arens had not offered a commitment not to attack, but it looked like a way for the administration to buy time. Even so, when Cheney reported on his conversation to the White House, Scowcroft was wary. If a team was sent, it should be a technical team, not a high-level political team, Scowcroft advised. The White House wanted to avoid any impression that Israel was a de facto member of the coalition.

Finally, at 10:40PM EST, Baker got hold of Shamir. By this time, the White House had learned that the early reports were wrong. There was no indication that the Scuds had carried poison gas after all. The Israeli prime minister said that the Scud attacks had not caused widespread deaths and did not mention the Cheney and Arens agreement to send a team of American experts. For the first time, it was clear that the Israelis would restrain themselves for the time being. After a tension-filled evening, Scowcroft and his aides were in almost a festive mood and sent out for burgers and sandwiches.

Cheney was advised not to push his plan for a technical team. Washington would operate on the basis of Baker's call to Shamir, not Cheney's call to Arens. As the White House saw it, there was no sense in cooperating with Israel any more than was absolutely necessary. The evening of frantic phone calls became known in White House lore as "Scud Thursday."[3]

At the Pentagon there was relief, but also concern. If Iraq had managed to fire seven Scuds on the second night of the war despite the bombing raids, there would undoubtedly be more. Cheney was not happy with the way CENTCOM had dealt with the Scuds that night. Schwarzkopf's air-war commanders had assured him that patrols of F-15Es would be airborne and ready to pounce on the Iraqi missile crews the first time a Scud was fired. But there had been no patrol that night; they had aborted their mission after they failed to hook up with their refueling tankers.

Keeping Israel out of the war was a touch-and-go proposition. It was important to keep the heat on. But it was not clear that Schwarzkopf got the message. Each day, CENTCOM sent the JCS a copy of its Air Tasking Order outlining the upcoming air strikes. When Powell's aides saw the Air Tasking Order for January 19, they could see that Cheney's unhappiness with Schwarzkopf was about to escalate. The order did not arrive until 4:30 or 5:00AM, and there was little time to review the plan before the missions were executed that evening, let alone propose changes to it. But the transmission of the Air Tasking Order helped to keep the Pentagon informed of Schwarzkopf's plans.

It was clear that CENTCOM was not making nearly enough of an effort to neutralize the Scuds to satisfy Cheney. The number of strikes on Scud launchers, production sites, and storage facilities — about seventy-five on the second night of the war — had dipped slightly. Only a small portion of these were dedicated to attacking mobile Scud launchers in the west.

Powell was quietly advised there was a problem. The question was could it be straightened out before Cheney concluded that the military was not following the guidance from its civilian masters. Any chance that the issue could be smoothed over evaporated at Cheney's morning briefing. As the military briefer began his presentation, Cheney interrupted with a question: how many sorties was CENTCOM flying against the Scuds?

The defense secretary rarely got angry in public; he was too self-contained and composed for that. Cheney's was a cool, icy, disciplined anger, not a hot, shouting rage. But after the briefer ticked off the modest number of Scud sorties, Cheney erupted. It was the only time during the war that Powell's men had seen Cheney vent his irritation.

"Goddamn it, I want some coverage out there. If I have to talk to Schwarzkopf, I'll do it," Cheney exclaimed, according to one of Powell's aides who attended the session. "As long as I am secretary of defense, the Defense Department will do as I tell them. The number one priority is to keep Israel out of the war."

Powell moved immediately to calm things down. The JCS chairman saw himself as the link between the policy-makers in Washington and the commander in the field. It was his responsibility to see that the military was responsive to the political leaders in Washington. Powell wanted to maintain control. He did not like the idea of Cheney getting on the telephone to upbraid the theater commander. All their aides were ushered out of the room and Cheney continued his meeting with Powell alone.[4]

Later that day, Rear Adm. Mike McConnell, the chief intelligence official for the JCS, called Buster Glosson to give him an alert. A reserved intelligence officer whose earnest manner served him well in Pentagon briefings for the press, McConnell had developed something of a friendship with Glosson during the general's two trips to Washington before the war. During the war, McConnell became indispensable to the Black Hole, providing important intelligence directly to Glosson while the intelligence bureaucracy in Washington and in Riyadh was regularly serving up dated intelligence assessments. In a natural expansion of his role, McConnell also provided political intelligence on what Washington wanted from CENTCOM as well.

McConnell said Washington wanted the Scud-hunting campaign stepped up. At the very least, Glosson needed to keep some American aircraft over western Iraq so that the Israelis could see them on their radars. That would show Jerusalem that the Americans were making a genuine effort. Sure enough, the official word was soon relayed by Lt. Gen. Charles Horner: CENTCOM was being asked to increase its anti-Scud campaign.

Even so, it did not look as if CENTCOM would be able to stop the Scud attacks anytime soon. After another barrage of Scud missiles hit Israel, David Ivri, the director general of the Israeli Defense Ministry, called Wolfowitz, saying Israel was planning an attack.

That weekend, President Bush and his top aides gathered at Camp David to review the bidding. Bush agreed on a two-track plan. Eagleburger and Wolfowitz, it was decided, would make a return trip to Israel to reinforce the message that Israel should stay out of the war. At Cheney's suggestion, Richard Armitage, a former Pentagon official in the Reagan administration, would be dispatched to Amman to meet with King Hussein. Washington needed to prepare Jordan for the possibility that Israel might strike Iraq.

When Eagleburger and Wolfowitz got to Israel, they decided to hold most of their consultations in Tel Aviv, which was being targeted by the Iraqis, rather than Jerusalem, which the Iraqis were deliberating avoiding, so as not to hit their Palestinian supporters on the West Bank. The idea was to show that the Americans were prepared to expose themselves to the same risk as the Israelis. But wherever Eagleburger and Wolfowitz went, the Scuds did not seem to fall.

As the Americans tried to reassure the Israelis that the American military was dealing with the Scuds, they discovered that Schwarzkopf had made their already difficult assignment that much harder. Israel had never been within CENTCOM's area of responsibility, and as a result the command had little appreciation for Israel's concerns and no real contacts in the Israeli military.

As the Scuds kept falling, Schwarzkopf kept telling the press that the Scud was not a militarily significant weapon. In minimizing the Scud problem, Schwarzkopf may have been trying to maintain CENTCOM's image of success and reassure his troops, but his comments were heard loud and clear in Israel as an expression of unconcern. Eagleburger complained to Washington. If Schwarzkopf could not stop the firings, he should at least stop belittling the problem.

Eagleburger and Wolfowitz were no more impressed with the way that CENTCOM was dealing with the Israelis in private. CENTCOM had dispatched a two-star Air Force general to Tel Aviv, Tom Olsen, to keep the Israelis informed on the air campaign, but he shared little with them about the Scud campaign. Some of the Israelis suspected that the Americans were being crafty, but Eagleburger and Wolfowitz concluded that the officer had little knowledge of what CENTCOM was actually doing.

The Israelis had been studying the Scud problem for a long time and had their own thoughts about how to neutralize the Scuds. If Israel was precluded from launching its own attack, the Israelis at least wanted an opportunity to influence the targeting process and suggested installing a liaison officer at CENTCOM, an impossible recommendation given the command's determination to maintain an arm's-length relationship with the Jewish state. Or, the Israelis suggested, an Israeli officer could be placed on board a U.S. Navy ship in the Red Sea to facilitate intelligence sharing and coordinate targeting. That, too, was more than the Americans were prepared to accept.

But after months of spurning Israeli proposals that the two sides cooperate on military planning, the Bush administration agreed to take some steps in this direction. After Eagleburger and Wolfowitz returned to Washington, the Pentagon dispatched Brig. Gen. Malcom B. Armstrong, one of Powell's deputies, to Tel Aviv. The Israelis would submit a target list to Armstrong and he would forward it via the Pentagon to CENTCOM. As the air war progressed, the Israelis nominated an array of targets, suspected Scud sites and hiding places. They proposed hitting culverts, railroad trestles, and bridges, which they thought Iraq was using to bring mobile Scuds into western Iraq. The Israelis also suggested that air strikes be launched against the Iraqi phosphate mines at Al Qaim, describing them as possible hideouts for mobile Scud launchers.[5]

Armitage's meeting with King Hussein was also productive. During the sessions, Armitage and Hussein agreed that if Israeli pilots flew certain attack routes over Jordan there would be little that Jordan could do about it. The understanding was never publicized. With a wink and a nod, the United States had cleared a possible attack corridor for the Israelis that would keep Jordan out of the war. But Washington still hoped it would not have to put that understanding to the test.[6]

Israel and Jordan were not the only countries Washington had to worry about. American intelligence noted unusually high activity by the Chinese technicians at the Saudi Arabian base for CSS-2 missiles, the medium-range missiles Saudi Arabia had bought from China in 1988. In Washington, Prince Bandar told Brent Scowcroft that some of King Fahd's advisers had recommended that the Saudis lob a few CSS-2 missiles at the Iraqis but that the monarch had rejected the idea. The Saudis would maintain the high moral ground. But it was something less than an ironclad promise. King Fahd's policy would be in effect as long as the Americans were making headway in hunting Scuds, the prince advised.[7]

PROBLEMS AT HOME

In Riyadh, the push to step up the Scud campaign did not go down well with Schwarzkopf. What Cheney saw as a necessary intervention to ensure that CENTCOM did not take an overly narrow view of its responsibilities, Schwarzkopf saw as meddling.

When Glosson sent Schwarzkopf a note outlining the next day's Scud-hunting missions to blunt the attacks on Israel, the commander wrote back: "Let's not let them forget that we must also protect our own troops and headquarters (Read: Saudis will go crazy if Scuds fall on Riyadh)."

On another occasion, the commander mused at a staff meeting how Alexander the Great and Napoleon had operated without the sort of interference that he had to endure, drawing a comparison between himself and those military commanders. Not everyone at the session thought the analogy appropriate. Schwarzkopf was not Alexander the Great and this was not a campaign to conquer the world. One of CENTCOM's tasks was holding the coalition together and that meant trying to keep Israel out of the war.

Some steps were taken. More F-15Es were put on airborne alert, and F-16s, equipped with LANTIRN targeting pods, were also sent on Scud-chasing missions. JSTARS radar planes were assigned to try to track mobile Scud launchers.

The Navy, for its part, found the Scud problem a convenient excuse for expanding the role of its submarines, a weapon system that was essentially irrelevant to the desert war. It argued successfully that a plant in northern Iraq that made fuel ingredients for the missiles needed to be destroyed. Then, a submarine in the Mediterranean received permission to fire Tomahawk cruise missiles that flew over Turkey into Iraq to hit the plant.

But there were limits on what Schwarzkopf was prepared to do for the Israelis, or Cheney for that matter. As the Black Hole stepped up the Scud-hunting campaign, Glosson presented Schwarzkopf with a dramatic option: divert all sorties for a massive three-day-long Scud hunt. The planes would hit everything that moved in western Iraq and everything that did not. Meanwhile, coalition aircraft would drop mines on the highway from Amman to Baghdad. Then CENTCOM would get on with the war.

Schwarzkopf rejected the plan out of hand. The commander did not want to shift the focus of the air campaign, even briefly, less than one week into the war. Instead of seeking a decisive victory over the Scud threat, Schwarzkopf wanted only to minimize it.[8]

Nor did CENTCOM take the Israeli target list very seriously. As far as the command was concerned, it was another example of interference. Some of the targets had already been hit, Horner and Glosson argued, and the others were no better than the ones American intelligence had identified. Nonetheless, the commander made sure that enough of the Israeli-nominated targets were hit so that nobody could accuse CENTCOM of ignoring the list.

If that was not good enough for the Israelis and they decided to launch air strikes, Horner had a plan to cope: he planned to pull all coalition planes out of western Iraq and let the Israelis have at it.[9]

Throughout the war, and even afterward, Schwarzkopf and his commanders complained that the Scud-hunting efforts had siphoned away a large number of missions that would otherwise have been directed at other key targets. But CENTCOM's own statistics show that the Scud-hunting effort was relatively modest.

Including attacks on Scud production facilities, about 1,460 strikes were conducted. The rest of the time, the planes launched did not find the Scud targets they were looking for and attacked other targets. The strikes were a small fraction of the 41,310 bombing attacks carried out during the Gulf War.[10]

Not only did CENTCOM exaggerate the magnitude of its effort, but it overstated the results. It was not a conscious act of deception. American pilots were reporting that they had found and destroyed Scuds. But in the rush to persuade the White House and the public that their Scud-hunting campaign was a success, Schwarzkopf and his air-war commanders were too quick to give credence to the "kills" instead of discounting them as the sort of excited report pilots sometimes make in the heat of battle while seeking confirmation from American spy satellites.

During a January 30 press conference, Schwarzkopf told the media that the air campaign had destroyed all of Iraq's twenty-eight fixed launchers. After the war, the Defense Intelligence Agency reported that as many as half of the launchers were never destroyed. And since Iraq never used fixed launchers to fire Scuds, the number of destroyed pads was irrelevant.

Schwarzkopf also showed a cockpit tape at that news briefing that purported to show F-15Es blowing up Scud launchers. As the tape rolled,

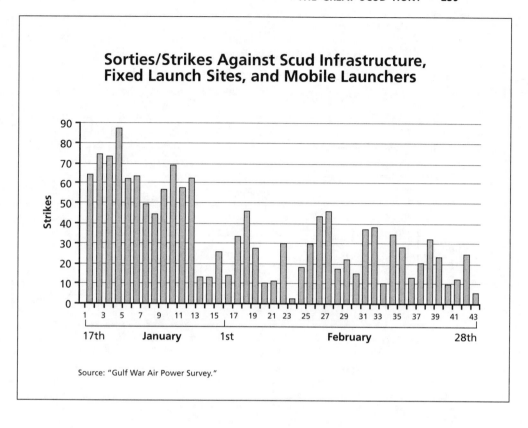

Sorties/Strikes Against Scud Infrastructure, Fixed Launch Sites, and Mobile Launchers

Source: "Gulf War Air Power Survey."

the commander hinted that there was some disagreement among intelligence experts on the nature of the targets destroyed. Later, intelligence analysts established that the F-15Es had blown up fuel trucks.[11]

The difficulty in hunting the Scuds was only part of the problem. The Patriots were having mixed success at best in fending off the Iraqi missile attacks. The Patriot had been designed to defend airfields and ports, not entire cities. More often than not, the Patriot missiles deflected the Scuds, leaving their warheads to fall where they might.

In the final analysis, CENTCOM's failure to snuff out the Scud firings not only threatened to undermine the coalition, it also posed a danger to American troops. In an unpublicized episode, a Scud missile hit the water 130 yards off the port side of the USS *Tarawa* as it docked in Al Jubail to unload its AV-8 Harrier planes. But the missile warhead did not detonate. A Scud missile that landed in Al Khobar, a suburb of Dhahran, on February 25 produced the largest single American casualty toll in the war. It killed twenty-eight troops and wounded ninety-eight others.[12]

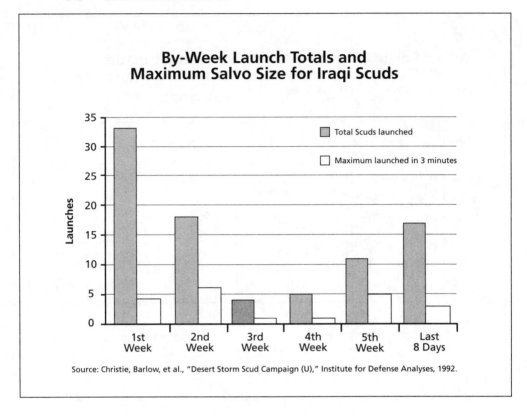

By-Week Launch Totals and Maximum Salvo Size for Iraqi Scuds

Source: Christie, Barlow, et al., "Desert Storm Scud Campaign (U)," Institute for Defense Analyses, 1992.

According to an internal Army report, the risk of even more substantial casualties was greater than generally realized. With the VII Corps deployment from Germany to Saudi Arabia behind schedule, huge numbers of Americans waited for their equipment in crowded camps near the ports at Ad Dammam and Al Jubail. It was not for nothing that the 1st Armored Division dubbed the camps at Al Jubail "the Scud bowl."

"Soldiers were put at risk in the densely packed camps for much longer than they should have been," the VII Corps noted in an internal report. "On the day the war started there were roughly 35,000 soldiers in camp. Security consciousness was high. Local security posed a substantial deterrent to terrorist or enemy special operations forces, and U.S. air defense was effective. However had the enemy possessed the capabilities or will to attack the camps with intensity, the very nature of the deployment could have changed to that of a national disaster. The loss of life that occurred in Beirut in 1983, or in Saudi Arabia in February 1991 from a Scud strike, might have been magnified many fold in the densely packed warehouses, tent camps and high rise apartments of December or January."[13]

In Tampa, Gen. Carl Stiner, the head of the Special Operations Command, watched the trouble CENTCOM was having dealing with the Scuds. With the pressure CENTCOM was under to stop the Scud firings, he figured, he might finally have an opportunity to get his men into the war.

RETURN OF THE "SNAKE EATERS"

A lanky Tennessean who helped engineer the invasion of Panama and whose nickname was "Country Carl," General Stiner had taken charge of the Special Operations Command in Tampa, Florida, before the Gulf crisis. From the start, Stiner was troubled about where special operations stood in CENTCOM's pecking order.

Schwarzkopf assumed his post at CENTCOM with a palpable skepticism of commando operations. American special operations had not been particularly successful in Vietnam, nor did commando teams acquit themselves well in the invasion of Grenada, where Schwarzkopf served as the deputy commander of the American forces. As far as Schwarzkopf was concerned, the "snake eaters" tended to exaggerate and get themselves in trouble.

Following Schwarzkopf's guidance, much of what special forces were doing was essential but noncontroversial. Special operations forces were manning reconnaissance posts along the border. As liaison officers with the Arab armies that had joined the anti-Iraq coalition, they served as CENTCOM's eyes and ears on the status of the allied forces. Special operations forces worked with the Kuwaiti resistance in Saudi Arabia, sending the Kuwaitis north of the Saudi border in bedouin caravans. They were also entrusted with search and rescue missions for downed American pilots. Schwarzkopf had agreed that when the ground war began special operations helicopters would lead Apache helicopters to attack the early warning radars the Iraqis had deployed along their border.

For all this, the Delta Force, Rangers, and other "black world" commandos, as they were known within the military, were forced to take a back seat. During the early part of the American troop buildup in the Gulf, American special operations forces commanded by Maj. Gen. Wayne Downing, the head of the Joint Special Operations Command, planned and trained for Pacific Wind, an operation to rescue the American diplomats who were then in Kuwait City. The complex operation, which was rehearsed at Eglin Air Force Base in Florida, would have used F-117 and F-15E strikes to block key roads, while Downing's commandos swept in and extracted the diplomats from the American Embassy. Schwarzkopf, however, never rated the operation's chance of success very high and breathed an enormous sigh of relief when Iraq freed the diplomats.

Tampa was a long way from Riyadh, but Stiner decided to try to do what he could to expand the role of special operations, as well as his own authority. The institutional position of special operations within CENTCOM was not strong. The commanders of the Army, Air Force, and Marine components were three-star generals, but the senior officer for special operations in the Gulf, Jesse Johnson, was a colonel. Stiner had four stars, and he proposed to join CENTCOM's staff as the senior commander of special forces.

It was not a proposal that attracted support in Riyadh or in Washington. Schwarzkopf did not welcome the idea of other four-stars trying to horn in on the act, but Stiner was persistent. When Schwarzkopf rebuffed Stiner by telling him that the Saudis would not welcome more than one four-star, Stiner offered to wear civilian clothes. Stiner also tried to open the command issue with Powell, but Powell backed Schwarzkopf. The JCS chairman informed Stiner there was room for only one four-star general in Saudi Arabia and Schwarzkopf was it.

Even though they could not get Schwarzkopf to let them set up shop in Saudi Arabia, Stiner and the other special operations generals kept hatching plans. Back at Fort Bragg, North Carolina, where his command was headquartered, Downing planned a number of sensitive "direct action" missions that targeted Iraqi leaders. Downing and his staff developed plans to send commandos into Kuwait City to ambush a convoy carrying the Iraqi chief of the security police, who was Saddam Hussein's half brother. "There was a very serious targeting of the Iraqi leadership in Kuwait City," one senior officer recalled.

Working with the CIA, Downing's team also spent long hours plotting ways to capture Saddam Hussein. They studied his network of palaces and bunkers in Tikrit and Baghdad. "He was very actively targeted," a senior officer remembered. "He proved to be a very tough target."[14]

The plans to attack the Iraqi leadership were presented to Schwarzkopf and Powell, but neither commander favored undertaking commando missions while a diplomatic solution seemed possible and while the Americans were still building up their forces. Provoking the Iraqis, the commanders feared, could prompt Baghdad to take military action before CENTCOM was ready.

"I did not want a bunch of guys running 'rambo-type' operations and have to divert forces from the real war to bail them out. I did not want a hostage situation," Schwarzkopf recalled.[15]

As the war approached, Stiner and Downing argued that the secret antiterrorist Delta Force should be deployed to Saudi Arabia in case the Iraqis launched terrorist operations. Still, Schwarzkopf was dubious. It seemed to him that Stiner and Downing were just looking for an excuse to get their commandos into the theater and eventually into the war. Again, Stiner was rebuffed.

While they were shut out of Saudi Arabia, Stiner and Downing managed to persuade the Pentagon to position their forces overseas so that they could respond if the Iraqis launched terrorist attacks elsewhere.

Special operations commandos were stationed at embassies that seemed to be particularly vulnerable targets and also shadowed suspected Iraqi agents. In addition, thirteen special operations helicopters were secretly deployed to England so that counterterrorism teams could respond to three simultaneous terrorist attacks in Europe or the Middle East.

In one previously undisclosed episode, ill-trained Iraqi agents tried to launch at least two terrorist attacks after the air war began. Iraqi agents in Manila and Jakarta blew themselves up trying to assemble bombs intended to blow up American commercial targets and government buildings, according to a senior American officer. "This told them there was some kind of problem with their equipment, and they were afraid or unable to find people to use it," he added.

But with the special forces barred from crossing the border prior to a war and no provision for using them to hunt Scuds once the war began, there was only a limited number of missions for the commandos.

The difficulty that the American special operations forces encountered with Schwarzkopf stood in marked contrast to the British. The senior British military commander in the Persian Gulf, Sir Peter de la Billière, had a background in commando operations. A veteran of the British Special Air Service, de la Billière lobbied Schwarzkopf to get the SAS into the war, the general argument being they could disrupt Iraqi military operations and provide reconnaissance.

According to de la Billière, winning Schwarzkopf's acquiescence was a protracted process, but as the war approached, the CENTCOM commander finally agreed. Turning down Stiner's brainstorms was one thing, but Schwarzkopf decided he could not afford to reject a request from America's most important military ally in the Gulf.

But the British SAS lacked the high-technology helicopters that the Americans possessed. They launched their Iraqi campaign by driving north from Saudi Arabia; but what they lacked by way of technology, they made up in grit and daring. Still, not even they had planned on hunting Scuds before the air war was launched.[16]

The American special operations forces were painfully aware of the difference in status. But with a little help from the Israelis that would change.

In late January, Moshe Arens, the Israeli defense minister, and Ehud Barak, the chief of staff of the Israeli military, flew to Washington to present their plan to put an end to the Scud threat once and for all. For months, Cheney had heard all sorts of war plans, but this one was different. Israel, Barak explained in a meeting at the Pentagon, wanted the United States' blessing to launch an air and ground operation in western Iraq using Israeli commandos.

The Israelis were not the only ones who were thinking in terms of a land operation to neutralize the Scuds. Henry Rowen, the assistant secretary of defense for international security affairs, who had inspired Cheney's Western Excursion, had also begun to counsel the defense secretary that the only way to put an end to the Scud firings was to go in on the ground.

After Cheney began to inquire about the role that the coalition's special forces might play in hunting the Scuds, he was surprised to learn that the British SAS had been in Iraq since the early part of the war. If British commandos were running around Iraq, why weren't their American counterparts doing the same?

The Bush administration had argued publicly that there was nothing that Israel could do to quell the Scud firings that CENTCOM was not already doing and, hence, no reason for Israel to enter the war. But in fact the Americans were not doing everything they could. They were not sending soldiers into western Iraq to hunt for the elusive Scuds. Only one plan had been considered to send American troops into western Iraq — Cheney's Western Excursion — and Schwarzkopf and Powell had rejected it because it did not contribute to their goal of destroying the Republican Guard.

Now, Israel's threats to take matters in its own hands gave Stiner and his commanders the opening they needed. Cheney was briefed by Downing on his men's Scud-hunting capabilities and gave his wholehearted endorsement. Prodded by the Israelis, Washington belatedly sent American special forces to join the great Scud hunt.

On January 30, Downing led a team of four hundred special forces to Ar'ar, a town in western Saudi Arabia where A-10 Scud-hunting planes and some of Jesse Johnson's search and rescue helicopters were also based. Downing and his men had only just arrived at the isolated desert base when there was a huge explosion, which sent the commandos scrambling. Some of the soldiers thought the base had been hit by a Scud missile, but it later turned out that a HARM antiradiation missile fired by an FA-18 had homed in on a radio navigation beacon at the airfield, which had been turned on to help guide the C-141s flying the commandos. It was not an auspicious welcome to the war.

The Americans and the British divided up the terrain. Equipped with helicopters with sophisticated navigational and targeting equipment, the Americans took the area near Al Qaim, including the stretch of highway between Baghdad and Amman. The British continued to operate in an area closer to the border.

The British had learned a few lessons about operating in Iraq the hard way and passed them on to the Americans. One tough lesson was just how cold the desert could get at night. The British commandos had worn a light set of clothes and some had died of hypothermia. There were also lots of bedouins in the desert, and the British had warned that hiding from them would not be easy.

The first American mission was not launched until February 7, when a team began a four-day-long hunt for Scuds. Over the next three weeks, the special operations forces conducted ground and aerial reconnaissance for Scuds, using specially equipped dune buggies inserted deep in Iraq by teams of Pave Low and Chinook helicopters and Hughes 500 helicopters that could be folded up and hidden during the day.

During the first mission, UH-60 helicopters operating 120 miles deep in Iraq reported blowing up three Scuds. After being briefed on the results, Downing was ecstatic, but intelligence analysts later determined the missiles were decoys.

The missions had their risks. On one occasion, a team of Delta Force commandos who were patrolling with vehicles stumbled into a group of Iraqis, and a couple of the commandos were wounded. A UH-60 helicopter that was sent to rescue the Delta Force team managed to navigate through the bad weather by following a Pave Low helicopter, only to crash while trying to land at Ar'ar, killing all aboard.

Some of the operations are still wrapped in secrecy. At a special operations base at Al Jouf, several Soviet-made Mi-8 Hip helicopters, with Iraqi markings, were kept under camouflage tarps.

After the war, the special operations forces initially reported that they had destroyed seven Scuds and called in air strikes on others. All told, according to classified testimony to Congress, they claimed a dozen kills.[17]

Only later would they concede that most, if not all, of their kills were decoys. Several years after the war, special operations officers still insisted that one Scud has been blown up by a helicopter. In another case, a team of commandos had called in air strikes by F-15Es, killing two or more Scuds, special operations officials asserted. But neither the CIA nor the DIA could verify those claims.

The commandos, however, were more successful in harassing the Iraqis. The commandos had the Air Force drop Gator mines in suspected Scud operating areas. They also discovered some of the sites the Iraqis were using to launch their mobile missiles and cut the cables that had been installed for firing the weapons. "We did make a difference," said Downing. "Scud launches were suppressed after we went in."[18]

Schwarzkopf's concern that special operations might take on unnecessary missions in order to have a piece of the action, however, was not without foundation. CENTCOM rejected Downing's proposal for a commando raid against an Iraqi terrorist training camp south of Baghdad.

But as the Scud hunt continued, Downing developed a plan for a secret Ranger mission. It was to be the first and only Army Ranger mission of the war. Escorted by F-15E Strike Eagles, the Rangers would be transported by helicopter to an Iraqi communications site near the Jordanian border. The F-15E would strike the neighboring antiaircraft artillery sites so that the helicopters could fly in unmolested. Then two teams of Rangers would land, take control of the radar site, and capture Iraqi prisoners.

When Glosson learned of the mission, he was dismissive. If CENTCOM wanted the site taken out, there was an easier and safer way to do it. Why have F-15Es escort the Rangers when the Strike Eagles could simply bomb the facility? But the commandos argued that bombing would not work; the Rangers wanted to exploit the mission for intelligence purposes. They would bring back captured documents that would show how the Iraqis were communicating with a secret network of agents in Jordan.

The mission did not go down as planned. The F-15E attacks on the triple A sites alerted the Iraqis and enabled them to escape. No Iraqis were captured or important documents retrieved. But at least there were no American casualties. The entire episode was confined to the classified annals of the conflict, but Downing had gotten the Rangers into the war.

After the war, the elusiveness of the Iraqi Scud threat became apparent. According to American intelligence, there is no proof that

CENTCOM succeeded in destroying a single Scud. Nor did the allies sever all of the command and control links to the Scud teams.

Still, the combination of air strikes and commando raids helped slow the rate of fire and forced the Iraqis to find new launch sites and new targets. Schwarzkopf's failure to make ground forces an integral part of the anti-Scud campaign from the beginning was a significant gap in CENTCOM's plan.

The Defense Intelligence Agency determined that the Iraqi Scud campaign could be broken into three phases. The first two weeks of the war was the active period. Between January 18 and January 27, Iraq launched twenty-five Scuds at Israel and twenty-four against Saudi Arabian and Persian Gulf targets.

From January 28 to February 10, as the air strikes and American and British special operations harassed the Iraqi crews, there were five launches against Israel and three against Gulf targets.

From February 11 to February 25, the firing picked up again as the Iraqis adjusted to CENTCOM's tactics. There were ten launches against Israel and nineteen against Saudi Arabia during this period. To elude attack, Iraq fired its Scuds from sites deeper in Iraq, and it changed many of its targets. Instead of aiming most of its missiles at Tel Aviv, Haifa, Riyadh, and Dhahran, it began to fire them at Hafar al-Batin, King Khalid Military City, and Israel's Dimona nuclear reactor.

"In spite of over a hundred claims of destroyed SRBM [short-range ballistic missile] mobile launchers, national intelligence resources did not definitely confirm any of the 'kills.' However, irregular SRBM launch patterns after 28 January indicated that the air campaign had an effect," the DIA stated.

"The threat of a Coalition air attack most likely reduced Iraq's opportunities to employ several mobile launchers for near simultaneous firing of multiple missiles, a method that could have increased damage and saturated Patriot defenses. The command and communication network supporting Iraqi SRBMs also may have suffered from the air campaign; but, the ability to change and retarget missile launch locations up to the end of the war suggests that such degradation was minimal," according to the classified DIA report.[19]

In what should surely be a cautionary note for the Pentagon's efforts to respond to the spread of ballistic missiles throughout the third world, a primitive rocket had come closer than anyone dared suppose to endangering the coalition and altering the course of the war.

Still, the Americans had made just enough of an effort to keep the Israelis out of the war. Washington had dodged a bullet. But Iraq had other tactics it would try to stir up problems for the coalition. It could capture allied pilots and display them to the world, just as North Vietnam had done twenty years earlier. And there was always the possibility of rattling the Saudis by launching air attacks against Saudi Arabia's oil complex.

12

With Friends Like These

*Syrian intransigence on over-flight delayed any effort at least 2 days.
Had they been amenable, search aircraft would have at least been
launched to Syrian airspace on night two to attempt to fix 03's position
and initiate a possible rescue effort.*

— Pentagon after-action report

L
T. GEN. CHARLES HORNER knew going into the war that he
was going to lose some pilots. But for political as much as military
reasons, CENTCOM needed to minimize the risks. Every dead
pilot was another debating point in Iraq's campaign to turn Americans
against the war. And every captured pilot was a potential POW that
Baghdad could parade across the television screen.

From Vietnam to Lebanon, the capture of American fighting men
had inflamed the public debate over war and peace. Hanoi used American prisoners as bargaining chips in its negotiations with the Nixon administration. Iran's seizure of American hostages helped destroy the
Carter administration. Syria's capture of an American pilot attacking a
pro-Syrian Lebanese faction — and his release to Jesse Jackson —
helped dissuade the Reagan administration from further military strikes
in Lebanon in 1983. Following the Gulf War, a Somalia warlord would
use the capture of an American helicopter pilot to hasten the withdrawal
of American forces from that East African nation. Seizing prisoners was
a more effective tactic than the American military liked to acknowledge,
providing the enemy had the time to mobilize public opposition and had

not been demonized to the point where the public was prepared to see the war through whatever the cost.

To hold down casualties, Horner and Glosson had mandated that most bombing raids be conducted at medium altitude, out of range of Iraq's antiaircraft guns. The special operations forces also developed an intricate plan to rescue the downed pilots before the Iraqis got hold of them. Warden had estimated that more than a hundred planes might be shot down, while Glosson had put the number at forty to fifty. Either way, CENTCOM wanted to ensure that as many pilots could be rescued as possible.

After some resistance from Saudi officials apprehensive about the intrusion of Americans in the Saudi desert, a system of special operations bases was established across the northern Saudi border. Merrill McPeak, the Air Force chief of staff, was worried that the search and rescue teams might take too many risks and themselves become casualties. "I don't want to trade three for one," he observed at one briefing. "We have plenty of pilots."[1] The search and rescue teams thought they could do the job, but the task was more complicated than it seemed.

Like transport ships and mine warfare, search and rescue was one of those essential but unglamorous areas that the military had neglected for years. One big problem was communications. A downed airman's radio was an absolutely critical piece of gear for a successful rescue.

According to their procedures for combat rescues, special operations forces had to make voice contact with the downed pilot to determine his location and confirm his identity. During the Vietnam War, the enemy had faked rescue calls to lure American search teams into a trap, and during the Gulf War the Iraqis tried the same tactic. The American special operations forces were determined to avoid an Iraqi ambush. But there was a mismatch between the communications gear used by the rescuers and the airmen flying the combat missions over Iraq.

Special operations teams had sophisticated PRC-112 radios that sent out encoded communications in a burst, thereby making it all but impossible for the enemy to decipher and perform "DF," that is, "direction finding" using electronic gear that pinpoint the source of a transmission. But the pilots of Air Force warplanes had the much more primitive PRC-90 radios, whose transmissions could be readily intercepted and "DF'd" by the Iraqis. The Air Force had spent billions on the B-2 bomber and MX missiles. It was going to war with laser-guided precision munitions. But it had never made the investment to replace the Vietnam War–vintage PRC-90 radios.

The irony was that the pilot's only link to his potential rescuers also gave away his position to the enemy. Sending out distress calls on the radio was like shooting a starting gun in a race. American special forces and the Iraqis were the contestants. The pilots were the prize.

The politics of the coalition was an issue as well. Iraq is a large country, and American warplanes planned to strike virtually every part of it. To conduct rescue missions, bases needed to be set up around the periphery of the enemy's territory, which was bounded by Saudi Arabia, Jordan, Syria, Turkey, Iran, and Kuwait. Setting up rescue bases in western Saudi Arabia, of course, was not a problem. But bases in Jordan were out of the question. Pilots were advised that there was a substantial risk that Jordanian soldiers near the border might turn downed Americans over to Iraqi authorities and that they might be attacked by Palestinian civilians.

Later, according to a classified Air Force report, there were intentional efforts to jam the search and rescue radio frequencies used by the coalition forces from eastern Jordan, which was "100 percent effective in obliterating all voice communications." The Air Force concluded that the jamming came from a truck that belonged to a Jordanian armored brigade in the eastern part of Jordan.[2]

According to classified guidance to the pilots, the Iranian government offered a secret assurance that it would assist Americans who escaped into its territory, although the Iranians suggested they would hold them until the end of hostilities. But with more than a decade of hostility between Teheran and Washington, no one at CENTCOM wanted to put their trust in the Iranians. And it was not reassuring that CENTCOM occasionally received intelligence reports that the Iranians had fired missiles at allied planes.[3]

Turkey was on board. In all, five Pave Low helicopters, as well as several C-130 refueling planes, were based at the huge American air base at Incirlik and at Batman in western Turkey. The rescue forces had the responsibility for picking up American pilots shot down in the northern part of Iraq, specifically north of 33 degrees, 30 minutes north.

But Turkey's assent was only part of what the special operations forces needed. To conduct the rescues, the special operations forces based at Batman would have to fly over a strip of Syrian territory. It was the fastest and safest way to go, reducing the exposure of the American rescue crews to Iraqi antiaircraft guns and missiles.

From the start, Syria's involvement was more a political than a military requirement. The Bush administration's effort to upgrade relations with Damascus began well before the war, as Washington opened a dialogue over Syria's involvement in Lebanon, the Middle East peace process, and the emigration of Syrian Jews. When Washington began to assemble a defensive force for Saudi Arabia after the Iraqi invasion of Kuwait, the Bush administration wanted to include as many Arab states as possible to demonstrate that the conflict was not between Iraq and the United States but between Baghdad and the world.

Egypt's participation was nailed down when President Bush called President Mubarak and offered to write off Cairo's multibillion-dollar debt to Washington. Both the Egyptians and the Saudis wanted to see the Syrians added to the coalition. Syria was one of the staunchest foes of Israel, and its involvement would insulate Cairo and Riyadh against charges they were doing the bidding of the neo-colonialists in Washington.

Damascus appeared to have something to gain, as well. Hafez al-Assad and Saddam Hussein were bitter enemies; the Saudis, Kuwaitis, and other Gulf states were offering billions of dollars in assistance; and the Americans were offering Syria a new international respectability on the world stage that it had lost because of its support for international terrorism. Further, the Bush administration had held out the lure of a postwar Middle East peace process, in which Syria might press its claims for the return of the Golan Heights, which Israel had captured during the 1967 war. Assad had a dim view of Iraq's military capabilities. During one of his private meetings with Baker, the Syrian president spoke mockingly of Saddam Hussein's bellicose threats to drown the coalition's forces in their own blood, according to aides to the secretary of state. Until you have fought the Israelis, you have not fought a real Middle East war, Assad observed.

But none of this meant that Syria would be a wholehearted member of the coalition. Bush administration officials were heartened when Syria sent two divisions, including the 9th Armored Division, which had been stationed facing the Golan Heights. But that force was sent to help defend Saudi Arabia, and as the war approached, it was far from clear whether the Syrians were willing to go on the offensive, which was important to the White House, as it was determined that the Arab members of the coalition should be the liberators of Kuwait City. After numerous entreaties at the ambassadorial level, and an unusual visit to

Damascus by Baker, it was left to President Bush to press the issue himself, which he did in a November meeting with Assad in Geneva.

Even after Assad had assured Bush that the Syrians were prepared to join the land offensive, however, there was a considerable amount of backsliding. In December, John Warden had told Cheney that the bombing would be so effective that the Arab members of the coalition might be able to liberate Kuwait on their own. But as the war approached, the Syrians got cold feet and CENTCOM cast them in a reserve role. The role of the Syrian army was so minimal, Schwarzkopf recalled, that he met the Syrian commander only one time — for a photo op.

The reluctance of Syria to commit its army to the land offensive had considerable significance for the Arab members of the coalition. With the Syrians hesitant to attack, the Egyptians became apprehensive about their mission to attack into western Kuwait. To ease the Egyptians' concerns, CENTCOM agreed to pare back their mission and delay their attack from G day to the second day of the ground war. That meant that the Egyptians would be hard put to protect the Marines' western flank, but at least it ensured they would be part of the land war.[4]

Syria was no more accommodating when it came to extending overflight rights. Before the war, the Bush administration asked for overflight rights for Navy attack planes based on aircraft carriers in the Mediterranean, Tomahawk cruise missiles fired from the Mediterranean, and search and rescue teams based in Turkey. The response in Damascus had been no to the first two requests and a noncommittal response on the search and rescue operations. There were disputes within the administration over how hard to push the Syrians. The Navy, which had already gone through the laborious process of programming some of its cruise missiles to fly over the swath of eastern Syrian desert south of Turkey, simply ignored Damascus and fired the weapons according to its original plan, according to a senior Navy official.

The arrangements for rescuing pilots in northern Iraq, however, remained uncertain. Syria agreed to grant overflight rights but only on a case-by-case basis. The procedure was potentially very time-consuming: a request had to be made for each planned rescue, and some military officials did not think that would prove practical. Syria argued that the procedure was necessary because it needed time to alert its antiaircraft gunners that the Americans were flying over the eastern slice of its territory so that there would not be any mistakes, but a cabinet-level Bush administration official later derided that argument as an "excuse."

In any event, the cumbersome procedure was not in place at the start of the air war.

"CORVETTE THREE"

All the technological and political problems came home to roost when Col. David W. Eberly took off on the third night of the air war. The deputy director of operations for the F-15E Strike Eagles in the Persian Gulf, Eberly had helped plan the Gulf missions. Two-seat air-to-ground versions of the F-15 fighter, the F-15Es had initially been based in Oman but had been moved to Al Kharj as the war approached so that they would be closer to Iraq. On the first few nights of the air war, F-15Es were sent after Iraq's fixed Scud launchers in the west in the vicinity of the heavily defended H-3 airfield, close to the border with Jordan and Syria, which was where Eberly was headed on his January 19 flight.

Eberly's mission appeared to be jinxed from the start. He had not been scheduled to go on the mission and bumped another pilot to go, which meant that he had to borrow another pilot's gear and fly with an unfamiliar squadron. When it came time to refuel enroute to his targets, Eberly told his Air Force debriefers after the war, the operation was "a goat rope at best."

When the war started, none of the F-15Es had been equipped with the special targeting pods that would enable them to do precision bombing, so Eberly was tasked to drop dumb bombs on three targets. Using its infrared radar, the F-15E's computer equipment would produce a map of the target on a cockpit display before the plane approached the area.

Eberly was about eight miles from the target when his radar warning receiver — the alarm that alerted pilots when they were being tracked by surface-to-air missile radars — sounded a "two-bar." The alarm sounded like a German ambulance siren; it was a terrifying sound for any pilot.

Looking over his right shoulder, Eberly saw an orangish object racing toward his plane from the ground. Then Maj. Thomas E. Griffith, his crew partner, saw a second orange spear rising through the sky.

Eberly made a hard right turn, called a "break turn," to evade the SAMs and the target came off his display. After dodging the missiles, Eberly was rolling left to get back on course to his target, when a third missile slammed into his plane. It felt, Eberly later recalled, like the worst car wreck in the world. Immediately after pulling the eject lever, Eberly blacked out.

Like many pilots, Eberly had dealt with the fear of being shot down through denial. He had been too busy before the war to take a refresher course in desert survival and escape techniques. And as he recovered from his blackout, Eberly was operating on instinct. Wrapping his parachute around his body for warmth, Eberly was sitting on the ground when the sound of a truck engine broke the still of the desert night. There were not too many good places to hide in the desert, but Eberly noticed an electrical tower about fifty feet away. He raced to hide himself behind the base of the tower before the Iraqi truck came over the rise. Crouching, Eberly could see the truck pull up, pause, and then leave. If the Iraqis were looking for him, it would not make good sense to hang around and wait to be captured. Eberly decided to head southwest, away from the Scud sites targeted by the F-15Es.

As he made his way south, Eberly turned on his PRC-90 radio, which he knew had to be used selectively so that he would not make himself a target for the Iraqis. As a security precaution, the pilot's call signs were changed for each sortie. Still suffering from the shock of being shot down, Eberly initially used a call sign from a previous mission: "Chevy." But then he caught himself and used his current call sign: "Corvette Three." There was no sign of a rescue attempt. But after walking south, Eberly used his radio to link up with Griffith, and the two airmen climbed onto a hill and settled in for the night. It looked like a good spot to get picked up if a rescue effort was mounted, and there was a small depression on the top of it, which would allow them to hide from the Iraqis during the daylight.[5]

Back at Horner's headquarters, the Tactical Air Control Center in Riyadh, word circulated quickly that "Corvette Three" had failed to show up for its scheduled rendezvous with a refueling tanker. But Eberly was not the only problem that weighed on Horner's mind.

The air-war commanders soon discovered that they had even bigger worries. Emboldened by their success on the first day of the war, Horner and Glosson figured they had done enough damage to Iraq's air defense that it was safe to dispatch nonstealthy bombers against targets in a "strike package" against Baghdad. This would enable the coalition to drop more bombs against targets around the Iraqi capital and keep the heat on during the daylight hours.

A strike package was the virtual antithesis of the F-117 raids. The support the F-117s had received from the Ravens in the opening attack was modest indeed, compared with a strike package, where dozens of bombers, electronic warfare planes, and fighter escorts were massed to bull their way into enemy territory. It was the difference between a rapier thrust and swinging a sledgehammer. The strike package included more than seventy F-16s, as well as F-15 escorts, EF-111 jamming aircraft, and F-4G Wild Weasel HARM-missile shooters.

Most of the planes would strike Tuwaitha, the nuclear research facility on the outskirts of the Iraqi capital. Protected by sand berms and batteries of SAMs and antiaircraft guns, Tuwaitha was considered to be the most heavily defended facility in Iraq. Several F-117s had already been dispatched to attack the nuclear research center and had bombed the reactors and a laboratory there. But Horner was determined to level the installation. The F-16s were to deliver a crippling blow. Some of the F-16s had also been assigned targets in Baghdad. The Iraqi Air Force headquarters had been repeatedly hit. While there was every likelihood that the building had been gutted inside, it was still standing. They were also assigned to hit the Republican Guard headquarters and an oil refinery on the outskirts of the city.

As the strike package headed north, Iraqi antiaircraft fire disrupted the formation. About a quarter of the planes broke off and, unable to rejoin their comrades, returned home.

As the F-16s approached Tuwaitha, it was clear that the Iraqis were trying to make a stand. Tuwaitha was surrounded by sand berms and the Iraqis had put out smoke pots, which sent up billowing clouds of haze. Then the Iraqis let loose with a withering barrage, firing antiaircraft guns. Twenty-seven SAMs were launched in the first three minutes.

The F-4Gs began firing back, launching their HARM antiradiation missiles. But with the smoke and bad weather, many of the F-16s could not identify their target. To avoid collateral damage, many did not drop their bombs.

As the rest of the F-16s headed toward their targets in Baghdad, the formation shrank. The F-4Gs had expended all their antiradiation missiles on the surface-to-air missile sites in and around Tuwaitha and they and the EF-111s turned away from Baghdad. The F-16s went into Baghdad on their own. The Kari system was disrupted, but the Iraqis used SAM batteries to set up a trap. As the F-16s flew by, the Iraqis fired their SA-6 and SA-3 missiles. Two F-16s were shot down and the pilots were captured.

In Riyadh, the episode was not regarded as one of the Air Force's finest moments. For all the planning that went into knocking out Kari, the Iraqi air defense system turned out to be more resilient than the air-war planners had anticipated. While American planes pounded the main Kari command posts, the Iraqis were able to put some back into operation, and use some SAM radars and batteries to maintain small pockets of their air defense system.

"Communications between Kari nodes proved harder to sever than anticipated, and some connectivity seems to have persisted through the end of the war," according to the "Gulf War Air Power Survey," a study commissioned by Air Force Secretary Donald Rice. "Granted, as more and more reporting posts, early warning radars and other sensor elements of Kari were eliminated, the operational utility of the system's residual capacity to pass tracking information on Coalition strike packages became less and less. Nevertheless, in Iraqi hands Kari exhibited an ability to regenerate portions of itself — despite the paralyzing shocks sustained during the first two Air Tasking Order days of the air campaign."

It was tough enough for a nonstealthy plane to operate over Baghdad with its antiaircraft defense escorts, but sending F-16s to Baghdad without any protection from the HARM shooters was tempting the fates. The F-16s wanted to go back, but Glosson and the air-war planners decided that it was the last time that nonstealthy aircraft would be sent on a bombing mission over Baghdad. Even a diminished air defense system could take its toll. Glosson sent out an order that, with the exception of F-15C air-to-air fighters, no nonstealthy aircraft were to go within thirty miles of Baghdad without explicit approval.[6]

The Americans were not the only ones having trouble. The British were also beginning to reconsider their bombing raids against Iraqi airfields.

Slung under the belly of each British Tornado bomber was the JP-233, a large cannister that dispensed hundreds of small bomblets. The bombs were released when the planes were streaking across the runways at low altitude, but that tactic meant the planes had to fly through walls of triple A.

To try to hold down their losses, the British experimented with a series of new tactics. On one occasion, J. A. Broadbent, a Tornado wing commander, devised a plan to stun the Iraqis so that the low-flying planes could drop their bombs and get out unscathed.

Under Broadbent's plan, two Tornados would drop their bombs. Then twenty seconds later, four Tornardos would each loft eight 1,000-pound bombs, which would explode in airbursts 100 feet off the ground, to shell-shock the Iraqis. Then forty seconds later, another pair of Tornados would rush across the airfield dispensing their bombs. For further insurance, the attack would be protected by American F-4Gs and EA-6B jammers.

The mission did not go as planned. As Broadbent's flight reached its target, an F-4G fired a HARM antiradiation missile at a radar, which tipped off the Iraqis that an attack was under way. After Broadbent and his wingman dropped their bombs, the lofters came in. But their maneuver took them closer to the target than they anticipated and was disorienting. The pilots were turned upside down with the flak coming up at them.

Broadbent finally prepared a memorandum for his superiors suggesting that they abandon the risky low-level Tornado attacks. The Iraqi air force did not appear to be flying. The risk was no longer worth the gain.[7]

The runway-busting missions were canceled, but six Tornados were lost. One crew was shot down on the first morning in a daylight attack; another flew into the ground. A third crashed while trying the lofting maneuver. A fourth was hit by a Roland missile while pulling up for a lofting attack. Two were also destroyed while flying at medium altitude.

After the war, the British air force argued long and hard that there was nothing wrong with the JP-233 system. But there was everything wrong with the tactics that were required to employ it.

Now, on top of the F-16 fiasco in Baghdad and the British casualties, Horner had to worry about the effectiveness of his search and rescue procedures. Eberly and Griffith were presumed lost, but western Iraq was a huge area and a rescue mission could not be launched until the airmen were located and their identities confirmed. CENTCOM also contacted the Syrians to get permission for overflight in case the crew was found, but the response was not encouraging. The Syrians took the request on board, but it was slow going. If there was going to be a rescue effort, it would have to wait another day.

On their second night in Iraq, Eberly and Griffith were waiting in their hilltop hideout for a message from a search and rescue team when they finally heard a friendly communication: "Chevy 54" was looking for "Corvette Three." The query had come from F-15Es on a bombing run.

"Let's get on with it," Eberly quickly radioed back.

Eberly spent the rest of the night with the radio's earpiece lodged in his ear but heard nothing. He had no idea if his response had been picked up or not. But Eberly's response had gotten through to the warplanes, and for the search teams in Saudi Arabia, it was what they needed to prepare the rescue mission. Finally, the special operations forces had a general fix on the airmen's position and had verified their identity.

The plan was clear. Eberly had gone down right near Syria. A Pave Low helicopter with HC-130 refueling tankers would take off from Batman in Turkey, fly over Syria, snatch the airmen, and get out of Iraq quick. The Batman base was put on alert, as special operations waited for overflight clearance from the Syrians. But there was no response. The alternative to launching a mission from Batman was to undertake a long and dangerous rescue mission from Ar'ar in western Saudi Arabia, which risked losing the search and rescue helicopter to Iraqi air defenses. The decision was made to give the Syrians another day to grant the clearance. As in every shoot-down, time was against Eberly and Griffith. But they would just have to tough it out.

As Eberly prepared for his third night in Iraq, he began to question his initial decision to wait for a search and rescue team. With radio contact limited to a single communication with the F-15Es, Eberly had no confirmation that a rescue mission had been launched.

The desert nights were so cold that Eberly could see his breath, and the two airmen had not eaten since they were shot down and had little water. The back of Eberly's neck was cut during the ejection and his ankles were bruised by the landing. Perhaps he and Griffith could commandeer a military vehicle and drive across the border, Eberly thought. But neither of the airmen spoke Arabic. How would they get through the border crossing? Walking hundreds of miles south to Saudi Arabia was out of the question. The only real alternative, Eberly figured, was to try to walk across an unguarded section of the Iraq-Syria border, which he estimated to be about eight miles away.

As Eberly was hatching escape plans, CENTCOM's rescue efforts were becoming confused. Three days after the shoot-down of Corvette Three, Syria had still not given the clearance for overflight. A Syrian liaison officer in Riyadh had suggested that Damascus might undertake the rescue. And word reached CENTCOM through American intelligence channels that "operatives" in Syria would carry out the rescue. Further clouding the picture, a bedouin had turned up at the American embassy in Amman, Jordan, with a "blood chit" from Corvette Three, according to one report. The report indicated that the bedouin was offering to trade the American aircrew for a Toyota pickup truck.

Meanwhile, American warplanes flying over western Iraq continued to receive garbled messages from Corvette Three but could not recognize Eberly's or Griffith's voice. The unsecure PRC-90 radios had thrown a monkey wrench into the rescue effort. Perhaps the Iraqis had heard Eberly's initial transmission and were imitating it, trying to ensnare the search and rescue teams. No one at CENTCOM was sure what to do, and the rescue effort went into a holding pattern just as Eberly's situation was becoming increasingly desperate.

Shortly before leaving their hiding place on their third night in Iraq, Eberly heard on the radio that a rescue mission was on for a downed Navy pilot and tried to contact the search and rescue team. But again he received no acknowledgment. Eberly figured that they would have to try to make it out on their own. The airmen tried to fashion Arab-looking garb out of their parachutes, stuffing the remains of the chutes into their flight suits for insulation against the cold. After sunset on January 22, they started walking, aiming for Abu Kamal, a Syrian border town.

As they walked through the desert, past large black bedouin tents, about a dozen fierce dogs suddenly raced out, barking and baring their teeth. Some downed airmen had been captured at gunpoint by tribes of bedouin, but no one came out of the tents. As far as Eberly knew, they were undetected.

A short time later, they were walking down a dirt road when a truck came roaring toward them. The airmen ran about twenty yards off the road and flung themselves to the ground, certain that they had acted too late. Again, there was no sign that they had been seen. Perhaps luck was with them after all.

As they approached the Syrian border, Griffith began to check the radio again. There was no sense taking on Iraqi border guards if a rescue effort was finally under way. Suddenly, a call came through.

"Mobile 41 looking for Corvette Three. What is your condition?"

They responded to the call, which had come from a combat plane. But again there was no answer. The airmen decided to rest and wait to see if there were any other messages. During the hour and a half they waited, lying in the desert scrub, the wind picked up and the chilly evening air seemed even colder. At last they decided to backtrack and take shelter in a building they had seen along the way. As Eberly approached, the building was dark and there were no signs of life. It was not much of a refuge, but at least they could get out of the cold for a while.

The colonel looked in one of the windows. Suddenly, the seemingly abandoned building exploded into activity. A dozen soldiers poured out of the structure, firing their AK-47s all around Eberly and Griffith. The soldiers appeared nervous and scared and clearly were not trying to hit the airmen. It was like standing in the middle of a room with firecrackers being set off all around, Eberly thought. The soldiers took the airmen inside and starting chanting: "Iraq. Syria. Iraq. Syria."

It was clear they were near the border, and Eberly thought they might have made it to Syria after all. But then he looked up and saw a picture of Saddam Hussein.[8]

CENTCOM, meanwhile, had begun to question the reports about "operatives" effecting the rescue. Combat planes had continued to pick up distress calls from "Corvette Three." Finally, a command decision was made: if Syria did not give overflight clearance for January 23, a rescue mission would be attempted from Saudi Arabia.

On the night of January 23, two Pave Lows and an HC-130 tanker stood on alert at Batman, waiting for the clearance from the Syrians. As the hours ticked by, the rescue team lost patience. For days, an American aircrew had been stranded in Iraq while the diplomats at the State Department had tried to win approval from a coalition member to save them. Nothing had happened. There were rules and procedures to be followed, but this was war.

The rescue team was launched without waiting for Syrian approval, which eventually came that night as they were in flight. The Pave Lows landed near the border and tried to contact Eberly on the nonsecure channels used by the PRC-90. There was no answer from the Americans, but every time the helicopers sent out a message, Iraqi antiaircraft fire ripped into the sky. The Iraqi gunners were listening to the broadcasts, too, and assumed that the radio broadcasts were coming from a loitering aircraft.

Eberly and Griffith spent most of the war in brick prison cells at the Baghdad headquarters of the Iraqi Intelligence Service, kept in isolation, maintained on a starvation diet, and subjected to physical abuse. On February 23, the headquarters was hit by 2,000-pound bombs dropped by F-117s, sending a thunderous roar through the cells and cracking their prison wide open. Almost miraculously, none of the coalition prisoners were killed in the raid, and they were soon repatriated.

After the Eberly affair, CENTCOM tried to improve its search and rescue procedures. Maj. Gen. John A. Corder sent a secret memo to the Pentagon:

1. Intelligence reports indicate that Iraqi forces are aggressively pursuing downed pilots and are homing in on the two guard frequencies used by downed airmen. This has made it increasingly difficult for our downed airmen to remain concealed and still communicate their position and condition to SAR [search and rescue] forces without being captured.

2. We desperately need a system that will give downed aircrews a selec-

tion of frequencies and a means of transmitting their position accurately without alerting enemy forces. I understand the PRC 112 survival radio and the compatible AN/ARS receivers will fill this void. I am aware that some SOF [special operations forces], Army and Navy units already have limited numbers of the PRC 112's and that a few SOF and Navy helos have been modified to receive the PRC 112's signal.

3. It would greatly enhance our rescue capability if all of our combat rescue helos in theater had this equipment installed and our aircrew had the compatible PRC 112. I am aware the modification program has already been funded and the aircraft can be fitted in the field. I also understand that roughly 1000 PRC 112 have been acquired (primarily by SOF). To be of maximum benefit in recovery operations, it is essential this limited stockpile of radios be temporarily distributed on a proportional basis to all high risk strike assets until more units become available. These modifications would greatly assist recovering our aircrews.[9]

In Feburary, some six hundred PRC-112 radios were transferred from special operations forces to the Air Force. There was no time to fully train the Air Force pilots on how to use the radio, and with the coalition flying some two thousand sorties a day over Iraq, there were not enough to go around. But it was better than nothing. Nonetheless, search and rescue remained an uphill battle. The search and rescue teams demonstrated great courage under difficult circumstances. The statistics in Air Force after-action reports, however, spoke for themselves. Thirty-five aircraft were lost in the war, leading to the downing of sixty-four airmen. Only nine of the sixty-four were on the ground longer than thirty minutes without being captured. Most that survived were picked up within two minutes of landing. Only four airmen were rescued by the special operations forces.

A Pentagon review of the rescue attempt for Corvette Three faulted the inferior radio equipment used by Air Force pilots, the misleading assurances from the intelligence community, about "operatives," and the lack of cooperation by the Syrians.

Complicating the entire effort were unreliable intel inputs. There was never an accurate position fix and only one radio call was ever received authenticating 03's status (on night 2). This is a result of no reliable, secure, radio/position locating device issued to aircrew or compatible aircraft mounted locating equipment with any range and accuracy.

Syrian intransigence on over-flight delayed any effort at least 2 days. Had they been amenable, search aircraft would have at least been launched to Syrian airspace on night two to attempt to fix 03's position and initiate a possible rescue effort.[10]

For search and rescue missions, where a downed pilot's ability to elude his Iraqi captors was often measured in hours, the two-day delay was critical, and made Eberly's apprehension all but certain. But the complaints about the Syrians were never officially aired. Indeed, the Pentagon's report "The Conduct of the Persian Gulf War," presented to Congress as an authoritative account of the lessons learned from the conflict, nowhere refers to the Eberly affair; nor does it acknowledge that a rescue was attempted from Turkey.

Syria might be an uncertain ally, but during the war the Bush administration decided that it needed as many Arab members of the coalition as possible. After the war, the administration had other reasons not to offend Damascus: its decision to put together a Middle East peace conference. American military officers who were unhappy with the role that Syria had played would have to keep their complaints under wraps.

GOING FOR BROKE

By late January, the Iraqis were in a fix. The Scuds they had fired at Israel had failed to provoke an Israeli attack. A few allied warplanes had been downed and their pilots captured, but the losses were not nearly large enough to provoke a public reaction against the war. The allies had begun to pound the Iraqi warplanes that had taken refuge in their hardened shelters, slowly decimating the Iraqi air force. Worse, there was no ground war in sight.

With its back against the wall, the Iraqi air force gambled by launching a potential headline-making attack against Saudi Arabia to make the costs of war visible to King Fahd. The January 24 Iraqi raid had all the earmarks of a well-planned operation, including a deception plan aimed at spoofing the American AWACS planes that monitored airspace in southern Iraq from the point of takeoff. The operation began when two Iraqi aerial refueling tankers left the Shuaiba airfield in southern Iraq and flew southeast of Tallil, where they met up with four Mirage F-1s. The aircraft flew together. But as the formation turned north, two of the Mirages broke away and fell in trail of an exiting American strike package, flying 10,000 feet below the Americans at their dead six o'clock. It was evident that the Iraqis had closely studied the American exit routes and were trying to make it look as if they were friendly planes returning from an attack in Iraq.

What the Iraqis could not have hoped to count on was the problem the Air Force and Navy would have in operating together. To protect its Persian Gulf fleet, the Navy kept aloft a Navy E-2C Hawkeye radar surveillance plane. Also scanning the skies was the USS *Bunker Hill,* a $1 billion Aegis air defense cruiser equipped with an array of sophisticated radars, stationed in the northern part of the Gulf. Any potential intruder over Gulf waters would be intercepted by a Navy combat air patrol, which flew twenty-four hours a day. To the west, the Air Force maintained a similar vigil, using its AWACS to monitor the air picture while American and Saudi planes guarded the airspace over eastern Saudi Arabia.

Well before the Gulf crisis, it had been decided that there would be occasions when the Air Force and Navy surveillance planes would need to share their tracking data. A secure communications channel, called Link 11, had been developed so that the computers on the two aircraft could talk to each other. But on January 24, Link 11 was out of order. The E-2C and the AWACS commanders could still communicate with each other by voice, but that was not an ideal arrangement, particularly for a situation in which an intruder could cross from the Navy to the Air Force sector at low altitude.

When the Mirages were over Bubiyan Island, the E-2C asked the AWACS whether it saw the potential bogies, military-speak for enemy planes. The AWACS was confused. It saw the returning American strike package flying at medium altitude but could not see the lower-flying intruders. There were miscues between the E-2C and the *Bunker Hill* as well. The air defense officers on the *Bunker Hill* initially found it difficult to believe that the Iraqi air force was launching a desperation strike at the Americans. Its crew initially assumed the two blips on the radar screen behind the strike package were Navy jets. When the two planes broke away from the strike package and set a course due south, the *Bunker Hill* became alarmed. The planes were declared to be "unknown, but presumed hostile."

The Navy was in a jam. Its combat air patrol consisted of Navy F-14 Tomcats and Marine FA-18 Hornets, sophisticated aircraft with well-trained crews that would be more than a match for the Iraqis. But the patrol was not in a good position to intercept the Iraqis. The Mirages had already flown under the patrol, which was circling over Bubiyan Island. It would not be possible for the Tomcats or the Hornets to intercept a receding Mirage flying at more than 500 knots. The Iraqis were splitting the seam of the Air Force and Navy defenses, flying along the fringes of the E-2C and AWACS radar coverage.

The Navy sent out an urgent call to the AWACS. Some way or other, the AWACS would have to orchestrate the defense, using whatever interceptors it could muster.

The AWACS, however, had its own set of problems. No Air Force planes had been scrambled to challenge the intruders. The only planes at the AWACS's disposal were four Saudi F-15s, which had recently relieved the Air Force patrol over eastern Saudi Arabia. Saudi pilots were American-trained and by third world standards highly proficient, but they were still regarded somewhat patronizingly by the Americans. The coordination between the two air forces was not always what it could have been, and the Iraqi gambit put them both to a real test. For any air force, it would have been a tough intercept. The Saudis would be racing to cut off the Mirages to their east. The first two Saudi F-15s overshot the projected Iraqi flight path. That left two Saudi F-15s between the Iraqi Mirages and coalition targets to the south. The American Hawk missile sites near Al Jubail were alerted. If the coalition could not stop the Iraqis in the air, it would have to try to shoot them down from the ground.

The remaining Saudi planes, flown by Capt. Ayedy Al-Shamrani and his wingman, also overshot the Iraqis but managed to recover. As the chase proceeded, the wingman began to run out of fuel, pulled his nose up, and lofted a radar-guided Sparrow missile before giving up the hunt and returning to base. The Iraqi planes were well out of range of the Sparrow, but the missile firing spooked the Navy. Watching the radarscope, the Navy could only conclude that the Mirages had fired Exocet anti-ship missiles and went to general quarters.

Al-Shamrani continued to pursue the Mirages, which jinked left to get away from the F-15 and dropped what appeared to be their fuel tanks to lighten their load. About forty miles north of Al Jubail, Al-Shamrani fired a Sparrow, but he, too, was out of range. The Saudi pilot continued to close on the Mirages and fired his last two missiles, two heat-seeking Sidewinders. Both Mirages were destroyed, and Al-Shamrani landed at Dhahran air base on fumes.[11]

After the war, American officials retrieved documents from Tallil that appeared to describe the strike. The plan described in the documents was to hit the Saudi oil complexes at Abqaiq and Ras Tannurah, which could have resulted in major damage to the Saudi oil infrastructure, as well as respresenting a political coup for the Iraqi military.[12]

After the episode, accounts circulated in the Western press that the Navy CAP (Combat Air Patrol) was restrained from attacking the Mirages so that the Saudis could get their first air-to-air kill. It was a distorted and ungenerous account of the episode, but a convenient one for the American military. With the Mirage attack, the Iraqis had come far closer to striking the heart of the Saudi oil network than CENT-COM ever acknowledged.

But the foiling of the attack marked the end of a chapter. The Iraqi air threat was finally neutralized. Iraq was running out of tricks. The next day, the Iraqis released millions of gallons of crude oil into the Persian Gulf. But even that did not provoke much of a response. On January 27, two F-111Fs from Taif used their precision-guided bombs to shut down the pipeline and stop the flow of crude to the sea from the Al Ahmadi refinery.

By the end of January, the Iraqis had concluded that if they wanted to strike at the alliance and provoke the long-awaited ground war, they would have to do so on the ground.

13

The Mother of All Battles

Preliminary reports indicate that there was contact with enemy forces at three different locations along the border. The contact began last night and continued until early this morning when contact was broken off.

— CENTCOM press release #01,91-62,
January 30, 1991

O N JANUARY 25, Walt Boomer received an unusual alert. For the past few days, American intelligence had picked up heightened enemy activity. Fifteen small Iraqi amphibious vessels were detected preparing to be put to sea below Kuwait City. The Iraqis were continuing the shell game with their Scud missiles. And an Iraqi armored column had been tracked by a JSTARS radar plane near the Kuwait border. Allied warplanes had been called in and had blasted fifty-eight of the seventy-one vehicles. CENTCOM had concluded that the Iraqis were moving to strengthen their border defenses. But now Boomer's intelligence briefer was suggesting a different reason for the Iraqi moves. The Central Intelligence Agency had passed on a tip based on one of its informants.

"The CIA reported yesterday there was a possibility of a ground attack by the Iraqis into Saudi Arabia," the intelligence briefer told Boomer. "There's a possibility we should watch out for some type of raid or ambush type thing by forces positioned just along the border against our OPs," the briefer added, referring to the old customs buildings along the border that the Marines were using as observation posts.[1]

Boomer ordered his staff to notify Maj. Gen. William Keys's 2nd

Marine Division to stay on its guard, but no extraordinary measures were taken. The Saudis, whose forces were stretched along the frontier of the kingdom, also picked up signs of Iraqi activity and wrote them off altogether.

Nor were Schwarzkopf and his intelligence experts in Riyadh worried that the Iraqis might take on the Marine and Saudi forces south of Kuwait. CENTCOM had not picked up any major signs of Iraqi attack preparations. And if the Iraqis really wanted to do some damage, the Wadi al-Batin in the west looked like a better place to attack. By rolling down the Wadi al-Batin, the Iraqis could catch the American XVIII Corps on the move, overrun King Khalid Military City, the Saudi military base south of Hafar al-Batin at the head of the wadi, and deal a blow to the arriving VII Corps.

For the first two weeks of the war, it had been the allies who had the initiative, and it did not look like that was about to change. In fact, despite the United States' best intelligence capabilities trained on Kuwait and with American planes flying over Iraq and the region at will, the Iraqis still had managed to move their forces unnoticed through the open desert into attack positions near the Saudi border. The battle of Khafji, the most important clash of the six-week Persian Gulf War, was about to get under way.

Khafji was one of a series of border engagements at the end of January that took Schwarzkopf and his top commanders completely by surprise. Although characterized at the time as a minor skirmish, the two-day clash was the war's defining moment. Schwarzkopf's failure to grasp the significance of Khafji was one of the general's greatest oversights. His war plan was never revised to take account of the lessons of the battle and that omission contributed mightily to the escape of the Republican Guard when the allies' land offensive was launched more then three weeks later.

SADDAM HUSSEIN BLESSES THE PLAN

To this day, Iraqi officials have never openly discussed their plan. But an analysis conducted by the CIA after the battle, as well as captured Iraqi documents and intelligence reports, makes clear that Iraq intended it not as a feint, but as a major attack. It drew on divisions from two Iraqi army corps. Maj. Gen. Salah Aboud Mahmoud, the head of III Corps and one of Iraq's most capable field officers, was to command the attack. The IV Corps would also provide troops.

The battle was viewed as so important that Saddam Hussein traveled to Basra on January 27 to go over the plan with his field commanders. It was a noteworthy visit in more ways than one. On the way back from Basra, two Air Force F-16s spotted his convoy and attacked it, but Saddam Hussein survived unscathed. Only later did American intelligence find out that the Iraqi leader was in the motorcade.[2]

The Iraqis planned a two-pronged attack with divisions of the III Corps. One prong would consist of the 3rd Armored Division, which would attack through the Wafra forest thirty-five miles inland from the coast. The border at this point was — for all practical purposes — undefended, with only light American and Saudi forces in the area. All major American and Arab forces were positioned well south of the border to avoid the possibility of a premature engagement. After breaking through the border, the 3rd Armored Division was to turn east and hit the Saudi port of Mishab, which the Marines were using to bring in supplies.

Because the Iraqis were uncertain of the exact whereabouts of most of the American units, they took special precautions to protect the 3rd Division against being outflanked. To deal with that possibility, the 1st Mechanized Division of the neighboring IV Corps was to move south and provide a protective screen between the "elbow" and the "heel," where the Saudi-Kuwaiti border angles to the northwest. From there they could protect the western flank of the two attacking divisions and engage any Americans it came across.

The other prong consisted of the 5th Mechanized Division, one of the III Corps's best units. It would attack south along the coastal highway, overwhelming the Saudi forces along the border at the northern Saudi Arabian town of Khafji, which had been evacuated of civilians before the war, and taking on any American forces that came to their rescue. The 5th Division would be supported by Iraqi commandos, who were to sneak along the Saudi coast in small boats and land south of the Saudi town. There, they would raise havoc throughout the rear area of the Saudi defenses and disrupt their lines of communication.

The Iraqi objective in launching the attack was both strategic and tactical. Convinced that the Americans would not tolerate heavy casualties, the Iraqis' hope had been to force a stalemate on the battlefield in which the Americans took steady losses, which would stir up political opposition to the war at home. But two weeks into the war, there were no signs of an allied ground offensive and Iraq was taking a one-sided pounding from the air. For Iraq's strategy to work, it needed the ground war soon. If the Americans would not march north to fight, the Iraqi army would go south and make them fight. By launching an attack,

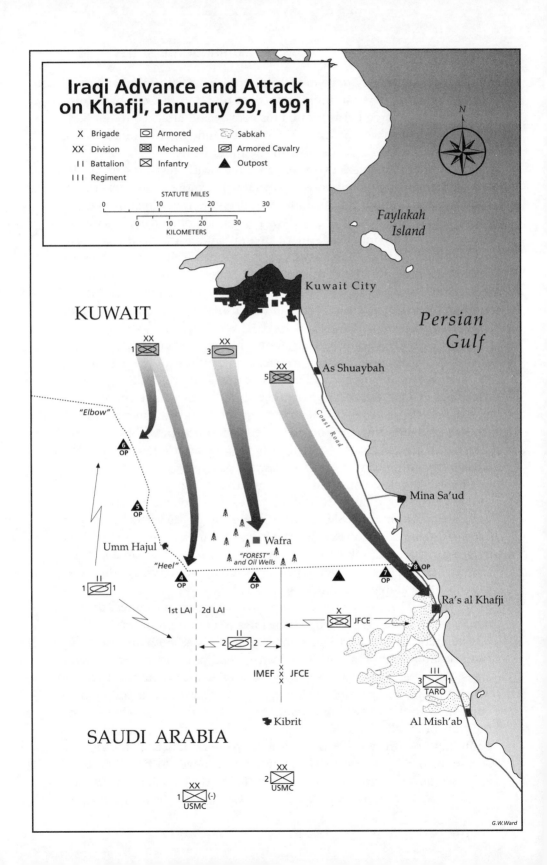

Iraqi Advance and Attack on Khafji, January 29, 1991

X   Brigade

XX   Division

II   Battalion

III   Regiment

Armored

Mechanized

Infantry

Sabkah

Armored Cavalry

Outpost

STATUTE MILES

0   10   20   30

0   10   20   30

KILOMETERS

N

Faylakah Island

Kuwait City

KUWAIT

Persian Gulf

As Shuaybah

Coast Road

"Elbow"

6 OP

5 OP

Umm Hajul

"Heel"

4 OP

Wafra

"FOREST" and Oil Wells

2 OP

1st LAI   2d LAI

1 II 1

2 II 2

Mina Sa'ud

8 OP

7 OP

Ra's al Khafji

X JFCE

IMEF   X   JFCE
        X

Kibrit

3 III 1

TARO

Al Mish'ab

SAUDI ARABIA

XX 2 USMC

XX 1 USMC (-)

G.W.Ward

Saddam Hussein could deliver a humiliating defeat on the Saudi forces guarding the border and inflict casualties on any American units coming to their aid. Once his offensive had spurred the coalition into a ground war, the Iraqis could withdraw behind their defenses, pulling the Americans after them and grinding them down.

Tactically, the attack would give the Iraqis the initiative. It would also enable them to disrupt the allied logistical preparations for a land offensive and gather intelligence on the location and battle readiness of the allied forces.

The success of the plan depended upon surprise. Because the Iraqis had pulled many of their troops back from the frontier to the interior of Kuwait as a defensive precaution, they calculated that their greatest problem was moving their forces into attack positions undetected.[3]

The Iraqis moved at night and under camouflage to minimize being spotted by allied aircraft. The intelligence the Reagan administration had shared with the Iraqis during the Iran-Iraq War also gave the Iraqis a few clues about how to outsmart the American spy satellites.

"The problem with overhead imagery, of course, is that it comes once or twice a day, that you don't have to be a rocket scientist to figure out when the imagery comes through," Gen. Joseph P. Hoar, Schwarzkopf's successor as CENTCOM commander, said after the war. "The imagery that we use had been shown to the Iraqis during the Iran-Iraq War. It was not given to them, but they were aware of the quality of the imagery and what it could be used for. There is every reason to believe that once they got a line on the satellite imagery they made their moves consistent with when the satellite was not there."[4]

It was impossible for the Iraqis to conceal all their moves, but without a framework for understanding the Iraqis, their troop movements at the end of January were shrugged off as minor and of little consequence to the ground campaign.

The night before the attack, a Marine reconnaissance team manning an observation post on the border spotted tanks and armored personnel carriers northwest of Khafji and detected a mechanized force in the Wafra oil field. The Marines called in air strikes on both columns, and the following morning flames and smoke from the burning tanks were still visible for miles.

The air strikes devastated the Iraqi brigade that was to spearhead the 3rd Division attack across the border at Wafra. But neither the Marines nor the American command in Riyadh thought an attack was about to begin. Col. Ron Richard, the chief operations officers for the 2nd Marine Division, told the pool of reporters attached to his unit that the

Iraqis had been conducting some kind of exercise to maintain their edge before the ground war and had been caught in the open.[5]

Instead of girding themselves for an Iraqi thrust, the Marines were focusing on their own offensive preparations. But as night fell on January 29, it was the Iraqis, not the Marines, who were planning on doing the attacking.

BATTLE AT THE POLICE POSTS

Lt. Stephen A. Ross was pulling reconnaissance duty at OP-4, one of the old police posts along the border, as darkness fell on January 29. Two-story stone buildings, the police posts looked like forts out of *Beau Geste* and, separated by fifteen miles, sat astride the routes into the Saudi kingdom. During peacetime, vehicles had to pass through the eight police posts, which were used for customs clearance in order to enter Saudi Arabia from Kuwait. Between the outposts ran a twelve-foot-high sand wall built to discourage smugglers.

When the air war began, the defense of eastern Saudi Arabia was the responsibility of the Marines and the Saudis. Each had its own defensive sector, and the relations between them were less than harmonious. Saudi and American air and naval gunfire spotters manned the outposts along the coast. But Saudi commanders had the main defensive responsibility for the area, leading a hodgepodge of Saudi National Guard units, regular army forces, Saudi, marines, and company-size units from other Arab states. None had ever trained together, and command relations were vague. The Saudis used roving mechanized task forces to guard the border and stationed a brigade just south of Khafji. The sector immediately to the west was entirely the U.S. Marines' responsibility.

Ross's police post, near the "heel" where the border slants to the northwest, was one of the most important. Ross's reconnaissance team had hidden their Humvees just behind the police post. In the event of an Iraqi attack, Ross's job was to sound the alarm and head south, leaving the initial fighting to the two Marine light armored infantry battalions equipped with their Canadian-made armored vehicles, called LAVs. The bulk of the Marine combat power was sixty miles to the south where the 1st Marine Division and the newly arrived 2nd Marine Division from Camp LeJeune, North Carolina, were in training.

Suddenly, at 7:26PM, Ross and crew members in one of the light armored vehicles behind the post spotted Iraqi mechanized vehicles on the Kuwaiti side of the berm. The enemy vehicles were three miles away and headed right at the outpost. Soon more vehicles appeared. The Iraqis were part of the 1st Division sent to protect the western flank of Mahmoud's III Corps attack against Wafra and Khafji.

Ross held his team in place and screamed into his radio. The Marines needed air strikes and fast. The Iraqis, however, knew that airpower was the Americans' strong suit and were jamming the radio frequencies. The United States had amassed the largest air armada in the history of warfare, but Ross would have to fight off the Iraqis without air support.

As Ross called in vain for air strikes, the alert was passed back to Col. Clifford Myers, who commanded the battalion of LAVs just behind the outpost. The outpost was under attack.

Capt. Roger L. Pollard, a company commander in Myers's battalion, moved his LAV forward and opened fire. But the Marines were outnumbered and outgunned. By 9:30PM the Iraqis had all but surrounded the outpost and threatened to overrun it. It looked as if Ross's team might be the first ground troops to be killed or captured by the Iraqis. With more than half a million allied troops, the fate of a few Marines would not be militarily decisive. But it would enable the Iraqis to draw American blood and give them a propaganda victory they were looking for.

As the beleaguered Marines tried to hold on, Ross heard two Marine attack planes finally roar over the battlefield. The tide of the battle was about to turn, but on the darkened, confused battlefield it would be hard to tell the Marines from the Iraqis.

Breaking through the Iraqi jamming, Ross called in air strikes against the tanks. The bombs came none too soon. An Iraqi tank directly in front of the police post was blasted apart by a bomb, and Ross took advantage of the explosion to beat a hasty retreat.

Pollard ordered his LAVs forward to cover Ross's withdrawal. But as the LAVs rumbled over the desert one of them suddenly exploded into flames, killing four of its crew. The armored vehicle had been destroyed by a TOW antitank missile fired by another LAV in Pollard's company. The first Marine casualties at the battle of Khafji had come at their own hands.

Pollard had to think fast. His LAVs were now the front line of the Marines' defense. He needed help from the warplanes circling above, but he did not need any more casualties from friendly fire.

Pollard ordered his LAVs to concentrate their 25mm cannon fire in the direction of the most threatening tanks. By keying on the stream of tracers, he hoped the pilots would spot the targets.

Tragically, the tactic did not work well enough for a flight of Air Force tank-busting A-10s. As they swept over the battlefield, they still could not see the Iraqi tanks. The A-10s dropped a flare virtually on top of the Marine positions and asked the Marines to designate targets in relation to the flare. But when one of the A-10s fired, a Maverick anti-tank missile malfunctioned and slammed into another LAV, killing seven and wounding two.

When the second LAV was hit, Pollard was not sure exactly what had happened. The Marines now had eleven dead as the result of friendly fire, but Pollard thought he had been outflanked by the Iraqis. He withdrew his company to rearm and assess his losses while another company moved up.

After almost five hours of fighting, however, the Marines had blunted the Iraqi attack. A captured Iraqi tank officer from the company attacking OP-4 told his interrogators that he had pleaded for support from his comrades, but it never came.

From the flash and glare of explosions on the horizon, the Marine reconnaissance team at OP-2, the neighboring post below Wafra, could see the police post fifteen miles to the west was under attack and decided to get out while they could.

The LAVs behind them, commanded by Lt. Col. Keith Holcomb from the 2nd Marine Division, became the first line of defense. Like the Marines at Ross's outpost, Holcomb's immediate worry was not the Iraqis but friendly fire. A mechanized battalion of the Saudi Arabian National Guard was supposed to be on Holcomb's right flank. But Holcomb had no means of making radio contact and had not seen the Saudis all day. After nearly six months in the Gulf, the Marines and the Saudis did not completely trust each other and cooperation between them was still flawed.

One Marine liaison officer to the Saudi command recalled the problem. Marine command messages were marked "SECRET-NOFORN" (no foreigners) and the Saudis, in effect, had "SECRET-NOAMER" (no Americans). "Since I was an American attached to Saudi forces, nobody told me anything," he added.

With his Saudi allies nowhere in sight, Holcomb ordered his companies to form a horseshoe defense. That way he could cover the border as well as both his flanks. Beyond the berm there was the grinding and clanking of the advance elements of Mahmoud's 3rd Armored Division, but Holcomb's men could not see them.

Finally, Corp. Edmund W. Willis III spotted four T-62 tanks coming toward his LAV. Willis fired a TOW antitank missile at the lead tank from almost 3,000 yards, which careened off the turret, leaving a deep scar. The other three Iraqi tanks then turned tail and fled. As important as the battle was to Baghdad, the Iraqi troops were fighting with something less than fanatical determination.

Holcomb called for air support. When the Air Force and Marine attack planes reported to him by radio, Holcomb turned on a strobe light on his command vehicle and gave the planes a direction and estimated distance from the strobe to the noise from the Iraqi tanks. In an age of precision-guided weapons, it was not the most sophisticated targeting technique. But it was the only way he had to hunt down Iraqi vehicles north of the border.

As Holcomb waited for the Iraqis to strike back, his men spotted mechanized vehicles to their east. The Marines fired illumination rounds from their mortars and prepared to fire. As the bursts lit up the desert, the Marines found a company of Saudis in armored personnel carriers aiming back at them. The Saudi battalion had fled when the first reports came in that Iraqis were attacking, but had worked up its courage to return north after the Iraqis were beaten back. That was Holcomb's last scare of the night.

At OP-6, the outpost northwest of Ross's police post, the Iraqis started lobbing artillery shells shortly after 1AM, lofted flares, and then moved in with a dozen tanks and armored personnel carriers. Iraqi soldiers scurried out of the vehicles, which withdrew to the open desert, and seized the post.

The Marines in the outpost got out in time. The Iraqis were not coming any closer. Instead, it appeared that they were trying to lure the Marines into attempting to retake the post.

Capt. Thomas Protzeller, the commander of a LAV company near the outpost, did not take the bait. Protzeller called in Marine and Air Force air strikes on the Iraqi mechanized force loitering in the desert. But as the warplanes swooped in, the Iraqi tanks laid down a smoke screen and the Iraqis laced the sky with antiaircraft fire.

Protzeller advanced to within 500 yards of the police post and started firing at the Iraqi defenders. Thinking the Americans were planning to take back the outpost, the Iraqi tanks revved up their engines and began rolling toward the Marines. But in a matter of minutes the Marines beat them back with a combination of TOW antitank missiles and air strikes. Under continuous attack from the air, the Iraqis then retreated across the desert. By dawn only destroyed Iraqi armored vehicles and surrendering soldiers remained at the police post. Protzeller's unit regained possession of the outpost and had suffered no casualties.[6]

*   *   *

Twenty miles south of the border, the fighting threw a scare into Brig. Gen. Charles A. Krulak, one of the Marines' top logistics officers. To ensure that they would have the fuel, food, and ammunition to carry out an offensive, the Marines had turned conventional wisdom on its head and were putting their supply base in front of the combat divisions. Boomer knew it was a calculated risk, but now it began to look like a real gamble.

For weeks, Krulak had been overseeing the construction of a logistics base at Kibrit, a sprawling facility nine miles long and four miles wide. The base was supposed to be a secret. But the Marines were so short of vehicles they were relying heavily on third world drivers supplied by the Saudis to deliver the supplies over the rutted desert roads built by the Marine engineers. Word of the supply base near the border was bound to have gotten around.

Krulak was convinced that the Iraqis knew about Kibrit and that their attack along the border was an attempt to destroy it. Kibrit was essentially defenseless; Krulak had only one infantry platoon equipped with two TOW missile launchers.

Krulak could see the Saudi battalion that was posted east of Holcomb's company fleeing south, the taillights of its vehicles flickering in the distance. A small group of Marines who were building a POW camp for Iraqi soldiers just north of Kibrit also fled, destroying caches of shotguns and other weapons before they left.

When Krulak called Bill Keys, the commander of the 2nd Marine Division, to ask for help, Keys ordered the Tiger Brigade to move one armored company in front of the base. With its M-1 tanks, the Army brigade was the heaviest unit Keys had. By midnight, the company was in place and Krulak breathed a little easier.[7]

The western prong of the Iraqi attack had already been stopped dead in its tracks. Along the coast, however, the Iraqis had more luck.

THE BREAKTHROUGH

As the moon climbed high in the eastern sky over the Persian Gulf, Capt. Douglas Kleinsmith had no idea that a battle was raging fifty miles to the west. At about 8PM, the Marine air and naval gunfire spotter located at one of two coastal posts just north of Khafji detected Iraqi artillery moving into position on the Kuwaiti side of the border. Kleinsmith speculated that the Iraqis planned a "shoot and scoot" artillery raid and called in an air strike. Bomb bursts lit up the night sky and the artillery fell silent.

Shortly thereafter, the Iraqi artillery that survived the air strikes sprang to life, lighting up the sky over the outposts with illumination rounds. Bathed in the pale yellow light, Kleinsmith saw Iraqi T-55 tanks emerging out of the darkness and heading south. It was the vanguard of the Iraqi 5th Mechanized Division, the second prong of the attack designed to start the ground war.

Kleinsmith and his team held their ground as the Iraqis raced past them, figuring they could call in air strikes and, if necessary, slip away later. When it became clear to Kleinsmith that there would be no immediate allied counterattack, he and his team evaded the Iraqis by going through a sabkah and rejoined Saudi forces the following day.[8]

The Saudi reconnaissance teams along the border and the Marines from an adjacent post beat a hasty retreat only to find themselves intermixed with the attacking Iraqis. With Iraqi forces all around, the Marine spotters raced to a "safe house" in Khafji, regrouped, and then headed to Saudi National Guard positions south of the city.

With the sounds of gunfire in the night, the Saudi marines guarding the beach north of Khafji also headed south. Fleeing in Toyota pickup trucks, they were not seen or heard from again until they showed up the next day at Mishab, thirty-five miles from their original positions.

Stripped of the thin screen of protectors north of them, American intelligence and special operations teams that had been secretly working with the Kuwaiti resistance from an abandoned desalinization plant north of Khafji also bolted. In their rush to leave, the Americans abandoned their cryptographic material for encoding radio messages and other classified items. Fortunately, none of it proved to be of interest to the Iraqi soldiers who overran the plant. The Iraqis placed greater value on sleeping bags and personal souvenirs, and when the desalinization plant was taken back a day later, the classified material was found undisturbed.[9]

An Iraqi mechanized battalion roared down the coastal highway into the center of Khafji and drove its tanks and armored personnel carriers through the streets of the town. The 800-man Iraqi advance guard drove past the Khafji Beach Hotel and the provincial governor's residence and into the center of the city, taking the five-story telephone exchange on the northern side of town. Within an hour the first stage of the battle for Khafji was over. The Iraqis' coastal attack had gained them a bloodless victory. They appeared for the moment content to occupy the town and made no attempt to go farther south.

Although the Iraqis did not know it, they were not alone. Two Marine reconnaissance teams had been sent into Khafji a day earlier by Col.

John Admire, the commander of the 3rd Marine Regiment farther south at Mishab. As the special forces and Saudis headed south, Cpl. Charles Ingraham, the leader of one of the teams, quickly consulted the other Marines and decided to stay to direct air and artillery strikes on the Iraqis. It was a high-risk decision. If the Iraqis swept through the town and withdrew, the Marines would be relatively safe. But if the Iraqis continued to attack south or simply remained in place, the teams would in time be discovered and the Iraqis would have some American prisoners.

Ingraham moved his team to the roof of a building, rigged claymore mines in the stairway, ordered his men to burn their address books, and put an orange cloth panel marking his position on the roof so that they would not be attacked by allied warplanes. As Iraqi troops ran through the streets below, he waited for the allies to counterattack.[10]

At the Tactical Air Control Center in Riyadh, Buster Glosson had checked after midnight to get a quick fill on how the night's sorties were going and was surprised by the reports that Iraqi forces were attacking along the border and had stormed into Khafji. It was hard to tell that CENTCOM was involved in a major battle from the way the air-war controllers at the twenty-four-hour operations center were responding. A business-as-usual attitude prevailed in the center.

Air strikes were being directed against the Iraqis, but they were only loosely coordinated. Virtually all the airfields in the Arabian Peninsula were chock-a-block with coalition aircraft, and the Navy had four aircraft carriers in the Gulf, but no effort was being made to mobilize a massive air bombardment. Lt. Gen. Charles Horner, the coalition's top air-war commander, had gone to bed before the first reports about the Iraqi attack and had yet to be alerted.

Glosson immediately called Horner to tell him that the Iraqis had charged into Saudi Arabia. Horner rolled out of bed and rushed into the TACC. Horner was not a great strategist, but he had long focused on how to stop an Iraqi attack on Saudi Arabia. The Khafji battle was a situation tailor-made for the general.

Horner began ordering up more sorties of Air Force, Marine, and Navy attack planes and JSTARS surveillance aircraft to track the Iraqi ground forces. Now that the Iraqis were out of their trenches and on the move, Horner planned to pummel them before they had time to exploit their breakthrough.

As the planes headed toward Khafji, Horner received an urgent telephone call from Prince Khalid, the commander of the Arab forces in the coalition. As Horner grabbed the phone, an aide told him Khalid was calling from a bunker near Khafji.

"Khalid, where are you?" Horner asked incredulously. Khalid explained that he was near Khafji visiting the Saudi forces when the Iraqis attacked and demanded B-52 strikes.

"Don't tell me how to do the job. Tell me what you want done," Horner replied. Whether it was Schwarzkopf or Khalid, ground commanders always thought B-52s were the answer to all their problems. But B-52s dropped "dumb" unguided bombs and Horner had hundreds of more useful aircraft to draw on.

Horner assured Khalid that he would support him 100 percent and jested, "By the way, Khalid, remember, you are in a bunker at Khafji. I am in a bunker in Riyadh."

The prince did not appreciate Horner's attempt to lighten the mood. Ever since the Iraqi invasion, King Fahd was insistent that Saudi territory could not be yielded. With the Iraqis in Khafji, the Saudi high command was on the line. After the war, Khalid issued a blistering statement, blasting the Americans for being slow to launch air attacks during the Khafji battle.[11]

While the allies' land and air forces were caught by surprise, their navies were more alert. Fifteen Iraqi patrol boats loaded with commandos were spotted along the coast by British planes, and Lynx helicopters from three British warships scrambled to intercept them. The British planes and helicopters destroyed most of the Iraqi boats and the few that escaped destruction headed for shore. The Iraqi seaborne attack was squelched so quickly that it was not until after the battle that the connection was made between the commando force and Khafji.

Even so, the sea-based operation was a relatively minor part of the Iraqi attack. The land assault down the coast was the main thing, and there was no denying the fact that the Iraqis were now in Saudi territory. No real damage had been done to the allies, but the Saudis' pride had been gravely wounded.

Horner summed up the whole, confusing evening with one blunt acknowledgment: the Iraqis were able to get "forward elements in town before we really knew what was happening."

A CHANGE OF PLANS

Unlike the early days of the American military deployment, when the threat of an Iraqi attack south was a real concern, the Saudi military had discounted the possibility of an attack from the north once the air war began. The Saudi military commanders had never rehearsed a defense of Khafji and did not have a plan to recapture it.

So Maj. Gen. Sultan Ibn Al Mutairi went to work. The commander of Joint Forces Command East, Gen. Sultan oversaw a 37,000-man Arab force. Cobbled together from brigade-size or smaller units, his force consisted of troops from Saudi Arabia, Oman, UAE, Qatar, Bahrain, Morocco, Senegal, Kuwait, and Bangladesh. Even a smattering of Afghan Mujahideen had been been dispatched in the name of Islamic brotherhood to Saudi Arabia and assigned guard duty.

The Saudi general had had the finest training that the American military could provide, having attended courses at Fort Bliss, Texas; Fort Sill, Oklahoma; and the Army War College at Carlisle, Pennsylvania. But his expertise was in air defense, which was of little use in armored desert warfare.

Sultan was not looking for a bloody house-to-house fight. At his headquarters near Safania, a small town on the road below the port of Mishab, he quickly drew up a plan to surround Khafji the following day, isolate the Iraqis, and persuade his fellow Arabs to surrender with honor.

Col. Turki Al Firmi, the commanding officer of the 2nd Saudi National Guard Brigade and the Saudi front-line commander, was to lead the attack. In addition to U.S. artillery to buttress Al Firmi's forces, Sultan counted on U.S. airpower to isolate the Iraqis by preventing any reinforcements from the north.

Sultan issued his orders to Al Firmi, and the Saudi and Qatari units earmarked for the attack began their preparations. But the Saudi commander soon learned that he had another problem on his hands.

Col. Admire, the commander of the 3rd Marine Regiment at Mishab, who had raced to the Saudi command post when he learned of the Khafji attack, informed Al Firmi that he had two Marine reconnaissance teams trapped in Khafji. The Marines were barely, just barely, managing to keep themselves hidden from the Iraqis. From the roof of one of Khafji's buildings, Corporal Ingraham had watched the Iraqis enter the structure and had seen the tops of their helmets in the stairwell as they searched the rooms below.

To encourage the Iraqis to move away from the building, he had called for artillery fire and air strikes on the street around him. "I called in artillery and close air support," Ingraham later recalled in a letter to his father. "On one of the artillery missions my assistant team leader got hit by shrapnel. He received a Purple Heart. I didn't know you could get one for 'friendly fire.'"

Admire judged that they could remain undetected for no more than forty-eight hours. He knew that he could bring his regiment north and drive the Iraqis out of Khafji, but that would be a blow to the Saudis' pride and might also sour American-Saudi relations. The colonel decided that the Marine role in the coming battle would be limited to providing artillery and air support and backing the Saudis up with anti-tank fire. It was, Admire said later, the most difficult decision he ever had to make.

Al Firmi was disturbed by the information about the trapped Marines but stuck with his original plan. Yet no sooner was the plan set for besieging the Iraqis when orders from on high changed everything.

Arriving at Sultan's headquarters late in the day, Khalid overruled the plan to lay siege to Khafji. It was not a matter of tactics, but a royal imperative. King Fahd considered the Iraqi attack an affront to his kingdom and a challenge to his role as the guardian of Saudi Arabia. A Saudi town, even one devoid of citizens, could not be allowed to remain in enemy hands. If his commanders failed to eject the invaders, he would find new commanders.

Khalid directed Sultan to launch a limited attack that night to allow the reconnaissance team to escape. Then the Arabs would get down to the bloody business of retaking the town.

Later that day, Al Firmi told Admire about his new instructions. Pointing on a map to one of his task forces just south of Khafji, he exclaimed, "We attack." The assault would be undertaken by a task force of Qataris and Saudis, led by Lt. Col. Hamid Moktar, a Saudi battalion commander.

As darkness fell on January 30, Moktar gathered his officers at a gas station a mile south of the town to go over the mission. The task force was made up of twenty-two Qatari tanks and a battalion of Saudi infantry in armored personnel carriers.

With no combat experience and only marginal training, the battalion's prospects for a difficult night attack against the Iraqis were dim. Moktar's unit did not have maps of the city and he had only the vaguest idea of what they would do once his men got there other than attack any Iraqis they could find. No plan existed to facilitate communication between the Saudis and the Qataris. Nor did the Saudis have a plan for directing artillery or air strikes — standard procedure for any professional military — even though American spotters were in Khafji.

Capt. Joseph Molofsky, a Marine liaison officer attached to the task force, suggested that Moktar delay the attack until arrangements were made for Marine artillery fire and air strikes. Ensconced on a rooftop in the besieged town, the Marine reconnaissance teams were in radio contact with their parent unit and reported that they were ready to control artillery and air strikes in support of the Arab attack. But the reconnaissance teams could not be of much use if the Saudis were determined to attack without support. However, Moktar had his royal orders — attack immediately — and that was what he was going to do.

At 10PM, the highway to Khafji was bumper to bumper with armored vehicles. The Qatari tanks were in the lead, with the lighter Saudi armored personnel carriers in train.

Without anyone giving the command, the Saudi APCs roared forward in a cloud of exhaust fumes. The Marine liaison officers were unsure whether the attack was on or whether a nervous driver had stampeded the column into action. So were the Qataris. The Qatari tanks in the lead pulled off the road and stopped. But the Saudi personnel carriers pressed forward nonetheless. Moktar's task force had not even gotten to the gates of Khafji and already it had lost its armored punch.

As the Saudis reached the outskirts of Khafji they were ambushed by the Iraqis. The attacking column broke up under Iraqi fire. Some entered the town, some swerved off the road, and some backed away. For half an hour both sides fired wildly and with little effect. Finally, Moktar broke off the attack and regrouped his forces. Some of the Saudis were still missing, but he was determined to try again, this time using the Qatari tanks.

The second attack, like the first, was also little more than a rush forward, and the results were similar. At 4AM the task force withdrew past a burning Qatari tank to its original position south of the city. The attack was a total failure.

The weary soldiers dismounted from their vehicles, lit fires against the cold, and brewed tea. A U.S. Army adviser found Moktar standing in the hatch of his command vehicle staring ahead in shock.

As the first light of dawn spread across the horizon, the Saudi armored personnel carriers, thought to have been lost in Khafji in the first attack, somehow managed to make their way out again and rejoined the task force. Miraculously, the two amateurish attacks had resulted in only two killed and four wounded. Although the casualties were light, the king would not be happy. The Iraqis still held Khafji.[12]

"THE MOTHER OF ALL BATTLES"

While the Saudis had been beaten back by the Iraqis, Horner had his warplanes at full throttle. The air-war commanders had gotten a slow start, but now aircraft ranged up and down the coast north of Khafji and across southern Kuwait. The Iraqis maintained their toehold in Khafji, but north of the Saudi border they were taking a vicious beating from the air.

According to a survey commissioned by the Air Force after the war, 262 individual air strikes were delivered against the Iraqis in the Khafji area between January 28 and 31. This included attacks by Harriers, A-10s, B-52s, and other planes, but not attack helicopters, for which no reliable figures were available.

The Iraqis were also being pounded north of the border, along the coastal road and near Wafra. On January 30, F/A-18s aboard the USS *Saratoga* delivered 100 MK-83 1,000-pound bombs on Iraqi positions in Kuwait, the largest bomb tonnage carried in a single naval mission.

The Iraqis' plan called for exploiting their early success by sending reinforcements streaming south, but with the severe allied bombardment they discovered that it was all but impossible to maneuver on the battlefield.

According to classified electronic intercepts of communications between Baghdad and the Iraqi III Corps command post on the coast near Mina Addallah, Major General Mahmoud, the III Corps commander, knew he was beaten early in the fight as air strikes caught his main force in the open moving south and repeatedly attacked them. The radio intercepts, which have never been officially disclosed, made it clear that the Iraqi high command was controlling the battle from Baghdad.

On January 30, Mahmoud requested permission from Baghdad to break off the offensive, but was told that he was in the "Mother of All Battles" and should continue the attack. He repeated his request twice more and received the same reply.

"The mother is killing her children," Mahmoud finally radioed back.

While the furious air attacks frustrated the Iraqi battle plan, they also produced the largest single American loss of the air war when Horner sent AC-130H gunships of the Special Operations Command against the Iraqis.

A combat variation of a conventional transport plane, the aircraft were equipped with 20mm guns, 40mm guns, and a 105mm cannon. While their guns were fearsomely accurate, the aircraft were also inherently vulnerable because of their size and slow speed. During the first few weeks of the air war, there had been considerable anxiety within the special operations community that Horner and Glosson were misusing the gunships by sending them into highly defended areas. One AC-130 maneuvered so violently to avoid an Iraqi surface-to-air missile that it suffered structural damage and had to be sent to Germany for repair, and some crew members even began refusing missions. Finally, the head of the Air Force Special Operations in the theater, Col. George Gray, had insisted on the right to clear all missions.

Khafji was the first mission that Gray had cleared in more than a week. In all, three AC-130Hs were sent into the fray above Khafji. The first two carried out their attacks and returned. Just before daylight, the third took off.

With the coming of dawn it was a potentially hazardous mission. At 5:30AM the special operations forces began asking for the plane to be recalled. The gunship received the order but was hitting the Iraqi forces hard and was reluctant to cut short its mission.

As dawn broke, the plane's silhouette was visible against the rising sun, making an easy target for the Iraqis. Struck in the wing by a shoulder-fired missile, the AC-130 fell into the waters of the Persian Gulf, killing its fourteen-man crew.[13]

It was the only air loss of the Khafji battle and the largest single loss for the special operations community during the war. CENTCOM was stung by the shoot-down, but the Iraqis were at the breaking point. It was a one-sided battle. The air attacks were weakening the Iraqis by the hour. American strike aircraft and helicopters were stacked above the battlefield waiting to be assigned a target.

While the air strikes cut off the Iraqi forces in and around Khafji from any reinforcements, the Saudis renewed their effort to gain control of the town. Two Saudi mechanized battalions swung around to the north to seal it off. When the battalions reached the desalinization plant that had been hastily evacuated by the Americans earlier, it was clear that most of the Iraqi force north of the town had cracked under the weight of the air assaults. The Iraqis were firing wildly into the sky with everything, including antitank rockets.

Soon white flags began sprouting from their vehicles, and by 11AM those who had not surrendered were in a disorganized rout north. Harried from above, the Iraqis left seven tanks and eleven armored personnel carriers burning in the bright morning sunshine.

In the joy of victory, the Saudi commander lost control of his forces.

Relieved that the tide of the battle had turned, the Saudis rushed forward to loot the Iraqi dead and rounded up seventy-five Iraqi prisoners, all the while firing their weapons in the air.

As they celebrated their victory, three Saudi vehicles, including an ambulance, suddenly blew up, killing eight and wounding four Saudi soldiers. The Saudis thought they had been blasted by two Marine Cobra helicopters which had reached the site, but this time friendly fire was not the problem. The Cobras reported they had not fired. A group of Iraqi diehards who were still hiding in the desalinization plant had hit the Saudis at the height of their victory celebration. The beleaguered Iraqis continued to pepper the Saudis with fire until two Marine AV-8 Harriers bombed the plant.

With the odds clearly favoring the allies, Al Firmi sent Moktar's task force into Khafji a third time. This time Moktar had arranged for American artillery and air support. The attack began at 7:30AM, when Marine artillery began pounding Iraqi defenses in and around the town. The sky was full of aircraft and attack helicopters, but they were of limited value in the confined battlefield of the town itself. Still, the presence of the helicopters flying at low level up and down Khafji's streets gave the Saudis and their Qatari allies a psychological boost and rattled the Iraqis.

As the shells fell around the Marines, the reconnaissance teams became worried that it was taking the Saudis too long to regain control of the streets and expel the Iraqis, who were still in sight. The teams decided to take advantage of the confusion and try to make their way back to friendly lines. Ingraham ordered his men to leave everything on the roof except their weapons. Then, carrying an M-16 rifle in one hand, a radio in another, and holding an orange cloth panel in his teeth to identify the team as friendly, Ingraham ran half a mile to the Saudi lines.

"We escaped, linked up, extracted when the Saudis and their V-150s were just on the outskirts of the city. Either an Iraqi tank or APC was burning on the side of the building when we hit the street," Ingraham later recalled. "The smoke and secondary explosions from it helped to cover our egress. We were very, very, very lucky throughout the whole ordeal."

With the allied bombs falling on the Iraqi reinforcements to the north and Marine artillery pelting Iraqi forces in Khafji, Mahmoud issued an order, at 10:50AM, directing his leading brigades to break contact and fall back to the interior of Kuwait, according to classified intercepts. By 1PM the Iraqi defense in the southern end of Khafji had all but collapsed.

When the firing died down, some of the Arabs took time out for belated noon prayers. While kneeling, one Saudi squad received some poorly aimed rounds of sniper fire from Iraqis holed up in a building about 400 yards away, none of which struck the Saudis. But they continued praying. At the end of prayers the Saudis had a meeting and agreed that only apostates would shoot at believers while at prayer. With that, one of the Saudi soldiers mounted his armored personnel carrier, aimed its antitank weapon at the building, and fired. A corner of one of the upper stories fell to the street along with three Iraqi soldiers.

The Saudi task force withdrew that afternoon, and it was not until that night that the Saudis reentered Khafji and permanently occupied it.

The cost to the Saudis and Qataris for liberating the city was not incidental: ten killed, forty-five wounded, and ten armored personnel carriers destroyed. But the stain on the Saudi honor had been removed and the Saudis showed their Western allies that they too could fight.

The cost to the Iraqis had been considerably higher. They lost ninety tanks and armored personnel carriers in and around Khafji itself. About a hundred Iraqi dead were counted by Americans accompanying the Saudi attack immediately north of Khafji, one of the few instances of body counting in the war. About a hundred Iraqis were reported taken prisoner. All of them were terrified by the air attacks.

The toll was much higher farther north, where Iraqi units were caught coming and going by American aircraft. One Iraqi captain who turned himself in to the Saudis had been part of a brigade that had tried to reinforce Khafji on January 30 but had been stopped short by air strikes and Saudi tanks.

He told his Saudi captors that his column was retreating in column through an Iraqi minefield when the Saudis fired a volley of rockets from their multiple-rocket launchers. One of the missiles hit the lead vehicle in the withdrawing Iraqi column, immobilizing it in the only cleared lane through the mines.

Allied warplanes immediately pounced on the column. The Iraqis abandoned their vehicles only to become casualties of their own minefield or of the strafing American aircraft. A veteran of the Iran-Iraq War, the captain said he saw more destruction in the fifteen minutes his column was snared in the obstacle belt than he did in his eight years in the war with Iran.

According to one communication intercepted on January 31, the Iraqi plan to send two divisions into Saudi Arabia had been abandoned after suffering 2,000 casualties and having 300 of their vehicles destroyed, mostly by air attacks.

But the pounding was not over. In the days following the Iraqi retreat, allied pilots had a field day hitting the Iraqi troops in southern Kuwait. Between February 1 and 3, attack pilots delivered an additional 554 attacks on the Iraqis, a level of intensity not repeated until the start of the ground war.

But the effect of Khafji on the Iraqis went beyond the count of destroyed vehicles.

The Iraqi plan for the defense of Kuwait called for a combination static and mobile defense. Successive lines manned by infantry in fortified positions were expected to trap and slow the Americans and their allies in barbed wire and mine-infested killing zones while artillery took its toll on them. When the location of the allies' main attack was identified, second-echelon reserves were to move forward in armored counterattacks to halt the allies. This done, Republican Guard armored and mechanized divisions located in southern Iraq would roar into battle and deliver the coup de grâce against the weakened foe. Rich in mobile antiaircraft systems, the Iraqis assumed they could neutralize low-level allied air attacks against their tanks — or at least stop the air attacks from seriously impeding their critically important armored counterattacks.

That is the way it had worked in the Iran-Iraq War. But to carry out this strategy, the Iraqi armored formations and their logistical trains had to be able to move freely and swiftly into battle and be protected from allied air attacks when they were on the move.

The theory was tested and was found wanting at Khafji. During the offensive, allied planes avoided Iraqi ground fire by flying above their range while still maintaining reasonable bombing accuracy. Allied air strikes disabled Iraqi artillery, immobilized or destroyed their armor and mechanized units, and knocked out their logistics.

Throughout the battle, the Iraqis had great difficulty in coordinating their actions. Allied signal intelligence revealed virtual command chaos. Iraqi unit commanders lost control of their subordinates and most of the time were unaware of events beyond their line of sight. Artillery failed to coordinate with ground attacks and was incapable of shifting fire in a fast-moving situation. Logistics were unresponsive to the needs of the combat units.

The Khafji battles also showed Iraqi commanders that it was one thing to draw up a plan for a multidivisional operation, but quite another to execute it. The Iraqi army's reputation as a tough, combat-seasoned force was destroyed. It was a bitter lesson in what allied airpower could do to an army stripped of air cover. The hold-and-counterattack strategy that had worked against ill-trained and poorly equipped Iranians was not going to work against a modern military rich in airpower.

At the tactical level, the Americans learned some lessons, too. Friendly fire had proved to be a bigger threat than the Iraqis. The difficulties in operating with the Saudis belied CENTCOM's assertion of an effective and harmonious fighting coalition. And as the result of Iraqi jamming, American intelligence shortfalls, and less-than-streamlined command relations, the conduct of the defense was clumsy and largely uncoordinated. Fighting had raged at OP-4 for hours without an alert being passed to the American and Saudi defenders along the coast, and air strikes were long in coming.

On the positive side, the Saudis, Qataris, and American ground forces did not collapse under the series of surprise attacks that hit them. Marines took the measure of the Iraqi fighting man and found that he was not very good. "Get in the first shot at him and the rest will run away," in the words of one young Marine. Marines who faced them during the Khafji battles had nothing but contempt for them thereafter.

But back in Riyadh, the larger strategic significance of the Iraqi defeat was missed. The details of Khafji were analyzed in isolation. Air Force planners believed the destruction of the two divisions was proof of what airpower could do to the rest of the Iraqi army. Marine planners also saw the battle as confirmation of Iraqi weaknesses. But the Army, which did not participate in the fight, ignored the battle almost entirely.

CENTCOM never recognized the enormity of the Iraqi defeat in the January border battles. The command did not see the whole of the operation for what it was: a well-planned major offensive involving three heavy divisions from two corps, designed to humiliate the Saudi army, start the ground war, and begin to bleed the Americans. Those on the ground saw only the tip of the iceberg because most of the Iraqi troops committed to the battle never made it to the front. And the ground generals who controlled the war — Schwarzkopf and Powell — were not inclined to accept the notion that an invading army could be destroyed from the air. Confounded by Khafji, CENTCOM did not make a single substantive change in its plan for a land offensive as a result of the battle. The consequences of the failure to appreciate the lessons of Khafji were to lead to an incomplete victory weeks later.

14

Back to the Drawing Board

We fought Desert Storm with a European Army.
We used European tactics.

— Gen. Colin L. Powell
September 1, 1993
Referring to the Army's VII Corps
during a briefing on the Clinton
administration's "Bottom-Up Review"
of military planning

THERE WERE LESSONS to be learned from the battle of Khafji, but neither Schwarzkopf nor Powell fully grasped them. When order was restored along the border, American intelligence agencies began to put the pieces together. In a top secret sixteen-page report completed after the war, the CIA correctly analyzed the scope and ambitiousness of the Iraqi attack. But, not everyone understood what the Iraqis were up to. Schwarzkopf believed that Khafji had shown the Iraqis' limitations but shrugged off the episode as of little consequence to the ground campaign. The CENTCOM commander described the Iraqi attack as about as significant as a pinprick on the hide of an elephant.

It was one of the major miscalculations of the war. Schwarzkopf's plan for taking the war to Iraq's Republican Guard and liberating Kuwait remained the same after Khafji, graphically illustrating his failure to appreciate the weakness of the Iraqis' position and their vulnerability to air attack.

As Schwarzkopf saw it, the Marines and the Saudis would kick off the ground offensive, assaulting the Iraqi forces in Kuwait to draw in and engage the Iraqis. Then, a day later, the main Army attack would begin to swing like a giant scythe. The Army surprise attack from the western desert would hit the Republican Guard and cut them down.

The Army move would take time, but it was assumed that since the Iraqis had tried to ride out the air war, they would be determined to stand and do battle with the Americans. If the Iraqis had lost the will to fight, as they had shown a propensity to do in Khafji, the Marine attack would not be a lure to set the Iraqis up for a surprise attack from the west. It would be a piston pushing the Iraqis north. The Iraqi army would be running away before the American Army was even off the starting blocks. The elite Republican Guard, which was already positioned just north of the Iraq-Kuwait border, would survive.

As he had done with the defense of Saudi Arabia, Schwarzkopf left the details of the operation to his Marine and Army commanders. And the tactics they developed would make it even more difficult to close the gate on the Republican Guard.

Bill Keys, the 2nd Marine Division commander, had his doubts about the fighting quality of the Iraqis, and the Khafji battle confirmed what he had long suspected: the Iraqis were vastly overrated. Most significantly, they lacked the tenacity of the North Vietnamese he had fought two decades earlier in the jungles of Southeast Asia.

A mountain of a man, with a shock of hair that looked as if it had been cut by a pair of sheep shears, Maj. Gen. William Keys lacked the polish and panache of some of the Marine commanders. Keys's radio code name was Pitbull. Despite his fierce appearance, Keys spoke softly, at times almost mumbling. But the general, a genuine hero from Vietnam, had enormous credibility within the Marine high command and particularly with Boomer. In a military increasingly dominated by paper pushers, Keys belonged to a vanishing breed: the warriors.

Keys did not care much for the war plan Lt. Gen. Walter Boomer and his staff had prepared to evict the Iraqi forces from Kuwait. Boomer wanted to rip a hole in the Iraqi fortifications and then push two divisions — 40 percent of the Marine Corps — in column through the gap, with each division alternating the lead. Keys thought this was too slow and possibly risky. If the Marine division at the head of the line became ensnared in the Saddam Line or was hit by a chemical attack, the Marine assault could grind to a halt.

Once the dust had settled after Khafji, Keys clamored for a radical overhaul of the Marine war plan. Each Marine division, he argued, should conduct a separate attack, hitting the Iraqis with simultaneous body blows. His plan embodied traditional Marine thinking. The way to win a quick victory and hold down losses was to push as much combat power through the enemy fortifications as fast as possible, bypassing pockets of enemy resistance and thrusting into the enemy rear. As conceived by Keys, the Marine attack would be like conducting its specialty, an amphibious assault, except it would be in the desert.

Keys's plan was not without its complications. One problem was the point of attack. Since Boomer had planned to attack closer to the coast, he had been trying to fool the Iraqis into thinking the leathernecks would be assaulting the Iraqi defenses between the heel and the elbow, where the Iraqi border angles to the west. As part of the feint, a mock logistics base was set up just west of the area near Al Qaraah. Marine light armored vehicles faked a reconnaissance mission, managing to draw Iraqi fire. Artillery raids were conducted against the Iraqi defenders in the area, and EA-6B electronic warfare planes conducted jamming missions there. The Marines advised the Kuwaiti resistance to avoid the area, on the assumption that the organization was penetrated by Iraqi agents, and staged a telephone communication in which Marine commanders discussed plans to cut through the sand wall there. In one of the more imaginative touches, a two-star imposter had driven up to the elbow area in Boomer's command vehicle. But the elbow was near to where Keys thought the two Marine divisions should actually launch their attack. If Keys's plan was carried out, life would be imitating art. The Marines would have to undo their deception operation. Otherwise, the Iraqis might be on to the plan.

The shortage of equipment to break through the Iraqi defenses was a more serious worry. Like drones and radios for pilots, mine-clearing gear was another area neglected in the Reagan administration's multibillion-dollar military buildup. Keys's division had arrived with so little mine-clearing equipment that only one of its regiments was able to practice breaching techniques, and his plan could not work unless he obtained more.

There was a solution for the equipment problem, but the politics of it were tricky. Col. Merrill Marapotti, one of the top combat engineers in the Marine Corps, knew exactly where the Marines could get what they needed. Years ago the Corps had considered buying breaching equipment from the Israelis, who manufactured some of the best in the world. The purchase never went through because of budget cuts. But with the ground war fast approaching there was no longer any shortage of funds.

The Israelis were happy to help. The reluctance was on the American side. CENTCOM was trying to hold the Western-Arab coalition together by keeping its distance from the Jewish state. For Keys's two-division assault plan to work, Schwarzkopf would have to be sold on the paramount importance of obtaining the Israeli mine-clearing equipment.

Keys was not worried about such weighty geopolitical concerns. He had to come up with the best, most aggressive strategy for the Marines. It was up to Schwarzkopf, as overall commander of the allied forces, to make sure what the Marines were doing fit with the allies' overall political and military strategy.[1]

Back at CENTCOM, Schwarzkopf seemed content to let the Marines make whatever adjustments they thought were necessary for their land campaign. His chief worry was over the interest the Marines had in preparing for an amphibious landing in the Gulf. In September and October, Schwarzkopf had confided to Buster Glosson and Robert Johnston, the Marine major general who served as the CENTCOM chief of staff, that he had no intention of allowing the amphibious Marines to hit the beaches in the Gulf. That, he felt, was an ill-fated idea, one destined to rack up heavy casualties. Importantly, Schwarzkopf knew that Powell felt the same way.

Schwarzkopf, characteristically, did not like the idea of imposing his sense of tactics on the Marines and never told the Navy and the Marines that. He hoped to wean them away from the plan without having to directly countermand them.

By early February, however, the Marines and the Navy were still planning an amphibious operation. While the Marines at sea were the strongest advocate of a landing, the top secret war plan Boomer distributed to his commanders on January 1 called for two brigades of amphibious Marines to seize the Kuwaiti port of As Shuaybah south of Kuwait City. Vice Adm. Stanley Arthur, the top Navy commander in the Gulf, also supported the idea of planning for a landing in case Boomer's forces on land got into trouble. For months, the Navy had observed the Iraqis seeding the northern Gulf with mines. Arthur had wanted to sink the Iraqi minelayers before the UN deadline for the Iraqis to leave Kuwait expired, but Schwarzkopf had vetoed the plan. He had not wanted to provoke the Iraqis for an operation of dubious importance while the Army's reinforcements were still en route to the Gulf. Now that the mines were laid, however, the Navy was facing an almost impossible task. Navy intelligence assumed the mines had been laid in the shallow waters near the Kuwaiti coast but was not exactly sure where. Nonetheless, Arthur was willing to consider an amphibious operation.

Three days after Khafji, Schwarzkopf flew to the USS *Blue Ridge*, Arthur's command ship in the Gulf, to meet with Arthur and Boomer. After arriving on the *Blue Ridge*, the commanders went into the admiral's briefing room. An aide laid out the amphibious operation. Entitled the "Role of Amphibious Forces in Support of the CINC's Campaign Plan," the briefing started off with a laundry list of everything that the amphibious Marines could do for Schwarzkopf.

Strategically, the preparations for an amphibious operation would keep the Iraqis looking east, instead of west, where the main ground attack was coming from. Tactically, the landing would help reduce the Iraqi threat to Boomer's force and provide a port for the long-term logistical support of the allied troops headed north.

But the briefing also contained a slide innocuously titled "Amphibious Assault Time Line," which was a showstopper. Schwarzkopf listened as the Navy explained that it needed up to twenty-eight days to prepare for an amphibious attack, a period that would necessitate a delay in the ground war. Silkworm missile batteries that could threaten ships off the coast of Kuwait had to be destroyed. Mines had to be cleared so that the amphibious landing craft and the battleships that would provide gunfire support could maneuver close to the shore. Those were not the only problems. To protect the landing force, the Kuwaiti shoreline needed to be pummeled. One sensitive target that was singled out for destruction in the proposed landing area was a liquid natural gas plant. The Marines were worried the plant could turn into a fireball with the explosive force of a small nuclear blast if it was blown up by the Iraqis or accidentally ignited during the landing. Before an amphibious assault was launched, the plant was to be destroyed.[2]

Schwarzkopf sat quietly through most of the briefing. In particular, the idea of wiping out the liquid natural gas plant did not sit well with the commander. The destruction of the plant was likely to be a sore point with the Kuwaitis, who would contribute little to the liberation of their own country, but were nonetheless worried that the allies would destroy much of the country in the process of liberating it. The media would be sure to highlight the attack. That was the sort of political consideration that the Marines did not have to worry about, but which Schwarzkopf had to deal with everyday.

"I do not want to destroy Kuwait in order to save it," Schwarzkopf said.

As the meeting drew to a close, Schwarzkopf brought the issue to a head. Concerned about excessive Marine casualties as well as damage to Kuwait, he asked Boomer if the Marines could manage without an amphibious landing.

It was clear to Boomer and everyone else on the *Blue Ridge* that this was the moment of truth, and the Marine commander paused for a long moment before answering.

"I think so," Boomer responded.

Boomer quickly added that if the Marines were not to land on the Kuwaiti coastline, it was vital that amphibious feints or raids be carried out to convince the Iraqis that the attack was still going ahead and to tie down the Iraqi forces along the coast. Soon after the meeting, Arthur instructed his staff to plan a raid on Faylakah Island, off the coast of Kuwait City. The code name for the operation was Desert Slash.

The meeting on the *Blue Ridge* was a turning point, and a disappointment for the Marines afloat. The months of Marine amphibious rehearsals on the beaches of Oman and in Saudi Arabia, the beach reconnaissance by Navy SEALs, the near doubling of the amphibious task force to a strength of more than 17,000 men, and the secret planning at Quantico and on the *Blue Ridge* would not yield a landing on the Kuwaiti mainland.

In retrospect, the decision not to conduct an amphibious attack was correct. The superiority of the coalition forces over the Iraqis made amphibious assaults, and the risk of casualties they implied, unnecessary. The port of As Shuaybah, a defended beach smack in the middle of an urban and industrial complex, did not lend itself to the choreographed water maneuver that the Marines had practiced in their training. Given the nature and location of the area, and the crowded battlefield behind it, there would be precious little room to maneuver. Mines, and the Navy's difficulties in dealing with them, were also a principal factor.

But if the Iraqis had put up a stiffer defense than anticipated and had bogged down the allies on land, it might have been a different matter. CENTCOM might have wanted to play the amphibious card to unhinge the Iraqi defenses only to find that it was in no position to do so. CENTCOM had opted to have the Marine amphibious force in the Gulf execute a giant deception plan. Schwarzkopf later took full credit as an example of his military brilliance. In fact, it was deception by default.

Two days after his meeting on the *Blue Ridge*, Boomer stopped by to see Keys. With the amphibious landing now off, proposals to improve the ground-war plan were more important than ever.

Keys began to sell his plan. Myatt's 1st Marine Division would attack first on the right, near the heel of the Kuwaiti border. Keys's 2nd Marine Division, which had the only M-1 tanks in the Marine Corps and was supported by the Army's Tiger Brigade, would carry out the main Marine attack on the left shortly thereafter. It would punch through the defenses near the Umm Gudair oil field, northwest of the 1st Marine Division, and then race up to the Al Jahrah intersection and Mutlah Ridge, the high ground just west of Kuwait City. There, Keys would cut off the escape route for the Iraqi forces in Kuwait City as well as those throughout southern Kuwait.

Khafji had persuaded Boomer that his initial hunch about the Iraqis was right. The Iraqis, he concluded, could not move, shoot, and communicate at the same time. And once they had their nose bloodied, they often lost their will to fight.

To Boomer, it looked like Keys would be taking on a lot. Boomer reminded Keys that the 2nd Division had been in Saudi Arabia only a short time while Myatt's division had been practicing the breach for months. But Keys exuded confidence and that meant a lot to Boomer. Keys was not fancy, but what he promised he delivered, and Boomer had not liked his one breach plan that much to begin with.

As the two commanders went over the new plan, Brig. Gen. Charles Krulak came by the briefing tent. Boomer looked up from the map and said that he was considering a new plan under which Keys's and Myatt's divisions would launch separate attacks between the elbow and the heel. Would the logistics work? Boomer asked.

Krulak was stunned. The son of Victor H. Krulak, a highly decorated Marine general, Krulak served as the Marines' logistics officer. He had been educated at Exeter before going to the Naval Academy. He had served for a year as Keys's assistant division commander and saw himself first and foremost as an infantryman who had been pressed into service as a logistician. It was Krulak's job to make sure that Boomer's forces did not run out of fuel, ammunition, and spare parts as they pushed north. He had just finished supervising the construction of a huge logistics base at Kibrit with a week's supplies to support an attack closer to the coast. Now he was being asked to hurriedly erect another base for an attack on the western side of Kuwait — except this time the problem was compounded. The logisticians would have to support two simultaneous attacks instead of one, and they would have only several weeks to get ready.

Krulak told Boomer that it was barely, just barely, doable, but work would have to begin immediately. Sand walls would have to be constructed to protect the base against artillery and rocket attack. Tons of ammunition and other supplies would have to be trucked over dirt roads and flown to airstrips that had yet to be built.

Boomer said that he and his top commanders would take up Keys's plan at a command meeting on February 6 at the Marine battle head-quarters at Ra's Safania. Until then, Boomer was reserving final judgment.

Krulak immediately dispatched a reconnaissance team to scout sites for a new logistics base, and they picked a location in a gravel plain, close to the point of attack. Kibrit was thirty miles from the port of Al Mishab and could be quickly resupplied from the sea. The gravel plain was eighty miles farther northwest of Kibrit. Resupply would be diffi-cult, so the Marines would have to stockpile fifteen days' worth of sup-plies there, not the seven days' worth the Marines had stockpiled at Kibrit.

The day of the commanders' meeting, Krulak ordered that the earth-moving equipment for building the logistics base be manned and ready to move at a moment's notice. He felt he could not lose even a minute if the base was to be built in time. Then he headed off for the commanders' meeting at Ra's Safania, with an aide, 1st Lt. Joseph W. Collins.

If Boomer decided on Keys's two-division breach, Krulak told Col-lins, he would leave the meeting and give a thumbs-up signal. Collins would relay the decision by radio to Kibrit to start the earthmoving equipment rolling.

As the meeting began, Boomer led off with a rambling discussion of possible Iraqi responses to a Marine attack. At 11:30AM the meeting broke for lunch with no decision. Exasperated, Krulak approached his commander and pressed him for an answer. If the Marines were to have any hope of carrying out Keys's plan, he said, they needed to begin work immediately.

"We will make a two-division breach," said Boomer tersely, settling the issue.[3]

Boomer had not yet cleared the plan with Schwarzkopf, but he did not think he would have a problem there. The CENTCOM commander believed in decentralized planning and was deferring to the Marines when it came to the planning what everyone agreed was supposed to be a "secondary" attack.

However, Boomer did have to secure Schwarzkopf's assent to dis-patch Marapotti to Israel to secure the mine-clearing gear needed for a double attack, and that was a sensitive matter. Hoping to score propaganda points, the Iraqis had charged that the allies were working hand in glove with Israel. Schwarzkopf had denied that the Israelis were in any way helping the allies during his first press conference in Saudi Arabia, and the Air Force had even gone so far as to forego the deployment of Israeli-made Hav Nap air-to-surface missiles it had purchased for its B-52 bombers before the Gulf crisis. Nonetheless, Schwarzkopf supported the Marines. If Israeli gear was what the Marines needed, they could have it, as long as they kept it a secret.

Krulak's Marines worked furiously to complete the new logistics base, which had to be up and running by February 20. Dubbed "Al Khanjar," Arabic for the dagger that Saudi men wore at their waist, it became the largest expeditionary logistics base in the history of the Marine Corps. Since the base was within range of Iraqi artillery, as well as Frog and Astro rockets, most of it was constructed underground.

Covering 11,280 acres, it had 4.8 million gallons of fuel and 1.2 million MREs, or field rations. The base included fourteen field hospitals, making it the third largest hospital in the Navy. To ensure that the detonation of one ammunition store did not set off the entire 17,000-ton ammunition supply, the nearly 1,000-acre ammunition storage area was divided into cells separated by blast-resistant sand walls.

Trucking the supplies to the base was an enormous undertaking. The Marines had started out with 450 trucks, including vehicles donated by the Saudis and driven by Filipinos, Pakistanis, and other third world drivers hired by Riyadh. But when it came time to build Al Khanjar, barely a hundred trucks were still operating. To fill the base with the necessary food, fuel, and ammunition, the Marine logisticians calculated that six truckloads an hour needed to make their way to Al Khanjar.

To rebuild their fleet of trucks, Marines went as far as Jiddah to hire vehicles and drivers. The fleet of trucks soared to 1,200. To keep the 500 third world drivers from abandoning the vehicles because of the skirmishing along the front, the Marines tried to motivate them with cash bonuses and gas masks and by showing them Kung Fu martial arts movies at night. As a stopgap, 900 Marine clerks, Navy dental technicians, and other personnel were given a crash course in driving trucks along the rutted desert roads. By late February, the nonstop driving had ruined the transmissions and engines on almost half of the trucks and 150 of the third world drivers had left, but the supplies had gotten through.

Navy Seabees and Marine engineers also built two airfields for the C-130s that brought in many of the supplies, and plowed lanes through the sand from Al Khanjar to the attack positions for the Marine divisions.

The biggest challenge was finding water. Without wells, the Marines would have to truck the water in on hard-packed desert roads, already clogged with vehicles. In an ideal world, Krulak would have determined that there was a water supply at Al Khanjar before adopting Keys's plan. But there had been no time for that.

By the end of the first week, just as the search for water had turned desperate, a truck driver reported a bright blue object just off the side of the two-lane sand road the Marines were using to haul their supplies to Al Khanjar. The Marine trucks had been driving past it for days without noticing what turned out to be an electric well with its own supply of fuel. When Krulak went to test it, he discovered that the key that turned the motor on was missing. But when Krulak pushed the "on" switch, it worked. The Marines later referred to it as the "miracle well." The Marines had the water they needed.

To keep the Iraqis from deciphering the new attack plan, the Marines stationed dummy tanks well to the east of the new point of attack and broadcast surrender appeals in the area. But Al Khanjar was such a massive enterprise that it was impossible to hide all the activity there.

As the countdown to the ground war continued, Al Khanjar was bathed in floodlights as the logisticians worked around the clock to get ready. Soon, a steady trickle of dispirited Iraqi line-crossers began turning themselves in to Marine guards outside Al Khanjar. The Iraqis explained they had been looking to give themselves up to the Americans and had been unsure where to go to offer their surrender, so they headed toward the light on the horizon.

As Al Khanjar rose out of the desert, Marapotti made two secret trips to Israel, flying by way of Europe. The Israelis gave the colonel thirty mine plows for the Marines' M-60 tanks, ten plows for Marine tractors, and nineteen large metal rollers, which would be used to pound down the sand and "proof" the lanes for unswept mines. Marapotti had the gear repainted with Marine Corps markings and phony identification numbers.

Some of the Israeli mine-clearing gear was provided free of charge. But Marapotti spent $100,000 on lumber for packing crates. Wood was in short supply in Israel, and with the ground war less than two weeks away, there was no time to shop around. Then the equipment was loaded on American C-5 planes, which flew over the Mediterranean before circling around and heading to Saudi Arabia, the better to support the cover story that their cargo was Marine gear delivered from the United States.

To complete the cover story, Marapotti flew back to the United States from Israel instead of returning to Saudi Arabia after acquiring the gear. CENTCOM had its list of politically correct allies, and welcome though its assistance was, Israel was not among them.

The Marines were not the only recipients of Israeli largesse. Before leaving for Israel, Marapotti had broached the issue of making the Israeli equipment available to the Saudis and their Arab allies, who had no mine-clearing gear of their own and who had been clamoring for help. Meeting with a Saudi brigade commander, Marapotti tried to be as diplomatic as he could, noting that some mine-clearing equipment would be soon available but it would be "coming from a country not even on your map." Then the colonel waited for a reaction.[4]

Almost immediately the Saudi commander smiled and said, "Now we will see our grandchildren."

The Marines had turned their entire plan inside out at virtually the last moment. The idea of an amphibious landing had been dropped in favor of a raid. The point of attack for the Marine land offensive had been shifted. More important, Boomer had accepted Keys's suggestion of undertaking a two-division breach.

The new attack would have its risks, but once it started it would go fast. Boomer estimated that the Marines would be at the gates of Kuwait City in three days. The only thing that could stop them would be a chemical attack. But Boomer was sanguine even on that point. "You know," he said later, "the Good Lord has a way of taking care of drunken sailors and pissed-off Marines. I just couldn't believe they would use gas against us, and if they did, they'd only piss us off more."

THE BATTLES THAT NEVER WERE

While Khafji had confirmed the Marines' low opinion of the Iraqis, the battle meant almost nothing to the Army commanders. Alone among the services, the Army began the countdown to the land war with no experience in fighting an Arab force. Its approach was not shaped by combat experience in the Gulf, but by two other conflicts: the twenty-year-old Vietnam War and the war they never fought with the Soviets.

After the trauma of Vietnam, the Army had attempted to transform itself. It had established the National Training Center in California's high desert, where it practiced desert warfare. It revised its doctrine, developing its Air-Land Battle doctrine, in which speed, synchronization, and maneuver would be used to defeat the enemy. It developed a new generation of high-technology and costly weapons. It abandoned its practice of rotating soldiers through combat units, which had made its forces less cohesive. This time, everyone who came to the desert would see the war through. If the Army went to war again, it would be with the best weapons the taxpayers could buy and with a well-trained and professional volunteer force.

The Army was also determined not to underestimate the enemy the next time around. American intelligence had painted a hazy picture of the Iraqis, and the Army had filled in the picture with threatening hues. With a few notable exceptions, the Army commanders saw a Soviet-trained and numerically superior force. They had an enormous regard for the larger Soviet army and its weaponry. Now, just as the Russian threat was beginning to evaporate, it seemed to the Army that it was about to fight an Arab version of its cold war foe.

While Schwarzkopf had good ties with the Marines, his relationship with the Army high command was troubled from the start. The Third Army, which oversaw the VII Corps and XVIII Corps, had never been a source of dynamism. The head of the Army in the Gulf was Lt. Gen. John Yeosock. Yeosock knew Saudi Arabia well from previous tours of duty training the Saudi army. But he had been assigned to head the Third Army precisely because the Army had not expected a Middle East war. Running the Third Army was a job the Army doled out to officers on the verge of retirement.

Yeosock had done a solid job overseeing the Army buildup in Saudi Arabia. Though a competent staff officer, he was not cut out to command the two corps. Almost everyone in CENTCOM and the Army knew it.

When Lt. Gen. Calvin Waller, the deputy CENTCOM commander, arrived in Saudi Arabia in December to help plan the upcoming offensive, it provided Schwarzkopf with the opportunity to develop a more effective chain of command by putting him in charge of all the American and other Western ground forces. Indeed, the idea of establishing an overall commander for the American ground forces was repeatedly suggested by Powell, who knew the Army leadership well and was concerned that the planning of the land offensive was consuming too much of Schwarzkopf's energy and time. Powell, Schwarzkopf recalled, kept saying "you need something between you and Yeosock."

Schwarzkopf never liked Powell's suggestion, but he discussed it with Waller, drawing an analogy from World War II. "Powell is Marshall. I am Eisenhower. Where is my Bradley?" he asked, referring to the American ground force commander for the European campaign.

But Waller told the CENTCOM commander that it was too late to establish another layer of command. There would be no Bradley in the desert. Waller instead encouraged Schwarzkopf himself to ride herd on his top Army and Marine commanders, Yeosock and Boomer. Yeosock, in turn, would ride herd on his corps commanders, the armor-heavy VII Corps from Europe headed by Lt. Gen. Frederick Franks, and the U.S.-based XVIII Airborne Corps, an eclectic organization commanded by Lt. Gen. Gary Luck and made up of a mechanized infantry division, an air assault division, an armored cavalry regiment, paratroops, and a light French division.[5]

Yeosock seemed to acknowledge the limited skills he brought to the job. He lived in fear of Schwarzkopf's temper and often sought to get Waller to run interference for him on minor questions. Yeosock also deferred to his corps commanders on strategy and tactics, each of whom reinforced the conservatism of CENTCOM's strategy.

With his gray hair and white mustache, Franks, whose VII Corps represented Schwarzkopf's main punch, was on a particularly weak footing with Schwarzkopf. Like Schwarzkopf, he had never wanted to be anything but a soldier. Growing up in a small town in western Pennsylvania, Franks had gone on to West Point, where he captained the baseball team. Like his contemporaries, he had gone to Vietnam, and the experience had left its mark. Young Major Franks was seriously wounded when a North Vietnamese tossed a grenade at him while he was trying to clear out any enemy from a bunker complex during the invasion of Cambodia. The explosion blew away most of his left foot. He spent twenty-one months in an Army hospital in Valley Forge, as doctors attempted one operation after another, vainly trying to save his leg.

Franks had fought hard to stay in the Army. He had commanded an armored cavalry regiment and made his mark in the intellectual side of the Army, serving in the Training and Doctrine Command and as the deputy commandant of the Command and General Staff College at Fort Leavenworth. Quiet, cautious, and a consensus builder, he helped redraft Army doctrine for a war against the Soviets and rose to become the commander of the VII Corps in Germany, one of the crown jewels of the Army, organized and equipped to fight the Soviets in Europe, where he assembled a staff that reflected his own training and outlook. Franks's chief operations officer was Col. Stanley Cherrie, who had also lost a leg and part of his hand in Vietnam and had fought to stay in the service. Franks and Cherrie used to joke that together they filled one pair of boots.

The VII Corps had long stood toe to toe with the Soviet army across the German border. It was very European in its style of warfare: methodical, deliberate, and trained to synchronize its every movement to maximize its combat power in a defensive battle against a larger foe. This was the combat philosophy that Franks embraced, and he was determined to concentrate his forces before doing battle with the Iraqis. Heinz Guderian, the successful World War II German panzer general, had preached the value of using massed armored forces to shock and shatter the enemy, or as Guderian put it, "fist not fingers." Borrowing the concept, Franks's style of attack was to "fist" the corps.

At the same time, as a European-based unit, the corps had given little thought to the logistical problems of fighting an offensive deep into enemy territory. "Here you've got essentially the corps support command that is designed around a concept where we are going to be defensive and we would fall back on top of our support structure as we thought in Germany," said one VII Corps officer. "A lot of it wasn't even mobile at all. It wasn't ever going to be moved." The European concept was a far cry from the reality of offensive war in the desert.[6]

In the weeks leading up to the war, the VII Corps plan suggested that Franks's attack would be anything but bold. The initial plan was to array virtually the entire VII Corps in column. After Col. L. Donald Holder's 2nd Armored Cavalry Regiment conducted a feint down the Wadi al-Batin to distract the Iraqis, the VII Corps would use massive firepower to stun and kill the Iraqi defenders farther to the west. Maj. Gen. Thomas G. Rhame's 1st Infantry Division from Fort Riley, Kansas, had lobbied hard to be at the head of the line and would punch a hole in the Iraqi fortifications.

Then the whole VII Corps would move through the gap in the Iraqi lines. The attack would be like one big arrow pointed north. Franks's aides justified the plan on the grounds that it would allow the corps to mass its striking power, would ease command and control, and would even enable the Army to put its field hospitals in one place. But some of the VII Corps's shrewder commanders were appalled. Pouring the corps through a single gap in the Iraqi defenses would be like trying to quickly empty a tube of toothpaste. Stacking up the divisions one behind another would produce a column sixty miles long. It was the same concern that Keys had for an attack in column by Boomer's two Marine divisions.

Holder was particularly distressed. His regiment was suited for fast-paced offensive operations, and he believed that the plan was ill conceived and a misuse of the corps's armored units. "We came away from

Left to right: Lt. Col. Ben Harvey, Col. John Warden, Lt. Col. Dave Deptula, and Lt. Col. Ronnie Stanfill in Riyadh when they unsuccessfully tried to sell "Instant Thunder" to Lt. Gen. Chuck Horner. (*Ronnie Stanfill*)

Lt. Gen. Chuck Horner, senior Air Force officer, who rejected Warden's "Instant Thunder" air plan only to later adopt it and claim credit for its success. (*Chuck Horner*)

Brig. Gen. Buster C. Glosson, chief of CENTCOM's offensive air campaign special planning group, reviewing the daily Air Tasking Order in the "Black Hole" in Riyadh. Glosson hoped to win the war through airpower alone. (*Buster Glosson*)

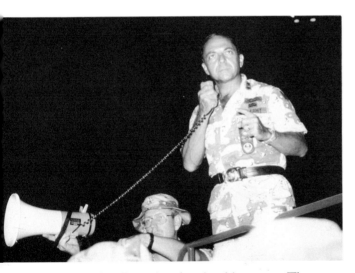

Lt. Gen. Gus Pagonis exhorting his troops. The Army's logistic magician kept CENTCOM's army fed, fueled, armed, and moving. (*U.S. Army*)

Lt. Gen. John Yeosock, the star-crossed Third Army commander who suffered from Schwarzkopf and a gallbladder attack. (*U.S. Army*)

Lt. Gen. Cal Waller, deputy CENTCOM, sharing a light moment with Colin Powell and Dick Cheney during their pre–G day trip to Riyadh. (*U.S. Army*)

Left to right: Maj. Gen. Paul Funk, 3rd Armored Division; Lt. Gen. Frederick Franks, Jr., VII Corps; Maj. Gen. Ron Griffith, 1st Armored Division; Maj. Gen. Thomas Rhame, 1st Infantry Division (Mechanized). Commanders of the powerful VII Corps "balled fist" that planned to smash the Republican Guard with a surprise attack from the western desert. (*U.S. Army*)

Gen. Norman Schwarzkopf (left) visiting Maj. Gen. Barry McCaffrey, who was to lead his 24th Mechanized Division on a wild charge into southern Iraq. (*U.S. Army*)

Lt. Gen. Gary Luck (left), commander of the XVIII Corps, meeting with Maj. Gen. Binford Peay of the 101st Airborne Division. Peay tried unsuccessfully to get Luck's permission for a helicopter assault north of the Euphrates. (*U.S. Army*)

Brig. Gen. Chuck Krulak, who created a massive logistic base in the desert to support the Marine attack into Kuwait. Shown with Col. John Woodhead, USMC. (*USMC*)

Maj. Gen. Bill Keys, call sign "Pit Bull," who commanded the 2nd Marine Division in its breakthrough and dash to Mutlah Ridge. (*USMC*)

Maj. Gen. Bill Keys (left) meeting in the desert with Army Col. John Sylvester, whose Tiger Brigade provided armor punch to Keys's 2nd Marine Division. (*USMC*)

MEF commander Lt. Gen. Walt Boomer, Maj. Gen. Bill Keys, and Maj. Gen. Mike Myatt, commanding the 1st and 2nd Marine divisions, flank Gen. Norman Schwarzkopf during his visit to the Marines just prior to G day. (*USMC*)

Maj. Gen. Mike Myatt, commanding general of the 1st Marine Division, conducts a sandtable briefing. (*USMC*)

The Navy changes command in the Gulf with Vice Adm. Stan Arthur (right) relieving Vice Adm. Hank Mauz. (*U.S. Navy*)

Brig. Patrick Cordingly, commander of the "Desert Rats," who resisted the reassignment of the British forces from the Marines to the Army. (*U.K. Embassy, Washington, D.C.*)

Lt. Gen. Peter de la Billière, British commander in the Gulf, at a planeside meeting with Maj. Gen. Rupert Smith, commanding the British 1st Armored Division. (*U.K. Embassy, Washington, D.C.*)

that thing saying, 'OK, our first mental task in this war is to change that plan. This is pretty broken,' " said a member of Holder's staff.

Holder quietly lobbied Franks to revise the plan and worked with Maj. Gen. Paul E. "Butch" Funk, commander of the 3rd Armored Division, to develop an alternative. Instead of a World War I plunge up the middle, Holder proposed that his regiment lead an armored column around the Iraqi fortifications, bypassing the Iraqi defenders altogether, and then race forward to take the war to the Republican Guard.

Under pressure from his commanders, Franks gradually modified his ideas, but he was too conservative to break completely with his original design. Franks's first instinct was to adjust the plan rather than overhaul it altogether. The VII Corps would line up in column. As the attack got under way, Holder would take his regiment west and do an end run around the Iraqi fortifications. If Holder did not run into much resistance, Franks would call an "audible" as a quarterback would in football and order Ronald H. Griffith's 1st Armored and Funk's 3rd Armored divisions to follow Holder. But that approach was eventually rejected as too tentative and complex.

Finally, Franks and his planners developed a two-prong approach. Holder's regiment would lead an armored column that included Griffith's 1st Division and Funk's 3rd Division west of the Iraqi frontline defenses. Meanwhile, to the east, Rhame's division would cut its way through the Iraqi front-line defenses and let Rupert Smith's British division pass through.

Franks was determined to create a three-division fist before taking on the Republican Guard. Franks was hoping that Schwarzkopf would give him operational control of Maj. Gen. John Tilelli's 1st Cavalry Division, which the CENTCOM commander was holding in reserve, so that he could beef up his corps. If Schwarzkopf didn't — and there was no guarantee that he would — Franks would have to reunite the two prongs of his attack. Rhame's division would have to conduct a breach, let the British through, and then catch up with the armored forces for the climactic battle with the Guard.

Franks's supporters insisted that his approach was a carefully thought-out design to defeat the Iraqis and hold down American casualties — a plan that reflected the ominous intelligence reports flowing into headquarters that the Iraqis planned to put up a stiff fight and use poison gas.

But critics within the VII Corps said that the plan revealed a lot about Franks's style of leadership. The development of the plan was not Pattonesque but a process of prolonged consultation within the corps. It was the work of an architect trying to address a variety of tactical and logistical considerations while satisfying his division commanders. There was something for everybody. Holder got his armored thrust, and Rhame got to conduct the breach. Maneuver warfare would be side by side with trench warfare. And if Rhame's division got bogged down, it could slow the entire corps attack.

The critics within VII Corps also thought the plan failed to sufficiently emphasize maneuver and fast-paced armored attacks. If it was possible to do an end run around the Iraqi fortifications, why not send the entire corps another twenty miles or so to the west and circumvent the front-line defenses? And if the Iraqi defensive lines were to be breached, why make it the VII Corps's main effort? In addition to its artillery units, the 1st Mechanized Infantry Division was given most of the corps artillery battalions, five in all, to break through the enemy lines. In contrast, the 2nd Armored Cavalry Regiment, the leading edge of the western VII Corps attack, was given only two artillery battalions and a battery of rocket launchers. To the critics, it did not make sense to weight the 1st Division's attack at the expense of the more promising advance by the 2nd Armored Cavalry Regiment.

When Franks was asked at one planning session why he had held to the initial plan of having Rhame break through the Iraqi defensive positions when they could be bypassed, he said that the plan was dictated by logistical considerations. Diesel fuel for the gas-guzzling M1 tanks and supplies for his units would be in demand. By cutting a path through the Iraqi fortifications, the corps could run its logistics straight north from the supply base it planned to construct northwest of Hafar al-Batin.

Franks's aides also argued that it was important to get the British forces into southern Iraq as soon as possible to guard the VII Corps's right flank against an attack by Iraq's tactical reserves and that cutting through the defenses was the most direct way to do it.[7]

As the metamorphosis of the VII Corps plan took place, neither the Army field commanders nor the Army leaders in Riyadh paid much attention to the changes taking place in the Marine planning. Carrying out Keys's proposals, the Marines had put their attack plan into fast-forward, while the Army stuck with its timetable of seven to ten days of highly synchronized maneuvers against the Republican Guard.

The previous October, Schwarzkopf's Jedi planners had had little confidence that a single Army corps could retake Kuwait and did not see how two Marine divisions could roll over the Iraqis now. Instead of considering how a Marine breakthrough could affect the Army schedule for destroying the Republican Guard, the Jedis fretted that the Marines might suffer heavy casualties unless their attack was scaled back.

As the Jedis noted in their classified log, "Adjusting the I MEF mission to a feint or limited objective attack will, the group believes, still accomplish the mission and reduce casualties."[8]

RIYADH MEETING

Ten days after Khafji, Cheney and Powell arrived in Riyadh for a status report on the air campaign and a final review of the land-war plan. It was an opportunity to iron out the disconnects between the services. But even among the top commanders there was little thought about how an adjustment to the Marine plan might affect the execution of the Army plan. Whatever the Marines did, they were still viewed as a holding force, ancillary to the main action by Yeosock's two Army corps.

In a lengthy presentation, Franks walked Cheney and Powell through his elaborate plan to take on the Iraqis. The VII Corps commander saw three fights: one to break through the front-line Iraqi defenses, a second with Iraq's tactical reserves, and then a decisive battle with the Republican Guard. No one could be sure what the Republican Guard would do, so a number of contingency plans were developed. But the guiding assumption was that the Republican Guard would stay put, which meant that the critical battle would take place 100 miles deep into Iraq. Massing the VII Corps before the key battles, continuous air support, and getting good intelligence "reads" at the critical points were the keys to success.

To the consternation of Schwarzkopf, Franks also appealed for more forces, specifically, Tilelli's 1st Cavalry Division. Schwarzkopf was furious with Franks for going over his head and raising the question of the 1st Cavalry Division in front of Cheney and Powell. Schwarzkopf had already rebuffed the VII Corps's request for the 1st Cavalry and was planning to use it as a reserve force in case the Egyptians got in trouble. But Franks believed that Cheney had asked for his honest assessment of his needs and he had given it.

One of Franks's commanders, Ron Griffith, the commander of the 1st Armored Division, also played the role of the squeaky wheel. Griffith said his division needed more sophisticated munitions and chemical-protective garments. Griffith felt that each soldier needed two chemical suits, so that they would have a fresh garment if they were hit with a gas attack, and "preferred" ammunition, like the tank-killing Sabot round.

The XVIII Airborne Corps's assessment contrasted sharply. That corps was represented exclusively by Maj. Gen. Barry McCaffrey, the most gung-ho of the Army division commanders. McCaffrey told Cheney that his 24th Mech would be in the Euphrates Valley in four days and ready to drive east to help destroy the Republican Guard. He accepted that his division would have to take its share of casualties to get the job done. The commander envisioned a war of one to four weeks with as many as 500 to 2,000 casualties in his division alone. But McCaffrey wanted Powell and his civilian master to know that even in a worst-case scenario he could accomplish his mission without major problems. When Cheney asked McCaffrey what worried him the most, McCaffrey paused for dramatic effect and said what troubled him was that nothing particularly worried him. The XVIII Airborne Corps, he said, had it all down.

When it was Boomer's turn, he said his main worry was the bombing campaign. The Marine commander wanted a lot more of it to make sure that the Iraqi artillery, particularly that capable of chemical attack, was neutralized before the ground war. He made it clear in side conversations with Cheney's aides that he was not happy with what he was getting from the Air Force. Glosson, he said, was still focusing too much on Baghdad and not enough on pounding the Iraqi troops in the field.

Speaking for the Navy, Arthur went over the war at sea and the planning for an amphibious raid at Faylakah Island. It was clear that that was not an option that appealed much to Cheney or Powell. To the Pentagon chiefs, the raid looked like a way to take casualties for a marginal objective. No decision was made on the raid.

The commanders then discussed the politics of the coalition. Schwarzkopf assured Cheney and Powell that all the Hebrew markings would be stripped off the Israeli gear that had been secretly brought into Saudi Arabia. The Saudi practice of squirrling away the Iraqi deserters they gathered up and keeping them away from the Americans was discussed. Although the move reflected a kind of Islamic solidarity, it was depriving the allies of important intelligence. But Schwarzkopf was not eager to press the Saudis on this point.[9]

After the meeting, Schwarzkopf and the Pentagon officials gathered in a small room to talk more privately. Schwarzkopf had not been the only one troubled by the contrast between Franks's and McCaffrey's performance. According to a senior military official, Cheney was also troubled by the methodical nature of Franks's plan and his anxiety about taking on the Iraqis.

"We've got the wrong man commanding the corps," Cheney observed, the military official reported. Cheney, for his part, said after the war that he could not recall making the statement.[10]

But neither Schwarzkopf nor Cheney had any intention of replacing Franks at this late stage. No one suggested any modifications to the VII Corps attack plan to speed up the pace of the attack. No one questioned how the rapid success of the Marine plan might undercut the plan to delay the main Army attack for a day.

The failure of the top commanders to grasp the potential contradictions between the Marine and Army planning emerged during their discussion of the timing of the land offensive. During his December trip to Riyadh, Wolfowitz had thought the longer the air war lasted, the better. Now Wolfowitz again posed a key question: what would be the effect of delaying the land war until March?

Powell cut that discussion short. The allies could not continue to sit in the desert indefinitely, he argued; they would lose their edge. It was a far cry from the opinion he had expressed to his British counterpart months earlier. But now that the war was all but won, Powell was prepared to use overwhelming air and particularly ground power to see it through.

Schwarzkopf went along with Powell. CENTCOM's recommendation was that the coalition ground forces be ready to go on February 21 or within several days thereafter. Schwarzkopf would later attack unnamed "Washington hawks" in his memoirs for pressing CENTCOM to launch the land war before the military was ready. But in front of the defense secretary and the chairman of the JCS, Schwarzkopf had been given an opportunity by one of the administration's more hawkish civilian officials to endorse an open-ended bombing campaign and had not done so.

After the meeting, Buster Glosson phoned David Deptula, who was anxiously awaiting word in the Black Hole, and told him the news was not good. Schwarzkopf, Powell, and the Army were determined to launch a ground war. The Air Force was losing the test of wills with the Army. In the final analysis, Schwarzkopf acknowledged later, the selection of the ground-war date was determined more by Army and Marine logistics than by a sense that the air war had exhausted its potential. Late February was the earliest possible date that the Army would be ready to attack, and attack it would.

Using Boomer's complaint, Wolfowitz again tried to raise the issue of prolonging the air war with Cheney and Powell on the flight home and was rebuffed again. The Marines, Powell explained, were only a holding action. If Boomer was worried that the air-war commanders were not dropping enough bombs on the Iraqi artillery in Kuwait, he did not need to rush to liberate Kuwait. The Marine action, the general added, was only supposed to be a "fixing action."

Wolfowitz argued that "fixing operations" to engage but not defeat the enemy was not the way that the Marines fought. The Marines might launch an all-out attack and get themselves in trouble. Powell replied that Schwarzkopf would make sure that the Marines did not get in over their heads.[11]

It was a revealing exchange. The Marines had considered many plans, but skirmishing along the border had never been one of them. Like the rest of the ground commanders, Boomer wanted the Air Force to do more bombing to hold down his losses, but once the Marine attack was under way there would be no turning back. Boomer's Marines were planning to get to Kuwait City in three days; the only question was the number of casualties if the Iraqis resorted to chemical weapons.

Powell had spent months scripting the Army's left hook but, like Schwarzkopf, he had not learned the lesson of Khafji and did not appreciate the effect the Marines would have on CENTCOM's overall plan to destroy the Republican Guard if Boomer's force blew through the Iraqis in southern Kuwait. The JCS chairman consistently thought of the Marine attack as a sideshow. When it came to military planning, Powell was not guilty of many lapses, but this was a major one.

15

Air-Land Battles

Air support related issues continue to plague final preparation of combat operations and raise doubts concerning our ability to shape the battlefield prior to the initiation of the ground campaign. Too few sorties are made available to VII and XVIII corps. And while air support missions are being flown against 1st echelon enemy divisions, Army nominated targets are not being serviced.

— ARCENT Situation Report
February 18, 1991

FOR THE AIR FORCE, Schwarzkopf's Riyadh meeting with Cheney and Powell was a major setback.

In three weeks of bombing, the air-war commanders had bombed Iraq's electrical grid and attacked Saddam Hussein's security services. They had turned Iraq's telephone exchanges into rubble and struck many of its bridges — all at a negligible cost to the allies. But Saddam Hussein had not fallen, and Iraq had not sued for peace.

The air commanders had not given up on their strategy. For centuries, land armies had demonstrated that brute force and the occupation of territory could deliver a decisive victory and overthrow an enemy regime. Buster Glosson was still determined to show that the new, precision-guided weapons the Air Force had fielded could accomplish the same result. He still thought the best way to win the war was by going after the brain of the Iraqi military, not just the troops in the field. But with a date set for the ground war, they were running out of time. Unless the Air Force broke the back of the regime over the next two weeks, it would be the Army, not the Air Force, that would deliver the coup de grâce to the Iraqis.

Glosson still had some leverage. While the air commanders had been unable to delay the date for the land war, they still dominated the targeting process and were determined to keep attacking Baghdad and other points deep in Iraq. But that put the air commanders on a collision course with the Army and the Marines, who wanted the warplanes to pound the Iraqi army before the ground war. Schwarzkopf's decentralized approach of letting services conduct warfare according to their doctrines, traditions, and planning was fine until they were at each other's throats. As in the case of the Army and Marine planning, CENTCOM was discovering that its military strategy was more joint in name than it was in fact.

Like much of the military structure, the system for running the air war was a direct reaction to the Vietnam War. During the Vietnam conflict, there had not been a unified air campaign. The Tactical Air Force controlled air strikes from South Vietnam while Strategic Air Command controlled the B-52 raids. The Navy orchestrated the attacks from carriers in the China Sea. Coordination of the overall effort was a hit-or-miss proposition.

The Vietnam experience and congressional criticism of the military's penchant to maintain peace in the family by giving all the services a piece of the action led the military to decide in 1986 on a new approach. No longer would each service fight its own war. The next big air campaign would have a single master. It would be run by a Joint Force Air Component Commander (JFACC), and he would almost certainly be an Air Force general. The Persian Gulf War was the first test of the new concept, and each service came with different expectations as to how it would work.

For the Air Force, the system reflected its ethos: airpower would function as an independent combat arm that could be massed for attacks anywhere in the theater. The Air Force generals who ran the air campaign would have the total view. Their vision would span from northern Iraq to the front lines along the Saudi border, and they would use their position at the top of a vast airpower pyramid to apply air strikes where and when they were needed most. Each service could "nominate" targets, but Lt. Gen. Charles Horner and his fellow Air Force planners would be the men who would decide what, when, and how they would be hit.[1]

For the Army, the JFACC system was a beast to be corralled and tamed. New technology had expanded the Army corps commanders' capabilities to look deep into the battlefield and identify enemy targets, and an Army corps commander was not concerned with the entire theater. He looked at the battlefield like a giant bowling alley. To move down the lane, the corps needed to sweep the obstacles from its path, starting with those directly in front of it and then those a day or two away. For the corps commanders, airpower was a form of flying artillery and should be on call immediately to support their attack.

For the Marines, the JFACC system was first and foremost a drain on their resources. The Marines did not have heavy ground forces, but unlike the Army, they had their own air wing to make up the difference. Warplanes were an integral part of Marine Corps combat power, no different from artillery and tanks. They were all organized and trained to operate as parts of the whole. That made the Marines less dependent than the Army on Air Force support of the land offensive. But it raised another point of tension.

The very fact that Marine air wings had been created to put a protective bubble over the Marine ground troops was contrary to the Air Force dreams of winning the war through strategic airpower. The patron saint of Marine aviators was not Billy Mitchell but Alfred A. Cunningham, who pioneered the use of close air support for the Marines as early as 1925 in Nicaragua. Any task that diverted Marine air from its battlefield mission was seen as a distraction from the main event.

Soon after the Marines deployed to the Gulf, Royal Moore, commander of the Marine air wing, and Buster Glosson worked out a Solomon-like solution to the Air Force and Marine dichotomy. Under the understanding, the Marines would cede all their A-6E bombers and EA-6B jamming planes and 50 percent of their FA-18 attack planes to Horner to use as he saw fit. But the Marines would retain control of the remaining FA-18s and all their AV-8B Harriers — close-air-support planes that took off vertically, had little range, and were of little use to the Air Force. In return, the Marines would be able to draw on the Air Force's assets, its B-52s and A-10s, to soften up the Iraqis for the eventual ground war.

The Marines, however, were never comfortable with the arrangement. Their attitude was best expressed by Col. Manfred Reitch, one of the Corps's most experienced commanders, who argued that Marine combat planes should not be assigned to drop a single bomb on a target in Iraq until the Marine ground forces had successfully launched their ground offensive in Kuwait.[2]

The centralized campaign orchestrated by the Air Force had its own procedures and rituals. Building one day's worth of attacks was, in theory, a three-day process, though adjustments could be made. Even as the bombs rained down on Iraq, planners would be looking seventy-two hours ahead, inserting targets in a Master Attack Plan. The plan would be transformed the next day into an Air Tasking Order (ATO), a massive document that would be messaged to the aircrews for execution the next day. It took hours to transmit the voluminous plan each day to air wings throughout the Arabian Peninsula and at sea. The order was sent in digital form in many cases, using personal computers, and a unit got the entire Air Tasking Order or it did not get one at all.

The process of transmitting the order was fraught with difficulties. The Navy did not have the software and computers to receive the order on each carrier, so the Navy representatives in the Black Hole had to work around the problem by phoning the missions to the carriers so that the aircrews could begin planning for their strikes while the document with the details was being flown out to the ships. Even some Air Force units had trouble receiving the ATO and had to have it flown to them.[3]

To supporters of the system, the transmission difficulties meant only that the communications technology was lagging behind the doctrinal advance of a centralized air war. To its critics, the problems were a symptom of a system that was overcentralized, unresponsive to the needs of the ground forces, and dominated by an Air Force general.

As long as the doctrinal differences among the services in peacetime were largely theoretical, they could be sidestepped. But now, with a date set for the ground war, that was getting more and more difficult to do. Even with all the airplanes CENTCOM had in the Gulf, there were only so many missions that could be launched, and the air and ground commanders had very different ideas of what the planes should be used for.

DECAPITATION

For Glosson and his planners, the answer was simple. As long as his pilots were flying, he wanted to keep the pressure on Baghdad. The strikes in and around Baghdad were an effort both to shut down the Iraqi command structure and to create the conditions for Saddam Hussein's overthrow by destroying the levers of power and stripping away the security forces that the Iraqi leader depended on for his own survival.

But the air campaign had unfolded more slowly than expected, and the Iraqis had been more resilient than the Air Force had anticipated. By late January, the Black Hole had planned to have carried out three hundred strikes against targets in Baghdad, sixty against targets in the vicinity of Basra, thirty against targets in the Mosul area, and thirty against targets in western Iraq near H-2 and H-3. But with the bad weather, the air war was well behind schedule. After two weeks only a hundred or so strikes, one-third the anticipated number, had been carried out in Baghdad.

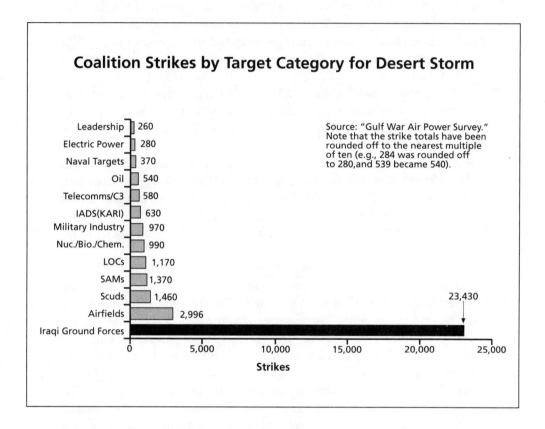

Coalition Strikes by Target Category for Desert Storm

Source: "Gulf War Air Power Survey." Note that the strike totals have been rounded off to the nearest multiple of ten (e.g., 284 was rounded off to 280, and 539 became 540).

Target Category	Strikes
Leadership	260
Electric Power	280
Naval Targets	370
Oil	540
Telecomms/C3	580
IADS(KARI)	630
Military Industry	970
Nuc./Bio./Chem.	990
LOCs	1,170
SAMs	1,370
Scuds	1,460
Airfields	2,996
Iraqi Ground Forces	23,430

Of all the bombing raids, the attacks on leadership targets were the most sensitive. According to CENTCOM statistics, the allies launched 260 bombing raids during the war against sites where they thought Iraqi leaders might be hiding and 580 attacks against command, control, and communications sites. The public line was that the coalition was targeting facilities, not individuals. There was nothing in the rules of war that precluded efforts to target enemy commanders, and as a commander in chief with a gun holster on his hip Saddam Hussein arguably fit that definition. But the assassination of foreign leaders was illegal.

Col. Michael F. Reavy, one of General Horner's top aides, put it this way: "Not to imply that we were trying to assassinate Saddam, but we were trying to kill him."

While Saddam Hussein survived the initial attacks on his Baghdad command posts, CENTCOM kept a watch out for the Iraqi leader. In late January, an employee of the Bluebird Company, an American firm that manufactured Winnebago-like vehicles, told American officials that it had sold up to a dozen Wanderlodges to Iraq in 1987 and 1988 and that Saddam Hussein had been photographed inside one of them. The vehicles were quickly added to the target list as likely command posts and attacked.

"We were told that Saddam had some RV type vehicles that he used as a mobile command post when he traveled," Reavy recalled. "We would, through intel channels, find them parked, and we would generate an air strike."[4]

On one occasion, CENTCOM received an intelligence report that Saddam Hussein would be using one of the Wanderlodges to take personal control of a Scud missile firing in western Iraq, a suspect report but one that the Air Force acted on nonetheless. F-15Es were dispatched, and the Winnebago was destroyed, but the Iraqi leader reappeared elsewhere.

On another occasion, according to a senior Air Force official, CENTCOM received a tip that a presidential motorcade would be moving between Baghdad and Tikrit at midnight. F-15Es were dispatched, but there was no motorcade. Three weeks into the war, F-117s used an innovative tactic to try to destroy the bunker under the Royal Palace in Baghdad. Buried deep underground and extending only ten feet beyond the palace itself, the bunker was hard to destroy. First, the F-117s dropped four GBU-10s, hoping that the bomb blasts would push aside the dirt covering the bunker. Then, the planes dropped two GBU-27 bombs, good for penetrating concrete, into the same hole. But there was no payoff. Nor did Saddam Hussein turn up after the air commanders received a report from a spy that he was hiding out in a residential area of Baghdad. American warplanes were mobilized and the area was put under surveillance, but the Iraqi leader was not seen.

One series of "decapitation" attacks that has never been publicly acknowledged involved repeated efforts to kill the top Iraqi ground commanders in Kuwait. At the behest of the Marines, several attempts were made to bomb Maj. Gen. Salah Aboud Mahmoud, the commander of the Iraqi III Corps. As the senior Iraqi leader responsible for the defense of southeastern Kuwait, Mahmoud was regarded as one of the most capable leaders in the force occupying Kuwait and was the officer who directed the ill-fated Khafji attack.

In their first and only daylight raid, Glosson ordered Col. Tom Lennon's F-111Fs to attack a polo club outside Kuwait City, where the Kuwaiti resistance had reported the Iraqi commanders to be gathering. To undertake the risky daytime mission, two F-111s circled off the coast of Kuwait, aiming their laser target designators at the club. Meanwhile, a pair of F-111Fs streaked along the coast and dropped GBU-24 laser-guided bombs and zoomed away. The club was blown up, but intelligence reports later indicated that the Iraqi III Corps commander survived the raid. After the war, however, Saddam Hussein stated that one of his top commanders died in a bombing raid in Kuwait.[5]

Other efforts to topple the Saddam Hussein regime were indirect. In addition to the military impact of knocking out Iraq's electrical power, recalled David Deptula, the air commanders hoped to send a signal to the Iraqi people: "Hey, your lights will come back on as soon as you get rid of Saddam."

The attacks on the Iraqi communications were intended not only to disrupt the command and control of the Iraqi military but "to put every household in an autonomous mode and make them feel they were isolated," Glosson recalled. "I wanted to play with their psyche."[6]

In all, allied warplanes carried out 890 strikes against electrical power and oil installations. The attacks were supposed to use precision-guided weapons so that the maximum military effort could be obtained with the smallest possible damage. That way Baghdad was to be able to rebuild in a matter of months, not years. Since the air commanders believed that Saddam Hussein could be overthrown with a properly orchestrated air campaign, they also assumed that the United States would be able to help with the rebuilding.

The electrical grid around Baghdad was knocked out in two or three days, as the special filament-carrying cruise missiles shorted out the power lines. Iraq, seeing that electricity was a target, shut down its national grid, which was designed to compensate for local shortages by directing electricity around the country, after twelve days. In the case of the oil installations, major refineries were destroyed in five days, and domestic fuel sales halted in seven or eight days. The CIA later concluded that the allies had knocked out more than 90 percent of Iraq's petroleum refining capability.

The theory of discriminate warfare, however, worked better in theory than in practice. In the case of electrical plants, the air commanders instructed the air wings to avoid attacking the generator halls, which American intelligence estimated would take years to rebuild. Instead, the nearby switching yards that carried electricity from the plants were to be bombed. But in an exception to that policy, Glosson directed that the electrical generators at the Al Hartha plant near Basra and several substations be leveled. He was worried that the facilities might be used to provide power to the pumping stations in Kuwait used by the Iraqi military to fill the "fire trenches" along the border with crude oil. The plant was bombed more than a dozen times. The Navy, in particular, used it as a "dump" target to dispose of any bombs its planes might still have on their way back to the carriers.[7]

Of greater significance, the philosophy of obtaining the maximum effect with minimum damage often did not penetrate the ranks of the pilots. In theory, the Black Hole provided the guidance to the Air Force intelligence shop in Riyadh, which picked the specific spots where the bombs were to hit. But due to a breakdown, the key guidance on limiting damage to the electrical installations was not passed down the chain of command to all the pilots. And without the guidance, the pilots attacked the installations the old-fashioned way: by bombing the larger generator halls. On a number of occasions, oil installations were attacked by planes, including F-16s and even B-52s, dropping unguided bombs.

By early February, it was clear that the verbal guidance was not being followed. Deptula drafted a memorandum for Glosson to send to the intelligence cell in Riyadh, stating again the philosophy behind the air campaign. The memo was backdated to early January to reflect the fact that the guidance was to have been in effect all along.

"Electrical targets will be targeted to minimize recuperation time. At electrical production/transformer stations the objective will be the transformer/switching yards and the central buildings in these yards," the memo said. "Boilers and generators will not be aimpoints. The objective at POL targets is to destroy refined product storage. Distillation and other refining areas will only be an aimpoint for military related fuel production refineries."[8]

By then, however, much of the damage had already been done. According to a survey commissioned by the Air Force after the war, the generator halls at twelve of fifteen major power plants were damaged, imposing an extra hardship on the Iraqi people the United States was trying to win over. After the war was over, a team of experts from the Harvard University School of Public Health asserted that the destruction of the electrical plants had hampered efforts to purify water and contributed to an alarming escalation in infant mortality rates. But the public health crisis was also a result of Saddam Hussein's ability to survive the war and his reluctance to comply with UN requirements for lifting the trade embargo: that Iraq's programs to develop weapons of mass destruction be dismantled and its ethnic groups protected. As it turned out, the damage done to the plants was not as lasting as many of the experts — and American intelligence — had anticipated. Even in the face of economic sanctions Baghdad announced a year after the conflict that it had rebuilt the Al Hartha plant.[9]

While the strikes against the Iraqi infrastructure were intended to undermine the Saddam Hussein regime, the allies failed to target Baghdad with an effective propaganda campaign making clear that the coalition's bombs were not intended for the Iraqi people and encouraging the Iraqis to take matters into their own hands.

The Air Force special operations troops in the Gulf were equipped with *Volant Solo,* a specially configured C-130 full of electronic equipment to broadcast radio and television pictures into enemy territory. *Volant Solo* could override enemy transmissions and send allied messages over the enemy airwaves. Even with air superiority, however, the Air Force considered *Volant Solo* to be a vulnerable aircraft and it never operated within broadcast range of Baghdad.

Acting with the support of the CIA, the Saudis ran a network of radio stations, dubbed the Voice of Free Iraq, which urged the Iraqi people to topple Saddam Hussein. But the range of the radio stations limited the broadcast to the Iraqi ground troops in the Kuwaiti theater of operations and to the Shiite-dominated area of southern Iraq, a group Washington knew little about and was reluctant to support.

Nor were many leaflets dropped in the capital city. Although tons of leaflets — the pilots called them "bullshit bombs" — were dropped on the Iraqi troops along the front urging them to give up the fight, only on one occasion did an F-16 drop the leaflets on the outskirts of Baghdad. Washington wanted to encourage a Baghdad-based coup against the Iraqi leader, but its propaganda was not reaching its target audience.[10]

Still, Glosson thought that if the allies kept bombing Baghdad and the Iraqi army it would be more than the country could take. And there was a good chance that sooner or later the Saddam Hussein regime would crack.

At the Army's Riyadh headquarters, Steven Arnold saw things differently. The Air Force had talked a great game, but how was the air campaign going to come close to meeting its goal of destroying 50 percent of the Iraqi tanks, armored personnel carriers, and artillery pieces in time? How much damage had the interdiction of fuel, parts, and supplies really done to the Iraqis? The Iraqis were not consuming huge supplies. They were hunkered down and not using their equipment.

With the most sophisticated planes committed to attacks deep in Iraq, the results of the bombing attacks against Iraq's troops were mixed. American warplanes had racked up a terrible toll during the battle of Khafji; four times as many kills were registered there than during the previous two weeks of the war. But attacking the troops when they were dug in was more difficult. The coalition was throwing dumb bombs at the Iraqi troops and doing so from medium to high altitude, tactics that minimized the risk to the pilots, but made it hard for the aircrews to see and destroy their targets. Tons of bombs were being dropped, but there were many more misses than hits.

To pin down the Republican Guard, the Air Force ran twenty-four B-52 sorties a day against the forces. But the results were not good. During the Vietnam War, B-52s had leveled whole sections of the jungle with their "Arc Light" raids. But to limit their exposure to Iraqi surface-to-air missiles, the B-52Gs in the Gulf were bombing in groups of three — half the size of a typical bombing cell during the Vietnam War. Nor were the B-52s dropping their bombs with much accuracy. The crews struggled with high winds. Worse, after several weeks of bombing, intelligence analysts discovered that the bombs dropped by the B-52s seemed to be falling 400 to 600 feet short of their mark.

In an effort to improve the B-52s accuracy, a team of experts was secretly dispatched from the Strategic Air Command to work out some fixes. Part of the problem, it was later determined, had to do with discrepancies between the B-52s' targeting system and the intelligence data that the Black Hole was using. Programmed into the B-52s' computers was a geodetic map, essentially a grid that covered the world. While the bombing coordinates provided by the Black Hole used a map developed in 1984, the targeting systems in the B-52s were based on an older geodetic survey. It was another example of Clausewitz's "friction," a small glitch that was enough to throw all the bombs off target. The problem was fixed, but none of the air-war commanders pretended that it would make the B-52 a precision bomber. In the end, the B-52 was primarily a means of terrorizing the Iraqi ground troops, not killing them.

The F-16s that were being dispatched against the Republican Guard had their problems, too. At medium to high altitude, the F-16s were not very accurate. The Air Force's A-10s were also affected by the altitude restrictions. During the first weeks of the war, the planes were used against the Iraqi front-line forces. They had to rely on their Maverick antitank missiles and were unable to use their Gatling guns that fired 30mm armor-piercing munitions.[11]

The Navy and Marine warplanes were not doing any better. The lack of good intelligence on the Iraqi positions was a major headache for the Marines. Months before the war, the Marines had retired their RF-4B reconnaissance planes as an economy measure, and that left the Marine airmen desperate for accurate and up-to-date targeting information.

The Marines' dilemma was described in an internal analysis prepared by the Marine Corps Research Center at Quantico after the Gulf War. "Target photos provided to the aircrew were days, weeks and many times months old. Without current aerial photos, it was extremely difficult for an aviator to find a target even in a totally permissive environment," the report stated. "Aircrews with dated intelligence were told to bomb point targets by latitude and longitude; an inherently inaccurate bombing technique."

When the Marines found their targets they could not be sure of hitting them. Only a quarter of Marine combat aircraft were equipped with the FLIR technology that enabled the planes to pinpoint enemy targets at night and in bad weather by the heat they generated. Even when the Marines dropped dumb bombs they ran into problems. When they dropped MK-20 Rockeye cluster munitions from high altitude, the weapons had fusing problems.

To expand their killing power, the Marines broke out their cache of Vietnam-era napalm as well as fuel-air explosives, which dispersed a gaseous vapor into the air, which then ignited, creating a huge concussion. The plan was to use the bombs to set off mines and kill Iraqi troops in their bunkers. But analysis after the war indicated that only half the fuel-air explosives detonated.[12]

Like the rest of the ground commanders, Arnold believed that Glosson was too absorbed in trying to win the war by going to downtown Baghdad. Too few of the Army's targets in Kuwait and southern Iraq were being hit.

To document his case, Arnold prepared a briefing entitled "AR-CENT's Plan to Shape the Battlefield Prior to G-Day." Yeosock and Arnold presented the brief to Schwarzkopf shortly after the battle of Khafji.

Following the Air Force's targeting procedures, Army commanders had submitted their lists of targets to the air-war commanders. But of the 1,185 targets that the Army nominated by the end of January, 202 (17 percent) had been included in the Air Tasking Order and only 137

(12 percent) had actually been attacked. Not only did the air campaign need to do better, but the Army would have to get priority treatment for the eight days leading up to the ground war so that the 50 percent goal could be reached.[13]

Vice Adm. Stanley Arthur, the senior Navy officer in the Persian Gulf, also joined the rebellion against the Air Force generals. The Navy had resented its subordinate role in the air campaign from the start. Arthur thought the whole targeting process was inflexible. Navy planes were identifying targets, but were having trouble getting them on the target list. Worse, Arthur recalled after the war, he was convinced that the Iraqis had figured out the system. His intelligence officers were telling him that the Iraqis were moving what combat planes remained in Iraq every day or so, having discovered that it took three days to get all but the most critical targets on the allies' target list.[14]

The Marines did more than complain about the system. They began to put limits on their involvement in the Air Force–dominated campaign.

After the air-war planners ordered a Marine strike on a Scud rocket motor plant near Baghdad, the first and only Marine air attack near the Iraqi capital, Boomer's command informed Maj. Jeffrey R. "Oly" Olsen, the Marine representative in the Black Hole, that its aircraft were no longer available for carrying out strikes in central Iraq. It was the first of a series of restrictions — the Marines called them "amendments" — that the Marines imposed on their participation in the Air Force–run air campaign. Eventually, they would try to withdraw all their aircraft from the Air Force campaign and conduct their own air war over southern Kuwait.[15]

Now that the ground war was approaching, the dialogue between the ground and air commanders soon began to look more like litigation than combined arms warfare, with each side marshaling its evidence and trying to score points.

With the complaints of the ground commanders echoing through CENTCOM, Schwarzkopf assigned his deputy commander, Lt. Gen. Calvin Waller, to set up a panel to adjudicate the dispute between his air and ground commanders over what targets should be hit. Schwarzkopf's staff had recommended precisely this before the war, but Schwarzkopf had rejected it, hoping that it would not be needed. As in his handling of the defense of Saudi Arabia, Schwarzkopf's preference was for his commanders to work their differences out among themselves.

Against the recommendation of the air-war commanders, who wanted to focus intelligence on Iraq's command network, facilities for making weapons of mass destruction, and military infrastructure, Schwarzkopf also asked Washington to shift more of the satellite coverage to Kuwait and southern Iraq so that the battlefield targets could be hit. To the frustration of the Black Hole, more than 75 percent of the satellite time was focused on stationary Iraqi forces, leaving the planners without timely battle damage assessment of some key targets in Iraq.

Waller's new role, however, did not put an end to the infighting. The deputy CENTCOM commander thought that the Air Force generals had a not-so-hidden agenda throughout the war — to wit, "victory through airpower" — and were not team players.

Glosson, Waller complained, pretended to cooperate with the Army. But the Air Force general did everything to build a case that air strikes were destroying the Iraqis and sought to go around Waller to Schwarzkopf to sell the Air Force strategy.

During the daily brief for Schwarzkopf, Glosson used a small briefing board depicting air planning that only Schwarzkopf and a few senior officers in the front row could see. Then Glosson would come out of the meetings and say that "the CINC wants this or that done," Waller recalled after the war.

Waller told Yeosock and Schwarzkopf that Glosson was trying to manipulate the system, but got nowhere. Finally, Waller got so furious with Glosson that he confronted him, charging that he was disobeying Waller's instructions.

Glosson professed loyalty, but Waller became so mad at one point that he ran up to "the duplicitous bastard" and threatened to "choke his fucking head off." Glosson saw it differently. As far as he was concerned, Waller was not a neutral arbiter but an Army general who was carrying water for the Army commanders. Schwarzkopf's targeting board did not resolve the situation; it simply imported it to a higher level of the command.[16]

NIGHT CAMEL

Little by little, the Air Force responded to the complaints about its obsession with deep strikes and began paying more attention to "shaping the battlefield" for the ground forces.

During the long lead-up to the war, the Air Force had given some thought to using the F-111Fs to attack the Iraqi army, although it had not done so at the outset of the air campaign. In December, American warplanes had participated in a mock battle in the Saudi desert, dubbed Night Camel, in which they searched for tanks. High-flying TR-1 and

U-2 reconnaissance planes had looked for Iraqi armored formations and passed the information to AWACS planes, which in turn directed F-111Fs, F-15Es, and F-16s to their targets. The F-111Fs were equipped with FLIRs (forward-looking infrared systems), which created images from the heat of ground targets. Since the Iraqi tanks would absorb the sun's energy by day, they ought to be plainly visible against the cool desert background on the FLIR screens at night. The idea was that if the aircraft could find the Iraqi forces, they could drop cluster bombs on them. Now Glosson wondered if the wing's F-111Fs could use their 500-pound laser-guided bombs to blow up Iraqi tanks.

The F-111F was designed to fly low and fast, streak past enemy air defenses, drop its bombs, and make a quick getaway. Trolling at 18,000 feet for tanks buried up to their gun turrets in sand was not one of the plane's traditional missions. But on February 5, Col. Tom Lennon, wing commander of the 48th Tactical Fighter Wing, led a two-plane mission over the Medina Division in southern Iraq to try to find out if the F-111F could perform such a maneuver.

Lennon's mission went a giant step beyond Night Camel. He did not have any spy planes to find the Iraqi tanks for him; if he did locate one, the weapons system officer, who sat in the right seat of the plane, would have to score a direct hit with a GBU-12 500-pound laser-guided bomb. The wing planned to use 500-pound bombs instead of 2,000-pounders not for any tactical reasons but because it had many more of them.

As Lennon cruised over Iraq, armored vehicles appeared on the FLIR screen, greenish blobs against a hazy background. Lennon's weapons system officer used his targeting device to direct the laser on the tanks and guided the GBU-12 at the crosshairs. They waited for several seconds, and then there was an enormous flash. Reviewing the tapes later that night at Taif, Lennon concluded that the two F-111Fs had blown up seven out of eight armored vehicles. The pilots later dubbed the technique "tank plinking."

The novel technique was limited by the weather. The lasers used to target the tanks could not penetrate cloud cover, but on clear nights the tactic was devastatingly effective. Word of the new capability soon spread through the Iraqi encampments. The first night Lennon detected no movement around the targets, but several nights later he saw tank crews run from the vehicles after the GBU-12s came whistling toward their mark. Still later, the FLIRs picked up the crews hiding in foxholes away from their tanks.

Before tank plinking, the air campaign had been way short of its goal of destroying 50 percent of the Iraqi armor. But now it appeared that, given time, the tools were available to make up the difference. To beef up the tank-killing force, Glosson ordered F-15Es and A-6s, aircraft that were also equipped with laser targeting systems, to join the F-111Fs. The Black Hole had stumbled onto a good thing and planned to press the advantage home.[17]

Tank plinking was not the only innovation. To improve the accuracy of the F-16s, the Falcon pilots were instructed to start bombing from 8,000 feet instead of 12,000 to 15,000.

The Air Force also revived the Vietnam War tactic of using airborne scouts. The tactic had not worked well in Vietnam — the losses were considerable, and it was difficult to find targets in the jungle. The Air Force had all but abandoned the concept, but the scouting technique was better suited to the Gulf, where the aircraft could fly at medium altitude with near impunity searching for Iraqi vehicles with no place to hide. To implement the tactic, all of Kuwait and southern Iraq was divided up into thirty-five "kill boxes" of thirty by thirty miles. F-16 "killer scouts" would patrol the zones and lead attack planes to the targets in the predesignated zones. The box system was borrowed from the Saudis, who used it as an air traffic procedure to ensure that Saudi and friendly Arab aircraft did not run into each other.

As the warplanes began to show some success against the Iraqi ground troops, the Air Force launched a campaign to head off, or at least delay, the ground war. Even before the Riyadh meeting, it was clear that it would be an uphill battle. On February 6, Gen. McPeak had alerted Glosson that the Bush administration was planning to launch the ground war between February 21 and 25. Glosson should do what he could to stop the Army commanders from launching the ground offensive too soon.

Glosson took his case to Schwarzkopf, and suggested that the air campaign be given at least three additional weeks to carry out its bombing attacks. That would, in effect, carry the air campaign through February and perhaps beyond. In Washington, Air Force Secretary Donald Rice argued that the air war should proceed as long as it was showing results, floating the recommendation to Vice President Dan Quayle, his golfing partner. Rice had his connections and was trying to work all of them.

The Riyadh meeting between Schwarzkopf and the Pentagon chiefs, however, cemented the decision on the start time of the ground war. And the Air Force's effort to win the war suffered another body blow several days later when the F-117s took off for what they thought would be another routine mission over Baghdad.

★   ★   ★

On their way back from reviewing the war plan in Riyadh, Dick Cheney and Colin Powell paid a quick trip to the Saudi air base at Khamis Mushait. Tucked away in southwestern Saudi Arabia, isolated from the inquiring media and well out of range of Iraqi Scuds, the ultramodern air base had been a good place for the F-117s. The two Pentagon chiefs were led into a concrete airplane shelter and mounted a small wooden podium. On the wall of the otherwise bare shelter was a notice board covered with the signatures of the top officials who had passed through Khamis, as well as the sort of slogans that depersonalized the enemy in a way that made the strategic air campaign appear to be an entirely everyday pursuit. "Bombs R Us" read one bold-lettered slogan; "We Live So Others May Die" read another.

Cheney and Powell delivered brief speeches to the pilots, maintenance personnel, and bomb builders, who attached the laser guidance systems to the bomb bodies, turning them into instruments of precision warfare. After their brief pep talks to the airmen, the two Pentagon chiefs inscribed separate 2,000-pound bombs.

"To Saddam, with fond regards," wrote Cheney.[18]

Three days later, the black jets prepared for another bombing raid on Baghdad. There were times that the Black Hole assigned targets to the Nighthawks at the last minute, rushing satellite photos that the stealth pilots would use to find their mark to Khamis in a C-21 jet. But there was nothing out of the ordinary about the preparations for the February 13 attack. The list had been received the night before and contained the usual array of military targets, including ones in Baghdad. The F-117s had hit bunkers in Baghdad before. The Al Firdos bunker would be just one more.

One of twenty-five facilities that had originally been constructed as air-raid shelters for the general population in Baghdad, Al Firdos had been upgraded by Western European contractors to serve as a hideout for the Iraqi leadership. The bunker had two stories, and according to CENTCOM's intelligence reports could shelter as many as 1,500 people.

The bunker had been considered to be a potential target since December. It was Charlie Allen, the National Intelligence Officer for Warning who had forecast the invasion of Kuwait, who pushed the Air Force to attack the facility. On the first few nights of the war, American intelligence saw that the Iraqis had sought to camouflage the roof. Sedans were also observed near the facility. Finally, American intelligence concluded that the facility was being used by the Iraqi Intelligence Service, located several blocks away, which was charged with quashing internal dissent. That made it a high-priority target for Washington's effort to knock the props out from under the Saddam Hussein regime.

Allen told Warden on February 10 that the facility needed to be struck. Warden asked if there was any possibility it was being used to shelter civilians. Allen replied that the evidence suggested it was not.

Three days later, F-117s were assigned to attack the facility. To ensure the job got done, two F-117s were each to drop GBU-27 bunker-busting bombs on the structure.

The mission went according to plan. It was only in reviewing the video recordings of the bomb drops that each aircraft made during its mission, used for bomb damage assessment and for critiquing the performance of the pilots, that F-117 commanders saw anything unusual about the facility. A number of vehicles, including what looked like buses, were parked near the bunker, which was located in the Ameriyya suburb of Baghdad. In reviewing countless videotapes, the wing's planners had never seen vehicles near Baghdad command bunkers before. Later that day, the news reports filtered in: Baghdad had announced that hundreds of civilians had been killed in the raid.[19]

The Pentagon handled the public relations. It insisted that Al Firdos was a command, control, and communications bunker that had recently become active and suggested it was being used to help direct the war. Pentagon officials even hinted darkly that Saddam Hussein might have allowed civilians into the facility, sacrificing them to influence world public opinion.

Meanwhile, Pete Williams, the Pentagon's top spokesman, placed a couple of quick calls. The unintentional killing of hundreds of civilians was bad enough, but Cheney and Powell's decision to sign the bombs was a potential problem. It was with relief that Williams later called reporters, saying that neither of the bombs signed by the Pentagon chiefs had been dropped on the bunker. The bomb signed by Cheney had been dropped by Maj. Wes Wyrich on a chemical bunker in northern Iraq. Wyrich's unit later sent the defense secretary a tape of the bombing with the inscription "When it has to be there overnight, count on 37th Aerial Delivery," referring to one of the 117 stealth squadrons. But by then the joke was no longer funny.

Although the Pentagon and CENTCOM circled the wagons, privately it was a different matter. It was clear that the bombing of the facility was an intelligence failure. Classified intelligence revealed that a senior Iraqi security official and a third of his staff had been killed in the attack. But the satellite reconnaissance had not picked up any indication that the families of the intelligence officials and perhaps other people from the Ameriyya suburb were being admitted into the facility each night.

Intelligence gathered after the war also suggests that the Al Firdos bunker was essentially a hideout for senior Iraqi officials. Allen later concluded that he had been mistaken in believing it was an important Iraqi command and control center. The bunker was equipped with an Erickson communications suite, which enabled Iraqi officials to keep in touch with developments, but was not nearly sophisticated enough to manage a war.

Nor is there a shred of evidence that the Iraqi government knowingly sacrificed the civilians in that shelter.

The attack was a major blow to the strategic air campaign. The White House, which had sought to limit the harm to innocent Iraqi civilians, was worried about the political fallout, and Colin Powell moved to rein in the air campaign. The word was passed to the Black Hole: the bombing of Baghdad would be the exception, not the rule.[20]

Up to then, the air commanders had enjoyed enormous leeway, but from now on its target lists would be scrubbed by Schwarzkopf and reviewed by Powell.

After the Al Firdos attack, Glosson was informed by Mike McConnell, the chief intelligence official on the JCS, and by Schwarzkopf that Powell had a lock on the Baghdad targets. No target in the Iraqi capital could be struck unless it had his specific approval.

"CINC has big concern over cities. Receiving pressure from Chairman not to hit urban areas in Baghdad or urban targets anywhere. Urban targets now being approved in Washington," an aide to Glosson wrote in his diary one day after the bombing of Al Firdos. "Take all F-117s off Baghdad targets."[21]

After the Persian Gulf War, the Pentagon would tout the war as a validation of the post–Vietnam War principle that Washington should establish the broad parameters of the war and leave the details up to the theater commander. But now Washington was picking the targets. To the Air Force it seemed as if the political fallout from the Al Firdos raid had accomplished what the Iraqi air defenses could not: downtown Baghdad was to be attacked sparingly, if at all. By placing the city off limits to American air strikes, the command was giving in to Iraq's propaganda campaign, the air-war commanders argued. Saddam Hussein had been put on notice that the Iraqi capital would not be a sanctuary. Powell's perspective was clearly different. He needed to hold together the allied war effort, but a few more strikes like that at Al

Firdos and the coalition would be undone. From his vantage point, Powell believed that the coalition had reaped most of the benefits from attacking the Iraqi capital and that the risks of continued bombing were not worth the gains.

"I had to start taking a closer look," recalled Powell. "They had a pretty free hand. After something like this, we did not need another situation where a large number of civilians were killed with Peter Arnett all over the place. We were a month into the war and our concentration was shifting to the battlefield. We needed to look at how many times we needed to hit the Baath Party headquarters and why."[22]

The Al Firdos episode came on the heels of another public relations setback. American intelligence received a report that the Iraqis were prepared to launch a pilotless radio-controlled MiG equipped with chemical weapons. SPEAR, the Naval intelligence cell, did not believe the report, but the Navy was ordered to attack the plane with Tomahawk cruise missiles.

Six missiles were fired in quick succession in the daylight raid. The February 1 attack was captured by CNN, and at least one missile was shot down. Powell, who believed the Tomahawk attacks were reaching a point of diminishing returns, ordered a halt to the daylight cruise missile attacks — the only daytime attacks that were being carried out in Baghdad.

Schwarzkopf characteristically yielded to Powell's guidance, just as he had on the development of the left hook and the prosecution of the Scud campaign. But the CENTCOM commander sometimes chafed under the second guessing in Washington.

"Powell," Schwarzkopf told his staff one day, "is a political genuis. But he lacks the stomach for war."[23]

To keep the deep attacks going, Glosson had a few tricks up his sleeve. Powell might have the authority for approving strikes in downtown Baghdad, but "downtown Baghdad" was in the eye of the beholder.

At the suggestion of his planners, Glosson took a map and drew a three-mile-wide radius around the center of Baghdad and colored it in. The international airport was outside the circle, and there were lots of targets in and around the airport that the Black Hole wanted to hit, including facilities for Saddam Hussein's security police. And on February 17, CENTCOM authorized the F-117s to attack Tamarya, a nuclear facility northeast of Baghdad that American intelligence had learned of from a defector. That raid served a double function: the coalition would take another swipe at a possible nuclear facility while keeping the heat on in the Baghdad area.

Glosson and his deputies also began to look for a way to get inside the circle. One way to renew the attack on downtown targets with little risk of collateral damage was to restrike targets that were already hit, and the planners proposed that attacks be launched against the International Communications Center (also called the AT&T building), the Al Kharj tower, and the Baath Party Headquarters. Militarily the strikes would not accomplish much, but at least psychologically they would show that the war was still on.

Meanwhile, Glosson, David Deptula, and Warden's team in Washington tried to lay the foundation for a major blitz against military targets and command centers in the Iraqi capital. A February 21 memo prepared for Horner to send to Schwarzkopf made their case:

> If any settlement results in Saddam remaining the titular head of Iraq, it may be prudent to render ineffective those facilities and personnel who may allow him to recapture control of the populace and subject them to the repression they apparently are close to shirking off. Targeting these facilities may further cripple the Saddam regime such that even with cessation of hostilities he may become impotent and subject to replacement.[24]

Horner and Glosson proposed targeting the Babylon Hotel, which intelligence indicated was being used as a residence by the Iraqi air force chief of staff, the intelligence chief of staff, and the defense minister. But in the wake of the Al Firdos bombing raid, Maj. Gen. Robert Johnston, Schwarzkopf's chief of staff, and Maj. Gen. Burt Moore, Schwarzkopf's chief operations deputy, were afraid that the attack would be perceived as bombing civilians and argued against the move.

The Black Hole planners also proposed bombing the Al Rasheed Hotel, the Baghdad base for foreign journalists covering Iraq, whose modern technology made it a node in the Iraqi communications network. The plan was to give the journalists and other occupants notice that the Rasheed was to be bombed and then strike several days later. Barring that, the planners wanted to target the bridges that spanned the Euphrates River, having concluded that they carried fiber-optic cables that the Iraqis relied on for communications.

In Washington, McPeak pressed to restart the Baghdad bombing campaign. He was particularly concerned about the bridges, and if he had his way, there would not be one left standing in Baghdad — they would all be in the water. McPeak lobbied Powell, but was rebuffed. Warden also tried to change Cheney's mind. The defense secretary was invited down to Checkmate for a briefing, where Warden made the point that a virtual halt had been called to the attacks on downtown Baghdad. As usual, Cheney played his cards close to his vest.

All the while that the Air Force was lobbying to renew the attacks in Baghdad, the Army was tugging the other way.

Several days after Cheney and Powell left Riyadh, Brig. Gen. John Leide, the chief intelligence officer at CENTCOM, directed that a U-2 fly across southern Iraq to develop a new battle damage assessment of the Tawakalna Division. The southernmost of Iraq's Republican Guard divisions, the Tawakalna had been within easy range of allied aircraft. There was every reason to think that the division had been badly damaged. CENTCOM's battle damage assessment put the Iraqi division at 48 percent. But after analyzing the U-2 data, Leide dramatically revised the BDA. The Tawakalna, Leide ruled, was at 74 percent strength.

The new estimate hit the Army like a thunderclap. If the earlier CENTCOM assessment had exaggerated the damage done to the Tawakalna Division, the estimates of the other Iraqi divisions were probably off as well. The ground forces could have a stiffer fight than they had been led to believe.[25]

Before the air campaign was launched, Horner had told Schwarzkopf that the Army could be the judge of the bombing campaign against the Iraqi ground forces. Now the Army decided to exercise its right. After the new intelligence reassessment circulated at CENTCOM, Brig. Gen. John Stewart, the chief Army intelligence officer in Riyadh, decreed that only half the kills reported by F-111Fs and F-15Es, which were recorded by the aircrafts' taping systems, would be accepted as legitimate. One-third of the A-10 kills, which were confirmed visually by the pilot, would be counted.

The Air Force saw the Army's new battle damage criteria as a slap at Horner and his generals. The Army was saying, in effect, that it did not trust the Air Force reporting. The F-111Fs had tapes of their missions, which were reviewed by an Army liaison officer. On February 13 and 14, when there was a break in the weather, the F-111Fs reported that they had killed 225 armored vehicles. The Army wanted the Iraqi front-line defenses softened up for the big ground war; but as the Air Force saw it, the way the air war was going there was not going to be a costly land offensive. The Iraqi army was coming apart at the seams. Battle damage assessment had started out as a way to gauge the strength of the Iraqis, but it had now become a political football. The Army was trying to use the battle damage criteria as a means of bending the Air Force to its will and inducing it to step up the bombing of Iraq's front-line forces.

The Army also made sure its unhappiness with the Air Force generals got back to Washington. Arnold typed out a short paragraph for the Army's classified SITREP (situation report). The SITREP circulated at the highest levels of the United States Central Command and the Pentagon. Within military circles, putting a complaint in the SITREP was the equivalent of going public. It was a sure-fire way to get high-level attention in Washington.

> Air support related issues continue to plague final preparation of combat operations and raise doubts concerning our ability to shape the battlefield prior to the initiation of the ground campaign. Too few sorties are made available to VII and XVIII corps. And while air support missions are being flown against 1st echelon enemy divisions, Army-nominated targets are not being serviced. Efforts must be taken now to align the objective of the air and ground campaign and ensure the success of our future operation.

In case anybody missed the message, Arnold repeated it in the Army SITREP the next day: "Our inability to control the air campaign continues, resulting in a great deal of uncertainty in shaping the battlefield."[26]

When Arnold's telephone rang, Horner was on the line. The Army general knew that the SITREPs had hit a nerve. The senior Air Force commander was in a rage and threatened to use his influence at CENTCOM to have Arnold run out of Saudi Arabia. Horner was convinced that airpower was extracting a terrible toll on the Iraqi ground forces. To the Air Force, the Army's complaints were a cheap shot, stimulated by Army field officers who neither understood the overall game plan for apportioning airpower nor appreciated the success airmen were having in whittling down the Iraqi army.

The exchange between Arnold and Horner was one of the sharpest between the Army and Air Force commanders. Following Horner's protests, Arnold was approached by Waller, who advised him to include a few words of praise for the Air Force in the next Army SITREP to defuse the tensions. Arnold complied; but the Army corps commanders continued their complaints until the day of the ground war.

After the war, CENTCOM's posture was one of unity. Congress was assured that the relationship between the Army and the Air Force had been a model of cordiality. "I cannot recall any divisive differences of opinion nor any inability to work any issue out on a very friendly basis," Horner told the Senate Armed Services Committee in May 1991. The bitter debate that buffeted CENTCOM throughout the war was swept under the rug.[27]

But behind-the-scenes sniping continued, for the confrontation between the Army field commanders and the Air Force was not so much about the performance of airpower as the Army's inability to control it. As the Air Force saw it, the Gulf War was a model for future conflicts. But neither the Army nor the Marines wanted to go to war that way again.

In the final analysis, the air war had confirmed the Air Force's growing ability to destroy targets deep in the enemy heartland and on the battlefields. By late February, however, airpower's success in crippling Iraq had not led to a political success comparable to its military success. Airpower had yet to do what ground power had habitually done — change the political equation as a function of that power. The air-war planners were frustrated by Powell's restrictions. Even so, Warden's grandest hopes for Instant Thunder had not been borne out in almost six weeks of bombing.

But while the air-war commanders had not won the war in downtown Baghdad, they devastated the Iraqi army. By depriving it of any help from the Iraqi air force, forcing it to dig in, eliminating the prospect of a mobile defense, and knocking out much of the Iraqi armor and artillery, the air campaign had all but won the war.

After the war, a panel of experts commissioned by the Air Force and a separate assessment carried out by the CIA concluded that bombing had destroyed one-quarter of the Republican Guard armor and much more of the equipment used by the front-line troops. That fell short of their goal to destroy 50 percent of the Iraqis' overall armor and artillery in southern Iraq and Kuwait. But the numbers game missed the larger point. CENTCOM had put the bar too high. The threshold for the disintegration of the Iraqi army was considerably less than 50 percent and was surpassed during the bombing campaign.

And while the collapse of the Iraqi army was not apparent to the U.S. Army, it was a growing concern for Iraq's long-time supporters in Moscow.

16

Second Thoughts

Theater Intelligence: Expect Significant Resistance.
Air Component: Regular Army Waiting To Surrender.
 RG No Longer An Effective Fighting Force
CINCENT: The Iraqi Army Is Ready To Collapse.

— Sign posted in the Black Hole

N MOSCOW, it was clear to President Gorbachev and his generals that the Iraqi army was being hit hard. Throughout the buildup to the war and during the fighting itself, Gorbachev played a double game, supporting the allied war effort while pressing the allies to pursue a diplomatic settlement that would shield Baghdad from the full humiliation of its defeat.

Gorbachev's stance was intended to placate conservative elements in Moscow, including the Russian military, which was loath to see its former client vanquished on the battlefield. The Russians had been rebuffed by both Washington and Baghdad when they sought to broach the idea of a cease-fire several days after the air war was launched.

By mid-February, however, Moscow could see that time had almost run out. The Soviet president ordered Yevgeni Primakov to go to Baghdad and explain the facts of life to Saddam Hussein. Iraq's army could escape a final, humiliating defeat, but Baghdad would have to act fast.

Primakov's journey was a memorable one. With the allied warplanes patrolling Iraq's skies, flying to Baghdad was not an option. So Primakov flew first to Teheran and then hopped a plane to Bakhtaran, near the Iran-Iraq border, where he was met by Iraqi officials and aides from Moscow's embassy in Baghdad. Primakov made the long drive to Baghdad in a car smeared with dirt. The Iraqis hoped that would camouflage the motorcade; Primakov was worried that the allied warplanes might be onto the trick and would swoop down on the procession.

The Iraqis put Primakov up in the Al Rasheed Hotel, and later that night the Soviet diplomat was taken for a meeting with Saddam Hussein. Primakov expected to be taken to a bunker. Instead, he was taken to a small house in a civilian area of Baghdad. Civilian areas were off-limits to allied planes, and the Iraqis knew that it was safer to hold a meeting there than in any underground command center. The house was equipped with a small stove and lit by a generator.

Primakov's first impression of the Iraqi leader was that he looked thinner, but otherwise he seemed to be bearing up. After unfastening his gun belt, Hussein attacked Moscow for supporting the allied war effort and boasted how Iraq had withstood the coalition's hammer blows. But Primakov concluded that the bravado was meant to impress the gaggle of Iraqi officers who accompanied the Iraqi leader.

After the Iraqi officers were dismissed and Hussein and Primakov were alone, the mood became more businesslike. Primakov made his pitch. The Americans were moving toward a ground operation. The Iraqi army would be crushed. The diplomatic options had narrowed with the decline of Iraq's fortunes on the battlefield. Politics was the art of the possible. It was imperative that Iraq declare that it was prepared to withdraw its forces in the shortest possible time frame.

The Iraqi leader absorbed the presentation. If the Iraqi forces withdrew, how could they be sure they would not be harried as they retreated? Would the economic sanctions against Iraq be lifted if Baghdad pulled its forces out of Kuwait? It was clear from his questions that Saddam Hussein was not rejecting a settlement out of hand.

It was agreed that Tariq Aziz, the Iraqi foreign minister, would go to Moscow to discuss the terms of a withdrawal. Baghdad Radio later announced that Iraq's Revolutionary Council had decided that Iraqi forces might withdraw if the United States promised to remove its troops from the Gulf and a solution was found to the Palestinian problem. With a land offensive only days away, the Iraqis were still trying to negotiate a deal.

Although the Russians thought that Baghdad was finally on the right track, they knew that the Iraqis had a weak hand and that the Bush administration was not in a compromising mood. There was no way that the Iraqis were going to get off scot-free. In effect, Moscow was advising the Iraqis to plea-bargain. Iraq was having a hard time accepting that it had lost the case, so Gorbachev would make the presentation himself.

When Aziz met Gorbachev in Moscow on February 17, the Soviet president said that it was time to stop the bargaining. The only guarantee Moscow could wangle from the Americans was that the withdrawing Iraqi forces would not be shot in the back. Like an attorney in a criminal case, the Russians were trying to get the best deal for their client.

In a separate meeting five days later, the Soviet president exhorted the Iraqis to cut down their timetable for withdrawing troops. The Iraqis said that they needed a minimum of six weeks — and preferably three to four months — to withdraw their forces. Gorbachev urged them to cut the withdrawal period in half. A three-week withdrawal with no strings attached, he reasoned, was a plan that Russia just might be able to sell to the Americans.[1]

In Washington, the White House was not enthusiastic about Gorbachev's peacemaking. White House officials talked about an "aperture" through which Saddam Hussein might avoid the humiliation of losing the war and hold onto his base of power. President Bush had supported Gorbachev, but he was determined to deny the Iraqi leader the opening.

Saying no to the Russians was not so hard. But Moscow was making noises about taking its plan to the Security Council, and some members of CENTCOM's coalition were already beginning to waiver. French President François Mitterrand had quietly proposed that the Americans put off the land offensive so that a diplomatic compromise could be explored. Egyptian President Hosni Mubarak joined in the appeal. Although the French and Egyptian forces were not critical in a military sense, the Bush administration wanted the land offensive to have a multinational cast. The French and Egyptian appeals were kept under wraps, but the Russian peace initiative risked a split in the coalition just as the war was reaching its denouement.

Paris and Cairo were not the only ones to have second thoughts. On February 21, William Webster, director of the CIA, went to the White House to deliver a sobering assessment. Throughout the Gulf conflict, the CIA had sought to guard its independence. The military had a penchant for exaggerating its successes, but the agency would tell the story straight.

During the Vietnam War, CIA analysts had challenged the body count the American military generated. Now Webster was challenging

CENTCOM's bomb damage assessment, and he was doing so virtually on the eve of the ground war. CENTCOM had reported that it had destroyed 1,700 tanks, 900 armored personnel carriers, and 1,400 pieces of artillery. Performing a battle damage assessment was not easy. If a bomb fell near a tank and scored a "mobility kill" by knocking off the treads or damaging the engine, there would be very little obvious damage for the spy satellites to pick up on the outside of the tank. The CIA chief told Bush that his agency could confirm only 470 of the armor "kills" recorded by CENTCOM. Webster's assessment had enormous implications. If the American military had badly underestimated the damage done to the Iraqis, it could suffer considerable casualties when it attacked.[2]

Numbers (Percent) of Reported Iraqi Equipment Losses as of 23 Feb. 1991 Briefing to the President

Organizations	Tanks	Armored Personnel Carriers	Artillery
JCS/CENTCOM	1,688 (39%)	929 (32%)	1,452 (47%)
Central Intell. Agency	524 (12%)	245 (9%)	255 (8%)
Defense Intell. Agency	685 (16%)	373 (13%)	622 (20%)

Source: "Gulf War Air Power Survey."

One intelligence official who was not impressed with Webster's analysis was Charles Allen, who had been working closely with Col. John Warden and other Air Force officers at their Checkmate office since the invasion. Allen did not accept the implication in Webster's assessment that the Iraqis were still a viable fighting force. The battle damage assessment Webster presented was a quantitative measure of the number of Iraqi weapons on the battlefield based on satellite photos and high-flying spy planes. It was not an assessment of how many Iraqis were still around to operate the equipment or of the declining state of their morale — what Allen called "invisible damage."

Getting information from deserters had not always been easy. The Saudis had declined to let the Americans interrogate the Iraqi deserters they apprehended, depriving CENTCOM of an important source of intelligence. The idea of Western officers interrogating Islamic soldiers, even enemy ones, was unacceptable to the Saudi military.

But from intercepts of Iraqi communications and from the deserters the Americans were able to get in their hands, there were clear indications that the Iraqi ranks were growing thinner by the day. The Iraqi front-line units were shrinking their "frontages" and protecting an increasingly smaller area.

One noteworthy intelligence report disclosed a platoon-size firefight between Iraqis trying to go AWOL and a death squad set up by the Iraqi high command to stop the exodus. There was also a report that one Iraqi commander had hung several Iraqi deserters and exhibited their bodies for days. One of the eeriest developments had to do with "cold spots," which had been detected by airborne sensors. Initially, American intelligence officials thought they signaled the presence of refrigerated storage sites for biological weapons. But DIA analysts eventually arrived at another explanation: the "cold spots" were twenty-nine-foot-long refrigerated vans used to transport the bodies of dead Iraqis to Baghdad, a practice the Iraqi military had used during the war with Iran.[3]

In mid-February, Allen circulated several memorandums to Pentagon officials, summing up his conclusions that the Iraqi army was in a state of rapid decay. One read:

> Tactical responses to coalition attacks have been generally inept or passive. Although digging in and going underground are appropriate responses to coalition air, helicopter and artillery attacks, the wholesale burying of heavy divisions unquestionably has a devastating psychological and physical effect upon a unit's mobility. Since their drubbing at Khafji, Iraqi reconnaissance operations have been timid and unrewarding. Their response to aggressive coalition raids, recons in force and artillery strikes has been conspicuously absent.

On February 21, the same day that Webster went to the White House, Allen briefed Pentagon officials that the Iraqi army was in a state of collapse and forecast that the allied ground offensive would be quick.

> As a result of this psychological damage to the Iraqi will to fight, any plan of maneuver that plays to coalition strengths, avoids Iraqi strengths, and forces the enemy to come to us is more likely to result in a rapid victory. An armored envelopment supported by airborne and amphibious assaults probably would cut off the bulk of enemy forces in the KTO within 5 to 10 days with a minimum of coalition casualties. We judge the majority of Iraqi forces will not have the will to leave their defensive positions and try to

prevent such an encirclement. Moreover, once aware that they are cut off, we believe the bulk of the Iraqi Army will surrender after a degree of resistance.[4]

Neither Cheney nor Rear Adm. Mike McConnell, the chief intelligence officer for the JCS, was inclined to give much weight to Webster's analysis. To Cheney, Webster's presentation looked like a typical cover-your-rear briefing. The CIA was taking the most conservative estimate of what the air war had accomplished. If the land war was tough, no one could say that the agency had failed to warn the president of the risks. Most important, President Bush was not persuaded either. The same day that Webster took his brief to the White House, President Bush expressed confidence to his family that the ground war would be relatively brief.[5]

On the weighty issues of war and peace, the White House found the CIA director to be a poor guide. He had failed to alert the White House in time to head off the Iraqi invasion of Kuwait. As Iraqi defectors made clear, his agency failed to uncover much of the Iraqi nuclear program. Now, he failed to discern the disintegration of the Iraqi army. Long and painful experience had persuaded Bush administration policy-makers that the CIA's advice was sometimes best ignored.

If Moscow was acting like Baghdad's defense counsel, Washington was the determined prosecutor who wanted to make sure that the Saddam Hussein regime received the stiffest possible sentence. The White House wanted to deliver the decisive blow on the ground. Some way would have to be found to rebuff the Soviet gambit without making Washington look bloodthirsty and bent on vengeance. Not only did the administration not want to delay the ground war, it was looking for a way to start it as early as possible.

In Riyadh, Schwarzkopf knew that Washington wanted to get on with the ground war and resented the pressure. When Cheney and Powell had visited Riyadh in early February, Schwarzkopf had rebuffed Wolfowitz's suggestion that the air campaign be extended into March. But a land war would put Schwarzkopf's strategy to a test and he was nervous about it.

As the tension built, even Iraq's failure to respond to the shift of Army forces to the west worried Schwarzkopf. Perhaps Iraq had a nuclear bomb after all, Schwarzkopf wondered, and planned to detonate it in the empty desert as the allies advanced.

While the White House saw the Russian involvement as a threat, Schwarzkopf saw it as an opportunity and defended Moscow's role in a telephone conversation with Cheney, describing it as the only plausible way for Baghdad to work out a face-saving compromise. A Russian-brokered compromise, however, would have enabled Baghdad to keep its Republican Guard intact and salvage most of its army, defeating one of CENTCOM's central objectives.[6]

With Washington interested in attacking early, Schwarzkopf called Walter Boomer, who was to kick off the coalition offensive, and asked if the Marines could launch their ground assault on February 22, two days earlier than planned. Schwarzkopf told Boomer that CENTCOM's weather forecasters were reporting that bad weather was moving in. If they attacked on February 22, the Marines could have three days of good weather, which was very important for the Marine helicopters and airplanes. By February 25, clouds would be drifting over the battlefield.

Boomer was not enthusiastic about the request. Frustrated with the absence of satellite photos of the Iraqi defenses, he had already sent reconnaissance teams through the Iraqi obstacles in southern Kuwait, and the Marines could not start softening up the Iraqis with artillery and air strikes until those teams made their way back to Saudi Arabia. Boomer also wanted to launch a final series of B-52 raids before unleashing his attack, and he also wanted time for Maj. Gen. Harry W. Jenkins, the commander of the Marines steaming in the Persian Gulf, to launch an amphibious feint. An amphibious landing was not in the cards, but Boomer was still planning on using amphibious raids to keep the Iraqis looking east.

After conferring with his commanders, Boomer told Schwarzkopf that the Marines could advance the time of the attack if necessary, but preferred to stick to their timetable. Boomer explained his decision in a memorandum for the record:

> These factors, plus many others, caused me to tell the CINC that while it would be possible to execute on the 22nd, my attack would be significantly degraded, perhaps as much as 25 per cent. I told him that my first choice would be to wait for three good days of weather. My second choice would be to go on the 24th and take a chance on bad weather on the 25th. My rationale is that on the 25th we would be through the barrier and have more room to maneuver, with less concern for artillery and chemicals. Finally, my last choice would be to go on the 22nd.[7]

Schwarzkopf told Boomer that he understood and would resist pressures to go early. However volatile he could be at times of stress, in the days leading up the ground offensive, the general was determined to let his field commanders be the judge of what they needed.

Schwarzkopf's willingness to hold up the land war until the Marines were ready made little sense to some administration officials. The Marines' role was to tie down the Iraqis while the Army swept around them, and the Marines could accomplish that by skirmishing along the border, the officials argued. But Schwarzkopf had long ago acceded to the Marines' insistence that they have an opportunity to play a major role in the liberation of Kuwait, and he was prepared to give them the time they needed to do it right.

As in early February, however, Schwarzkopf was still troubled by the plan for an amphibious operation, even one limited to a brief raid on an offshore island. When Stan Arthur and Harry Jenkins flew to Riyadh in mid-February to discuss the plan, Schwarzkopf subjected them to a barrage of skeptical questions. The Navy and Marine commanders assured Schwarzkopf that a raid on Faylakah Island was needed to reinforce the deception that the Marines intended an amphibious landing on the Kuwait mainland. They argued that the action need not divert too much of the Navy's airpower or risk too many casualties: the Marines would have a two-to-one advantage on the western part of the island, where they planned to attack.

After hearing the pitch, Schwarzkopf turned to Jenkins and raised a more political issue. If, as the plan stated, the Marines seized the island and then withdrew, the world might have the impression that the Marines were driven off the island by the Iraqis. Schwarzkopf had spent considerable energy burnishing the image of the military and had little tolerance for negative press.

"Our media beats their media to the punch," Jenkins replied. If the American press was told the purpose of the raid beforehand, they would accurately describe the purpose of the operation, he reasoned.

As the Riyadh meeting came to a close, Schwarzkopf told the Navy and Marine commanders that he agreed with their plan but stopped short of giving his final approval.

"I really think you ought to do it," Schwarzkopf said. "But I've got to tell you I am going to have one hell of a time selling it in Washington," he added in an oblique reference to Powell. Before Jenkins left, Schwarzkopf pulled him aside and told him he should be prepared to carry out the raid by February 22.[8]

GIVING THE ULTIMATUM

With the Russians, Iraqis, and Americans involved in their triangular diplomacy, Schwarzkopf's commanders made their final war preparations.

In the days leading up the ground war, the air-war commanders turned their full attention at the Iraqi front-line positions. Lennon's F-111Fs were pulled off their tank plinking for two days of attacks on Iraqi artillery positions, including the Iraqi 47th Division near the VII Corps. F-117s were assigned to attack heavily defended command and control positions in Kuwait and southern Iraq.

When the ground war began, Horner planned to step up the pounding. The Air Force ordered that the altitude restrictions on the pilots be lifted as soon as the land offensive was under way. Flights of aircraft would be directed over the battlefield on a continuous basis so that the Army might call for close air support whenever it needed it. But the Army was still worried that the Air Force was overstating its capabilities and underestimating the Iraqis.

Even with a 116,000-man corps, the promise of air support, and open desert almost devoid of enemies before him, Lt. Gen. Luck, the XVIII Airborne commander, was nervous. By late February, the Army field commanders had been given the authority to run raids across the border. In addition to providing the ground forces with a long-awaited chance to gather intelligence, it was an opportunity for the young, all-volunteer force to gain a taste of battle. The XVIII Corps's probes showed western Iraq to be largely a strategic void. The corps's most celebrated probe came on February 21 when Apaches from Peay's 101st took fire, engaged a bunker, and mounted a heliborne assault in southern Iraq, taking 406 prisoners, including an Iraqi battalion commander. Nonetheless, there were apprehensions.

In the fall, Luck had told Wolfowitz that the liberation of Kuwait was not worth the life of a single American soldier. Now, as the ground war approached, the XVIII Corps's apprehension jeopardized the secrecy of the left hook. Concerned that Iraq's 54th Division in far western Iraq might move east and interfere with the corps's attack, Luck's staff designed a ploy to freeze the division in place. Pakistani troops, American helicopters and trucks, and mock-ups of armored vehicles were moved to Ar'ar, the town in the far western part of Saudi Arabia that Maj. Gen. Downing's commandos were using as a base in their Scud hunt. Then the XVIII Corps broadcast radio conversations to create the impression

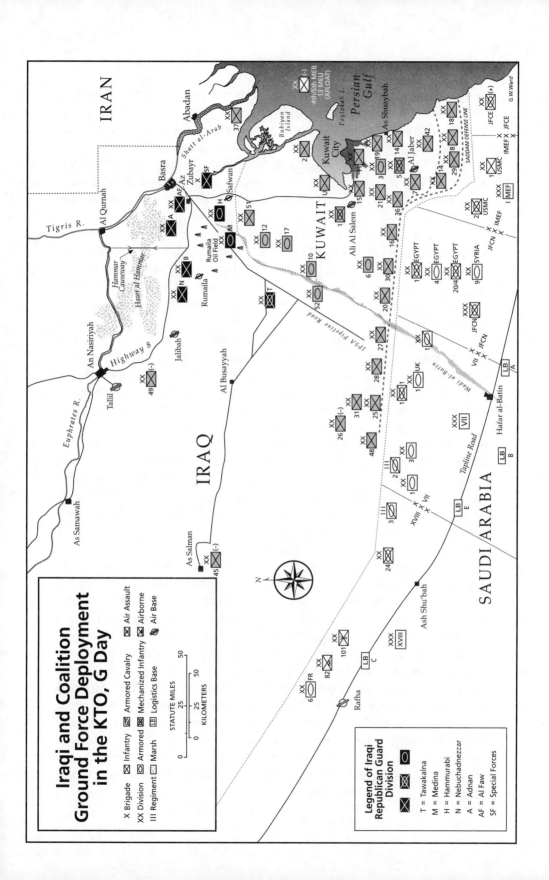

Iraqi and Coalition
Ground Force Deployment
in the KTO, G Day

X Brigade   ⊠ Infantry   ⊠ Armored Cavalry   ⊠ Air Assault
XX Division   ⊘ Armored   ⊠ Mechanized Infantry ⊠ Airborne
III Regiment   ▨ Marsh   ⊡ Logistics Base   ✈ Air Base

STATUTE MILES
0   25   50

0   25   50
KILOMETERS

**Legend of Iraqi
Republican Guard
Division**

T = Tawakalna
M = Medina
H = Hammurabi
N = Nebuchadnezzar
A = Adnan
AF = Al Faw
SF = Special Forces

IRAN

Abadan

Persian Gulf

Bubiyan Island

Faylakah I.

As Shuaybah

Shatt al-Arab

Basra

Al Qurnah

Tigris R.

Az Zubayr

Safwan

Kuwait City

Al Jaber

Ali Al Salem

KUWAIT

SADDAM DEFENSE LINE

Hammar Causeway

Hawr al-Hammar

Rumaila Oil Field

Rumaila

An Nasiriyah

Talil

Euphrates R.

Highway 8

Jalibah

Al Busayyah

IRAQ

IPSA Pipeline Road

Wadi al-Batin

Hafar al-Batin

Tapline Road

As Salman

As Samawah

SAUDI ARABIA

Ash Shu'bah

Rafha

N

G. W. Ward

that the Americans had stationed an armored brigade in the town with the mission of attacking Baghdad.

Steven Arnold, Yeosock's operations deputy, observed after the war that had he known about the ruse he would not have permitted it to go forward. The deception operation was at cross-purposes with what much of the VII Corps was doing. Franks's commanders did not want the Iraqis to have a clue they were about to be attacked from the far west.[9]

Luck was also worried about how well his corps would do when it encountered the Republican Guard. In the days before the ground war, Luck sent a still-classified message to Waller appealing for more forces and more area in which to maneuver. Luck wanted CENTCOM to take one of Franks's divisions, the 1st Armored, and put it under the control of the XVIII Corps.

"To accomplish our mission in this [contingency plan] requires more combat power," Luck wrote. "The Hammurabi is at the highest strength of any RGFC division. The proposed plan calls for us to attack the Hammurabi with our single heavy division corps after having suffered through the attrition of defeating two-three RGFC infantry divisions."[10]

The VII Corps was concerned, too. For Franks, his probes and feints were not the confidence builders they were intended to be. Franks concluded that the Iraqis could inflict considerable casualties if his troops were caught in the Iraqi killing zones. American intelligence officials have an expression for the process used to impose order on raw data — "template." The Army had its template when it came to the Iraqis, and it was that the troops across the border could be a tough match. At VII Corps, every piece of data fit into this mold.

One of the most striking pieces was a February 19 raid to gauge the Iraqi capabilities and create the false impression that the corps intended to attack down the Wadi al-Batin. The "Black Jack" brigade from the 1st Cavalry Division crossed into Iraq to attack an infantry battalion. A Vulcan air defense gun and two Bradley fighting vehicles were destroyed in the fighting, and A-10s were called in to pound the Iraqis. Three American soldiers died in the fighting, which, according to Army estimates, produced more than 170 Iraqi casualties. CENTCOM withheld any announcement of the action or the casualties, ostensibly to avoid giving Baghdad the impression that the ground offensive had begun and thus kick off the land war prematurely. But some senior American officials saw another motivation: the command did not want to alarm the troops by suggesting that the Iraqis had drawn blood in one of the first Army attacks of the war.

The final preparations also created some tension between the two corps. Some VII Corps officers complained after the war that Luck had undercut their plan. Like a partly lit neon sign, the XVIII Corps had signaled its presence in the far west. Not all the letters were visible, but the message could be interpreted by the discerning foe. In the XVIII Corps sector, going from west to east, Luck had launched the deception and was herding up prisoners. McCaffrey's 24th Mech was trying to keep a low profile, but Doug Starr's 3rd Armored Cavalry Regiment was firing on the berm near the border for target practice. Meanwhile, immediately to the east, in the VII Corps's sector, the 2nd Armored Cavalry Regiment was so security conscious that it was using messengers instead of radios for communication.[11]

Luck's appeal for the 1st Armored Division also strained relations between the two corps. Franks's officers countered by asking for control over McCaffrey's 24th Mech. Both appeals were rejected. As many forces as the Army field commanders had at their disposal, they had a seemingly insatiable appetite for more.

While the Army was preparing for battle, the Navy had a bruising encounter with the Iraqis. To keep open the option of an amphibious raid and get its battleships into position to support the land offensive, the Navy needed to clear away the mines.

The Navy's mine-clearing effort was under the command of Capt. G. Bruce McEwen, commander of the USS *Tripoli*. Before the Gulf War, McEwen's only experience in mine warfare had been in dropping them from his A-7 during the Vietnam War. It was not until late January that McEwen was told the *Tripoli* would serve as the command ship for the allied mine-clearing effort. The *Tripoli*'s Marines, helicopters, and other war-fighting equipment were unloaded and McEwen took on board a squadron of minesweeping MH-53 Super Stallion helicopters.

McEwen had his work cut out for him. There was no hard intelligence on the Iraqi minefields, but the general presumption was that they were laid in the shallow coastal waters near the bay of Kuwait. Mines, however, were not the only threat. The Navy also had to contend with Iraq's Silkworm missiles. Despite the air attacks along the Kuwaiti coast, the Chinese-made anti-ship missiles remained one of the Navy's biggest worries. To help defend against the Silkworms, Arthur ordered the USS *Princeton,* an Aegis air defense cruiser, to the northern Gulf, instructing it to take up a position between the suspected Silkworm batteries on the Kuwaiti coast and the coalition minesweepers farther out to sea. Chock-full of sophisticated radar equipment, the $1 billion

Princeton had been built to deal with just this sort of sea-skimming threat. If Silkworms were launched, the *Princeton* would try to shoot them down with its own missiles, much as the Army's Patriot shot down the Scud missiles aimed at Saudi Arabia. Like the Patriot antimissile system, the Aegis's ability against sea-skimmers had never been tested in combat before the Gulf War.

But as the mine-clearing operation was under way on February 18, McEwen received an urgent alert. The Navy had ordered "air warning red." The Navy faced a possible Silkworm missile attack. As a precaution, the *Princeton* and the *Tripoli* moved away from the coast, with the *Tripoli* taking the lead. The tallest ship in the group, the *Tripoli*'s lookouts searched the waters for random floating mines, which Navy intelligence had reported were the greatest threat to ships outside Kuwait's coastal waters.

McEwen was working in his sea cabin just off the bridge at 4:36AM when there was a huge explosion. The spine of the *Tripoli* jerked back and forth like a dog shaking its back. McEwen had a sick feeling. The command ship of the coalition's mine-clearing effort had struck a mine.

The engineers shut down the boiler to prevent an explosion. But one of the backup emergency diesel generators was flooded. There was no power in the forward part of the ship. Worse, the blast had ripped a hole in the tanks that carried the JP-5 fuel for the Sea Stallion helicopters and blown apart buckets of noxious gray paint in a main storage area. The entire forward part of the ship had filled up with explosive fuel and paint vapors. McEwen was afraid that a spark could ignite the fumes with catastrophic consequences for the crew and the ship. The *Tripoli* had been sent to clear a path for others, but now all its energy was needed to save itself.

The crew formed a human chain to unload ammunition near the storage area, while water-powered exhaust fans were used to blow away the fumes. Crew members furiously cut timber to shore up damaged bulkheads. Meanwhile, a diver was sent overboard to inspect the damage. What he reported was disturbing. The mine had blasted a sixteen-by-twenty-six-foot hole well below the waterline. There was no way that the damage could have been done by the floating mines McEwen had been warned about.

The *Tripoli* had, in fact, struck a more powerful, moored "contact" mine, floating unseen below the surface of the water. Soon sonar reported possible mine-link objects in virtually every direction. The *Tripoli* had been zigzagging through an Iraqi minefield for hours. The surprise was not that the *Tripoli* was damaged but that it had not struck a mine sooner. McEwen was worried that another mine explosion would sink the vessel.

At 7:15AM, the *Princeton* was rocked by an Italian-made "influence mine," detonated by sound or the magnetic properties of the ship passing overhead. The mine was directly underneath the cruiser when it detonated. Moments later, another mine detonated 300 yards off the ship's starboard bow. The blasts damaged the *Princeton*'s superstructure and jammed its rudders. The radar and missile systems were knocked out, making the ship a sitting duck for the Iraqis. If ever there was a time for the Iraqis to launch a Silkworm missile, this was it. But the Iraqis missed their opportunity.

In two hours, the crew of the *Princeton* managed to get the radar and missile systems back on-line and ready to shoot. That gave the *Princeton* a defensive capability against anti-ship missiles, but the ship was even more seriously damaged than the *Tripoli*. A third explosion might have sunk the ship altogether.

As the USS *Beaufort*, a salvage ship, steamed to the aid of the *Princeton*, a Canadian exchange officer aboard the *Tripoli* looked at the sonar readings indicating mine-like objects and calculated that the *Beaufort* — a relatively small vessel that could be blown out of the water by a mine blast — was heading into a line of mines. The *Beaufort* was alerted and abruptly changed course, missing a mine by four feet. The mine-clearing effort was barely under way and already it was dead in the water.

After the war, the Navy captured an Iraqi map showing an elaborate multi-tiered minefield. The Navy had assumed that the Iraqi mines were laid in the shallow waters close to shore. Instead, the Iraqis had constructed two mine belts farther out to sea, a seaward extension of the twin obstacle barriers that Iraqi combat engineers had constructed across southern Kuwait. The outer mine belt extended almost thirty miles into the Gulf, swinging northeast in a wide arc to block the approaches to southern Kuwait and Kuwait City. Five miles wide, the belt contained over 1,000 mines, laid in three rows.[12]

The Marines felt the impact immediately. The day after the blasts, Jenkins received a message from Arthur instructing him to scale back his plans for the raid. It was another graphic example of how the Iraqis could create trouble for the allies with low-technology systems. Jenkins still thought the raid was a "go." Neither Arthur nor Schwarzkopf and his aides again told him otherwise. As Jenkins planned his raid, the Marines along the Kuwaiti border also began to lay the groundwork for their offensive.[13]

TASK FORCE GRIZZLY

The first operation of the land war actually began two days before the official start of the ground offensive when Col. Jim Fulks secretly led a task force code-named Grizzly into Kuwait. The infiltration, which began one minute after midnight on February 22, was an integral part of the Marine strategy. The commander of the 1st Marine Division, Maj. Gen. Mike Myatt, wanted his division to push past the Iraqi fortifications as quickly as possible, establish a lodgment beyond them, and then thrust into the rear before the Iraqis could organize an effective counterattack.

To meet the anticipated allied offensive the Iraqis had set the main line of their defense opposite Myatt's division back from the Saudi border, behind the second of two belts of minefields and obstacles. The mission of Grizzly and Taro, its companion task force to the west, was to sneak past the first set of barriers, clear out whatever Iraqi troops might be there, and grease the way for the main division attack. If discovered, the task forces would be supported by two 155mm artillery battalions that were also to slip into Kuwait. Myatt had insisted on the infiltration against the advice of some of his officers, who were afraid that the task forces might get trapped in the obstacle belts.

Rain was falling as the task force set out, which Fulks thought was all to the good, since it would mask the sound of the Marines moving north in the darkness. None of the Marines in the 1,600-man task force was wearing the suits that protected them from poison gas attacks, which made American troops look like men from outer space. Infiltrating the Iraqi lines was difficult enough without donning the cumbersome garb.

After a long night of slogging through the desert, the Marines in Grizzly halted within two miles of the first set of barriers, dug six-foot-deep fighting positions in the sand, and covered themselves with camouflage nets. The task force spent the next day sleeping, writing letters, and cleaning its weapons. But when the Iraqis starting firing mortars and artillery shells, it was clear that they had been detected.

The main problem, however, was political, not tactical. Only hours after the infiltration got under way, Gorbachev called Bush to press his latest proposal to arrange an Iraqi withdrawal from Kuwait over a twenty-one-day period. Moscow was trying to bail out the Iraqis just as the allies were moving to deliver the final blow.

As Bush administration officials debated how to respond, Schwarzkopf ordered the Marines not to get tied up fighting the Iraqis. Time was quickly running out, but CENTCOM needed to be able to put its war preparations into reverse gear.

"My instructions were to do nothing that is irreversible but to be able to execute," Myatt recalled. "I was a little concerned because I already had Task Force Grizzly and Task Force Taro in Kuwait. But I thought that is all reversible. We can just bring them out."

Some of the Marine commanders believed that there was no going back. As he ate his lunch with a pocketknife, Col. Carlton W. Fulford, the commander of one of Myatt's mechanized task forces, shrugged off reports about the Russian diplomacy. "The toilet's flushed," Fulford said.[14]

But for Fulks, Moscow's move was a complication. When Fulks requested permission to move his task force through the first set of obstacle minefields, Myatt demurred, citing Schwarzkopf's orders not to become entangled with the Iraqis. So Fulks restricted his task force to calling in artillery barrages and broadcasting surrender appeals.

Soon a company of seventy dispirited Iraqis emerged from their shallow trenches and gave themselves up, braving mines and mortarfire from other Iraqi units trying to prevent them from surrendering. The Iraqis said that many of the Iraqis along the front had abandoned the Al Jaber air base. Citing the Iraqis, Fulks persuaded Myatt to permit the task force to make its way through the first defensive line, though Myatt restricted their role to marking lanes through the minefields and capturing some nearby bunkers.

The Iraqi prisoners helped the task force find a lane through the antitank mines. They did not, however, know the way through the antipersonnel mines behind their own defensive positions. They had been walled in by their commanders, who were afraid they would retreat. And on February 23, the last evening of Grizzly's three-day infiltration, Sgt. Charles Restifo, a combat engineer from Phoenix, Arizona, began probing for the antipersonnel mines the old-fashioned way, by using a bayonet as a probe while a rifle company provided cover for him.

After clearing out a single lane, the task force used explosive charges and blasted a larger path for vehicles. Abandoning any pretence of secrecy, two infantry battalions, one artillery battalion, and the regimental headquarters then moved through the lanes. With the war still a day away, the Marines already had thousands of troops miles into southern Kuwait. The movement through the minefield was particularly eventful for one Marine who was trying to bring ammunition to the other side of the minefield. Uncertain of how to make his way through the Iraqi minefield, he used antitank mines as stepping stones, figuring that his weight could not be enough to set off a blast. By keeping to the antitank mines he avoided the antipersonnel mines. All told, Grizzly destroyed three tanks and an artillery battery and captured more than 540 Iraqi prisoners while carrying out its "secret" infiltration mission.

To the right of Grizzly, Taro, commanded by Col. John H. Admire, whose regiment had supported the Saudis in their recapture of Khafji three weeks previously, moved north to open another gap in the Iraqi defenses. Taro's infiltration, however, came at a cost. During its move north a grenade on one Marine's belt got caught on a truck as the men dismounted from the vehicle, pulling out the safety pin. There was nothing for Pvt. 1st Class Adam T. Hoage to do but step away from his fellow Marines as the grenade went off, killing him. Things went from bad to worse when a HARM antiradiation missile fired by a Marine plane homed in on a radar that the task force used to pinpoint Iraqi artillery, blowing up the Humvee carrying it and killing a Marine.

By the evening of February 23, however, Grizzly and Taro had completed their work. Two Marine regiments were in place. They had opened the door into southern Kuwait with surprising ease. All that was needed now was the attack order from CENTCOM the next day and the 1st Marine Division's mechanized task force, code-named Ripper, would go roaring through on the way to Kuwait City.

While Myatt's infiltration teams tangled with the Iraqis, Bill Keys's 2nd Marine Division was also skirmishing with the enemy. From his attack position northwest of Myatt's division, Keys had an entirely different tactical problem. Iraq's front-line defenses were shallower than the ones that confronted Myatt but more dense. The Iraqi combat engineers had constructed a 550-yard-long trench that they filled with oil and intended to set ablaze as soon as the Marines advanced. The fire trench tapered off into a latticework of oil pipes and pumping stations in the Al Minisha oil field.

Keys did not want his men to sneak past the Iraqis; he wanted to attract their attention. The plan was to fool the Iraqis into thinking that the Marines were attacking the fire trench and prompt the Iraqis to fire their artillery. Marine Harriers and FA-18s would then bomb the Iraqi gun positions. After the Iraqis had been weakened, Keys would attack where the Iraqis least expected it: pushing his division through the narrow gap near the network of oil pipes.

On February 23, Lt. Col. Keith Holcomb led a company of light armored vehicles and Humvees into Kuwait and began racing along the fire trenches, daring the Iraqis to fire. The operation was officially dubbed a reconnaissance mission, but Keys actually had a small war going. The Marines destroyed more than twenty Iraqi tanks, knocked out twenty-five other Iraqi vehicles, and took more than three hundred Iraqi prisoners. Two Marines narrowly escaped when they were thrown clear of their Humvee after an Iraqi artillery round landed in the back of their vehicle, turning it into a jagged mass of metal.

With the Iraqis knocked off stride, Keys began to move his artillery into southern Kuwait. Putting vulnerable artillery battalions in front of their heavier mechanized forces was not the way the Marines had been taught to fight. But the Marine guns could not fire as far as the South African and Soviet artillery pieces in the Iraqi inventory, and Keys needed to ensure that his artillery could cover his forces when they launched their main attack.

Captured Iraqi officers later told the Marines that the Iraqi defenders had taken Holcomb's skirmish for the real thing and concluded that they had repelled the Marine attack. In Baghdad, the Iraqi commanders thought much the same. Baghdad Radio announced that they had repulsed the opening attack of the ground war. Boomer himself confessed after the war that he was not aware of how intense the fighting became during Keys's "recon" mission.[15]

While the Marines attacked, Washington debated how to counter the Russian-brokered Iraqi proposal. It was not just the French and the Egyptians who wanted to explore Moscow's move. Adm. David Jeremiah, the vice chairman of the JCS, said that Washington owed it to the military to explore the Soviet compromise if there was a chance it could save American lives. To the end, there was a schism between the men in uniform, wary that the war could go wrong, and the policy-makers, who were determined to teach Iraq a lesson it, and the other third world countries watching the conflict, would never forget.

The Bush administration developed a counterproposal: Iraq would have seven days to pull out of Kuwait unconditionally, not the twenty-one days it had proposed. To prevent the Iraqis from stalling for time, the administration set a deadline for beginning the withdrawal. The State Department favored issuing a seventy-two-hour ultimatum, which would delay the ground war a couple of days. But Cheney and his civilian aides wanted to move with more dispatch.

As senior civilian and military officials discussed the issue, Dennis Ross, Secretary of State Baker's head of policy planning, told Wolfowitz he was perplexed. Before the war began, Wolfowitz had seemed apprehensive about kicking off a casualty-producing ground war. But Wolfowitz explained he was now persuaded by the intelligence that the collapse of the Iraqi army was at hand and now saw a major strategic benefit from humiliating it in a land war so Baghdad could never make the claim that it fought the Americans to a standoff.[16]

Ironically, while Moscow's diplomacy hindered the Marines' infiltration, their forays along the Kuwait border helped tip the balance within the administration against giving Iraq more time. As the Marines attacked, Iraqi troops set Kuwait's oil fields ablaze. Intended as a tactical move to neutralize the Americans' high-technology weapons systems by blinding them, the oil fires strengthened the hand of the hard-liners, who wanted to get on with the war.

On February 22, the White House delivered its ultimatum, demanding that the withdrawal start by noon EST on February 24. The noon deadline was picked so that the ground war could be launched early the next morning, as planned, if the Iraqis did not respond.[17]

While the White House and Pentagon policy-makers believed the Iraqis were teetering and were about to collapse, the Army was girding itself for a real fight. With Webster arguing that the Iraqi field army was intact and Allen insisting it was a defeated force, American intelligence was in a state of total confusion. Schwarzkopf was all over the map. Days before he had publicly pronounced the Iraqi army to be on the brink of collapse, but his plan to destroy the Republican Guard assumed the Iraqis would stand and fight.

At CENTCOM, the status of the Iraqi army was evaluated in terms of percentages that made the estimates appear to be misleadingly exact. The command's battle damage assessment for February 23 indicated that the front-line forces opposite the U.S. Army were at 33 percent strength, with the second echelon at 55 percent. The Iraqi forces in the areas of Marine operations were at 78 percent. The Republican Guard was rated at 66 percent strength.[18]

An analysis posted in the Black Hole summed up the debate:

Theater Intelligence: Expect Significant Resistance.
Air Component: Regular Army Waiting To Surrender.
  RG No Longer An Effective Fighting Force
CINCENT: The Iraqi Army Is Ready To Collapse.

Only the Iraqis knew the real story. While the allies were preparing for a land war, many Iraqi soldiers put their trust in a political settlement, hoping that their deployment to the desert was no more than an elaborate bluff. Using their transistor radios, they listened hopefully to the reports about Moscow's new peace plan.

THE OTHER SIDE OF THE HILL

The commander of Iraq's 48th Infantry Division was not a happy man. Two days before the air war began, he had been pulled out of his command on the Iranian border and transferred to the front. Morale was low, spare parts were hard to come by. Under the allied bombardment, his already weakened division was shrinking by the day.

For months, the Iraqi high command had been waiting for their opportunity to engage the allies and inflict casualties during the ground war. But their defense plan was flawed and the forces that might execute it were battered and demoralized.

After the war, the deterioration of the Iraqi army was documented in a report by the U.S. Army's 513th Military Intelligence Brigade blandly entitled "The Gulf War: An Iraqi General Officer's Perspective." Based on interrogations of senior Iraqi officers captured during the war, the report, which has never been publicly released, raises sensitive issues for the U.S. Army. The report confirms that before the ground war was launched, the bulk of the Iraqi army was all but broken by poor morale and the unrelenting assault of allied warplanes.

Even before a shot was fired, the Iraqi field force was far smaller than the 540,000-man army of occupation Schwarzkopf and the Pentagon described. The Iraqi army was riddled with dissent, not because the Iraqis had qualms about invading Kuwait but because the long desert duty took its toll. To shore up morale, Baghdad granted a week's leave to the troops every twenty-eight days, a policy it had also implemented during the Iran-Iraq War. But many of the soldiers who left never came back.

When the bombs began to fall, desertions increased. The F-111Fs' tank-plinking attacks against the Iraqi armor had a devastating psychological effect on the Iraqis, making them afraid to sleep in or near their vehicles. Although the B-52s did not drop their bombs with much accuracy, the planes terrorized many of the troops.

"Logistical support beyond food, ammunition and water was weak, particularly in the area of spare parts and replacement vehicles. There was apparently no functioning replacement system for the massive personnel losses (often 50 percent) resulting from the wholesale desertions and casualties caused by the air attacks," the American interrogation report noted.

The numbers in the intelligence reports told an astounding story. While the allies debated over when and whether to launch the land war, much of the Iraqi army was already going home. There were still thousands of armored vehicles in southern Iraq and Kuwait, but in many cases there was nobody in them.

The 48th Division, for example, had started out with 5,000 men, but 400 had been killed and wounded during the air war and many more had deserted. By late February, the division was down to 3,100 soldiers. Nor did it have a clue as to where allied troops were deployed. If it had, its despair would have turned to alarm for the 48th Division was directly in the path of the U.S. Army's VII Corps.

It was not an isolated case. Iraqi officers reported the following losses in their front-line and second-tier defenses:

27th Infantry Division: 8000 men deployed and about 3000 deserted. During the air war, 108 were killed and 233 wounded, leaving 4659 at the time of the ground war. Of 17 tanks, 8 were destroyed.

48th Infantry Division: 5000 men deployed and 1000 deserted. During the air war, 300 were killed and 800 wounded, leaving 3100. Of 25 tanks 18 were destroyed.

30th Infantry Division: 8000 deployed and 4000 deserted. During the air war, 100 were killed and 150 wounded, leaving 3750. All of its 14 tanks were destroyed.

31st Infantry Division: 8000 deployed and 4000 deserted. The number killed and wounded during the air campaign is not known.

3rd Armored Division's 8th Mechanized Brigade. 2300 deployed. 520 deserted. Some 1000 were killed and 250 wounded during the air war, leaving 1480. Six of its 35 tanks were destroyed.

52nd Armored Division's 52nd Armored Brigade: 1125 deployed. 550 deserted. 35 were killed and 40 were wounded, leaving 500 by the time of the land war. Of its 80 tanks, 62 were destroyed.

Hammurabi Republican Guard Division: 10,000 deployed, 5000 deserted. 100 were killed and 300 were wounded, leaving 4600 on G day.[19]

Nor did the Iraqi commanders make good use of the forces that remained. Reflecting Soviet doctrine and the autocratic nature of the Iraqi system, the command structure was a rigid one. The Iraqi military leadership was seeded with officers picked not so much for their skills as their loyalty to the Iraqi regime. Much of the regular army was not trusted by Baghdad and was excluded from military decision-making.

Orders came directly from Baghdad, and the Iraqi army failed to establish forward headquarters close to the front lines. There was little if any understanding of the problems plaguing the Iraqi forces along the front lines. The Iraqi division commanders near the front were one-star generals, but they functioned more like captains in the American Army. The commanders had little autonomy and rarely saw their corps commanders to review the planning and solicit support.

From what they could divine of the allied strategy, the Iraqis expected an attack into southern Kuwait in conjunction with an amphibious landing on the coast. They also expected an attack in the west down the Wadi al-Batin in the direction of Basra.

The Iraqi strategy was defined by the road network that criss-crossed the barren desert in Kuwait and southern Iraq. The Iraqis found it hard to navigate far from the roads and assumed that the Americans had similar difficulties. In fact, maneuvering in the open desert was an easy proposition for the Americans, who used handheld devices to query navigational satellites. The Iraqis could have tapped into the American satellites, too, had they bought the commercially available receivers. But the Iraqis never caught on. Although the troops were on their home turf, Iraq's technological gap left them without the home-field advantage.

The Iraqis never detected the telltale hints of an American shift in the desert, although they had managed to piece together a list of the allied troops from listening to BBC and Voice of America radio reports. Impressed by the Americans' high-tech weapons, the Iraqis assumed incorrectly that they would give away their location if they tried to intercept allied communications, thus depriving themselves of a potentially important source of information.

"Vague references to Egyptians, Syrians, U.K., Kuwaiti, and American forces somewhere across the border were the best they could muster. None of our sources had seen in reality the coalition deployment of the XVIII Airborne Corps far to their right flank; all believed firmly in the inevitability of a coalition amphibious assault against Kuwait City, supported by an attack on the Wadi al-Batin," the interrogation report stated.

By the Iraqis' own account, however, Baghdad would not have been able to put up an effective defense even if it knew the allies' attack plan. More important, the air strikes had the Iraqis pinned down.

American intelligence had predicted that the Iraqis would use chemical weapons, citing the testimony of deserters that some artillery units were segregated for that purpose from the rest of the force. But deterred by the American threats to retaliate massively against any chemical use, the Iraqis never moved chemical munitions toward the front. Many of Iraq's ground forces in fact had shoddy chemical-protective gear and were ill-equipped to survive on a chemical battlefield.

American Army intelligence summed up the results: "From figures provided to us by our sources, it appears that the average front line and second echelon division was deployed at no more than 80 per cent strength, in some cases as low as 60 per cent, and then lost 50 per cent of its already depleted numbers, through desertions, AWOL and casualties. Divisions ranked 4000 men or fewer, and consisted by G-day of dispirited officers and men who had silently conspired in many cases to surrender upon the first smell of gunpowder. We do not have a wide enough sample to provide a definitive estimate that would survive the scrutiny of a statistician, but if the situation described by our Iraqi general officer prisoners is representative of the Iraqi Army in the Kuwaiti Theater of Operations, the 42 division force so accurately tracked by the ARCENT G-2 could well have consisted of 200,000 by G-day."

"In summary," the report added, "our prisoners describe an Iraqi army whose composition closely fits the picture developed by all-source intelligence, but whose size and morale had eroded steadily until it became literally combat ineffective. Notwithstanding the extensive stocks of ammunition in the possession of Iraqi units and the advantages inherent to the defense, this was a defeated force that lived in dread of the prospect of combat with the VII and the XVIII Corps."

The Army report, as well as other postwar intelligence, settles some of the military's bitterest disputes. While American intelligence concluded later that the air campaign fell short of its goal of destroying half the Iraqi armored equipment, CENTCOM had put the bar too high. The Iraqi army had already begun to disintegrate. Physical and psychological effects of the bombing had turned the first and second tiers of the army into a hollow force. The Republican Guard was in somewhat better shape. Since they were farther back from the front, they were bombed less and had shorter supply lines. But even that force was degraded.

As the ground war was about to begin, it was being planned on two different planes. CENTCOM stood ready to smash the Republican Guard if it stood and fought. But the question was not whether the allies would win. They had the full might of the American military, and the Iraqis were already a defeated force. It was what would happen if the Iraqis offered perfunctory resistance and then left. Would the American command be able to adjust and catch the Iraqis before they escaped?

Schwarzkopf and Powell were about to discover that the plan they had developed would make it difficult to close the door on the Iraqi army.

17

The Fifty-Hour War

The faster the attack, the fewer the soldiers it costs. By making your battle short you will deprive it of the time to rob you of many soldiers. The soldier who is led in this manner gains confidence and exposes himself gladly to all danger.

— Frederick the Great

A T 3:59AM on February 24, Walt Boomer received the long-awaited order to launch the ground war. Boomer's mobile command post was little more than a tent filled with communications gear, a table strewn with nerve-gas pills, a map of the attack drawn on a huge bedsheet, and a small battle staff — all of whom planned to squeeze into a handful of armored personnel carriers and Humvees and follow behind the combat forces.

As certain as he was of a quick victory, however, it was an emotional moment for the Marine commander. Khafji had shown that the Iraqi fighting skills were limited, and the infiltration his divisions had carried out had already given the Marine high command some reassurance that the Iraqi front-line infantry was demoralized. Still, the Marines were about to undertake the largest and most complicated Marine offensive since World War II. The Marines also faced armored and mechanized divisions and a formidable concentration of Iraqi artillery at the Al Jaber airfield. American intelligence had flatly predicted that the Iraqis would use chemical weapons.

Boomer was also worried about the weather. CENTCOM's weather forecasters monitoring meteorological patterns over the Mediterranean had predicted a break in the rainy and overcast weather over the Arabian Peninsula. But the clouds had lowered, a cold rain fell, and the acrid smoke from the fires the Iraqis had started in the oil fields began to obscure the crescent moon that hung in the sky. Boomer's plan depended heavily on airpower, and the low clouds and gray haze created by the fires would make it tough to call in the air attacks. However, the Marines had gotten one break. During the long months of waiting for the ground war to begin, the wind in Kuwait had generally blown north to south, but now the wind was blowing in the opposite direction. The billowing columns of black smoke from the oil fields would be drifting into the faces of the Iraqis, not the Marines.

For the young Marines in the attack positions along the border, expectation was blended with hope and fear. They were the ones who would clear the mines, drive around the fire trenches, and navigate among the burning oil wells to put the Marines' strategy to the test. It was almost two weeks since Valentine's Day, and many of the Marines had spent the day reading the cards that had been delivered on the final mail call. Now they were sitting on hard metal benches in crowded amphibious tractors, or Amtracks, buttoned up in tanks, and waiting in trenches for the call to go forward.

After a short pause for reflection, Boomer signaled his two divisions to attack according to plan. Immediately after Mike Myatt's 1st Division rushed through the gap created by his infiltration, Bill Keys's 2nd Marine Division, Boomer's left flank unit, would push through the Iraqi defenses between the Al Minisha and Wafra oil fields.

Myatt's division would cover Keys's main attack by punching through the Iraqi defenses to the east and seizing Al Jaber airfield, which served as the main Iraqi artillery fire base. The Iraqis also used the base as a headquarters in southern Kuwait. After taking the installation, Myatt was to advance toward the airport on the outskirts of Kuwait City while Keys raced north up to the high ground of Mutlah Ridge west of Kuwait City to cut off the Iraqi army to the southeast. Then the Marines would wait for the Arab members of the coalition to make their way to Kuwait City and occupy it. According to Schwarzkopf's script, the Marines would blaze the path, but the Arabs would be the "liberators" of the city.

After receiving Boomer's order, the Marines waited for the B-52s to pound the Iraqi front-line defenses for one last time. After the bombs shook the desert, the Marines began to charge ahead, while loudspeakers from an Army psychological warfare unit attached to the Tiger Brigade blared the Marine Corps Hymn. After almost seven months of preparation, appeals to Schwarzkopf for a piece of the action, and countless revisions to the war plan, the Marine ground war was finally under way.[1]

Standing up in his tank, Gunnery Sgt. John D. Cornwall, a forty-six-year-old reservist from New Albany, Indiana, could see that the Iraqi trenches had been worked over by the allied bombing campaign. The desert looked like a giant rake had gone over it. Vehicles were upended. There was bomb debris everywhere. Nothing was in a straight line.

Cornwall's Marine reserve unit has been mobilized and sent to the Gulf to help fill out Keys's division. The M-60A1 tanks his battalion was driving were older than the tanks the Egyptians were using. Like the scales on some sort of prehistoric beast, reactive armor covered the front of the M-60 tanks. This armor contained explosive charges that would go off when the tank was hit by an antitank weapon, deflecting the blast before it could penetrate the crew compartment. It was a technique the Israelis had devised to protect their tanks. Unfortunately, many of the metal boxes on Cornwall's tanks were empty. There was not enough of the explosives to go around.

Attached to the 6th Marine Regiment, Cornwall's platoon of reservists had the job of protecting combat engineers from Keys's 2nd Division as they forged a path through the Saddam Line. All told, the engineers were to clear six lanes, which would be marked with plastic garbage cans painted red, blue, or green, the traditional colors used to mark assault beaches in an amphibious landing.

Even with the gear secretly acquired from the Israelis, mine clearing was a time-consuming process. An M-60 tank with a steel plow mounted on its front drove to the edge of the minefield with an Amtrack, which was equipped with rocket-propelled line-charges — heavy cords festooned with explosives. After reaching the minefield, the Amtrack would fire the line-charge and detonate the explosives, blowing a line through the mines four yards on either side of the line. The tank would then "proof" the lane by plowing through it, pushing aside any mines that might remain. Combat engineers disposed of any of the missed mines by blowing them up with explosive satchel charges.

Cornwall's platoon covered the engineers as they cleared the "blue lanes" and prepared to lead the charge through the gaps in the Saddam Line. Keys was confident the regiment could hold its own, but Cornwall figured his platoon was at the front because its old tanks made it expendable.

When the engineers cleared the lanes, the M-60s went forward in a

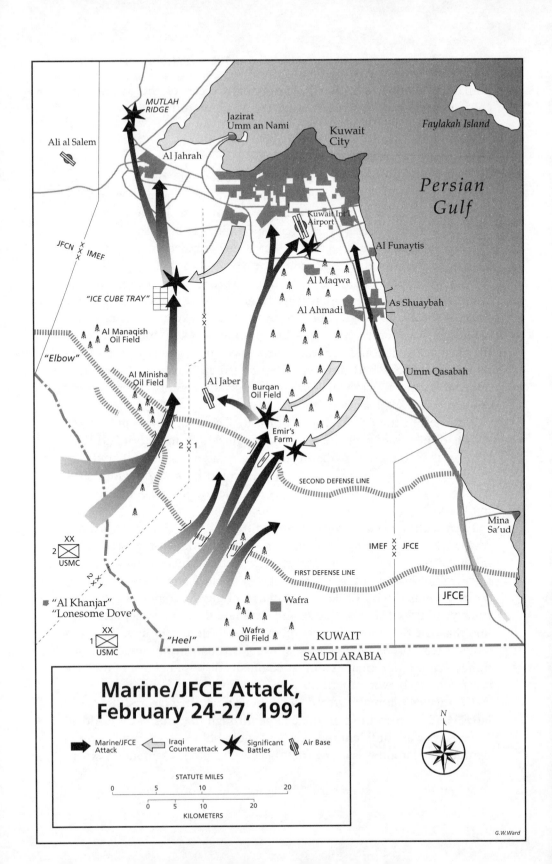

Marine/JFCE Attack, February 24-27, 1991

MUTLAH RIDGE

Ali al Salem

Al Jahrah

Jazirat Umm an Nami

Kuwait City

Faylakah Island

Persian Gulf

JFCN IMEF

Kuwait Int'l Airport

Al Funaytis

"ICE CUBE TRAY"

Al Maqwa

As Shuaybah

Al Manaqish Oil Field

Al Ahmadi

"Elbow"

Al Minisha Oil Field

Al Jaber

Burqan Oil Field

Umm Qasabah

Emir's Farm

2 X 1

SECOND DEFENSE LINE

Mina Sa'ud

IMEF JFCE

XX
2 USMC

FIRST DEFENSE LINE

JFCE

2 X 1

"Al Khanjar" "Lonesome Dove"

Wafra

XX
1 USMC

"Heel"

Wafra Oil Field

KUWAIT

SAUDI ARABIA

Legend

Marine/JFCE Attack

Iraqi Counterattack

Significant Battles

Air Base

STATUTE MILES
0   5   10   20

0   5   10   20
KILOMETERS

N

G.W.Ward

wedge formation, blasting the Iraqi bunkers with machine-gun fire. As rocket-propelled grenades whizzed by, Cornwall concluded that the Iraqi fire was too hot. He clanked down the lid on his tank. From inside, the only sound Cornwall could hear was the ping of bullets ricocheting off his M-60 as it approached the Al Minisha oil field.

Navigating from inside the tanks was like traveling in the middle of a dark bubble. The M-60's night-vision system was more primitive than the M1's used by the Army. Instead of creating images from the heat of objects in its field of view, the M-60's system amplified available light. But with the oil-fire clouds and bad weather, there was barely enough light for the night-vision system to work. The tank crews were used to attacking tanks at 1,700 to 2,800 yards, but they could see only about 300 yards forward and back. The battlefield looked dark, darker, and darker still.

As the tanks made their way forward in the darkness, Cornwall's gunner thought he saw an Iraqi tank. "Shoot it," yelled Cornwall.

The M-60 fired a round at the shadowy object. When the round hit, thousands of golf-ball-size slags of metal flew through the air. Then the tank rounds in the destroyed tank started going off like skyrockets. Smoke started pouring out and an orange flame shot 100 feet in the air.

As Cornwall's tank moved onto the crest of a bunker, a stick with a white bag on it was raised into the air. Dozens of Iraqis popped up out of their trenches waving white pieces of paper. The Iraqis later told the Marines that they had planned to get back into tanks they had abandoned and shoot the Marines from the rear after they passed. But after seeing a few tanks explode, the Iraqis lost their stomach for battle.[2]

While the 6th Marine Regiment passed through the "blue" and "red" minefield lanes with little trouble, the 8th Marine Regiment was stymied as it tried to clear the "green" lanes. The regiment was equipped with new M1 tanks, but the minefield it faced was filled with a dense array of sophisticated British-manufactured "Bar" mines, designed to elude mine-plowing gear.

First, a Marine Amtrack lobbed a line-charge only to have it become entangled in a high-tension wire. Then, several tanks equipped with mine plows ran into mines and were stopped dead in their tracks. It was 1:45 PM before one of the "green" lanes was cleared, more than seven hours after the 2nd Marine Division began its attack. The regiment abandoned its effort to clear the second "green" lane. The entire process took so long that the gas-guzzling M-1 tanks ran low on fuel and Lt. Col. Bruce Gombar, who was commanding the lead battalion, had to bring up the fuel trucks and replenish the tanks while they were between the first and second mine belts, a potentially risky maneuver.

Schwarzkopf later described the initial Marine assault as a "textbook operation," but the Marines were more critical. Had the Iraqis worked harder on their minefield and been better skilled at directing their artillery to cover the minefield with fire, they might have exacted a high toll from the Marines. "We have all kinds of smart guys developing all kinds of smart weapons, but nobody really developed good mine-clearing techniques," said Gombar. "Mine technology is way ahead of countermine technology."[3]

Nonetheless, Keys's division had five of the six lanes it needed, and its combat units began to pour through the narrow gap in the Saddam Line. The weeks of bombing and artillery fire had taken the fight out of the Iraqis. Keys's decision to attack along the pipes of the Al Minisha oil field had also surprised the Iraqi defenders. The Marines later discovered that the Iraqis had sited their artillery to fire to the west of Keys's point of attack where they expected the Marines to attempt a breakthrough.

With bomb debris scattered across the battlefield and geysers of burning oil spewing flames seventy-five to a hundred feet in the air, Col. John Sylvester's Tiger Brigade navigated slowly through the tangled terrain. Of all the units in Boomer's attack, the Army's Tiger Brigade was the most potent. Formed by General Patton during World War II, the brigade had the key mission of guarding the left flank of the entire Marine offensive. As Marines, their faces sooty from the oil smoke, gave the thumbs-up signal, the soldiers heard a deafening explosion: one of the Tiger Brigade's military policemen had driven over a mine and was killed in the blast. Even with Iraq's defense collapsing before them, the Iraqis' low-tech weapons could exact a price.[4]

As Keys attacked to the west, the low growl of M-60 tanks and Amtracks reverberated across the desert as Myatt's division pressed ahead. His infiltration forces, already well into Kuwait, had done their work well. Fulks's Task Force Grizzly was behind the first set of barriers, and he reported that the Iraqis were not putting up much resistance.

The first real fight for Myatt's division began at 11:25 AM, when the Marines began to attack the second Iraqi obstacle belt. They pounded the Iraqis with artillery shells and covered their attack with a smoke screen while their engineers rushed to clear the mines. Within fifteen minutes, they fired green and white signal rockets into the air, indicating that they had opened a path through the mines. Then Colonel Fulford's mechanized force, Task Force Ripper, began to push forward, using its counter-mortar radars to pinpoint Iraqi artillery so that the Marines could shell the enemy guns.

While Myatt's infiltration plan had speeded up the assault, it was not without incident. As Fulks's task force exchanged fire with the Iraqis, tank rounds and artillery shells began to hit his Marines from the southeast. Fulford's task force had mistaken Grizzly for a retreating Iraqi unit. And unlike most of the Iraqi fire, the Marine barrage was accurate. The blasts destroyed two trucks and damaged an Amtrack, killing one of Fulks's men and wounding three others. Again, friendly fire was as great a threat as the Iraqi defenders.

By the evening of G day, Myatt's division had a solid hold beyond the Saddam Line. Fulford's tanks had rolled west to Al Jaber. On Myatt's right the division's light armored vehicles had raced northeast and skirted the burning Al Burqan oil field. The most serious worry came when the crew of a German-made chemical-detection vehicle accompanying the 1st Division reported that a chemical mine had gone off as the Marine engineers cut a path through a minefield. It was the first of several false alarms that caused the nervous Marines to don their gas masks and bulky antichemical suits. The only breakdown in the overall plan was the cancellation of an attack by Myatt's heliborne task force, code-named X-Ray. It was to take up a blocking position to cover the right flank of the division in case the Saudi attack on the flank faltered. Bad weather and fear that Iraqi antiaircraft guns were hidden beneath the smoke made the prospect too risky and the operation was canceled.

Myatt traveled with his attacking units in a militarized version of a Chevrolet Blazer. After rolling through the Saddam Line, he ordered that his command post be set down in a clump of trees at the "Emir of Kuwait's farm." This was a cultivated area southwest of the Al Burqan oil field that was kept green through irrigation. As the command group pulled up, a Marine accidentally fired his weapon. Suddenly, a group of Iraqis hidden in the trees jumped up with hands in the air and surrendered. Myatt saw it as a good omen. Many of the Iraqis were determined to give themselves up at the first opportunity, but not all.[5]

At his Riyadh command post in the basement of the Royal Saudi Ministry of Defense, Schwarzkopf could tell he had a problem on his hands. The Marine and Army timetables were out of synch. The plan had been to keep the Iraqi forces focused on the fighting with the Marines in Kuwait so that the Army could surprise them from the west. The Marines would hold the Iraqis by the nose so that the heavy Army forces could blindside them from the rear. To allow time to draw the Iraqis into the net, the main Army attack was not scheduled until the day after the Marine assault.

Schwarzkopf had figured that the Marines would proceed slowly, but now that they were racing ahead, Schwarzkopf was worried that Boomer's forces might run into more of a fight than they bargained for. They would be taking on the full wrath of the Iraqi army while the Army was still revving its engines in Saudi Arabia. The Egyptians were supposed to be on the Marines' left flank, but they were not scheduled to attack until the following day. The arrows on the map in Schwarzkopf's command center suggested that the Marines might be getting too far out on the limb with a vulnerable left flank.

In reality, Schwarzkopf had an even bigger problem, though it was not fully apparent to him. If the Marines moved too successfully, the logic of his strategy to destroy the Republican Guard would be turned on its head. Instead of holding the Iraqis in place, so that the Army could destroy the Guards, Boomer's forces would act as a piston, pushing the Iraqis north before the Army could get to them.

Schwarzkopf called Boomer during the early afternoon to express his concern for the Marine flank and tell him he was thinking of advancing the time of the main Army attack. Boomer agreed. He thought that the entire Iraqi army was about to break and run. If the Iraqi defenders in the west retreated through Kuwait, it would put them on a potential collision course with his Marines.

The CENTCOM commander called Prince Khalid and asked him if he could get the Egyptian forces, which were west of the Marines, to move. This would alleviate the threat to Boomer's left flank and free him to concentrate on the battle immediately to his front. But the Saudi prince reported that the Egyptians could not attack because of bad weather. Coalition warfare was great, Schwarzkopf thought, until you were in a pinch. The Marines were attacking in bad weather, too, and they were making a beeline for Kuwait City.[6]

Then Schwarzkopf called Lt. Gen. John Yeosock, who was running the Army side of the war from Lucky Main, the Army's Riyadh command center at Eskan Village, a modern apartment compound on the outskirts of Riyadh that the Saudis had built for the bedouins but which the desert nomads had refused to occupy. Schwarzkopf told Yeosock he was considering advancing the time of the main Army attack.

The call came as a surprise to the Army general. Neither Yeosock nor his operations deputy, Brig. Gen. Steven Arnold, anticipated that the Marines would be making such good time. After consulting with his corps commanders, Yeosock reported back to Schwarzkopf. The VII Corps and the units the XVIII Corps was holding back for February 25 were ready to attack on two hours' notice. At 1PM, the Army got the call to battle. The attack would begin at 3PM.

As night fell, the Marines halted their advance and moved into a defensive crouch. They were not well equipped to fight at night: Boomer's entire force of 85,000 Marines had only 1,100 sets of night-vision goggles.

The Marines were exhausted by the long day and overwhelmed with thousands of prisoners: more than 8,000 Iraqis had been captured during the first hours of the war. The human flood had clogged up the attack routes and forced them to use the Saudi buses they had set aside for mass casualty evacuations for prison convoys. The mass surrenders turned the no-holds-barred assault into the Iraqi defenses into a strange new brand of warfare. The young Marines were confused as to what to do about their foes, who sometimes fought and sometimes quit. One grizzled gunnery sergeant finally gave them a practical rule of engagement: "If they stand up, don't shoot. If they don't, shoot."

The reports flowing into Schwarzkopf's headquarters recounted the Marines' success. They had accomplished the first half of their mission. They had launched a frontal assault into the teeth of the Iraqi defenses and made it through the Saddam Line. The Iraqi artillery had been neutralized. Most of the rounds the Iraqis had managed to get off were almost aimless, and the Iraqis had not resorted to chemical weapons. Radar images taken by the JSTARS surveillance plane showed long lines of Iraqi forces fleeing north from Al Jaber as the Marines closed in.[7]

Exhilarated by his success, Boomer, however, worried about becoming complacent. In his evening meeting with his officers, the Marine general said his staff needed to "keep 'worst-casing' it." The attack, he added, "was going too well." Hours later, the Iraqis struck back.

BATTLE OF BURQAN

As the first day of the ground war drew to a close, Maj. Gen. Salah Aboud Mahmoud, the Iraqi III Corps commander, was determined to delay the American attack. Mahmoud had orchestrated the battle of Khafji and had survived several Marine and Air Force attempts to "neutralize" him in a bombing attack. The American high command had developed a grudging respect for the wily Iraqi commander.

After the disastrous fight at Khafji, American intelligence reported that Mahmoud had been summoned to Baghdad, and some American commanders thought that after Saddam Hussein got through with him he would never be heard from again. But Mahmoud had returned to oversee the defense of southern Kuwait, and he had a plan. As in the case of Khafji, his plan was a desperate effort to bloody the Americans. This time, however, Mahmoud hoped to outwit the allies.

To erase the Americans' high-technology advantage, the Iraqis had torched the Kuwait oil fields. There were not many opportunities for a surprise attack in the open desert; obscuring the battlefield with smoke from the burning oil wells was the Iraqis' best shot. Contrary to Marine expectations, Mahmoud did not intend to defend the Iraqi fire base and command center at the Al Jaber airfield, which was bracketed by Keys's and Myatt's divisions. His plan was not to meet the Marine attack head on, but to attack out of the flames of the Burqan oil field, hitting the Marines' right flank as they headed north and catching them by surprise. Contemptuous of the Saudi attack on the coast, the Iraqi general oriented his force for an attack to the west.

While the Marines were pushing through the Iraqi fortifications, Mahmoud assembled his force for the counterblow. The oil fields burned like pyres, the smoke rising in concealing black billows. Mahmoud's 3rd Armored Brigade and 8th Mechanized Brigade took up positions in the southern part of the oil field. Other Iraqi units stationed themselves on the flanks and to the rear of the oil field, poised to exploit any success the Iraqis might have in attacking the Americans. Mahmoud planned to strike at dawn.

The Marines had war-gamed their campaign time and time again. Every contingency had been played out — or so they thought. But an Iraqi counterattack out of a flaming oil field was something the Marines had not anticipated. Myatt had expected most of the fighting to take place at the Al Jaber air base and was surprised at the little resistance the Marines had encountered there. He had even located his command post just shy of the Burqan oil field on the assumption that the boiling inferno would protect his right flank.

Some of his planners were suspicious of the oil field complex because the Marines had received unconfirmed intelligence reports that the Iraqi troops were moving in and around the oil field during the day. But Marine light armored vehicles had raced into the oil field earlier in the day to check. They had seen nothing but an oily, black cloud hugging the ground and quickly left. The first day of the ground war came to a close with Mahmoud's plan still a secret.

On February 25, at 1:09AM, Myatt got his first tip about the Iraqi plan. A Kuwaiti interpreter traveling with Fulford's task force translated captured Iraqi documents taken from the command center at Al Jaber that revealed that the Iraqis were using the Burqan oil field as a staging ground for a major counterattack.

Myatt had to do something and fast. He ordered his two mechanized task forces, Fulford's Ripper and Col. Richard W. Hodory's Papa Bear, which had charged north behind Ripper, to set up a defensive screen with their light armored vehicles and scouts. The Marines put their anti-tank missile teams at the front. Unlike the M-60s, the TOW missiles had infrared targeting devices that would help the Marines pick out targets in the inky darkness.

Meanwhile, Myatt ordered more protection for his command post, which was virtually defenseless: he called for a company of light armored vehicles and a platoon equipped with TOW antitank missiles.

The commander of Bravo Company and a former lineman for the Washington State Huskies, Capt. Eddie S. Ray was not happy about the call to duty. A hulk of a man whose nickname was Swamp Thing, Ray had spent more than six months in the desert but had somehow missed most of the fighting at Khafji and had not seen much action on the first day of the ground war. Now, he was worried he would miss out again. The rest of the division would be headed north, and Ray would be pulling guard duty for Myatt's CP. Ray grumbled, but an order was an order.

As dawn approached, electronic intercepts picked up more indications that two mechanized brigades, some 250 vehicles in all, were preparing to attack at daybreak. Myatt still was not sure the Iraqis were in Burqan, but he was not taking any chances. If they were there, they could attack at any moment. Myatt wanted to strike first and scramble their attack.

At 7:53AM, Myatt ordered the 11th Marine Artillery Regiment to fire on the oil fields. With the Iraqis presumably ready to pounce, the wait for the Marine fusillade was "agonizingly slow," Brig. Gen. Thomas V. Draude, Myatt's second in command, recalled.

Finally, twenty-four minutes later, the guns began to fire. The regiment fired 244 rounds at the oil field. Then it shifted a bit to the right and fired another 496 rounds. Myatt sat in his command tent with the sides rolled up and waited to see what would happen. Suddenly, it was like a beehive that had been hit with a stick. The Iraqis came streaming out of the darkness racing toward Myatt's CP.

Ray's LAV company began launching antitank missiles at the Iraqis and peppered them with their 25mm guns. After an hour-long firefight, the Iraqis retreated into the oil field, only to launch a second attack.

By that time, Cobra helicopter gunships were on the scene. They hovered over the battlefield and also began firing TOW antitank missiles at the enemy. As the Iraqis continued to advance, the Cobras pulled back until they were firing from directly over Myatt's CP at Iraqis who were only four hundred yards away. As expended machine-gun casings fell around him, Myatt turned to his operations officer and observed wryly, "You picked a good spot for the CP."

The defense around the command post bent but did not break. For the rest of the morning, the Iraqis darted in and out of the oil field, firing their weapons and then seeking shelter behind the oil cloud. The Marine TOW platoon continued firing into the smoke until it was clear that Myatt's command post was out of danger.[8]

As the Marines beat back the attack on the command post, the Iraqis launched a parallel attack against Hodory's 3,500-man task force, which anchored the division's right flank south of the oil field.

After being alerted about a possible attack, Hodory had summoned his commanders, but the fog and smoke were so thick the officers found it difficult to even find the headquarters. The Marines could not see as far as the next tank. As Hodory waited to see what the Iraqis might do, one of his officers noticed something move: armored vehicles were slowly entering the perimeter of the Marine command post.

"Is that one of ours? That's not one of mine," said Mike Gephart, a tank commander.

A T-55 and two Soviet-made armored personnel carriers emerged out of the fog, pulled up about fifty yards from the command post, and Major Adai, the commander of the 7th Regiment, 22nd Brigade of the Iraqi 5th Mechanized Division, got out.

"I surrender, but I think the rest of my regiment is attacking you," he said.

No sooner had the Iraqi major spoken than Hodory's command post came under tank gun and automatic weapons fire. Tracers streaked across the desert floor at knee level. Between the gaps in the smoke and fog, the Marines could see a gaggle of Iraqi tanks and armored personnel carriers advancing. The Iraqis were firing wildly in every direction and at everything in sight.

The Marines started shooting back with everything they had: antitank guns, 50 caliber machine guns, even small arms. After a ten-minute fusillade, the Iraqis withdrew.

As the Marines waited for another Iraqi charge, a Marine OV-10 reconnaissance plane found a break in the clouds and smoke and reported a buildup of Iraqi forces to the northeast, near Burqan. Hodory called for air support and Cobra helicopters buzzed in.

The Cobras were armed with Hellfire laser-guided missiles. But unlike the Army Apache helicopters, most of the Marine Cobras did not have laser systems to designate their targets. To help direct the missiles to their target, a forward air controller attached to the division, Cpl. Bryan R. Freeman, jumped into the fight. The Cobras hovered overhead, where Freeman used his laser designator to guide their Hellfire missiles at Iraqi tanks 2,600 yards to the front.

As the Cobras blasted the tanks, they came under fire from Iraqi antiaircraft guns 7,000 yards to the east. For Freeman that presented a problem. The range of his laser designator was only 6,000 yards, so Freeman took a chance and ran 1,000 yards in front of the Marine positions with his designator so the Cobras could fire three Hellfires at the Iraqi guns.

During the next three hours, Hodory counterattacked. With the smoke from the oil field, both sides were virtually blind. The battlefield was chaotic. At one point artillery fire called for by Hodoroy hit Fulford's task force by mistake, injuring one Marine and killing two Iraqi prisoners.[9]

Two Marine planes were also lost during the brawl. A Marine OV-10 observation plane was shot out of the sky, and its crew lost. Capt. John A. Walsh, a Harrier pilot, was luckier. As he streaked across the battlefield, a heat-seeking missile slammed into his plane. Walsh tried to land at Al Jaber, which he hoped had been taken by the Marines, but his controls froze. Parachuting into the melee below, he hid in a trench until a Marine Humvee emerged through the smoke and rescued him.

Elsewhere, Myatt's division continued to press the attack. With fighting raging around the Burqan oil field, Fulks moved half his task force to Al Jaber, which the Marines hoped to use as a helicopter base.

After the Marines fired mortars at the base, Iraqi artillery north of Al Jaber began firing rockets, and for once the Iraqi fire was accurate. Twenty-four rockets rained down on the advancing Marines, killing one and wounding twelve. It was one of the heaviest Marine tolls during the ground war.

Fulks did not want to lose any more men in seizing the base and asked for permission to use tear gas to force the Iraqis out of hiding. But Boomer's command rejected the request. The Iraqis had not used chemical weapons, and the Marine commanders feared that the use of nonlethal gas would cross a threshold and prompt the Iraqis to turn to poison gas. Only after the war would the Marines learn that American intelligence reports had been wrong: the Iraqis had not deployed significant quantities of chemical weapons in Kuwait.

A shift in the wind sent a dense cloud of oil smoke over the base and temporarily forced a suspension in the fighting. Even with night-vision goggles, the Marines could not see their hands in front of their faces. Unable to see and afraid of booby traps, Fulks held up the attack, planning to take the base the next day. That night, Fulks's men shivered in the desert chill as a cold drizzle fell on the task force. The chemicals spewing out from the petroleum fires kept setting off the chemical alarms, and Grizzly's men spent much of the night in their charcoal-lined chemical warfare suits. It was a long, miserable night, but it was also the last gasp for the small Iraqi contingent defending the base.[10]

Myatt's division had beaten back the largest Iraqi counterattack of the war and suffered relatively few casualties doing it. "The III Corps commander was the only one who really fought," Lt. Gen. Horner later observed. Mahmoud had tried his best to disrupt the Marine advance with the lastest version of the "Mother of All Battles." Like Khafji, however, the Burqan oil field attack was a failure and the Iraqis continued their retreat.[11]

While Myatt's division consolidated its position, Keys pushed ahead, setting his sights on a collection of buildings to the north between Al Jaber and Kuwait City that the Marines dubbed the "ice cube tray" because of the way the area looked on the reconnaissance photos.

The Iraqis, Sylvester's Tiger Brigade discovered, fell into a pattern. They would take a tank round from the brigade's 120mm tank guns from 3,000 yards away, fire a token round back, and then give up. By late afternoon, Sylvester's main problem was coping with the 1,100 Iraqi prisoners they had collected. The brigade started taking ammunition off its trucks and putting prisoners on them so that they could move the POWs to the rear, away from the battle. The Iraqi prisoners confirmed the location of their defenses on documents the Americans had captured, but the attack was moving too fast to make any use of the information.

Meanwhile at sea, Maj. Gen. Harry Jenkins finally received a long-awaited order. Jenkins had been primed to carry out an amphibious raid on Faylakah Island. But now CENTCOM was switching signals on him: Jenkins received an urgent order to send his helicopters to conduct a fake amphibious attack against the Kuwaiti coast and the offshore islands. CENTCOM had had six months to decide how it wanted to employ the amphibious forces, but the command had not made its intentions clear to the Marines afloat until the second day of the ground war.

Jenkins launched ten helicopters from the USS *Okinawa* on a grueling 110-mile round-trip flight toward Kuwait. Flying in the pitch darkness two hundred feet over the water, the helicopters carried specially config-ured electronic emitters to suggest the presence of a large heliborne force. They approached the southern Kuwaiti port of As Shuaybah, then turned away at the last moment and returned to the ships.

The Iraqis, expecting an amphibious landing on the Kuwaiti coast, responded by launching two Chinese-made Silkworm anti-ship missiles at the allied flotilla. One of the Silkworms was shot down by HMS *Gloucester,* a British vessel, as it headed toward the battleship *Wisconsin.* The other fell harmlessly into the Gulf.

After the war, Jenkins told Boomer about the feints that he had carried out on short notice. Boomer was surprised: he had thought that there was more to CENTCOM's plan to fake an amphibious attack. The Iraqis had been fooled into anticipating an attack against the Kuwaiti coast, but many of the Iraqi defenders had already been routed by the time the feints were launched.[12]

The fighting at Burqan, the bad weather, the smoke from the oil field fires, and Schwarzkopf's nervousness about the Marines' salient all con-spired to arrest the Marine advance on the evening of February 25.

The attack out of Burqan had delayed the Marines' advance, but as evening fell, the significance of Mahmoud's failed counterstroke against Myatt's division became apparent. At 8PM seismic devices used by Ma-rine intelligence began recording large-scale Iraqi troop movements. Fifty minutes later the Kuwaiti resistance reported by phone to Buster Glosson in the Black Hole that the Iraqis were pulling out of Kuwait City. At 9:20, Mike McConnell, the chief intelligence officer for the JCS, notified Glosson that the Iraqis were retreating en masse. Forty minutes later, CENTCOM received confirmation from JSTAR and A-6E planes equipped with infrared night-vision systems.

American intelligence also intercepted Iraqi communications at the same time indicating that Baghdad had ordered a general withdrawal of its forces, with priority going to commanders and their staffs. By with-drawing their headquarters first, the Iraqis hoped to reconstitute their forces north of the Euphrates. It had been thirty-nine hours since the Marines had been told to launch the ground war and the Iraqis had ordered a general retreat.

Glosson immediately called the F-15E commanders at Al Kharj. Manned by two crewman, the F-15E was one of the Air Force's most accurate and modern bombers, but the F-15E pilots had just returned from a mission and were getting ready to hit the sack. The only F-15Es still in the air were the four in the west that were hunting Scuds.

Glosson told David E. "Bull" Baker, the vice wing commander, that he wanted twelve F-15Es to get airborne right away. The planes had to stop the escaping Iraqi convoy that was racing out of Kuwait City. Glosson instructed that the F-15Es be armed with MK-82 bombs or cluster bombs.

With the cloudy weather, the planes would have to fly low, making them potentially vulnerable to SA-16 and SA-9 surface-to-air missiles, and Glosson figured that as many as three of the planes might be shot down.

He told Baker to write a memorandum for the record, noting that it was Glosson who had ordered the crews to fly with no rest. Such a memorandum was a standard way for officers to protect themselves in case a mission went awry. But Baker insisted it was not necessary. "The day I have to make a memorandum for the record during a war, I'll quit," Baker said.

For the rest of the night of the 25th, allied warplanes pounded the Iraqi columns fleeing from Kuwait City. By bombing the lead vehicles, the F-15Es helped create a huge traffic jam. The air-war commanders attacked the Iraqis with abandon. Navy planes were reloaded with the first available munitions and took off again.[13]

By the next morning, Mutlah Ridge was a two-mile-long stretch of burned-out and abandoned vehicles, almost all of which were civilian cars and trucks stolen from the Kuwaitis. According to intelligence photos, the column included more than 1,400 vehicles, but only 28 tanks and armored personnel carriers. Two to three hundred dead Iraqis were later found at the scene. Press reports greatly exaggerated the loss of life along the highway, but the scene of wholesale destruction later emerged as a major factor in the decision to end the war.

The Defense Intelligence Agency later concluded that one of the critical events of the war came when the Iraqi III Corps failed to pull off its coordinated attack against the Marines near the Burqan oil field. Despite the oily black shroud the Iraqis pulled over the battlefield, they were not able to maneuver effectively. The Marines had put up helicopters to boost their firepower and their ground fire had been painfully accurate. From then on, the battle was almost a repetition of Khafji. Forced out of their defensive positions, the Iraqis were easy prey for allied warplanes. The Iraqi army was no longer trying to defend Kuwait, it was trying to escape from the American attack.

That night, Schwarzkopf sent a message to the JCS, tersely summing up the lessons of the day. The Iraqi army could not conduct a coordinated defense. Its corps commanders were controlling only the movement of brigades and could not execute a division-level attack.

"LAND OF DARKNESS"

Traveling just behind Keys's units, Boomer deployed his mobile command post at the southwest corner of the "ice cube tray" only to find himself surrounded by armed Iraqi soldiers trying to give themselves up. It was clear to Boomer that the only major resistance he could anticipate would be on the outskirts of Kuwait City and at Al Jahrah, at the head of the Gulf of Kuwait, as the Marines sought to get astride the Iraqi escape routes and take the airport.

But the Marines were also fighting the perpetual night. With thick smoke blotting out the sky, some Marines slept with their hands outstretched so they could find their comrades. The smoke even blacked out the navigational satellites that they used to fix their position. Many units were relying on compasses and odometers. Oil-rich Kuwait was the prize, but the Marines began calling it the "land of darkness."

At 4AM on the 26th, Boomer ordered the attack to press ahead. Moving on the Kuwait International Airport, Myatt wanted as much combat power as he could muster. But the Marine Cobra attack helicopters lacked the night-vision equipment the Army had and were stymied by the darkness.

Lt. Col. Michael M. Kurth stepped in to get the Cobras back into the war. Kurth's father-in-law, who worked for a defense contractor, had given him a FLIR night-vision system before he went to Saudi Arabia, and Kurth had installed it in his Huey chopper.

Kurth flew the Huey through the oily muck to guide five Cobras to the Al Jaber air base, which had been occupied by Fulks's task force. Bringing in fuel, the Marines used Al Jaber as a refueling point to support their offensive.

Then Kurth flew north, sometimes moving just a few feet off the ground, hovering underneath electrical wires to guide another Cobra to the front. Kurth designated targets with his laser so that the Cobra could take on the Iraqi tanks. It was a jerry-built system and another example of the lengths the Marines had to go to compensate for their limited technology and cope with Iraqi tactics. By the afternoon of February 26, Myatt had sealed off the Kuwait International Airport in the suburbs of Kuwait City.[14]

★   ★   ★

Keys's division, meanwhile, had moved toward the high ground at Al Jahrah, the critical junction on the Iraqi escape route just west of Kuwait City. To the east, Bruce Gombar's 8th Marine Regiment traded artillery barrages with the retreating Iraqis. After sparring with the Iraqis all night, Gombar was having a cup of coffee at dawn with Capt. Mark Ettore, his fire support officer, whose call sign was "Evil One."

Ettore, figuring that the Iraqis were also using the time to regroup, got up and called in a furious artillery strike. The shells fell on the Iraqis as they were getting ready to move back, blowing up their vehicles and lighting up the horizon with explosions.[15]

To the west, the 6th Marine Regiment churned ahead, with Cornwall's units still at the front. The Tiger Brigade, which held up the left flank, was also making good time. All three units were to cut off the routes leading out of Kuwait City, with the Tiger Brigade taking up positions in Al Jahrah to put the stopper in the bottle.

Rolling north, the Tiger Brigade rumbled along the Mutlah Ridge toward Al Jahrah until it collided with a column of eighteen Iraqi tanks that were trying to escape. After the brigade blew up the first three tanks in the column, the rest of the column surrendered. Then the brigade's soldiers assaulted the Mutlah police post, fighting room to room, killing or capturing forty Iraqi soldiers.

The brigade's last casualty came just as it was about to savor its victory: Sgt. 1st Class Harold Witzhe was shot in the leg by a sniper and bled to death before the medics could rescue him. As Keys had forecast, the Iraqis had lacked the fighting will of the North Vietnamese. But it took only one bullet to add to the toll of fallen troops.

As promised, Boomer had made it to Kuwait City in three days. The brigade the Army reluctantly attached to the Marines had its moment of glory at Mutlah Ridge. It closed the door on the remaining Iraqis in southeastern Kuwait. Those who had not escaped north of Al Jahrah by the time the Tiger Brigade seized Mutlah Ridge had no choice but to surrender or fight to the death. They elected the first option. What was left of Saddam Hussein's conquering army in Kuwait raised white flags and went into allied POW compounds. After six months of preparation and five weeks of bombing, Kuwait was liberated.

Much of the country was a wreck. Its oil fields were in flames. The few livestock the Kuwaiti elite possessed roamed the battlefield. The carass of a British 747 — blown apart by Marine aircraft during the weeks of air strikes leading up the ground war — was strewn across

Kuwait International Airport. The city itself had been looted, but most of its buildings were remarkably intact.

By the evening of February 26, the Kuwaiti resistance, wearing red and orange armbands, began linking up with the Americans. Twelve Marines from 1st Force Reconnaissance snuck into Kuwait City to raise the flag over the American embassy only to find it was still flying. It was an unauthorized act of mischief, which was captured by the journalists who made it into the city early and which upstaged the ceremonies planned at the embassy the following day.

Now that the Iraqis had been expelled from Kuwait City, the Marines had to wait for the Arab members of the coalition. CENTCOM's plan called for the Marines to throw the Iraqis out of Kuwait, but the Arab forces were to be the "liberators" of Kuwait City.

The 1st and 2nd Marine Divisions rested on their arms and waited for the Egyptians to make their appearance from the west to participate in the Arab "liberation" of the Kuwaiti capital. They failed to appear. Finally, Boomer received a call from Sylvester, the Tiger Brigade commander.

The Egyptians had finally shown up at dawn on February 27. But there was a hitch, Sylvester explained. The Egyptian commander had refused to enter Kuwait City.

"He said that he had no orders to go into Kuwait City, and he is not going, period," Sylvester reported.

"I do not know what to tell you. My clear understanding is that he is to move into Kuwait City," Boomer replied.

The Egyptians fussed and fumed for several hours, while Boomer called CENTCOM in Riyadh to explain the problem. The Arab delivery of Kuwait City from the aggressors was a scripted bit of political theater custom made for television, but now one of the major Arab allies was balking.

Finally, the Egyptian division commander received a call from the Egyptian liaison officer in Riyadh, who relayed an order from Cairo: Mubarak was ordering the Egyptian forces into Kuwait City. After an embarrassing interlude, the Egyptians marched in parade formation with other Arab contingents of the coalition and officially decreed Kuwait City liberated.

After the Arabs entered Kuwait City, Boomer entered the city to check it out. Boomer later sent an emotional message to President Bush, praising his leadership and giving a stirring account of the joyous reception the Marines had received from the Kuwaitis when they arrived in the city.

Schwarzkopf severely reprimanded his Marine general. As far as the

CENTCOM commander was concerned, communications with the White House were for him to handle.

But the larger question was whether the Marines had been too successful in their stunning attack. Schwarzkopf recalled after the war that he had assumed the Marine attack would set up the Iraqis for a knockout blow. But the Marines had routed the Iraqis so quickly that the Army had not yet built up a head of steam for what was to be the main attack. The outcome of the offensive to liberate Kuwait was a foregone conclusion. The question now was whether the Army would be able to destroy the Republican Guard before the war's denouement.[16]

18

Fragplan 7

VII Corps Destroys RGFC NLT EENT 27 FEB
[VII Corps Destroys Republican Guard Forces Command Not Later
Than Nautical Twilight, Feb. 27].

— Third Army
Order to VII Corps, February 25

W HEN THE MARINES began their attack on the Saddam
Line, John Yeosock was overseeing preparations for the
Army attack from Lucky Main, the Army's command post
in an apartment complex on the outskirts of Riyadh. The three-star
general looked haggard and drawn. Yeosock had been flown to Germany in mid-February for emergency gall bladder surgery and been
temporarily replaced by Schwarzkopf's hard-charging deputy, Lt. Gen.
Cal Waller. But Yeosock had insisted on getting out of his hospital bed
and returning to Riyadh for the war. After all the months of preparation,
he was not about to miss the main event. To Schwarzkopf, letting Yeosock resume his post seemed to be the right way to reward him for his
loyalty, but the decision would rebound in ways the commander could
not foresee.[1]

To Yeosock and his chief operations deputy, Steven Arnold, it looked
like it was going to be a long week. Each of the services was running its
own style of race. While the Marines had planned a sprint to the gates of
Kuwait City, the Army foresaw a marathon; it had farther to go and was
convinced it was about to lock horns with the premier fighting force in
the third world.

As the battle staff assembled at Lucky Main, the acetate overlays draped over the maps of Iraq indicated that the allies had outsmarted the Iraqis, who had anticipated that they would be attacked along the Wadi al-Batin, as well as from the sea and the allied positions near the Saudi-Kuwait border.

To defend against such an attack, the Iraqis stacked five Republican Guard and regular army armored and mechanized divisions, as well as lesser units, on either side of the wadi along its entire route. To protect the vital communications hub at Basra, three Republican Guard infantry divisions covered the western approaches to the city, with a heavy guard division, the Hammurabi, deployed in reserve. It was a well-laid-out defense against an enemy that was determined to attack along the wadi and which depended largely on ground power. But it was totally inadequate against an alliance with total air superiority that planned to attack from the western desert.

Taking the floor, Arnold explained to the battle staff that the Army campaign to destroy the Republican Guard would take seven to ten days. In keeping with Schwarzkopf's plan, elements of the XVIII Airborne Corps in the far west — the 82nd Airborne, the 6th French Division, and the 101st Airborne — had already begun to move north. To get astride the potential escape route along the Euphrates River in the west, CENTCOM figured, the allied forces in the west would need all the time they could get, so they began their assault on the morning of the Marine attack. John Tilelli's 1st Cavalry Division had also begun to attack the Iraqi defenses at the wadi, but his assault was only a feint, designed to reinforce the Iraqis' mind-set that the wadi was the main avenue for the American attack.

The Army units that were to take the battle to the Republican Guard — the XVIII Airborne Corps's tank-heavy 24th Division, the 3rd Armored Cavalry Regiment, and Franks's VII Corps — were not scheduled to kick off their attack until the morning of February 25, the idea being that the delay would fool the Iraqis into thinking the main attack was to the east.

To coordinate the Army's destruction of the Republican Guard, Arnold told his staff that he planned to fly to the front on the third day of the ground war with an updated "conplan," contingency plan. That way, the Army, based on the latest intelligence, would have time to organize its attack for the climactic battle.[2]

It was only hours after Arnold outlined the timetable when Schwarzkopf called. With the Marines bursting through the Iraqi defenses, the CENTCOM commander wanted to know if Yeosock could launch his entire force on February 24. In all its contingency planning, the Army had never anticipated that it would have to speed up its attack plans because the Iraqi defense would collapse in the face of the Marines' attack.

Yeosock immediately relayed the request. At 9:30AM, Yeosock placed separate calls to Luck and Franks, asking whether their corps could attack on two hours' notice.

As nervous as he was about taking on the Iraqis, moving up the attack was no problem for Luck. The reconnaissance mission he had ordered had shown the desert in front of his XVIII Airborne Corps to be largely devoid of enemy soldiers, and much of his force was already on the move.

But the way Franks had planned the VII Corps attack, slamming the Army attack into fast-forward was not going to be easy. Franks's two-pronged plan to assault the Iraqi front-line defenses west of the Wadi al-Batin, launch a parallel armored attack west of these fortifications, and unite the forces in a three-division fist to take on the Republican Guard required careful synchronization. Convinced he was outnumbered, Franks wanted to mass his forces before the VII Corps got into some heavy fighting, and he did not want the outside armored divisions to get too far ahead of the inside divisions as they made their way through the Iraqi defenses. The VII Corps commander saw the Iraqis as an Arab version of the Soviet Army and planned to fight them just as he would take on the Red Army, with massive firepower and careful coordination. He would maneuver his forces into position, concentrate the corps, and attack. Franks expected to take two days to fight his way through the Iraqi front-line defense and another six days to destroy the Republican Guard and mop up any enemy forces that remained.

Franks gave a tentative yes to an early attack, but consensus builder that he was, launched into a hurried series of consultations with his commanders, before giving the final okay. He had counted on daylight to breach the Iraqi fortification and hoped the assault could get under way as soon as possible. It would be getting dark by 5PM.[3]

As the troops waited to launch their long-planned attack, soldiers burned envelopes from home, preferring to sacrifice the mementos than risk having them fall into the hands of an Iraqi captor.

Finally, after Schwarzkopf consulted with Washington and the Arab members of the coalition, the word came down: the attack was to begin at 3PM. There would not be much daylight, but the VII Corps would make the best of it.

*   *   *

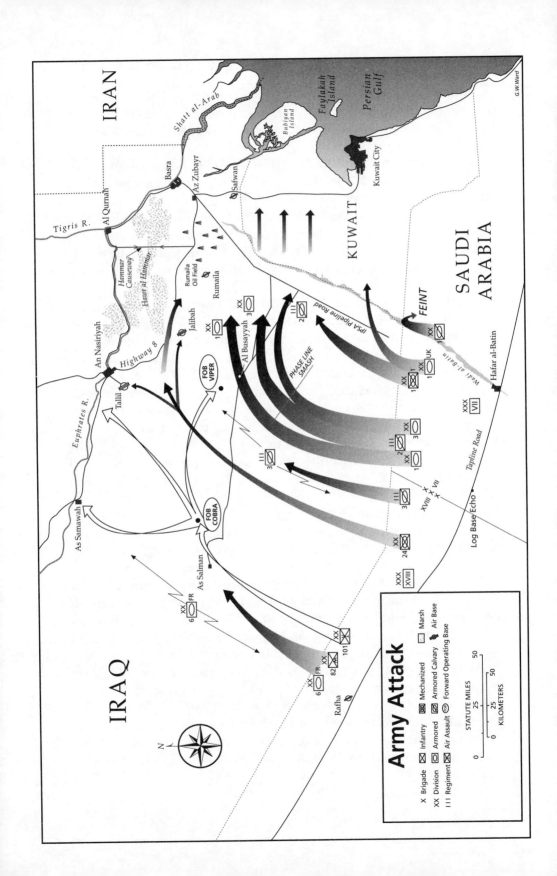

IRAN

Shatt al-Arab

Basra

Al Qurnah

Tigris R.

Az Zubayr

Safwan

Faylakah Island

Bubiyan Island

Persian Gulf

Kuwait City

G. W. Ward

KUWAIT

SAUDI ARABIA

Hammar Causeway

Hawr al Hammar

Rumaila Oil Field

Rumaila

Jalibah

An Nasiriyah

Highway 8

Talil

FOB VIPER

Al Busayyah

PHASE LINE SMASH

IPSA Pipeline Road

FEINT

Hafar al-Batin

Wadi al-batin

UK

VII

Tapline Road

Log Base Echo

XVIII

Euphrates R.

As Samawah

FOB COBRA

As Salman

Rafha

FR
6

FR
6

82

101

24

3

3

3

2
1

1
1

3

2

1
3

IRAQ

N

Army Attack

X   Brigade   ▨ Infantry   ▨ Mechanized   ▲ Marsh
XX   Division   ▨ Armored   ▨ Armored Calvary   Air Base
III Regiment   ▨ Air Assault   ◉ Forward Operating Base

STATUTE MILES
0   25   50

KILOMETERS
0   25   50

Major General Rhame's 1st Mechanized Infantry Division struck the first blow for the VII Corps. At 2:30PM, Rhame's five artillery brigades unleashed a furious barrage against the poorly manned and ill-equipped Iraqi defenders west of Wadi al-Batin. It was one of the most intense bombardments in modern warfare. For half an hour, the din of exploding shells rocked the desert. The brigades fired 6,136 artillery rounds and 414 rockets to smother any Iraqi artillery pieces that might somehow have escaped the allied air bombardment. Then the corps's combat engineers moved in to cut twenty-four lanes through the minefields and fortifications.

Under Franks's plan, Rhame's division would lead the eastern prong of the corps's attack: a headlong plunge into the Iraqi fortifications. Then Rupert Smith's British 1st Armored Division would exploit the breach made by its American cousins, pass through Rhame's lines, and attack to the east to protect the VII Corps's right flank. As Rhame's division pummeled the Iraqis, Smith's Division drove fifty miles to the edge of the battlefield, abandoning earlier plans to haul the armor to the battle area on tank transporters to save wear and tear on the engines.

The western prong of the VII Corps's attack, led by Col. Donald Holder's 2nd Armored Cavalry Regiment, swept around the Iraqi fortifications. Ron Griffith's 1st Armored Division and "Butch" Funk's 3rd Armored Division followed behind, their brigades in single file in a huge armored column that was twenty miles wide and forty miles long.

To keep up morale and soothe the soldiers' nerves, Funk arranged for the 3rd Armored Division Band to serenade the armored column as it rumbled through the Saudi berm. Dressed in the bulky chemical-protective suits, the band played "In the Mood" and the theme music from *Lawrence of Arabia* and *Patton*. With only little opposition directly ahead, the apprehensions about the Iraqis gave way to relief that the long wait was finally over.

As night fell, Franks faced his first critical command decision: whether to press ahead or pause until morning. The main problem was not the Iraqis: they were putting up a meager resistance. The difficulties arose from a battlefield strewn with exploded debris and unexploded munitions, the haunting worry about friendly fire, and a war plan that had never been practiced in darkness. Rhame's 1st Mechanized Infantry Division and Smith's 1st British Armored Division had conducted a full-scale dress rehearsal of the complicated maneuver of having British forces move through the American lines, but they had never practiced it at night.

For a VII Corps staff that had an almost obsessive concern with holding down casualties, that was a major worry. Col. Stan Cherrie, Franks's chief operations officer, worried that the attack on the Iraqi fortifications was getting to be "too hard." In the darkness, one of Rhame's tanks had already fired off a round at Funk's 3rd Armored Division and an Apache helicopter had fired back. Cherrie recommended that the VII Corps halt its attack for the night and renew it at first light. Not everyone in VII Corps agreed with the delay. Brig. Gen. John Landry, the VII Corps chief of staff, was frustrated. The attack had just gotten under way and now Cherrie was talking about stopping for the night. But Franks supported Cherrie. Tomorrow would be another day. Franks would rather be safe than sorry.

With Franks determined to concentrate his forces, his decision to hold up Rhame's attack affected the entire VII Corps. Franks decided to halt the western prong of his attack — Holder's 2nd Armored Cavalry Regiment and the armored divisions rolling behind — as well. He was waiting for the slowest piece to get through the gap.[4]

Cherrie called Arnold later that night and informed him the VII Corps was suspending the breach of the obstacles until dawn of the next day because of the difficulty in operating in the dark. Arnold concurred. The ground war was still young and there was no need to take unnecessary risks. Arnold reported his decision to Yeosock and instructed his staff to pass the word to Schwarzkopf's headquarters.

But Arnold recalled after the war that he did not realize that Franks was planning to suspend his entire attack. He thought that Franks intended to allow Holder's regiment to press on and clear the way so that Griffith's and Funk's armored divisions could leap ahead the next day. There was a disconnect between the VII Corps command in the field and their Army superiors in Riyadh.

That Franks was not prepared to launch his attack at night is surprising given that the Army had long concluded that American superiority in night-vision technology made night attacks preferable to daylight ones. Coordinating a night attack with a foreign ally, even a NATO member that the Army had worked alongside for years, was no easy task, but it was doable. The larger problem was that Franks had built an overly elaborate plan for a two-pronged attack that could not be easily adapted. Another problem was that nobody bothered to tell Schwarzkopf about the decision, setting the stage for one of his volcanic eruptions.

TROUBLE AT THE TOP

The next morning when Schwarzkopf's staff assembled in the war room at the Saudi Ministry of Defense, Lt. Col. Joe Purvis was puzzled by the map. The Marines were racing ahead.

Gary Luck's XVIII Airborne Corps was also leaping through western Iraq. The immediate impediment for the XVIII Corps was not the Iraqis, but weather, logistics, and the generous supply of cluster munitions the Air Force had sprinkled through Iraq. Unlike Franks, Luck had no compunction about splitting up his combat forces in the strategic void that was western Iraq.

The French 6th Division, reinforced with the 82nd Airborne, was attacking in the far western desert to secure the flank. Maj. Gen. Binnie Peay's 101st Airborne had flown north to Cobra, a fire base it set up ninety-three miles deep in Iraq. Fog had briefly delayed the 101st jump to Cobra. But by the end of G day the division had moved 200,000 gallons of fuel to the fire base, using not only all of its helicopters but a huge convoy from Saudi Arabia. It was the largest air assault in Army history and gave the division a staging area for launching attacks in western Iraq and attacking Highway 8, the east-west route along the Euphrates.

Racing ahead with his fuel trucks, McCaffrey's division was roaring northward, with the 3rd Armored Cavalry Regiment providing protection to its flank. McCaffrey was speeding toward the Euphrates River at a remarkable thirty miles an hour over rocky terrain. McCaffrey was hurrying to link up with Peay's 101st, cut Highway 8, and then turn east to attack the Republican Guard.

It looked like just about everyone but Franks was attacking. The VII Corps positions had not moved overnight.

Purvis approached Tim Sulivan, the British member of the Jedi team. Sulivan, Purvis said, should find out why the British 1st Armored Division was still in Saudi Arabia. Schwarzkopf would want to know why the attack was not going forward. Sulivan made a quick check and was relieved to find out the problem was not with the British. They were waiting for the Americans to finish cutting a path through the Iraqi defenses.

When Schwarzkopf entered the war room at 8AM and saw that the VII Corps battle lines had not changed, he exploded. Get Yeosock on the telephone, the commander barked. Schwarzkopf demanded to know why the VII Corps forces were not deep into Iraq. Schwarzkopf had been angry with Franks before but now his frustration was boiling over. There was a fundamental discrepancy between the ways Schwarzkopf and Franks saw the battlefield. From his vantage point in Riyadh, Schwarzkopf was receiving reports from across Iraq, and it was clear the Iraqis were cracking. By staggering the Army attack to follow the Marines, Schwarzkopf had started late. He was now flogging the VII Corps as hard as he could to make up the lost ground. If Franks was not capable of keeping up the pace, Schwarzkopf would replace him with a commander who was.

Yeosock deflected Schwarzkopf's anger on VII Corps. He never mentioned that the Army higher-ups in Riyadh had approved Franks's decision to suspend Rhame's breach or suggested that there had been any confusion in the calls between Franks's staff and Arnold.

The VII Corps was not Schwarzkopf's only worry. He was also concerned about the Egyptians. When the Egyptians attacked on G day, the Iraqis lit fire trenches in front of them, which had enough crude oil left in them to create an intimidating flaming wall. For the Egyptians, there was only one thing to do: wait for the trench fire to burn itself out. They were moving more slowly than the VII Corps, and there was no chance that they could help protect the Marines' left flank. As unhappy as he was with the performance of the Egyptians, Schwarzkopf felt there was little he could do about it.

Schwarzkopf turned to Sulivan. Could the British sweep across southern Kuwait after they passed through Rhame's lines and pick up the slack from the Egyptians?

Sulivan went off to discuss the matter with Peter de la Billière, the senior British commander. But the British commanders were not eager to take on the mission. They figured it would strain logistics, open the British flank to a potential counterattack by the Republican Guard, and create political problems within the coalition. After he returned, Sulivan told Schwarzkopf that the British did not favor the idea but would make sure the mission was accomplished if Schwarzkopf ordered it.

Schwarzkopf deferred to the British. The Egyptian attack would go forward, but at its own pace, despite the fact that this left the Marine flank unprotected. Schwarzkopf had not expected much from the Egyptians and they had proved him right.[5]

At Franks's command post, in the early morning of February 25, word began to filter in that Schwarzkopf was not happy with the pace of the attack. Franks, however, was not worried about the heat from Riyadh. Yeosock indicated to Franks that he could handle Schwarzkopf. The VII Corps commander figured his problems were in front of him, not back in Riyadh.

As dawn broke, Rhame's 1st Mechanized Infantry Division cleared lanes through the minefields and instead of sending troops in to clear the trenches of Iraqi soldiers, Rhame sent armored bulldozers to plow over the trench line, entombing any Iraqis who resisted or were too slow to surrender.

The armored bulldozers were not a novel killing machine. They were used in both World War II and Vietnam for the same purpose. Nor were they more brutal than the pounding the Iraqi front lines took from artillery, tons of bombs, fuel-air explosives, and napalm used by allied forces. The division's efforts to publicize its exploits after the war backfired when news reports said that thousands of Iraqi troops might have been buried alive. A classified log prepared by the division officers at the time, however, put the number of Iraqis buried at 150, and after the war, the Iraqis managed to unearth only several dozen bodies.[6]

With the way cleared by Rhame's men, Smith began to move the British 1st Armored Division through the gaps in the Iraqi defenses. The maneuver was complicated in the best of circumstances. In column, Smith's division covered an area about forty miles long and fifteen miles wide. Moving that big a force through the breach sites was like pouring a bucket of water into a small funnel, but it became even more difficult after Franks came on with a new plan to build up his force for the expected encounter with the Republican Guard.

Franks had hoped that after the start of the ground war Schwarzkopf would put Tilelli's 1st Cavalry Division under his control, but Schwarzkopf was not convinced that Franks needed the division and was holding it in reserve in case the Egyptians faltered. The CENTCOM commander felt Franks's appetite for additional combat power was insatiable. Like the Civil War general George B. McClellan, he always painted his enemy ten feet tall.

Denied the 1st Cavalry, Franks improvised. Helicoptering in, he met Rhame and told him that instead of guarding the gap in the Iraqi fortifications he would be heading north to join the attack on the Republican Guard. That was welcome news to Rhame, who desperately wanted to keep his division in the fight. Yet it meant that two divisions, not one, would have to share the lanes the combat engineers had cleared through the Iraqi defenses. To accommodate the change in plans, Smith cut his division in half. He sent his combat forces through and held up moving his logistical units so that Rhame could begin to move his combat units.

The result was not pretty, Smith recalled after the war. The British forces in the breach shifted to the eastern part of the opening, and Rhame's division began moving through the lanes in the west. The result was a huge rolling traffic jam. There were columns of vehicles going in all directions. All told, it would take the British fourteen hours to get all of their units through the breach.[7]

But it was the western prong of the corps's attack that saw the first real action. Holder's regiment had barely begun to lead the armored column north when the VII Corps received the initial intelligence that the Iraqis were beginning to respond to the allied ground attack. A photo from a JSTARS radar surveillance plane showed an Iraqi brigade moving westward along an oil-covered sand road toward the desert town of Al Busayyah. The information was sent to Franks's command at 6:35AM.

According to VII Corps logs, Franks's command interpreted the movement of the brigade as an indication that the Iraqis had identified the VII Corps as the allies' main effort and were rushing to block their advance and defend the western flank of the Iraqi army. Interrogations of Iraqi officers by Army intelligence after the war, however, showed that the Iraqi countermove was extremely modest, based on a total misreading of the allied strategy and all but impossible to execute in the face of allied airpower. Sending the brigade forward to stop the allies was like waving a handkerchief to ward off a blow from a sledgehammer.[8]

The forty-two-year-old colonel who commanded the brigade from Iraq's 52nd Armored Division told his American captors that all his battalion commanders were reservists and his brigade had had no artillery or helicopters. The brigade had launched its counterattack because of a report that the Iraqi front lines had been breached by a French force of eight tanks and four armored personnel carriers and had no idea that it was on a collision course with Holder's 2nd Armored Cavalry Regiment. His plan was to block one of the roads from Al Busayyah, a town to the west that was defended by a small Iraqi commando force. To defend the flank, the Iraqis planned to put brigades on both sides of the road from Al Busayyah, facing due west. That meant the Iraqis were perpendicular to the direction of the allied attack.

Thinking he was taking on a relatively light force, the Iraqi brigade commander had moved his speedier armored personnel carriers to the head of his force, holding his tanks back for the next morning. But American A-10s found the brigade's armor and blasted a battalion of T-55 tanks.

Racing up the road in the driving rain, Holder's regiment surprised the Iraqis as they were trying to dig in with picks and shovels and quickly destroyed what was left of the hapless brigade. According to the CIA, the Iraqis lost fifty-one armored personnel carriers, twenty-two tanks, and one ZSU-24 antiaircraft gun.

The devastation of the brigade pointed to an underlying problem with the Iraqi army's tactics for fighting in the desert. Many of the Iraqi forces were anchored on the few roads interlacing the area, which they used to orient themselves in the desert and distribute supplies. They assumed that since it was hard for them to navigate far from the roads, there was no possibility the allies could do so either. And with the first reports that the allies were attacking in the west, the Iraqis rushed to defend the east-west roads. That the Americans could launch an attack across the open desert seemed too fantastic to be taken seriously.[9]

While Holder's regiment made short work of the Iraqis, some of the armored forces traveling behind him were far more cautious. As the most western division in the VII Corps's attack, Griffith's 1st Armored Division had the farthest to go to get to the Republican Guard. It was like the outer ring of a great wheel rolling east.

But unlike Holder, Griffith fought a very deliberate war. After the division had rolled over the understrength Iraqi 26th Division, there was only one real enemy position standing in its way to the Republican Guard positions: the town of Al Busayyah.

Al Busayyah had been turned into a massive logistics dump and stocked with 100 tons of ammunition, enough for six months to a year of fighting for the nearby Iraqi divisions. Army intelligence had identified it as the headquarters of the 26th Division.

The beleaguered town had been blasted by the division's Apache helicopters. Griffith could have surrounded the town with a small detachment and ordered the rest of the division to bypass it. But as he came upon the town on the afternoon of February 25, he decided to seize it, even if it meant holding up his entire division — more than 8,000 vehicles and 17,000 soldiers — to do it.

Hoping to hold down casualties, Griffith told Franks that instead of taking the town right away he wanted to pummel Al Busayyah throughout the night and occupy it at daylight. Franks approved the attack plan. As in his decision to suspend Rhame's attack on February 24, Franks preferred waiting to fighting at night.

That night, the 1st Armored unleashed a massive barrage, which reached a crescendo at 6AM. Al Busayyah was pounded with 1,500 artillery shells and 350 rockets. In the morning, Griffith launched a two-brigade attack on what was left of the town. By 9AM, however, the town was still not declared secure; so Griffith ordered a task force to mop up and resumed his march.

The division later dubbed the engagement the "Battle of Al Busayyah" and churned out elaborate graphics detailing the attack. However, the official U.S. Army history later referred to the engagement more accurately as "little more than a skirmish."

The enemy, it was later determined, did not amount to much: one Iraqi infantry battalion, one commando battalion, and one company of

T-55 tanks. All told, the 1st Armored Division had destroyed eleven T-55 tanks, six armored personnel carriers, and eleven trucks, and had captured ninety-four prisoners.

Griffith explained after the war that he had wanted to ensure that the Iraqis in Al Busayyah would not be able to lash out and disrupt the corps's supply line. But some of Holder's officers were frustrated. To pound an insignificant town into submission, Griffith had slowed the VII Corps attack.[10]

As the VII Corps kept up its methodical attack, the XVIII Airborne Corps was continuing to make good time. The 101st's mission was to prevent the Iraqis from sending reinforcements into the battle area or to stop those in the battle area from trying to escape by going down Highway 8, paralleling the Euphrates River. Peay's Screaming Eagles, or at least a small portion of them, were astride the road by the end of G day.

With the wind and rain interfering with helicopter flights, Peay's initial blocking force — an anti-armor company, two TOW infantry companies, and some field artillery — numbered no more than 1,000 soldiers. The soldiers attacked a few light trucks along Highway 8, but there was no substantial enemy resistance when they cut the road. Peay had barred one of the Iraqis' possible escape routes. But another escape route to the interior of Iraq was open through Basra or over the nearby Hawr al Hammar causeway if the Iraqis decided to retreat. Whether the Republican Guard would stand fast and fight, launch a counterattack, or make a run for it was not yet clear to the XVIII Airborne commanders.

As for Franks, his VII Corps had a number of contingency plans to deal with possible Iraqi responses to the Army attack. Fragplan 7 was his plan to take the battle to the Republican Guard if they stood and fought. Instead of continuing on a northwest heading, the VII Corps would pivot, head due east, and slam into the Iraqi divisions.

To help decide what plan to use, Franks arranged for an update from Army intelligence on the status of the Republican Guard on the afternoon of February 25. But before the intelligence came in, the VII Corps received an order from the Third Army: "VII Corps Destroys RGFC NLT EENT 27 FEB."

The VII Corps had been ordered to destroy the Republican Guard forces not later than nautical twilight on the evening of February 27. Franks had not yet tangled with the Republican Guard or even selected a contingency plan for attacking them, and the commanders in Riyadh were telling him that the Guard had to be destroyed in the next two days.

In Riyadh, the reason for the order was clear. Under the pressure of the Marine attack, Baghdad had begun withdrawing its forces from Kuwait. To cover the withdrawal of their field army, the Iraqis hastily deployed a blocking force to the west. It was imperative that Franks move aggressively before the Iraqis could escape.

The western flank of the Iraqi defenses began to look like a giant fishhook. Brigades of the Iraqi 52nd Mechanized Division, 12th Armored Division, and the Tawakalna Republican Guard Division moved to hastily prepared defensive positions just east of the IPSA pipeline road, the main north-south road, to form the shank of the fishhook. Like the ill-fated brigade destroyed by Holder's regiment, the Tawakalna Division covered all the minor roads coming east from Al Busayyah. The Medina Republican Guard Division, deployed to the right rear of the new defense line, formed the hook.

The defensive line was spotty, lacked depth, and was laid out in a way that made it difficult for the divisions to support each other. It was little more than a thin line of tanks and armored personnel carriers punctuated with gaps. Little artillery was shifted to support the defense. The Iraqi emergency plan, which had completely reoriented the direction of their defense, was no longer to draw the Americans into a prolonged and bloody ground war; the Iraqis were trying to buy time for an escape.

Schwarzkopf knew the Army was pursuing a defeated foe, but Franks was convinced that the Republican Guard was determined to stand fast and slug it out with the Americans. As much as ever, Franks was determined to pull together his three-division fist before slamming into the Republican Guard.

FIRST BLOOD

At 5:22AM on February 26, Holder's regiment in the vanguard of the main American force received the long-awaited message over E-mail: Fragplan 7 was now in effect. The Americans may have outgunned the Iraqis, but the Army's communications network was an antiquated pastiche of technologies, more suited for defensive operations than for supporting lightning thrusts into enemy territory. The Army's FM radios were thirty-five to forty years old and had limited range.

As a result, the VII Corps Tactical Operations Center sent messages by electronic mail, using microwave antennas that were erected in the desert as the American forces advanced. The message was received on a cellular phone hooked into a computer.

But E-mail had its limitations. The communications link was easily

Euphrates R.

An Nasiriyah

Tallil

XVIII
CORPS

Highway 8

24 XX

Jalibah

101 XX (-)

1 XX

3 XX

Al Busayyah

2 III

1 XX

VII
CORPS

45 XX

1 UK XX

46 XX   31 XX 25 XX

IPSA Pipeline Road

Wadi al-Batin

EXPECTED AMERICAN ATTACK

N

STATUTE MILES
0   25   50

0   25   50
KILOMETERS

Al Qurnah

Tigris R.

IRAN

Hammar
Causeway
Hawr al Hammar

INTENDED AIR ASSAULT BY 101ST DIVISION

INTENDED
ATTACK

Basra

Shatt al-Arab

RUMAILA
OIL FIELD

XVIII
XXX
VII

Rumaila

MEDINA
RIDGE

73 EASTING

XX T

12 XX

52 XX

10 XX

17 XX

KUWAIT

36 XX

Safwan

XX M   H XX

XX N

XX AF

51 XX

Bubiyan
Island

Faylakah
Island

XX A

Kuwait City

Persian
Gulf

36 XX

Ali al Salem

6 XX

15 XX

11 XX

As Shuaybah

21 XX   1 XX

20 XX 30 XX 16 XX   36 XX

3 XX   14 XX

7 XX   Al Jaber   2 XX

"Elbow"

14 XX   3 XX   42 XX

29 XX   3 XX   18 XX

"Heel"

SAUDI
ARABIA

Iraqi Retreat and
Hasty Defense to the West
G+3/4, February 26 and 27, 1991

X   Brigade   ◎ Armored   ⊠ Overrun Positions
XX   Division   ⊠ Mechanized   ⚐ Air Base
⊠   Infantry   ⊠ Air Assault   Armored Cavalry
                                     Regiment

**Legend of Iraqi
Republican Guard
Division**

⊠ ⊠ ◎

T = Tawakalna
M = Medina
H = Hammurabi
N = Nebuchadnezzar
A = Adnan
AF = Al Faw
SF = Special Forces

G.W.Ward

broken. The VII Corps headquarters rarely called on the field telephone to see if the E-mail messages were received, and there was no system of electronic confirmation to ensure that the communication had gotten through. The main communications channel the Army used to give its attack orders was not as good as a modern office fax.

Holder thought the VII Corps attack plan was perfectly suited for his regiment. In Europe, the role of the regiment had been to slow down a Warsaw Pact onslaught. Under Fragplan 7, the regiment's role was reversed. It was to find the Iraqis so that the corps's heavy divisions trailing behind could roll over them. But Franks did not want the regiment to impale itself on the superior force.

Holder used the concept of aircraft carrier warfare as a model for his tactics. Long-range helicopters would fly in front, much as the Navy's F-14s would fly combat air patrols ahead of a carrier battle group to protect it from attack. Then the regiment's ground forces would advance along a nineteen-mile front. Scouts in Bradleys, like destroyers at sea, would range ahead as the tanks followed behind. The regiment was to retain the freedom to maneuver and, if need be, be prepared to fall back. Not everyone in the Army believed that the regiment could perform such a delicate task without being eaten up by Iraqi armor. Holder had argued that it could, and now he would have to make good on that prediction.

With the 2nd Armored Cavalry Regiment as the vanguard, Funk's 3rd Armored Division and Griffith's 1st Armored Division would wheel to the east, while Rhame's 1st Mechanized Infantry Division moved north from the breach site to come on line with the two armored divisions. All three divisions were to then position themselves for the final eastward assault along a line in the desert the VII Corps dubbed Smash. When Holder found the Republican Guard, Franks's three heavy divisions would be coiled and ready to strike the Iraqis with a balled fist. The British were to engage the Iraqis north of the breach site to protect the exposed right flank of the corps.

Before turning east, Holder ordered his staff to make sure the British had also been notified that Fragplan 7 was in effect. Under the plan, Holder's sharp turn east would cross into the northern part of what would otherwise have been the British zone. The last thing Holder needed was to send his regiment crashing into the British force.

Holder was told it was a good thing the regiment had contacted the British. They had not yet gotten word of the change in plans. Army command and control was becoming a problem for fast-paced offensive operations in the vast desert.

★   ★   ★

The pivot east was the beginning of what was to become one of the VII Corps's most intense fights. As the regiment rolled east, the weather soon became a big problem. With the clouds and blowing sand, the regiment's aviation squadron was grounded about half the time. This deprived the regiment of the air scouts it needed.

Adding to the confusion, the VII Corps maps did not show the IPSA pipeline road, the shank of the fishhook just to the rear of the Tawakalna Division where the Iraqis had anchored their hasty defense. The road had been bombed for weeks by the Air Force, but Holder did not know that the road existed. Because the Iraqis always established their defensive positions close to the few roads in the desert, that was an important gap in the Army's intelligence.

"In the corps's terrain analysis and my own maps, it did not appear," recalled Holder. "Mapping was a problem."[11]

Step by step, the regiment began to feel its way, moving eight troops abreast. The commander of Eagle Troop, Capt. H. R. McMaster, had his men in the standard formation. The scouts in the Bradley fighting vehicles were in the lead, looking for the enemy. The tanks and artillery followed behind.

As the regiment rolled forward, the sun broke through the clouds. But the wind was whipping the sand so hard it was difficult to conduct long-range observation, even with the thermal sights on the Bradleys and the M1 tanks. Soon, McMaster saw the telltale signs that the regiment had entered the Tawakalna security zone. A handful of Iraqi armored personnel carriers, presumably a reconnaissance force for a larger formation to the rear, was detected and attacked. But not knowing about the IPSA pipeline road, the regiment could not say where or when it would run into the main force.

McMaster alerted his men that they could be running into the Iraqis at any moment.

"We attack in five minutes to the Seventy Easting," he said, referring to the longitudinal line on the Army maps. "This is the moment we have all waited for."

"What kind of contact can we expect?" asked Lt. Gauthier, the third platoon leader.

"Enemy contact," McMaster replied, stating the obvious. It was clear to the soldiers that the intelligence left something to be desired.

Just on the other side of a small crest in the sand was the 18th Brigade of the Tawakalna Division. The Tawakalna was supposed to have been hit hard during the air war. But it had not been easy for the Air Force to isolate the Tawakalna from the jumble of Republican Guard units and tactical reserves near the Wadi al-Batin. The 18th Brigade had emerged from the air war with twelve of its eighteen tanks intact.

Trying to take advantage of even the smallest change in terrain, T-72 tanks were dug in quickly so they could get off the first shot at the coalition forces as they came over a rise. Behind the tanks were an ammunition depot, a field hospital, and a supply base.

As Eagle Troops' Bradleys approached the incline, they came under fire from Iraqi artillery and were peppered by small arms fire from several seemingly abandoned buildings. McMaster ordered his tanks to fire. Nearly simultaneously, the tanks fired 120mm shells into the building, devastating the structure.

McMaster shifted the more vulnerable Bradleys to the rear and moved the tanks into the lead, taking the point position in a nine-tank wedge. As his tank crested the rise, his gunner yelled out, "Tanks direct front!"

Eight Iraqi tanks were dug into fighting positions behind large earthen berms. It was like jumping into a foxhole and finding it filled with enemy soldiers. Both sides seemed surprised by the sudden confrontation.

With the rest of the Eagle Troop wedge still on the other side of the rise, McMaster's tank used its laser range finder to fix the position of the Iraqi tanks.

"Fire, Sabot," the gunner yelled.

A Sabot round made of depleted uranium shot out of the barrel at one mile per second. As the barrel recoiled, the T-72 exploded in a shower of fire and sparks.

McMaster's tank turned its turret to take on another T-72. The stabilizers in the M1 enabled the gunner to train the main gun on an enemy tank even as he churned forward. McMaster's gunner let fly another Sabot round, knocking the turret off a second T-72. All told, McMaster's tank fired for six or seven seconds before the rest of the tanks drove across the ridge.

While Eagle Troop was rolling forward, its executive officer, 1st Lt. John Gifford, radioed McMaster. "Seventy Easting was the limit of advance," Gifford said, referring to the north-south grid line that was to mark the regiment's farthest point of penetration.

"We are still in heavy contact, advancing to the seventy-three," McMaster replied. "Tell them I'm sorry."

Having locked horns with the Iraqis, he had no time to wait for Rhame's 1st Mechanized Infantry Division to come up and finish the job. There was only one way to go now: forward.

Eagle Troop's tanks kept grinding along with the M1s blasting away with their 120mm guns. The troop's Bradleys fired TOW antitank missiles and raked the backs of the American tanks with machine gun fire to keep Iraqi soldiers from trying to sneak up on the M1s and blasting their more vulnerable rear with rocket-propelled grenades. The most unusual kill came when a Bradley used a TOW missile to knock out a Soviet-made ZSU-234 antiaircraft gun that the Iraqis were using to sweep the battlefield.

Eagle Troop finally halted on a small hill from which the soldiers could look out several miles. McMaster called each platoon to see if they had made it through and was relieved to find out that the troop had not suffered any losses.

Not all of the regiment was so lucky. Ghost Troop and Iron Troop had also clashed with the Iraqis, and one of Ghost Troop's Bradley gunners was killed when his 25mm gun jammed and he was hit by Iraqi fire as he got out of his Bradley to try to fix it. To the south, the regiment's troops had easier going, tangling with elements of Iraq's 12th Armored Division.

After the sun set, the regiment continued to pound the Iraqis from afar, firing artillery at truckloads of fleeing Iraqis. By 10PM the weather had cleared enough to allow the VII Corps's aviation brigade to launch two Apache helicopter raids. The glow of the burning vehicles reflected off the clouds while secondary explosions from the artillery strikes sent towers of fire shooting up to the sky along the horizon. Finally, Rhame's 1st Infantry Division arrived. Like a relay racer picking up the baton, it passed through the regiment's position at 11:11PM and continued to press the attack.[12]

The regiment later dubbed its fight the Battle of 73 Easting. The battle with the Tawakalna Division had been unplanned and ran counter to the guidelines it had received from Franks not to get tangled up with the Iraqis. But it was one of VII Corps most important victories. If three troops from an American Cavalry regiment could destroy an Iraqi brigade at little cost, perhaps the Republican Guard was not the vaunted fighting force Franks had assumed it to be. But there was no time to absorb the larger military lessons of the battle. The regiment had its piece of glory and the rest of the VII Corps plowed ahead.

While Holder's regiment was heading into the fray, Funk's 3rd Armored Division was also moving toward the IPSA pipeline road to continue the attack against the shank of the Republican Guard positions.

As Funk attacked, Army intelligence officers picked up a heated argument over the radio between the commander of the Tawakalna Division and other Iraqi commanders. When the lower-ranking commanders complained that the Tawakalna commander was talking on an uncoded radio broadcast, they were angrily rebuked. The Tawakalna commander was desperately trying to pull together a defense against the unexpected allied attack from the west in the fastest way he could. He had no time for security procedures and announced he was assuming control over the other divisions in the area.

Funk attacked two brigades abreast, drawing on firepower from the Special Operations AC-130 gunships, A-10 attack planes, and F-16s. But friendly fire led Funk to suspend the attack that night. Identification in the desert was difficult.

The decision was made after the division mistakenly raked one of its Bradley fighting vehicles with 25mm fire, killing a scout, and some of Funk's soldiers lost contact with Holder's brigade to the south. In the darkness, three of the division's Bradleys were hit by friendly fire and two more soldiers were killed. Navigation in the desert was difficult.

Meanwhile, immediately north of Funk's brigade, Griffith's division, having taken Al Busayyah, was again moving eastward toward the hook of the Iraqi defenses. But the 1st Armored Division was having trouble keeping pace as it moved to fill out the three-division VII Corps "fist" for attacking the Republican Guard.

Griffith's problem was not the Iraqis, but fuel. The Army's turbine-powered M1 tanks that were pulverizing the Iraqi T-72s were gas-guzzlers and needed to be topped off every eight or nine hours.

Griffith also had more ground to cover than the other divisions, and like much of the VII Corps, he had planned on getting a breather before setting off after the Republican Guard. He figured that he would have about thirty-six hours to refuel and rearm. But with Schwarzkopf demanding that the corps press on, there would be no pause. Adding to Griffith's problem, the thirst of his division had been increased by Franks's decision to switch the 75th Artillery Brigade from Rhame's 1st Infantry Division to Griffith's division. Franks made the switch to increase Griffith's firepower before his confrontation with the Republican Guard, but the brigade needed fuel to keep it going.

Quenching the VII Corps's thirst for fuel was the task of Brig. Gen. Robert P. McFarlin, Franks's chief logistics officer. McFarlin had worked day and night to come up with a system to keep the attack rolling, but he was not confident about how well it would work. McFarlin had advised Franks before the ground war that there was a high risk that VII Corps would literally run out of gas on the third day of the ground offensive despite the best efforts of the logisticians.

There was no shortage of fuel. Sitting in Saudi Arabia, the Army had plenty of that. The problem was trucks. The Army depended largely on 5,000-gallon trucks that worked well when its forces were moving along the autobahns of Europe, but the fuelers were not designed to travel off roads or through deep sand.

Under pressure from Les Aspin, the Wisconsin chairman of the House Armed Services Committee, the Army had purchased HEMTTs. The large eight-wheeled trucks, which were manufactured in Aspin's home state, could carry 2,500 gallons and could maneuver in bad terrain. They had achieved a brief moment of notoriety when George Bush cited them as a blatant example of Democratic pork-barrel politics during his 1988 debate with Michael Dukakis. But by the time of the Gulf War, the Army's only complaint was that they did not have enough of them. The VII Corps had received forty-seven HEMTTs just before the war, and McFarlin ordered that they be loaded with fuel as a reserve.

To ease the strain on resupplying VII Corps, McFarlin established a number of logistical bases along the route into Iraq as the VII Corps divisions advanced. That way, the trucks that refueled the VII Corps juggernaut would not have to make their way all the way back to Saudi Arabia to take up a new load of fuel and then head north again. One base was at Nelligen, a patch of sand some twelve miles into Iraq, which was named after a town in Germany. Another was Buckeye, established by a National Guard unit from Iowa.

With the VII Corps rolling forward, however, McFarlin could see that a serious fuel problem was developing. Trucks were going out with fuel and not coming back. There were reports of fuel tankers getting lost or stuck in sand.

The 1st Armored Division borrowed some fuel from Funk's 3rd Armored Division and, with three brigades abreast, headed toward the Medina Division, which was rushing into new positions to defend its western flank. In the process, Griffith's division collided with remnants of the Tawakalna Division, which was trying to make its way north, and a brigade from the Adnan Division, a Republican Guard infantry unit.

But the fuel provided by Funk's division was just a stop-gap measure. Unless more fuel was made available to the 1st Armored Division, Griffith would be forced to leave a brigade behind and continue his attack with a reduced division.[13]

To get the trucks rolling again, McFarlin turned to Steve Walker, a twenty-eight-year-old tobacco-chewing captain from Memphis, Tennessee. Assigned to the VII Corps's 16th Support Group, Walker had a lot of practical experience in Army logistics.

McFarlin told Walker he could take the HEMMTs if only he could find someone to drive them. Virtually all fuel truck drivers were driving somewhere in Iraq or with the logistics trains following the divisions. Walker had to assemble the emergency fuel convoy to keep the corps attack rolling.

Within five hours, Walker had formed a transportation company of eighty volunteer drivers — cooks, clerks, NCOs, chemical decontamination specialists, and the like. About three-quarters of them had never driven a HEMTT before, and only five of them had ever discharged fuel from the vehicle. Leaving at 5:30PM, the convoy drove for eighteen straight hours over the dirt paths plowed by the combat engineers. After arriving, the drivers took out their technical manuals and began to pump the fuel as they read how to do it. At that time, Griffith's 2nd brigade had only one hour of fuel left.[14]

THE BOBBY KNIGHT PRESS

While the VII Corps was trying to keep pace, Yeosock again alerted Franks to the bad reviews he was getting in Riyadh. Schwarzkopf was still unhappy with the pace of the attack, Yeosock told Franks on the morning of February 26. The CENTCOM commander thought the corps was moving too slow and wanted Franks to explain the reason.

Franks said he thought things were going fine and would call Schwarzkopf to square things with him.

That was not the only message Yeosock had for Franks. Yeosock was also worried about the logistics problem and suggested that the VII Corps open up a new and more direct supply route. The British were slashing through the Iraqi units to their east. If Smith's 1st Armored Division turned south and cleared a path through the Iraqi fortifications from the rear, the Army could shorten the fuel runs by sending its trucks from Log Base Echo near Hafar al-Batin to the IPSA pipeline road that ran along the Wadi al-Batin.

Franks did not like the idea. The VII Corps had attacked west of the Wadi al-Batin precisely to avoid the Iraqi minefields and fortifications along the border there. He did not want to change the direction of the British attack by ordering them to attack the fortifications from the rear.

But after getting off the phone, Franks nonetheless gave a "warning order," or alert, to Smith to plan an attack south. Franks intended it as a simple notice about a decision that was not yet made. But in the British staff system, warning orders were not taken casually. The British commander was not happy about the order, but he prepared to carry it out.

Smith took all his combat engineers, attached them to Chris Hammer-bech's 4th Brigade, and began to prepare for an attack south.

Once again, Yeosock had sent Franks a mixed message. He had re-layed Schwarzkopf's frustration, but then burdened the VII Corps com-mander with the problem of planning an attack to the south.

While Schwarzkopf was berating Yeosock he was also looking over his shoulder at Powell. Now that an Iraqi order to withdraw had been an-nounced by Baghdad, it was beginning to influence the political equation. Powell raised the issue of a cease-fire in a telephone call. Schwarzkopf said he was planning to destroy the Republican Guard in the next two days. If the coalition called a cease-fire, CENTCOM would not accomplish its mission. Powell told Schwarzkopf to stick with the current plan.

Despite Powell's response, Schwarzkopf was worried the war might be ended prematurely. That afternoon, at 1:30PM, Schwarzkopf spoke with Sir Patrick Hine, the senior British official who was based in Lon-don, who also mentioned the possibility of a cease-fire. The Russians were planning to call a Security Council meeting to push for an end to the fighting, Hine advised.

At 1:46PM, Schwarzkopf passed the word to Yeosock. Pressure was building for a cease-fire. At 2:25PM, Schwarzkopf talked again to Pow-ell. The JCS chairman had to buy CENTCOM some time, Schwarz-kopf implored. The wadis were filling up with rain and the going was rough. Powell said that Schwarzkopf would have to keep the VII Corps moving. Schwarzkopf replied that he might have to get rid of Franks to do so. Under tremendous pressure to get the job done, Schwarzkopf began to take things directly into his own hands.

Stan Cherrie was in the VII Corps "jump" Tactical Operations Cen-ter when a call came through from CENTCOM headquarters. The for-ward TOC was not the best way to run the war. The entire command center was nothing but two armored personnel carriers filled with com-munications gear. The main TOC had much better communications capabilities, but one of the APCs that was moving it forward had thrown a track and was stalled somewhere in Iraq.

Right away, Cherrie could tell he was talking to a high-level headquar-ters. The line was crystal clear, not scratchy like the tactical radio nets.

Col. B. B. Bell, Schwarzkopf's executive assistant, was on the line. Schwarzkopf was calling for Franks. Cherrie explained that Franks was not there; he was off talking to Funk at the 3rd Armored Division com-mand post. Suddenly, the phone at the other end of the line changed hands.

"Who is this?" a familiar voice yelled.

Cherrie identified himself and gave a quick rundown on the status of the VII Corps attack.

"I want to keep pushing. We got a full court press on. I want the Bobby Knight press. You know who Bobby Knight is? Keep moving!" Schwarzkopf yelled again.

After Franks returned, Cherrie told him that Schwarzkopf had called, barked at him, and then hung up.[15]

Franks called Riyadh and got Schwarzkopf on the line. He figured that things were going pretty well. Step by step he was moving his divisions into place to attack the Republican Guard. Franks said he was turning the corps 90 degrees to attack to the east. The 2nd Armored Cavalry Regiment was making short work of the Iraqis at 73 Easting. The 1st Armored Division had taken Al Busayyah. Two corps artillery brigades were being shifted from the breach sites to beef up Griffith's division. The VII Corps was working the 3rd Armored Division into the fight. The British were attacking Iraq's second echelon.

Then Franks mentioned that he was thinking about sending the British south, without saying that the idea had originated from Yeosock.

Schwarzkopf erupted. "Christ, don't do that," he exclaimed. The enemy was to the east, not the south, the CENTCOM commander shouted.

Franks had assumed that since the Republican Guard was not fleeing eastward toward Basra and the causeway over the marshes west of the city they planned to stay and fight. The VII Corps commander had reasoned that he had time to synchronize his attack against the Republican Guard.

But Franks was looking at only a small piece of the battlefield and missed the larger significance of the Iraqi tactics. From Riyadh, it was clear that the Guard was just trying to hold the line while the rest of the Iraqi army escaped. Ever since Baghdad has ordered a general withdrawal of its forces in Kuwait, it was only a matter of time before the protecting Republican Guard followed.

Schwarzkopf told Franks that intelligence showed that the Iraqis had sent transporters to pick up the Hammurabi Division tanks. The Medina had also been ordered to pull out. The VII Corps needed to press the attack. Schwarzkopf did not tell Franks that he was considering relieving him.

"Wilco," said Franks. He would press the attack all night, including scheduling a deep attack with Apaches.

"You will have good shooting tonight," Schwarzkopf yelled. "You may have fog tomorrow morning, so you must shoot now."

It was the only time that Franks talked directly to Schwarzkopf during the ground war. Afterward, Franks called his staff together. It was time to crank up the heat.[16]

That night, Franks sketched out his plan for the final battle with the Republican Guard. Drawing his plan in the sand, he proposed a double envelopment of the Iraqi forces. Griffith's 1st Armored Division, which had quenched its thirst for fuel thanks to Captain Walker's emergency caravan, would form part of the pincer in the north.

After two days of importuning by Yeosock and Arnold, Franks had finally been given operational control of John Tilelli's 1st Cavalry Division. It had taken fifteen hours longer for the VII Corps to get control of the 1st Cavalry than Army commanders had anticipated. Desperate to join the battle and relatively fresh, the 1st Cavalry was making a forced march north. Tilelli's division was to slip around the 1st Armored Division and continue to hit the tottering Republican Guard forces after they had been pummeled by the 1st Armored Division. Filling out the northern envelopment, Funk's 3rd Armored Division would continue to attack to the west.

The southern arm of the pincer, Franks initially decided, would be made up of Smith's British 1st Armored Division. Franks told the British that they should drive to the sea north of Kuwait City. Then, after reaching the coastal highway, the British should pivot north and roll to the Iraq-Kuwait border. After Franks learned that Rhame's 1st Infantry Division was making good progress, however, he decided to substitute the American division for the British 1st Armored.

It was not the first time that the British had to take a back seat to the Americans. The British attack against the Iraqi tactical reserves on the first two days of the ground war was described by one senior CENTCOM official after the war as "holding the door open for the Army" so it could pursue the Republican Guard. After the war, the British would tout their role in the war. Britain had insisted on joining the "main" Army attack for prestige and to hold down the casualties they expected if they joined the Marine attack into Kuwait. But Britain had become little more than a junior partner in a methodical Army assault and had given up a mission that would have afforded the British division a more central role and more glory — the liberation of Kuwait.

After nailing down the plan with his commanders, Franks thought he had the battle in hand. The VII Corps would scoop up much of the Iraqi Army that was south of Basra. This whole thing is going to work, Franks said he thought at the time.

But the sands of time had run out on VII Corps. The collapse of the Iraqi defense and the flight of the Iraqis north were changing the relative priority of the corps's attacks. For the first three days, the VII Corps had done most of the Army's fighting. The main impediment to the neighboring XVIII Corps had been weather, logistics, and the generous supply of cluster munitions the Air Force had liberally sprinkled throughout the desert.

Now Luck's XVIII Airborne was beginning to assume the main role. Peay's 101st Airborne Division was hopscotching its way to the east, and Barry McCaffrey's 24th Mechanized Division was also rolling east on Highway 8.[17]

The "Mother of All Battles" had turned into a race to the Euphrates, and the Iraqis had a big head start. The question was whether CENTCOM could catch the Iraqis and whether it would have time to fight them if it did.

19

"The Gate Is Closed"

Question: You said that gate was closed. Have you got any ground forces blocking the roads to Basra?
Answer: No.
Question: Is there any way they can get out that way?
Answer: No. (Laughter) That's why the gate's closed.

— CENTCOM news briefing
Gen. H. Norman Schwarzkopf
Riyadh, Saudi Arabia
February 27, 1991

ON THE MORNING of February 27, Barry McCaffrey flew to Jalibah airfield to meet with his commanders. Located thirty miles south of Highway 8, the east-west road that ran to Basra, Jalibah had been one of Iraq's main airfields during the war. But now it was pockmarked with the burned and twisted wreckage of Iraqi MiG-29s and other fighters that McCaffrey's 24th Division had blasted in a four-hour fight to seize the airfield.

After leaving his helicopter, the general made his way over to Col. Paul Kern, the commander of the division's 2nd brigade. Kern had deployed his command post — two M-577 armored personnel carriers full of communications equipment — within a protective cordon of M1 tanks and Bradley fighting vehicles, which guarded the perimeter of the airfield.

No general was more aggressive than McCaffrey. He had been badly wounded in Vietnam, but it had not shaken his confidence or his ardor for battle. Unlike the VII Corps planners, McCaffrey was not in awe of the Iraqis. Dug into their fighting holes and with no air force to protect them, the Iraqi army was like a bunch of "tethered goats," McCaffrey recalled after the war.

Schwarzkopf had a soft spot for the general, who commanded his old unit. Just before McCaffrey's division moved to its attack positions in the Saudi desert, Schwarzkopf flew up to give a pep talk to one of the division's reconnaissance teams. Before returning to his helicopter, Schwarzkopf grabbed McCaffrey by his uniform. With tears welling in his eyes, the commander told McCaffrey that once the ground war started there would be no stopping until the Army had destroyed the Republican Guard. President Bush had assured Schwarzkopf of that. That moment was chiseled in McCaffrey's memory.

When it came time to launch the ground war, McCaffrey issued a top secret attack order that seemed like a call to a holy war and alluded to the assurance he had received from Schwarzkopf. "Soldiers of the Victory Division — we now begin a great battle to destroy an aggressor army and free two million Kuwaiti people," the order read. "We will fight under the American flag and with the authority of the United Nations. By force of arms we will make the Iraqi war machine surrender the country they hold prisoner. There will be no turning back when we attack into battle."

For three days of battle, he had methodically maneuvered his corps into position, hoping to carry out his double envelopment. Worried about dispersing his force, he had tugged on the reins of the VII Corps, trying to make sure that one of his lead charges did not out-gallop the others. But McCaffrey had operated under no such constraints.

McCaffrey's thrust into Iraq had resembled one of Jeb Stuart's wild rides during the Civil War. McCaffrey's division — a potent force of 26,000 soldiers and 8,600 vehicles — had driven through a blinding sand and rain storm, over rough, corrugated terrain, to race north to the Euphrates. The toughest part of the drive came when McCaffrey squeezed his division through a narrow series of wadis that ran toward the Euphrates — an area McCaffrey nicknamed "the great dismal bog." Operating under the protective umbrella of allied warplanes, and with the desert largely devoid of enemy, the division's trucks had driven through the night with their headlights on and the warning lights on their tails blinking in the darkness.

Fuel had been his main worry. McCaffrey had brought hundreds of fuel trucks with him to help keep his grueling pace of fifteen miles per hour. Schwarzkopf wrote after the war that he had held up McCaffrey's advance so that he would not arrive at the Euphrates well ahead of Franks. But that was not how McCaffrey remembered it: he had stopped only long enough to replenish his division and move on.

To his rear, the logisticians also pulled out all the stops so that the 24th Mech and its sister units in the XVIII Airborne Corps — Binford Peay's 101st Airborne Division, Doug Starr's 3rd Armored Cavalry Regiment, and James Johnson's 82nd Airborne, which had earned the sobriquet "82nd truckborne" because it was driving well behind the main thrust — would have enough fuel and supplies to finish the war. As the combat engineers plowed dirt roads from the huge supply base near Rafha to As Salman and beyond, an overzealous aide to Lt. Gen. William G. Pagonis, CENTCOM's top logistician, sent sixty-three Saudi fuel trucks with third world drivers north into Iraq. That violated the coalition's political injunction that the Arab members of the coalition and their vehicles were to be limited to the attack on Iraqi forces in Kuwait (the liberation of an Arab country) and were not to enter Iraqi territory (an attack on a fellow Arab country). When the third world drivers returned, the logisticians informed them that they had never been to Iraq.

As McCaffrey's division hit Highway 8 on February 26, it encountered its first real opposition. After an artillery duel in which it used its radar targeting devices to locate Iraqi guns, the division overran a detachment of Iraqi special forces and straddled the route. With both the 101st and the 24th astride Highway 8, there was no hope of an Iraqi escape to the west. McCaffrey then sent one of his units — 197th Brigade — to seize Tallil airfield to the west, while the rest of the division rolled west toward Jalibah. Some of McCaffrey's critics later complained that the assault on Tallil diverted forces from the main event — finding the Republican Guard. But McCaffrey insisted it did not slow the 24th's attack.

The next day, Paul Kern and Col. John LeMoyne, the commanders of the 24th Mech's 1st Brigade, kicked off their attack on Jalibah at 6AM, pounding the air base with their artillery and sending in their armor. The Iraqis responded to the fusillade by firing antiaircraft artillery straight up into the air. The idea that an American armored division might have snuck up on them from the west was inconceivable to the Iraqi troops; they thought they were being bombed. By 10AM the base was in American hands.

But Jalibah was just a waystop.

While the bulk of their force had been routed, the Iraqis were making one last desperate effort to delay the allies' advance so they could use the two remaining escape routes: the Hawr al Hammar causeway, which crossed the marshes west of Basra, and the routes over the canal to the east and through Basra itself.

Hastily constructing a defensive line, the Iraqis took up positions that ran from the causeway to the Rumaila air base to the south, drawing on soldiers from two Republican Guard infantry divisions and two armored brigades from the Hammurabi Division. The Iraqis had depth to their position. Allied maneuver room was restricted by the latticework of pipes and pumping stations in the Rumaila oil field.

McCaffrey was in the best position to cut off the retreating Iraqis, which was just what he proposed to do. Meeting Kern at his M-577 command vehicle, McCaffrey outlined his plan to slam the door on what was left of the Iraqi army.

Together with Starr's 3rd Armored Cavalry Regiment, the 24th would pound the Iraqis with artillery and then shoot forward across the Rumaila oil field toward Basra. By doing so, virtually all the Iraqi army remaining in the Kuwaiti theater of operations would be cut off. Whoever wanted to go north thereafter would have to get off their armored vehicles and walk.

The 24th Mech, McCaffrey told Kern, would continue on to the bridges crossing the Basra canal on the southern outskirts of Basra. Kern's brigade was to take the airfield. Then almost as quickly as he had come, McCaffrey was on his way.

The general had not yet persuaded the cautious Luck, his XVIII Airborne commander, to let him march to Basra. McCaffrey had planned to tackle that task later in the day.[1]

While McCaffrey was positioning his division for its final battle, Maj. Gen. Binnie Peay of the 101st Air Assault Division also had a plan to help shut the gate on the Iraqi army.

An ardent proselytizer for the Army's helicopter assault capabilities, Peay argued that the military experts who thought only in terms of heavy armored divisions with their concentration of tanks too often failed to appreciate the mobility and destructive power of the helicopter-laden divisions.

Like McCaffrey, Peay knew that the real action was to the east — which was where he was headed. After being the first to cut off the Iraqis' escape route in the west along Highway 8, Peay took control of the 12th Aviation Brigade, the XVIII Airborne Corps's reserve of Apache helicopters, and moved some of his helicopters southwest of Jalibah to a piece of desert near Tallil air base that the Iraqi air force had used as a bombing range in earlier days.

While McCaffrey pushed east toward Basra, Peay planned to airlift an entire brigade across the Euphrates by Chinook and Blackhawk helicopters and plunk it down north of the critical city. Three infantry battalions with antitank missiles and 105mm artillery pieces — three thousand men in all — would be astride the route north of Basra protected by Apache helicopters and Air Force warplanes.

It would be the most forward-deployed combat brigade in Iraq and the only one on the north side of the Euphrates. American forces would be bracketing Basra. Whoever slipped through McCaffrey's grasp would be blocked by the 101st. Between the two of them they would close the back door on the Iraqis.[2]

After a shaky start, the Army was beginning to build up some real momentum. The 24th Mech and 101st were ready to deliver a roundhouse punch on both sides of the Euphrates. To the south, the VII Corps was getting ready to catch any Iraqis that were still south of the XVIII Corps in a pincer.

For four days, Schwarzkopf had been complaining that his field commanders were not aggressive enough. Now he had two of his most hardcharging generals within striking distance of Basra. CENTCOM would not be able to stop all the Iraqis from getting away. It could get many of them, however, if the commanders in Riyadh and in Washington gave them the time to deliver the coup de grâce.

A CALL FROM HOME

At the Pentagon, the focus was not on the American divisions that were closing in on Basra. It centered on the pummeling the Iraqis had taken on Mutlah Ridge when they fled Kuwait City on the evening of February 25.

Throughout the war, Powell had been the voice of caution and restraint. All along, his reservations about the war had been political as well as military. During the buildup he had advised Sir Patrick Hine that a war with Iraq could spark a backlash against the West throughout the Middle East. No backlash ever materialized. Still, by February 27, Powell was again concerned. Once the Iraqis were out of their holes and on the move, they were easy prey for the Air Force, Navy, and Marine attack planes. During Khafji, allied warplanes had pounded the Iraqis with much the same results, but the press had not been in Kuwait to record the scenes of destruction. But now news reports were beginning to refer to a "turkey shoot" of the retreating Iraqi forces. It was as though the victimizer had suddenly become the victim. The effectiveness of the air strikes was threatening to bring an end to the land war before the ground forces had fully come into play.

At 3:05PM on February 27, Powell called Schwarzkopf. Powell had broached the subject of a cease-fire before. Now he began to prod Schwarzkopf to begin seriously thinking about wrapping up the war.

Powell told Schwarzkopf that CENTCOM was entering a "window" in which to end the war. Schwarzkopf agreed.

"What are your plans for tomorrow?" Powell asked.

Schwarzkopf had talked to Yeosock earlier that afternoon and Yeosock had said that the Army needed one more day. Schwarzkopf jubilantly reported that the Iraqis had been pushed into a box near Basra. By the evening of February 28, CENTCOM would have destroyed the Republican Guard.

"Do you realize if we go until tomorrow night that will be five days? The five-day war. Does that have a good ring to it?" Schwarzkopf asked.

Powell was noncommittal.

Schwarzkopf also broached the idea of a five-day war with his staff. That would beat Israel's 1967 war with the Arabs by one day. The Arab-Israeli war had not been preceded by five weeks of bombing, but nobody dared to make that point to the CENTCOM commander. By the afternoon of February 27, Schwarzkopf saw an advantage in ending the war quickly. Schwarzkopf wanted to hold down casualties, but he also wanted to win bragging rights for himself and the U.S. Army.[3]

That afternoon, Schwarzkopf's spokesman, Navy Capt. Ronald Wildermuth, contacted Pete Williams, Dick Cheney's chief spokesman. Wildermuth said that CENTCOM knew there had to be an end-of-the-war briefing, and Schwarzkopf wanted to be the one to give it. Schwarzkopf had not liked the idea that Powell's deputies were regularly briefing the news media in Washington. Detailing the progress of the war, Schwarzkopf felt, was CENTCOM's prerogative, and he was determined to deliver the finale.

Williams conveyed Schwarzkopf's request to Cheney and Powell, and they approved the idea. Schwarzkopf made plans to give his windup briefing that night.[4]

Meanwhile, Col. B. B. Bell, Schwarzkopf's executive assistant, telephoned Glosson and said that the Air Force should count on the 27th being the last night of the air war. No final decision had been made yet, but the handwriting was on the wall. If Schwarzkopf was to have his five-day war, it could end before the evening of the 28th.

While the commanders in Washington and Riyadh were talking about when to end the war, McCaffrey had halted his advance to refuel and regroup just out of range of the Iraqi artillery protecting the approaches to Basra. The laptop computer that the division used to map the battle-field told the story. Rather the worse for wear after bumping along the western desert for more than 200 miles, the computer screen was nearly obscured by a milky film. By pressing down on the screen, McCaffrey's aides could just make out the characters being transmitted to them by the division's intelligence officers back in Saudi Arabia. They were sending the coordinates of the fleeing Iraqi units, derived from a JSTARS surveillance plane.

With the JSTARS data and other intelligence on the Hammurabi Division in hand, McCaffrey was lobbying hard to pour it on. In their own way, Luck and his top aides were every bit as cautious as Franks. After the war, McCaffrey observed that Luck's caution went back to Vietnam. As a young commander, Luck had seen most of his unit chewed up in a fierce battle with the North Vietnamese army. Luck did not like to take unnecessary chances — or casualties — and he was nervous about Mc-Caffrey's plan to attack to the outskirts of Basra.

When McCaffrey had discussed the issue before the land war, Luck and his G-3, or chief operations officer, Col. Frank H. Akers, had fret-ted that the Iraqis would use chemical weapons when their backs were against the wall. They also argued that it would be hard for the 24th Division to navigate amid all the oil pipelines in the Rumaila oil field.

Akers was even worried that the Iraqis might torch the Rumaila oil field, turning it into a huge fireball that would consume McCaffrey's division, McCaffrey recalled. McCaffrey had already consulted ARAMCO oil engineers, who assured him that the idea of turning the oil field into a raging inferno was preposterous.

One by one, McCaffrey had tried to dispose of the arguments ad-vanced by his command and his staff. Since the Iraqis were not using helicopters and their artillery was notoriously inaccurate, McCaffrey ar-gued that the chemical weapons would not be a major threat to the Americans. To reassure his superiors about the Rumaila oil field, Mc-Caffrey said he would fire artillery into it before he advanced. If it was possible to ignite the oil field, McCaffrey would make sure it was the Iraqis who were incinerated, not the 24th Mech.

After a long conversation with Luck over the tactical radio, Mc-Caffrey finally persuaded the commander to let him attack east. Luck also gave him operational control over Starr's 3rd Armored Cavalry Regiment to help him do it. Luck had agreed that the 24th Mech and the 3rd Cavalry should begin their drive to the outskirts of Basra, start-ing at 5AM the next day.[5]

Peay was also pushing the war as hard as he could. By the afternoon of February 27, Peay had four attack helicopter battalions flying north of the Euphrates River blasting the retreating Iraqi columns.

As he waited for the final approval for his plan to put a brigade north of Basra, the 101st commander flew toward his eastward base of operations near the Tallil airfield just before darkness. When the command helicopter landed, the pilot unknowingly set it down in a field of unexploded Air Force cluster bombs but luckily none exploded. Peay huddled up in the helicopter and tried to catch a few hours' sleep before orchestrating the end game in the morning.

But while McCaffrey had won approval for his attack, Peay's plan was too daring for his superiors. After the war, Akers said that the XVIII Airborne command had no intention of letting Peay carry out his plan, and Steve Arnold said he had never been told that the 101st wanted to put ground forces north of Basra. Schwarzkopf also said he had not been made aware of the plan and would never have allowed Peay to carry it out had he known.[6]

As the XVIII Airborne Corps maneuvered to his north, Franks finally had the divisions he wanted in order to take the war to the Republican Guard — or those of them that still remained in the VII Corps's zone of operation. Refueled and rearmed, Ron Griffith's 1st Armored Division was heading east with Tilelli's 1st Cavalry to join in the attack. Just to the south, Funk's 3rd Armored Division was pressing ahead. Rhame's 1st Infantry was also making good time. Franks's pincer movement was unfolding.

The afternoon of February 27 saw some of the VII Corps's most intense fighting. Hoping to delay the allied advance, an armored brigade of the Medina Republican Guard Division set up a six-mile-long skirmish line on the far side of a low hill. The Iraqis hastily dug fighting holes for their T-72 and T-55 tanks and surrounded them with sand berms. The Iraqi tank crews were ready to strike the American forces as they came rolling over the ridge.

The tactic worked better in theory than it did in reality. As the M1 tanks of Col. Montgomery Meigs's 2nd Brigade of the 1st Armored Division crested the ridge, they halted their advance. The Americans had a high-technology advantage and were determined to exploit it. Unlike the M1 targeting system, which created images from heat given off by the Iraqi tanks, the T-72's targeting system depended on available light and was less effective at long range, assuming the Iraqi guns could even reach their targets. Meigs was determined to do whatever shooting was necessary at long distance.

Lodged on the crest of the hill, the Americans attacked the dug-in Iraqi tanks from 2,500 yards. Instead of blocking the Americans, the Iraqis had succeeded only in transforming their armor into vulnerable pillboxes. The sand had been so hastily pushed against the sides of the tanks that it left the turrets and some of the top decks unprotected. The M1s pumped one Sabot round after another into the Iraqis, knocking the turrets off the tanks and sending the rounds through the makeshift sand walls, turning the Iraqi tanks into fireballs.

Unable to spot the Americans with their targeting system in the overcast weather, the Iraqis in desperation aimed their guns at the muzzle flashes of the American tanks. But the American tanks were out of range, and the Iraqi rounds fell short. Even if the Iraqis had been able to score a direct hit, they were not likely to have destroyed their enemy. American intelligence reported before the war that the T-72 tank rounds could not penetrate the frontal armor of the M1 tank.

Even by the grim standards of the Persian Gulf War, it was an impressive tableau of destruction. The battle was the biggest armor engagement of the war. In forty-five minutes, American tanks and aircraft had destroyed sixty T-72 tanks, nine T-55 tanks, and thirty-eight Iraqi armored personnel carriers. It was more like a one-sided clay pigeon shoot than an armored battle.[7]

In the Black Hole, Buster Glosson and his deputies were also pressing the attack. With the onset of the ground war, Powell and Schwarzkopf had finally given the air-war planners the green light to resume hitting targets in Baghdad. Schwarzkopf figured that the strikes would make it that much more difficult for the Iraqis to coordinate the defense of Kuwait. But for Glosson, it was an opportunity to make one final push to undermine the Saddam Hussein regime, which was already under maximum stress. If ever there was a time that strategic bombing might cause the regime to collapse, he figured this was it.

Glosson pressed the attack on downtown Baghdad against the Iraqi leadership's suspected command posts, political structures, intelligence services, and praetorian guard. He targeted the Baath Party headquarters, a huge structure that had survived the cruise missile attack on the opening night of the war. He also hit the Presidential Guards at Abu Ghurayb, Baghdad's Special Security Service headquarters, the new Presidential Palace, and the Iraqi leader's residence in Tikrit.

The renewal of the attacks had a special significance for Col. Eberly, who had been held captive since the failed effort to rescue him. On February 23, the F-117s had hit the intelligence service headquarters where Eberly and other POWs were being kept. No one at CENTCOM had a clue that allied prisoners were there. Fortunately for the prisoners, the F-117s blew open the entranceway to the headquarters without killing the prisoners.

Eberly felt the building shake as the bombs crashed through the entrance to the headquarters, rocking the floor. Eberly was scared out of his wits when the F-117s blasted his prison. He had been beaten, starved, and abused since his capture more than five weeks earlier and felt he was barely hanging on. With the destruction of the headquarters, the POWs were transferred to another facility and put under the less harsh custody of the Iraqi army. After the war, Eberly concluded that the Americans that had nearly killed him might have saved his life.

Now that the Army was pressing its attack, CENTCOM received an intelligence report that the Iraqi president might be preparing two aircraft to fly his family, his closest advisers, and himself out of Iraq in the next forty-eight hours to Mauritania, Moscow, or some other refuge. To prevent this, Glosson ordered the F-117s to destroy the jets at the Muthena airfield. After the war, Bush administration officials considered whether to turn a blind eye if the Iraqi leader went into exile. But in the frantic final days of the war, the air-war commander was not just trying to topple the Iraqi leader, he was also trying to trap him.[8]

Drawing on new intelligence from defectors from the Iraqi weapons programs, who were beginning to make their way out of Iraq, the air-war planners also put At Tarmiyay and Al Altheer, two previously unknown nuclear facilities, on the target list.

At Khamis Mushait, the F-117 base near the Red Sea, some of the pilots were worried that Glosson was pressing his luck by sending them back to Baghdad. The weather was interfering with the attacks in the Iraqi capital, and with the war winding down, Glosson had directed them to fly lower — lower than they had flown during the entire war.

The F-117 pilots were not happy about the order or with the decision to hit the Baath Party headquarters, which had already been damaged in the war.

None of the F-117s had suffered a scratch during war, but now that the fighting was reaching its denouement, friction was taking hold and some odd things were beginning to happen.

An F-117 piloted by Maj. Lee Gustin had a close call when its bomb-bay door failed to shut after he dropped his bomb, making the plane detectable to Iraqi radars. The Iraqis launched an SA-3 missile at him, but after a few nervous seconds the bomb-bay door closed and the missile missed its mark.

On his first attempt to attack Baghdad at the lower altitude, Lt. Col. Ralph Getchell also had a close call. He was backlit by the moon, the dark silhouette of the plane clearly visible. The Iraqis fired a burst of 57mm fire that streamed by the tips of his plane. Then an SA-3 was launched at his F-117. When Getchell maneuvered out of the spotlight, the shooting ceased but it was not a good omen.

Taking risks to hit a political target in the waning days of the war seemed to be a questionable proposition to the F-117 pilots. If the Iraqis managed to down a stealth fighter, thought Getchell, it would do a lot more for their propaganda than putting a few bombs in a party headquarters would do for the allies. Not everyone in the Air Force believed that bombing political targets could change governments, but they were not giving the orders. Two more waves of F-117 attacks were scheduled for the night of February 27 and early morning hours of the 28th.[9]

One of the Air Force's most secret weapons, however, was not intended for Baghdad. To penetrate the Iraqis' hardened command bunkers, the Air Force had launched a crash program to build a new bomb. Using howitzer gun tubes from the Watervliet Army Arsenal in upstate New York, the Air Force Systems Command had manufactured a huge, 4,700-pound laser-guided bomb, which it dubbed the GBU-28. By mid-February a test bomb had been dropped at Eglin Air Force Base, and the Air Force had watched in wonder as it drove itself deep into the ground like a stake. The goal had been to build thirty of the bombs, but only two were ready in the waning days of the war.

Tom Lennon's F-111Fs were to deliver them. To prepare for the delivery of the GBU-28, Lennon had picked out four of his best crews and given them two days' rest. With only a pair of bombs in Saudi Arabia, the mission was scaled back from four F-111Fs to two.

When the bombs were unloaded at Taif, they were still warm to the touch from the tritenal, the molten explosive that had been poured inside. The Air Force had sent only a single bomb-loading crew with the weapons, so the F-111s had to be loaded one at a time. To prevent the plane from listing with the weight of the GBU-28 on one wing, a 2,000-pound bomb was placed on the other wing.

There had been three possible targets: Taji One and Taji Two, command bunkers dug deep underground about fifteen miles northwest of Baghdad, and a command post underneath a palace in downtown Baghdad, in which, according to a defector from Saddam Hussein's security service, the Iraqi leader was spending most of his evenings following the bombing at the Al Firdos shelter.

Glosson, urged by Deptula, weighed the idea of striking the Baghdad compound with the GBU-28, but opted to go after the Taji bunkers. The idea of dropping a 4,700-pound bomb in the heart of Baghdad on its combat debut was too much even for Glosson. There was no reason to think that Saddam Hussein was at Taji, but it was a major Iraqi command post and undoubtedly housed some of Iraq's senior commanders.[10]

The strikes in and around Baghdad, however, were only part of the story. The air-war commanders had unleashed a torrent of air strikes when the Iraqi forces fled Kuwait City. But as the allied armies pressed their attack, allied warplanes were having a hard time stopping the Iraqi ground troops from fleeing from the battlefield and heading north of the Euphrates.

The attack order CENTCOM drafted in December directed the air commanders to destroy all the bridges and roads across the Euphrates. But Lt. Gen. Horner later recalled that the Iraqis proved to be more ingenious at repairing the bridges than the allies had anticipated. When the allies hit a bridge over the canal on the outskirts of Basra, the Iraqis pushed earth into the waterway and kept going. The causeway proved to be a particularly difficult target.[11]

Air strikes were also hampered by the civilian houses near Basra. The Iraqis were able to salvage some of their war machine by moving tanks and armored vehicles into residential areas west of Basra and driving the vehicles into the streets of the city, knowing that the allies would not go after armor in civilian areas. Bad weather and concerns about overflying Iranian territory also inhibited allied warplanes near Basra.[12]

Another major complication was confusion between the ground and air commanders. To prevent allied ground forces from being bombed by their own air forces by mistake, the military drew a dividing line on its maps, dubbed the Fire Support Coordination Line, or FSCL for short. Enemy forces in front of the line could be bombed with abandon. But no air strikes could take place inside the line without coordinating the strike with nearby allied ground units.

According to military doctrine, the location of the line was determined by the ground commander. As the Army advanced, it kept pushing the boundary in front of it farther out so that it could operate its helicopters and move its forces more freely.

"Our problem was not how much air we had," recalled Col. Michael F. Reavey, who worked in Horner's operations center. "Our problem started to become how much airspace we had and wedging what we had into that piece of airspace."

The issue came to a head on the morning of the February 27 when Luck moved the boundary north of the Euphrates so that Peay's Apache helicopters could attack the causeway and the roads north of Basra. By midafternoon, however, Horner was furious. Only a handful of Apache attacks had been carried out, and moving the line had prevented the Air Force from launching strikes against the Iraqi forces that were escaping across the Euphrates. Iraqi forces had been traveling down a major road north of the river that connected An Nasiriyah and Basra for eight hours with virtual impunity. Horner decided that the line should be shifted south to the Euphrates.

"The Army was moving the FSCL well out past where they were going to impact on anything," Reavey said. "When they did that, they took away airspace and ground area for us to hit."[13]

A similar confusion arose the same day with the VII Corps. As the corps moved forward, Franks and Cherrie were worried that the divisions were about to break through the Iraqi defenders and rush to the coast, where the Air Force was attacking the Iraqis freely. To avoid a possible friendly fire incident, Cherrie directed Maj. David Rhodes, an Air Force officer assigned to VII Corps, to inform the air-war commanders in Riyadh that the boundary was to be shifted east of the coastal highway leading north from Kuwait City. That meant that allied warplanes could not bomb Iraqi troops as they streamed up the coastal road.

After directing that the line be shifted, the VII Corps staff discovered that Franks's attack had bogged down again. Rhodes called Horner's operations center and said it might be necessary to shift the line back to the west so that the Air Force could resume its strikes. But Rhodes was told that CENTCOM had decided to leave the boundary where it was. No official reasons were given. But one of the center's officers suggested to Rhodes that the politics of creating another "turkey shoot" in addition to the "Highway of Death" were getting too hot to handle.

At 7PM CENTCOM clarified the boundaries. The FSCL would run along the Kuwait coastline, up the Euphrates River, and then out to the west.[14]

After the war, it became clear that the positioning of the boundary was one of the most important miscalculations in the final hours of the war. Moving the line east and north was correct if the Army followed through on the ground. But if the Army attack was delayed, the line should have been moved back so that the allied warplanes could concentrate their firepower on the fleeing forces. CENTCOM did neither. As a result, much of the Iraqi army was shielded from the sort of punishing bombing raids it endured during Khafji and its retreat from Kuwait City.

A doctrinal technicality and inertia took precedence over common sense. The Army and the Air Force had trumpeted their ability to coordinate the "air-land" battle. In the final fourteen chaotic hours of the war, however, the FSCL had been pushed back and forth as the two services sought maximum flexibility for their own forces. After the war, Schwarzkopf said he knew little about the debate. It was another example of how joint warfare fell short and how the services' ability to work together suffered from Schwarzkopf's inattention.

THE MOTHER OF ALL BRIEFINGS

In Washington, Bush, Cheney, Scowcroft, Powell, and Baker were huddled at the White House. President Bush was about to meet with Douglas Hurd, the British foreign minister. Hurd thought the war might take another couple of days. And in London, John Major's national security adviser, Sir Charles Powell, was dubious that it was time to end the war. But it was the Americans who were carrying the fight to the Iraqis now, and the government of John Major was prepared to defer to the Americans. Margaret Thatcher had left office in November and the departure of the hard-line prime minister from the political scene loomed large in the calculation. Thatcher had reinforced Bush's tougher instincts in August, when Washington had to make the fateful decision to roll back the Iraqi invasion of Kuwait, as Cheney had suggested, or draw the line at the invasion of Saudi Arabia, as Powell argued. And she had argued to Prince Bandar that allied forces should occupy the Rumaila oil field until their postwar demands were met. But the "iron lady" was no longer part of the allied team.[15]

The decision was, in effect, Bush's to make.

Hurd's White House visit began just after 1PM when he met with Brent Scowcroft, Robert Gates, and other top officials. The meeting was a prelude to the foreign minister's session with Bush, and it provided the two sides with an opportunity to discuss how the war was going and talk about a possible cease-fire.

As the meeting began, Scowcroft suggested that the allies should take the initiative and declare cease-fire terms instead of waiting for Iraq to put forth its conditions for ending the war. As it had been throughout the preparation and fighting of the war, Washington was in no mood to bargain with Iraq.

Hurd agreed, but argued that any cease-fire that was arranged had to guarantee that the allies got their POWs back and needed to ensure that the Iraqis did not fire any more Scud missiles.

The Americans agreed that securing the release of the allied prisoners was a priority. "Especially down the hall," Gates said, alluding to Bush.

It was not just an American and British concern, Scowcroft said. The Iraqis might also have thousands of Kuwaitis, perhaps 25,000 to 30,000.

The allied prisoners were not the only problem. The coalition had tens of thousands of Iraqi prisoners on their hands. Gates suggested that the allies might have to encourage some of the prisoners to return home. But Hurd said the allies needed to take account of the "cossack factor." That was a reference to the forced repatriation of Russian prisoners — anti-communists, cossacks, and German collaborators — following World War II, an ignominious chapter in British history.

The larger issue, however, was the future of Iraq and its ability to regenerate its military capability. Scowcroft said that he thought Iraq's capability to develop weapons of mass destruction had been largely destroyed. The United States knew that Iraq still had stocks of chemical weapons, but did not think they would use them now. Only later would American intelligence learn that many nuclear and some key biological weapons targets had not been hit.

Iraq was still a potential menace. With Thatcher out of power, however, the British had little appetite for an extended military operation to influence developments in Baghdad.

Hurd said that sanctions were of limited value in influencing Iraq before the war, but now that Iraq had been weakened by air and ground attacks, the situation was different. Using sanctions as the allies' leverage was better than sitting in Basra, the British foreign minister asserted.

The British diplomat also raised the subject of a possible UN force to police the Kuwaiti border. Scowcroft thought that Arab troops — Egyptian, Saudi, and Syrian forces — might stay in Kuwait for a while, maybe joined by American and British troops. But he made clear that Washington was not interested in a long-term ground presence. Bush, the national security adviser said, was adamant that ground troops had to be returned.

Then the discussion moved to the Oval Office. Bush was on the verge of deciding the American position on the cease-fire and the British would be part of the deliberation.

Bush said he was very pleased with the way the war had gone. The allied forces, Bush confidently stated, were destroying the remnants of the Republican Guard. The war might go on another day, but at some point, Washington might be accused of butchering the Iraqis, Bush warned, according to notes taken by a participant.

As the officials pondered when to end the war, James Baker said that new information had just come in from the United Nations. The Iraqis had agreed to the demands issued by the United Nations Security Council resolution before the war.

At that point, Bush said it was time for Cheney and Powell to join the meeting.

Bush framed the decision. What do you need? he asked. The president would allow the top generals in the Pentagon and in the Gulf to determine when to end the war. From start to finish, it would be the generals' war to win or lose.

Cheney, reflecting Powell's assessment, said that the allies had all but completed their objective. "We are basically there," the defense secretary said. "It could be over by now or maybe by tomorrow."

Powell then explained that American forces were still in contact with the Hammurabi Division, but that should be finished soon, perhaps in a matter of hours.

Bush said it was important to pinpoint when the war might be brought to a close.

"We'll talk to Norm," Cheney said.

Powell broke in. Before the ground war began, Powell had told the press that a land offensive would not be like the air campaign. The battlefield would be a swirl of dust and confusion. And the debate between the intelligence agencies over battle damage assessment had borne Powell out. Even when the Iraqi forces were stationary, it was hard to determine just how much damage they had suffered. With the Iraqi army on the run and with bad weather, it was virtually impossible to specify exactly what was happening.

But Powell was relying on his intuitions as a soldier, Schwarzkopf's reports from Riyadh, and, most important, his political instincts. The press reports about the "Turkey Shoot" on the "Highway of Death" were an important consideration, he recalled after the war.

"I did talk to him," Powell said, referring to Schwarzkopf. "He said we are at most twenty-four hours away. There are three thousand destroyed tanks. We are in the home stretch. Today or tomorrow by close of business."

Powell said that most of the Iraqi forces had been pushed near Basra. "There is just one battle left. Norm and I would like to finish tomorrow, a five-day war."

Bush asked Hurd what the British assessment was, and he said that the British commanders thought it would be possible to end the fighting in another day or two.

It was a political as well as a military call now, Powell reminded the group.

Bush was weighing the political factors. "We do not want to lose anything now with charges of brutalization, but we are also very concerned with the issue of prisoners," he said. "The issue is how to find a clean end. This is not going to be like the battleship Missouri."[16]

Baker reinforced the argument for stopping the fighting. "We have done the job. We can stop. We have achieved our aims. We have gotten them out of Kuwait." But the secretary of state acknowledged that there was "unfinished business" about the future of Saddam Hussein's government and the embargo.

Powell suggested that the allies use the threat of air strikes to ensure that the Iraqis complied with the cease-fire, and Bush agreed.

Then Bush added: "Why do I not feel elated? But we need to have an end. People want that. They are going to want to know we won and the kids can come home. We do not want to screw this up with a sloppy, muddled ending."

Bush suggested a speech, winding up the war, which Scowcroft was to write.

After some discussion, Bush and his aides agreed to end the war at 100 hours, the timing being more a matter of public relations than anything else.[16]

"In the final hours, we were told that the ring had not yet been completely closed but that, of all the Iraqi divisions inside the ring, only a tiny fraction still maintained unit cohesion and could be considered 'fighting forces.' My recollection is that the number amounted to two or three divisions. I do not recall whether any of the divisions still thought to be cohesive were Republican Guard divisions," Bush observed after the war. "We were concerned principally about two aspects of the situation. If we continued the fighting another day, until the ring was completely closed, would we be accused of a slaughter of Iraqis who were simply trying to escape, not fight? In addition, the coalition was agreed on driving the Iraqis from Kuwait, not on carrying the conflict into Iraq or on destroying Iraqi forces."[17]

At 9:00PM, Schwarzkopf bounded into the briefing room at the Hyatt Regency Hotel in Riyadh to deliver his report to the nation. He started off by saying that Cheney had asked him to give an overview of the plan, even though he was the one who had initiated the idea. Then he took command, running through the plan as Lt. Col. Purvis, the chief Jedi, flipped the charts.

In devising their strategy, the CENTCOM commander claimed, the allies had faced a daunting military problem. Outnumbered three to two by troops in heavily fortified positions, CENTCOM had to come up with some kind of way to make up the difference. To weaken the Iraqis before the ground assault, the allies had pounded them from the air while the Marines tied down Iraqi divisions along the coast by practicing their amphibious operations.

CENTCOM had further confounded the Iraqis by launching the Marine attack first and focusing the Iraqis' attention to the south before ordering the XVIII Corps and the VII Corps into the fray, the general explained.

The roundhouse punch from the west had moved the Screaming Eagles from the 101st Airborne Division to Highway 8, a mere 150 miles from the Iraqi capital. The allies could have gone to Baghdad, but that, Schwarzkopf explained, was never the allies' purpose. Describing the ongoing attacks, Schwarzkopf described a solid wall of Army forces attacking the Iraqis in a "classic tank battle." Of Iraq's 4,000 tanks, 3,700 had been destroyed, he said.

"We almost completely destroyed the offensive capability of the Iraqi forces in the Kuwait theater of operations," the general exclaimed. "The gates are closed."

"When I say the gate is closed, I don't want to give you the impression that absolutely nothing is escaping," he continued. "Quite the contrary. That doesn't mean that civilian vehicles are not escaping, that innocent civilians aren't escaping, or unarmed Iraqis. That's not what I'm talking about. I'm talking about the gate being closed on their military machine."[18]

The briefing had been an effective advertisement for CENTCOM's plan. But much of the information in the brief had been misleading. With the desertions and the bombing attacks, the ranks of the Iraqi army had been reduced by half before the land offensive took place, which meant that it was the Americans, not the Iraqis, who had the numerical advantage.

Far from fixing the Iraqis in place, the Marine attack had rousted them out of the Kuwait theater, undermining the Army attack plan, which Schwarzkopf himself believed had been too slow. The Navy and Marine operations in the Persian Gulf had led the Iraqis to anticipate an amphibious landing, but the amphibious feint said as much about the allies' limitations as it did about their ingenuity. With their poor mine-clearing ability and the failure to destroy Iraq's Silkworm missiles, an amphibious landing was out of the question.

Although some of the Iraqis had stayed and fought, there had not been any classic tank battles. The largest armored confrontation — the 1st

Armored Division's battle at Medina Ridge — saw M1 tanks pummeling the immobile tanks of the Iraqi covering force from a distance. More important, the gate was not shut. Iraqi units were still streaming north through Basra and over the causeway across the Euphrates.

Glosson and his Black Hole planners were furious. Schwarzkopf's briefing, Glosson exclaimed, "was one of the most dishonest presentations" he had ever heard. The allies had been bombing the Iraqis for six weeks. The air-war planners had not won the war single-handedly, but Schwarzkopf was trying to make the ground war look more difficult than it was. "It was pure and simple an unethical briefing," Glosson told his Black Hole planners.

In Washington, Paul Wolfowitz was dismayed by Schwarzkopf's declaration that the allies had no intention of going to Baghdad. That was true, but why should Schwarzkopf tell that to the Iraqis? The civilians were still hoping for a coup and wanted to keep the psychological pressure on.

More important, Schwarzkopf had fortified Powell's position that the war needed to be brought to a close by portraying it as a one-sided rout. Schwarzkopf was planning a five-day war, but he all but declared victory a day early. The press was beginning to ask what was to be gained by continuing the fighting.

At 10:30PM Powell called Schwarzkopf in his sleeping quarters, and this time the JCS chairman was more direct. Powell told Schwarzkopf that the White House was considering imposing a cease-fire as early as 5AM in the Gulf. Things were getting difficult back in Washington, Powell said, referring to the press reports about the "Highway of Death" on Mutlah Ridge. The JCS chief was moving to bring the war to a close.

The plan was to have President Bush ask the Iraqis to abandon their vehicles and walk north. That would prevent Iraq from salvaging its military equipment, and no one could accuse the Americans of shooting an Arab army in the back. But with the Iraqis on the move, it was unclear how the allies would get the word out.

Schwarzkopf told Powell that he could accept the decision, but cautioned him to be sure to put words in the president's statement to the effect that CENTCOM would continue to destroy the Iraqis if allied forces were attacked.

"You can go with that unless I get back to you quickly," Schwarzkopf said. "They are running and we are chasing."[19]

Powell said that Washington was thinking about arranging a meeting of military commanders on both sides to sort out the cease-fire arrangements, but Schwarzkopf dismissed the possibility.

"I can't see their military leaders coming to meet us under any circumstances, and I do not want to go to downtown Basra," Schwarzkopf observed. Then Schwarzkopf turned to the more immediate problem. If Washington was looking at establishing a cease-fire at 5AM Gulf time. Schwarzkopf told Powell, CENTCOM had only six hours and twenty minutes to bring the fighting to a halt.

Schwarzkopf called Yeosock, Horner, and Boomer and asked if they had any problem with a cease-fire at 5AM. For everyone but Yeosock, the war was already virtually over.

It was clear to Army commanders at Lucky Main that the XVIII Airborne and the VII Corps had not wrapped up the war. A strong-willed and confident commander would have challenged Schwarzkopf on this point at the risk of being put down. But Yeosock had been worn down by months of tirades and was not looking for any more trouble. The consequences of letting Yeosock reclaim his post from the more assertive Waller were looming larger and larger. The war was coming to an end before the job was completed, but nobody with enough rank to change that decision objected.

Yeosock began to alert the corps commanders that Washington was preparing to call a cease-fire, but he was not asking for their opinion on the wisdom of ending the fight. He only wanted their sense of when it could be feasible for them to disentangle themselves from the Iraqis so that the offensive could be halted.

For the XVIII Airborne Corps, the possibility of a cease-fire came at just about the worst possible time. The corps's two most aggressive commanders were preparing to shoot forward the following morning.

McCaffrey was stunned. It never occurred to him that CENTCOM would cut off the war before the Army had finished the job. The XVIII Airborne Corps had spent hours getting into position for the final battle but would not be able to follow through. The call from Yeosock also torpedoed Peay's plans.

At the VII Corps, Franks was also thrown off balance. After four days of taking abuse from the rear, he had synchronized his attack for the final battle, hoping to destroy whatever Iraqi forces were still south of McCaffrey's position.[20]

Even with all the criticism from Riyadh, Franks had continued to approach his task cautiously and methodically. He was determined to succeed while minimizing losses from the enemy or from incidents of friendly fire, which had become a bigger worry than the Iraqis. And as the VII Corps grappled with the confusion on the battlefield, he slowed both prongs of his attack and stopped the air-war commanders from pounding the Iraqis in the path of his divisions as well.

When Griffith's 1st Armored Division was caught up in a series of small engagements just beyond Medina Ridge, Franks had held off on bringing the 1st Cavalry Division into the fight, figuring it would be best to undertake the maneuver in daylight. As on the first day of the ground war, Franks was still wary of carrying out complicated divisional maneuvers at night.

Fear of friendly fire had also led Franks to halt the southern prong of his attack. Worried that the tip of Funk's 3rd Armored Division might collide with Rhame's force as it moved north, Franks ordered Rhame to halt at 7PM. Little was moving on the VII Corps front as widely separated commanders wondered what was to become of their classic double envelopment. Rhame was still in a holding pattern when Yeosock called with the first word of a possible cease-fire.

Franks still hoped to entrap the Iraqis in his zone, but to the end he had moved deliberately according to his own timetable. The Iraqis and Washington, however, were operating on a quicker schedule.

Yeosock told the VII Corps to begin winding down and advised the corps to halt its deep Apache attacks. Protecting the force was now the paramount consideration. Franks continued with his preparations for an advance but put the word out: there was to be no attack after 5AM.

As the Army offensive stalled, Maj. Gen. Burt Moore, Schwarzkopf's chief operations deputy, called the Black Hole. There was to be no bombing after 5AM. That would force Glosson to cancel the last wave of F-117 attacks. The air-war commanders would have to squeeze in as many attacks as they could before that hour.

The first wave of F-117 attacks was assigned to attack Muthena airfield, Iraq's chemical plant at Salman Pak, and to make a final run at the Baath Party headquarters. Glosson had ordered the F-117s to fly low to attack the Baath Party headquarters, but since those attacks had been inhibited by bad weather he was now ordering them to fly even lower. Fortunately for the F-117s, the pilots got a break in the weather. Seven F-117s each dropped two bombs on the Baath Party headquarters, but failed to cause major damage to the vast structure. The second and final wave of F-117s attacked the Al Musayyib missile factory.

North of Baghdad, the F-111Fs proceeded with their attack on the Taji command post.[21]

Each of the two command bunkers at Taji was about the size of a football field and was buried deep underground. To drop the GBU-28 bombs, the F-111Fs would have to turn on their afterburners. With the streams of fire shooting out of the afterburners, the planes would be lit up like Roman candles and easily identifiable to the Iraqis.

The plan was for Lt. Col. Ken Combs and Maj. Jerry Huss to drop their bomb on Taji Two, as Lt. Col. Dave White and Capt. Tom Himes followed behind. Each plane was to guide its bomb down with its own laser. The trailing plane would be in position to shine its laser on the bunker if the lead plane failed to find its target. Then the two planes would reverse the order and circle around to attack Taji One.

As Combs approached Taji Two, Huss was having trouble picking out the command post on the targeting system. Both bunker complexes were linked by roads and had large doors, but they blended in with the rest of the terrain. Huss misidentified the target and dropped the first of the bombs on an open field.

Now, White and Himes would have to go after Taji Two with the remaining deep-penetration bomb. With their afterburners blazing, they flew toward the target. But Himes could not find it. The scope on the Pave Tac system was a maze of green lines. They would have to go around in a racetrack pattern and try again.

"Come on, Tommy. You've got to find the target," said White. He did not like the idea of flying over the northern suburbs of Baghdad with his plane glowing in the sky.

As they swung around, Himes finally picked out Taji Two. There was no visible damage from the attacks the F-117s had carried out earlier in the war using 2,000-pound bombs.

Dropping the GBU-28 was tricky. There was no computer software to deliver the weapon. The bomb had to be delivered manually. Himes punched in the projected time of fall and then pressed the release button as the plane approached the target. The bomb fell. White and Himes waited. Fifteen seconds. Twenty seconds. Forty seconds. Fifty seconds. White stopped counting.

"Shack," White called out, meaning that the bomb had hit its DIMPI (designated mean point of impact). Seven seconds later a little puff of white smoke came out one of the doors. It had taken that long for the blast to come to the surface. The bomb had gone down a long way.[22]

Meanwhile, the F-111Fs at Taif received an emergency assignment. As a member of a quick-reaction F-111F team, Capt. Mike Russell was used to getting difficult missions. But this one was straightforward: go as fast as you can to the Iraqi causeway over the Euphrates and take it out. For all the bombing, the allies had not knocked out all the escape routes over the Euphrates.

The F-111Fs had put together aircrews that specialized in knocking out bridge spans with laser-guided bombs. But no sooner would the bridges go down than the Iraqis would erect pontoon bridges and they had also been rebuilding the causeway west of Basra with dirt. Now that the Iraqis were streaming north, CENTCOM determined that it was more important than ever to knock out the remaining bridges and the causeway west of Basra and keep them down. The ground forces had not blocked the routes north. Shutting the door would be left to the aviators.

Since the early days of the war, the F-111Fs had been operating at medium altitude. But Col. Tom Lennon, the wing commander, told the airmen the last night of the war that they could fly at low-level if they thought that was the best way to carry out the mission of cutting the escape routes.

Dodging thunderstorms, Russell's flight of F-111Fs zoomed to take out the causeway, dropping below 4,000 feet to approach their target. The 48th Tactical Fighter Wing did not have any photographs of the causeway, and they were searching for it in bad weather. Because of the poor visibility, the planes would have to fly directly over the causeway, drop the bombs ballistically, and then turn on their laser target designators and hope that they could guide them in the final seconds before they struck. The F-111Fs had attained good results with their laser-guided bombs, but this was not the scientific way to go about bombing.

When Russell and his wingman spotted the huge earthen and stone bulwark, it was clear to them they were not going to be able to take it out with the eight 2,000-pound bombs they were carrying. The airmen quickly decided to fly four racetrack patterns, circular maneuvers over the target area, dropping a single laser-guided bomb each time they came to the causeway. Ordinarily, it was not a tactic that any pilot liked to execute. Attacking a target four times from the same angle made the planes vulnerable. But the airmen figured since there was no hope of dropping the causeway into the river, the flash and bang from eight discrete explosions might deter the Iraqis from trying to cross. Although some of the bombs found their mark, the pilots were under no illusions that they had destroyed the causeway. The Air Force could not put the cork in the bottle, and the Iraqis continued their flight north.[23]

At 2AM, Riyadh time, Schwarzkopf got another call in his sleeping quarters from Powell. The decision was now final. President Bush had decided to announce a cease-fire. But it had been moved to midnight EST, which would be 8AM in the Gulf.

How does that sound to you? Powell asked.

Schwarzkopf had no problem with the change. If Washington wanted to run the war for an even 100 hours for public relations purposes, so be it. That would not make an appreciable change on the battlefield.

As he emerged from his room, Schwarzkopf informed Waller that Washington had decided to announce a cease-fire. Waller was astounded. The last he had heard, the cease-fire was a matter for discussion, not a fait accompli. Waller knew that the war was coming to a close, but now was not the time to end it. From an operational point of view, the war should not have ended until both escape routes were blocked by allied ground forces and the Republican Guard destroyed. Bombing at the choke points would not suffice.

"You have got to be shitting me. Why a cease-fire now?" Waller asked.

"One hundred hours has a nice ring," replied Schwarzkopf.

"That's bullshit," Waller exclaimed.

"Then you go argue with them," replied Schwarzkopf.[24]

The brief exchange summed up the debate. In recommending an end to the war, Powell was motivated by considerations that went beyond military concerns. Determined that the military would erase the stain of Vietnam and come out of the Gulf War victorious with its honor intact, the JCS chairman wanted to avoid the impression that the United States was piling on and killing Iraqis for the sake of killing them. If that meant erring on the side of caution, Powell was prepared to live with that. Powell consulted with his fellow chiefs, but he had long established himself as the dominant voice of the military and none challenged his assessment. Only Merrill McPeak, the Air Force chief of staff, thought it was premature to end the war, and he kept his views to himself.

Schwarzkopf, like the chiefs, also took his cues from Powell's judgment. To his staff, Schwarzkopf could be hell on wheels, but he was not prepared to fight superiors in Washington. For months, he had said that the overriding goal was to destroy the Republican Guard. But throughout the planning and execution on the war, Schwarzkopf had yielded to Powell, whether the question was the development of the left hook, the number of reinforcements to be sent, or the decision to suspend air strikes in downtown Baghdad following the raid on the Al Firdos bunker. Now that the Iraqis were being routed, Schwarzkopf was prepared to subordinate the final destruction of the Republican Guard to the administration's political goals. Protecting the United States military against the charge of brutalization and holding down American and Iraqi casualties in the final days of the war were becoming the main measures of merit in Washington. After the war, Schwarzkopf observed that he was never quite sure in talking with Powell when the general was offering him a personal view or representing the views of the White House. "I never knew what was Powell, what was the NCS, what was the NCA [National Command Authority]," Schwarzkopf said. "I never had the ability to sort out what was Powell, what was Scowcroft, what was Cheney, what was the President." Either way, Schwarzkopf was prepared to go with the flow.[25]

As for the senior civilians in the Bush administration, including Scowcroft and Cheney, they too saw an advantage in avoiding the impression that the United States was piling on. But they were also laboring under a misimpression. After hearing Powell's presentation, Scowcroft and Wolfowitz thought the Republican Guard was essentially cut off and all but destroyed.

After the timing was set at the White House, Cheney called Wolfowitz to inform him of the move. Wolfowitz was disturbed by the symbolism. The 100-hour war had a meaning in Arab history, Wolfowitz argued, and it was not a happy one. After President Nasser of Egypt nationalized the Suez Canal in 1956, Britain, France, and Israel had launched a lightning 100-hour war to seize the waterway, only to stop in the face of American pressure. The 100-hour war was synonymous in the Arab world with Western and Israeli aggression. Wolfowitz told Cheney that anything would be better than 100 hours.

Cheney conferred with Scowcroft and came back with a quip. Would Wolfowitz be happier if the war was ended at 99 hours? The Bush administration had not been aware of the historical associations and did not think the American public would care either.

Wolfowitz also questioned whether it was wise to announce a ceasefire. The allies wanted to keep the pressure on Saddam Hussein and encourage a coup. The allies could stop their advance without broadcasting that fact to the world. By telling the world that the ground war was over, the allies would in effect issue a reprieve to the Iraqi leader.

Cheney reminded Wolfowitz that Schwarzkopf had boasted in his briefing that the allies could have gone to Baghdad but had no intention to do so. The damage was already done.

Spotty intelligence, no doubt, played a role in the decision. Only after the war, when spy plane and spy satellite imagery was fully analyzed, would it become clear that half the Republican Guard equipment had not been destroyed and that the vast majority of the fleeing Iraqi army was still south of Basra in the path of the Army's planned advance when the war ended.

Even so, at the CIA, it did not look like the job had been done.

Charles Allen's office received a call from Ron Stanfill, who was working for Warden in Checkmate. The White House had decided to end the war.

Lt. Col. Michael Tanksley, an Army officer who worked on Allen's warning team, threw up his hands in frustration. "One goddamn day too soon," Tanksley exclaimed.

Allen immediately called Richard Kerr, the deputy CIA director, but Kerr did not know anything about the decision to end the war.

Even with limited intelligence and the veritable "fog of war," the war looked different in the Euphrates valley than it did at the White House. The closer one got to the battlefield, the more questionable the decision to end the war seemed. Neither McCaffrey nor his key commanders thought the entire Republican Guard had been destroyed. Nor did they believe that driving to the Basra canals to cut off the fleeing Iraqis would produce inordinately high American casualties or result in the wholesale slaughter of the Iraqi army. Much of the Iraqi force would have been bypassed and many would have been given a chance to offer their surrender. But the commanders who knew the most about the battlefield were not asked for their views.

"There was a sense of success and a sense of concern at the same time," recalled Col. Paul Kern, McCaffrey's 2nd Brigade commander, who went on to become the senior military assistant to Defense Secretary William J. Perry. "My sense was we would have been able to continue the attack at about the same rate as the previous day. I figure we would have been there by early afternoon.

"You are prepared to go. You are ready to go, and you have a good plan. Everything is in your favor. And then you stop and say why?" Kern added. "I knew that this would be a military decision that would be debated for years to come in terms of where we stopped. The sense was there: 'success but.' "[26]

Steven Arnold, who had labored months over the war plan and overseen the XVIII and VII Corps attacks, was blunter still. "I hated to see us end the war when we did," he recalled.[27]

Within minutes, however, it was clear that Washington's plan for ending the war would have to be modified. Reconnaissance missions were reporting that substantial numbers of Iraqis with their equipment were continuing to escape. With the FSCLs moved north to the Euphrates and east to the coast, and with the Army still forty miles from the outskirts of Basra, Iraqi tanks were rolling over pontoon bridges and the causeway.

Schwarzkopf called Powell at 2:55AM and told him that if a cease-fire was announced, they would see T-72 tanks crossing the river. The Bush administration had to be made aware of that.

Powell told Schwarzkopf he would remove the condition from the president's statement ordering the Iraqi soldiers to get off their vehicles and walk north. If Washington had thought about the end game in advance, it might have announced that stipulation to the Iraqis in the weeks leading up to the war. But it was impossible to get the word out now. Unless the Bush administration adjusted its demands, the Iraqis would be violating the terms of the cease-fire and the war would have to go on.

As far as Powell was concerned, the war was virtually over and the last-minute military activity was largely irrelevant. But Schwarzkopf was not happy with the exodus, and the XVIII and VII Corps received another call from Riyadh. Instead of shutting down the attack as Yeosock initially suggested, Schwarzkopf wanted the attack to be speeded up. Switching signals, Yeosock now told them he wanted maximum pressure; the corps should push as far as they could get — until 8AM, that is, when offensive operations would be abruptly brought to a halt. After being advised to wind down its attack, the Army was now being urged to start it up again.

In his command post near the Euphrates, McCaffrey roused his division. When the first word of a possible cease-fire had trickled down to his command, the general had delayed his artillery attack. But at 4AM he began a mammoth artillery barrage, shelling the Iraqis as they fled into the distance. McCaffrey himself was stunned by the whoosh of an ATACMS surface-to-surface missile as the rocket flew off into the sky. The roar was so loud McCaffrey thought the division was being hit by an incoming Scud.

When the dust cleared, McCaffrey dispatched a reconnaissance patrol forward to just west of Rumaila oil field. It stopped at Phase Line Crush, a boundary the general had hoped would be the jumping-off point for his rush to the gates of Basra but which was now almost the outer limit of his advance. McCaffrey's soldiers stopped short of the causeway, which McCaffrey assumed had been thoroughly destroyed by allied warplanes. In fact, the causeway was still standing, and the Iraqis were using it as their escape route through Basra to withdraw their forces from Kuwait. In the final frantic hours, the left hand had not known what the right was doing. It was another failure to coordinate between the Army and the Air Force.

At Franks's headquarters, the VII Corps also moved to jump-start its delayed attack. Griffith's 1st Armored Division let loose with everything it had, firing a violent artillery barrage and sending his Apaches forward.

While the attack divisions pawed the sand like impatient stallions, Yeosock called Franks with another mission: seize the Safwan road junction astride the intersection of the north-south route between Basra and Kuwait City. Safwan was close to where VII Corps forces would have ended up if they had completed their planned double envelopment, but Safwan crossroads itself had never been an objective. CENTCOM, however, had received reports that Iraqi vehicles were streaming north through the town.

"Wilco," said Franks. Franks huddled with Cherrie. It was already 3AM. Time was running out. The commanders discussed sending Rhame's 1st Infantry Division to take the road junction. But the division was still frozen in place because of the VII Corps's earlier concern over friendly fire. Somehow, in all the excitement, VII Corps had not lifted the restriction on the 1st Division.

At 4AM, Franks ordered Rhame to restart his attack and interdict the road junction.

The division responded, breaking its nine-hour standstill. Its helicopters got there in two hours, but the pilots saw only a handful of vehicles driving north. If Safwan had been an important escape hatch, it was not any longer.

By 7:30AM the VII Corps put a hold on all firing after reports of another fratricidal incident. Half an hour later, the radio nets came alive. The cease-fire was in effect. Amidst the confusion, Franks assumed that Rhame's force had taken the road junction and that information was relayed to Yeosock. Only later would the VII Corps commander learn that he had misunderstood Rhame's situation report and that Rhame's ground forces never made it to the crossroads.[28]

At 8AM the Army guns fell silent. The last hours had been a confusing series of stop and start orders that had left the field commanders wondering whether they were to make a maximum effort to protect their troops or an all-out effort to destroy as much of the Iraqi army as they could. Uncertain about its ultimate objective, the Army had staggered to a halt, short of the finish line.

The victory in the ground war had been dramatic and Kuwait had been wrested back from the Iraqis with minimal casualties to the allies. Yet even as CENTCOM basked in the glow of victory, it was evident that the allies had not accomplished all their goals.

In briefing the American commanders in October, Schwarzkopf had left no ambiguity about the Army's mission. The Republican Guard were not to be routed, they were not to be made "combat ineffective."

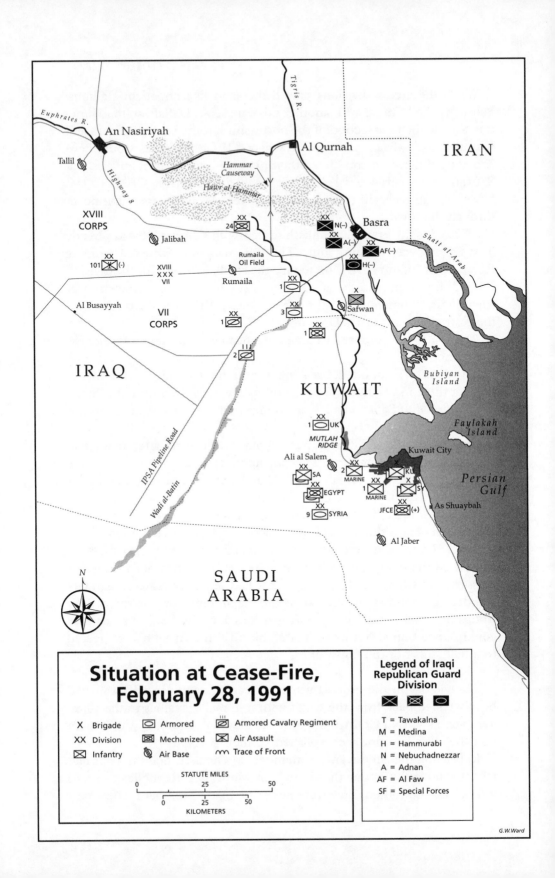

Euphrates R.

An Nasiriyah

Tallil

Tigris R.

Al Qurnah

IRAN

Hammar Causeway

Hawr al Hammar

XVIII CORPS

24

Basra

XX
N(—)

XX
A(—)

XX
AF(—)

XX
H(—)

Shatt al-Arab

Jalibah

101 (-)

XVIII
XXX
VII

Rumaila
Oil Field

Rumaila

1

3

Safwan

Al Busayyah

VII
CORPS

1

1

2

IRAQ

Bubiyan Island

KUWAIT

Faylakah Island

1 UK

MUTLAH RIDGE

Kuwait City

Ali al Salem

SA

2
MARINE

KU

SY

EGYPT

1
MARINE

9 SYRIA

JFCE (+)

As Shuaybah

Persian Gulf

Al Jaber

N

SAUDI ARABIA

Situation at Cease-Fire, February 28, 1991

X	Brigade	Armored	Armored Cavalry Regiment
XX	Division	Mechanized	Air Assault
	Infantry	Air Base	Trace of Front

Legend of Iraqi Republican Guard Division

T = Tawakalna
M = Medina
H = Hammurabi
N = Nebuchadnezzar
A = Adnan
AF = Al Faw
SF = Special Forces

STATUTE MILES
0   25   50

0   25   50
KILOMETERS

G.W.Ward

They were to be destroyed. Yet after six months of planning, the coalition's ground offensive never reached its logical culmination. Neither the ground offensive nor the bombing fully destroyed the Iraqi field forces, nor did they cut off the Iraqi escape routes out of southern Iraq and Kuwait.

On March 1, after the cease-fire, the American surveillance photos showed that 842 Iraqi tanks, a quarter of Iraq's tanks in southern Iraq and Kuwait, and 1,412 Iraqi armored personnel carriers and other armored vehicles, half of all its APCs in the theater, had escaped.

But it was more than a matter of equipment. According to the CIA analysis of the photos, at least 365 of the tanks that escaped were T-72s that belonged to Saddam Hussein's Republican Guard. By the CIA's count, the Republican Guard divisions had begun the war with 786 tanks. That meant half the Republican Guard armor got away. Since the Tawakalna and Medina divisions sought to hold off the Americans, Pentagon intelligence analysts later concluded that the Hammurabi Division escaped largely intact. According to intelligence estimates by the Defense Intelligence Agency, 70 percent of its troops managed to make their way north of the marshes.

Other Republican Guard and Army units escaped a company or a battalion at a time. Most important were the senior headquarters, which made it safely across the Euphrates and took charge of the routed Iraqi army, whipping it into shape and reconstituting the force so that it could suppress the Shiite uprising in the south. Notably, of the senior Iraqi officers captured during the war, only one was a Republican Guard officer. The devastation on the battlefield was considerable, but it was evident that the gate had never been closed and a lot of the horses got out.

To this day Schwarzkopf blames Franks for being too slow and letting too many Iraqis escape before the cease-fire. With Schwarzkopf's unhappiness with Franks echoing through the Army, the Jedis prepared a classified study of the CENTCOM rates of advance. The Army attack had not been far off schedule. It had taken the VII Corps about ten hours longer to engage the Republican Guard than had been projected, not a huge delay given the daunting logistics and the challenges of maneuvering a large armored force in the desert, but enough to enable the Iraqi army to get a head start in its escape north.

There is little doubt that Franks, however, could have been more aggressive. But Schwarzkopf had the advantage of seeing the big picture. Information from the Marines and intelligence from a variety of

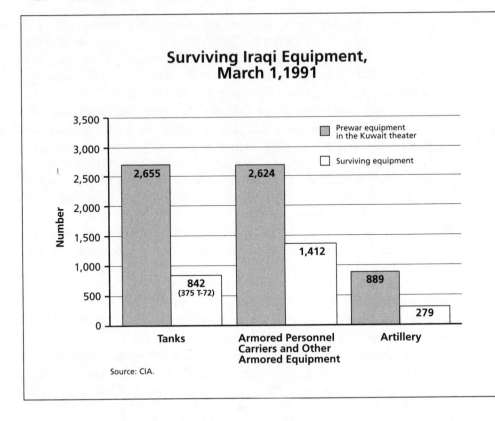

Surviving Iraqi Equipment, March 1, 1991

Source: CIA.

sources made him aware that the Iraqis were fleeing north and likely to escape the Army's wide envelopment from the western desert.

The disconnect between Schwarzkopf and his corps commander might have been avoided if CENTCOM had established a better command structure. It was Yeosock's responsibility to keep the two corps in harness and driving forward, but he was reluctant to assert his role as commander of Army ground forces and was thoroughly intimidated by the CENTCOM commander. In dodging his responsibilities, he frustrated Schwarzkopf, who felt compelled to deal directly with the corps commanders. Schwarzkopf's jumping in and out did nobody any good and confused command relations during critical periods of the offensive.

Schwarzkopf had a golden opportunity to rid himself discreetly of his ineffectual commander when Yeosock suffered a gallbladder attack in mid-February. The logical move was for Schwarzkopf to name Waller, his deputy, to take Yeosock's place. But Schwarzkopf's sense of loyalty took precedence over his military judgment. For all his bombast, Schwarzkopf was not tough enough.

Having made the mistake of retaining Yeosock, Schwarzkopf compounded it on the eve of the ground war. He knew that Franks was not the aggressive commander he wanted to lead the main attack, but instead of sending the Third Army commander forward to the front lines to oversee his performance and that of Luck's XVIII Airborne Corps, Schwarzkopf permitted Yeosock to run the war from his headquarters in Riyadh, more than three hundred miles behind the front. When the offensive kicked off, there was no senior field commander on top of the two attacking Army corps. Waller saw the weakness in the command arrangements and had earlier recommended that Yeosock or his staff go forward. Being Schwarzkopf's deputy he was reluctant to suggest that he be the one. He later regretted that he did not press the issue with Schwarzkopf.

Schwarzkopf, however, also bore considerable responsibility for the failure to destroy the Republican Guard. He failed to "read" his enemy and fell into the very trap he sought to avoid, that of being mechanical in his planning. A key assumption in his plan was that the Iraqis would stand and fight as they had done during the Iran-Iraq War. By G day there was sufficient evidence to question that assumption. The battle of Khafji demonstrated that the Iraqis would not be able to maneuver in the open desert in the face of American airpower and that their defensive strategy was doomed. Further, after the Iraqi defeat at Khafji, and intelligence reports of desertions and demoralization of the Iraqi field forces, there was reason to believe that the Iraqis would not defend in place, but retreat as soon as the Marines launched the ground campaign.

But no significant changes were made to the ground-war plan after the Khafji battle. Dominated by the massive logistical requirements of moving hundreds of thousands of men and tons of war material into position into the desert, CENTCOM lost track of the big picture. The command's military planning had become essentially an industrial enterprise.

Schwarzkopf stuck with the plan to lead with the Marine assault and launch the main Army attack against the Republican Guard the next day. While he was concerned over the deliberate pace of the VII Corps attack, Schwarzkopf never insisted that the plan be changed. He accepted the Army's plan for a ponderous seven- to ten-day operation without demurral. No alternate plan was developed in the event the Iraqi defenses collapsed.

When the Marines attacked and the Iraqis broke, Schwarzkopf's strategy for destroying the Guard and the Iraqi field army unraveled. The Marine attack prompted the Iraqis to signal a general retreat while the Army attack was barely under way. When he tried to speed up the VII Corps attack, the Army plan proved to be inflexible. Improvisation proved to be no substitute for good preliminary planning.

McCaffrey argued with some justification after the war that it would have made more sense to launch the XVIII Airborne attack two days before the rest of the allied offensive and limit the Marines to skirmishing along the border for several days. Only after the Army left hook was well under way should the Marines have been allowed to undertake their dash to the gates of Kuwait City, McCaffrey said. That would have enabled the allies to steal a march on the Republican Guard.

But in Schwarzkopf's command, the war plan was joint more in name than in fact. Each service was allowed to attack the way it preferred, with little thought about how an attack in one area would affect the fighting in another. Schwarzkopf yielded too unthinkingly to the Marines' demand that they be given a major piece of the war and accepted more than he would later acknowledge Franks's mind-set that the Iraqis were a determined enemy that was prepared to stand and fight.

Nor did Schwarzkopf have a plan to reap the full fruits of victory as he brought the war to a close. Had McCaffrey and Peay been allowed to carry out their plans to bracket Basra with American forces — even if Schwarzkopf had to stand up to Powell, Cheney, and the White House to get time to do it — CENTCOM would have been able to bottle up most of the escaping Iraqis and force them to surrender their weapons before marching north.

"The end game: it was bad," recalled McCaffrey after the war. "First of all, there was confusion. The objectives were unclear. And the sequence was wrong. They probably should have sent us forty-eight hours before the Marines."[29]

But even as the fighting drew to a close, the sparks from the Persian Gulf War ignited an uprising that spread across northern and southern Iraq. One war was over, but another war — the one between Saddam Hussein's regime and his own people — had just begun.

20

"I Survived Desert Storm"

Kuwait destroyed by Saddam. Iraq destroyed by combined forces. But Saddam is still in his chair.

> — Mehdy Nathil
> April 3, 1991
> Interviewed at an abandoned
>   cement plant near Highway 8, Iraq

Question: I'm struck by how somber you feel. And I was wondering, aren't these great days?

Answer: You know, to be very honest with you, I haven't yet felt this wonderfully euphoric feeling that many of the American people feel. And I'm beginning to. I feel much better about it today than I did yesterday. But I think it's that I want to see an end. You mentioned World War II — there was a definitive end to that conflict. And now we have Saddam Hussein still there — the man that wreaked this havoc upon his neighbors.

> — President Bush
> Press conference on the Persian Gulf War
> White House,
> March 1, 1991

N AN NAJAF, the news spread quickly. Allied forces were sweeping across southern Iraq and the Iraqi army was on the run. An Iraqi soldier had aimed his machine gun at one of the ubiquitous portraits of Saddam Hussein as his unit retreated through Basra and fired away. There was a power vacuum along the Euphrates.

Like the Kurds to the north, the Shiites had suffered decades of oppression at the hands of Baghdad. Before the war, Saddam Hussein wrapped himself in the mantle of Islam, even ordering that Allahu Akbar ("God is Great") be added to the Iraqi red, white, green, and black flag. In fact, the Iraqi leader, like many of his top aides, was a power-hungry secularist who fancied military uniforms and symbols over religious ones. Saddam Hussein was also a Tikriti, born in Sunni country, a hundred miles north of Baghdad. The Baghdad regime viewed the Shiites, who lived in the marshes along the Euphrates and outnumbered the Sunnis, as a potential internal threat to be closely monitored by the secret police.

Over the years, Saddam Hussein tried to coopt the Shiites by appointing them to government and military posts and by embracing Islam. But when power and privilege could not buy obedience, Baghdad did not hesitate to crack the whip. The Shiites had a history of asserting themselves when they thought there was a weakening of central authority — sometimes with disastrous results to themselves. Throughout the 1970s, antigovernment demonstrations in the Shiite cities along the Euphrates were brutally put down, Shiite clerics and their families were executed, and tens of thousands of Shiites were exiled to Iran.[1]

The Gulf War heightened the Shiites' grievances toward Baghdad — and emboldened them. From their bunkers in Baghdad, the Iraqi leadership had been defiant. But when the allied bombs began to fall, the price of flour began to soar and the salaries of workers in the cities along the Euphrates were suspended. Electricity and telephones were cut off. Little gasoline was available, and the only water supply came directly from the river. It seemed as if Iraq had been propelled a hundred years back in time, the leaders of the Shiite rebellion later recalled.

Before the ground war, there had been manifestations of dissent in An Najaf, one of the holiest of Shiite towns. In February, Yusef al-Hakim, a Shiite religious leader, died. As the funeral procession moved through the An Najaf streets on February 13, crowds began chanting: "There is no God but God" and "Saddam is the enemy of God." Iraqi secret policemen stalked the procession and rounded up hundreds of Shiites.

Now with the Iraqi army in full retreat and the allies marching ever closer, the Shiites' brewing resentment was boiling into a case of full-fledged insurrection.

The Shiites had turned to Western radio broadcasts because they believed that it was the allied powers that would decide the future of Iraq. With Iraq's electrical grid shut down, Baghdad's jamming of foreign radio stations had also ceased and the broadcasts were coming in clearer than ever.

On the Voice of America, Radio Monte Carlo, the British Broadcasting Company, and clandestine radio stations, like the CIA-equipped but Saudi-operated Voice of Free Iraq, the Shiite leaders in An Najaf learned both of the magnitude of the Iraqi defeat and President Bush's call for the ouster of Saddam Hussein. For the long-suppressed enemies of the Saddam Hussein regime, it looked like the moment to strike. In An Najaf, Karbala, An Nasiriyah, and Basra, the planning for a Shiite revolt shifted into high gear. In the Kurdish regions of northern Iraq, the Kurds also saw an opportunity to break away from Baghdad's domination.[2]

Iraq did not have enough forces to put down the Kurdish and Shiite rebellions simultaneously. It did, however, have somewhat more than CENTCOM had thought. The devastation on the battlefield was considerable. But when the dust cleared, no American forces were astride the Hawr al Hammar causeway east of Basra. No American forces were sitting astride the Basra canals. The gate had never been closed.

At his command post south of the Euphrates, Barry McCaffrey was already beginning to pick up reports that an insurgency was brewing to his north. But McCaffrey was not focusing on the turmoil in Iraq. He was still looking at the Iraqi army that had escaped to the east.

When the cease-fire was declared on the morning of February 28, McCaffrey's most forward troops were at the edge of the Rumaila oil field. Their final battle had been west of the causeway — one of the Iraqi military's principal escape routes — at an artificial boundary dubbed Phase Line Knife.

Even though President Bush had proclaimed a cease-fire, McCaffrey's officers wanted to continue the advance. Col. John LeMoyne, the commander of the division's 1st brigade, went to McCaffrey on two occasions and told him the 24th needed to keep rolling forward, LeMoyne recalled after the war.

It was clear to LeMoyne that the military's task was not done. Soon after the cease-fire was declared, some of the fleeing Iraqis began doubling back and retrieving the weapons and equipment they had abandoned. By continuing the march, LeMoyne also figured the forward troops from the 24th Mech could make sure that the Iraqis could not set up artillery positions within range of the Americans.

McCaffrey finally agreed to LeMoyne's request. The aggessive general had a liberal interpretation of the cease-fire arrangements and it did not include staying in place. "We continued to press on to clear the zone out in front," recalled Col. Paul Kern, the commander of the division's 2nd

Brigade. "There was no limit or boundary designated, only that we were to stop shooting. Our view was that we would continue to move forward as far as we could and clear as much zone in our area as we could."

In the day following the cease-fire, McCaffrey's 24th Mech, Starr's 3rd Armored Cavalry Regiment, and the division's artillery advanced about five to ten miles beyond Phase Line Knife, aligning themselves just to the west of the causeway. Meanwhile, McCaffrey's reconnaissance units began patrolling an area that extended to Phase Line Crush, a limit of advance the division set to the east of the causeway.

After the war, McCaffrey said he had not attached any particular strategic significance to his advance. He had assumed wrongly that the causeway had been destroyed by allied bombing. But in creeping forward, McCaffrey had aligned his forces along one of the Iraqi main remaining escape routes and inadvertently set the stage for a confrontation with the Iraqis. One of the Army's biggest clashes was about to begin, but it would not take place until after the war.

That the battlefield was still chaotic was clear. The battered Iraqi force was operating without reliable intelligence and was not sure just where the Americans forces were. On March 1, there was light skirmishing as the Iraqi forces tried to escape the Americans' clutches but instead blundered into them.

At 1AM, soldiers from LeMoyne's brigade confronted a busload of Iraqi soldiers driving west on Highway 8. Panicked by the Americans, the Iraqis started shooting at point-blank range. LeMoyne's troops returned fire. Seven Iraqis were killed and six wounded in the exchange. LeMoyne's troops also exchanged mortar and artillery fire with the Iraqis. That, however, was just a portent of what was to come.

It was on March 2 at 3AM that LeMoyne began to sense that something bigger was brewing. His scouts were reporting that enemy vehicles were moving along their front, and the alert was confirmed by OH-58 Delta helicopters and a JSTARS radar surveillance plane. The Iraqi force was sizable, consisting of hundreds of vehicles, including trucks, T-72 tanks, Frog missile launchers, and armored personnel carriers. LeMoyne's 1st Brigade, the northernmost of McCaffrey's unit, which was deployed astride the approaches to the causeway, appeared to be in the Iraqis' path.

Having done their best to escape the allied onslaught, the Iraqis were not looking to launch a headlong attack into an American mechanized division. With Basra jammed with fleeing Iraqi soldiers, they were trying to find an alternative route home over the causeway. But to LeMoyne, the Iraqis' intentions were unclear.

"We did not know about the causeway," LeMoyne recalled. "We thought: where are these guys going?"

With the Americans unaware that the causeway was intact and the Iraqis operating with poor command and control, and neither side sure of the other's intentions, it would not take much to set off a fight.

At 8AM, the first shot was fired when an Iraqi outpost protecting the Rumaila oil field saw an American Bradley fighting vehicle, got scared, and fired a rocket-propelled grenade. The Iraqi troops who fired the grenade surrendered almost immediately. But a column of Iraqi tanks to their rear saw the action and began to fire their guns and antitank missiles.

That was enough for McCaffrey. After four days of traversing terrible terrain in wind and rain, but with only sporadic action, the 24th Mech was ready to pounce on any Iraqi forces at the first indication that they were not complying with the cease-fire.

The Americans launched a merciless attack. LeMoyne ordered Apache attack helicopters to fly north of the causeway and seal off the Iraqi escape route. Then, five battalions of McCaffrey's artillery fired mines and other cluster munitions at the causeway as well as to the south of the Iraqis, bracketing the enemy.

The Air Force was eager to join in the fight, but this was one battle the Army was determined to handle by itself. Although the Americans refrained from attacking Iraqi armored concentrations north of the Euphrates or southeast of the battle area, the trapped column of Iraqi forces near the causeway was deemed to be fair game. With the Iraqis boxed in, the division polished off the enemy. All told, 346 armored vehicles were destroyed, including thirty T-72 tanks. It was one of the most intense and one-sided fights of the war. Overwhelmed by the American fire, hundreds of Iraqis abandoned their vehicles and fled into the marshes, leaving muddy footprints in the sand.

McCaffrey and his aides insisted that they were not trying to provoke a fight. Yet they acknowledged, in retrospect, it was clear that the Iraqis were not looking to do battle with the allies.

The Iraqi armored columns "either did not know we were there or thought they could drive through us under terms of the cease-fire agreement," McCaffrey said after the war.

Added Kern, "I think they just blundered in. They had very poor intelligence and poor leadership."

But some of McCaffrey's fellow Army officers in the nearby VII Corps thought the general had used a relatively minor exchange of fire as an excuse to pummel the Iraqi forces that had been put off-limits by the early cease-fire. Colonel Cherrie, the VII Corps operations officer, believed that the VII Corps rules of engagement would have precluded it from continuing to move its troops forward or launching the disproportionate fusillade ordered by McCaffrey.

Asked what led to the battle, one senior Army officer in Riyadh aptly expressed the view of much of the Army leadership. "I do not know, and I do not want to know," he said. With misgivings among the Army commanders over the premature decision to end the ground war, senior officers were not inclined to second-guess McCaffrey's attack.

Only later would McCaffrey's commanders learn that they might have dodged a bullet. During the fight at the causeway, LeMoyne was alerted by the Air Force that several Iraqi helicopters were flying southeast toward Basra. Since Iraq had not flown helicopters throughout the war and the helicopters were not a direct threat, LeMoyne advised that the Air Force leave the helicopters alone, and the choppers landed at the Basra airfield. Later, he was told that the helicopters might have been carrying the Iraqi generals for the cease-fire negotiations at Safwan.[3]

While McCaffrey was edging forward, Franks was not looking to expand his turf. The VII Corps commander had made it through the war with relatively few casualties and was determined not to suffer any unnecessary losses on the munitions-laden battlefield. He had frozen his forces in place.

But while McCaffrey was pummeling the wayward column of Iraqi troops after the cease-fire, it became clear that it was Franks who had the problem in Riyadh. With the land war over and victory declared, Schwarzkopf had been searching for a place to conduct cease-fire negotiations with the Iraqi generals.

The symbolism was important. The political prerequisite was that the negotiations site be in Iraq, not in Kuwait City, as the Iraqis hoped. It had to be clear to the world that the Iraqis had been forced out of Kuwait and that it was the allies who were dictating the terms in Iraqi territory. There were a number of possible sites, but Schwarzkopf liked Safwan, just north of the Iraq-Kuwait border. Schwarzkopf had not ordered Franks to take the Safwan road junction until the last night of the war, but Safwan was at the nexus of two major highways, near an airfield, and represented one of the Army's deepest penetrations into Iraq — or so Schwarzkopf thought. Based on reports from VII Corps, a 1st Infantry Division symbol had been placed squarely on the road junction near Safwan on the Army maps in Riyadh.

Schwarzkopf told Washington that cease-fire talks would be held there and the VII Corps was informed. Franks had not attached any special urgency to the CENTCOM request to take Safwan, but he believed Rhame's 1st Infantry Division had taken the objective. Almost immediately, Franks, who had suffered through four days of second-guessing in Riyadh and Washington, received more bad news.

With the cease-fire deadline looming, the hard-charging Rhame, who had insisted on being the first in the VII Corps to take the war to the Iraqis and lobbied hard to play a major role in Franks's attack over the next four days, had not actually taken Safwan. Franks had assumed that Rhame had his tanks at the road junction. But as it turned out, time ran out on the VII Corps attack, and the 1st Infantry Division had settled for flying helicopters there instead.

The episode crystallized all the confusion within the Army about the abrupt end of the war. CENTCOM had the Iraqis on the run and could have ended the war at any point and time of its choosing. It could have waited until McCaffrey's 24th was at the Basra canal, Peay's brigade north of Basra, and Rhame's force at Safwan before stopping. However, it was the top generals in Riyadh and Washington, not the field commanders, who had determined when it was time to stop the war. The war had been concluded by setting an arbitrary time for ending hostilities. Powell had become concerned how the one-sided rout might appear in Washington and to the world. He did not wait until the ground commanders had their objectives in hand before calling it quits. The decision to end the war was determined more by political than military considerations.

The divergent interpretations of the postwar rules of engagement only compounded the problem. While McCaffrey had used the cease-fire to take more ground, Franks's punctilious observation of the cease-fire left his corps short of Safwan.

When Franks was informed by his staff that Rhame had not seized Safwan, the usual gentlemanly Franks got on the phone to 1st Infantry Division commander. Erupting in a rare paroxysm of anger, Franks demanded to know who had reported that Safwan had been captured, according to an officer present.

In military terms, there had been nothing critical about capturing the site. By the time of the cease-fire, Safwan was no longer a key choke point in the Iraqi escape north. Most of the fleeing Iraqis were already north of the town, and the Republican Guard tanks and armored personnel carriers, not dependent on using the roads, were driving over the hard-packed desert. But politically, the failure to occupy the road junction was a visible reminder that the allies had fallen short of their goal and a gross embarrassment to Schwarzkopf. The CENTCOM chief had told Powell that the road junction was in American hands and the information had been conveyed to the White House. Not only had the allies failed to shut the gate but an Iraqi brigade still occupied the airfield near town, where the victorious coalition commander planned to deliver terms to his defeated opponent.[4]

Schwarzkopf might have charitably chalked the matter up to the fog of battle and proposed another site. Franks, for one, suggested that the armistice meeting be held at the site of the battle of Medina Ridge, where Griffith's tanks had blasted the Iraqi armor. It was one of the VII Corps's biggest triumphs, and the rows of burned and exploded Iraqi tanks provided a good photo op for the media. But Medina Ridge was far from the major roads. And Jalibah airfield, which Schwarzkopf later told the Iraqis had also been considered as a negotiation site, was covered with unexploded cluster bombs.

The CENTCOM commander felt he had been misled into believing Safwan was in American hands and ordered Franks to submit a written explanation of the incident. Still, Schwarzkopf wanted more than an explanation; he wanted action. Schwarzkopf was determined to negotiate a termination of the war at Safwan even if he had to start the war up again to do it.

On March 1, Schwarzkopf told Yeosock that the VII Corps was to take the road junction and airfield, forcing whatever Iraqi soldiers were there to leave. Franks and his aides scrambled to put together a plan. Cease-fire or not, the war was not over for Rhame. He had not taken the road junction before; now he would have to fix it. A-10s and F-16s would back up a cavalry squadron beefed up with extra attack helicopters. The Americans would surround the Safwan airfield, then issue an ultimatum. The Iraqis would have to be out by 4PM.

At 6:15AM on March 2, a squadron of Rhame's soldiers drove north, two troops abreast and with reconnaissance helicopters to the front, hoping to secure the negotiation site with some old-fashioned persuasion. But when they got to Safwan, the news was not good. The airfield was defended by five Iraqi battalions equipped with T-72s, T-55s, and ZSU-24 antiaircraft guns, and they had no intention of leaving.

The American troops tried to break the ice with the Iraqis by offering them food. Then, at 9AM, the Iraqi commander of the units approached Capt. Ken Pope from "A" Troop.

Pope delivered the message to the Iraqis: they had to leave. The Iraqi colonel was defiant and confused by the request. He asked the Americans if they were aware they were in Iraq.

Pope said yes. He was there to secure the site for the cease-fire negotiations.

The Iraqi officer was both surprised by the reply and offended that the Americans were offering his men food. He ordered his men to prepare tea for "A" Troop to show that they were hosts in their own country. The Iraqi said that he had assumed the cease-fire talks would be held in Kuwait City.

The word went up the chain of command. The Iraqis outnumbered the Americans at Safwan, and they said they would not leave without orders from on high. McCaffrey was already tangling with the Iraqis, but he had the excuse that his forces had drawn Iraqi fire. Did the Army really want to risk another clash to take the road junction in the VII Corps zone?

When Yeosock spoke to Schwarzkopf, he cautioned that it could take a while to pry the Iraqis out of Safwan. The Iraqi commander had reported that his men were dug in and had been there for a long time, Yeosock explained, according to a confidential Army memorandum of the conversation. Afraid of angering Schwarzkopf, Yeosock noted in his memo that he did not say that the Americans had been feeding the Iraqis.

But Schwarzkopf was insistent. The JCS were upset that Safwan had not been taken, Schwarzkopf explained. The seizure of the town had been briefed to the White House by Powell. The matter had to be straightened out quickly. CENTCOM did not want any Iraqis near that location.

Schwarzkopf ordered Yeosock to send overwhelming force to surround the Iraqi commander and his troops. "Try to do it by a show of force to capture them or get them to withdraw," Schwarzkopf ordered. "Capture him if he refuses to withdraw. If he attacks you, then return fire.

"Ensure that Lieutenant General Franks understands the mission; not sure of his ability to understand mission," Schwarzkopf said acerbically. Then Schwarzkopf told Yeosock to directly explain the operation to Rhame. "You have an entire corps to work with," Schwarzkopf said. "Use attack helicopters."[5]

The standoff continued until midmorning when a flight of A-10s zoomed past the airfield. Pope told the Iraqis that the planes would attack unless the Iraqis left. Finally, the Iraqis gave in. By noon, most of the Iraqis were on the road moving toward Basra.

After the episode, Franks wrote Schwarzkopf that there was no intent to disobey his orders or mislead him, but acknowledged that VII Corps had unintentionally submitted an erroneous report. Franks protected the VII Corps staff and Rhame's staff and took responsibility for the decision.

With time running out before the cease-fire, Franks wrote, Rhame had taken the road junction "from the air." The helicopters saw six tanks but did not fire. The VII Corps had ordered a halt to shooting in Rhame's area because of concern over friendly fire and in the confusion had failed to authorize Rhame to fire at any Iraqi targets at Safwan.

The explanation only made Schwarzkopf angrier. "There is not a military commander in the entire world who would claim he had taken an objective by flying over it," he recalled.

If Franks had reported up the chain of command that he did not have time to occupy the road junction, Schwarzkopf later said, "I would have said you do not have to shoot but keep driving until you get there. I want it physically occupied."

In Schwarzkopf's command, it was better to play a little loose with the rules, as McCaffrey had done, than to be overly cautious. Schwarzkopf later unsuccessfully urged Powell to block Franks's promotion to head of the Army's Training and Doctrine Command, suggesting that Waller, an aggressive, if not particularly intellectual, officer, according to other Army officers, be given the position instead. Franks's caution on the battlefield was not an example the Army should point to with pride, Schwarzkopf said, and when the controversy over Franks's performance became known, the Army would be embarrassed.

"Colin said 'You are right, I agree,'" Schwarzkopf recalled. But Franks, like Schwarzkopf, was a protégé of Gen. Carl Vuono, the Army chief of staff. Franks's appointment, Powell explained, was a matter for the Army to decide.

While Schwarzkopf was worried about how the position of his troops on the battlefield would look in Washington, the commander in chief was having his own second thoughts and, in his own manner, was expressing them openly.

The air and land campaigns had been designed to weaken the Iraqi leader's hold on power, although Washington had been ambivalent about making the overthrow of Saddam Hussein an objective. Bush had talked with Douglas Hurd, the British foreign minister, about having war crimes trials for the Iraqi leadership. And for the air-war planners, Saddam Hussein had been a target of opportunity and the destruction of his regime a goal. But since Washington had decided against sending ground troops to Baghdad, there was no guarantee that the war would topple the Iraqi leader.

Still, the war had been less decisive than President Bush had hoped.

Saddam Hussein was defeated on the battlefield and discredited in the eyes of military professionals. But the Iraqi leader held fast to the reins of power in Baghdad.

When President Bush announced the Safwan meeting in a March 1 news conference, he said that "nobody can be absolved from the responsibilities under international law on the war crimes aspect of that."

Bush also repeated his call for a rebellion: "In my own view, I've always said it would be — that the Iraqi people should put him aside and that would facilitate the resolution of all these problems that exist, and certainly would facilitate the acceptance of Iraq back into the family of peace-loving nations."

The inconclusive ending of the war seemed to weigh heavily on the president's mind. "You know, to be very honest with you, I haven't yet felt this wonderfully euphoric feeling that many of the American people feel," President Bush confessed to a surprised White House press corps. "And I'm beginning to. I feel much better about it today than I did yesterday. But I think it's that I want to see an end. You mentioned World War II — there was a definitive end to that conflict. And now we have Saddam Hussein still there — the man that wreaked this havoc upon his neighbors.

"I just need a little more time to sort out in my mind how I can say to the American people it's over finally — the last 'T' is crossed, the last 'I' is dotted," he added.[6]

SAFWAN SNAFU

Once Safwan was secured, Schwarzkopf was eager to get on with the job of cementing the truce. The negotiations themselves were to be held in a large tent near the Safwan airfield.

The first efforts to arrange a meeting faltered when Prince Khalid complained that the Iraqi delegation to the meeting was too junior and not befitting a meeting with the allied high command. Schwarzkopf had been willing to go along but had deferred to his Saudi counterpart. Now that the allies had their victory, Schwarzkopf was eager to conclude an agreement that would allow him to expeditiously withdraw his troops.

Finally, the Iraqis proposed a high-level team. It was sending Lt. Gen. Sala Abud Mahmoud, Iraq's III Corps commander, who had planned the battle of Khafji, and Lt. Gen. Sultan Hashim Ahmad, the chief of staff of the Ministry of Defense. The III Corps commander had survived the allied attempts to bomb him; he had survived Baghdad's unhappiness with the battle of Khafji, and he had survived the ground war. Now, he had a lead role in making peace with the Americans.

Back in Washington, Cheney's top civilian aides were uncomfortable about the way the cease-fire arrangements were being handled by the generals. There was a long tradition in the American military of treating a vanquished foe with respect, but it was not very Middle Eastern. The coalition had sought for six weeks not only to liberate Kuwait, but to "incapacitate" the Saddam Hussein regime and loosen its hold on power. But Schwarzkopf was not trying to put the Iraqi military in its place. The CENTCOM commander had already announced that the allies were not going to Baghdad. Now he seemed very eager to get to Safwan. For Schwarzkopf, diplomatic concerns were subordinated to the need to work out an understanding to repatriate the allied prisoners and go home.

The White House took the view that the generals were engaging in mere technical talks on cease-fire lines and did not need to be told how to negotiate with the Iraqis. Flush with self-confidence, Schwarzkopf did not seek any political guidance from Cheney or his aides.

When Schwarzkopf flew to Safwan, there was no senior administration civilian to accompany him. "Norm went in uninstructed," a senior Bush administration official said. "He should have had instructions. But everything was moving so fast the process broke down. The generals made an effort not to be guided. It was treated as something that was basically a military decision, not one to be micromanaged."

As the Iraqis approached the negotiations tent, Schwarzkopf insisted that everyone be searched for weapons before entering the tent and went first as an example.

Schwarzkopf raised the first issue: prisoners of war, according to a transcript of the meeting. It was a natural concern for a military that had seen its prisoners used as diplomatic bargaining chips by the North Vietnamese. But the Gulf War was not Vietnam. Iraq's holding of allied prisoners was an open invitation for the coalition to continue the war. The Iraqis immediately agreed to allow Red Cross representatives to visit the prisoners and then to exchange them. The Iraqis had only a handful of allied prisoners. The allies had an estimated 60,000 Iraqis.

The Iraqis also agreed to provide the allies with the locations of their minefields on land and at sea. General Ahmad told Schwarzkopf that Iraq had never deployed any chemical weapons or other weapons of mass destruction in Kuwait and assured the CENTCOM commander that Iraq would not launch any more Scud missiles.

Then Schwarzkopf shifted the discussion to ways to prevent another clash between the forces, like the one between McCaffrey's division and the retreating Iraqis the day before.

"We would now like to talk about safety measures since our troops are still close together. We had an unfortunate incident yesterday where our troops got in one more battle that we did not need," Schwarzkopf said.

Ahmad complained about McCaffrey's attack. "The ones you shot were drawing back," the general said, referring to their attempt to maneuver across the causeway.

"Well, unfortunately, they shot first. But that is something we could argue about until the sun sets," Schwarzkopf replied.

There was little to be gained by arguing over the fight and the two sides discussed cease-fire lines to prevent a repetition of the incident. Schwarzkopf pulled out a map of the allied positions and proposed a narrow mile-and-a-half buffer zone along the forward line of the allies' advance.

The Iraqis agreed on the condition that it was not a temporary cease-fire line and that the allies would withdraw from Iraqi territory.

"Absolutely," replied Schwarzkopf. "I assure you it has nothing to do with borders."

But the Iraqi general was not very happy about the allied occupation of southern Iraq, however temporary, and protested that the allies had continued their offensive after the Iraqis had signaled a general retreat on the evening of February 25.

"After we have withdrawn from Kuwait and announced it on the television and radio, we did not hope or think that you would step in the Iraqi territory," Ahmad said. "We are sure you know now how much we paid after we announced the withdrawal on the radio and television, casualty-wise I mean."

Schwarzkopf replied, "A lot of people paid with casualties for a very long time, that is not the subject we are here to talk about now. I think that we will leave that to history. I would also like to make sure we don't accidentally shoot . . ."

Ahmad interrupted, "I have just mentioned this for history."

"Again, history will be written long after you and I are gone," Schwarzkopf responded.

The CENTCOM chief then broached the subject of Iraqi aircraft flights. Allied warplanes were still patrolling Iraq's skies, and safety precautions needed to be taken to ensure that the coalition did not shoot down innocent aircraft.

Ahmad wanted to know why it was important for the allies to fly over Iraq at all.

"It is purely as a safety measure to make sure that we do not have any hostile aircraft attack us. It has no offensive intention at all. It is a defensive measure only," Schwarzkopf said. With each comment, Schwarzkopf was reassuring the Iraqis that they could breathe easy.

Then Khalid interjected, asking for a pledge that Iraqi border troops would never again cross into Saudi territory. "We will stop our soldiers and yours," Ahmad replied, striking a defiant tone.

Schwarzkopf asked solicitously if there were any additional matters the Iraqis wanted to discuss.

"We have a point, one point," Ahmad said. "You might very well know the situation of the roads and bridges and communications. We would like to agree that helicopter flights sometimes are needed to carry some of the officials, government officials, or any member that is needed to be transported from one place to another because the roads and bridges are out."

Schwarzkopf magnanimously conceded the point. To CENTCOM, helicopters had never been much of a threat. With the allied jets dominating the skies, the Iraqis had been afraid to fly helicopters against allied forces through the ground war.

"As long as it is not over the part we are in, that is absolutely no problem," Schwarzkopf said. "So we will let the helicopters, and that is a very important point, and I want to make sure that's recorded, that military helicopters can fly over Iraq. Not fighters, not bombers."

The Iraqi general seemed surprised that he had so easily obtained the concession and made it clear that the Iraqis wanted to fly armed helicopters. "So you mean even the helicopters that is armed in the Iraqi skies can fly, but not the fighters?" he asked somewhat incredulously.

"Yeah," Schwarzkopf answered. "I will instruct our Air Force not to shoot at any helicopters that are flying over the territory of Iraq where we are not located. If they must fly over the area we are located in, I prefer that they not be gunships, armed helos, and I would prefer that they have an orange tag on the side as an extra safety measure."

What CENTCOM had agreed to was better than anything the Iraqi negotiators might have reasonably expected. While the helicopters were of little concern to the Americans, they were a fearsome weapon as far as the Shiites and the Kurds were concerned. Helicopters had been a punishing weapon against the Mujahideen in Afghanistan, and unlike the Afghan rebels, the Shiites and the Kurds had not been equipped by the CIA with Stinger antiaircraft missiles. By attacking the insurgents with helicopters, the Iraqi army could panic their adversary and range deeply to strike at civilians far from the front lines.

The decision reflected Schwarzkopf's surprising disinterest in the internal situation in Iraq. The entire focus of the discussions had to do with the risk the Iraqi forces posed to the allies, not with the fighting in Iraq.

Ahmad immediately responded by assuring Schwarzkopf that Iraqi helicopters would not venture near the allies and by giving the Americans a breakdown of the forty-one allied prisoners held. The Iraqis, he said, had only 2,098 Kuwaitis, a far cry from the 30,000 Kuwaiti prisoners the Americans believed Baghdad was holding.

After a short break to look at Schwarzkopf's map, the Iraqis raised a sensitive point. The Iraqi general complained that the Americans had inched forward after the cease-fire. Safwan itself, Ahmad noted, had been under Iraqi control at the end of the war. Now, Schwarzkopf was including the newly seized territory on the allied side of the cease-fire line.

Schwarzkopf sought to cut off the discussion of what was an embarrassing issue for CENTCOM by offering a blanket assurance. "There will not be one single coalition force member in the recognized borders of Iraq, as soon as, as rapidly as we can get them out," Schwarzkopf said. "I know the general understands that sometimes it takes a little bit longer to move out then it does to move in, because we will have gasoline trucks, petroleum, ammo, but we will move out, and you have my guarantee."[7]

It was an extraordinary assurance. The United States might have used its occupation of southern Iraq to press for further demands. It might have insisted that the Iraqis reach a new political accommodation with the Shiites and Kurds, or at least not attack them. It might even have pressed for the removal of the Saddam Hussein regime. But it did none of this.

Before she left the post of prime minister, Margaret Thatcher had suggested to Prince Bandar that the allies might occupy and exploit the Rumaila oil field until they had recouped the cost of the war and had their other demands met. Having fought his way to the Rumaila oil field, McCaffrey did not see why allied forces should not sit on it until the allies' demands were satisfied, even if took five years.

Barring such bold diplomacy, the allies might simply have fudged the question and avoided offering the Iraqis any assurance that the coalition force would rapidly withdraw and would refrain from interfering with helicopter operations inside Iraq. With two Army corps deep in Iraq, command of the skies, and the Iraqi military in a state of disarray, Washington would never again be in such a strong position to press its demands. Yet Schwarzkopf, and his civilian masters in Washington, let the moment pass.

Still, there was plenty of second-guessing behind the scenes in Washington of Schwarzkopf's performance. "I did not like it," recalled Brent Scowcroft, referring to the commander's decision to grant an exception for helicopter flights. "My inclination was to repudiate it. But the majority did not want to do that. That would be a major repudiation of Schwarzkopf."[8]

At the Pentagon, Paul Wolfowitz thought that Safwan had been a lost opportunity. "The thing that disturbed us was that Schwarzkopf was ready to meet at the junior level until Khalid put his foot down," Wolfowitz recalled. "The military's attitude was we have won. Let's cut this cleanly and not let the civilians load us with a lot of missions. Safwan was too hasty and too dignified."[9]

In Riyadh, Buster Glosson told his aides who were dismantling the Black Hole that Safwan was the handiwork of Army generals who were preoccupied with drawing cease-fire lines in the sand and establishing terms for the withdrawal of their ground forces — and who were blind to the use of airpower and the broader political and diplomatic ramifications of the Iraq conflict.

After the war, Glosson reflected: "The only reason we gave them permission was that there was no airman in the tent at Safwan. If Horner had been at Safwan, he would not have given the Iraqis permission to fly, except a few flights around Baghdad. We would not have agreed to give them a field day against the Shiites."[10]

It did not take long for the Iraqis to take advantage of the loophole they wrung from the allies at Safwan. For the first three days after the ground war, the Shiites encountered little organized resistance to their anti-Saddam demonstrations and rebellions across the Euphrates valley.

But soon after the Safwan meeting, Saddam Hussein began to crack down in earnest. Not only had the Iraqi commanders salvaged half of the Republican Guard and many of their other units from the Kuwaiti theater of operations, but they had saved their command headquarters units. That enabled them to quickly organize the remnants of their field army into a cohesive force.

Because the Iraqi military was stretched thin, Baghdad decided to take on the insurgent forces sequentially. First, they would suppress the Shiite revolt. Then they would concentrate on the Kurds in the north.

Along Highway 8, the east-west route that ran from An Nasiriyah to Basra, the American soldiers could tell that Saddam Hussein was mercilessly putting down the rebellion. By day, refugees were streaming south, looking for medical aid and shelter, seeking protection in the shadow of the American Army and telling tales of atrocities in Basra, Karbala, and An Najaf. At Checkpoint Bravo, which Ron Griffith's soldiers had established along the highway, the tales at the medical tent had a common theme: indiscriminate fire at men, women, and children, the destruction of Islamic holy places, in which the Shiites had taken refuge, helicopter and rocket attacks, threats of chemical weapons attacks.

Iraqi special forces and regular army troops attacked Karbala on March 8, using mortars and tanks. The Shiites fought back, using rocket-propelled grenades and light arms that had been stored by the Iraqis in the town as a precaution against an allied attack. But they were quickly overwhelmed when Saddam Hussein's forces struck back with artillery and helicopter gunships, forcing thousands of Shiites to flee.

An Najaf, which many of the leaders of the Shiite Intifadah had made their home base, was hit the next day. The Shiite defenders tried to resist, using the light arms stored at the Training Center for Enlisted Men, but were overcome.

Shiite leaders from An Najaf headed south to seek support from the allied liberators of Kuwait. But when some of the Shiites reached the American lines, they were puzzled at the Americans' refusal to get involved. Instead of providing the Shiites with arms, the Americans were blowing up the arms caches in southern Iraq. That was in keeping with Schwarzkopf's order to shrink the Iraq arsenal, but it deprived the overmatched Shiites of one of their few means of obtaining weapons.

The Shiites went to look for the French, finally finding them near As Salman. But they were not interested in helping either, and some of the Shiites eventually joined the exiled Iraqi resistance in London.[11]

In Washington, the war had simultaneously done more and less than the administration had hoped. During the long months leading up the war, Bush had portrayed Saddam Hussein as worse than Hitler and described the liberation of Kuwait as a battle between good and evil.

Washington had not been willing to take the risk of sending its troops to Baghdad. Instead, the Bush administration sought to undermine Saddam Hussein through air attacks on Iraq's command centers, communications, and electrical system, and ground attacks on the Republican Guard, hoping for a coup from the ranks of the Iraqi military.

The goal was the replacement of one Iraqi dictator by another Iraqi strongman committed to holding Iraq together. One reason for insisting on the rapid exchange of prisoners, recalled Gordon Brown, Schwarzkopf's foreign policy adviser, was the calculation that the tens of thousands of returning Iraqi prisoners would spread the word about Baghdad's humiliation on the battlefield and undermine the Saddam Hussein regime. Instead, the allied attacks had sparked two ethnically based uprisings that the Bush administration neither wanted nor anticipated. And while the Iraqi leader was discredited in the eyes of military professionals, he was still in control and determined to ruthlessly suppress any challenges to his authority.

While the Bush administration knew little of the Shiites and was wary of them, the rush of pathetic refugees, all pledging their implacable opposition to Washington's most disreputable foe, to allied controlled territory gave them an international audience.

Safwan was soon overshadowed by a crowded camp of 11,500 refugees in the heart of the town. Desperate to avoid repatriation to Iraq, the refugees posted signs throughout the town begging the Americans not to leave and they staged noisy demonstrations for the reporters who ventured north from Kuwait.

As the refugees continued to stream toward Safwan, American soldiers along Highway 8 urged them to return home. But with the Iraqi army at their backs, the Shiites explained they had nowhere to go. Some of the Shiites produced military identification cards and demanded to be taken prisoner. Others camped near the roadside, waiting to see if Washington would change its mind and telling the press of the Iraqi attacks on their families and holy sites.

In a dilapidated trailer off Highway 8, Mehdy Nathil, a Shiite who had fled from Saddam Hussein's troops, said, "Bush told us to revolt against Saddam. We revolt against Saddam. But where is Bush? Where is he?"

Four days after the Safwan meeting, Secretary of State Baker flew to Saudi Arabia with some ideas about how to secure the peace. The plan Baker carried was developed by Robert Kimmitt and Thomas Pickering, Washington's ambassador to the United Nations. Pickering had proposed that a demilitarized zone be established by the United Nations in southern Iraq, putting all of Iraq south of Basra off-limits to Iraqi forces, and that allied troops patrol the area.

Pickering was confident that he could get the idea through the United Nations. The Deputies Committee, an interagency panel of high-ranking officials that included Adm. David Jeremiah, the vice chairman of the Joint Chiefs of Staff, discussed the idea for two days.

The plan had a military and political component. Militarily, any Iraqi intrusion into the zone would provide Kuwait and Saudi Arabia with substantial early warning in case the Iraqis ever again tried to threaten the Gulf states. Politically, the establishment of the zone would diminish Iraqi authority over southern Iraq, including its Rumaila oil field. The allies would have leverage over Baghdad's future oil production. The zone would also cover part of the highway from Amman to Baghdad, allowing the allies to crack down on sanctions busting from Jordan.

But the scope of the newly minted plan was still a matter of debate, and it had its critics within the administration. When Lt. Gen. Howard Graves, the JCS representative on the trip, received a call from the Pentagon on the flight to Riyadh, it became clear to Paul Wolfowitz that the JCS was having second thoughts about the idea of establishing a demilitarized zone, seeing it as a potential snare in its effort to expedite the withdrawal of American forces.

Nor was the State Department enthusiastic about the idea of helping the Shiites. Wolfowitz argued that the Shiites of Iraq were different from the Shiites of Iran, the point being that affording a measure of protection to the Shiites of Iraq would not encourage the expansion of anti-American Islamic fundamentalism. "For one thing, they're Arabs, not Persians," he told John Kelly, the senior Middle East official at the State Department. But Kelly stopped him short.

"So are the Hezbellah," quipped Kelly, referring to the Lebanon-based terrorists. The State Department's top Middle East hands tended to associate the Iraqi Shiites with the Iranian fundamentalists to the east.

In fact, the State Department policy-makers knew little about the Iraqi Shiites. Iraq's Shiites had been loyal members of Baghdad's army in Saddam Hussein's eight-year war with Iran and, with some notable exceptions, did not favor attaching their region to Iran.

It was Schwarzkopf himself who delivered the mortal blow to the plan for a security zone. Having promised the Iraqis that the allied forces would withdraw, which he wanted to do anyway as soon as possible, the CENTCOM commander was dead set against the demilitarized zone. When he met with Baker, Schwarzkopf argued that a security zone would have no military value and would delay the withdrawal of American forces from the region.[12]

After meeting with Schwarzkopf, Baker huddled with his team. Robert Kimmitt and Wolfowitz disagreed with the commander's assessment, but the top generals had made their objections known and the civilians were reluctant to challenge them.

Pickering's proposal for a security zone died at birth. But it was not the only plan to challenge Saddam Hussein's authority that was rejected by CENTCOM's senior leadership. One day after Baker arrived in Riyadh, Steven Arnold put the finishing touches on "The Road to Baghdad." As the Army's chief operations officer, Arnold knew the civilians needed alternatives in case they wanted to help the Iraqi insurgents topple the Saddam Hussein regime and seize Baghdad.

The goal, Arnold wrote in the still-secret plan, would be to remove Saddam Hussein and the Baathists from power, install a friendly political regime, stabilize the situation, and "increase US/Western influence in SWA [Southwest Asia]/Middle East through long-term military presence in the region." Iraq would be left with a sufficient defense capability to ward off encroachments by Syria and Iran, but the forces loyal to Saddam Hussein would be destroyed once and for all.

Arnold outlined three possible routes for a march to the gates of the Iraqi capital, using Civil War names to mark the possible lines of advance. The Army's VII Corps would oversee the attack, though some of the forces could be drawn from the XVIII Airborne Corps as well. Logistics would be stretched. But Arnold figured that no more than two Army divisions and one armored calvary regiment would be necessary to surround the city, and he believed that the Army had enough fuel, trucks, and bridging equipment to pull it off. None of the American units would enter Baghdad. That would be left to American special forces and the insurgents.

Accompanying the plan was a prospective order:

USARCENT ATTACKS ON ORDER ACROSS THE EUPHRATES RIVER AND SEIZES KEY TERRAIN VICINITY BAGHDAD TO PROVIDE LEVERAGE TO POLITICAL CEASEFIRE NEGOTIATIONS.[13]

When Arnold showed the plan to Yeosock, he was aghast. Yeosock told Arnold to stop working on it. Why plan for renewed hostilities when the campaign had been declared a brilliant and unqualified success? The very existence of "The Road to Baghdad" implied that the triumph had been less than complete. While it raised the possibility of a decisive victory, it also opened the door to a protracted occupation of Iraq, which was not the kind of war Powell or Schwarzkopf wanted. What was done was done. The Army really had only one plan now: to sit

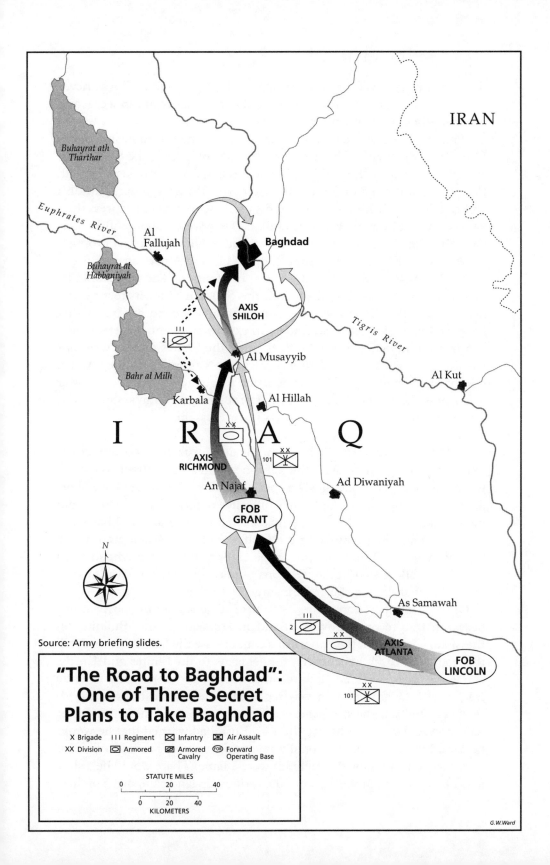

IRAN

Buhayrat ath Tharthar

Euphrates River

Al Fallujah

Baghdad

Buhayrat al Habbaniyah

AXIS SHILOH

2 III ⊘

Al Musayyib

Tigris River

Bahr al Milh

Al Hillah

Al Kut

Karbala

I R A Q

XX ◎

AXIS RICHMOND

XX ⊠ 101

An Najaf

Ad Diwaniyah

FOB GRANT

N

As Samawah

2 III ⊘

XX ◎

AXIS ATLANTA

FOB LINCOLN

XX ⊠ 101

Source: Army briefing slides.

"The Road to Baghdad": One of Three Secret Plans to Take Baghdad

| X Brigade | III Regiment | ⊠ Infantry | ⊠ Air Assault |
| XX Division | ◎ Armored | ▣ Armored Cavalry | FOB Forward Operating Base |

STATUTE MILES

0   20   40

0   20   40

KILOMETERS

G.W.Ward

tight until it deployed back home. "The Road to Baghdad" was never shown to Baker's team and was relegated to the archive of top secret and never-used contingency plans.

With the generals reluctant to take on any new responsibilities in Iraq, it was the Saudis who kept alive the idea of helping the Shiites and trying to overthrow the Saddam Hussein regime. When Baker met with Prince Saud, the Saudi foreign minister, and Prince Bandar, Riyadh's ambassador to Washington, the Saudis used the meeting to express their concern about how the war was ending. They were unhappy that Saddam Hussein was still in power and wanted to launch a covert program of weapons deliveries to the Shiites, much like the American support to the Afghan resistance during the Soviet occupation. The goal would be to stir up trouble for Baghdad until the Saddam Hussein regime was overthrown. The Americans, the Saudis argued, should not worry that supporting the Shiites would lead to an expansion of anti-American and pro-Iranian influence in the Gulf, because the Shiites of Iraq were not like the Shiites of Iran, the Saudis explained. Not only were they Arabs, but they had supported Saddam Hussein throughout a bitter eight-year war against Iran. The Saudis had their problems with Iran's Shiites, but they were more concerned about Saddam Hussein.

As Baker returned to Washington, the administration was at a crossroads. It could go along with the Safwan formula and extract American troops from the Gulf as quickly as possible. The allies would have liberated Kuwait and diminished Iraq's offensive potential. But there would be no guarantee that the regime that started the war and still harbored hopes of militarily dominating the Gulf would fall. Washington would have to rely on United Nations inspections to prevent Baghdad from reviving its effort to develop weapons of mass destruction. Washington would be abandoning the Iraqi insurgents to their fate.

Or the administration could try to take advantage of the postwar upheaval in Iraq to overthrow the Saddam Hussein regime. Building on the Saudi suggestion, the Americans could revise the Safwan accord, tell the Iraqis not to fly helicopters, funnel arms to the Shiites and Kurds, create military-protected enclaves in the south and north, and squeeze Iraq until Saddam Hussein was replaced. The administration had already established the predicate for further action. In the letter Baker had showed Tariq Aziz before the war, Bush had warned that he would hold Saddam Hussein personally responsible if the Kuwaiti oil fields were torched, and now the oil fields were aflame. There would be a slow and steady closing of the vise, not the furious air-land campaigns orchestrated by Powell and Schwarzkopf. The failure to close the gate on the Iraqi army would make this approach that much more of a challenge. Victory would not be assured and there would be no date certain for ending the war. But if the plan worked, the White House and its Saudi ally would have the definitive end it was looking for. The Saddam Hussein regime would be done for and would never again threaten the Gulf.

Bush, for his part, was initially pulled both ways. He wanted to bring Saddam Hussein to justice, but he had little ardor for continuing the fight. He did not want the Iraqis to attack the Shiites and Kurds with impunity, but he was afraid of the possible breakup of Iraq.

As the postwar arrangements were debated, the president and his men put aside the Saudi proposal for a covert program of assistance to the Shiites. Instead, the debate centered on the relatively narrow issue of whether the allies should impose a ban on helicopter flights.

During a March 13 visit to Ottawa to meet with Canadian Prime Minister Brian Mulroney, President Bush publicly denounced the Iraqi helicopter attacks on the Shiites as a violation of the cease-fire. The attacks had to stop, he warned, before there was any "permanence to the cease-fire." But after the press conference, Scowcroft and Haass quickly got Bush aside and explained that the Safwan accord did not ban Iraqi helicopter flights after all. Schwarzkopf had given the Iraqis a loophole.

For days afterward, administration officials continued to debate the pros and cons of repealing the Safwan exemption to fly helicopters.

The Bush administration was split. Wolfowitz favored action. F-15 pilots patrolling southern Iraq were watching helplessly as the Iraqis launched helicopter strikes against the Shiites. It did not matter what was agreed at Safwan. It was the allies who had won the war. If the military was worried about getting entangled in the fighting inside Iraq, the United States did not need to publicly take on the role of protector of the Shiites. Its public stance could be simply that it was rigorously enforcing the ban on postwar flights, he argued.

Cheney was sympathetic to the idea of shooting down the Iraqi helicopters, but more wary than his civilian aide of being drawn into the fighting inside Iraq.

Scowcroft, while unhappy that Schwarzkopf had allowed the Iraqis to fly their helicopters, was concerned that the insurgents might be too successful. When asked why the United States did not help the Shiites after the war, Scowcroft said the reason was "geopolitics."[14]

Just as he did before the Iraqi invasion of Kuwait, Scowcroft saw Iraq as a buffer against the expansion of Iranian power. "My view is there was a real danger in the first few days that the country would fall apart and I was fundamentally not interested in seeing that. But I did not want to see the converse: that the Iraqis should be able to go after the Shiites," Scowcroft recalled.

Baker was also notably unenthusiastic about getting involved in the fighting in Iraq.

Powell's position was clear. He did not want additional missions, and argued that stopping the helicopter assaults would not stop the fighting. If the American military was called on to stop air attacks, would it next have to stop ground attacks? Powell wanted to extract the American military from Iraq as quickly and cleanly as possible. To support the push for a speedy withdrawal of American forces from Iraq, Schwarzkopf publicly portrayed the fighting inside Iraq as an ancient quarrel with no heroes or villains, ignoring the fact that Iraq and Kuwait also had a long history of grievances.

Administration officials continued to debate the pros and cons of repealing the Safwan exemption to fly helicopters until Wolfowitz received an angry call from Powell, who complained that Pentagon civilians were telling the press that the question of enforcing a total ban on Iraqi helicopter flights was still open.

Shortly after that, the issue was closed. The Bush administration decided to pocket its battlefield success and let the fighting in Iraq run its course. Reporters were told that the White House had ruled out any intervention in the fighting inside Iraq, on the grounds that it would be opposed by the Arab allies even though it was Riyadh who wanted to pursue Saddam Hussein to the point of arming the Shiites. Reporters were also told that Turkey's president, Turqut Ozal, opposed continuing efforts to topple Saddam Hussein when Ozal's views were exactly the opposite.

"It was never our goal to break up Iraq. Indeed, we did not want that to happen, and most of our coalition partners (especially the Arabs) felt even stronger on the issue," Bush insisted after the war. "I did have a strong feeling that the Iraqi military, having been led to such a crushing defeat by Saddam, would rise up and rid themselves of him. We were concerned that the uprisings would sidetrack the overthrow of Saddam, by causing the Iraqi military to rally around him to prevent the breakup of the country. That may have been what actually happened."[15]

The president and his men had not given up on the "definitive" solution they were looking for, but they were not willing to take any further military action to achieve it. American casualties had been much lighter than expected. There had been 613 casualties from the fighting:

146 American soldiers were killed in action, 35 by friendly fire; 467 had been wounded, 72 by fire from friendly units. In the weeks after the war, top officials predicted that Saddam Hussein would be overthrown within a year. The expectation was that the Iraqi leader would be deposed but that no American lives or treasure would have to be risked to make it happen.

After the parades and celebrations were over, however, the Bush administration found that the war had not really ended. CENTCOM's war in the desert was over, but the confrontation between Washington and Baghdad persisted.

After pummeling the Shiites into submission, the Iraqis turned their full attention to the Kurds. By April, under pressure from Britain and Turkey, which wanted to avoid an influx of new Kurdish refugees, the United States established a militarily protected enclave for Kurdish forces in northern Iraq to stop Iraqi attacks in that part of the country. American air and ground forces were now committed to the defense of the Kurds in northern Iraq.

Frustrated by Saddam Hussein's tenacious hold on power, the Bush administration said in May 1991 that economic sanctions would be maintained until Saddam Hussein was out of power.

Only after the war would Washington discover from Iraqi defectors that the Iraqi program to develop weapons of mass destruction was more extensive than it had anticipated. The economic embargo and the United Nations monitors became the main barriers to the rebuilding of Iraqi military power.

"Saddam Hussein's plan to acquire nuclear weapons had been slowed, not halted, and Iraqi leaders are firmly committed to rejuvenating it," the Defense Intelligence Agency noted in a March 1991 classified assessment. With 2,000 foreign-trained scientists, 18,000 engineers, and a network of Jordanian front companies, it was not a threat to be taken lightly. "Should sanctions and intrusive U.N. inspections cease, Iraq could produce a nuclear weapon in 2 to 4 years," the DIA report said, and added that "despite war losses, Iraq still has a number of TU-22 Blinder bombers and MiG-25/Foxbat fighter-bombers with sufficient ranges and payloads to deliver nuclear weapons in theater."

The DIA forecast that in the absence of economic sanctions and United Nations inspections it would take three to five years for Baghdad to reconstitute its chemical weapons program and five to eight years to rebuild its program to develop biological weapons. As for Iraq's Scud

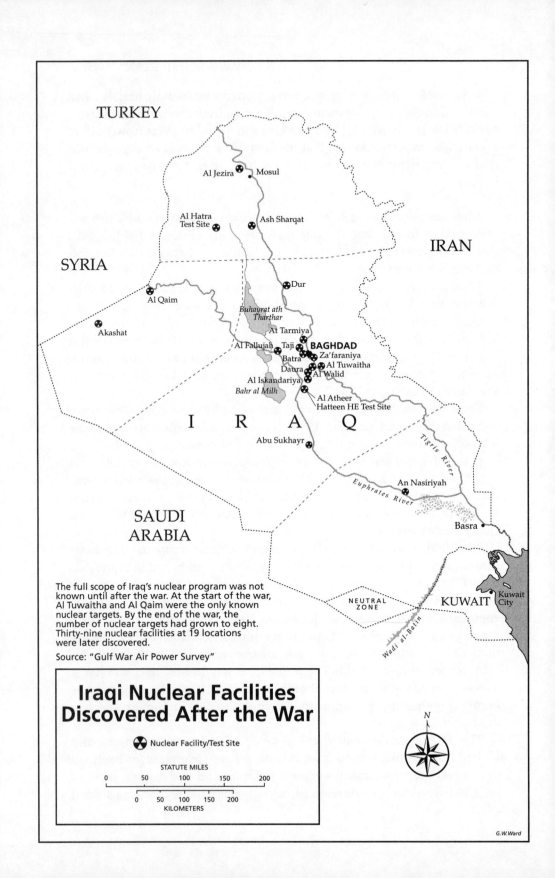

TURKEY

Al Jezira   ● Mosul

Al Hatra
Test Site ☢   ☢ Ash Sharqat

SYRIA

☢ Al Qaim   ● Dur

☢
Akashat

*Buhayrat ath
Tharthar*

At Tarmiya

Al Fallujah ☢ Taji ☢   **BAGHDAD**
Batra ☢   ☢ Za'faraniya
Daura ☢   ☢ Al Tuwaitha
☢ Al Walid
Al Iskandariya ☢

Bahr al Milh

Al Atheer
Hatteen HE Test Site

I R A Q

IRAN

Abu Sukhayr ☢

Tigris River

Euphrates River   An Nasiriyah ●

SAUDI
ARABIA

Basra ●

The full scope of Iraq's nuclear program was not
known until after the war. At the start of the war,
Al Tuwaitha and Al Qaim were the only known
nuclear targets. By the end of the war, the
number of nuclear targets had grown to eight.
Thirty-nine nuclear facilities at 19 locations
were later discovered.

NEUTRAL
ZONE

KUWAIT   Kuwait
City

Source: "Gulf War Air Power Survey"

Wadi al-Batin

Iraqi Nuclear Facilities
Discovered After the War

☢ Nuclear Facility/Test Site

N

STATUTE MILES
0   50   100   150   200

0   50   100   150   200
KILOMETERS

G.W.Ward

missiles, American intelligence concluded after the war that Iraq had hidden many of them.[16]

In the immediate aftermath of the war, Iraq also tried to rebuild its conventional forces. Its army had shrunk from seventy to thirty-one divisions. The Republican Guard was reduced from twelve divisions to seven, most of which were garrisoned near Baghdad. Even so, the Iraqi divisions were not at full strength.

While the offensive potential of Iraq's army against its neighbors was limited, the forces were sufficient to keep Saddam Hussein's enemies at bay.

"Because much of its repair/rebuild infrastructure received little or no damage during the war, Baghdad has been actively repairing its ground equipment," the DIA noted in a classified assessment. "The Iraqis appear to have an adequate supply of munitions supplemented by production from undamaged ammunition plants and damaged facilities that have been rebuilt. Moreover, Baghdad has started reconstructing its artillery production facilities, and portions of its military electronics production plants may be operational."[17]

Just as Iraq sought to rebuild its military capability, it repaired much of the civilian damage. The damage done to Iraq's electrical grid was repaired far more quickly than the West anticipated. The Al Hartha plant near Basra, for example, was rebuilt in 270 days, less than the three years originally projected by the Iraqis.[18]

In January 1992, the Pentagon completed a report on Iraqi war crimes, which alleged that 1,082 Kuwaitis had been killed by execution and torture during the Iraqi occupation. The report also stated that Iraq had abused all the prisoners of war it captured, making a special effort to ferret out Jewish prisoners. Iraq also damaged the environment by releasing oil into the Perian Gulf and destroying Kuwaiti oil wells. But the Bush administration never released the Pentagon report, thus avoiding focusing attention to the fact that Saddam Hussein was still in power and that there was little Washington could do to bring him to justice.

Finally, a year and a half after the Bush administration decided not to help the Shiites in the south, it reversed itself and imposed a no-flight zone in southern Iraq to protect the Shiites from air attack and demonstrate that Iraq would not have full sovereignty over its territory as long as Saddam Hussein remained in power. But unlike the enclave for the Kurds, the measure fell short of what was needed to protect the Shiites. Circumventing the flight ban, the Iraqi army began draining the marshes in the Euphrates valley and used its ground troops to press the attacks on the Shiites. More than 10,000 Shiites had sought refuge in

Saudi refugee camps after the war. Although some were resettled in the United States, Amnesty International later reported that many had been repatriated to Iraq by the Saudis against their will.[19]

In its last weeks in power, the Bush administration engaged in a series of attacks on Iraqi air defense sites and on a military factory in Baghdad that made components for Iraq's nuclear program after Baghdad challenged the no-flight zones in northern and southern Iraq and sought to block demands for United Nations weapons inspections. But the style of the allied military attacks communicated caution as much as strength. The tit-for-tat strikes bore little resemblance to the punishing, all-out, day-and-night attacks of the Gulf War. The strikes were not militarily decisive, nor were they always well planned. Much of the operational art that went into the elaborately planned air campaign appeared to have been forgotten.

Worried about the Iraqi air defenses, CENTCOM's new commanders — Schwarzkopf, Horner, Glosson, and the other top military officers had either retired or moved on to other assignments — restricted the time the warplanes spent over the targets. The first attack, which was launched on January 13, 1993, against air defense targets in southern Iraq, was compressed into fifteen minutes. By limiting that attack to a single, brief raid, the American planes were forced to lob two laser-guided bombs at once, a procedure that increased the number of errant bombs. Three of the four surface-to-air missile batteries the Americans tried to destroy were missed, forcing the allies to go back almost a week later to hit the targets again.

Even the cruise missile attack against the Za' Faraniyah complex, which made machinery for Iraq's nuclear program, launched four days later, sent a mixed message. By launching the attack, the United States showed that it was willing to bring the fighting to the outskirts of the Iraqi capital. But the White House explained that cruise missiles were used because Washington feared that using planes might result in the loss of a pilot, thus highlighting American worry about challenging Iraq's rebuilt air defenses. And in launching the cruise missile attack on the factory, the Navy failed to coordinate the launches from the Red Sea and the Persian Gulf so that the Tomahawk missiles would arrive at the same time. This gave the Iraqis an opportunity to shoot down one of the missiles. It crashed into the al-Rasheed Hotel, destroying part of the structure and giving Baghdad a propaganda coup.

During the 1992 election campaign, candidate Bill Clinton criticized Bush for not pursuing war crimes trials against the Iraqi leaders. But when he was elected, he had no better plan for influencing developments inside Iraq and curtailing the Saddam Hussein regime's attacks on the Shiites than did his predecessor.

Clinton insisted that the sanctions be maintained, against the increasing opposition of France, Turkey, and Russia, and carried on the Bush administration's pattern of limited strikes. After American intelligence determined that Saddam Hussein had launched a plot to kill former President Bush during a visit to Kuwait, Clinton ordered a cruise missile strike on Baghdad's intelligence headquarters, which had already been attacked during the war.

The low-intensity military campaign against Saddam Hussein was not without cost. In April 1994, two F-15Cs mistakenly shot down two Army helicopters ferrying allied officers to meet with the Kurds in northern Iraq in one of the military's worst episodes of friendly fire.

CENTCOM's lightning war was over. It had been billed as a 100-hour blitz, but three years later it was still an unfinished war.

Recalled Gordon Brown, the foreign service officer who served as Schwarzkopf's chief foreign policy adviser at CENTCOM, "We never did have a plan to terminate the war."[20]

Epilogue

THREE WEEKS after the war ended, Schwarzkopf went to visit Walt Boomer and the rest of the Marine high command for an off-the-record discussion.

The war was over, but a new battle for the public mind had begun. The CENTCOM chief had worked hard to shape the public's impression during the war. The press has been controlled and the Iraqi threat painted in the darkest hues. Schwarzkopf had even weighed the public relations factor in planning military operations: he had told the Marines that one drawback of a Marine raid on Faylakah Island was that the media might portray the quick insertion and withdrawal of an amphibious force as a defeat for the allies.

Now Schwarzkopf was determined to come out ahead in the public relations battles. The general recalled how the book writers and the journalists had dissected the Grenada operation and highlighted its faults.

"Watch out what you say. Why do I say that? Because we have people interviewing everyone they can get their hands on. They are out writing their books," Schwarzkopf warned, according to a transcript the Marines kept of the meeting. "Just think of the reputation of the United States military, what it is today, compared to what it was six months ago. I think we ought to be very proud of what we did here, and don't allow those bastards to rob us of that."[1]

With their place in the history books at stake, the commanders sought to shape the war's legacy. So did the military services, as they struggled over the declining military budget.

Having urged his commanders not to cooperate with authors,

Schwarzkopf turned around and wrote a book, which gave himself the lion's share of the credit for the allies' success. He also told subordinates that he had not second-guessed his commanders once the war was under way, ignoring his upbraiding of Franks. "I am a centralized planner and a decentralized executor. Just that simple," Schwarzkopf boasted to Boomer and his staff. "You have to have confidence in your subordinates. If you don't have, you get rid of them, and get someone that does. You don't micromanage on the battlefield because nobody has a better idea than the guy fighting the battle."

But even with the benefit of reflection, Schwarzkopf's book failed to recognize the significance of the battle of Khafji and how it had challenged CENTCOM's basic assumption that the Iraqis would stand and fight. Nor did it acknowledge how his plan to let the Marines launch an all-out attack to the gates of Kuwait City while holding back the main Army attack made it easier for the Iraqis to get away. Instead, he blamed Franks for the failure to complete the destruction of the Republican Guard.

For Powell, the Gulf War was a way to restore the prestige and status the American military had lost during the Vietnam War. After the war, Powell oversaw the publication of the Joint Chiefs of Staff manual on military doctrine that touted the Gulf War as a "triumph of joint operational art." Powell was right that there was much of which to be proud. But when embarrassing examples of problems began to surface, Powell privately cautioned one Pentagon-based general against revealing disputes within the military family.

Neither Powell nor Schwarzkopf, however, had the last word, and the plethora of competing accounts from within the military establishment soon produced a cacophony.

The Army responded to Schwarzkopf's criticisms in a book-length account, entitled *Certain Victory,* that defended Franks's generalship and suggested that any misunderstandings stemmed from Schwarzkopf's inability to grasp the complexity of the battlefield from his distant Riyadh command post.[2]

To Schwarzkopf's consternation, the Army ignored his recommendation that Waller, not Franks, later be made the four-star head of the Army's Training and Doctrine Command. ("History is being revised to cover up the fact that Franks was not a very aggressive commander," Schwarzkopf said later, referring to the official Army accounts of the war. "It makes you feel bad that the institution you are serving is stretching its integrity."[3])

In an attempt to magnify the Army's accomplishments and minimize its shortcomings, the Army study claimed that airpower had had little effect on the Republican Guard. The Army account also asserted that most of the Iraqi army was north of Basra before the XVIII Airborne and VII Corps had a chance to cut it off. But that analysis was contradicted by a comprehensive CIA assessment, based on surveillance photos, that showed that the bulk of the Iraqi force that escaped was still south of Basra and in the Army's path at war's end.

The Air Force, for its part, portrayed the war as a vindication of the long quest to achieve a victory through airpower, boasting that airpower had destroyed Iraq's weapons of mass destruction, severed its lines of communication, and cut off the Iraqi troops. Lt. Gen. Charles Horner also sought to burnish his own record. The Air Force commander, who had rebuffed John Warden's Instant Thunder plan, never acknowledged Warden's role as an architect of the air campaign. Horner also told Congress that he was not aware of any disputes within CENTCOM, overlooking his threat to have Steve Arnold evicted from the Kuwaiti theater because of his complaints that the Army-nominated targets were not being hit.

On the whole, however, the Air Force was much more forthright than the Army. Air Force Secretary Donald Rice commissioned an independent survey of the use of airpower during the war — the "Gulf War Air Power Survey" — which in a scholarly and analytical way dissected the lessons of the war and defined airpower's limits. The study's analysis of the problems in hunting Scud missiles, neutralizing the Iraqi command structure, and destroying Iraq's weapons of mass destruction were not welcome by everyone in the Air Force. In an April 1993 memo, the official Air Force historian, Richard Hallion, himself the author of a book touting the use of airpower in the Gulf, suggested that the report be withheld. But the Air Force leadership, to its credit, ignored Hallion's suggestion and published the lengthy critique.[4]

The Marines, whose success had surprised Schwarzkopf and unintentionally contributed to the unraveling of CENTCOM's plan, also engaged in a measure of self-criticism. In a series of unclassified after-action reports, the Marines discussed their problems in clearing minefields and acknowledged their limited ability to use precision-guided weapons. The tensions between the Marine commandant and the Corps's top commander in the Gulf, however, was kept under wraps.

Navy officials, resentful at being overshadowed by the Air Force, were quick to highlight the glitches in the centralized system the Air Force generals established for running the war. Still, the service quietly acted on the lessons of the Gulf conflict. Navy officials acknowledged that their decision to stay aloof from joint military operations and to command its Gulf force from sea, instead of from Riyadh, was a mistake. Soon after the war, the Navy moved its one-star representative to CENTCOM from Honolulu to Tampa. More significantly, it revised its doctrine, deciding to concentrate on littoral warfare instead of using its carriers primarily to mount strikes deep into the enemy homeland.

It was not only the military leaders who tried to shape history. The civilian leadership of the Pentagon oversaw the official Defense Department history of the war. The politic document steered clear of the war's sharpest controversies. All services were afforded equal billing in what was deemed to be an unqualified victory, and the report sidestepped the issue of whether the war was ended prematurely before the military objectives were reached. When a senior civilian official, I. Lewis Libby, interviewed Schwarzkopf, he pointedly avoided the issue of termination.

The American defense establishment was not alone in its concern with the verdict of history.

Prince Khalid also sought to embellish the history of the Arab members of the coalition. In a long statement — "The Gulf War: Setting the Record Straight" — Khalid rejected any claims of faint-heartedness by the Syrian members of the coalition, made by Schwarzkopf publicly and privately by other American officers, and claimed that CENTCOM failed to provide adequate air support during the battle of Khafji.[5]

In Iraq, Saddam Hussein sought to capitalize on his defeat, restoring the morale in his army with lavish pay and awards and blaming Iraq's deteriorating economy on the American-inspired sanctions, not on the war. Turning history on its head, the Iraqi leader held up the war as a victory, boasting that he fought a brilliant delaying action in Kuwait, thus preventing the allies from crossing the Euphrates into Iraq's interior. What other army but the Iraqi could have achieved such a feat? he boasted. In the face of over half a million enemies, Iraq's army was still intact and the nation was still under the leadership of Saddam Hussein.

Emboldened by his ability to hold on to power, Saddam Hussein also claimed in the months after the war that his principal mistake was that he was not audacious enough, citing his failure to invade Saudi Arabia to preempt the American military buildup and his failure to exploit the hostages. But those remarks showed that the Iraqi leader still failed to appreciate the extent of his miscalculation.

If Saddam Hussein had been less audacious and contented himself with seizing the Rumaila oil field or the Bubiyan and Warbah islands, he probably could have pressed the Kuwaitis into making financial concessions, intimidated Saudi Arabia, and undermined the United States' credibility in the Gulf while avoiding a direct confrontation with the American military, Schwarzkopf and other American officials acknowledged. But by seizing all of Kuwait he overplayed his hand. He provoked Washington at an ideal time for U.S. forces. The American military had reached a high level of training and technological proficiency to counter the Soviets only to see its enemy disappear, but had yet to undergo the deep cuts mandated by budgetary pressures in Washington.

Even the Russians sought to redefine the war. In their study of the war the Russian military vigorously assailed any suggestion that Iraq's Soviet-supplied weapons were ineffective as a "propaganda trick by the West" and blamed Iraqi incompetence for the defeat. The Russians acknowledged the value of the allies' high-tech weapons systems, surveillance planes, and spy satellites, but also underscored their limitations.

"Reconnaissance data did not always reflect the actual Iraqi armed forces losses and deceived the higher political leadership of the United States relative to the level of Iraq's combat potential, which led to adoption of incorrect decisions," the Russian report stated. "Thus, basing itself on this very reconnaissance data concerning the 'unacceptable losses by Iraq in men and materiel,' U.S. President G. Bush made the decision to halt military actions on the ground, literally four days after they had begun. All this speaks to the underestimation of the capabilities of the enemy due to the low reliability of intelligence information."[6]

As for George Bush, he portrayed the Persian Gulf War as the prototype of the post–cold war conflict. Bush predicted that future adversaries who studied it would think twice before challenging the United States.

"I think because of what has happened, we won't have to use U.S. forces around the world," Bush said the day after the war. "I think when we say something that is objectively correct, like don't take over a neighbor, or you're going to bear some responsibility, people are going to listen because I think out of all this will be a newfound — put it this way, a reestablished credibility for the United States of America."

To some extent, Bush was right. The respect for American military technology and the quality of American troops was greatly enhanced.

In the Middle East, where the nations had the closest view of the fighting, the conflict had a profound influence on the region. As a consequence of the air and ground campaigns, and the regimen of United Nations inspections, postwar Iraq was no longer an imminent nuclear menace and a threat to its neighbors. The United States had sent a message that oil was the lifeblood of the modern world and that Washington would do whatever was necessary to make sure it flowed.

Still, the failure to topple the Saddam Hussein regime meant that Iraq was still a potential menace to the Kurds, whom Washington had promised to protect, and a daily threat to the Shiites, who were afforded only partial protection, and to other states in the region. Nearly four years after the war, the United Nations embargo on Iraq was coming under increasing challenge in the Security Council from Turkey, France, and Russia, who saw economic benefits in dealing with Baghdad. The difficulty in sustaining the embargo and the cadre of trained scientists in Iraq posed the risk that Baghdad might be able to revive its programs to build weapons of mass destruction.

And while American ties to the Persian Gulf states were strengthened, the resistance to an overt American role in the region continued. The Saudis blocked the Bush administration's plans to store a division's worth of American armor equipment at King Khalid Military City and declined to acknowledge publicly that American Air Force planes were launching patrols of southern Iraq from Saudi airfields. CENTCOM's plans to establish a forward headquarters in Bahrain or other Gulf states were quietly dropped.

More broadly, despite President Bush's hope that the Gulf War would send a message of American resolve to troublemakers around the world, the conflict has become an anomaly in a world dominated by small wars in Somalia, Bosnia, and other distant trouble spots in which American credibility has been an early casualty.

But the legacy of the Gulf War will be determined not only by the actions of its generals, but by its implications for the future. If the conflict in the Gulf was not the war to end all wars, it has had enduring consequences and offered military and political lessons. It was a laboratory for the American military's new weapons and fighting doctrines, a test of the services' abilities to work together, an object lesson in the failure of deterrence and in the problems of war termination.

LIMITATIONS OF THE POWELL DOCTRINE

Shaped by the Vietnam experience, the American military fashioned a winning strategy. Overwhelming force would be used. The enemy would be given no sanctuary; nor would there be any diplomatic pauses to let enemy forces catch their breath. It would be the generals, not civilian targeteers in Washington, who would pick the targets. A decisive victory would be achieved and American forces would be quickly withdrawn so as not to become entangled in the war's messy aftermath.

American power, it was said, would be like a raging thunderstorm, not a steady shower. The doctrine was applied in the invasions of Panama and Grenada with good results. Powell and Schwarzkopf made sure that it was applied to the Gulf as well. There was much in the approach that contributed to the success in the Gulf. With their unrelenting air and ground attacks, the allies seized and maintained the initiative. The air strikes against Baghdad and other targets in central Iraq and the armor operations deep into the Iraqi desert surprised and confounded the Iraqis. The Iraqi military was defeated at an astoundingly small cost in allied lives.

But the iron link between the use of military force and a decisive outcome had its political costs. First, it inhibited the Bush administration in August 1990 from maneuvering military forces in the Arabian Sea and Persian Gulf to deter Iraqi attacks on Kuwait and contributed to the failure of deterrence. When civilians at the State Department and the Pentagon recommended such demonstrations of American power, Powell fended them off.

Second, the Powell doctrine contributed to the decision to bring the war to a premature close and to the muddled ending and left Washington without a means for influencing events in postwar Iraq.

The military impulse to end the war as soon as a "victory" was achieved, to get out as quickly as possible, and to view support of the insurgents in southern Iraq not as a way to squeeze the Saddam Hussein regime but as a snare limited American military power as an instrument for shaping and enforcing the peace. Powell's all-or-nothing doctrine of decisive force not only is insufficient for many of the smoldering conflicts the United States faces today, where the military is called on not to win a decisive "victory" but to support diplomacy, protect peacekeepers, or carry out humanitarian tasks, it also has its limitations when it comes to ending major "high-intensity" wars.

UNREALISTIC EXPECTATIONS ABOUT CASUALTIES

The Gulf conflict created new expectations for low casualties in warfare in the mind of the public and within the military establishment. Historically, the United States has been willing to shed considerable blood to win what it viewed as "wars of survival," such as World War II.

Loss was incidental to the mission. The United States liberally sacrificed its own sons and had no compunction about destroying its enemies. But one question raised by the Gulf War is whether commanders can be ruthless enough to pursue the enemy to the limit in the television age when the stakes are less than national survival.

In overseeing the air and ground campaigns, Powell and the White House were concerned not only about holding down American losses and civilian casualties, but about limiting the destruction of enemy combatants, as was evident in Washington's concern over the press reports about the "Highway of Death" and the Bush administration's decision to end the ground war at 100 hours and abjure going to Baghdad. This decision helped the American public lose touch with the reality of war — a grim, ghastly, and bloody affair. The American military has become a victim of its own success.

Concern over holding down casualties — from enemy attack and friendly fire — has become a constant in American planning for war. The assumption in the Pentagon today is that any military incursion must be low in cost to be politically feasible. While low casualties are desirable, the expectation that losses will be minimal on a fluid battlefield may inhibit the future use of force as an instrument of national power.

The expectation of low casualties has also undermined President Bush's hope that the Gulf War would send a message of American resolve to troublemakers around the world. In Somalia, Gen. Mohammed Farah Aidid used Saddam Hussein's strategy of trying to draw out the confrontation, bleed the Americans, and wait for public opinion to turn against military involvement. With no oil supplies at stake and the Americans supporting the mission more out of charity than animus toward a third-world tyrant, Aidid's approach worked. In Bosnia, Serb forces tightened their hold on the territory they wrested from the Muslims, knowing that NATO would limit itself to episodic threats to launch air strikes.

THE ALL-VOLUNTEER MILITARY IS A SUCCESS

The war confirmed the military's personnel policy of relying on a well-trained volunteer force. The power and effectiveness of American troops, weapons, and equipment was so impressive as to leave no doubt that the United States is the most powerful military nation on earth. The United States brought to the battlefield an integrated system of sensors, stealth, electronic suppression techniques, and precision munitions designed to counter Soviet-style warfare on the European continent. It proved its worth in the desert. High technology was key to American military dominance.

The other strong suit the United States brought to the battlefield was the quality of its armed forces. Never in the history of the republic has a more competent and proficient military been fielded. The high quality displayed by all the services is a function of four things: high-caliber personnel, professional education, realistic and continuous training, and leadership.

The United States military operates with a pyramidal organizational structure. But while the structure is rigid, the execution is flexible in that subordinates are expected to take the action necessary to meet the mission goals. This fosters innovation and creativity.

The effectiveness of this system was demonstrated in countless ways during the Gulf War as service personnel coped with the unexpected. Without such a system of leadership, even the best weaponry and equipment in the hands of well-trained troops would not have been brought to bear effectively. As the result of this system, the logistical and operational deficiencies that emerged during the course of the deployment and war were solved by the initiative of scores of unnamed, unknown, and frequently unrewarded enlisted men and women and junior officers.

MILITARY REFORMS TO ENCOURAGE JOINT SERVICE WARFARE ARE INCOMPLETE

"Jointness" became the military's mantra after the passage of the Goldwater-Nichols Act in 1986. There was no intent to erase the differences in service philosophies and cultures. The idea was that the unique characteristics and strengths of each service could be molded to complement one another so that the whole would be more than the sum of its parts.

The reforms also strengthened the role of the chairman of the JCS and of field commanders. As a result, Powell wielded power and influence beyond that exercised by previous chairmen. His fellow members of the Joint Chiefs were relegated to onlookers who simply provided the forces. As for Schwarzkopf, he was the king of his domain. During the war, no serious attempt was made by any of the services to go around Schwarzkopf. A service chief could not even visit the Gulf without his permission.

But the Gulf War showed there is much to be done if the services are to operate in a truly joint manner.

At the outset of the Gulf crisis, Schwarzkopf himself violated the spirit of jointness. He imported a special team of planners — the Jedis — to draw up the ground offensive strategy. They initially excluded a Marine representative, even though the Marines had almost all of their combat forces committed to the campaign, but they invited a British officer. It was not a deliberate slight, but an unconscious reflection of service culture. For decades, the Army had focused on Europe. It had more in common with a long-standing NATO ally than it did with a service with which it rarely associated.

The air war was also riddled with interservice tensions. To run the air war, a Joint Forces Air Component Commander was created. The Air Force dominated the process. Its planners believed in centralized control of airpower and attacks against targets critical to the overall campaign, but the Army, Marine Corps, and Navy were unhappy with the system. The Air Force believed it was weakening the enemy by hitting Iraqi forces at home and within the "kill boxes" it drew on battlefield maps, but the Army and Marines complained that specific targets were ignored that they wanted to be hit. With the services at odds, the Marines tried to cut some corners by withholding planes from the Air Force–run campaign. And in the final days of the war, the Air Force was frustrated when the Army moved the Fire Support Coordination Line, which defined the area in which air strikes could not be carried out without coordination of ground commanders, so far forward that aircraft could not freely attack targets fleeing from the advancing allied troops.

At sea, the Navy and the Marines had their differences. The Navy was oriented around the aircraft carrier and had little interest in planning amphibious operations. The Marines had to dispatch a special team of amphibious planners from the United States to get the Navy to think seriously about attacks from the sea.

Even within the Army, there were differences that influenced performance. Heavy in armor, the Germany-based VII Corps was organized, trained, and equipped to fight the Soviet Army. Meticulous planning and deliberate synchronization were its hallmarks. Based in the United States as a central reserve, the XVIII Corps was not NATO-oriented, but ready to go anywhere in the world against any enemy.

The cultural differences between the services and Schwarzkopf's decentralized command policy, which gave maximum freedom of action within the framework of his overall plan, combined to frustrate the allies' carefully crafted strategy to destroy the Republican Guard. The problem was compounded by Powell and Schwarzkopf's failure to see Khafji as the defining moment in the war and by the services' differing interpretations of the battle. The Air Force was convinced that Khafji showed the failure of the Iraqi army to maneuver on the battlefield in the face of allied air superiority. The Marines were convinced of it too. They had taken the measure of the Iraqis at Khafji. But the Army, and the CENTCOM staff, continued their preparations as if the Iraqis were determined to put up a stiff fight.

CENTCOM planners counted on the Marines holding the enemy in place in southern Iraq so that VII Corps could launch its planned seven-to-ten-day offensive on the following day. But the rapid Marine advance on the first day of the ground war knocked the VII Corps's timetable into a cocked hat. The Marine action should not have been a surprise given the commitment the Marines have to offensive operations. Either Schwarzkopf should not have yielded to the Marines' entreaty that they be allowed to undertake a major ground offensive against the Iraqi forces defending Kuwait, or the Marines should have been held back until the main Army offensive was under way.

Doctrinal differences among the services still exist and are frequently papered over. The services that depend most on support from their sister services — the Army is a prime example — champion jointness, at least as long as their central role is preserved. Services capable of semi-autonomous action, like the Air Force, tend to go their separate ways. While the differences among the services are often an asset, it is not enough to let the services fight as they see fit. An effort must be made to harmonize their plans and operations.

THE POTENTIAL AND LIMITATIONS OF AIRPOWER

Since the dawn of military aviation, airpower advocates have sought victory through airpower. Appalled by the carnage of trench warfare, they looked to the airplane as the key to future warfare.

Conventional airpower played a critical but unfulfilled role in World War II and the Korean War. Airpower never severed supply lines during the Vietnam War. When it came to the Gulf War, however, airpower advocates claimed that technology had finally caught up with doctrine and that air warfare would finally make good on its potential. With the advent of new and precise systems to acquire and destroy targets with a single missile, Air Force theoreticians and strategists maintained that the war could be won entirely through the air. Billy Mitchell's dream would be fulfilled.

The air campaign was impressive. Even though the air traffic within the theater was extremely heavy, with different types of aircraft and helicopters from different services and countries flying to and fro, the airspace management systems were effective and remarkably, there were no mid-air collisions during the war.

The Air Force did deliver on its promise to make any ground offensive a walkover. Several factors contributed to the collapse of the Iraqi army, including poor leadership and lack of motivation in the face of the international coalition. Nonetheless, the air attacks made it impossible for the Iraqis to mount an effective defense. Airpower crippled the Iraqi war machine. It neutralized sophisticated air defense systems, destroyed bridges and road junctions, destroyed the Iraqi artillery, and made it difficult for Iraq to maneuver forces on the battlefield. While the success of the bombing campaign against the Iraqi forces varied from unit to unit, it delivered a devastating psychological blow. Airpower did this at negligible cost to itself. The ground war was won in four days; but it was preceded by five weeks of bombing.

But the air campaign was not perfect, and it did not fulfill the Air Force dream of victory through airpower. The Iraqis proved adept at deception and camouflage. An air campaign can be no better than the intelligence it is based on, and the intelligence community was unaware of the extent of Iraq's nuclear program and facilities. The same was true of its Scud inventory. And as it turned out, more damage was done to the economic infrastructure than was intended. Electrical systems that were critical to Saddam Hussein's command and control were also critical to civilized urban life.

More important, if war is an extension of politics, it should have achieved a political success comparable to the military one, defeating Saddam Hussein as well as his army. The air-war planners aimed at winning the war by destroying Iraq's governing infrastructure and causing Saddam Hussein's overthrow.

The air-war planners chafed under the restrictions imposed by Powell on bombing missions in Baghdad. Even so, the air campaign was much more intense and sustained than John Warden's Instant Thunder plan. Saddam Hussein survived the war with his political and security apparatus intact. The Gulf War confirmed the Air Force's ever-increasing ability to destroy military things and people. But airpower had not demonstrated an ability to change governments.

FOR WANT OF A NAIL

In war, as in other human affairs, it is the little things that count. Benefiting from the Reagan military buildup, the military used the most advanced high technology against the Iraqis. It used F-117 stealth bombers, surveillance drones, cruise missiles, and "fire-finder" radars that pinpointed enemy artillery and diesel-powered tanks. The widespread use of handheld global positioning system devices enabled the Army to determine its position in the vast Iraqi desert, a feat that eluded the Iraqis.

The high-tech weapons were not perfect. Some "smart bombs" missed their targets. But they succeeded beyond any reasonable expectation and helped the allies trump their enemy. The criticism that America's weapons were too complex and fragile to work in war was dispelled.

But the weak side of the Reagan military buildup was also exposed. In its single-minded pursuit of high-tech weaponary, the military ignored some unglamorous but essential areas.

The Marines lacked the mine-clearing gear they needed to breach Iraqi fortifications. Given the proliferation of mines around the world, it was a glaring deficiency and the Marines were forced to turn to the Israelis for help.

The Navy also lacked the capability to sweep mines at sea, which would have made it difficult to carry out an amphibious landing had one been required. Its recommendation was to destroy the Iraq minesweepers before the mines were laid — a preemptive policy that was politically infeasible as a matter of coalition politics and was a poor substitute for counter-mine capability.

Nor did the Navy have a sufficient number of ships to rapidly transport American forces to the distant Gulf.

Air Force pilots lacked radios to communicate with search and rescue teams without giving away their positions. And pilots were captured as a result. Had the Gulf War occurred just a few years later, the service would have been without the F-4Gs that contributed mightily to the air campaign. The Air Force plan — since revised — was to retire the planes.

The Army had plenty of 5,000-gallon fueling trucks, but not enough HEMTTs, special vehicles that could plow through the desert to deliver fuel to thirsty divisions. Its communications were distressingly fragile for fast-paced armor operations.

Ever-declining military budgets raise the risk that deficiencies will be compounded, not fixed. Mundane areas of national defense, which do little to burnish the services' prestige and force structure during peacetime, are vital during war.

WAR TERMINATION

The untidy end to the conflict showed that it is not enough to plan a war. Civilian and military officials must also plan for the peace that follows. Civilian policy-makers also had not given much thought to the possibility that Iraq might break apart, let alone to the prospect that Saddam Hussein's foes might call on the allies for protection. Their failure to anticipate the upheaval in Iraq, their ignorance of the Shiites, and the White House's ambivalence about committing itself to toppling Saddam Hussein reflected the administration's absence of a clear political strategy for postwar Iraq — all of which was reflected in the negotiations at Safwan.

The decision to end the war can be analyzed at several levels. In terms of CENTCOM's military objectives, the decision to terminate the ground war at 100 hours was too hastily made amid the confusing swirl of battlefield events. From the start, CENTCOM's objective was not just to defeat the Republican Guard, render it "combat ineffective," or chase it out of southern Iraq, but to destroy the force. But that goal was not fulfilled. Half of the Republican Guard got away.

Bush administration officials later explained the allied advance was halted to avoid — as Cheney put it — the spectable of "piling on" and to hold down American casualties. American field commanders later said, however, they could have driven to the gates of Basra and cut off much of the Iraqi army without a wholesale slaughter. The Iraqis could also have been encouraged to abandon their vehicles and walk north if the word had been passed to them in time. Instead, one day's worth of news reports about the Iraqi soldiers caught on the "Highway of Death" helped persuade the Bush administration to end the war.

Some senior administration officials said that they would not have supported ending the war so soon had they been informed that half of the Republican Guard tanks were likely to escape. But obtaining accurate battle damage assessments had been a problem throughout the war when the Iraqi troops were hunkered down and even more of a problem once the American and Iraqi troops were on the move. Powell and the White House decided to end the war based on initial, fragmentary intelligence reports instead of waiting for a fuller accounting.

In terms of the administration's overall political strategy, the premature end to the war was defensible if the goal was restricted to liberating

Kuwait, blunting Saddam Hussein's offensive power, and allowing his government to use his diminished military to prevent the breakup of the country. But if the administration's aim was also to undermine the Saddam Hussein regime and afford a measure of protection to the Shiites, two objectives Washington specifically embraced after the war, the failure to complete the destruction of the Republican Guard detracted from those goals since it gave Saddam Hussein more loyal troops to suppress his enemies.

The United States also erred in renouncing any intention of going to Baghdad, a reassurance aimed at our Arab allies. This self-denial simplified things for Saddam Hussein when the ground war got under way. A "survivor," he then knew that he did not have to worry about the allies toppling him. All he would have to deal with was any internal disturbance. This he could do if his political, military, and security infrastructure remained in place even if he did lose Kuwait. This dictated that he simply salvage as much of his field army as possible for use at home.

Importantly, the decisions on ending the war also highlighted the failure to keep political and military objectives in synch. In summoning the nation to war, Bush had described Saddam Hussein as "worse than Hitler" and painted the conflict as a Manichaean struggle between good and evil. But when it came to waging war against the new "Hitler" the allied armies, as it were, stopped at the Rhine. The Bush administration ruled out the occupation of Baghdad, stopped the Army and Air Force assault before it had completed its destruction of the Republican Guard, interrupted the air war in downtown Baghdad after the destruction of the Al Firdos bunker, and failed to protect the insurgents or arm the resistance.

The Bush administration's ambivalence over the postwar settlement was revealed when it took the position after the war that economic sanctions were to remain in place until Saddam Hussein was removed from power. Washington, in effect, made the removal of the Iraqi leader an explicit goal of its policy, but not until its military forces were being withdrawn. Then eighteen months after abandoning the Shiite insurgents in the south, the Bush administration reversed itself and established a no-flight zone in southern Iraq to protect them.

Bush may have made his generals more comfortable by exercising restraint. But he failed to exploit the benefits that accrue to those who exercise overwhelming power. It allows those who exercise it to set the agenda and the course of the future on their own terms.

Notes

Numerous books have been written about the Persian Gulf War. But a surprisingly large amount of original source material has remained classified or been overlooked.

The following notes cite classified as well as unclassified government reports obtained by the authors. They also reference articles, studies, and books by experts outside government.

In writing contemporary history, a growing number of authors have relied heavily on background interviews. We, too, have done many interviews on a background basis, but when possible we have identified our sources.

PREFACE

1. Notes of the meeting were taken by Philip Zelikow, director for European Security Affairs, National Security Council, and now an assistant professor of public policy at Harvard University's John F. Kennedy School of Government. The official record of the meeting has never been made public, but Zelikow kept his notes and made them available at the authors' request.

2. "Operation Desert Storm: A Snapshot of the Battlefield," Directorate of Intelligence, Central Intelligence Agency, September 1993. This accounting of the Iraqi equipment is unclassified but has not been widely disseminated.

3. "Joint Warfare of the U.S. Air Forces," National Defense University Press, November 1991. The publication was widely distributed throughout the Pentagon after the Gulf War to underscore Powell's message that "Joint Warfare is Team Warfare." The Gulf War was discussed on pages 63–69.

4. See Public Papers of George Bush, Book 1, January 1 to June 30, 1991, "The President's News Conference on the Persian Gulf Conflict," March 1, 1991, p. 201.

1: WAR BY MISCALCULATION

1. This account is based on interviews with current officials and former Bush administration officials.

2. "Capabilities for Limited Contingencies in the Persian Gulf," a classified study prepared in 1979 for then Defense Secretary Harold Brown. An unclassified version was supplied by the Defense Department at the authors' request. On pages 7–9, the report notes:

> The emerging Iraqi threat has two dimensions. On the one hand, Iraq may in the future use her military forces against such states as Kuwait or Saudi Arabia (as in the 1961 Kuwait crisis that was resolved by timely British intervention with force). On the other hand, the more serious problem may be that Iraq's implicit power will cause currently moderate local powers to accommodate themselves to Iraq without being overtly coerced. The latter problem suggests that we must not only be able to defend the interests of Kuwait, Saudi Arabia, and ourselves against an Iraqi invasion or show of force, we should also make manifest our capabilities and commitments to balance Iraq's power — and this may require an increased visibility for U.S. power.
>
> Another basic problem is that Iraq has a sizable army close to where it would be employed (e.g. Kuwait City is only 50 nm from the Iraqi border, and Saudi oil fields are within 300 nm). . . . The figure and related analysis suggest:

> - If the U.S. were to intervene at all, it would be desirable to do so early in the crisis, before hostilities began, and while escalation might still be avoided.
> - If Iraq precipitated a crisis with Kuwait or Saudi Arabia, it would be totally dominant until U.S. force arrived.
> - Without forward deployments, the U.S. could not get significant ground forces to the region for 10–20 days at best, and force ratios would be worse than 2:1 for at least 25 days; furthermore, U.S. buildups would depend upon the uncertain availability of ports and airfields. However, in the absence of opposition, Iraq could conquer Kuwait, seize Saudi oil fields, and capture critical airfields and ports within a week or two.
> - Although the U.S. would have the advantage in training, troop quality, and equipment, Iraq would have much heavier forces and greater familiarity with the climate and terrain.
> - The pro-Iraq asymmetry in ground forces would have to be compensated by U.S. tacair, especially during the first 25 days or so. The deterrent value of U.S. tacair could be a critical factor.

> Although there are other considerations that go beyond the scope of the present study, the above points argue for the U.S. having substantial in-place forces such as a carrier task force, and perhaps an Amphibious Ready Group.

3. Interviews, Harold Brown and Paul Wolfowitz.

4. Interview, Zalmay Khalilzad. Khalilzad served as the head of the Defense Department's office of policy planning during the Persian Gulf War and is now a researcher at the Rand Corporation.

5. Interview, Dennis Ross.

6. Interview, Richard Kerr.

7. "Rise of Third World Threats," Appendix B. This Pentagon study was prepared during the early part of the Bush administration and classified secret. It has been obtained by the authors.

8. "Prelude to War: US Policy Toward Iraq 1988–1990," pp. 7–8. This case study, which is a good account of the Bush administration's policy toward Iraq prior to the Gulf War, including the preparation of NSD 26, was prepared by Harvard University's John F. Kennedy School of Government. It was written by Zachary Karabell and edited by Philip Zelikow.

9. See "U.S. Plan for Iraq in 1990 Revealed," by Michael R. Gordon, *New York Times*, August 5, 1992.

10. Interview, aide to Dick Cheney.

11. "Security Environment 2000: A CENTCOM View," May 21, 1990. This study was disclosed by the "Gulf War Air Power Survey," an independent study commissioned by the Air Force. It was directed by Dr. Eliot A. Cohen and published in 1993. Vol. 1 (Planning and Command and Control), p. 202.

12. The meeting between Mack and al-Mashat is recounted in a confidential State Department cable entitled "Iraqi Letter to Arab League Threatening Kuwait." The cable, no. 235637, was sent to American embassies in the region on July 19. The cable has been obtained by the authors.

On July 24, 1990, Baker sent another cable, no. 241042, entitled "U.S. Reaction to Iraqi Threats in the Gulf." The cable repeated the July 18, 1990, press guidance and urged ambassadors in the region to press the point in their respective countries. The cable also included this instruction: "While we take no position on the border delineation issue raised by Iraq with respect to Kuwait, or on other bilateral disputes, Iraqi statements suggest an intention to resolve outstanding disagreements by the use of force, an approach which is contrary to UN-charter principles."

13. Allen's role was discussed by current and former officials. The watch notices from the Defense Intelligence Agency were declassified at the authors' request. The warnings of war issued by Allen were described by intelligence officials.

14. The discussion of the administration's consideration of military deployments is based on interviews with Gen. Colin Powell, Adm. David Jeremiah, Robert Kimmitt, Paul Wolfowitz, and Gen. H. Norman Schwarzkopf.

15. The Bush administration's press guidance that stipulated that Washington had no treaty commitments in the Gulf was prompted by an article in the *Washington Post* that quoted Cheney as saying the United States would come to the aid of Kuwait if the Gulf state was attacked. Cheney denied the quote, and John H. Kelly, the assistant secretary of state for Near Eastern and South Asian Affairs, used a July 31, 1990, hearing with the House Foreign Affairs Committee to clarify the episode. Kelly and Lee Hamilton, the chairman of the panel, had this exchange:

> HAMILTON: What is precisely the nature of our commitment to supporting our friends in the Gulf? I read a statement, an indirect quotation in the press from Secretary Cheney, who said the United States commitment was to come to Kuwait's defense if it is attacked. I am not sure that is an

accurate statement, but that is just what I read in the press. Perhaps you could clarify for me what our commitment is?

KELLY: . . . We have no defense treaty relationship with any Gulf country. That is clear. We support the security and integrity of friendly states in the region . . .

HAMILTON: If Iraq, for example, charged across the border into Kuwait, for whatever reason, what would be our position with regard to the use of U.S. forces?

KELLY: That, Mr. Chairman, is a hypothetical or a contingency, the kind of which I can't get into. Suffice it to say we would be extremely concerned, but I cannot get into the realm of "what if" answers.

HAMILTON: In that circumstance, it is correct to say, however, that we do not have a treaty commitment which would obligate us to engage U.S. forces.

KELLY: That is correct.

16. Glaspie's account of the meeting is detailed in her cable to Washington entitled "Saddam's Message of Friendship to President Bush." The cable, numbered Baghdad 04237, was sent on July 25, 1990, and was obtained by the authors. Glaspie also sent a summary of the meeting entitled "Ambassador's Meeting with Saddam Husayn," numbered Baghdad 94235.

Iraq was the first to disclose the substance of the meeting, releasing a transcript of the exchange. Glaspie argued that the Iraqi account was misleading. She told the House Foreign Affairs Committee on March 21, 1991, for example, that Saddam Hussein had said that he "would not pursue his disputes with Kuwait in any violent way" (United States Iraqi Relations, Hearing before the Subcommittee on Europe and the Middle East of the Committee on Foreign Affairs, House of Representatives, March 21, 1991). But her own cable largely supports the Iraqi version of the meeting and contradicts her congressional testimony. According to Glaspie's cable, Saddam Hussein never promised not to attack Kuwait, but said he would not act if, in his negotiations with Kuwait, "the Kuwaitis will at last give us some hope."

17. The presidential message was sent in a cable entitled "President Bush's Response to Saddam Hussein's Message." The cable, sent on the morning of July 28 and numbered Baghdad 247990, has been obtained by the authors. The Pentagon's effort to block the message was discussed by Henry Rowen and other former Defense Department officials.

18. Interviews, current and former administration officials.

19. Interview, Schwarzkopf.

20. "Watch notice," declassified by the DIA at the authors' request.

21. Interviews, Richard Kerr, Robert Kimmitt, administration officials.

2: DRAWING THE LINE

1. The account of the Iraqi invasion is provided by the Defense Department's final report to Congress on "Conduct of the Persian Gulf War," April 1992, chapter 1: Invasion of Kuwait.

2. The account of the August 2, 1990, meeting between Cheney and Powell is based on

notes taken at the session by a participant, who asked not to be named. The notes were made available to the authors.

3. Baker and Ross's role is described in "The Gulf Crisis: The Road to War," a three-part television series, conceived and arranged by the American Enterprise Institute.

4. Interview, Jack F. Matlock, former U.S. ambassador to Moscow.

5. Powell's and Pickering's positions at the NSC meeting were described by a participant.

6. Thatcher memoirs (*The Downing Street Years*, by Margaret Thatcher, HarperCollins, 1993), pp. 816–822. According to Thatcher, she told Bush that the invasion was unacceptable, that the Iraqi pipelines through Saudi Arabia and Iraq needed to be shut down. The rewriting of the State Department briefing papers before the meeting was described by Zelikow.

7. Interview, Eagleburger. Also see "The Gulf Crisis: The Road to War."

8. This account is drawn from interviews with the participants.

9. "Appendix A: The Chairman's National Military Strategy," submitted by Adm. William Crowe, August 25, 1989. It read:

> In protecting our far-flung interests while prosecuting a global war, the United States is constrained by potential threats, alliance commitments, limited resources, and the historic placement of forces and infrastructure. We cannot initially field sufficient forces to ensure prompt defeat of all enemies in all theaters. Further, we don't know where or how war will break out, and our current force deployments will constrain somewhat the reactions of all theater CINCS. This means that we must achieve our objectives sequentially and prepare campaign plans accordingly. The final decision on priorities and sequencing will be made by the NCA [National Command Authority] depending on the existing circumstances.
>
> Our foremost interest remains the defense of the North American continent (including Hawaii, Alaska, the friendly nations of the Caribbean and Central America, the interconnecting LOCs [lines of communications], and the Panama Canal). Regardless of where war begins, the United States is firmly committed to the defense of Western Europe and the Atlantic LOCs in accordance with our NATO obligations. Similarly, we must aid in the defense of our Pacific allies and protect the LOCs to them. Access to Arabian Peninsula oil and the critical natural resources of South America and Africa will also be high priorities.

Crowe then outlined theater strategies for North America, NATO, and East Asia and the Pacific.

10. Memorandum, FY 1992–1997, Defense Planning Guidance, January 24, 1990, classified "secret," from Dick Cheney to service secretaries, JCS Chairman, and other top officials. In a classified section of the memo, Cheney wrote: "The Secretary has increased the relative priority of Southwest Asia by making explicit that the region ranks above South America and Africa in terms of global wartime priorities and by outlining an initial theater strategy."

He also wrote: "In Southwest Asia, we should concentrate our resources on the defense of the Arabian peninsula and freedom of passage in the Persian Gulf in order to ensure continued access to increasingly important energy resources. We should retain our capability to defend there against either a Soviet-led or Soviet-supported contingency or a robust regional threat. We must also continue to keep in mind the strategic importance of Iran."

11. The schedule for completing CENTCOM's plan is recounted by the "Gulf War Air Power Survey." According to the survey, "The planning assumptions set forth in OPLAN 1002-90 were deficient in regard to warning time, presidential willingness to authorize military actions before hostilities, cooperation among friendly regional states and the willingness of Middle East political leaders to ask for visible U.S. military assistance, and the size and complexion of the U.S. military response." Vol. 1 (Planning and Command and Control), pp. 36–37.

12. Hoar's account is taken from a transcript of a lecture he delivered following the war. The transcript was made available by the Marine Corps Historical Center.

13. Interview, Gordon Brown.

14. This account was provided by a participant at the meeting.

15. An account of the Camp David meeting is provided in Schwarzkopf's *It Doesn't Take a Hero* (Bantam Books, 1992), pp. 298–300.

16. Interview, Scowcroft.

17. Hoar transcript.

18. Gen. Hansford T. Johnson, Commander in Chief, United States Transportation Command and Air Mobility Command, in an oral history conducted by Dr. James K. Matthews, Office of History, United States Transportation Command, and Dr. Jay H. Smith, Office of History, Air Mobility Command, Scott Air Force Base, Illinois, December 1992.

3: CROSSED SWORDS

1. Interview, Col. Ron Rokosz.

2. Interview, Schwarzkopf.

3. H. K. Park, unpublished manuscript on sealift capabilities.

4. Gen. Hansford T. Johnson, Commander in Chief, United States Transportation Command and Air Mobility Command, in an oral history conducted by Dr. James K. Matthews, Office of History, United States Transportation Command, and Dr. Jay H. Smith, Office of History, Air Mobility Command, Scott Air Force Base, Illinois, December 1992.

5. See interview with Maj. Gen. John I. Hopkins, U.S. Naval Institute proceedings, November 1992. This account is also based on an interview with Gen. Boomer.

6. See *Certain Victory: The U.S. Army in the Gulf War*, Office of the Chief of Staff, United States Army, Washington, D.C., 1993, pp. 87–88.

7. 101st Airborne Division Command History, pp. 9–10.

8. Interview with A-10 pilots. Those were not the only problems. According to the command history of the 48th Tactical Fighter Wing, whose F-111Fs were sent to Saudi Arabia:

> The initial flow of intelligence information was slow at best, forcing decision makers to refer to alternate means of acquiring information, most commonly, via Cable News Network. Two major factors mitigated against the

48th TFW receiving the latest intelligence information. First, the 48th TFW is primarily committed to NATO, with no tasking for the CENTAF area, or indeed anywhere outside of the European theater. Second, in the early portion of August, the 48th TFW had not received any official notification of tasking to the Desert Shield theater. Essentially, the 48th, with no tasking and no commitment, would rank low on any priority list for current information.

9. Interview, F-117 commanders.

10. Interview, Lt. Gen. Jimmy D. Ross, the chief Army logistician at the Pentagon during the Gulf War.

11. Interview, senior intelligence official.

12. Interview, Schwarzkopf.

13. Interview, Schwarzkopf.

14. See "No War Unless Iraq Strikes, U.S. Gulf Commander Says," by Michael R. Gordon, *New York Times,* September 1, 1990.

15. Interview, Arnold. The "Gulf War Air Power Survey" noted, "Like many other 'operations' plans, UNCINCENT OPLAN 1002-90 primarily was a deployment plan, geared heavily toward logistic support and troop deployment considerations with only a broad concept of combat operations. Central Command planners' thinking about precisely how forces might be deployed had not been committed systemically to paper." Vol. 1 (Planning and Command and Control), p. 38.

16. This information comes from a participant in the meeting.

17. Interview, Schwarzkopf.

18. Interview, Wolfowitz.

19. Interview, Schwarzkopf.

20. Interview, Arnold.

21. Interview, Rokosz.

4: INSTANT THUNDER

1. Interview, Schwarzkopf.

2. See *The Air Campaign,* by John A. Warden III (Washington: National Defense University Press). The portrait of Warden is based on interviews with Air Force officials.

3. Interview, Dugan.

4. The account of the August 10 and 11, 1990, meetings is based on the notes of a participant.

5. A copy of the Instant Thunder plan was made available to the authors.

6. The account of the August 17, 1990, meeting is based on notes taken at the time by a participant.

7. An account of the confrontation with Horner was provided by participants.

8. Diary made available to the authors by a participant.

9. Interview, Glosson.

10. Interview, Vice Adm. Stanley Arthur.

11. According to the command history of the 48th Tactical Fighter Wing, there were a number of serious limitations. The report noted:

> When the first wave of F-111s shattered the early morning peace around RAF Lakenheath at 0700 on 25 August, the Statue of Liberty Wing was ready for war. Twenty-four jets were launched to ensure the 18 primary aircraft reached Taif. These primary aircraft were loaded with a full complement of LGBs since there were no "smart" bombs available on the ramp in Saudi. A week later, another 14 fully loaded aircraft were deployed, with many of the 494 TFS aircrews who had been recalled from their deployment in Spain. In a remarkable performance by the maintainers, every primary aircraft in the two deployments reached Taif, and none of the air or ground spares were needed to full a gap.
>
> . . . For supply, business began very slowly. Fortunately, there was very little flying at first because it took almost two weeks for all of the WRSK [war reserve] pallets to arrive.
>
> . . . For fuels personnel, flying into Taif meant starting with virtually nothing. The only fuels function at Taif was set up at the civilian airport. Total JP-4 [jet fuel] storage capacity was approximately 250,000 gallons. There was no Saudi military fuels section to speak of, and aircraft refueling was accomplished by contractors. Needless to say, this situation had to change to be able to sustain a war effort. There were no R-9 refueling vehicles, no storage bladders, no laboratory equipment. The immediate concern was getting this equipment in place and set up. The bottom line was that jet fuel was in critical storage and would have severely hampered combat operations if they were required in the first weeks.
>
> . . . Faced with the possibility of launching aircraft against alert targets at any time, the lack of a communications center and timely, relevant intelligence presented a major challenge to the initial cadre, who relied on sparse secure telephones and message traffic couriered by C-21 [planes] from Riyadh.

12. Interview, Rice. For additional details on the "limfacs," see "Gulf War Air Power Survey."
13. Transcript, Dugan interview with news reporters.
14. Interviews, Dugan. Transcript of Scowcroft appearance on "Meet the Press," September 9, 1990.

5: KARI

1. History of Strike Projection Evaluation and Anti-Air Warfare, provided by Navy public affairs.
2. Interview, senior Air Force official.
3. The Kari system was described by officials familiar with the SPEAR analysis.
4. Memorandum on "interdiction tasking" reviewed by the authors.
5. "Poobah's Party" was described by military officials familiar with the program. Also see "U.S. Decoys Covered for Allied Aircraft by Saturating Iraqi Defense Radars," David A. Fulghum, *Aviation Week and Space Technology*, July 1, 1991.

6. The problems with the Tomahawk cruise missile program were described by military officials. Also see "Secret Carbon-Fiber Warhead Blinded Iraqi Air Defenses," David A. Fulghum, *Aviation Week and Space Technology*, April 27, 1992.

7. "Stealth in the Storm: Sorting the Facts from the Fiction," by Lt. Col. Ralph W. Getchell. In his unpublished paper, Getchell wrote:

> On the eve of Desert Storm, the F-117A, like most of the pilots who flew here, was unproven in battle. From the exhaustive classified test reports available, we knew the aircraft's low observable characteristics would give us a substantial advantage over the Iraqi interceptors, surface-to-air missiles (SAMs), and anti-aircraft artillery (AAA) which was ready to oppose our attack. But the F-117 is LOW observable, not NO observable. In planning our attack routes, we carefully took advantage of our strengths to minimize the times during which we could possibly be detected and tracked. However, there would be significant risks even if both the aircraft and the enemy performed as expected.
>
> In wartime, the unexpected sometimes happens. Maintenance access panels inexplicably come off in flight, bomb bay doors fail to close, or an enemy SAM proves more capable than previously thought. . . . It was the prospect of friction which prompted our unit to request EF-111 Raven jamming support for the first nights' operations. Based on peacetime exercises such as Red Flag, we knew enemy radar operators usually try to counter electronic jamming by reducing the sensitivity or "gain" of their radar receiver. Any reduction in gain would cause the small radar blip of a malfunctioning F-117 to disappear from the scope.
>
> To the Stealth planners, Raven jamming seemed like good insurance. CENTAF agreed. But jamming would only be provided around the Baghdad area, which was defended by an estimated 60 SAM batteries and 1800 AAA guns. F-117s attacking less heavily defended targets were not directly supported by the Ravens.
>
> EF-111 Ravens were never tasked to escort the F-117s per se. As a practical matter, it was extremely difficult, if not impossible, to fly formation with the F-117, which is designed to be visually as well as electronically elusive at night. Further, the close proximity of the non-stealthy Ravens would have helped the enemy predict our proximate location and attack route. Instead, the EF-111s entered enemy airspace on their own and began jamming at the agreed upon time and place. At the end of the alloted time, the Ravens turned off their electronic jammers and proceeded to other jamming assignments to support non-stealthy aircraft. The F-117s and EF-111s never saw or heard each other over Iraqi territory.
>
> Further, since EF-111 jamming was a precaution not a necessity, no provision was made to cancel the attack or even notify the attacking Stealth Fighters should the Ravens be forced to abort their mission. Sometimes you have to live without insurance. . . .

8. "Tactical Deception Plan," classified "secret." The plan, obtained by the authors, provided for the following sequence:

H-5 Hours: AWACS to AWACS Call initiates effort.

H-4 Hours: HC-130 appears on scene to assist talks to AWACS.

H-3 + 10 minutes: HC-130 Divert to TURAOF to Refuel.

H-2 + 45 minutes: 2 HH-60s (Navy) take off to assist SAR [search and rescue] from Tabuk.

H-2 + 10 minutes: HC-130 takes off from TUFAIR to scene.

H-2 + 05 minutes: AWACS to ABCCC hand off AWACS net.

H-1 + 45 minutes: HC-130 goes off to notionally search. Actually descends down to refuel strike helos at H-1 + 30.

H-50 minutes: HC-130 returns to Al Jouf and refuel stand alert.

H-50 minutes: ABCCC continues SAR radio traffic established in H-Hour orbit to control helo strikes.

H-22 minutes: Helos commence strike.

6: "HIGH DIDDLE DIDDLE"

1. Interviews, Lt. Col. Joseph Purvis and CENTCOM officials.

2. The development of the ground-war plan is described in a confidential chronology of the Jedi planners, obtained by the authors.

The October 6 entry noted: "CINC approved COA 1 and directed development of concept of operations. Observations from CINC: Main attack is to be west of the elbow to seize an objective on N/S Loc 60 Km North of Kuwait City; 0/0 continue north to seize the Raudhatain oilfields and secure the northern Iraq/Kuwait border. Mission at risk due to unfavorable force ratios, but force not at risk."

Also see, "From the Top: How Commanders Planned Operation Desert Shield," by Tom Donnelly, *Army Times*, February 24, 1992.

3. Transcript, Boomer staff briefing, Marine Corps Historical Center.

4. Interview, Schwarzkopf.

5. Interview, member of briefing team Schwarzkopf sent to Washington.

6. Interview, Sir Patrick Hine.

7. The account of the JCS meeting is based on interviews with participants. The confidential Jedi chronology for October 9 offers a terse summation of Washington's negative reaction: "Observations made during and after the briefing: Plan attacks into the enemy strength. Breach operations will be extremely tough."

8. Interview, Schwarzkopf.

9. Interviews, Donald Rice and Air Force officials.

10. The account of the White House meeting is based on interviews with participants.

11. Written response to authors' questions, George Bush.

12. Interview, senior military official.

13. Interview, military official.

7: "THE WESTERN EXCURSION"

1. Interview, Schwarzkopf.

2. Interview, member of Jedi planning cell.

3. Interviews, Henry Rowen and Paul Wolfowitz.

4. Interview, aide to Powell.

5. According to the October 16 Jedi planning chronology: "Developed three COAs based on two U.S. Army corps. Began to design what the new corps structure would be for planning purposes. Asked J-2 for a new projected defense for planning. The current objective defense was valid through December and we projected the additional corps would take 90 days to arrive (mid-January)."

The entry for October 17 noted: "The planning effort which was previously restricted to a small group was opened up to some degree. Briefed U.K. and ARCENT commanders at separate times on both the one corps concept and initial work on a two corps concept."

The entry for October 21 noted: "CINC approved two U.S. Army Corps as the main effort west of Kuwait border. CINC modified the concept to reflect a continuation of the attack to destroy the RGFC [Republican Guard Forces Command]." Among the issues discussed was "Proper role for MARCENT (MARCENT's mission was LOC security for ARCENT due to the need for combat power in the main attack and the lack of an appropriate amphibious mission)." MARCENT referred to the Marine command; ARCENT to the Army command.

6. Interview, Schwarzkopf.

7. Arnold's analysis argued that the Western Excursion would be too risky and would divert forces that were needed for the left hook. Specifically, he argued that the "XVIII ABN Corps cannot accomplish objective if either the 3rd ACR or the 82ABN div is taken from their task organization." He also noted that it would take forty-two C-141 sorties to bring the equipment for a parachute drop, straining airlift capabilities.

The "H-2/H-3 Ground Battle Assessment," obtained by the authors, contained the following slide.

"Future Operations H2/H3, Considering Principles of War"
Objective: Does Not Attack Center of Gravity
Offensive: Requires Execution and Accomplishment of Air Campaign, Phase 1
Mass: Does Not Achieve Decision Results (Does Not Support Principle of Objective)
Economy of Force: Once Initiated, It Further Reduces Combat Power Required for Ground Offensive
Maneuver: Increases Vulnerability in East and Reduces Flexibility
Unit of Command: Does Not Insure Unity of Effort (ARCENT/ CENTCOM Focus Diluted)
Security: Risk to Employed Forces on H2/H3 Mission
Surprise: Tips Off Iraqis of Willingness to Attack into Iraq
Simplicity: Complex Air LOCs and Command Control

8. Interview, Schwarzkopf.

9. October 31, 1990, entry in Jedi planning chronology.

10. Interview, Robert M. Gates.

11. Interview, Powell.

12. Written response to authors' questions, George Bush.

13. Interview, Dennis Ross. The account of Baker's meeting also comes from "The Gulf Crisis: The Road to War."

    According to a three-part article in *Pravda* by Yevgeni Primakov, "The War Which Might Not Have Been," during Gorbachev's meeting with Bush, Marshal Sergie Akhromeyev "told Americans in Bush's entourage that a military outcome in the region would bring tremendous devastation and human casualties; that it would not prove possible to end the war with a one-shot air attack to fully disable Iraqi control centers and that losses in the event of a clash between the two sides' ground forces were inevitable."

    Primakov also met with Prince Bandar. "Bandar categorically disagreed that the military operation could lead to grave consequences. 'Your words are clearing an exaggeration,' he said. 'I am a military pilot and I can say with authority that in the event of an attack, if, of course, Iraq refuses to withdraw its troops, everything will be over in a couple of hours. Do not overestimate the possible number of casualties. The operation will be supported by the most modern electronic equipment and will be 'surgical in nature.' "

    The articles were published on February 28–March 2, 1991.

14. Interview, Powell. Powell's description of the episode raises questions about a previous account. In his book *The Commanders* (Simon and Schuster, 1991), Bob Woodward wrote: "Surprised that Crowe had come down so hard for sanctions, Powell vowed that when he left office, he would not publicly second-guess his successors and would not appear voluntarily before Congress. They would have to subpoena him" (p. 332).

15. According to the November 15, 1990, entry in the Jedi chronology, "Feedback we received from the Commander's Conference. A heavy division will be the theater reserve. XVIII Corps will be in the west (vicinity As Salman to As Samawah). British forces remain with MARCENT. . . . Focus of the ground campaign is to destroy the RG (VII Corps is the main effort). Be ready mid-January."

8: TELL IT TO THE MARINES

1. According to the November 3, 1990, entry in the Jedi chronology, Colonel Majchrzak was briefed on the concept for launching a two-corps attack in the west. "Major concern with Marines' mission in the west (triborder area) is that this moves them away from MARCENT's logistical support. The plan would be to place the Marines FSSG at the doctrinal distance from Marine forces and have ARCENT provide logistics to the FSSG. Marine air is also an issue. It will take longer to reach the Marine forces in the West but the group did not feel that time was not operationally significant."

   Also see "U.S. Marines in the Persian Gulf, 1990–1991: With the I Marine Expeditionary Force in Desert Shield and Desert Storm," History and Museums Division, Headquarters, U.S. Marine Corps. Washington, D.C., 1993. It noted:

   > The Marines became concerned. It seemed that the CENTCOM planners were developing a concept of operations that treated I MEF as if it were an Army Corps. Much of the 3d Marine Aircraft Wing's offensive air assets

might be used in theater support of non-Marine units . . . Upon hearing of these developments, General Boomer directed his battle staff planning group under Majchrzak not only to develop MARCENT plans, but also to provide prompt and appropriate inputs to General Schwarzkopf's planners as well.

2. Interview, Jedi planner. According to the November 6, 1990, entry in the Jedi chronology, "CINC is very concerned with the deception effort, focus is to keep the threat oriented inside Kuwait. Concept was too detailed. CINC guidance was to give components more flexibility. CINC directed that Marine forces attack in the east closer to the coast. (Our concern was that the threat in the heel was not as relevant as that to the west. We positioned only the EAC in the 'heel.' ")

3. MARCENT Command Brief, slide 18.

4. Transcript, Boomer staff briefing, November 2, 1990, Marine Corps Historical Center. The intelligence official noted: "The Iraqi soldiers, members of the party, have been given orders to shoot anyone, regardless of his rank, that was not strictly adhering to party policy. . . . Also we have had observers indicate some of the Iraqi soldiers are wearing white T-shirts. We have also had other reports that they are carrying white flags and in the event the multinational forces cross the border that they will surrender."

5. Boomer letter, made available to the authors.

6. Interviews, Tim Sulivan, Patrick Cordingly, and Gen. Peter de la Billière.

7. Interview, Boomer.

8. Interview, Khalid.

9. Interviews, Marine planners.

10. Interviews, Boomer, Schwarzkopf, and Marine officers.

9: "THE MAILED FIST"

1. Testimony to the Senate Armed Services Committee.

2. Interviews, Pentagon officials.

3. Also see, "Iraq's Strategic Mindset and the Gulf War: Blueprint for Defeat," Norman Cigar, *Journal of Strategic Studies*, March 1992, pp. 1–29.

4. This information is drawn from the Defense Department's final report to Congress on "Conduct of the Persian Gulf War" and from the "Gulf War Air Power Survey."

5. Report by Defense Intelligence Agency, obtained by the authors.

6. Interview, official of the United Nations Special Commission for the disarmament of Iraq.

7. Report, United Nations Special Commission.

8. "The Gulf War: An Iraqi General Officer's Perspective," March 11, 1991, Memorandum for Record. This classified assessment, obtained by the authors, was prepared by the Army's 513th Military Intelligence Brigade, but was never publicly released.

9. Information Memorandum for the secretary of defense, deputy secretary of defense, March 28, 1990, "Analysis for Defense Planning Options: the Defense Planning Options: the Potential of Air."

10. A copy of Warden's Checkmate briefing was obtained by the authors. To strengthen the Air Force's case that it could single-handedly win the war, Warden's Checkmate office asked the Rand Corp. to prepare an analysis of a possible peace treaty. The Rand study, obtained by the authors, was entitled "Winning the War — and the Peace: The Termination of Hostilities with Iraq." It noted:

> Given Iraqi conduct, some might feel justified in demanding not only that Iraq withdraw from Kuwait, allow its former government to return, commit itself not to reinvade, and release the hostages, but also that Iraq agree to pay reparations and accept Nuremberg-style trials for its leadership as preconditions for ending the war. But insisting on the latter two conditions is likely to prolong the war: the Iraqi leadership would be much more likely to fight on rather than accept what amounts to unconditional surrender. Such a degree of resolve may oblige us to occupy Iraq — thus increasing substantially the costs, casualties and duration of the war. Threats such as reparations and trials might have some useful deterrent value in affecting some Iraqi actions in Kuwait before war breaks out — but insisting on them after war begins might well become counterproductive. Because of this concern, the proposed Post War Armistice Agreement with Iraq has not dealt directly with the issues of reparations and trials. Instead, we have approached these issues indirectly and ambiguously — leaving them to be settled between the Kuwait and Iraqi governments.
>
> The idea of forcing Iraq to pay reparations is enticing: however, Iraq is not in a financial position to pay larger reparations — unless it commits its income from oil sales for an almost indefinite future. Imposing reparations will delay to the point of danger Iraqi's recovery from the effects of war and also from the effects of Saddam Hussein's gross mismanagement of the economy over the last decade. Since our aim is a long-term peace and movement of Iraq toward a stable, non-aggressive, and democratic government, it is imperative that we eschew reparations that may block realization of our real interests in the area. No one needs an impoverished Iraq that becomes a hot bed of revanchism. . . .
>
> On the disposition of the Iraqi heavy equipment — armored vehicles, artillery and other weapons — in Kuwait, we should demand that it be left behind. It is possible such a demand might increase the incentive of officers in the field or the leadership in Baghdad to fight on. However, it is likely to be a marginal factor in affecting the Iraqi incentives to fight on.
>
> As far as future stability of the region is concerned, U.S. and allied attacks will seriously weaken the military and economic power or Iraq and humiliate its leadership. The full range of potential internal and regional consequences of such a development are very difficult to predict. Some weakening of Iraq and punishment for its aggression can increase regional stability. Iraqi military preponderance and the absence of a balance of power in the Gulf contributed to the invasion.
>
> Conversely, while some weakening of Iraq is in our interest, the total destruction of Iraqi power is not; a militarily devastated Iraq would be unable to balance Iranian power. This in turn might encourage Iran or some of Iraq's

other neighbors to become aggressive and might result in the dismemberment of Iraq. This would almost certainly increase regional instability.

11. Pentagon officials and "Gulf War Air Power Survey."

12. Interview, Horner.

13. Interview, Wolfowitz.

14. Interview, Pentagon officials. Also see "VII Corps Debarkation and Onward Movement," 1st Infantry Division (Forward) Desert Shield/Storm After Action Report, May 30, 1991. While the VII Corps blamed ocean transport for many of their delays, the Transportation Command found fault with the VII Corps.

    See TRANSCOM's oral history with Gen. Hansford T. Johnson: "When Phase II began, we were ready to move but more quickly than the troops were. Because the unit equipment wasn't ready to move, the VII Corps was not as prepared to move as other U.S. units that have an active mobility requirement day-to-day, and we couldn't fully use the capability that we had . . . as it was, each unit looked at 15 January and based their departure planning on meeting that date, so the big push didn't come until well after Thanksgiving. Consequently, we lost a full month's worth of move time."

15. Interview, administration official.

16. Primakov provided this account to a diplomat.

17. See Public Papers of George Bush: Book 1, January 1 to June 30, 1991, "Statement by Press Secretary Fitzwater on President Bush's Letter to President Saddam Hussein of Iraq," January 12, 1991.

    Mr. Bush's letter, dated January 5, 1991, read:

    Mr. President,

    We stand today at the brink of war between Iraq and the world. This is a war that began with your invasion of Kuwait; this is a war that can be ended only by Iraq's full and unconditional compliance with U.N. Security Council Resolution 678.

    I am writing you now, directly, because what is at stake demands that no opportunity be lost to avoid what would be a certain calamity for the people of Iraq. I am writing, as well, because it is said by some that you do not understand just how isolated Iraq is and what Iraq faces as a result. I am not in a position to judge whether this impression is correct: what I can do, though, is try in this letter to reinforce what Secretary of State Baker told your Foreign Minister and eliminate any uncertainty or ambiguity that might exist in your mind about where we stand and what we are prepared to do.

    The international community is united in its call for Iraq to leave all of Kuwait without condition and without further delay. This is not simply the policy of the United States: it is the position of the world community as expressed in no less than twelve Security Council resolutions.

    We prefer a peaceful outcome. However, anything less than full compliance with UN Security Council Resolution 678 and its predecessors is unacceptable. There can be no reward for aggression. Nor will there be any negotiation. Principle cannot be compromised. However, by its full compliance, Iraq will gain the opportunity to rejoin the international community. More immediately, the Iraqi military establishment will escape destruction. But unless you withdraw from Kuwait completely and without condition, you will lose more than Kuwait. What is at issue here is not the future of Kuwait — it will be free, its government will be restored — but rather the future of Iraq. The choice is yours to make.

The United States will not be separated from its coalition partners. Twelve Security Council resolutions, 28 countries providing military units to enforce them, more than one hundred governments complying with sanctions — all highlight the fact that it is not Iraq against the United States, but Iraq against the world. That most Arab and Muslim countries are arrayed against you as well should reinforce what I am saying. Iraq cannot and will not be able to hold on to Kuwait or exact a price for leaving.

You may be tempted to find solace in the diversity of opinion that is American democracy. You should resist any such temptation. Diversity ought not to be confused with division. Nor should you underestimate, as others have before you, America's will.

Iraq is already feeling the effects of the sanctions mandated by the United Nations. Should war come, it will be a far greater tragedy for you and your country. Let me state, too, that the United States will not tolerate the use of chemical or biological weapons or the destruction of Kuwait's oil fields and installations. Further, you will be held directly responsible for terrorist actions against any member of the coalition. The American people would demand the strongest possible response. You and your country will pay a terrible price if you order unconscionable acts of this sort.

I write this letter not to threaten, but to inform. I do so with no sense of satisfaction, for the people of the United States have no quarrel with the people of Iraq. Mr. President, UN Security Council Resolution 678 establishes the period before January 15 of this year as a 'pause of good will' so that this crisis may end without further violence. Whether this pause is used as intended, or merely becomes a prelude to further violence, is in your hands, and yours alone. I hope you weigh your choice carefully and choose wisely, for much will depend upon it.

George Bush

18. Interview, Scowcroft.
19. Iraq published a four-part transcript of the Aziz-Baker meeting one year after the session in the English-language *Baghdad Observer*. The account was published in the January 9–12, 1992, editions.
20. Interview, Ross.
21. Interview, Air Force official.
22. Interview, Air Force official.

10: FRICTION

1. Interview, Lt. Col. Jay Beard.
2. "Tactical Deception Plan," interview, Air Force officers.
3. "Apache Attack," by Richard MacKenzie, *Air Force Magazine*, October 1991, pp. 54–60. "First Shots Fired in Anger," *Soldiers*, April 1991, pp. 21–24. Also see command history of the 101st Airborne Division, p. 25.

4. Interview, Maj. Greg Feest, other F-117 pilots.

5. Interview, Lt. Col. Dennis Hardziej. See Silver Star citation awarded to Hardziej. The F-15C pilots were dubious of Hardziej and others' claims that they were being chased by Iraqi planes equipped with spotlights.

In an after-action report, the F-15C pilots included this poem on "Baghdad Billy."

> I'm an F-111 jock, and I'm here to tell
> Of Baghdad Billy, and his jet from hell.
> We were well protected, with Eagles in tight.
> But that didn't stop, the man with the light.
> RJ, AWACS — they didn't see
> As Baghdad Billy snuck up on me.
> Then I found a spotlight shining at my six.
> And my whoozoo said, Holy S _____ !
> I popped some chaff and I popped some flare
> But that Iraqi bandit, he didn't care.
> I had tracers on my left, and tracers on my right.
> With a load of bombs, I had to run from the fight.
> I rolled my Vark back to Taif and gave this rap.
> CENTAF said, I was full of C _____ !
> I'm here to tell you the God's honest truth,
> That Iraqi bandit, he ain't no spoof.
> You don't have to worry, there is no way
> You'll see Baghdad Billy if you fly in the day.
> But listen to me son, for I am right,
> Watch out for Baghdad Billy if you fly at night!!!

6. Interview, Lt. Col. Ralph W. Getchell, who commanded the 415th Tactical Fighter Squadron, one of the two F-117 squadrons in the Gulf. Also see Getchell's paper: "Stealth in the Storm: Sorting the Facts from the Fiction." Getchell wrote:

> As the war continued, the Ravens were occasionally tasked to provide stand-off jamming for F-117 attacks. These missions were not tasked to counter the SAMs (which failed to demonstrate any real capability against the F-117) but to elicit a poorly timed response from the hundreds of AAA guns which protected important targets. Many of Iraq's AAA batteries lacked radar for detection and tracking, but opened fire on cue from the more sophisticated systems or from listening posts on the outskirts of town. . . .
>
> After the first few days of combat, we discovered that well-timed jamming by the Ravens caused the gunners to fire blindly into the air until they ran out of ammunition or overheated their barrels. When the firing died down, the F-117s could then attack with much less risk of damage from unaimed flak. "Flak baiting" became a secondary or tertiary mission for the EF-111 crews, who spent most of their time providing jamming support for non-stealthy strike aircraft.

Also interviews with Col. Al Whitley, the commander of the F-117 wing, and other F-117 pilots.

7. Interview, Navy officials. Also see an article on the episode by Mark Crispin Miller, *New York Times,* September 15, 1992, op-ed page. Miller asserts that American military authorities sought to cover up the fact that Speicher's plane may have been downed during a dogfight. But Pentagon officials publicly acknowledged that possibility during and immediately after the war.

8. The data on the performance of the F-117s is contained in "Nighthawks over Iraq: A Chronology of the F-117A Stealth Fighter in Operations Desert Shield and Desert Storm," Special Study 37 FW/HO-91-1. Office of History, Headquarters 37th Fighter Wing, 12th Air Force, Tactical Air Command. Data were also obtained from interviews with intelligence officials.

9. Interview, Schwarzkopf.

10. The information on the near shoot-down of the Saudi plane is contained in the Distinguished Flying Cross the Air Force awarded Capt. Getnar Drummond.

11. Interviews, Lt. Col. Denny Ertler, Maj. Keith Zuegel. Also see their Silver Star awards.

12. Interview, Lt. Gen. Frederick Franks. Also see the 1st Infantry Division's "Operation Desert Shield and Desert Storm, Chronology of Events, March 14, 1991." The entry for January 17, 1991, reads:

> Air operations commence against Iraq at 0200 local. Later, reports are received of two groups of Iraqi forces penetrating Arab forces to our north. One group of approximately 50 tanks was reported to be attacking the 3 (EG) AD command post and moving south. The other group of tanks was moving from the south east corner of Kuwait, moving toward Log Base Alpha. The division's combat power was almost nothing, amounting to only a tank battalion with a total of 9 HEAT rounds per tank on board. Subsequent reports identified these forces as an Egyptian tank battalion which a pilot had misreported and a LAV [light armored vehicle] battalion from the Marine Corps operating as part of the MARCENT deception plan. This "non-battle" had a positive aspect in that it provided a quick shake out of procedures in the TOC [tactical operations center] and energized plans for upload of tanks and local defense in the TAA. This occurred during the jump of the main command post, while the Battle Center was in the process of moving to its new location. The jump was subsequently called off.

13. Interview, White House official.

11: THE GREAT SCUD HUNT

1. Interview, Maj. Gen. Giora Romm, Pentagon officials.

2. "Iraqi Short-Range Ballistic Missiles in the Persian Gulf War: Lessons and Prospects," Defense Intelligence Memorandum, March 1990, classified "secret." That report noted:

> The Coalition anti-Scud campaign significantly reduced but never neutralized Iraq's ability to employ short-range ballistic missiles . . . Initial expectations were high that the 28 operational fixed launchers in western Iraq would be destroyed quickly, but the intelligence community was concerned

that mobile SRBM [short-range ballistic missile] launchers would present a more difficult targeting problem . . . Prewar estimates of the size of the Iraqi SRBM force reflect significant analytical uncertainties. The SRBM inventory was estimated at between 300 and 700 missiles. The breakdown of the force between the standard Soviet-supplied 10.9 meter SS-1C/SCUD Bs and indigenously modified longer range variants (10.9 meter Al Husayn and 12.2 meter Al Abbas) was unknown. The number of mobile launchers was estimated to be 22 Soviet-supplied MAZ-543 transporter-erector-launchers and up to 14 indigenously produced mobile-erector-launchers, for a total of 36. . . .

3. Notes, White House official. This account is also based on interviews with Eagleburger, Haass, Schwarzkopf, and Cheney.

4. Interview, Powell aide.

5. Interviews, Wolfowitz, CENTCOM officials.

6. Interview, senior diplomatic official.

7. Interview, Saudi official. The Saudis suggested including their CSS-2 medium-range missiles in the American air-war plans prior to the war. Some targeteers in the Black Hole even drew up contingency plans for firing the missiles prior to the war at targets near Saddam Hussein's home town of Tikrit. But the missiles were never formally incorporated into the plan.

8. Interview, CENTCOM officials.

9. Interview, Lt. Gen. Charles Horner.

10. The Scud data is drawn from the "Gulf War Air Power Survey," pp. 330–341.

11. Transcript, CENTCOM briefing, Schwarzkopf, January 30, 1991. The destruction of the fuel trucks was described by an intelligence official.

12. According to the 5th Marine Expeditionary Brigade after-action report, "On 15 February, the USS *Tarawa* docked in Al Jubail, Saudi Arabia, to off-load Harrier aircraft. During the early morning hours of 16 Feb, Al Jubail came under an Iraqi Scud missile attack. The Scud missile impacted the water 120 meters off the port side of the USS *Tarawa*. Luckily, the missile warhead did not detonate."

13. "VII Corps Debarkation and Onward Movement," 1st Infantry Division (Forward) Desert Shield/Storm After Action Report, 30 May 1991.

14. Interview, senior special operations official.

15. Interview, Schwarzkopf. According to transcripts at the Marine Corps Historical Center, Schwarzkopf complained vociferously to Boomer and his aides after the war about the Scud intelligence, particularly the American intelligence community's assessment that the Scud carried chemical warheads.

You got a tremendous dump of information but you never got an analysis. By the time you got an analysis. it was so hemmed and safe-sided on all sides so they could never be accused of being wrong. It was absolutely useless at my level. I'm talking about the national product, and I never really got any estimates, any analysis or anything like that that was worth a damn. The best example is the chemical capability of Scud missiles. For two years, I had been guaranteed that they did not have a chemical capability. The day the war started, their estimate shifted, and by one month later it was they probably did have a chemical warhead on a Scud missile, and nothing had changed out there in the way of occurrences or events. All they were doing is the bureaucracy there decided: "well, they may shoot a chemical missile, so we will cover our butts by saying they may have it." So we went to the "definitely do not," to "maybe," to "do have" in a period of two months.

16. Also see *Storm Command: A Personal Account of the Gulf War* by General Sir Peter de la Billière (HarperCollins, 1992).

17. Classified briefing presented by the Special Operations Command to the Senate Armed Services Committee after the war.

18. Interview, Maj. Gen. Wayne Downing.

19. "Iraqi Short-Range Ballistic Missiles in the Persian Gulf War: Lessons and Prospects," Defense Intelligence Memorandum, March 1990, classified "secret."

> The Coalition's inability to neutralize Iraq's SRBM capability illustrates the difficulty of locating and destroying relocatable targets. This underscored the effectiveness of Iraqi denial and deception techniques, including launching under the cover of darkness or clouds and excellent communications security, which was largely successful in hiding SRBM mobile launchers from Coalition discovery and air attacks. The use of decoy equipment figured prominently in this effort. Iraq also successfully concealed its deployed missile fueling equipment and its stocks of reload missiles. The success of these operational security measures contributed significantly to Iraq's ability to continue launching till the end of the war and preserved some essential components of the SRBM force . . . The Coalition's inability to permanently degrade SRBM command and control is also significant, despite determined efforts to incapacitate Iraqi military and civilian national networks. Even in the last days of the war, Baghdad retained a sufficient capability to initiate firings from new launch areas and to retarget SRBMs from urban to military and high-value targets, such as the Dimona nuclear reactor.

According to an Air Force report after the war — "Reaching Globally, Reaching Powerfully: The United States Air Force in the Gulf War" — American warplanes stopped a mass launch of Scud missiles in the final days of the war. UN inspectors visited the supposed site of the strike and found no evidence of destroyed Scuds.

12: WITH FRIENDS LIKE THESE

1. Interview, Air Force officer.

2. Transcript, Boomer staff briefing, Marine Corps Historical Center.

3. Classified search and rescue guidance to pilots. According to Marine officials, the Iranians also occasionally fired missiles at American warplanes. See Boomer's command briefings: "Of note, also in air defense activity, an Iranian I-Hawk locked onto and fired on a flight of F-18s from MAG-11 moving up past Basra. They fired one I-Hawk. The EA-6 and F-18s were able to defeat the I-Hawk and continued on to complete their mission."

4. The classified Jedi log notes in its entry for December 31, 1990:

Possibility has arisen that Syria will not participate in offensive operations. Egyptians raised the following concerns: Relative combat power in Egyptian Corps without 9th Syrian division. Location of breach. Need to breach further west now that 9th Syrian Division will not attack. Help with counter obstacle equipment. Not tied to Syrian issue. Ongoing concern. Role of 1 Cav in NAC [Northern Area Command] sector. Need for combat power to replace 9th Syrian Division.

To compensate for the loss of the Syrians, the Jedis changed the Egyptian mission. The Egyptian attack was delayed a day and its mission was limited. As the Jedis noted, "Change in NAC mission (more conservative and closer to VII Corps east flank). Mission changed from 'destroy force in zone' to 'protect right flank of VII Corps by the occupation of a blocking position vicinity Al Abraq.' "

5. Interview, Lt. Col. Dave Eberly. This account is also based on a Pentagon after-action report on the Eberly episode, which was made available to the authors.

6. The F-16 episode was recounted by some of the pilots who participated in the raid and is described in the "Gulf War Air Power Survey."

7. Interview, John Broadbent. Also see, *Thunder and Lightning: The RAF in the Gulf: Personal Experiences of War,* by Charles Allen (London, HMSO).

8. Interview, Eberly. After-action report.

9. January 23, 1991, memo from Maj. Gen. John A. Corder on "Downed Aircraft Recovery." Classified "secret."

10. After-action report on the Eberly episode. Also see "No USAF Combat Rescue Aircraft in Gulf; It Took 72 Hours to Launch One Rescue," Benjamin F. Schemmer, *Armed Forces Journal International,* July 1991, pp. 37–38.

11. The F-1 attack was described by CENTCOM and intelligence officials. It is also recounted in the transcript of Boomer's staff briefing at the Marine Corps Historial Center.

12. Interview, CENTCOM intelligence official.

13: THE MOTHER OF ALL BATTLES

1. According to Boomer's command briefing for January 25, 1991, his intelligence officer made the following report: "Yesterday across the border on enemy capabilities, the CIA reported yesterday there was a possibility of a ground attack by the Iraqis into Saudi Arabia. It was from an unreliable HUMINT [human intelligence] source of undetermined reliability, but you couple that with the Scud activity and the sighting of a MEL [mobile erector launcher] out west, the naval activity, dispersal of naval craft, if not an actual sortie to conduct offensive ops, and it stacks up to a push by the Iraqis."

2. Interviews, Air Force officials.

3. The account of the Iraqi plan is based on accounts of officials familiar with the CIA analysis of the battle.

The account of the sea-based element of the Iraqi plan comes from Sir Patrick Hine, the British air chief marshal and the joint commander of Operation Granby. He wrote in the official British after-action report: "The first anti-surface action occurred on 29 January when RAF Jaguars detected Iraqi fast patrol boats heading off the Kuwaiti coast as part of a combined operation to attack the port of Al Khafji. Lynx from HM Ships *Gloucester, Cardiff* and *Brazen* were launched to locate and engage the enemy flotillas with Sea Skua missiles, leaving two sunk or damaged and scattering the remaining, which were attacked by fixed-wing aircraft as they sought shelter along the coast."

4. Hoar transcript, Marine Corps Historical Center, 1991.

5. Interview with Col. Ron Richard, CENTCOM media pool.

6. Details of the outpost battles were based on interviews with the main participants, after-action reports, and oral history accounts made immediately after the events. Also see the after-action report for the Marine support command, specifically the entry for January 30, 1991: "CSSD-91 conducts tactical evacuation of EPW [enemy prisoner of war] facility in the face of Iraqi movement in Southern Kuwait. Destroyed armory with 32 shotguns, 4 sets of night vision goggles and other miscellaneous equipment in order to avoid capture by the enemy."

7. Interviews, Brig. Gen. Charles Krulak and Maj. Gen. William Keys.

8. Interview and journal, Capt. Douglas Kleinsmith.

9. Interview, Lt. Col. John Meagher, the Marine liaison to Prince Khalid, Joint Forces Command.

10. The account of Ingraham's experiences is from a letter he wrote, which was forwarded by his father to Brig. Gen. J. H. Admire. It is also based on an unpublished manuscript by Jim Michaels, a reporter for the *San Diego Union*.

11. Interviews, Glosson and Horner. Also see "The Gulf War: Setting the Record Straight," General Khalid bin Sultan, 1992, in which Khalid says: "Schwarzkopf asserts that, after the Iraqis seized Khafji, he and I were in contact during the battle to retake the town. In fact, I had no secure means of communication with him during the battle and did not call him at all. I can now reveal that the reason Iraqi forces managed to take the town in the first place was because of delays in giving our forces the American-controlled close air support they had called for."

12. Details of the fighting inside Khafji are based upon interviews with the participating Americans, military logs, message files, and record of interrogations of the captured Iraqis.

13. The downing of the AC-130, code-named Spirit 03, led to charges that the Air Force had misused the plane and sent it on an unnecessary risk mission. But military officials said that the downing of Spirit 03 was primarily the result of the crew's failure to leave the area at the approach of daylight. See "Death at Daylight," *Pensacola News Journal*, February 23, 1992.
According to Boomer's command briefing for February 2, the Marines took the further precaution of laying explosive charges in a culvert south of Khafji to block the highway if the Iraqis succeeded in making their way south.

14: BACK TO THE DRAWING BOARD

1. Interviews, Maj. Gen. William Keys.

2. Interviews, Arthur and Boomer. This account is also based on the briefing "Role of

Amphibious Force in Support of the CINC's Campaign Plan," which was made available to the authors.

The problems that mines posed for amphibious operations were also underscored by the after-action report by the 5th Marine Expeditionary Brigade. It noted:

> Another planning challenge was that of Naval mines. The mine threat did have a substantial negative impact on the planning for an amphibious assault. With the extent of the Iraqi naval mining unknown, but presumed significant, the seaward portion of the AOA [amphibious objective area] was shrunk. . . . It was estimated that it would have taken 17 days to clear the sea echelon areas and fire support areas at Ash Shuaybah, to an 80 per cent mine free reliability. To achieve this estimate, it required employing both a smaller than usual sea echelon area and smaller than usual FSA's [fire support areas]. The situation meant a longer time to build combat power ashore and the potential for constrained naval gunfire support.

3. Interviews, Keys, Boomer, and Krulak.
4. Interviews, Marine officials.
5. Interview, Waller.
6. Interview, Army officer, conducted by Tom Donnelly, *Army Times*.
7. Interview, VII Corps officers.
8. Entry, February 16–19, 1991, Jedi chronology.
9. Interviews, Schwarzkopf, Maj. Gen. Ronald Griffith, Maj. Gen. Barry McCaffrey, and Boomer.
10. Interview, senior military official.
11. Interview, Wolfowitz.

15: AIR-LAND BATTLES

1. Briefing on the Joint Forces Air Component Command prepared after the war by David Deptula.
2. Marine after-action report.
3. Interviews, Navy officials.
4. Tactical Air Command, USAF Air Warfare Center, oral history interview with Col. Michael F. Reavy.
5. Interview, Col. Tom Lennon, commander 48th Tactical Fighter Wing, F-111 pilots.
6. Deptula and Glosson, as quoted in the "Gulf War Air Power Survey."
7. Interview, Air Force officials.
8. Memo, reviewed by the authors.
9. "Electrical Facilities Survey," by Walid Doleh, Warren Piper, Abdel Qamhieh, Kamel al Tallaq, October 1991.

> Generating stations were intensively targeted during the early days of the air war. The southernmost stations were especially hard-hit . . . At least ten of 16 stations visited were bombed on 17 January, the first day of the war. Several were hit first with metallic threads, which short-circuited the network and prevented transmission, including Beiji and Musayeb, the largest

generating stations in Iraq. At least, fourteen were hit multiple times, many after they were shut down. Al Hartha in Basrah was hit 13 times, from the morning of 17 January to 15 minutes before the cease-fire.

10. Classified Special Operations Command briefing to Senate Armed Services Committee.

11. Interviews, Air Force officials.

12. "Aviation Operations in Southwest Asia," Marine Corps Research Center, Research Paper, 92-0003, Battle Assessment Team, Southwest Asia Aviation Study, June 15, 1991. The paper noted:

> Ground communications capability was severely strained during Marine Corps operations in SWA. Ineffective tactical communications, unreliable High Frequency radios and the large theater of operations were almost communication show stoppers. The timely "open market" purchase of handheld radios, use of available satellite communications (SATCOM) and employment of Marine Corps couriers prevented a communications breakdown. Procurement of modern, reliable communications equipment compatible with sister services is needed. . . . Routinely, Marine Corps air control agencies could not consistently communicate with Marine Corps aviation assets. . . .
>
> Air intelligence could not provide real feedback to air groups, squadrons and aircrew. Pilots quickly learned that the best intelligence was obtained from a fellow aircrew returning from a strike mission. Lack of photo imagery and other tactical reconnaissance data, further hindered Marine Corps attack aircraft effectiveness. . . .

13. Interview, Arnold. According to a paper prepared by Glosson's staff, "On Jan. 29 Gen. Schwarzkopf commented on lack of BDA [battle damage assessment] concerning Republican Guard. Stated system is broken and should use pilot reports. Commented vehicles must be on back like dead cockroach before J-2 would assess kill. On 31 Jan. Lt. Gen. Yeosock briefed the CINC that the Republican Guard strength was 99 per cent."

One problem in developing accurate battle damage assessment was the Pentagon's decision to retire the SR-71 spy plane. Senior Army intelligence officials believe the plane, which provided wide area coverage, was needed. One senior official said that the plane was requested "big time" by CENTCOM. But Cheney, who had supported the retirement of the SR-71 as a member of the House Intelligence Committee, was not sympathetic.

Also see "Intelligence Successes and Failures in Operations Desert Shield/Desert Storm," House Committee on Armed Services, August 1993, p. 15.

14. Interview, Arthur.

15. "Persian Gulf Campaign: U.S. Marine Corp Operations," an after-action briefing prepared by Boomer. Slide B/U 29 lists the 3rd MAW Amendments. Before the war, A-6Es were tasked for night-only missions. And when additional squadrons of aircraft arrived at 3rd MAW, they were not added to the numbers of sorties to be shared with the JFAAC, the briefing noted. As the ground war approached, the briefing added, "3rd MAW made a concerted effort to disengage from the JFAA

process." Specifically, seven days into the air campaign, the Marine wing requested a "three package limit per day with no A-6E's scheduled." Twelve days into the air campaign, the Marines said they would only attack "targets which had impact on MEF concept of operations." Twenty-two days into the air war, the Marine air wing gave "priority to targets in immediate Marine frontage." At twenty-three days, the Marines effectively stopped their "participation in the offensive air campaign" directed by Horner and Glosson and concentrated on their own targets.

Deptula was disturbed by the Marine move, but Horner decided that the Air Force had enough warplanes and decided not to make an issue of it.

16. Interviews, Waller and Glosson.

17. Interview, Lennon. The tank-plinking innovation was regarded as so important that news organizations were urged not to publish details of the technique. The *New York Times* refrained from publicizing the breakthrough, but it was later disclosed by ABC News. Cheney decided against publicly criticizing the network for fear that it would draw more attention to the tactic. Despite the disclosure, there is no evidence that the Iraqis were aware of the news reports or used them to counter the American bombing strategy.

The tank-plinking effort did not put an end to the infighting between the Army and the Air Force. According to a paper prepared for Glosson, "On 9 Feb. F-111 reported 100 destroyed armored vehicles. None were accepted. ARCENT agreed to count BDA only if each claim was verified by the GLO [ground liaison officer, an army officer attached to Air Force units]."

18. Author gathered this information while traveling with Cheney and Powell, February 1991.

19. Interview, F-117 strike planner.

20. The bombing of Iraq's "baby milk factory," identified by American intelligence as a suspected biological warfare plant, also caused controversy.

According to the House Armed Services report on intelligence operations in the Gulf, the plant was identified as a potential biological warfare site for eight years. The report noted that the plant did not have the sort of containment system that would be needed to handle dangerous biological agents, but said this might be an indication of poor safety practices in Iraq. It did have a manned security gate. According to the report:

> Over the years, data on the milk plant mounted. Some evidence pointed to the plant as a biological site. But other evidence, which remains classified because it involves sensitive sources and methods, was contradictory. Long into Operation Desert Shield, it was still listed simply as a potential manufacturing plant.
>
> Then, in December 1990, the Iraqi authorities began applying a mottled camouflage scheme to the roofs of two confirmed biological sites. At the same time, the same camouflage scheme was applied to the roof of the milk plant. The site was immediately shifted from the potential to the confirmed list and made a target for the air campaign that was to begin in just two weeks.
>
> Today, almost two years after the end of Operation Desert Storm, we still do not know with absolute certainty whether the plant that was bombed was a biological site or a legitimate baby milk plant.

See House Armed Services Committee report, "Intelligence Success and Failures in Operation Desert Shield/Desert Storm," pp. 37–38.

21. Interview, aide to Glosson.

22. Interview, Powell.

23. Interview, senior military official.

24. Air Force memo, reviewed by the authors.

25. According to a staff paper prepared for Glosson: "On 15 Feb. DIA reassessed Tawakalna RG divison 26 per cent greater strength than CENTCOM estimate (74 per cent versa 48 per cent). Target assessed using overhead and medium altitude sensors."

26. Arnold memo. The criticism was also reflected in the Jedis' log. They noted: "Apportionment for PHASE III still does not appear to be where it should be to best support the ground commanders' schemes of maneuver. The group's analysis of the ATO indicated that even when kill boxes are included, battlefield prep sorties account for less than 40 per cent of the total. The concern with kill boxes is that they may not be where they can best support the ground scheme and pilots may not be going after the right targets."
   The Army also stated its case in a briefing prepared after the war, called "Air-Ground Operations Operation Desert Storm: A Closer Look," which was prepared by a VII Corps officer.

27. Horner's testimony to the Senate Armed Services Committee, "Operation Desert Shield/Desert Storm": Senate Armed Services Committee, 1991, p. 247.

16. SECOND THOUGHTS

1. "The War Which Might Not Have Been," a three-part article in *Pravda* by Yevgeni Primakov.

2. Air Force staff paper, obtained by the authors. "On 21 Feb, as G-Day approached, the CIA became nervous about CENTCOM claiming 1700 tank, 900 APC, and 1400 artillery kills. Took briefing to the President saying they could only validate 500 kills. Fortunately, DIA, Admiral McConnell, and SECDEF had seen F-11I VTR tank killing tape and supported CENTCOM's BDA count," the paper noted.

3. Boomer command briefing.

4. Interview, Pentagon official.

5. Bush's attitude is recorded in notes taken by a White House official.

6. Schwarzkopf, *It Doesn't Take a Hero*, pp. 441–42. Schwarzkopf wrote that after one conversation with Powell he called his staff together and outlined the Soviet peace initiative. "If it had been up to the veteran military men in the war room, they'd have been thrilled to see Saddam accept a cease-fire and walk off the battlefield — not that anyone believed he would. People winced when I described Washington's response; Bob Johnston, whose son was on the front lines, shook his head: 'The Soviets are talking about getting us exactly what we asked for, and we summarily turned them down.' "

7. Boomer, February 19 "Memo for the Record." The full text read:

I was called by the CINC at approximately 1000, and he asked if it were possible to move G day to the 22nd of February vice 24 February. He asked the question because his weather forecaster predicted low ceilings and rain on the 25th, bad weather on the 25th, and good weather again on the 26th and 27th. When he discussed the matter with Washington, he anticipated that they would ask if he could go early, therefore he was calling to get my reaction to such a suggestion. I told him that I needed to check with my commanders, but that I would get back with him in a couple of hours. I polled the Division Commanders and the DSG Commander. After studying the situation, they all came back and told me they could execute on the 22nd, but not without some degradation in the attack. This was the same assessment that I received from my staff.

After reflecting on it, I felt there were several factors involved. First and most important, the fact that we have built an intricate timetable in terms of our fire plan, and it would have been very difficult to recover much of that had we gone two days earlier. The whole thing was tied together very tightly. For example, there are recon teams across the barrier which we are going to extract on the 19th and the 20th. We had gotten them through as far as the second barrier. Of course, there had to be a restricted fire plan developed for their safety. As a result, we are not going to be able to put fire right along the barrier until the 23rd and 24th. It was such things as this which cause me to believe that in many small ways our whole plan would be degraded.

There were numerous other things that went into our recommendation to the CINC, such as the fact that we were offloading bombs today and it would be more difficult to get them into the bomb dumps in time, had we gone earlier. We are studying imagery on artillery sites in order to refine our targeting. B-52 strikes were planned for G-minus-2. These would have to go at 0300 on the 20th, and getting that changed through CENTAF would have been difficult. It also would have been questionable as to whether or not the amphibious feint could have been accomplished.

These factors, plus many others, caused me to tell the CINC that while it would be possible to execute on the 22nd, my attack would be significantly degraded, perhaps as much as 25 per cent. I told him that my first choice would be to wait for three good days of weather. My second choice would be to go on the 24th and take a chance on bad weather on the 25th. My rationale is that on the 25th we would be through the barrier and have more room to maneuver, with less concern for artillery and chemicals. Finally, my last choice would be to go on the 22nd.

The CINC replied that he understood, and that he would use the information that I had provided him when he discussed the matter with Washington. I told him that if we were going to go on the 22nd, that I would need to know this afternoon. He said that he would resist going early and to continue to plan to go on the 24th; he would still continue to seek three good days, but worst case we would take three good days of weather on the 22nd, 23rd and 24th, and then take our chances with weather on the 25th.

8. Interview, Brig. Gen. Harry W. Jenkins.

9. Interviews, Col. Frank Akers, chief operations officer for the XVIII Corps, and Steven Arnold.

10. Luck's memo to Waller, sent several days before the ground war, was obtained by the authors. The full text is reproduced below:

> Message personal for Lt. Gen. Waller from Lt. Gen. Luck. Subject: ARCENT Conplan for attack on RGFC division defense.
>
> I do not agree with the current ARCENT Conplans for phase three D of operation Desert Storm. My disagreement is based on a clear difference between my understanding of your intent about our operational maneuver and the intent which is portrayed in the current ARCENT Conplan. I have three principal objections. First, Conplan tasked us to penetrate the RGFC Infantry. This is a costly and unnecessary tactic which fails to exploit our superior capability to destroy by fire. Second, we need more room to maneuver. The proposed boundary is too restrictive, particularly with respect to maneuvering logistics. Finally, to accomplish our mission in this Conplan requires more combat power. The Hammurabi is at the highest strength of any RGFC heavy division. The proposed plan calls for us to attack the Hammurabi with our single heavy division corps having suffered through the attrition of defeating two-three RGFC infantry divisions.
>
> Recommend ARCENT rethink the Conplan concept.
>
> (a) Penetration requirement. We do not need to penetrate in order to defeat the RGFC infantry. . . .
>
> (b) Maneuver space. We do not have the terrain on which to fix and maneuver around the RGFC infantry in order to focus on the Hammurabi. . . .
>
> (c) Combat power. Establish an on order task for the VII Corps to provide 1st AD to reinforce XVIII Airborne Corps. By reinforcing XVIII ABN Corps with a heavy division . . . we establish a focused theater main effort to destroy first the Madinah, and then the Hammurabi. Concurrently, the 101st Airborne Division (AASLT) can provide the Corps with the right combat power and maneuverability to isolate the RGFC infantry in an economy of force mission.
>
> 3. The linkage between our strategic goals in the current course of action is missing. The COA is not acceptable cost for fight with the RGFC infantry that we do not want or need. We should capitalize on our positional advantage, our maneuverability, and our superior firepower. Recommend we set the terms of battle for this operation — fight the battle at the time and place of our choosing. We would much prefer a boundary further south which allows the XVIII Airborne Corps more maneuver space. However, a boundary must be cut now so that we can prepare the battlefield with deep operations.
>
> Finally, give us the combat power required to execute the mission.
>
> 4. Respectfully, Gary.

11. Interviews, VII Corps officers.

12. Interview, McEwen.

13. Interview, Jenkins.

14. Interviews, Maj. Gen. James M. Myatt and Col. Jim Fulks. Also see Myatt's testimony to the Senate Armed Services Committee. "Operation Desert Shield/Desert Storm": Senate Armed Services Committee, pp. 65–67. Fulford's comments are taken from a press pool report.

For details on the infiltration, see "U.S. Marines in the Persian Gulf, 1990–1991: With the 1st Marine Division in Desert Shield and Desert Storm."

15. "Persian Gulf Campaign: U.S. Marine Corp Operations," a briefing prepared by Boomer, p. 49. "Starting G-3, both divisions began extensive recon inside Kuwait to prep for the breach. 1st Mardiv had recon 20 km into Kuwait for last 3 days prior," the briefing noted. "2nd LAI BN conducted a 3 day recon that Baghdad radio announced as the start of the ground war. Total take was over 20 tanks, 25 vehicles, and more than 300 EPW's."

16. Interviews, Bush administration officials.

17. See Public Papers of George Bush: Book 1, January 1 to June 30, 1991, "Remarks on the Persian Gulf Conflict," pp. 165–166 and 168–169. On February 22, 1991, Bush said:

> Needless to say, any conditions would be unacceptable . . . More importantly and more urgently, we learned this morning that Saddam has now launched a scorched-earth policy against Kuwait, anticipating perhaps that he will now be forced to leave . . . Indeed, they're destroying the entire oil production system of Kuwait. At the same time that that Moscow press conference was going on and Iraq's Foreign Minister was talking peace, Saddam Hussein was launching Scud missiles.
>
> After examining the Moscow statement and discussing it with my senior advisers here last evening and this morning, and after extensive consultation with our coalition partners, I have decided that the time has come to make public with specificity just exactly what is required of Iraq if a ground war is to be avoided.
>
> Most important, the coalition will give Saddam Hussein until noon Saturday to do what he must do: began his immediate and unconditional withdrawal from Kuwait. We must hear publicly and authoritatively his acceptance of these terms.

The statement released that day by White House Press Secretary Marlin Fitzwater outlined the following conditions:

> First, Iraq must begin large-scale withdrawal by noon, Feb. 23. Iraq must complete military withdrawal from Kuwait in one week. Given the fact that Iraq invaded and occupied Kuwait in a matter of hours, anything longer than this from the initiation of the withdrawal would not meet Resolution 660's requirement of immediacy.
>
> Within the first 48 hours, Iraq must remove all its forces from Kuwait City and allow for return of the legitimate government of Kuwait. It must withdraw from all prepared defenses along the Saudi-Kuwait and Saudi-Iraq borders, from Bubiyan and Warbah Islands and from Kuwait's Rumaylah oilfield within the 1 week specified above. Iraq must return all its forces to their positions of August 1st, in accordance with Resolution 660.
>
> In cooperation with the International Red Cross, Iraq must release all

prisoners of war and third country civilians being held against their will and return the remains of killed and deceased servicemen. This action must commence immediately with the initiation of the withdrawal and must be completed within 48 hours.

Iraq must remove all explosives or booby traps, including those on Kuwaiti oil installations, and designate Iraqi military liaison officers to work with Kuwaiti and other coalition forces on the operational details related to Iraq's withdrawal, to include the provision of all data on the location of any land or sea mines.

Iraq must cease combat aircraft flights over Iraq and Kuwait except for transport aircraft carrying troops out of Kuwait, and allow coalition aircraft exclusive control over and use of all Kuwaiti airspace.

It must cease all destructive actions against Kuwaiti citizens and property and release all Kuwaiti detainees.

The United States and its coalition partners reiterate that their forces will not attack retreating Iraqi forces and, further, will exercise restraint so long as withdrawal proceeds in accordance with the above guidelines and there are no attacks on other countries.

Any breach of these terms will bring an instant and sharp response from coalition forces in accordance with United Nations Security Council Resolution 678.

18. According to an Air Force staff paper, "Corps Air Support at Desert Storm," on February 11, the Battle Damage Assessment at CENTCOM rated the Republican Guard at 82 percent, the operational echelon at 71 percent, and the front-line troops at 45 percent. The total was 67 percent. On February 23, the CENTCOM Battle Damage Assessment rated the Republican Guard at 66 percent, the operational reserves facing the Army at 55 percent, and the front-line troops at 33 percent. The average was 53 percent.

The Iraqi forces facing the Marines were rated at 78 percent, a surprisingly high figure that reflected the difficulty in gathering BDA in the Marine sector.

19. "The Gulf War: An Iraqi General Officer's Perspective," March 11, 1991, Memorandum for Record. This classified assessment, obtained by the authors, was prepared by the Army's 513th Military Intelligence Brigade, but was never released.

The disintegration of the Iraqi Army is also recounted in "Analysis of Source Debriefings," March 15, 1991, and other documents prepared by the military intelligence brigade, which have been obtained by the authors.

17: THE FIFTY-HOUR WAR

1. Interview, Boomer.

2. Interview, Sgt. John D. Cornwall.

3. Interview, Lt. Col. Bruce Gombar.

Also see "Breaching Operations in Southwest Asia," Marine Corps Research Center, Lt. Col. G. W. Enders and Maj. J. P. Carothers, July 1991. Page VIII of that report provided a highly critical account of Marine Corps breaching capability:

The Marine Corps does not possess the required countermine/ counterobstacle equipment to provide the MAGTF with a capability to execute breaching operations. The bulk of the countermine/ counterobstacle equipment employed by the I MEF was not Marine Corps equipment. Equipment fielded to support combat operations was provided in the final weeks, days, and hours prior to "G-day." This countermine/counterobstacle equipment was on temporary loan, open purchased, or prefabricated from raw materials. Many of the items were in varying stages of the research and development process. Because training with most of this equipment was conducted in the "11th hour," skill levels, confidence, and equipment performance were considered marginally satisfactory.

According to the report, Belgian, British, Chinese, Czechoslovakian, French, Italian, Iraqi, Jordanian, and Soviet mines were used by the Iraqis.

4. "Actions of the 1st (Tiger) Brigade, 2nd Armored Division, during Desert Shield/ Operation Desert Storm 10 Aug 90–1 March 91," an after-action report by the brigade.

Also see "Eye of the Tiger," J. Paul Scicchitano, *Army Times,* June 10, 1991, and "U.S. Marines in the Persian Gulf, 1990–1991: With the 2d Marine Division in Desert Shield and Desert Storm," by Lt. Col. Dennis P. Mroczkowski, U.S. Marine Corps Reserve, 1993.

5. "U.S. Marines in the Persian Gulf, 1990–1991: With the 1st Marine Division in Desert Shield and Desert Storm."

After-action report by 11th Marines Regiment, Col. P. G. Howard.

6. Interview, Schwarzkopf.

7. After-action report by marine combat engineers: "CSSD-91 had a difficult night receiving an influx of approximately 8,000 EPWs. A sandstorm, strong winds, and rain added to the problems that night, blowing over the chowhall and contributing to a near riot among the starving EPWs."

8. Interview, Myatt. Also see testimony to the Senate Armed Services Committee by Myatt and Capt. Ed Ray. "Operation Desert Shield/Desert Storm," pp. 72–74.

9. After-action report Task Force Papa Bear.

10. See "U.S. Marines in the Persian Gulf, 1990–1991, With the I Marine Expeditionary Force in Desert Shield and Desert Storm," by Col. Charles J. Quilter II, U.S. Marine Corps Reserve.

Also see Jim Michaels, "War Diary: A Historic Ride With Task Force Ripper," *San Diego Tribune,* February 28, 1991.

11. Interview, Horner.

12. Interview, Jenkins.

13. Interviews, Glosson and Horner.

14. Interview, Kurth.

15. Interview, Gombar.

16. Interview, Boomer.

Also see "U.S. Marines in the Persian Gulf, 1990–1991, Anthology and Annotated Bibliography," compiled by Maj. Charles D. Melson, U.S. Marine Corps (Retired), Evelyn A. Englander, and Capt. David A. Dawson, U.S. Marine Corps.

18: FRAGPLAN 7

1. See Schwarzkopf, *It Doesn't Take a Hero,* pp. 438–39. Prior to the ground war, Schwarzkopf went to see Yeosock, who had been hospitalized with pneumonia and a gallbladder condition. Schwarzkopf explained that Yeosock needed to be sent to Germany for surgery and that Waller would serve as the Third Army commander in the meantime. "Yeosock did not say a word," Schwarzkopf wrote. "Tears ran down his cheeks."

2. Interview, Arnold. Also see videotape of the Third Army Command Center, declassified by Pentagon at the authors' request.

3. Interview, Franks. Also see *Certain Victory: The U.S. Army in the Gulf War,* Office of the Chief of Staff, United States Army, Washington, D.C., 1993.

4. Interviews, Franks and Cherrie.

5. Interviews, participants in meeting. Also see "The Generals' War," Tom Donnelly, *Army Times,* March 2, 1992.

6. The entombing of the Iraqi soldiers is described in a chronology prepared by the 1st Infantry Division. It noted that "over 500 enemy prisoners were captured, who were broken in spirit and readily surrendered to our leader brigades. Some 150 enemy soldiers, who chose to resist, were plowed under their trench lines by tanks equipped with mine plows and M9 ACEs." The chronology is entitled "Operation Desert Shield and Desert Storm, Chronology of Events," March 14, 1991, Ar Rawdatayn, Kuwait, and is classified "secret."
According to a report by the VII Corps—"Operation Desert Storm: A Fire Support Perspective"—the military used overwhelming firepower to attack the front-line defenses facing the American army units. Between February 20 and 23, the Air Force launched thirteen B-52 attacks, dropping 754 750-pound bombs for a total of 565,500 pounds. It also dropped surrender leaflets followed by two 15,000-pound bombs. The artillery preparation was just as fierce. Between February 20 and 23, 9,208 rounds and 1,606 rockets were fired into the breach area. In the 30-minute prep before the attack, 6,136 rounds and 414 rockets were fired there.

7. Interview, British military officers. For more information on the British operation, see *The Shield and the Sabre: The Desert Rats in the Gulf, 1990–1991,* by Nigel Pearce (London: HMSO, 1992), p. 92.

8. See "Operation Desert Storm, 2ACR Operations Summary," 23 February–1 March 1991.

9. This is drawn from "The Gulf War: An Iraqi General Officer's Perspective."

10. "The Battle of Al Busayyah, Operation Desert Storm, 24–28 Feb. 1991," 1st Armored Division. Also see *Certain Victory.*

11. Interview, Holder.

12. "The Battle for the 73 Easting," Capt. H. R. McMaster. Also see "The Battle of 73 Easting," Michael D. Krause, U.S. Army Center of Military History, and "A Swift Kick," by Steve Vogel, *Army Times,* August 5, 1991. The Institute of Defense Analyses has developed a computer reconstruction of the battle.

13. Interview, General McFarlin.

14. Interview, Steve Walker.

15. Interview, Cherrie.

16. This account is based on interviews with Schwarzkopf and VII Corps officers.

17. XVIII Airborne Corps, Operation Desert Shield and Operation Desert Storm, Briefing Book, Major General Scholes, Deputy Commanding General.

19: "THE GATE IS CLOSED"

1. Interviews, McCaffrey, Col. Paul Kern, and Col. John LeMoyne. Also see General Order to Attack, 15 February, 1991, Barry R. McCaffrey, and Operation Desert Storm Post-Attack Summary, 22 March 1991, 24th Infantry Division (Mechanized).

2. 101st Airborne Division command history, p. 59: "The division was fortunate not to lose any soldiers in another incident on the 27th. The division Assault Command Post (ACP) had arrived at Objective Tim by air in the night. In the morning, they realized they had set down in the middle of a cluster bomb unit minefield. They carefully relocated. No one was injured."

3. Interviews, Schwarzkopf and Powell.

4. Interview, Pete Williams.

5. Interview, McCaffrey.

6. Interviews, Akers, Arnold, and Schwarzkopf.

7. Interview, Col. Montgomery Meigs and soldiers from the 2nd Brigade. After-action report on the Battle of Medina Ridge by the 2nd Brigade.

8. Interview, Glosson.

9. Interviews, F-117 pilots.

10. Interview, Lennon. Also see "Genesis of Bomb," *Dallas Morning News,* June 30, 1991.

    A widely circulated account, *Triumph Without Victory* (Times Books, 1992), by the staff of *U.S. News and World Report,* holds that the dropping of the GBU-28 was an attempt to kill Saddam Hussein. Saddam Hussein was a target of opportunity, but senior Air Force generals say that they had no reason to think he was at the Taji command post when the order was given to attack. To the contrary, the Iraqi leader was believed to be hiding out in a bunker in Baghdad. But downtown Baghdad was an unlikely first target for an experimental 5,000-pound bomb.

11. Interview, Horner.

12. "Gulf War Air Power Survey."

13. The placement of the fire support coordination line north of the Euphrates is discussed in an oral history with Col. Michael F. Reavy prepared by the Tactical Air Command, USAF Air Warfare Center. Reavy was sharply critical of the Army for seeking to move the coordination line north. He said:

    The Army would attempt to coordinate an FSCL move with us without really thinking through the impact what that was going to do with our campaign and our ability to support them. . . . The Army was moving FSCL well out past where they were going to impact on anything it seemed to us, and when they did that, they took airspace and ground area for us to hit . . . They did not have anybody out there that could coordinate with us, so those areas, in essence, wound up not being hit. . . . I made a note in the big green log that General Horner kept that, at one point in time, the safest place for an Iraqi to be was just behind the FSCL because we couldn't hit it. . . .

By the time that we realized how bad off we were regarding the Army working on the FSCL stuff, the war was over.

The VII Corps's request to move the FSCL to east of the coastal road is based on interviews with Air Force officers. Also see "8th Air Support Operations Group After Action Review, Operations Desert Shield/Storm," which notes that "an error to the conservative prematurely pushed the FSCL beyond the strategic road between Kuwait and Basra the last evening of the ground battle."

The differences between the Army and the Air Force over the coordination line are also discussed in "The Fire Support Coordination Line: Is It Time to Reconsider Our Doctrine?" a thesis presented to the faculty of the Army Command and General Staff College by David H. Zook III, Maj., USA (Fort Leavenworth, KS, 1992). Also see Maj. John M. Fawcett, Jr., "Which Way to the FEBA (And FSCL, FLOT, Troops in Contact, Etc.)?" *USAF Weapons Review*, Fall 1992.

14. Interviews, Air Force officials.

15. In her memoirs (*The Downing Street Years*, HarperCollins, 1993, p. 828), Mrs. Thatcher wrote:

One of my very few abiding regrets is that I was not there to see the issue through. The failure to disarm Saddam Hussein and to follow through the victory so that he was publicly humiliated in the eyes of his subjects and Islamic neighbors was a mistake which stemmed from the excessive emphasis placed right from the start on international consensus. The opinion of the U.N. counted for too much and the military objective of defeat for too little. And so Saddam Hussein was left with the standing and the means to terrorise his people and foment more trouble. In war there is much to be said for magnanimity in victory. But not before victory.

16. The White House account is based on the notes of a participant.

Bush announced the suspension of offensive operations at 9:02PM EST. See Public Papers of George Bush: Book 1, January 1 to June 30, 1991, pp. 187–88.

Bush said that Baker would be traveling to the Middle East for consultations on the peace process and outlined the following conditions for maintaining the ceasefire.

Iraq must release immediately all coalition prisoners of war, third country nationals, and the remains of all who have fallen. Iraq also must inform Kuwaiti authorities of the location and nature of all land and sea mines. Iraq must comply fully with all relevant United Nations Security Council resolutions. This includes a rescinding of Iraq's August decision to annex Kuwait and acceptance in principle of Iraq's responsibility to pay compensation for the loss, damage, and injury its aggression has caused.

The coalition calls upon the Iraqi government to designate military commanders to meet within 48 hours with their coalition counterparts at a place in the theater of operations to be specified to arrange for military aspects of the cease-fire. Further, I have asked Secretary of State Baker to request that the United Nations Security Council meet to formulate the necessary arrangements for this war to be ended.

This suspension of offensive combat operations is contingent upon Iraq's not firing upon any coalition forces and not launching Scud missiles against any other country. If Iraq violates these terms, coalition forces will be free to resume military operations.

At every opportunity, I have said to the people of Iraq that our quarrel was not with them but instead with their leadership and above all Saddam Hussein. This remains the case. You, the people of Iraq, are not our enemy. We do not seek your destruction. We have treated your POW's with kindness. Coalition forces fought this war only as a last resort and look forward to the day when Iraq is led by people prepared to live in peace with their neighbors.

We must now begin to look beyond victory and war. We must meet the challenge of securing the peace. In the future, as before, we will consult with our coalition partners. We've already done a good deal of thinking and planning for the postwar period, and Secretary Baker has already begun to consult with our coalition partners on the region's challenges . . .

The war is now behind us. Ahead of us is the difficult task of securing a potentially historic peace . . .

17. Written response to questions on the Gulf War. In his response, Bush also gives a somewhat different account, saying it was Schwarzkopf, not the White House, that asked for a few additional hours to pursue the war, making the land offensive a 100-hour war. Bush also wrote: "On the last day of the war, I was debating this very issue with my advisors in the Oval Office. There was a genuine sentiment that we had accomplished our objectives, but I asked General Powell to call General Schwarzkopf. He did so immediately from the secure phone on my desk. Schwarzkopf concurred that our objective had been met and a cease-fire was appropriate, but asked for a few more hours to clean up a few loose ends. On that basis, the conflict was ended."

18. Schwarzkopf briefing, February 27, 1991.

19. Interview, Schwarzkopf.

20. Interview, McCaffrey.

21. "Nighthawks over Iraq: A Chronology of the F-117A Stealth Fighter in Operations Desert Shield and Desert Storm," Special Study 37 FW/HO-91-1. Office of History, Headquarters 37th Fighter Wing, 12th Air Force, Tactical Air Command.

22. Interview, Lt. Col. Dave White.

23. Interview, Capt. Mike Russell.

24. Interview, Waller.

25. Interview, Schwarzkopf.

26. Interview, Kern.

27. Interview, Arnold.

28. Interview, Cherrie, VII Corps officer.

29. Interview, McCaffrey.

20: "I SURVIVED DESERT STORM"

1. Interview, Iraqi Shiite leaders.

2. Transcripts of radio broadcasts, prepared by the Foreign Broadcast Information Service.

3. Interviews, McCaffrey, Kern, and LeMoyne. Also see 24th Mechanized Infantry Division Combat Team, Historical Reference Book, Compiled at Fort Stewart, April 1991.

4. Interview, VII Corps officer.

5. The exchange between Schwarzkopf and his top commanders is reflected in several memoranda for the record, "Situation at Safwan 1 March," prepared by top Army commanders.

One memo recounts the following conversation between Yeosock and Schwarzkopf:

> 10:45, ARCENT commander called CENTCOM Chief of Staff, said tell CINC orders to destroy radars had not been followed. . . . LTC Wilson requested Iraqis withdraw from area. So far not done. Did not destroy radars because of delicate situation. CINC directed BG Carter to get Iraqi vehicles to withdraw. CINC mission to find a place in Iraq where we can bring the Iraqis to humiliate Iraqi forces at the negotiations by being in an area under our control.

Another memo recounts the following conversation between Schwarzkopf and Yeosock:

> 13:36 ARCENT Commander discusses situation with the CINC: If Iraqi brigade will not withdraw as we request commit overwhelming force to surround them. Use attack helicopters. Talk to him, and capture him if he refuses to withdraw. If he attacks you return fire.
> COMMANDER: May not happen immediately.
> CINC: Get me timelines.
> COMMANDER: Do not know size of enemy force total. Only provided what has been reported. Iraqi commander says they are in dug-in positions and have been there for a long time. (I did not say that they had been feeding the Iraqis.)
> CINC: Want them to withdraw or bring into custody. Ordered by the JCS.
> COMMANDER: Finding another place in Iraq at this time.
> CINC: Too late for that. JCS upset that road junction was not taken. Briefed to the White House. Must straighten out quickly.
> CINC: Don't want any Iraqis near the location. Try to do it by show of force to capture them or get them to withdraw. A delicate situation. Must get them to withdraw, if needed will do so myself. Want someone to do it smart, not stupid. Want to be posted.
> CINC: Ensure the LTG Franks understands the mission; not sure of his ability to understand mission. Therefore, make sure you tell MG Rhame. Tell Iraqi general that if he doesn't withdraw then he will be captured.

Critical to the security of our mission. Must accomplish without a shot fired. Get the force on the ground ASAP.

COMMANDER: My mission is to go into the Safwan Safreh airfield with overwhelming combat power to surround the Iraqi force, to have the Iraqi force withdraw, be captured . . . without the use of offensive operation. We'll need to have help determining size of the enemy force.

CINC: Have an entire corps to work with. Use attack helicopters.

6. See Public Papers of George Bush: Book 1, January 1 to June 30, 1991, p. 201.

7. "Cease-Fire Discussions with Iraqis at Safwan Airfield, Iraq," obtained from the United States Central Command through the Freedom of Information Act.

8. Interview, Scowcroft.

9. Interview, Wolfowitz.

10. Interview, Glosson.

11. Interview, Shiites.

12. Schwarzkopf's support for a rapid withdrawal from the Gulf is clear in the after-action report he sent to Cheney in April 1991. In that report, Schwarzkopf wrote:

War termination: The rapid success of the ground campaign and our subsequent occupation of Iraq were not fully anticipated. Thus, some of the necessary follow-on actions were not ready for implementation. The prolonged occupation of Iraqi territory, necessitated by the absence of a formal cease-fire agreement, has been further complicated by the unforeseen civil unrest that has occurred throughout Iraq since the cessation of hostilities. Documents for war termination need to be drafted and coordinated early. This could well serve to expedite a formal cease-fire agreement, thus minimizing our obligations to take post-war EPWs and care for dislocated civilians . . . There must be early coordination with a plan developed and approved to allow the rapid withdrawal of the occupying force.

13. The plan, obtained by the authors, contains the following slide:

The Road to Baghdad, Mission Analysis.

Specified Task — Attack North of Euphrates River to Control Baghdad.
Implied Task
    Seize Key Terrain to Control Baghdad
    Cross Euphrates River
    Establish and Secure Theater Locs
    Establish Communications and Coordinate with Insurgents and Kurds
    Prevent Escape of Saddam and Baathist Regime
    Coordinate/Assist SOCCENT [Special Operations forces with the Central Command] with Provision of Arms, Equipment and Training to Insurgents/Kurds with Follow on Training/Advisor Assistance to New Iraqi Army

Another slide covers the planning assumptions.

Planning Guidance
Develop courses of action to seize control of Baghdad
VII Corps as Controlling HQ
Use VII Corps Heavy Forces
Forces Available
  One ACR
  One Heavy Division and One AA Division or Two Heavy Divisions

14. Concern over the fragmentation of Iraq was reflected in this memo by Zalmay Khalilzad, the director of policy planning, to Wolfowitz.

Subject: Winning the War — and the Peace: Adaptive Strategies in Case of War with Iraq.

It is possible that once war begins Iraqi nationalists in the armed forces might see the fate of their country at risk because of his reckless ambition and might move against Saddam to save their country. It is not out of the question that even Saddam's Takritis might decide to turn on him. They might calculate that if another group overthrows Saddam they all would be collectively at risk. It is possible that defeat in Kuwait can lead to the unraveling of his regime. The regime's internal security apparatus — which we should target — is very effective and feared. The degradation of this apparatus can itself encourage those opposed to Saddam to move against him . . . The new regime will require external assistance in repairing the damage done to it by war and it will need food and medicine. It might well seek our assistance. We should respond positively and seek to develop a good relationship with the new Iraqi government. . . .

There is a danger that the overthrow might be followed by more substantial instability and chaos. This can happen if the armed forces disintegrate and different factions fight each other. Ethnic groups such as the Kurds might declare independence from Iraq. Iraq's neighbors such as Iran, Syria, and even Turkey might either seize parts of Iraqi territory or establish governments to their liking in areas adjacent to them — in effect partitioning Iraq into several countries. The most dangerous of these would be the Iranian occupation of any part of Iraqi territory. And, should Syria and Turkey take over parts of Iraq, it is likely to be very difficult to stop the Iranians from doing the same.

The partitioning of Iraq will not serve our long-term interests. Iraqi disintegration will improve prospects for Iranian domination of the Gulf and remove a restraint on Syria. It will sow the seeds for future wars. Should Iraqi forces begin to disintegrate, we might become the principal power interested in maintaining Iraq's territorial integrity. We will need a strategy for deterring Iraq's neighbors from invading it while waiting for the Iraqis to sort things out for themselves. We might well have to be prepared to deploy U.S.-led allied military units to parts of Iraq where they will not be in a hostile local environment and can deter Iraq's regional rivals from partitioning it. Sending Arab forces to establish order would not be a good idea. The Iraqis are likely to resent that more than if we go in, since other Arabs have their own rivalries with Iraq and these will further complicate the issue.

15. President Bush's written response to Questions Regarding the Persian Gulf War, June 13, 1994. The full text of Bush's response reads:

> While some of the escaped Iraqi forces were apparently used against the Shiites in the south, most of the forces employed were those not engaged in the conflict in Kuwait. It was never our goal to break up Iraq. Indeed, we did not want that to happen, and most of our coalition partners (especially the Arabs) felt even stronger on the issue. I did have a strong feeling that the Iraqi military, having been led to such a crushing defeat by Saddam, would rise up and rid themselves of him. We were concerned that the uprisings would sidetrack the overthrow of Saddam, by causing the Iraqi military to rally around him to prevent the breakup of the country. That may have been what actually happened.
>
> I prefer not to comment on the helicopter question except to note that, as it was, helicopters were not significantly involved in the fighting against the Shiites at that time. When the Iraqis did begin to use helicopters against the Shiites in a big way, the following year, I got from the Security Council a ban on Iraqi flights in the southern zone, to match that imposed in the north to protect the Kurds.

Bush's statement is not precisely correct. When the Bush Administration imposed a flight ban in the south, it cited previous U.N. Security Resolutions urging Iraq not to repress its people, but the Security Council did not specifically approve the ban.

16. The Defense Intelligence Agency's March 1991 assessment, entitled "Iraq's Nuclear Program," reads as follows:

> Saddam Hussein's plan to acquire nuclear weapons has been slowed, not halted, and Iraqi leaders are firmly committed to rejuvenating it. Should sanctions and intrusive U.N. inspections cease, Iraq could produce a nuclear weapon in 2 to 4 years.
>
> Had the Persian Gulf war not occurred, Iraq could have produced its first nuclear weapon in early 1993. Iraq began a nuclear program in the early 1970's. . . .
>
> Despite sanctions, Baghdad can easily reestablish procurement networks or create new ones — many front companies are small, unstaffed offices. So far, Iraqi agents apparently have not reestablished a network in Europe. Instead, they are using Jordanian firms as front companies through which nuclear-related goods could be transferred to Iraq via Jordan's free-trade zones.
>
> Iraq continues to administer the largest and most capable concentration of nuclear scientists in the Arab world. Some 2,000 mostly foreign-trained Iraqi scientists and engineers and 18,000 technicians are posed to resurrect the Iraqi nuclear program as soon as conditions allow. Although the existing scientific cadre is large enough to support progress at a reduced rate, postwar efforts to train and recruit nuclear scientists suggest that Iraq needs even more personnel to sustain a long-term nuclear weapon program. In the wake of known defections and information leaks, Saddam Hussein almost certainly has intensified already-tight security measures to prevent scientists from escaping. . . .

Iraqi scientists and engineers have not yet designed a nuclear weapon tailored to a specific delivery system. Before the war, they were conducting exploratory work on several short- and medium-range ballistic missile systems. Further modification of these systems would have allowed them to carry a 1,000 kilogram payload to distances in excess of 500 kilometers. Until such missiles are produced, however, the most likely delivery platforms will be medium-range bombers. Despite war losses, Iraq still has a number of TU-22/Blinder bombers and MiG-25/Foxbat fighter-bombers with sufficient ranges and payloads to deliver nuclear weapons in theater.

. . . As soon as intrusive U.N. inspections cease, Iraq is expected to reestablish its covert uranium enrichment program and accelerate its nuclear weapons development. Based on DIA's current knowledge of Iraqi capabilities, Baghdad could (using previously known technology) produce sufficient fissile material, complete design work, fabricate components, and assemble its first nuclear weapon in 2 to 4 years.

According to this report, "Iraq's chemical and biological warfare capabilities have been significantly degraded but not eliminated. Should the Iraqi leadership again decide to develop these forms of unconventional warfare, they have an important part of their chemical infrastructure intact and the basis for a biological warfare capability, albeit at a greatly reduced level. Complete reconstitution to prewar levels, however, will take a minimum of 3–5 years for the chemical program and a minimum of 5–8 years for the biological program."

"Iraq's Chemical and Biological Warfare Capabilities: Surviving Assets and Lack or Use During the War." Defense Intelligence Agency report, March 1991.

17. On the subject of "The Iraqi Army's Uneven Recovery," the DIA report noted:

While protecting Saddam Hussein's regime against Kurdish and Shia insurgent threats, the Iraqi Army has managed to reorganize into 31 understrength divisions since the war.

Maneuver brigades in armored and mechanized infantry divisions generally have 70 per cent of their estimated total authorization for armored vehicles.

. . . The Iraqi Army's most pressing requirements have been to repair battle-damaged equipment and to acquire spare parts, uniforms, and other expendable items. Iraq had only partially succeeded in domestically fulfilling these needs. While large numbers of Soviet-designed armored vehicles have been repaired, Iraq's limited military spare parts production capability will be unable to satisfy the Army's requirements.

Because much of its repair/rebuild infrastructure received little or no damage during the war, Baghdad has been actively repairing its ground equipment. The Iraqis appear to have an adequate supply of munitions supplemented by production from undamaged ammunition plants and damaged facilities that have been rebuilt. Moreover, Baghdad had started reconstructing its artillery production facilities, and portions of its military electronics production plant may be operational.

The regular Army, occupied with efforts to reconstitute its units, is shouldering the burden of internal security operations in the north against the Kurdish insurgency and in the southeast to contain the Shia population.

Some improvements have been noted in Iraqi unit organization, use of artillery, and armed helicopters during counterinsurgency operations. However, in the course of scattered, bitter clashes with Kurdish and Shia insurgents, regular Army units usually have suffered excessive losses and sometimes have exhibited a lack of fighting spirit. The heaviest buildup of regular forces is in the north — a situation that has resulted in considerable thinning of forces in the major Shia operating area of southern Iraq.

The report contained the following chart:

IRAQI ARMY STRENGTH		
	Current	Pre–Desert Storm
Personnel	*300,000–500,000*	*900,000–1.2 million*
Regular army divisions	24	59
	3 armored	
	3 mechanized infantry	
	18 infantry	
Republican Guard divisions	7	12
	3 armored	3 armored
	1 mechanized infantry	2 infantry
	3 infantry	6
		1 Sp. Ops.
Tanks	2100	5800
Armored personnel carriers	3350	5100
Artillery pieces	1100	3830

Also see testimony by Rear Adm. Edward D. Sheafer Jr., Director of Naval Intelligence, before the House Armed Services Subcommittee on Seapower, Strategic and Critical Materials, February 5, 1992. In that testimony, Admiral Sheafer noted that Iraq's "KARI Air Defense Network . . . is still operationally effective."

18. "Electrical Facilities Survey," by Walid Doleh, Warren Piper, Abdel Qamhieh, Kamel al Tallaq, October 1991. This team visited Iraq between August and September and found that electrical generation had been restored to about 68 percent of 1990 peak load and about 37 percent of installed capacity. About 75 percent of the transmission lines were operable. Lack of spare parts was the primary limitation on reconstruction.

19. "Saudi Arabia — Unwelcome 'Guests,' The Plight of Iraqi Refugees," Amnesty International, May 10, 1994. According to this report, 32,000 Iraqi refugees were sent to two camps after the Gulf War and held at two camps: Rafha and Artawiyya. Khalid said in an interview soon after the war that Riyadh's plan for handling the refugees was to return them to Iraq following Saddam Hussein's ouster, which he predicted would happen in about six months. But by April 1994, there were still 23,000 Iraqi refugees in Saudi Arabia. "Hundreds of Iraqi refugees who sought

shelter in Saudi Arabia after the war were arrested, tortured, killed or forcibly returned to Iraq," the report notes.
20. Interview, Gordon Brown.

EPILOGUE

1. "A Line in the Sand," prepared by the Marine Corps Combat Development Command and available from the Marine Corps Association, Quantico, Virginia.
2. *Certain Victory: The U.S. Army in the Gulf War,* Office of the Chief of Staff, United States Army, Washington, D.C., 1993, pp. 314–315.
3. Interview, Schwarzkopf.
4. Memorandum from Richard Hallion, the Air Force historian, April 30, 1993.
    The "Gulf War Air Power Survey" contradicted much of what Hallion wrote in his own book, *Storm Over Iraq* (Smithsonian Institution Press, 1992). In his memo, Hallion wrote that he was "increasingly concerned that the actual accomplishments of airpower in the Gulf War will be distorted or misinterpreted by the upcoming GWAPS report in much the same way that the lessons learned and the accomplishments of airpower in the Second World War were distorted by the Strategic Bombing Survey. Further there is the potentiality that even the positive statements that the GWAPS report states will be gradually lost in much the same way that those of the USSBS [U.S. Strategic Bombing Survey] were in the 1950's."
    Hallion urged that the Air Force "seriously consider the implications of releasing this report."
5. "The Gulf War: Setting the Record Straight," General Kahlid bin Sultan, 1992.
6. Soviet Analysis of Operation Desert Storm and Operation Desert Shield, translated by the Defense Intelligence Agency, p. 32.

Acknowledgments

When we began our research for *The Generals' War* four years ago, we knew that the book would be a large undertaking.

From the start, our hope was to understand how each of the services planned and fought the war — and how those plans did and did not fit together. To the extent possible, we planned to cite our sources on the record and to draw on classified and unclassified documentation.

To try to get at the "ground truth" of the war, we interviewed administration officials, diplomats, allied military officers, and intelligence experts, some more than a dozen times.

Many senior commanders and planners were interviewed in Saudi Arabia and the other Persian Gulf states during the planning for the war. They were also interviewed during the war and in the conflict's immediate aftermath when the coalition forces occupied southern Iraq and were deployed in Kuwait. To prepare our account, we visited some of the main battle sites, talked to the airmen, soldiers, Marines, and sailors who did the fighting.

Away from the battlefield, we conducted numerous after-action interviews at military bases throughout the United States and Europe. In Washington, we talked to a broad range of policy-makers at the Pentagon, the White House, the State Department, and the various intelligence agencies.

We also interviewed foreign diplomats and talked to Iraqi Shiite leaders and refugees in their exile in Europe and in southern Iraq, as they fled the Iraqi onslaught after the war.

With each month of interviews, the story of the planning and execution of the war turned out to be more fascinating and complex than the initial briefings and news reports suggested.

Some American and allied officials, who were often on opposing sides of the debates that raged behind the scenes in Riyadh and in Washington, shared their private papers and notes so that we could more fully reconstruct the history of the war. Some talked on the record; others on a not-for-attribution basis. Some reviewed portions of our manuscript. Each stone overturned suggested another lead. And often the real story was starkly at odds with the first accounts.

Our interviewees are by no means responsible for our conclusions or for any errors of fact, but *The Generals' War* would not have been possible without their cooperation.

First, we would like to thank President George Bush, who agreed to share his recollections about the key turning points in the planning and execution of the war.

Other top Bush administration officials were also generous with their time. We benefited from interviews with Dick Cheney, Gen. Colin L. Powell, Brent Scowcroft, Lawrence Eagleburger, Paul Wolfowitz, Robert Kimmitt, Richard Haass, Dennis Ross, Henry Rowen, Zalmay Khalilzad, and other ranking civilians and military officials. We would like to thank Pete Williams for helping to declassify the Pentagon's 1979 study of contingencies in the Persian Gulf, which pointed to a possible Iraqi attack on Kuwait.

Within the intelligence community, we would like to thank Robert M. Gates, Richard Kerr, Walter P. Lang, Charles E. Allen, Ken Pollack, and others who prefer to be unnamed. The Defense Intelligence Agency declassified its July and August 1990 "watch notices" at our request and the Central Intelligence Agency provided a copy of its definitive and unclassified account of the battle damage assessment following the Gulf War.

Gen. H. Norman Schwarzkopf and the deputy CENTCOM commander during the war, Lt. Gen. Calvin C. H. Waller, spoke to us at length and on the record. Thanks to Lt. Gen. William "Gus" Pagonis, who ran the enormous logistical operation in the Gulf. The United States Central Command also facilitated interviews with its top officials and their aides, both in Riyadh and in Tampa, Florida.

The Air Force story is an important but complex one. We would like to thank Gen. Charles A. Horner (Ret.), Gen. Merrill A. McPeak (Ret.), Gen. Michael Dugan (Ret.), Donald B. Rice, Lt. Gen. Buster C. Glosson (Ret.), Col. John A. Warden III, Col. David A. Deptula, Col. Ben

Harvey, Col. Ron Stanfill, Col. John Barry, Lt. Col. Richard P. King, Lt. Col. Mark "Buck" Rogers, Maj. Randy O'Boyle, Maj. Bill Brunner, among many others.

The pilots and commanders also provided us compelling and vital firsthand accounts. Brig. Gen. Thomas J. Lennon and the airmen from the 48th Tactical Fighter Wing at Lakenheath, England, explained their bombing missions, as did commanders and airmen from virtually all of the other types of aircraft that flew in the Gulf. Lt. Col. Jay Beard helped us describe the first use of air-launched cruise missiles in combat. Col. "Orville" Wright described the F-16's first, and only, attack on Baghdad. Col. Alton C. Whitley, Lt. Col. Ralph Getchell, and Lt. Col. Greg Feest, among others, helped us understand the contribution made by the F-117.

The Army was of enormous help, facilitating interviews in Iraq and Kuwait immediately following the war with many of its key commanders and with its troops. We benefited from interviews with Gen. Carl E. Vuono (Ret.), Gen. Frederick Franks Jr. (Ret.), Gen. Gary E. Luck, Gen. Barry R. McCaffrey, Gen. J. H. Binford Peay 3rd, Lt. Gen. John J. Yeosock (Ret.), Lt. Gen. Steven L. Arnold (Ret.), Lt. Gen. Paul E. "Butch" Funk, Lt. Gen. Ronald H. Griffith, Lt. Gen. James Johnson (Ret.), Maj. Gen. L. Donald Holder, Maj. Gen. John F. Stewart Jr., Brig. Gen. Robert F. McFarlin, Col. Joseph H. Purvis, Brig. Gen. Ronald F. Rokosz, Brig. Gen. Stanley F. Cherrie, Brig. Gen. Frank H. Akers Jr., Lt. Col. Douglas E. Lute, and many others.

The VII Corps — and in particular, the 1st Armored Division and the 3rd Armored Division — were gracious hosts in occupied Iraq and Kuwait in the weeks following the war. The Army's Center of Military History provided access to important after-action reports as did the units.

The Marines made all of their top commanders and many of their key records available. Thanks to Gen. Walter E. Boomer (Ret.), Gen. Alfred Gray (Ret.), Lt. Gen. Charles C. Krulak, Lt. Gen. William M. Keys (Ret.), Maj. Gen. John M. "Mike" Myatt, Maj. Gen. Harry W. Jenkins (Ret.), Maj. Gen. Matthew P. Caulfield (Ret.), Col. John Meagher, Col. James A. Fulks (Ret.), and Col. Cliff Myers. We gratefully acknowledge Gen. Keys's cooperation in hosting us during his deployment in Kuwait. The 1st Marine Division was most cooperative in its desert encampments in Saudi Arabia and at its home base in California.

The Marine Corps Historical Center provided us access to after-action reports and access to transcripts of Boomer's command meetings.

The Navy granted interviews with Adm. Stanley R. Arthur, Adm.

Henry H. Mauz, and numerous pilots, seamen, and planners. Capt. G. Bruce McEwen helped us tell the story of the war at sea, while Rear Adm. Lyle Bien helped us understand the Navy's role in Riyadh. Thanks also to Capt. Michael "Carlos" Johnson and the Navy's Office of Public Affairs for helping us document SPEAR's contribution before the war.

Many allied officials were also helpful, including Gen. Sir Patrick de la Billière, Sir Patrick Hine, Sir Charles Powell, Douglas Hurd, Lt. Gen. Rupert Smith, Maj. Gen. Patrick Cordingly, Brig. Christopher Hammerbeck (Ret.), and Maj. Gen. Tim Sulivan.

Lt. Gen. Khalid Bin Sultan al-Saud and Prince Bandar helped us understand the Saudi point of view. Israeli military officials also provided us with accounts of the Scud problem and of cooperation between Jerusalem and Washington.

The United Nations Special Commission on Iraq, which has been entrusted with dismantling Iraq's arsenal of weapons of mass destruction after the war, helped us understand the Iraqi weapons program and their postwar status. We would like to thank Rolf Ekeus, Robert Gallucci, Karen Jansen, and others.

We also benefited from a number of key studies. One of the most important is the "Gulf War Air Power Survey." Commissioned by Air Force Secretary Don Rice, it is one of the most independent and informative analyses to be produced on the war.

Thomas Donnelly, who broke the story of Schwarzkopf's displeasure with Franks for the *Army Times,* and did other important reporting on the ground war, was helpful. Not only did his and other articles by the *Army Times* facilitate our understanding of the land offensive, but he made available his voluminous documents and notes of interviews.

Philip Zelikow shared his study of the Bush administration policy before Iraq's invasion of Kuwait and helped us correct our account of key meetings. William Arkin also made available his prodigious library of Gulf war documents.

A book, of course, is more than a collection of interviews. It is a project that requires time, intellectual and moral support, and funding.

Our appreciation goes to Arthur Sulzberger, the former Publisher of the *New York Times,* and to Joseph Lelyveld, the Executive Editor of the *Times,* who supported the effort and gave us time to launch this project.

Stephen Engelberg of the *Times's* Washington Bureau read, edited, and helped organize the book. We are much indebted to his patient efforts and to the support provided by the Washington Bureau. Matthew Gordon helped review the manuscript.

H. K. Park, our researcher, gathered valuable information on the deployment of American forces to the Gulf and other important subjects. We would also like to thank Barclay Walsh, the supervisor of the *Times*'s Washington library, Monica Borkowski, and Marjorie Goldsborough for help with the research.

The book would not have been possible without the generous support of two institutions.

The Woodrow Wilson Center for International Scholars helped underwrite the effort and provided research facilities for our initial effort. We would like to thank Charles Blitzer, the Director of the center; Samuel F. Wells, Jr., the Deputy Director; and Robert Litwak, the Director of International Studies.

We would also like to thank the Carnegie Corporation of New York, for helping us pursue our work. Our appreciation goes to David Hamburg, the President of the Carnegie Corporation, Jane Wales, Carnegie's program officer, and the Henry L. Stimson Center, which administered the grant.

Finally, thanks to our wives, who endured a project that lasted years longer than the American military operation in the Gulf itself.

Index